the group in *inverting* their gaze upon the parts they have played in their difficulties. As the group progresses, the boys' own efforts to solve their internal problems while maintaining social equilibrium offer moving evidence of what can be done by delinquents who have too often been "written off" as hopeless.

Part One explores the theoretical background of the study. The sources and meanings of the "delinquent act" are analyzed; then the characteristics of the boys are delineated, including such elements as their orality, narcissism, sadism, and self- and social alienation. Particular problem areas are also explored, followed by the author's explanation of the new techniques and a description of reactions to them by the boys and their parents.

Part Two comprises the session-by-session reports of the demonstration group, supplemented by the author's comments and intermediate progress reports on each of the boys.

In Part Three, Mr. Slavson evaluates the treatment results and offers his general conclusions and recommendations for future dealing with and prevention of delinquency.

Reclaiming the Delinquent

Earlier Works by S. R. SLAVSON

Science and the New Education, 1934
   (edited with Robert K. Speer)

Creative Group Education, 1937
   translated into Japanese

Character Education in a Democracy, 1939
   also in Braille

An Introduction to Group Therapy, 1942
   translated into German and Japanese

Recreation and the Total Personality, 1946

The Practice of Group Therapy, 1947
   (with collaborators)

Analytic Group Psychotherapy, 1950
   translated into French and Japanese

Child Psychotherapy, 1952

Re-Educating the Delinquent, 1954
   translated into Italian

The Fields of Group Psychotherapy, 1956
   (with collaborators)

Child-Centered Group Guidance of Parents, 1958

A Textbook of Analytic Group Psychotherapy, 1964

Reclaiming
the Delinquent

by

Para-Analytic Group Psychotherapy

and the Inversion Technique

S. R. Slavson

THE FREE PRESS, NEW YORK

Collier-Macmillan Limited, London

ACKNOWLEDGMENTS

THE AUTHOR wishes to acknowledge his gratitude to the many individuals, too numerous to list, who have helped in a variety of ways during the conduct of this study. The staffs of the different departments of The Children's Village have at all times cheerfully co-operated. I wish particularly to give recognition to the group therapists and the other members of the clinical staff—caseworkers, supervisors, psychiatrists, psychologists, and child care supervisors—who were most involved with this study.

I owe special thanks to the Board of Directors, to Mr. Joseph F. Phelan, director, to Mrs. Dorothy Orr, former director of child guidance, and to Mr. Barney Rabinow, the former administrative director—all of The Children's Village. I owe further thanks to the "Thursday Club of Irvington-on-Hudson, New York" for help in initiating the project and to Miss Estelle Whelan of The Free Press for her devoted and meticulous editorial assistance during the transplanting of the rather long manuscript to the printed page. My gratitude also goes to Mrs. Teresa Scribner, head of secretarial services, whose painstaking interest has carried her through the tedium of typing and retyping a rather complex manuscript.

Finally, I wish to record my indebtedness to Mr. John G. Byler and Miss Adelle W. Morrison and to the Board of Directors of the Grant Foundation, Inc., for their steadfast financial support of this and some others of my projects and particularly for the special grant that enabled me to bring this book within reach of all professional workers.

S. R. S.

CONTENTS

PART THREE.   Conclusions

The Scope and Setting of the Study

The Scope of the Study

THE ESSENCE OF EFFECTIVENESS in psychotherapy lies in the proper matching of the patient's problems and personality with the treatment procedures suitable for correction. No craftsman can expect success in his work if he does not understand the potentials and limitations of the materials he employs. The good carpenter knows the best use to which he can put the various kinds and grades of wood, and the tailor knows which of the many textiles will serve different needs to obtain best results. Each will deal with a material according to its nature.

These general considerations of the carpenter and tailor are equally vital to the behavioral or, better, the *mis*behavioral sciences, which are concerned with management and/or correction of human behavior. Understanding of the nature of personality and underyling motivational impulses and their sources is the *sine qua non* of fruitful guidance and psychotherapy.

Much work has been done by many workers to plumb the depths of motives for asocial and antisocial behavior on the part of young people, and many valid and insightful formulations have resulted from these efforts. Most of the available studies that uncover reasons for deviant conduct are the result of systematic *observations* of behavior and of conclusions drawn from them. Other formulations have been derived either from voluntary communications of individual subjects or from responses to questions asked by investigators or questionnaires. Much understanding has also been derived from the theoretical constructs, postulates, and assumptions that currently govern a great deal of the work with wayward youth.

As we shall see further in this volume, adolescence is a major period or phase in the continuum of the maturing process of the individual, who at this stage is most vulnerable to losing his way in the prevailing complex milieu. Torn in many directions by biological urges, psychological strivings, physical needs, and social demands, the adolescent requires guidance of a most sensitive and skilled kind to support culturally valid and useful trends within him and to diminish or wither those trends that are antithetical to his future best interests and those of society. Needless to say, such props are often lacking and always difficult to supply. Some subcultures of our society rather buttress than counteract the primitive and the antihumanistic trends in children.

The present volume is a *study in action and in depth* of the content of wayward youths' unconscious determinants for their seeming harshness and their deviant values—which in most instances serve as defenses against overwhelming fear, anxiety, and guilt—and of methods by which these determinants can be used to reclaim such youths for constructive participation in life.

The aim of the six-year study on which this volume is based was to uncover the less obvious and mostly unconscious inner dynamisms of the delinquent boy in our culture. At first the objective was to find an effective procedure for reclaiming comparatively hardened delinquent boys. But it soon became evident that if we were to do so we would first need to plumb the depths of the conscious aims and unconscious motivations that activate delinquent boys to follow a path in life contrary to, or inconsistent with, the ethos of their time. We felt that objective tests and interview techniques left much unrevealed in the subjects' psyches, and that much of the information so obtained was spurious as supplied by the subjects to the interviewers and therapists. The youngsters somehow knew the "right answers"—those that adults expected of them. What was needed, instead, was a free-flowing self-revelatory process in which the young people would lay open to their own and our view what they had always concealed from themselves and from others. We wondered what were the fantasies, relationships, perceptions, attitudes toward self and others, distortions, and compulsions and needs of the wayward youth; we wished to learn what were the internal and external forces that mold the delinquent's ego function and character—not in general, sterile, and stereotyped terms, but rather in specific and detailed dynamic processes and states. To achieve this goal we eschewed statistical and socioeconomic interpretations. Rather, we felt that the process needed to be reversed, that the understanding of the psychic dynamics of delinquency might more reliably lead us to the causative interpersonal and social conditions that give rise to them than would a study beginning with social forces.

As the reader will find from studying the text and especially the protocols of sessions in Part Two of this volume, our efforts were fully rewarded in this regard. We succeeded, by strategies detailed in the group protocols and the comments following each of them, in putting the boys in what can be termed an "analytical" or "introspective" mood, which is the essence of the "inversion technique" to be described later in this book. In this state, the boys revealed matters pertaining to their backgrounds, preoccupations, fantasies, fears, anxieties, and attitudes toward self and others that unveiled to us the mystery behind their self-destructive life aims.

This advance was made possible by the relaxed, comfortable, and secure climate of the group, the catalytic influence of its members upon one another, and the therapists' genuinely understanding and empathetic, as well as sympathetic, identifications with the boys. Not only did the boys communicate matters of which they were aware; the unconscious, as well, was tapped through spontaneous and voluntary sharing during discussions of nocturnal dreams and of past feelings, wishes, and thoughts that had molded the boys' characters and given meaning to their acts.

Thus the boys discovered that their first disclaimers of rage against their parents and the accompanying declarations of affection for them were spurious; that their feelings of power and potency were rooted in the quicksands of weakness; that their belief in predestination and abiding convictions of being doomed had no bases in fact; that their over-powering guilts (which finally came to light) had ontogenic bases and were phylogenetically derived; that their sexual transgressions (which they came to recognize as stemming from conditions in their lives as well as from their biological natures) were transitory and could be overcome (as all the boys actually did overcome them). The boys discovered through their intellectual interaction with one another and the guidance of the therapist that their past conduct had brought them only short-term spurious gratifications leading eventually to pain and disaster, and they thus came to recognize the importance of selectivity in conduct and of self-control.

The evolution of these and a great many other lines of thought—as well as the emotional reliving of the past in the light of more mature per-spectives—are recorded step by step in the protocols of the seventy-five sessions of one group of seven boys fifteen to sixteen years of age. Thirty-four boys were involved in this part of our study, but we con-centrated on this particular group because it was one of the "delin-quency-saturated" groups for which membership was unselected. We accepted boys as they came.

Out of the welter of the ideas and thoughts suggested by the boys themselves after a trying and prolonged period of resistance ranging from distrust to violence, stubbornness to arrogance, and passivity to rowdyism, general observations emerged and some fundamental concepts were formulated. These are detailed in the record material of the group sessions, as well as in the theoretical part of this volume. Concepts like the *doom motif*, which we found to be characteristic of delinquent boys, the *onto-archaic mind* as differentiated from *new concepts*, various significances of the delinquent act, outer versus inner threats, and many others emerged. We have preserved in our records and reproduced in this volume the often vile language the boys employed. To do this was essential, for language mirrored the boys' conditions. They initially employed vulgar, obscene, and downright putrid words and images, which later gave way to a more cultured and even scientific vocabulary.

As a result of this work we have arrived at new and what seem to be basic conclusions. One of these, which is of paramount pertinence in attempts to rehabilitate asocial adolescents, is that their problems—complicated as they are in their organopsychosocial connotations—proceed in essence from their immaturity. Because of the manner in which the youngsters had been dealt with in their families, they remained fixated in early childhood or even infancy and showed the indiscriminate aggressions of the small child in his oral phase of development. It was therefore our problem to find means of advancing the psychologic maturity of our boys as part of the therapeutic efforts. Out of these efforts emerged what we term *para-analytic psychotherapy* (in our case "group" psychotherapy) and the *inversion technique*. These receive careful elucidation in the theoretical part of the book, but what is more important, in our view, is the detailed account of how these concepts gradually evolved and how they apply to therapy.

Every effort was made to make this book one of *utility to practitioners* and to mental hygienists. *It must be kept in mind throughout that the protocols of the sessions reflect the gradual unfolding of the personalities of the boys,* their evolving social and personal values, the steps by which they unraveled their confusions and evolved awareness of self and their motives. *As such the protocols are the core of this book* and, in our view, offer an unfailing armamentarium for the treatment and prevention of delinquency if properly and sensitively employed. It is for this reason that frequent reference to the protocols is made in subsequent pages. The aim is to impress the reader and the student of the importance of these protocols and thus motivate them to study these records *in toto* and in detail.

The Setting of the Study

It was with the attitudes and assumptions briefly outlined that the study of the applicability of group therapy in the residential treatment of "neglected" and "delinquent" adolescent boys was undertaken at The Children's Village early in 1957. The Children's Village is an open residential treatment center for emotionally disturbed, delinquent, and dependent boys. The court-committed boys are placed for indeterminate terms.

At the time when the study was undertaken, the institution operated through four major departments: Child Care; Child Guidance; Community (recreation and clubs) Center; and Education (school). Each of the departments was headed by a director, with a number of assistants and a working staff.

1. The Child Care Department consisted of a director, eight "child care supervisors," each in charge of two cottages, eight cottage-parent couples, and male "associate cottage parents" who relieved the regular cottage parents on their days off and during vacations.

There were sixteen resident cottages, each accommodating eighteen to twenty boys. The child care supervisors were professionally trained caseworkers whose function was to aid on a professional level the cottage parents, who were not so trained, toward better understanding and management of their charges.

2. The Child Guidance Department included, in addition to a director, a casework supervisor, four caseworkers, and a psychiatrist for each of four "cottage units." Each unit consisted of four cottages of boys of approximately the same age and school placement. A staff of psychologists was attached to this department.

3. The Community Center was in charge of a director who had a staff of specialists in club leadership, sports, gymnastics, free-time activities, and R.O.T.C.

4. The academic school, headed by a "School Counselor" (principal), had a complete staff of classroom teachers, a number of vocational and arts and crafts teachers, and a psychologist. This personnel was under the jurisdiction of the State of New York Departement of Education. Within the cottage units, students were grouped in accordance to their capacities for academic achievement.

Goals and Methods

The original aims of the Evaluation Project were *1]* to explore the applicability of Activity and Analytic Group Psychotherapies, as formulated by the present author, to residential treatment of delinquent boys; *2]* to derive judgments as to the responses of staff and the boys to these procedures; and *3]* to determine the effects of the freedom within the therapy groups on the total institutional community. Because each therapy group was initially planned to continue for the duration of one school year only, it was not envisaged that observable changes would occur in the boys either behaviorally or psychodynamically. However, as an afterthought, and to test the effectiveness of analytic group therapy, we extended the life of one of the analytic groups (C) to two years.[1] As indicated, the report on this group *in extenso* forms the body of this volume.

It was envisaged at the outset that departures from the standard or traditional group therapeutic techniques would probably be necessary to suit the particular boys in the Village setting and that procedures for "accountability" might have to be modified. A peripheral study introduced later was the evaluation of the response of mothers of the boys in the Children's Village to child-centered group guidance of parents[2] as part prevention and treatment of delinquency.[3]

After the five months during which the first groups met, the personnel involved in the project were impressed with the obvious improvements in the appearance and behavior of the boys in both activity and analytic groups, and especially with the absence of any negative effects on their conduct in the Village community. The group therapists—the caseworkers who had seen the boys on a reduced-frequency basis, the psychiatrists who had interviewed the boys periodically, the teachers, the cottage parents, and the child care supervisors—all reported impressive improvements in the boys' attitudes and behavior.[4] These changes, observed as they had been by independent sources, made it clear to us that the original research design to evaluate only *response* to group treatment ought to be extended to a study of the intrapsychic changes in the personalities of the group members. A facility for doing this was accordingly established to ascertain the effectiveness of the analytic type of group psychotherapy as a *therapeutic armamentarium* for work with delinquent adolescent boys.

1. This group, C, and also group D will be referred to as "demonstration" groups throughout this book. Groups A and B, which were limited to one school year in duration, will be identified as "observation" groups. All the boys in all the therapy groups were court-committed cases.

2. This guidance concept was formulated by the present author in his *Child-Centered Group Guidance of Parents* (New York: International Universities Press, 1958).

3. An attempt was made to organize such groups in various neighborhoods in New York, but the parents failed to respond and the plan was abandoned (see Chapter 9). Thus, no guidance or therapy for parents was available to buttress the treatment of the boys beyond occasional interviews with some parents by caseworkers after the boys' discharges from the Village, and these, too, were in most cases strenuously resisted by them.

4. These are described in this volume in the successive "progress reports" on each boy obtained from the various staff members, including psychological tests and psychiatric examinations. See Chapters 12, 14, 16, and 18.

The design of the evaluation closely paralleled the therapeutic process in the groups, this correlation being an essential characteristic of
"action research." The outline we projected consisted of eleven distinct
steps:

1. gathering of complete anamneses on each boy and his
family, including a social history;
2. obtaining information from the courts, hospitals, and social
agencies, including psychological and psychiatric reports and
diagnoses, and statements on the boy's precommitment problems;
3. studying Children's Village "work-up" and intake studies,
which included psychiatric and diagnostic evaluations and psychological tests (a) at the point of admission to the Village and
(b) at the point of joining the group;
4. studying the adjustment of each boy in his cottage, in the
school, in recreation, and in the (institutional) community at the
point of placement in a group;
5. studying the casework history at the Village and the boy's
attitudes and relations at the point of joining the group;
6. summarizing the recorded behavior of each boy at each
session of the group from the group therapist's protocols;
7. holding periodic "integration conferences" or follow-up
interviews with caseworkers, cottage staff, academic school personnel, and psychiatrists during each boy's career in the group;
8. studying adjustment of the boy in all the areas enumerated
above at the close of the group experience;
9. giving psychological tests at termination of the group and
comparing them with the initial tests at the time the boy joined
the group;
10. collating and arranging all material in sequence in temporal
and psychological relatedness;
11. editing and preparing each case with a view finally to
relating the group experience of each boy and its impact upon
him, with attention to whether that impact produced or failed to
produce desirable corrective results.[5]

The groups met once a week, the analytic groups for an hour and a
half and the activity groups for two hours.[6] Detailed process protocols
were dictated by the group therapists and transcribed by the secretarial
pool in time to reach the present writer (who planned and directed the
project and functioned as supervisor of the therapists) for review before
the next weekly group session. The protocols usually took eight to ten
double-spaced typewritten pages. These were analyzed in detail with
the respective group therapists in terms of the characteristic reactions of

5. Only one example of this sequence is given in this volume (see pp. 62-90).   6. Only the analytic groups are discussed in this volume, however.

each group member, the nature of his participation, and its meaning in terms of his "nuclear" problem and the positive or negative effects the group had on him. Nonverbal responses by act and grimace, as well as the interactions among the boys, received consideration, as did verbal formulations. These and other intangibles served as cues for the content of future sessions and were emphasized by the director of the project. However, because all responses and conduct on the part of therapists flow from their understanding of the total climate of the group and its various phenomenological aspects, the therapists' insights, attitudes, therapeutic orientation, value systems, and life philosophy (*Weltan-schauung*) also received consideration from the supervisor.

It is of utmost importance in work with groups where emotional intensification and contagion are unavoidable, especially in the potentially explosive setting of a commitment institution for disturbed adolescents, *to anticipate developments* and to prepare therapists to deal with eventualities. In the analytic groups, cues and clues had to be followed with precision and the therapists prepared to "pick up," "lead on," or "deflect" the interviews toward significant outcomes and conceptual formulations that would lay open feelings. Although the original plan was to devote one hour between group meetings to supervisory discussions of each session, very often these discussions extended to two and not infrequently to three hours, for it was not sufficient to confine analysis exclusively to that of the recorded reports. The nuances, the subtle reactions and interactions, and the latent content of verbalizations also had to be understood. This necessity invariably led to relating such nuances to sociological, anthropological, philosophical, and psychological concepts and formulations, and even to political and economic areas—all of which served to broaden the horizons of the therapists.

Unlike most other professionals, psychotherapists have to possess, in addition to sensitivity and perceptiveness, wide understandings and a catholicity in knowledge, which at first may seem unrelated but which actually are of inestimable help in clarifying the wide variety of patient's feelings and thinking. The concatenation of events in living and of the human condition had to be recognized and involved in the course of our group treatment. These recognitions and involvements are recorded in the protocols included in this volume.

The staff of the project consisted of the director, who, as already indicated, served also as supervisor of the group therapists; two therapists—one for the activity groups and another for the analytic groups—who were selected for their personality fitness after interviews with a number of the casework staff; a part-time research associate whose functions included summarizing group records for each boy and gathering information on them from various staff members; a leader for the mothers' guidance groups; a coordinator whose functions were to act as liaison with the Village staff and assume charge of all such arrangements as securing meeting rooms, purchasing materials for the activity groups, keeping accounts, coordinating the project with individual caseworkers as this became necessary, arranging conferences for the director of the study with professional and administrative staffs, and carrying out other administrative details; and a secretary to type records of the sessions, memoranda, and progress and other reports.[7]

Thirty-five boys initially referred by the casework staff as suitable for group therapy were reviewed in conference by the director and the referring caseworkers. Out of these, twenty-four were found suitable for therapy groups. Fourteen were chosen for immediate placement in either an "activity" or an "analytic" group. The remaining ten formed a pool from which would be drawn replacements should vacancies in the groups occur. The range of ages of the boys who were candidates for the activity group was from 10.6 to 12.6 years (from the "lower unit"). Boys from 13 to 14.6 years of age (from the "middle unit") became candidates for the analytic group.

Note must be taken that after the first, "observational," analytic groups, A and B, *no criteria for selection were employed for the later groups*, which were dubbed "delinquency saturated" by a staff member, and that the boys ranged around fifteen to sixteen years of age. The detailed studies of the actual process of one of these groups (C) will be found in other parts of this volume.

7. This function was assigned to the "secretarial pool" of the Village.

PART ONE

THEORY

Some Meanings
of the Delinquent Act

IT IS NOTEWORTHY that predelinquent and delinquent behaviors most often appear at the onset of puberty. In a large majority of cases the problems are first noted in school maladjustment and underachievement. Although in many instances delinquent boys (and many girls) have had histories of interpersonal conflicts and social maladjustments in their earlier years, their major difficulties set in at puberty and continue until they come to a head in the period customarily called "adolescent turmoil." This period is characterized by profound inner conflicts, uncertainties, and diffuse resentments. Much that parents and the community have attempted to inculcate becomes tenuous, doubtful, and endowed with negativism. In fact, so intense is this revision of feelings and values that the idea of a "psychosocial moratorium" (Erikson) has been suggested. Certainly great understanding and tolerance on the part of adults are needed to guide the adolescent through this period and into adulthood undamaged.

Developmental Crises

It may be of some benefit to approach these particular crises from the perspective of other crises that, in modern societies, the individual experiences during his development. Crises occur at specific periods in the psychosexual and psychosocial evolution of the individual, confronting him with new difficulties and sets of experiences, usually accompanied by anxieties of varying intensities. If these difficulties are dealt with appropriately, they are either sloughed off or incorporated healthfully into the final character structure of the individual. Crises are inescapable in the orderly development of the human personality, for they are byproducts of, and inherent in, organic, psychic, and social maturation. Some of these crises have distinct characters and fall into one of two categories: *developmental* and *relationship* crises.

The former arise from the sequence in organic development; the latter, which are inevitable and essential for the individual's personality formation and for his survival as a social unit, arise from his relationships with others. As maturational and social elements coincide in point of time and quality of response, some crises fall indistinctly between the two types, and others belong to both.

Because the second category is scrutinized throughout this work, we shall concentrate our discussion at this juncture on developmental crises. First among these crises is the so-called "birth trauma," which is believed by "depth" psychologists to result from the shock and attendant *organic anxiety* of the sudden change from the prenatal to the neonatal physical milieu. Those who are inclined toward this holistic concept of the unity of the biological and the psychological (as well as the cultural) life hold, with seeming justification, that the birth trauma is a major crisis in the psycho-organic experience of the individual—one that is intensified by the slapping of the newborn infant to induce breathing via crying and by the handling of him by doctors and nurses.

The second observable crisis is the so-called "eight-month anxiety" of the baby. At this stage he displays increased sensitivity to stimuli and envinces fear and keener responsiveness, with marked signs of anxiety. The causes of this phase are obscure, but we can assume that, because of neuronic maturation, awareness of the external world and reactions to it are intensified. Objects, persons, and phenomena are seen as new and strange and therefore cause anxiety. At this period and until he becomes accustomed to the impact of the external world and especially to the impact of persons upon him, the baby requires special protection and security measures. Through such measures, the basis for a healthy personality is laid. The attitudes, responsiveness, and manner of the adults who are handling the baby physically become even more egoplastic once this increase in sensitivity has set in.

Perhaps the most crucial developmental crisis, as far as future adaptations to social and interpersonal relations are concerned, is the "two-year negativism." This is the phase in development at which the monosyllable "no" becomes predominant in the child's vocabulary. The word is, however, not merely symbolic of the child's general self-assertiveness, of his insistence upon having his own way, of having things according to his whims. It is symbolic of the beginnings of individuation, the dawn of awareness of *self*, with diminishing dependencies and conscious assertiveness emerging as a result of increases in organopsychic strengths. This period—a trying one for the parents—usually extends into the fourth year of the child's life and presents mothers, especially, with trials and tensions. The manner in which the child's strivings for individuation and assertiveness are dealt with at this critical period of his normative development, despite the irritations they cause, lays the foundations for interpersonal relations in the family and later in the larger world. The foundations for relatedness and isolation, hostility and friendliness that characterize adult relations are determined certainly to a telling degree at this early period.

The Oedipal conflict, a result of the child's perceiving his parents not as separate, unrelated individuals but as a couple in an intimate relation, is the next psychic crisis, which begins at about the age of four or five years. So much has been written about this particular phase and its importance and about the role each parent plays in the emotional organization of the future adult that we shall omit even a cursory consideration of it here. This period is followed by a latency period, when the child assimilates his infantile identifications and self-perceptions and moves out of the family circle toward a new identity. This is also the period of accelerated intellectual growth, or cerebration.

At twelve years or thereabouts the Oedipal urges begin to reappear, but they now assume a different character. In the earlier Oedipal period the parent of the opposite sex is the child's "sexual aim," and the other parent is a restraining, threatening symbol. In this second period the feelings for the opposite-sex parent as "sexual object" have strong incestuous overtones. The same-sex parent therefore becomes an ally to whom the child ambivalently turns as a defense against his prohibited, anxiety-evoking incestuous urges, and a new type of identification takes place. At fifteen or sixteen and until the individual reaches young adulthood, these feelings grow to a climax. Defenses against them are sought in the extrafamilial arena, first in homoerotic relations and later in drives toward heterosexual outlets.

Of all the tensions during the various developmental crises, those that appear at adolescence are the most disturbing to the subject and the most threatening to adults. This fact is due partly to the psychodynamics of adolescence, but even more to the interpersonal and social implications that stem from them. Some of the characteristics that dominate the youth during this transitional period are *1]* fluid and shifting identifications which require alignment because of his changing role and his place in society, since the new position enhances his susceptibility to emotional infection; *2]* the sharpening conflict between dependence and the changing image of himself as an independent entity; *3]* the conflict between his "reproductive and inadequacy constellations" (Spotnitz), for

while the sexual (reproductive) drive makes its appearance with a compelling urge, the boy is uncertain of his potency and the girl is unsure of
her capacity to function adequately as a mother; *4]* homoerotic
responses, as a defense against feelings of inadequacy, which progressively yield to heterosexual inclinations and are accompanied by guilt
(since the basic sexual urges are directed toward the parent of the opposite sex, who unconsciously abets them); and *5]* the flight of the
adolescent into the peer group as a means of self-protection and as a
defensive maneuver.

Dealing with the Adolescent

The most direct threat that adolescents offer to society stems from
this flight into the peer group. It is the grouping of adolescents that holds
the most serious challenge to the constituted social order. Adolescent
groups are the most cohesive in our society. Because adolescents are preoccupied with, and are motivated by, many of the same strong needs and
impulses, in groups they manifest a high level of empathy and mutual
identification. Emotional *induction, interstimulation,* and the resulting
emotion and action *intensification* are correspondingly high, as is susceptibility to emotional *infection.* This leads to group and even mass
synergy, and should this synergic quality turn to aggression, it can
seriously threaten the orderly pursuits of adult society.

To be constructive and socially wholesome, a group must contain
among its number *neutralizers,* who exert a balancing influence upon it
and diminish its overintensified synergic activity or urge. This process
we have described as *neutralization.*[1] Groups lacking such factors to neu-
tralize the basic aggressions and resentments of congregated adolescents
become impulse ridden, acting out entities which are a threat to law,
order, mores, and tradition. The evil in this situation lies in the fact that
adults and their constituted regulative agencies deal with these manifestations repressively and punitively, with both individuals and groups.
What is needed, instead, is to normalize these aggregates by a planful
shift in centrality from destructive to constructive leadership, which can
be provided, in part, by personally equipped and educationally qualified
adults such as teachers, recreationists, and social group leaders. They can
not only direct the groups into constructive channels, but can also serve
as neutralizers to hostile and aggressive urges.

1. For a further elaboration of these other group dynamics see S. R. Slavson, *Character Education in a Democracy* (New York: Association Press, 1939), Chapter IV; or Slavson, *A Textbook of Analytic Group Psychotherapy,* (New York: International Universities Press, 1964), Chapter II.

Adults, by and large, refuse to accept the fact of futility in repressive measures and blanket punishments, which obviously fail. The community insists on these traditional approaches, which have their origins among primitive societies as well as in the basic, pervasive hostility in man. The assertiveness of the early adolescent was cut short in primitive societies. The younger teenagers were sequestered from the community, starved for prolonged periods, then circumcised en masse. These ritualistic practices, supervised and executed by the constituted authority of the gens or clan, were palpable assertions that the youth was not an independent entity, an island to himself, but belonged to his society (gens or clan). After the completion of these sadistic, humiliating, and impotenizing (castrating) rituals, the youngster was fully accepted into the fraternity of the males in his community.[2] He had equal status with his elders in the "men's house" and participated on an equal basis with them in hunts and wars.

Obviously, civilized societies cannot employ such stringent methods of subduing the rebellious spirit of youth. But our current attitude of suspicion toward adolescents is not in consonance with civilized living. The fact that the very word *adolescent* implies an onus and stigma in our unconscious deserves exploration.

Adults' Attitudes toward Adolescents

The reawakened incestuous strivings of adolescents toward their parents in Western society do not continue unrequited. In the unconscious of parents, too, there are present sexual urges toward their children. In the vast majority of people these are repressed, but they are frequently evinced in "innocent" jokes and "teasing"; in unwarranted interest in the amorous affairs of teenage offspring; in unmistakably provocative maneuvers, such as playfulness, wrestling, and in other forms of bodily contact; and in less obviously seductive attitudes and acts. In extreme cases incestuous wishes are actually acted out. Thus the defensive, reactive aggressions against prohibited urges and feelings are not limited to youth alone; they are present also in adults, and punitiveness often stems from them as a denial of these guilt-evoking feelings.

There is also unmistakable jealousy and envy on the part of adults toward younger people; they are jealous of the young people's virility,

2. In some tribes beheading a member of an enemy tribe or the killing of an edible wild animal singlehanded was also required. Obviously the aim was to assure the tribe's survival. The "con-firmation" rituals among Christians and *bar mizvah* among Jews at the end of pubertal years are survivals of the ritualistic practices of these earlier societies.

their zest for life and capacity for enjoyment, and the fact that life, experience, and pleasures are still ahead of them. An added element in this situation is the fact that parents are likely to remember their own adolescence vividly. In their minds are the suppressions and prohibitions to which they were subjected and the guilt they felt at that period of their lives as a result of committing "prohibited" acts and entertaining "bad" thoughts. Consequently, some pass on their confused feelings to their children, while others seek to deny those feelings by repressive measures against their offspring. The underlying resentment and distrust which result from these conflicting inner states are very intense indeed. However, the conflict between children and their elders stems also from the fact that children live in the present, while their parents envisage current events in the perspective of the past.

The cultural residue of the primitive's ways of dealing with adolescents that persists in modern society is one of harshness, but the status affirmation and group acceptance afforded to youth in the past are not forthcoming in current cultures. It is characteristic of Western technological cultures to nurture the dependencies of children rather than to encourage independence and self-reliance. Whether in the home or school or in the community, adults plan and legislate for, and direct, children and young people, who are forced into the role of recipients of "benevolence" and protection at the price of obedience, conformity, and submission.

Prolongation of obvious dependency is particularly damaging to the adolescent because it re-enforces his "inadequacy constellation"; it brings into focus the very feelings of "self" of which he wishes to be rid, namely, inadequacy and weakness. It is, therefore, understandable that adolescents should be filled with resentment and rage, and that they should indulge in retaliatory and self-maximization fantasies and acts— acts which are greatly intensified and exaggerated in the so-called delinquent.

Social Status of Adolescents

One of the striking features of our culture is that adolescents are, to all intents and purposes, the forgotten segment of the community. While young children occupy a special *protected status* and adults an *authority status*, adolescents have no defined position in current society. One adolescent boy, accused of an infraction of the codes of the institution in which he resided, complained that younger boys were "protected" by the staff, while the older boys had no status: "The kids are protected here. We are on our own. We have to take care of ourselves."

Adolescents have neither protection nor authority nor any other status of their own. This leaves them without anchor or function or feeling of belonging to the community, giving rise to understandable rancor which serves as an added source of resentment and aggression. This lack of social status is one factor that drives adolescents into compact group associations of their own that meet their needs for status and belonging, in addition to giving them a (transient) identity.

Western society has continued the primitive's authoritarian aspect of control of adolescence, but has not adopted or adapted the second aspect of their practice, *status affirmation.* One way in which adolescents' tensions can be reduced and the incidence of violence diminished is to give them status and respect. Family, school, recreation groups, and community might very easily find means to do so if adults would rid themselves of their fantasies of superiority (by virtue of age and experience) and of their distrust and latent hostility toward the young. Participation and responsibility are not only the preconditions for emotional maturity, but are also indispensable in eliminating or reducing tensions.

In a project to rehabilitate adolescent delinquent boys and girls in a residential setting (with no facilities for direct psychotherapy or guidance), introduced in 1934, the technique of status affirmation proved of singular effectiveness. Despite the fact that the residents were in the throes of a violent riot of six weeks' duration, calm group controls and cooperation emerged in a matter of a few days and later led to self-imposed group discipline. In less than a year the social and creative activities of an institution housing about 190 boys and girls were largely planned and conducted by them, with staff members serving only in advisory and supervisory capacities.

The significant element in this development was that the most delinquent and most violent boy, aged sixteen, became the leading force in establishing law and order in the school community. Before the transition from adult control and discipline to pupil participation was made he had physically attacked adult staff members and was the mastermind of three small gangs who broke into and stole from staff apartments. Despite the efforts of staff and state police, the young perpetrators could not be identified. The gang leader not only dissolved his own predatory groups but, through his physical strength and superior status with the boys, ended *all* acts of vandalism and destructiveness. He was able to accomplish this more readily, however, since the attitudes of the entire population, including staff, had grown more friendly and benign.[3]

This reaction can be understood in sociological terms as a response to being accepted by the staff and community: The boys and girls were,

3. Slavson, *Re-educating the Delinquent through Group and Community Participation* (New York: Harper and Brothers, 1954; Collier Books, 1961).

therefore, able to accept the milieu in which they lived. Such is the case in any democratically conducted group or society. But the life pattern that emerged was also the result of a changed self-perception, a new identity—temporary as it may have been in some instances—because the adults *trusted* the youngsters; the desire to be "trusted" was a major theme in the interviews of the groups with which the present volume deals.

Of no small value in effecting the change was the fact that, as the frustrating and punitive operations by staff were eliminated, the adolescents' accumulated hostilities and vengefulness decreased, and finally were entirely eliminated in nearly all of them. Once their status and self-identities in relation to their environment changed, they grew inwardly free to assume a new role in daily life.

Parents, teachers, and recreationists overlook vast opportunities to foster self-reliance and responsibility potentials in the young by failing, beginning with early childhood, to accord them the *respect* they need and to which they are entitled, and by failing to have faith in their latent capacities. From very early years children can, and should, take on responsibilities of graded difficulties and complexities so that their powers and judgment and, above all, their self-esteem are strengthened.

Sources of Adolescent Hostility

Facts can be taught, but character must be demonstrated. Character is built like a painting. A work of art is painted by minute and often imperceptible strokes, and it is the minutiae of living and experiencing that mold the human personality. But it is customary for adults to concentrate on the gross and massive, forgetting that participation and responsibility in small matters beget the strength and maturity for larger concerns later in life.

The feelings toward adults that the boy and girl carry into adolescence determine relations between them, and the resulting attitudes are transferred to school, peers, and society generally through the herostratic (displacement) tendency. Noxious attitudes especially are carried over to the therapeutic encounter between the adolescent and his therapist. The essential ingredients of therapeutic effectiveness are the transferential feelings of the patient toward his therapist, his trust and suspicions, his love and hate, his anger, his realities and his fantasies. These he redirects from the adults in his past and displaces upon the therapist, projecting upon the latter the images the youth has internalized and inadequately tested in reality. By and large, the images lodged in his unconscious range from negative to insidious. At best, the adolescent's unconscious automatically perceives adults' attitudes of mistrust and wariness toward him and recognizes their defensive restrictions and suppressions of his strivings for individuality. He perceives adults as agents bent on denying pleasures and frustrating consummation of sexual urges, which are now at their height. He views adults as determined to restrict his awakening strivings for self-direction and autonomy. While the adolescent attempts to defend himself against infantile strivings, he also feels with increasing anxiety the strain and pressures of making his way into the wider world of which he knows he must become a part.

It is understandable that the adolescent should view adults and their world with suspicion and hostility—and these attitudes he also carries over into the therapeutic relation. This condition often creates an insurmountable impediment to individual psychological treatment, for the teenager views the therapist as a replica and representative of his natural enemies, the adults and their world. The adolescent finds it sometimes almost impossible and always difficult to enter into the close and warm emotional relation required in individual psychotherapy. Instead of the transference being basically positive with periodic exacerbations of negative feelings, which is the normal course in psychotherapy, the transference in the treatment of adolescents tends to be predominantly negative, thus rendering therapy a tenuous and often indifferent experience. Group therapy resolves some of these difficulties because, in a group, the therapist is not the libidinal focus, as is the case in individual treatment. The group provides a milieu of benignly disposed peers in empathic relation, with an element of commonality, sharing, and mutual support.

Another element that obstructs therapy with adolescents lies in their defensiveness against feelings of inadequacy, their fear of being damaged. During the transitional period from childhood to adulthood the personality is in a nascent state, identifications are fluid, and powers have still not reached their fullness. There is doubt about sexual and social adequacy, and self-regard is at a low ebb. To a large extent the adolescent adopts as a defense against these self-doubts a stance of self-maximization and employs antiphobic attitudes of omnipotence so that he may maintain an image of strength. He thus wards off hopelessness and depression. To admit to doubts, vacillation, conflicts, and especially inability to deal with problems on his own, and to have to seek help, constitutes a source of severe narcissistic injury against which the adolescent defends himself. This complex of feelings constitutes one of the main sources of resistance to therapy, only second in intensity to the rise of awareness of inadequacy.

Apart from the almost negligible number of constitutionally predisposed individuals who are unable to adjust to the restrictions of social living and who of necessity adopt an asocial life pattern, delinquency is shaped during the impressional and formative years by excessive and virulent errors of parents, schools, the regulative agencies in the community, by the mass media of communications, and by the profit-motivated pandering of private entrepreneurs.

Gradations in "Delinquency"

For effective treatment and control of delinquency, the generic term "delinquent" needs to be understood in its psychodynamic and sociolegalistic meanings. The term as commonly employed in the United States[4] refers to an individual who violates the sense of propriety or breaks the constituted laws of a given population living under a specific consensus as to probity, legality, and normality. Young persons whose acts are so deviant or destructive in their effect as to present a problem to the community are stamped as "delinquent." But to understand adequately the sociodynamics and psychodynamics of these phenomena, a differentiation has to be made between *incorrigibles, vandals,* and *delinquents.*

Incorrigibles are the nonconforming, disobedient to the authorities who by tradition are in control, such as parents, teachers, and the police. In the category of vandalism fall acts of destruction of property belonging to individuals or the municipality which have no significance or aim beyond the act itself. Within certain limits, incorrigibility and vandalism are part of growing up. If not too violent and prolonged, a modicum of incorrigibility is expected as inherent in the process of individuation—of becoming an independent, self-reliant individual. It is a step toward throwing off submission and dependence, and if exercised within limits leads to a rather constructive maturity. Only when incorrigibility is overintense and persistent, when flaunting authority and disregard for all regulative principles in interpersonal and social living become a life style, does it threaten the integrity of the evolving individual and become a potential threat to the group. Ego strengths and sturdy character reflect inner controls against such "acting out" which originally derived from internalizing outer controls from significant persons. Every child does this, if the controls are not applied too severely and too peremptorily. For psychic maturity, both obedience and rebellion in proper balance and relationship are essential. When disobedience or rebellion becomes a

4. In England the term designates the deviant behavior of adults as well, to which the appellation of "criminal" is given in the United States.

permanent life pattern and extends to areas that undermine the healthy development of the personality through self- and social alienation it can be considered undesirable.

As already indicated, vandalism is an act of destruction of property which has no discernible aim beyond the destructive act itself. However, a deeper look at such acts reveals that vandalism serves as an exhaust for overflowing unconscious and sometimes conscious anger against real or fancied oppression, cruelty, and injustice. It is in a real sense a mental-health safety valve. The destructiveness usually appears in isolated acts and can be tolerated when mild and infrequent; but when it becomes a set and habitual pattern of violence, it ultimately leads to delinquency. Therefore, should correctives be indicated on the part of society, they should be directed not toward the acts as such, but rather toward the intrapsychic sources from which they flow.

"Delinquency" may be understood as having one of two meanings: it may be confined to occasional acts legally defined as "delinquent," or it may refer to a set pattern of personality organization. The delinquent act serves to discharge inner tensions in defiance of individuals who represent the prevailing code of society. The psychological significance of such acts will be explored elsewhere in this volume; indeed, it has been studied by many writers and investigators before. Here we shall consider the delinquent act in the light of its meaning in interpersonal and intrasocial phenomenology.

By its very nature the delinquent act abrogates the codes that regulate conduct as it relates to and affects other humans in the environment. Whether the acts result in injury to persons, as in assault, or involve property, as in stealing and robbery, they endanger the welfare of the community and, therefore, action is taken by the community to block and prevent recurrence. In other types of disturbing acts, less concerted and less rigid steps are taken by society as compared with the steps taken against delinquency, because delinquency is most often the forerunner of adult crime. In considering delinquency it is necessary to differentiate between the legalistic and psychological meanings of the term. The traditional legal criterion for delinquency is the antisocial act. The psychological approach embraces the motivations and the intrapsychic states that produce them. In the course of development from childhood to adulthood, few are innocent of having at some time or another committed an act or acts that can be appropriately characterized as delinquent, just as each has also sometime in his life been incorrigible and may occasionally have committed an act of vandalism. In the orderly development of the personality inner needs for such acts are sloughed off, and the individual then pursues a socially acceptable life pattern. There are some, however, whose life conditions so anchor them to deviant behavior in their character organization that they are propelled toward asocial or antisocial conduct.

All three unsocial patterns of conduct—incorrigibility, vandalism, and delinquency—are derived in the first instance from the assertiveness and individuation trends. All three serve the child's and adolescent's needs to project his individuality, detach himself from dependencies, and attain self-identity. While the delinquent act has a variety of meanings, its major significance is that the individual seeks self-identity through it. One who commits an isolated antisocial act is not of necessity psychologically a delinquent, nor can all who are addicted to such acts be treated alike. Unlike the criminologist and the penologist, who concentrate on behavior and its effects on others, the psychoclinician directs his attention to psychic sources of behavior, its conscious and its unconscious significance. It may be more correct to differentiate between "delinquents" and persons who commit "delinquent acts." Delinquent acts may be committed only as irregular reactions to intolerable and morbid life conditions, and given up as the stress factors are eliminated or diminished; for the true delinquent, however, committing such acts is a way of life emanating from the structure and cravings of the personality.

Elementaristic versus Holistic Approach

An "elementaristic" (J. M. Murray), as differentiated from a holistic, approach to a problem is one which views the problem in the light of the *elements* and forces inherent in it. An illustration is found in nuclear physics and chemistry. As long as physicists adhered to the doctrine propounded by the Greek philosophers that the "atomics" were the primary indivisible unit of the physicochemical world, they were prevented from carrying forward their endeavors. Rutherford's discoveries of the elements that make up the atom opened to the scientist new and immensely important vistas. Since that investigation revealing the proton, electron, and neutron within the atom, even smaller particles have been found in subsequent decades, giving the scientific worker not only better insights, but also incomparably more effective means for utilizing nature's forces.

Such an elementaristic approach is of vast importance also to the solution of problems of the sociologist and the psychoclinician. As in medical practice, the curative steps the psychotherapist takes are determined by the presence of specific elements involved in the pathologic complex and their interaction and influences upon each other. The enlightened psychotherapist does not overlook life setting and the "total personality." To be effective, he needs also to understand the patient's milieu and its effect upon his development, to view the patient in his historic perspective in assessing his strengths and weaknesses. Nonetheless, the major attention of the psychotherapist will always be focused upon those noxious forces that contribute to, or constitute, the pathology. While a holistic view of the total somatopsychosocial phenomenology is of great help in planning and conducting psychotherapy, too wide an inclusiveness and blanket formulations, even with regard to diagnoses, may obscure the elementaristic intrapsychic conditions that require therapeutic attention and resolution.

The elementaristic approach needs to be employed with persons who have become victims of an antisocial life pattern. Enlightened criminologists have come to recognize that delinquent acts, consistently repeated, have a variety of sources within each individual and peculiar to him. Criminotic and delinquent behavior may be a means for discharging overriding hostile, retaliatory feelings against society (as a displacement of feelings toward parents and other persons in authority—which we referred to as the herostratic tendency); it may resolve inner conflicts, fulfill a neurotic need to be punished, act as ego and superego defense, serve as a means for gaining status and recognition, compensate for a deflated self-esteem, or give a feeling of self-identity through the grandiosity implicit in the delinquent act. Antisocial behavior is frequently a means of fulfilling an unconscious wish of a parent, or a demonstration to denigrating parents of a child's ability for achievement (in this case by flouting authority), despite their lack of confidence in his powers. Sometimes delinquency represents an effort to gain attention (love) from an otherwise rejecting parent, usually the mother.

The challenge of authority involved in delinquency counteracts feelings of weakness and inadequacy and instead generates fantasies of power and strength. A boy with feminine identification or one with feelings of impotence may indulge in delinquent acts to satisfy a neurotic, impelling need to create the illusion of himself as adequate and potent. A girl whose identity is one of being undesirable or unattractive is likely to become a sexual delinquent and join antisocial gangs, both as a denial of her feelings and as a means for attaining status. An emotionally deprived girl may become a sexual delinquent as a consequence of an unfulfilled craving for tenderness and acceptance. Delinquent acts may be a natural development in a life pattern of ingratiation, submission, and masochistic, self-punishing needs. In girls, unconscious masculine strivings, with feelings of castration and the resulting sense of incompleteness are among the many reasons for entering upon the path of delinquency as a way of correcting a defective self-image.

The striving for status among friends and playfellows in the neighborhood or school group serves as a legitimate motive for attention-getting and bizarre behavior. Youngsters come by their delinquency in a "natural way," as a result of the character-forming influences and adaptive needs in the family and the neighborhood, which at once mold the ego and determine its functioning. These deviancies are further buttressed by value systems of peer groups and the rationale prevalent in the microculture. Where the desire for status and a feeling of belonging (social hunger) is more easily satisfied by antisocial acts and values, such values will be incorporated by the child and will permanently stamp (imprint) the complexion of his personality. Delinquent "character" may also stem from constitutional and organic deficits, defects, and abnormalities, such as diminutive size, various organ deformities and inferiorities, mental deficiency, epilepsy, or schizophrenia and other psychotic states.

Delinquent acts, especially vandalism committed against property, incorrigibility, and stealing frequently have a restitutive character. The underlying attitude of large numbers of delinquents, verbalized in group discussions, was that what they had done was their right. They sometimes specified, and always implied, that they had been deprived of their just due, and that their acts served to compensate for these deprivations. Laying aside for the moment the deeper psychic meanings and determinants of this restitutive attitude, its conscious sources have a socioeconomic base, as well. Contemporary economic perquisites and differential standards have an important conscious and unconscious effect upon the individual's expectations of what he considers to be his right. If the degree of social permissiveness generally sanctioned for attaining pleasures and status is not adequately available to the less economically or culturally favored, the deprivation begets resentment. This resentment may overflow in the committing of antisocial acts. The delinquent act satisfies the narcissistic, acquisitive needs of the child—needs that are strengthened by affect deprivation. As is well known, stealing by a child, especially when it involves the mother's possessions, has the implicit meaning of taking the love which has been denied him.

Delinquency, therefore, can be normal, accidental, neurotic, or psychotic. Where the normal code of the general culture and value systems of a community or the microcultures of the home and the neighborhood condition the individual in a type of behavior that is antisocial in character, delinquency can be viewed as normal. In view of the fact that human behavior and character are molded by the inexorable influences, pressures, and demands of the environment, the resulting product cannot but be rationally viewed as normal. When a criminotic or delinquent act is episodic or is the result of special pressing or temptational circumstances, traditionally such an isolated misconduct is, in modern, more humanistic penological practice, overlooked. Courts dismiss such cases of "first offenders" or where "extenuating circumstances" exist.

When criminal or delinquent acts stem from neurotic conflicts or tensions and serve unconscious needs, the perpetrator of such acts can be classified as a neurotic delinquent requiring corrective professional intervention. Similarly, when antisocial acts and attitudes are determined by nonvolitional organic or psychic pathology, the culprit is viewed and treated as a sick person, and in certain instances sequestration may be indicated. Whatever the classification, and insofar as the antisocial act serves the individual who commits it as satisfaction of an inner need or as a relief from tension and stress, it is *clinically* viewed as auspicious and as a form of self-therapy.[5]

Treatment of "Delinquents"

The correction of the personality organization of the delinquent can be achieved in some instances through a planned, conditioned milieu in which the prevalent human relations and the total social climate counteract the noxious attitudes and impulses and cause the latter to wither, as it were, by disuse; the other procedure involves a psychotherapeutic regimen through which intrapsychic changes are effected, disposing the individual toward more benign attitudes and feelings, through resolving conflicts and engendering a more wholesome identity.

In actuality, both approaches conducted simultaneously are needed for effective and lasting results. However, the first procedure, commonly referred to as "milieu therapy," is suitable for persons whose deviant behavior is a reaction to unfavorable life conditions and where the need for such behavior has as yet not been internalized—that is, it has not become *structured in character*. Various mild character disorders, such as faulty identifications, may respond favorably to a conditioned environment. In such instances, the experiencing of friendly and comforting relations and the feeling of being accepted alter attitudes and the "feeling tone," resulting in a more favorable and more integrated personality.[6] However, where resentments and hostilities have been structured in the psyche through prolonged repetition of traumata with intense affect and conflict, psychotherapy in addition to a therapeutic social climate is necessary. This relation will become clear from the main part of our study. We have found that properly conducted group psychotherapy can

5. See also section entitled "Identification, Identity, and Alienation," p. 34 *et seq.*
6. See Slavson, *Re-educating the Delin-* *quent through Group and Community Participation.*

counteract even deeply ingrained neurotically virulent attitudes in adolescents and render the youths capable of enduring and dealing with the unwisdom and hostility of adults in an unfriendly milieu.

The essential characteristic of this therapy consists of engendering attitudes, transferentially, that favor assimilation of components of the therapeutic experience and the giving up of paranoid-like sensitivity and impulsivity. The central aim in the treatment of delinquent youth is to motivate them toward change. This can be achieved only if they can be made to recognize, and consciously accept, a *purpose* in the treatment. Without this state of mind, therapy may be well-nigh impossible. The establishment of a favorable attitude toward the treatment situation should, therefore, be the first concern of the therapist. Primarily, this attitude flows from positive transferential feelings, but it is also determined by the setting in which the corrective effort is attempted. For example, relations, aims and process are at great variance when therapy is conducted on an in-patient basis, in an out-patient clinic, in a private office, in a military setting, or in restraining institutions such as prisons or so-called industrial (reform) schools. The inherent elements in each are in a measure different, and factors secondary or incidental in one setting may be of major or primary importance in another.

However, it is not the setting alone that determines attitudes toward psychotherapy and inner change. Character rigidities, neurotic defensiveness, insecurity, and the value system to which each individual is subject play even more important parts. These can be dissolved and altered only through a specific relation and a specific process, the description of which forms the bulk of this study. But because we are concerned here with the corrective process in residential treatment or school communities, some thought need be given to the structure and quality of a school community and the quality and qualifications of the persons who staff it. At the moment, our task is to single out and describe the direct, clinical psychotherapeutic procedures that have proven effective with the type of boy under consideration. It need be said, though, that the setting of the school community envisaged here, one which would buttress and make clinical effort most fruitful, should conform to the general principles of a true democracy, which are freedom, status, participation, and responsibility.

FREEDOM

The degree of freedom permitted must obviously be graded in a progressive manner to accord with the readiness of the residents to make constructive use of it for their growth and the creation of a wholesome social milieu. Freedom in a democracy does not mean blanket license to act out impulsively. Controlled spontaneity is both a sign of maturity in an individual and the source of a rich and colorful body politic. Individual freedom must always be conditioned by the freedom, convenience, and happiness of others. Limitations to liberty are inherent in all group and mass living, and emphasis must be made on this fact in re-education, both in the setting and in the discussion.

STATUS

A corrective environment must provide status for the individual, and a feeling of self-value. One's natural trends to self-regard as an individual entity and as a social organism must be adequately supported. Some of the means by which esteem can be provided are through satisfying occupations, the opportunity for successful achievement, and the feeling that one is an acceptable and respected part of the community. It is not enough to provide facilities and activities. The aim should be to engender the feelings of importance and belonging that active and honest participation yields. The attitude of the staff in this matter is a determining factor. Resentful, punitive, or derogatory attitudes, even if well concealed, counter the recuperative trends of children and young people; they rather intensify hostility and negative attitudes.

PARTICIPATION

True democratic living is achieved through spontaneous, as well as planned, participation in the life of the school community, in constructive living relationships, and in supportive educational and creative activities. Reconstructive participation must be genuine. Pretensions at democracy may prove more detrimental than frank authoritarianism. Frankness gives the residents security. Pseudo-democracy, wherein the decisions of the group are manipulated behind the scenes or are reversed, vetoed, or negated by persons in authority, creates insecurity and, what is even more destructive, resentment. It militates against a full-hearted feeling of belonging and trust. For practical reasons, democratic participation may have to be encouraged in specific areas of the school-community life and withheld or modified in others as expediency and readiness of participants indicate, but to whatever extent or areas it is employed, democracy must be genuine and honest.

RESPONSIBILITY

Responsibility, whether in the home or in the community, is a product of social living. Normally, a well-ordered home provides this as a beginning. Later other group experiences in schools and in the larger community help this process through work and play and through the demands and limitations imposed during an active group life. Reconditioning the personality and motivating it to act responsibly constitute, perhaps, the major tangible aim in rehabilitating the criminotic individual. But attention needs be given to the fact that responsibility cannot be inculcated by direct means. It is, rather, a by-product of specific attitudes and values in the *process* of living.

2

First Steps
and Early Observations

Some Mechanisms of Our Boys

ACTIVITY GROUP THERAPY, which is based upon unimpeded acting out, can be expected to prove disturbing to an institutional milieu, since there is the possibility that the young residents may carry over the impulsive and random behavior from the group to the institutional community and create disturbances in the cottages, school, and on the campus generally. The result of this could be a climate full of tensions and disorganization, with adverse effects upon the therapeutic atmosphere of a residential treatment facility. Freedom, though essential in therapy, can be constructive only when it is practiced upon a background of orderly and organized community life. When serious stresses prevail, neither clinical nor milieu therapy efforts can be effective.[1] It could also have been expected that the boys in interview (analytic) groups would hesitate to reveal their shabby backgrounds, ignoble acts, and deviant impulses and strivings in the presence of fellow residents.[2]

Socially deviant acts generate guilt in the neurotic, for they are ego-alien and, therefore, give rise to guilt and remorse. To our boys, this

1. This caution proved unfounded. Instead, the boys who had been carefully chosen for activity therapy groups by standard criteria have uniformly shown behavioral and character improvement. We plan to report these developments in a separate volume.

2. This assumption was made as a result of an experience with one group of adolescent girls in a re-educative, co-educational correctional institution. The girls, in this case, rigidly defended themselves against revealing their personal lives, their backgrounds, and past behavior that might have affected their status in the school community. See S. R. Slavson, *Analytic Group Psychotherapy* (New York: Columbia University Press, 1950), Chapter XIII.

behavior was acceptable to the ego and superego; that is, it was ego-syntonic. Under ordinary circumstances, a patient who is not normally guilt prone is not accepted for psychoanalytically oriented out-patient group therapy, for it is usually impossible to make any inroad into his psyche and reconstitute it along more benign lines. To reach our boys we found it necessary to make drastic modifications in our traditional techniques, though still retaining their essential nature. The outcome of these modifications is a system which we term "para-analytic" group psychotherapy.

The boys viewed their destructive, antisocial, and often brutal acts with ease and surface calm and recounted them with bravado. They seemed to derive an image of self-worth and a feeling of status through the voluminous and graphic narrations at the group discussions of orgies and escapades in which they had participated. For a time this indulgence was puzzling, until it occurred to us that, having failed to establish a self-identity in the past through early family relations, and with no other sources at hand for deriving corrective identifications later in life, the extraordinary nature of the behavior that made the boys stand out and attract attention in their environment served to give them a feeling of self, a (special) identity. Another outstanding characteristic that appeared to be universal among our boys was an inordinate tendency to project blame upon persons and conditions in their environment for the very conduct of which they seemed so proud, and a seemingly complete unawareness of their own part in such conduct.

While American adolescents in the subculture[3] from which our boys were drawn are generally devoid of contemplation or introspection, our boys seemed particularly illiterate in matters of psychologic understanding. The compelling need to project defensively and displace and the absence of even a most rudimentary effort at understanding proved to be the greatest blocks to our therapeutic effort for which we had to find a solution. As we worked with these boys, it became compellingly obvious that, as long as they continued in these projective attitudes of blaming others and thus remained unable to recognize and *accept* their parts

3. All the boys in our para-analytic groups came from low-income, socially disadvantaged homes, usually with crowded living quarters, in congested, squalid neighborhoods. (The one exception was the son of a middle-class white-collar worker whose parents had a higher level of education. This boy, however, was not a member of the "demonstration group" with which this volume predominantly deals.) As will be seen from the case histories (Chapter 8), the families from which our boys came were devoid of cultural influences, of exposures to art, even of the most primitive nature, and lacked an ideational and ideological climate. The boys were reared in atmospheres of varying degrees of violence, universal gruffness, mannerlessness, and "unrefinement." Training in self-control, sublimation of primary impulses, and allotropic empathy were minimal.

in their antisocial life patterns, no therapeutic inroads could be made with them. This recognition, and the resulting procedures that we evolved to counteract the boys' externalization mechanisms (which we have characterized as the "inversion technique") proved to be at once the most important steps in our therapy and the most difficult ones.

At first glance the mechanisms of projection and the absence of psychologic understanding did not appear to be defenses against guilt and anxiety (which would invariably be true in psychoneurotic and neurotic patients). With the exception of a few cases, these projection mechanisms rather appeared to be the results of deeply entrenched cultural conditioning in the family and the neighborhoods from which the boys came; they seemed to flow from the prevalent value system in these cultures. With no exception, the values, clearly revealed in the group interviews reproduced in this volume, seemed to be common to all our boys.

All took personal pride and derived self-esteem from their blustering "courage," physical strength, and sexual acting out; all complained of being victims of the injustices of others. These mechanisms, though fairly common in the general population, both among adults and the young, differed in nature and dynamics with our boys. The difference lay in the different quality of the character disorders and the neuroses. In the character disorders the mechanisms described constitute a character armor, and as such are admittedly difficult and more often impossible to affect in individual as well as in group psychotherapy, though they are more accessible in groups. Since character defenses and the resulting resistances require direct confrontation and mirror reactions, the therapist in individual treatment would become involved in polemics with his patients, thus vitiating and even abrogating the transference relation, and thereby losing his charismatic image and often also his patients. Groups have been found more effective with character-disorder patients, because the confrontation originates among peers (fellow patients) without involving the therapist, and is therefore more acceptable, the factor of authority (parent surrogate) being bypassed. The neurotic, on the other hand, possesses awareness (though it is vague at times) and feels guilty and anxious even when he defends himself against narcissistic injury. Herein lies the very important difference: the impenetrable armor of the character-disorder patient and the near-the-surface, easily aroused anxiety of the neurotic.

While paranoid-like sensitivity to real or fancied criticism is on the increase among all adolescents, in the case of our boys this defensiveness reached a rather high level of intensity. Even a slight suggestion that would throw light on their motivations or conduct was taken as an attack. Another area of extreme defensiveness involved attitudes and feelings toward parents. For many months, our boys were bent upon maintaining an image of their parents as perfect individuals. These attitudes were not apparent in relation to siblings. The boys were rather quick to blame and find fault with the latter. It seemed as though they had to cling to the conviction that their parents were perfect and blameless. This conviction seemed to bolster their self-esteem.

At first the boys presented complaints almost exclusively against the institution and its staff and concentrated on current and past common events. They stumbled over each other in their haste to recount violent occurrences in which they were involved both in the Village and in their homes and communities. The "here and now" motif was prevalent, and the need for introducing reflection and perspective upon these events became increasingly apparent to us if the group interviews were to move beyond trivia.

During the early group discussions the boys verbalized intense, almost murderous, hostility toward, and great distrust of, all adults, and especially the Village staff, whom they envisaged as brutal oppressors, and expressed hatred toward the social workers in their communities, whom they viewed as treacherous and dishonest. These themes were recurrent in all the early sessions of all our analytic groups. The boys would also detail injustices and cruelties (most of them seemingly fancied) they had to endure from the (nonprofessional) staff members, and the misunderstanding by, and inadequacies of, the caseworkers and psychiatrists at the Village. Of interest was the fact that hardly any complaints had been leveled at the academic school. Our impression is that the boys expected from the nonacademic staff the love, protection, and instinct gratification one seeks from parents, while by contrast the academic school was accepted in the light of traditional expectations. The clinical staff at the Village were seemingly blamed for the separation from family and community, while the cottage staff appeared to the boys as failing in meeting affectional and protectional cravings. The academic school did not seem, in the boys' minds, to be involved in either of these deprivations.

A constantly recurring subject, along with their suspicion of adults, was reflected in the complaint that the boys were not "trusted" by the very adults whom they themselves so severely distrusted. This belief, like many of their other convictions and feelings, had at least a partial basis in reality, but it was the exaggerations that concerned us, for we were convinced that as long as the boys persisted in and believed their projections, very little progress could be made in their social rehabilitation. However, while the need to project was extremely intense and was of an infantile dependency nature, the boys yearned to be "trusted," and felt that all adults mistrusted them. On further reflection it became clear that the phrase "being trusted" often meant "being respected," and the longing to be able to trust adults meant a desire to have the security of their protection. It was the feeling that they were not respected that caused narcissistic injury and undermined their already tenuous and defective self-esteem even further. We considered this attitude to be in part, at least, a striving for maturity, spurious as it may have been, and as will be seen from the protocols in another section of this volume, we gave it special attention as the group interviews unfolded in scope and depth.

The suspicion and hostility evinced against adults extended to include peers. All residents in the Village were viewed as potential rivals, enemies, and informers. Everyone had to be on the alert against confiding in, or revealing oneself to, any other boy. It took considerable time and subtle maneuvering to have the members of our groups believe the reassurances that personal revelations were confidential and safe within the confines of the group. While sibling rivalry and antagonisms are inherent in the Western family structure, the degree and intensity of such feelings in different families reflect the hostility and distrust of parents toward each other and toward their children. These pernicious attitudes are displaced upon all persons and upon society generally. We recognized that helping our boys to overcome this diffuse and generalized distrust was one of our major responsibilities. Our therapists were alerted to this need and various steps for dealing with it were indicated. This subject was one of many we thoroughly discussed on numerous occasions during the weekly supervisory conferences. The approaches to this and other crucial issues are demonstrated in the group protocols.

Some Characteristics of Our Boys and Therapeutic Measures

Some of the characteristics of our boys, as we have observed them, and the therapeutic orientations and techniques evolved on the basis of these observations are described in the following section.

ORALITY

As already mentioned, we found all our boys fixed on, or regressed to, the pregenital level, which stamped their characters in a number of respects and determined much of their conduct. One of the outstanding features was the oral fixation which, as is known, gives rise to infantile dependence and lays the foundations for an inadequate identity and ego weakness later in life. In all our groups, food had been a special problem. The boys demanded that they be given food and seemed to gain great satisfaction and inner comfort from it, which they frequently verbalized. The group situation seemed to evoke and reactivate memories and anxieties of earlier childhood and the stresses the boys had experienced in the original groups, their families. Food appeared to allay these and to assuage cravings for sustenance (love and manifest interest in them) rather than physical hunger, since the analytic groups met in the evenings directly after dinner and the boys could not have been actually hungry.

Theoretically, supplying of food in analytic groups is counterindicated, since it favors the type of regression that leads to acting out rather than reflection and prevents expression of hostility toward the therapist as a parental figure, which in psychotherapy should not be withheld. We applied this rule to the analytic (but not to the activity) groups at the Village. However, we soon discovered that this principle could not be imposed, for the boys put up a rather intense and persistent struggle to satisfy their oral needs. The details of such a protracted struggle in one of the groups, which we have dubbed "the battle for food" follow.

When the boys in this group first asked for food, their request was referred by the group therapist to the "club department" for decision and for funds to meet the cost. The response to this "request" was delayed for several weeks in the hope that the boys' interest in the subject would abate, but instead they raised the question at each subsequent session. Finally, we were forced to give the boys a definite answer, which was that no funds were available for victuals. Not to be denied, some of the boys brought small quantities of instant coffee from their cottages, using the clinical staff's pot and electric plate in the preparation of coffee. The following week the boys found the electric outlets not in working order, for we had disconnected the wires in one of the outlets. Into the other outlet in the room, from which the faceplate could not be removed, we stuffed rubber bands to serve as insulators. One of the boys made a thorough search of the room, however, and discovered an electric outlet hidden from view that we had not known existed. Coffee-brewing then proceeded at each of the next several sessions.

Our next step was to disconnect a wire in the electric heating plate, which prevented the current from passing through the coils. The same boy who had discovered the hidden wall outlet proceeded to fix it. After taking it apart, he found that he could not reassemble it. This greatly disturbed him and he gathered up the pieces to work on the next day in the auto repair shop where he did part of his industrial training. The following session he turned up with the repaired electric stove. Our next step was to remove the pot to prevent heating water. When asked by the boys where the pot was, the therapist conjectured that some staff member must have taken it away. Another boy then ran to his cottage, which was some distance away, and brought back a pot he had borrowed. Not being able to repeat this in subsequent sessions, the boys took to using hot water from the tap in the adjoining wash-room. One evening one of the boys brought with him a small jar of instant coffee and some crackers. We were unable to ascertain where or how he obtained these. (There was always the possibility that he had purloined them from his cottage, but it was equally possible that the cottage parents had donated these to the "club," which they greatly favored.)

Because the plumbing in the building was far from new, we were loath to have the boys continue using tap water, and the therapist announced a few weeks later that the "club department" had found necessary funds for coffee and cookies for the group. We had lost the "battle," but gained many friends.

The foregoing events took place during the early part of the group's life, and it was natural for us to consider the boys' insistence on food as part of the resistance to "talking" and as a rebellion against the therapist. We were in a sense justified in considering these events in this light because they occurred during the period of severe acting out. However, the feelings of satisfaction that pervaded the group once they were given food suggested that the food had deeper meaning than we at first suspected. On a number of occasions, boys remarked how pleasant it was "to sit around, drink coffee, and talk." Some compared the atmosphere to a "home." Serving food aided the cohesiveness in the group [4] and gave the boys an area for exercising responsibility. At each session one boy or another prepared and poured the coffee for the therapist and the other boys, though at times individuals would go to the corner of the room where the water was boiling and fetch his own. However, most often one of the boys took charge of brewing and distributing the beverage while he or another boy would distribute the cookies and cigarettes. The room was put in order after the session on the boys' own initiative.

At first the process of distributing the food was somewhat chaotic and served as an escape and resistance, but in time it had become an

---

4. Group cohesion is undesirable in true analytic group therapy, for it involves giving up individuality and emphasizes submission to the therapist. However, in para-analytic therapy with adolescents, relationships of this order are of extreme value and highly therapeutic in their effect. See Slavson, *A Textbook of Analytic Group Psychotherapy* (New York: International Universities Press, 1964), pp. 50–52.

incidental chore causing no distraction. Cigarettes, coffee, and simple cookies became an integral part of the setting, without a hitch, though at times of heightened anxiety some of the boys would stroll over for an extra cup of coffee (while others would in the same circumstances smoke excessively or leave the room). As treatment progressed, the therapist would point out the meaning of the behavior shown, thus extending the boys' "psychologic literacy," or understanding of their feelings and behavior. The steps that were taken to accomplish this are reflected in the protocols later in this volume.

From the very outset a package of cigarettes was supplied to the group at each session. This gesture was designed to demonstrate the therapist's acceptance of the boys, as a step in recognizing their "maturity" (we knew that all the boys smoked), and to allay mounting anxiety by oral gratification. At first the cigarettes were left on the table in the package intact and one or another of the boys would usually tear it open and distribute its contents equally among those present. (When a group member was absent, his share was distributed equally among those present.) In the early sessions clashes often arose as to the number of cigarettes each was entitled to. They would grab and haggle, so that the scene resembled one of pirates sharing spoils. When this pattern persisted for some months, we suggested that the therapist procure a cigarette tray into which he would empty the package before the boys arrived. This setting changed the behavior toward more conformity with social amenities, and the distribution of snacks and cigarettes assumed a more mature pattern.

NARCISSISM

Because the boys had been disappointed in their strivings for love from their mothers (and fathers), they had withdrawn their libidos from them as love objects, and simultaneously from all others, and instead remained in a state of infantile primary narcissism. Sometimes children so deprived "invent" imaginary persons who become their "friends," that is, their love objects, or they attach themselves to animals, as was the case with some of our boys. As the boys grew older, however, those who did not become victims of severe neuroses as a result became antisocial and delinquent. The major function of the therapist, whether in individual or group treatment, and of all other staff members in an institution for emotional rehabilitation, is to reverse this process, namely, to help the delinquent youth turn back to love objects that are human, and thus to the human community.

The resulting state of inner satisfaction, which is referred to as "being happy," permits the centrifugal flow of the libido toward external objects and relations, and favors reality-testing, hence, personality growth and maturity. Frustration, on the other hand, fixes the libido upon the individual himself, centripetally, thus damaging the ability to establish relations with the outer world, inhibiting development toward maturity, and perpetuating infantile narcissism. The raw pleasure urges and the compelling need for immediate gratification of them, without envisaging consequences, is part of this syndrome. Magical thinking and lack of imagination also result from it.

Every healthy child gives up his pre-Oedipal narcissistic (destructive) tendencies in exchange for the love of his parents (which is the basis for self-discipline). But where the child has been deprived of basic love and failed to internalize the parental ego and superego and develop an identity as he grew older, he remains in a state of primitivism, a victim of anarchic impulses.

These theoretical formulations are amply supported by developments as reflected in the protocols of the group sessions. One of the striking characteristics of our boys was their rather surprising capacity to form, under favorable conditions, ready attachments to the group therapists. One may have expected that their capacities to relate were so profoundly damaged that they would not be able to establish ties with other humans, particularly adults. This was not the case. Though at first the boys in all the groups viewed the therapists with suspicion and distrust, once they were convinced, after a variety of protracted testing maneuvers, of the therapists' benign attitudes and understanding, the boys grew intensely attached to the therapists and concerned about their welfare and happiness.

This phenomenon had different meanings for different boys. Some had the basic requirement for relating through having experienced at least partially gratifying relatedness in early childhood, however ambivalent it may have been.[5] Others responded to the therapists' nonjudgmental, accepting, and benign feelings, because these met infantile cravings for unconditioned acceptance and love to which they now responded with an avidity of small children for food and emotional sustenance. It was, therefore, our task to aid maturity and self-dependence by restitutive emotional relations which would help establish adequate mature identities.

IMMATURITY

Our boys had displayed in their thinking all the characteristics of the defective perception of reality found in pre-Oedipal children. They

5. Slavson, *Introduction to Group Therapy* (New York: International Universities Press, 1942), pp. 197 *et seq.*

perceived the outside world in terms of themselves, their needs, and their impulses. They projected their own feelings upon the world; they were in the throes of wishful thinking, and the feelings of omnipotence that some of them entertained were characteristic of early childhood, rather than middle adolescence.[6] Their sexual development, despite the experiences they had had, was extremely unsophisticated and, psychologically, actually pregenital. From our earlier "observational" groups, we clearly saw the need to provide our boys with whatever maturing influences we had at our disposal. Among these were transferential identifications with the therapists and the consequent internalization of their manner, values, conduct, and attitudes. We recognized that the content of the group discussions had to be reality-oriented and had to deal with the immediates in the boys' lives and with their feelings and thinking, which would gradually lead them on to wider horizons.

They had to be made aware of their herostratic displacement (displacement of personal feelings on society) of feelings toward parents, teachers, policemen, and all other adults and toward society and its regulations. After overcoming resistances to doing so, they had to recognize their transferential distortions—characteristic of all delinquents—and accept the realities which they were perceiving in a parataxic pattern. It is incumbent upon all staff members of re-educative and therapeutic agencies not to reinforce by repressive measures the hostilities with which delinquents come to them. Rather, institutions need to demonstrate to delinquents benign relationships that will evoke latent constructive attitudes. In many instances a favorable milieu alone (in which adults play a pivotal role) is sufficient to effect corrective outcomes by maturing personality,[7] but where an intense unresolved Oedipal conflict is involved, transference therapy is essential, not infrequently of an individual psychoanalytic type.

However, as the story of our treatment procedure unfolds, it will become clear that, because we were dealing with acting-out patients, our therapy was directed predominantly to ego-functioning and character structure. The psychoneurotic elements were treated less intensively, largely because of the limited time span, but even so, these elements were sloughed off with the strengthening of the boys' egos and the improvements in their self-images.

Correctives for habitual delinquency are best supplied within a residential setting. Out-patient therapy with acting-out delinquents, where character disorders predominate, cannot be effective because of

6. These qualities are characteristic also of psychotics, though quite different quantitatively and especially qualitatively.

7. This type of institutional milieu and ac-

tivities is described in detail in Slavson, *Re-educating the Delinquent through Group and Community Participation* (New York: Harper and Brothers, 1954; Collier Books, 1961).

the continuing stresses in the home and in the community which not infrequently overtly and covertly sanction the deviant behavior. In this process, parents' fantasies and unconscious wishes, and the peer culture as well as adult standards, reinforce immaturity and delinquent acting out. This climate negates therapeutic effort, while the climate of a re-educative residential community can be conditioned and regulated so that as essential restraints to antisocial acting out are applied, they at the same time lay foundations for more constructive values. It is assumed, of course, that "restraints" in a therapeutic community would not do violence to the adolescent's self-respect nor enhance his resentment and hostility. Residential treatment has the added value in that it prevents escapes from treatment which are ever at hand in out-patient clinics. Runaways from an insitution are episodal escape events, while in *in situ* treatment, opportunities to escape, psychologically and physically, are present as soon as the patient emerges from the interviewing room.

LANGUAGE AND DEVELOPMENTAL PHASES

Closely allied to characteristic food anxiety and oral dependence in our boys was the language they employed. The use of obscenities was not as much of a problem in the early "observational" groups because they consisted of selected patients. It was a considerable factor in the "delinquency saturated" groups. Because the boys for the former groups had been selected on the basis of neurotic components, it could be expected that their superegos would be more restraining and that they would be more mature than the boys in the unselected groups. This proved to be the case, and the difference was strikingly reflected in the language they used. Profanity and obscenity were rare in the selected (observational) groups, while in the unselected (demonstration) groups, the language was often very vile. As they discovered the permissiveness of the therapists (and possibly also with a desire to challenge, test, and annoy them), the boys let loose with shocking descriptions of sexual practices and orgies, using four letter words in endless profusion. The usual epithets and profanities, and many newly coined words and phrases as they are used in gangland, were employed. Many of these are recorded in the protocols in Part Two of this volume.

The therapists maintained a studious air of indifference. They did not react to the obvious abuse of freedom; however, as a result of the boys' emerging maturity, they gradually modified their language. The discussions had progressively become more serious and dignified in content, and words that so graphically and forcefully characterized and reflected thoughts of infantile anal and sexual preoccupations did not serve the boys' more mature ideas. As the boys matured, obscenity no longer met

infantile fixated needs and atrophied through inappropriateness and disuse. Nonetheless, on rare occasions expletives which were still part
of the boys' cultural backgrounds persisted in emphasizing affect-laden
ideas even at the end of treatment.[8]

While the boys' language was conditioned by their culture, we were
aware that, in the ongoing group therapy process, it had many and special
meanings. The image of "toughness" it conveyed was one; another was
its origin in anal-sexual fixations of these highly immature youngsters.
But of no small value was its potential in aggression toward, challenge
to, and provocation of the therapists as representatives of adult mores
and as parent surrogates. We urged the therapists to be particularly
aware of the latter and warned them against falling into the trap of reacting to the obscenities and thus justifying the boys' hostilities toward
them. The therapists were rather advised to use the boys' own colloquial-
isms occasionally (but never profanity with sexual or anal connotations).
This placed the therapists within the boys' social orbit, though not on
an equal level.

The last step in elimination of profanity occurred when sexual matters came under serious consideration and appropriate scientific terminology was used by the therapists in explaining the illustrative charts
and photos used during these sessions. In fact, in the nineteenth session
of group D, our most highly delinquency concentrated group, the boys
were discussing perversions, and one of them asked the therapist to
repeat the scientific terms so that he could write them down. When he
was finished, terms such as homosexuality, heterosexuality, anus, fellatio,
sodomy, and others were on his list. The need to compile these terms
might have various significances if it were not that the boy in question
was the brightest in the group, with a high IQ (though despite it, his
school achievement was very low at the time of his commitment to the
Village). His wish to acquire the new vocabulary was apparently motivated by a desire to obviate any future need to use coarse expressions,
which were the only ones he knew. The desire to use more acceptable
language may be a step in a boy's identification with the therapist favor-
ing maturity and ego integration. As such it is an important instrumentality in psychological and social rehabilitation.

This episode may also indicate a need "to be fed," in this instance
words, as the boys were fed edibles and cigarettes at the sessions, and
hence, be part of the oral-dependence syndrome. An act of this nature
is one means of symbolically acquiring a father, and the need to be given
to by him may include information as well as things. (The boy in ques-

---

8. Changes in the use of language could serve
   as a measure of maturity and impulse control.

tion had an outstandingly cruel and despotical father and a rather complicated family situation that started with his birth out of wedlock to slave laborers in Nazi Germany.)

DEVELOPMENTAL SEQUENCES

Analysis of the group interviews unmistakably reveals the developmental sequences of the oral, anal, and genital phases as described by Freud. The oral phase was reflected in inordinate dependencies and yearnings for approval and acceptance, which the boys made known by endless complaints against the inconsiderateness and harshness of adults, unfounded dissatisfaction with the food at the cottages, insistence on being given food at the group sessions, and in the inordinate value attached to cigarettes. The many other forms of infantile dependence were relived in the groups in other forms, such as provocativeness, regressive acts, demands for special privileges, and finally by the intense emotional ties to, and the deep affection for, the therapists.

The fixation at the anal phase took the form of profane and obscene language and, while our boys did not pass flatus, which frequently occurs among aggressive delinquents, they made identical sounds by mouth and through slits in pieces of paper and frequently resorted to "the Bronx Cheer."

In the next phase, the genital phase, similar disorders were observed. The boys' "loose talk," their boastful descriptions of unrestricted transitory sex experiences, the orgies in which they claimed to have been participants, the prevalence of homosexuality, and the nearness to the surface of incestuous strivings all stamped their sexuality as infantile and not adequately differentiated.

The genital phase, which in various forms extends throughout life, is the period when the integration of the total personality occurs. Genitality is the ultimate end in nature, for through it procreation and the survival of the species are achieved. When God banished Adam and Eve from the Garden of Eden he bid them to discharge two functions: to labor and to procreate. This admonition has its parallel in the psychological nature of man. Both the biological and psychological functions demand the integration and coordination of all of man's inner resources, as seen in work and marriage and in maintaining a family in a societal setting. In psychotherapy, working through sexual confusions and anxieties and fears generated by social mores and prohibitions is essential in the treatment of all categories of emotional disturbances and social maladjustments. We recognized, therefore, that, when our boys could vicariously live through the uncompleted infantile phases in which they remained fixed, they would make long strides toward maturity.

DEVELOPMENTAL DICHOTOMIES

As the interviews in the analytic groups progressed, it became clear that, while the boys revealed idiosyncratic as well as common intrapersonal and interpersonal problems, the most universal and basic difficulty with all of them was arrest in their psychosocial and psychosexual development. Though all of them had attained adequate physical growth, and many exceeded the norm, their psyches had not kept pace. Thus athletic prowess and physical strength enormously exceeded judgment and controls. This dichotomy created an imbalance also in their functioning. Chronologically the boys had reached a stage at which society demanded suitable conduct and achievements. Psychologically, the boys were unable to meet these demands. Strengths necessary to buttress and direct psychic (ego) forces to meet these expectations were lacking. Narcissism; impulsivity; considerable polymorphous perversity; unbridled spurious pleasure urges; the explosive urge for immediate (egotropic) gratification; oral dependence; weak—or absent—allotropic (interpersonal, social) feelings of love and tenderness; self-alienation; magical thinking and superstition; projections; narcissistic distortions; and unintegrated and uncontrolled appetites of various kinds, as they were re-revealed in conduct and verbal communications, convinced us that the core of our boys' difficulties was immaturity and that our therapy had to be directed not toward specific syndromes, as would be the case with psychoneurotics, but rather toward *maturing the total personality*.

However, we were aware that, unlike the usual procedure employed of attempting to "implant" standards, inculcate values, and convey or teach desirable "ideas," emotional maturity can be attained only by a life process, not by funneling percepts and knowledge. The principle which gradually grew out of our experience with the earlier experimental (observational) groups taught us that before we could help our boys attain a more socially acceptable orientation and functioning, they would have to be allowed to act out freely their *true* selves at *their* level of development without guilt, fear, or anxiety. The therapists were, therefore, warned that for a long period the slightest signs of surprise or disapproval expressed or implied by word, grimace, or gesture would vitiate the therapeutic effort. Even objective interpretations or explanations would be perceived as disapproval and criticism.

We could not envisage the length of the period during which full, unconditioned acceptance and permissiveness were essential or how soon this policy (namely, absolute permissiveness) could be modified and finally abandoned. In this respect these conversational groups were temporarily similar to activity therapy groups (in fact, "acting-out" groups). The resemblance was more than superficial, for every criminotic person acts out of a character or ego deficiency, even when the deeper source is neurotic tension. The true psychoneurotic develops symptoms, while in the "delinquent" the neurotic tensions are transformed into a life pattern and are acted out. Identifications with the therapist and the resulting improvement in self-identity are steps in character repair. These steps cannot be taken by patients unless they are at first unconditionally accepted and understood, for only then will they accept the therapist and internalize his values and conduct. Only then could the underlying neurotic mass, which was later uncovered, become available for corrective therapeutic measures, as shown in the protocols.

Status and group participation are in some cases sufficient in themselves, and a properly conditioned institutional milieu, therefore, can be very effective in altering attitudes and behavior. With some reactive delinquents, respect from adults is a potent maturing influence and character corrective. But for the vast majority of youngsters who have reached the point of court commitment, the alteration of behavior has to proceed rather from changes in psychic operations and in affect. As long as the internal drives remain unchanged, behavior will be reactivated as soon as the individual is removed from either the external controls or benign influences of the institution, as the case may be. Recidivism can be understood in these terms: the offender changes his conduct in the institution, but he remains psychodynamically unchanged, which propels him to repeat the offenses when the external controls (threats) are removed.

We, therefore, understood our task as being not only to alter behavior through imposed discipline or by inculcating moral and ethical precepts, but also to create a setting in which *basic* feelings, attitudes, and values would be healthfully experienced, a process through which personality matures. We repeatedly sought to impress our therapists with the fact that we had to do for our teenage boys what their parents should have done for them when they were little children, though the process can be telescoped as it gradually leads them toward psychological maturity.

IDENTIFICATION, IDENTITY, AND ALIENATION

The foregoing concepts fitted well into our conclusion that the delinquent's sources of identity were basically drawn from their alienation, not from the integration of the psyche and a wholesome awareness of the "self." They were derived mostly from negative identifications with outer objects and events. Having been debilitated by noxious relations and influences and severe rejection, the delinquent grew dependent to a massive degree upon externals, rather than growing into a self-reliant entity with awareness of his own strength and a sense of security in it. While every person acquires and lives out his identity through, and in relation to, others, in normal development a reservoir of energy is built up within the ego and superego upon which one draws later in life. In the pathognomic personality this reservoir is very limited, and the individual "feels" identity only in action and in negativism, or in dependent relationships. This type of identity can be characterized as a *reflected identity*. In the case of the delinquent and the criminotic, particularly, actions and relationships are of a morbid nature.

Thus, the antisocial individual "feels" his *being* only when he feels hatred, anger, and rage at others, when he verbalizes or acts out hostilities, or commits antisocial acts. As we came to know the inner life of our boys, we could recognize, in addition to other benefits, the therapeutic value of their virulent acts and pronouncements. Through them the boys were acquiring status in their own eyes and in the eyes of those in alliance with them. Griping, boasting, grandiosity, and fantasies of omnipotence were not only means for awareness of the self (or self-identity), but they also satisfied the needs for group status and recognition (or reflected identity). A degree of negativism, the oppositional stance, is characteristic of all adolescents. It is a form of assertiveness that begets awareness of self in the healthy personality; it is the road to inner identity and self-reliance. The negative stance is exaggerated and intensified in the delinquent. In most instances, it is a reaction formation to failure in acquiring individualization in significant areas of life and, as a result, the quantitative mass of negativism, arrogance, and acting out becomes part of the delinquent's autarchy. We can understand the delinquent act only when we recognize it as a means of seeking identity, a self and group status. As such it is a step in self-therapy for the individual.

In the light of this understanding, the gang appears to be a reinforcement instrument in the pursuit of identity, as are also the special insignia in these groups. Rooted in hostility though they are, group-idiosyncratic style of clothing, mannerisms, language, and diversions oppositional to the social norms serve these ends. Having been rejected by the prevailing society (via families and later by other social instrumentalities), the members of a gang have not been able to establish constructive identifications with the norms of society and, therefore, remain not only without an anchorage but also without the self-identity that in normal growth occurs through internalization of outer values seen in significant persons. The delinquent has only one recourse left to him, and that is to create in the company of others of his own ilk a social milieu with which he can identify and be at one.

Beyond the reinforcement of negativism (characteristic of all adolescents), one of the noxious aspects of the society which delinquents create for themselves is overidentification with their newly created culture. Since the members have previously been deprived of the sense of belonging, the gang becomes an extraordinarily close-knit and immensely cohesive social 'group. The intermember loyalties are of an extremely high intensity, and disloyalty to the group may lead to extermination of the culprit. Transgression against the gang code is a threat to all its members, for the dissolution of the group (gang) would leave each of its members without an anchor in life. Lacking a self-identity and being alienated from the environment in which he lives, the delinquent sees the death of his gang as the vicarious death of himself. The demand for rigid loyalty and adherence to the group is a reaction to the fear of being let loose upon the buffeting waves of life without a secure and protective anchorage.

A large number of gang members do break away as they grow into adulthood, and many of them become socially acceptable, though usually in a menial and simple life pattern. This they achieve when through a combination of circumstances they have found a new anchorage and new identifications. At times the family setting alters; the former delinquent feels more accepted and his role thereby sustains a favorable change. In some instances, marriage and a tolerable job helps to "settle" him in a socially approved role as his autarchic characteristics become modified by new relationships and the new self-image that results from them. In the group discussions our boys frequently spoke of marriage and having children as a means of attaining love and solving their problems. Nonetheless, the functioning and the general characteristics of the reformed full-blown delinquent only occasionally reach high levels. His sublimatory mechanisms always remain weak; he remains violence-prone.

The more we have probed into the personality structures of our boys, the more convinced we have become that the source of the criminosis which is designated as delinquency (from other than constitutional and psychotic causes), is an overwhelming sense of pervasive alienation. The words of a Greek philosopher come to mind in this connection: "Man is nothing without the work of man," which can be paraphrased to "everything that is human in us is given to us by other humans." It is through relationships with persons from the moment of birth until death that feelings, attitudes, and values are conditioned and activated. The quality of these relationships determine not only social adaptations but also the self-image, the awareness of the self, and the total character.

SELF-ALIENATION

Self-images can be integrative or alienative. In the former the individual feels himself capable and self-reliant; he is allotropic and optimistic. But when his background has been an emotionally morbid one, he feels himself defeated, unworthy, hostile, and unrelated to his family and his society. Alienation has been variously described as powerlessness, meaninglessness, normlessness, isolation, and self-estrangement. Alienation is characterized by feelings that one has toward himself and toward persons around him: family, neighbors, society, and mankind generally. "Alienation lies in every direction of human experience where basic emotional desire is frustrated, every direction in which the person may be compelled by social situations to do violence to his own nature. 'Alienation' is used to convey the emotional tone which accompanies any behavior in which the person is compelled to act self-destructively . . . its dimensions will be as varied as human desire and need."[9] The background of every delinquent clearly indicates that he has sustained deprivations of the essential needs for emotional, and usually also physical, sustenance; that his ego was not nurtured and his ideas and values, which are forged predominantly in latency, were molded by inadequate or defective persons, or both.

One of the chief characteristics of self-alienation that we found common to our boys was the compelling need for self-injury or self-destruction, of which they became aware as treatment progressed. Accident-proneness, psychic and physical masochism, homosexuality, habitual seeking of punishment and of rejection from others, depression, withdrawal, fear of success, inability to love, suicide fantasies—all were brought out during the group discussions, often quite bluntly, but sometimes in a disguised form. In all situations in which self-alienation was involved, the individual did not utilize the potentials for positive outcomes to himself and others.

SOCIAL ALIENATION

Social alienation proceeds from self-alienation as night follows day. Self-alienation, being a product of alienative experiences with other persons and of damaging relationships, is inherently socially alienative. In many instances, however, the social setting itself generates alienation by preventing identification and empathy and by divorcing the individual from his basic instinctive needs. Noxious relationships in childhood beget diffuse anger and rage, are structured into the ego, and beget diffused antagonism that consumes much of one's ego energies. The hostile attitude and conduct of the alienated person arouses counterhostility in all with whom he comes in contact. When he tries to disguise his emotional orientation, he only delays revealing himself. Actually, most people perceive, even though vaguely, the basic

9. Lewis Feuer, "What Is Alienation? The Career of a Concept," *New Politics,* Spring, 1962, p. 132.

nature of the alienated person and feel uncomfortable in his presence. As recorded in the protocols, these facts had been brought forth in the group discussions and formulated rather clearly by the boys themselves in their own simple language. Negative reactions to himself which he himself invokes are perceived by a neurotically alienated individual as attacks upon himself initiated by others, and which he uses to feed his hostilities and manipulations further. His superego guilts are thereby assuaged, for his ego recognizes only the aggressions and resentments of others, not his own. The lack of empathy and identification characteristic of alienation blinds him to the feelings of others and his own effect on them.

The alienated individual participates in group activities and social movements only if they meet his unconscious needs for self-destruction and the resultant wish for injury to others. Individuals whose identities are negatively directed may join frankly hate organizations, which provide for the alienated person a field where he can work out his negativism to the full and silence his rather weak superego by justifying it as being in the service of a noble effort.[10] In the case of our boys, various gangs and mob action served this purpose.

SELF-ALIENATION VERSUS SOCIAL ALIENATION

To a definite degree self-alienation is inherent in the essential nature of man, but this is not so true of social alienation. The true personality of man, as of all animals, lies in instincts, and as these instincts are modified, controlled, or repressed, a degree of alienation with respect to his biological nature necessarily occurs. His biological nature is transformed by culture and education into a "spiritual" entity with strivings and values alien to his "raw" instincts. He acquires, as he should, through training and exposure, group-imposed sublimations and derivative wishes that place him on a "higher" plane than his biological nature intended him to be. The more some of the basic instinctual urges are sublimated and repressed, the "higher" the plane the individual, and thereby also the race, reaches. This is at once man's glory and his burden, for it is by this that his life is enriched and also that his basic neuroses are generated.

Interpersonal or social alienation, on the other hand, is contrary to the natural order, for survival of the species in the animal world depends in varying degrees on cooperation. Individual survival as well depends upon concerted action by numbers.[11] Integration with a species group is nature's device to assure perpetuation of life. Man is the only animal who,

---

10. Witness those who justify segregation of Negroes as the "will of God revealed in the Bible."

11. See Slavson, *A Textbook of Analytic Group Psychotherapy*, Chapter I.

by modifying his instincts, abrogates these laws of nature in many important areas, though sacrificing of life by individuals for the group (as for one's country or a principle in crisis situations such as revolutions, disasters, and war) is in keeping with the order in nature. However, the fact remains that despite the problems man has created for himself by alienation from his biological instinctual nature, he has been amply compensated for his "loss." Art, science, and culture, and all the works of civilization are a result of transmuting his "raw" nature into intellectual and spiritual achievement. One can muster an array of supportive arguments in favor of man's primary alienation, for without it he would have become alienated from his potentials (beyond organic survival) and remained primitive and impoverished.

A fact pertinent to our central topic is that alienation has quantitative and directional elements which in the delinquent and criminotic is quantitatively great and directionally destructive. Self-alienation is not the concern of the police and legal authorities, though it presents an area of concern to the mental hygienist, the medical professions, and the behavioral sciences. The legal and penal communal instrumentalities come into play only when alienation propels an individual to acts that abrogate the security and "rights" of the community. Every attempt to rehabilitate the criminal is an attempt to counteract his alienation and instill into his psyche relatedness to the self and to others via the therapist and transitional small groups. For such total relatedness we suggest the term *alliance* in opposition to *alienation*.

ALIENATION AND REALITY

Another area in which alienation was made apparent in our boys was in their reality perception. At the beginning, the actualities of the adult world in which they physically lived but which they did not accept were perceived and understood in infantile, narcissistic images and in terms of primary elaboration or process. They rejected the values of the world partly because they rejected the adults in that world, but also because they did not understand the *raison d'être* of its mores and regulations. The utility of these regulations had to be explained to them during the group discussions, as the boys developed in emotional maturity and grew receptive to such learnings. However, despite their vehemence and ravings against all restraints and controls, the boys felt anxious and guilty underneath for their transgressions.

As poorly as their parents and others may have represented the adult ethos, the boys were aware of their estrangement even early in the group interviews and attempted to allay guilts by overvaluating their parents and by professing admiration for and loyalty to them. It was only after a prolonged period of therapy, when the boys were freed of these guilts and the concomitant fears of losing their parents, that they were able to evaluate the latter objectively. This was the first step toward understanding them; now they had to (emotionally) accept them and, in the sense of Goethe, "forgive" them. This was also the first obvious step toward accepting the adult world of which the parents were representatives. The protocols clearly show how the boys freed themselves to a point where they were able to criticize their parents and, as a result, view other life areas objectively as well. Another source for the superego's permission to be objective about their parents lay in the fact that as the boys grew more mature they grew also less dependent upon, and more detached from, the parents. Once this step was made, our protocols show that the boys were able to re-evaluate other areas of their world realistically—staff members in the institutions, siblings, their own futures, school, jobs, their home neighborhoods, friends—and above all, their own deficiencies, attitudes, needs, and possibilities.

Among the mechanisms of social alienation, magic and omnipotence played an important role with our boys. The "primary process" is natural to the young child's pregenital phase. It is the natural adaptive mechanism to an overwhelming adult-created world of imposing and frequently threatening actuality, which has to be replaced during latency through cerebration and expanded capacity for reality-testing. In our boys the transition to the "secondary process" or elaboration was blocked due to a barren economico-cultural milieu, on the one hand, and through the frustrating treatment by parents and teachers on the other. The boys, therefore, continued to fantasy magic and miracles so as to relieve themselves of their stresses and give them respite for the future. In most delinquents and criminals the persistent infantile belief in magic begets unfounded superstitions, which dominate much of the criminotics' awareness. The adherence to magic extends to the conviction that transgressions, particularly, will not be discovered. Magic served as a conscious defensive tool for our boys, which they proceeded gradually to give up through their therapeutic experience, but as the fantasies of magic were punctured, they were replaced by *expectations of disaster and doom*.[12] When in later sessions, and quite on their own, the boys proceeded to make plans for their futures after leaving the protective arms of the institution, they spontaneously and reasonably faced each other with the unreality of some of their visions of future possibilities and opportunities. They became reality-oriented to the degree that they recognized the importance of a high-school education for occupational opportunities and discussed steps for obtaining a job, for evading gang affiliations, for achieving self-control, while recognizing their individual

12. The "doom motif" received special attention, as will be seen from the protocols. We considered this form of mass depression an impediment to mobilization of powers for recovery.

limitations and capacities. They even informed themselves on income taxes, and how to report them.

ALIENATION AND OMNIPOTENCE

Feelings of omnipotence are greatly enhanced during adolescence as a reaction to the underlying "inadequacy constellation" that plagues all young people during that period of life. Omnipotent feelings are reaction formations to doubts as to sexual potency and they may also be residues of fantasies of infantile magical powers. In delinquents, however, these feelings reach overhigh intensity. For them it is the means of silencing misgivings and offering hope for the future. In the average adolescent who has some supportive guidance from parents and other benevolent adults, the magic feeling is dissipated and replaced by a gradually increasing sense of reality (reality-testing). Not so with the delinquent, whom the tension factors and pressures of the emotional and actualistic environment force more and more to separate himself from reality and escape into a realm he can control by his own powers, that is, by feeling omnipotent.

We doubt if we have been successful in significantly reducing these feelings in our group members to the same extent as other of their pathognomic areas, such as impulsivity, defensiveness, denial, and alienation. Perhaps if the groups had met longer we might have made greater headway in this area, but in view of the naturalness of the feelings at the age of our boys, it may have been just as well that we did not. In working educationally, or therapeutically, with people, one needs to keep in mind that the feeling of omnipotence at the appropriate period in life is father to strength, security, and hope. If we have succeeded in lastingly correcting the ego reserves and ego strengths and diminishing the magical trends in our young patients, the likelihood is that omnipotence feelings will be sloughed off with age and reality-testing, unless the pressures of the environment activate them again as an implacable defense.

In the pervasive narcissism and autarchy which dominated the thinking of our boys, as conveyed by their grandiosity, boastfulness, and claims to power and prowess, there was discernible an underlying insecurity, self-hatred, and at times even self-contempt. (These are clearly reflected in the protocols.) Unless the delinquent is psychotic, mentally defective, or organically deficient, he is vaguely aware of his atypicality as a person and of the unacceptability of his conduct, despite the defensive façade he presents. Having been subjected to incessant correction, strict discipline, and severe punishment by parents and the criticism and sermons of relatives, neighbors, ministers, and teachers, his unconscious has stored up the ability to discern between proper and improper behavior, even though he consciously continues with his stored up negative and autarchic propulsions. His alienative condition produces in him a codeless orientation (except, of course, for the codes of the gang) that feeds on his anarchic pattern and egotropic feelings, with a resulting feedback from power and ego satisfactions.

The Matter of Love

It is customary to emphasize in educational, psychological, and psychiatric literature the importance of the child's receiving love, protection, and security. Frequently, however, the fact is overlooked or, at least, underplayed that being given love must lead to an ability and a desire in the recipient to give love. Remaining on the receiving end only reinforces native narcissism and self-centeredness. In human relations, love needs to be bidirectional: centripetal and centrifugal.

Centrifugal love, however, is made possible only where the needs to be loved (and protected) have been adequately met, namely, where centripetal love was experienced. The period in which centripetal love is inherent is infancy and very early childhood, but it cannot remain one-directional without damage to the personality later in life as well. When the centripetal phase—that of receiving love—is fulfilled, the child at appropriate periods normally attempts to reverse the parent-child roles. He wishes to do things for the mother, especially, and needs to be encouraged in this by *proper* emotional and material rewards to motivate further emerging allotropic feelings and relatedness. This process is one of the foundations of a wholesome identity.

No one can bestow on others that which he himself has not received. Not having received love, one is bankrupt in that area and cannot dispense it to others. Our boys were particularly pauperized in this regard, and having been denied the love from others, they have given "love" to themselves, rendering them egotistic, self-centered, narcissistic, and falsely omnipotent. The delinquent act, viewed from this perspective, is an act of restitution through which a deeply deprived individual seeks his own redemption.

The protocols of the demonstration group contain passages that reveal the unmistakable emergence of centrifugal love for the therapist at first, then for each other, and finally more benign feelings for persons outside the group. The increased capacity for loving, or at least for concern for the welfare of the therapist, was made manifest at various points in the shorter-lived groups as well. When the weather was inclement during the winter months, for example, the boys would warn the therapist to "drive carefully" after the session. And when a boy would complain about a session's being omitted because of a holiday, others would resentfully admonish him: "Don't you think Mr. _____ is entitled to a holiday?" The records frequently described the touching manner in which the boys would express their affection for the group, its members, and the therapist.

Receiving love is essential for wholesome personality development, and a measure of egotropism is unavoidable and necessary for physical and emotional self-preservation; yet, it has to be tempered and balanced with allotropic feelings and eventually extended to socially motivated urges. A basic characteristic of a corrective relation is the restitutive love from a therapist and others involved—fellow group members and members of an institutional staff—which ultimately can lead to the development of centripetal love and allotropism. The balance between these two forces is the precondition for the prevention of alienation from self and society. The protocols and the case histories of the boys show that this balance did not originally exist in our boys, but gradually made its appearance as therapy proceeded, reaching rather dramatic heights toward the end.

3

Sex and Homosexuality

The Problem of Sexuality in Delinquency

AS THE IMMATURITY in our boys was being decreased, though slowly, through the ongoing group process, their improved identifications, corrective interpersonal interactions, and gradually emerging self-identities, the most urgent preoccupation that contributed to their stress was evidenced by their sex tensions. The salutary effect of the group on character generally was strikingly exemplified by the reaction of several of them, whose use of vile language had only recently abated, to overhearing profane expletives uttered by an unskilled laborer on the grounds of the school. The boys were taken aback by it and discussed it in the group. The reaction was epitomized by the statement: "A long time ago when we came to the Village we used to talk like that, but we don't talk that way anymore; and the Village hires somebody who talks worse than the kids."

Such change could not have occurred automatically in the area of sex, a frequently recurring subject during the group interviews. We did not, however, go into this subject, paramount to all adolescents and especially our boys, before we were convinced that they were ready to sustain the anxiety and guilts that would be associated with the discussion. Proper timing is of the essence in all psychotherapy, in fact in all human relations, but it is never as pivotal as in dealing with a subject so highly charged as sex. We, therefore, allowed the boys to verbalize freely their interests and feelings and bided our time until they gave us a cue to readiness.

Both from theoretical considerations and experience with delinquents,

45

we were aware of the importance of working through sexual pressures and confusions. This is the most disturbing problem, and one that commonly, though not exclusively, leads to social maladjustment and asocial acts. The inhibition in modern societies of the matured sex impulse at the apex of sexual virility, which is reached in adolescence, creates unsurmountable tensions in all young people, more especially in boys. These tensions have been justifiably compared to an "actual (organic) neurosis." Young people whose ego development has been adequate can control or regulate the impulse. Where the ego development is inadequate and the total personality remains on a comparatively infantile level, or where the individual has been subjected to sexual overstimulation (which was the case with most of our boys), the urge often proves uncontrollable. The resulting tensions may seek release in various forms of acting out, because psychic and somatic energies are mutually transmutable. Thus, acting out is an indication that the regulative inner forces for dealing with this and other impulses are insufficient and have to be strengthened by a maturing ego and psycho-organic integrative processes, rather than being dealt with by adults repressively and punitively. We therefore delayed addressing ourselves to this problem directly until a stage of comparative maturity was reached by the boys in our groups and the follow-up studies of their conduct in the school community justified our approach. In all cases, homosexual activity was diminished or had entirely disappeared, and the staff reported also simultaneous character changes in the boys involved.

As will be made clear in the group protocols, the boys voluntarily made known their preoccupations and revealed their confusions in the area of sex as the group discussions progressed. Not infrequently they talked openly about their heterosexual and even homosexual activities, but more often these communications were disguised and in indirect terms. While they felt that their practices were sanctioned and encouraged by their peer microculture and, in fact, served as a badge of prowess and a passport to gang status, nonetheless, below the veneer of superciliousness, banter, and boastfulness, there was buried an awareness of the wrongness of their conduct. As the boys, planfully encouraged by the therapists, continued the discussions, it became clear that their conflicts basically stemmed from Oedipal guilt, for these boys have redirected their libidinal strivings toward nonincestuous sexual objects less than does the average adolescent. The case histories of every one of the boys in all of our groups revealed gross disturbances in psychosexual development caused by overstimulating sleeping arrangements in crowded homes, highly seductive and promiscuous mothers, latent homosexual and delinquent fathers, and unenlightened parent-child relations, generally, that favored libido fixation on infantile levels. Due to infantilization and the absence of a life sphere favorable to personality growth and psychological integration, the etiological factors militated against the emergence of nonincestuous sexual aims, which normally begin in adolescence. The resultant inadequate repressions and sublimating processes contrary to the social mores begot confusion and inner conflict that was a major factor in our boys' difficulties.

Because the periods of existence of the earlier observation groups were so brief, intensive or exploratory discussions of sex never occurred, though the subject was often touched upon. As indicated, these groups met for periods shorter than a school year, and their membership was recruited from among boys with some neurotic difficulties, whose sexual fantasies had, therefore, been under better control. Our demonstration groups, on the other hand, consisted of unselected, more sexually acting-out youngsters. In group D (the most delinquency-saturated group), for example, four of the eight members were known to have regularly indulged in homosexual activity, while some of the others were suspected of it.

How the Delinquent Perceives Sex

When the opportune time came for discussions of the subject, our orientation was first to dwell on the normal, healthy aspects of sex and reproduction as phases of biological, organic, and social development, but we were also prepared to answer any questions of a pathologic nature that the boys might ask. As anticipated, despite their sexual acting out, including cohabitation with "girlfriends" and rapings, before coming to the Village and on their periodic visits home, all the boys without exception had no knowledge or understanding of the sexual act beyond the sensations derived from it. Group discussions revealed that the boys were full of underlying fears and guilts, misconceptions, and superstitions that could not but cause great anxiety. Though they all indulged in masturbation, all the boys believed it led to insanity. Some believed that a strong desire to masturbate resulted in one's becoming homosexual; others were convinced that sodomy (among males) can result in pregnancy, and that the "scum" (semen) goes to the brain of the recipient and causes him to become insane; a few were in dread that they would impregnate the girls with whom they had intercourse.

The neighborhood cultural values were revealed by several who wondered why girls were hesitant about unrestricted sexual intercourse. They were genuinely puzzled as to why a girl who "goes out" with a boy, goes to the movies with him and partakes in after-theater refreshments, should refuse to have intercourse. None of the boys was to a slightest degree aware of the personal, aesthetic, and affectional factors in the sex act. Apparently in the environment in which these boys had been reared, tenderness was lacking in man-woman relations, and virginity was no consideration.

In the demonstration group (C), on which a full report appears in a later part of this volume, a full discussion of sex did not arise before the twenty-fourth session. But in the group (D) with the most severe delinquency and character disorders, in which there were four active homosexual boys, the subject was introduced as early as the fifth session. Although the group spent an unconscionably long time on the subject, homosexuality was only hinted at. At the sixteenth session, one of a pair who were known to be homosexual mates violently attacked the other, calling him "faggot, dirty prostitute, whore," and the two proceeded to accuse each other of pederasty and fellatio.

Approaches to Sex Education

Our initial approach was the elucidation of normal sexuality in nature. We had prepared in advance necessary visual aids, such as books on anatomy and pictures of male and female reproductive organs, of an embryo and fetus *in utero*, and so on, but this particular group of high delinquency saturation continued to return to the subject (as a stereotype) session after session.[1] They kept hinting at homosexuality and inquired as to the reasons for it.

Remarks concerning sex, both facetious and serious, had been made at various points in many sessions in all the groups, but the problem seemed so pressing in this particular group, and the boys appeared so confused, that we felt it appropriate to deal with it, even though it seemed to us too soon. We did not wish to appear evasive or reluctant. The repeated return to the subject was a signal that homosexuality was a problem. An answer was imperative, albeit unconsciously so, and the group could not move forward therapeutically until the matter was cleared up. Therefore, we decided that the therapist should bring the subject into the open, head-on, thus diminishing the stigma and guilt attached to it and ending the secrecy that served only to perpetuate it.

When the time seemed propitious, we suggested to the therapist that he ask the group what their thoughts were on homosexuality, since they had brought the question up at a number of meetings. The consensus was

1. One of the meanings of such a stereotype is the demand for clarification of a specific cathected subject. Patients become blocked unless these subjects are clarified. See S. R. Slavson, *A Textbook of Analytic Group Psychotherapy* (New York: International Universities Press), pp. 161–162, 360–362.

that the absence of girls in the boys' milieu and their intense sexual urges drove them to practices that relieved them of the tension. These activities they freely narrated. During the discussion, one of the group graphically described his observations on homosexual male prostitutes in Times Square in New York and the strategies they employ for attracting attention. In response to questions from the boys, the therapist explained the conditions that produce confirmed (real) homosexuals. After the explanation was made, one of the boys remarked: "I always wondered what made somebody 'queer' but nobody really told me and I don't know why not. It's not so terrible; all they have to do is come to a group and talk about it."

Another complained that adults never explained matters relating to sex to their children: "They just tell you what you should and should not do." A third wished that his parents had talked to him about "these things." All said that they "picked up" their information; their fathers had never told them anything about it. (This, by the way, was the universal complaint of all the boys in all our groups—that their fathers gave them no sex information—and they declared that they only now came to recognize through the group discussions how erroneous the information they "picked up" on the streets was.)

We are going to reproduce three of the sessions of Group D, consisting of the most delinquent boys, in which the developments of the discussions around sex and homosexuality are detailed, and their effects upon the boys' conduct in the Village as a result revealed.

Discussions of Sex in Group D

SESSION NINE

At session nine, Umberto stated that he was looking forward to going home during the approaching week-end holiday to see a movie in a Harlem theater which dealt with unmarried mothers. He said: "You know what the movie is about?" Fritz innocently responded: "No, tell us about it, Umberto." Umberto explained it was "about" girls who . . . ," and then beginning to search self-consciously for words to finish the sentence, repeated: "—girls who . . . ," and finally blurted out: "who have babies without getting married." Ray asked ironically: "You mean you're going to see how to do it?" There was a burst of laughter from the group. Umberto said seriously: "No, they don't show that." Ray baitingly said it was a "shame." Jerry remarked that it was "disgusting" to show such a movie. There was disagreement on the part of Fritz and then the subject of censorship arose. When asked what they thought about such movies, David said maybe it was in order to have "the facts about bad girls." Fritz interrupted: "So that when we grow up we won't get into trouble with these bad girls." The therapist wondered whether what they were trying to find out was some facts about sex. David said that he thought it was "a good idea to have all the facts." Randy and Fritz asked what facts he was talking about. David glared at them and said: "You know what facts I'm talking about." Ray claimed he did not know, and why didn't David tell them what they were. Steve declared that probably David was ashamed to talk about these matters, and Umberto announced that he knew what David was talking about and so did everybody else and why didn't they quit "fooling around."

Jerry (who is known to have participated in homosexual acting out more than most boys and was suspected of being a borderline schizophrenic and suicidal) leaned forward and told the therapist: "You know, my eyes really hurt me tonight and so does my head," and he started to rub his eyes. Fritz tried to divert the discussion by getting up and walking around the room, throwing paper clips at David. The therapist said that the discussion of sex seemed to disturb the boys and he called attention to Fritz's behavior as well as the distractibility of the other boys. Umberto suggested that the group should "get rid" of some of the members if they had to "fool around all the time."

Ray denied that this distractibility had anything to do with the discussion of sex, and that it was rather due to the idea of going home for the (approaching) Thanksgiving holiday. Jerry repeated again that he did not feel well and did not feel like talking, and Julius (who had been a victim of extensive homosexual attacks before he entered the group) fell silent. The distractibility continued, with Randy quitting the meeting and Umberto suggesting that Randy should be "kicked out of the club." Ray was throwing empty paper cups into the wastepaper basket, while Umberto started a small fire in the ash tray, using some paper napkins.

Jerry said he'd heard a "good" joke and, speaking very rapidly, told a somewhat obscene story, the punch line of which had to do with the practice of fellatio. Fritz said he, too, wanted to tell a joke. Randy said that he would tell Fritz's joke. Fritz said no, he wanted to tell it himself. Randy chased Fritz around the table, and Fritz attempted to tell the story as he was running. Finally David ordered Fritz to sit down and let Randy tell the joke, which Randy did.

In the joke he used the words *pussy, prick, screw,* and others of the same genre. Occasionally he would substitute phrases such as "and then the man got started" or "started to work on the girl" instead of "screw." The group laughed at this. The therapist remaked that he felt that the boys were embarrassed talking about "these things." Randy said that the therapist was an "adult" and "you feel kind of funny when you talk about sex [in the presence of an adult]." Fritz said boys have their "own language." It's different when they talk among themselves. The therapist expressed wonder as to why they thought they could not talk about sex in the presence of an adult. Sex was something that "everybody knows is around. It is here." The boys broke into laughter at this formulation. Randy said that he thought adults did not want to talk to boys about it because they wanted to treat them like babies. He became quite agitated as he said this and repeated the statement several times. Finally he said: "They think if we talk about it and we learn about it, we're going to be homosexual maniacs."

This statement seemed to unleash intense anxiety among all the boys, and it continued throughout the rest of the session. Randy, David, and Fritz were vocal throughout, while Umberto and Julius remained passively attentive. Jerry, on the other hand, withdrew, and in fact left the table and sat behind the therapist. Ray, at one point, said that he was warm and tired and crawled under the table, where he remained for a short period. At one point he began unnecessarily to adjust his trousers and facing Jerry unzipped them, ostensibly to push his shirt in. He and Jerry then became involved in a conversation about clothing as Jerry expressed admiration for Ray's attire. There was a definite flavor of homosexual interplay between these two boys.

When the phrase "homosexual maniacs" was uttered by Randy, David said that he thought everybody was afraid they might become "sex hot" and have relations "all over the place." The therapist asked Randy what he meant by "homosexual maniacs." Randy replied: "Just what David meant. Everybody goes around "pluking" [having intercourse with] all the girls. Once somebody had intercourse, "you've got to have it again and the adults think if they don't tell us about it we won't do it." He went on to say that he felt that his father kept "these things" from him because his father was afraid to treat him like a man. "He wanted to keep me a baby, but it didn't do him any good, because I learned from the guys on the street." David said, "That's the way I learned too." Julius: "Nobody ever said anything about sex with me and I would never talk to my father about it."

The therapist wondered why. Randy commented he thought he knew why, but he didn't want to say it. David wanted to know why he would not. Randy laughed and said: "Because my mother had seven children." Julius (who had ten siblings) said that Randy had said something about Julius' father "being busier than his father." This evoked laughter from all the boys present. Randy: "Oh, I might as well tell you. I think that maybe some of the people think it's dirty and they don't want to tell us about it." In his excitement, he stood up as he was speaking and continued: "That's what I don't understand. On the one hand, they don't want us to know; they think it's something wrong and dirty, but they can do it [have intercourse] all the time. That's why I think they want to keep us as babies." Julius: "Well, what good would that do them?" Randy: *"If we're babies then we won't be on our own.* We have to keep going to them to ask for things."

Randy now began walking around the (large) conference table,[2] as he was saying: "You know what happened to me? I was in school and this friend of mine and I were writing each other jokes; everybody does this." Addressing the therapist: "Probably you did it, too, when you were my age." Then to the group: "Then what happens? One of the teachers finds the story and wham-bang he takes it away from me and hits me. You know what I did then? I wanted to get out of the state [New York]. I wanted to get away from home. I couldn't face anybody, particularly my mother and father, so I tried to steal or do something because I didn't want to face them. Also, I think I wanted to get back at the teacher, get him into trouble, too. I just wanted to get away." Therapist: "What happened?" By this time Randy had walked completely around the rather large conference table and stood next to the therapist. "I guess," he said, "*I* got into trouble and I only got myself deeper into trouble; instead of getting even on the right person. I'm the one that got stuck with it." He turned and said he had to take coffee down to the night telephone operator. "But," he said, "don't continue talking until I get back." He filled a cup with coffee and ran out, saying: "This sure was one of the better discussions!"

David said that things worked out sometimes for him the way Randy described. He said, "The thing that I don't understand is this homosexual stuff."[3] Fritz: "You mean one guy pluking the other guy?" "Yes," said David, "that's what I mean. The thing that is terrible about it is that if that happens to you the thing (semen) will go into you and hit your brain cell and that's going to destroy you."

Therapist: "You know, David, one of the things that is becoming clear tonight is that because you fellows weren't really given a chance to learn about sex, some ideas you have are wrong. You have a lot of misinformation." The therapist then explained that feelings about sex come from within, and also that sperm could never "hit the brain." "What is a homosexual, then? What about masturbation?" demanded Fritz. "If you screw a girl and you come, does that mean she's knocked up?" Randy had returned to his seat by this time. He said, "Yeah, let's get some of

2. Due to construction in their own room, this group met temporarily in the large conference room in the administration building.

3. David had been the object of rather severe homosexual attacks by many boys when he first came to Children's Village. According to reports from cottage staff, he successfully resisted these advances as the discussion in the group progressed.

these things straightened out. What about when you jerk off into some-body's mouth, does that mean he's going to be insane?" He went on to say that his social worker was talking to him about "this stuff" but he did not think she knew anything. The therapist explained about masturbation, sexual play between two boys, and the normal development of the feeling of love between a man and a woman and its culmination in the sex act; that while the boys were now in a difficult situation, when they got older they would be in a position to enjoy sex without fears or worry.

Randy sat back at this and said: "Gee, why didn't my father talk to me like this?" David: "Well, maybe because he finds it hard to talk to you because, as you said before, maybe he's scared of you that you're going to grow up; that he doesn't want to look at the fact that you may be coming of age to have sex. My father didn't tell me either. I think it's because he's ashamed of talking to me because of the way *he* feels about it." The therapist suggested that there were still many things about sex which they did not touch upon and they could talk about it more. Sex is part and parcel of the total functioning of a person, but when it is "kept in the closet" it becomes different and separate, and maybe, then, problems arise.

Randy said it was past quitting time already, and three of the boys who were scheduled to be at the dance (held in the gymnasium) said that they were late. David said he was glad he hadn't missed the session. (On the evening of this session, three of the boys were scheduled to attend a dinner and dance of their "unit" at which a visiting group of girls were present, but instead left soon after the meal to come to the group.) Randy suggested that the group continue the discussion the following week.

SESSION TEN

At the start of session ten, Fritz recalled the discussion of the preceding week and suggested: "Let's talk about it more." After a brief period of giggling by the boys, in their discomfort, Fritz said, referring to the therapist: "Quiet, fellows, who do you think would sit and talk to us about this? That's why we feel this way." David and Randy agreed and Umberto wondered: "How come you didn't know about these things?" to which David responded: "Well, maybe nobody ever told us." He proceeded to ask the therapist the following question: "If your scum (semen) is in a woman's pussy (vagina) sometimes she will have a baby and sometimes she won't have a baby. Why is it, if your scum is in a woman's pussy?" Julius picked this up and wanted to know how a woman knows that a baby is coming, and Ray inquired whether a woman can "piss" when she is pregnant. Jerry expressed surprise at this lack of knowledge of how things happened and explained that "scum" gets into the woman's "stomach."[4] At this point the therapist said that he had a book with some pictures that would answer some of the questions. All expressed enthusiasm at the prospect. The therapist left the room to fetch the books from the building housing the clinic, and when he returned found the boys sitting in the same seats in absolute silence and expectancy. As he sat down, the boys clustered around him. Pictures of the male reproductive organ were shown and explained in simple terms, as was the phenomenon of "wet dreams," to which the boys referred as "pissing dreams." There was some confusion among the boys as to whether a male can have three testicles, or not, which was explained to them, too.[5] The boys also seemed confused between the nature of nocturnal emissions and the emissions caused by masturbation. The difference was made clear to them. Special curiosity was displayed about the spermatozoa, their appearance and propulsion. As the therapist used scientific terms to describe these facts, David said he rather liked the idea of using the words "scum, pussy, and prick," because "it's something I know." Later he used the word "bone" to describe an erection.

The pictures of the female reproductive system were then shown and the various organs pointed out: the vagina, the cervix, the uterus, the Fallopian tubes, the ovaries, and how and where the "eggs" come from and where they are fertilized. Displaying real understanding, Randy pointed to the urethra and the vagina and explained to Ray how a woman could urinate while she was pregnant, because of the two different "openings." Fritz wanted to know how a baby was born and Julius asked to be enlightened on the process "when a lady bleeds." The group led by the therapist spent time discussing the menstrual period, emphasizing that it was part of the preparation for motherhood, and the normality of the phenomenon. The therapist spoke in a manner that would help the boys divest themselves of their feelings of repugnance toward menstruation which they openly expressed. The phrase, "the body prepares itself for procreation" was frequently employed. Randy volunteered that he had once seen a large picture of it in one of his father's books, but his father never allowed him to see that book again. Maybe when he goes home he will be able to look at it now. Menstruation, particularly, seemed to arrest the boys' attention. Julius asked whether one could have intercourse during that time, and Ray wanted to know whether there was pain attached

4. As the boys began to reveal their preoccupation with intercourse, we suggested to the therapist that he have in readiness the books which we had obtained from the resident nurse and one of our psychiatrists for use in group C (on which a detailed report is included in this volume) and use the books at the appropriate time.

5. Of note is the fact that in some Latin countries a man of power and potency is described as one who "has three balls."

to the menstrual flow. Fritz inquired where women wore their napkins. All these questions were answered, and when it was necessary the therapist drew diagrams to illustrate his explanations.

The fertilizing of the ovum and pregnancy was another center of interest. Again diagrams drawn by the therapist were employed to supplement those in the book in tracing the stages in the development of the embryo and fetus. The therapist was impressed with the clarity with which Fritz grasped the metamorphosis and development of the embryo. Fritz remarked that the embryo was like a fish "because it breathes through its gills and not through lungs." When a drawing of the fetus was made, Julius at once remarked that that was the position in which he himself slept.

When the question of birth was raised, Randy appeared to know a great deal about its mechanics and explained that the baby's head came out first, but he did not know why. Ray was concerned about the vaginal tissues and how it must hurt the woman during parturition. The therapist explained to him how the tissues stretched, why they had this capacity, and how rarely tissues were actually damaged. Again the normality of these functions was stressed. Some were concerned also about birth abnormalities, the "freaks," as David called them, who were born "with five legs" or otherwise disfigured. The therapist explained some of the anomalies and stressed their rarity as compared to normal births. What impressed the boys greatly was the umbilical cord. Each pulled up his shirt and examined himself. They could not get over the fact that their navels were the remnants of the cord which "tied them" to their mothers.

The group ran fifteen minutes overtime. Steve announced the time and said he was expected at his cottage. He and Jerry left while the rest remained and helped clean up. As they did so they continued to ask about the birth process, the role of the doctor, and the life of the fetus while it was still in the uterus. The therapist suggested that if the boys had any more questions, they could talk about them the following week.

SESSION ELEVEN

At the beginning of session eleven Randy inquired whether the therapist had brought "the book" with him. The therapist gave him the textbook on anatomy. Umberto joined Randy in examining it. Their curiosity was aroused by the development of the fetus at the various stages from five weeks to nine months. Randy was curious as to what organs developed first. Jerry mentioned that he had seen a fetus in a museum floating around in "alcohol." He said that it was alive but Steve corrected him, saying, "This was impossible. You mean it was preserved." Jerry nodded, saying, yes, that was what he meant. The therapist outlined briefly and very sketchily the sequence of fetal development. Randy then asked: "Well, how do you prevent people from getting pregnant?" Julius said: "You use—a big word—they call the rubber something big." The therapist volunteered the term, condom. Julius smilingly said, yes, that was what he meant. Jerry: "You know they don't sell them to boys, and sometimes it is not easy to get them."

At the supervisory conferences, as these discussions proceeded, we had suggested that since the educational phase would soon be coming to an end, the therapist should go further and explore the boys' feelings associated with sex, for the questions they had been raising readily offered such an opportunity. Taking his cue at this point, the therapist asked Jerry how he felt about such a restriction, and why he thought prophylactics were not sold to boys his age. Instead of Jerry, Randy responded by saying that "they did not want boys to have sex [intercourse] but that was stupid because everybody has sex." The group giggled at his remark. From then on only Randy, Ray, and Jerry participated in the discussion, while the rest sat and listened closely. Even Ray's participation was minimal, although he seemed to be the most interested among the boys.

Therapist: "Well, it seems that you are saying that adults, parents, seem to have some kind of feelings about boys and girls having sex at this age. What do you think of that?" Randy: "I don't understand this because they [the parents] do 'it' yet they don't want us to do it. Maybe that's why they don't talk to us about it." He turned to Jerry and Ray and asked them if their fathers ever talked to them about sex. Everyone agreed that this never happened. Therapist: "Randy, you are telling us really that parents don't talk to you about sex. Why do you think they don't talk about it? Why do you think they and other grown-ups make these restrictions?" Randy: "Maybe they had some ideas that it [sex] is bad, not just for us but for them, too." He sat back and, speaking with ease, went on to say that he felt that maybe his father "and the other people" had really never gotten used to sex or were unable to see it as "something normal," and so they never wanted to talk to children about it. It really did not make sense to him because his father and mother had sex. He knew it; his father did "it," but he seemed to want to hide it from Randy.

Julius said it could not be hidden very well because of all the brothers and sisters that he had (ten). There was laughter at this, and Randy said the same thing applied to him because of his brothers and sisters (seven). Therapist: "Well, it seems to me that what we are saying is that adults have feelings about sex which they can't seem to handle, and, as Randy said, they feel bad about it inside." Jerry said: "You mean, you have to be married to have sex?" At which point Randy declared: "Rape is a crime," while Ray said something about girls and boys being "underage." Randy thought that "maybe some of the un-written laws that we are talking about had to do with the parents' feel-ing badly inside and that this has something to do with how they talk about it and how they look at sex by boys. . . ."

Ray suddenly asked what the therapist told his own children about sex. Randy said: "How do you know he has children?" Ray: "I just sort of figured he did." When the question was repeated, the therapist said that he had three children. The boys asked what their ages and gender were. The therapist said he had three boys whose ages were twelve, ten, and five years. Randy: "What do you tell them?" Therapist: "I answer them whatever they ask me about sex. For example, when my young-est boy was born, the other two asked about how the baby 'got there,' and I explained to them in the same way as we did it here, but in simple terms since they were much younger. They don't understand like you do and when you, too, get older you will understand more." Randy: "I understand what you are driving at. You mean that when we get older and get married and have babies, and maybe it might be better to wait [to have sex relations] until then, if you can." Ray nodded his head and said: "That's what I said before."

The group again ran over its time by fifteen minutes, but the boys continued to talk. Ray wanted to know what made somebody "a rapist" or caused a person "to expose himself." Discussion of such pathology was underplayed, but the therapist explained that all human functions, physical and mental, can go awry—eyes can go bad and so forth—and that the sex impulse, too, can be distorted. Randy said: "You mean that the guy who is showing his [penis] has a problem; that it is just like anything else. He has to have help [treatment]?" Ray suggested seri-ously that "maybe he could come to the Village and be in the group." (Though this remark evoked some laughter, it seemed to us as very significant; it was a declaration as to how much the boys learned and possibly gained from the discussions.) Jerry said: ". . . the only thing that happens to those guys is that they get into jail." Despite the late-ness of the hour, the boys stayed on. The therapist put the room in order, and the boys voluntarily helped. All exchanged holiday greetings with the therapist. Ray kept saying that the therapist should be sure to give Ray's regards to his family.

Follow-Up Interviews

As a test of the effectiveness, if any, of the discussions and ven-tilation of feelings concerning sex and behavior regarding it, we ar-ranged follow-up interviews on the boys with the milieu personnel after

eighteen sessions and compared the information with the group preplacement data. The following changes in the boys' sexual adjustment
were reported by the staff.

Ray: Cottage staff reported in Ray's group-preplacement statement
that although there had not been any definite information regarding his
homosexual activity, the staff felt that it was occurring on a rather
regular basis. The cottage parents and the cottage life supervisor declared
that Ray's femininity and infantile character "placed him at the mercy
of the more sexually aggressive boys." They suspected that Ray provoked this type of aggression. Although no concrete evidence of sexual
activity in the academic school was available, the education supervisor
felt that the scatter in the boy's achievement, his hyperactivity in the
classroom, and his persistent attempts to get out of the room may well
have been a way of running away from sexual invitations or attacks from
other boys.

After eighteen sessions in the group, the cottage parents and cottage
life supervisor felt that sexual play and activity had definitely stopped.
Cottage personnel attributed this to the change in Ray's "general development," in that he was "more masculine and more aggressive and
seemed to be able to protect himself more adequately." The school
reported that there seemed to be none of the previously described behavior, nor were there any difficulties in relationships with peers,
which had been a rather serious problem for the boy in the past.

Jerry: Jerry was known in the Village as being active sexually, inviting other boys to participate. This was reported from all areas, including school and cottage. Just prior to his entrance into the group,
there appeared to be some reduction of his attempts to get close to
the cottage father (who was a strong figure).

According to school and cottage personnel, Jerry's sexual activities
had greatly decreased since he joined the group. At a conference on
Jerry, the child care (cottage) supervisor stated that staff members
reported no sexual activity taking place now.

(Jerry narrated in the group a highly symbolic dream which seemed
to keep him awake. The dream involved a tree that sank into the ground
and then came up again. The tree had a lot of eyes which were looking
at him and its branches attempted to clutch at him. He also dreamed of
his dead grandmother. Despite the apparent improvement, it was our
feeling that Jerry was basically schizophrenic, and might become a sexual
pervert later in life unless he received intensive treatment—which still
might not prevent it.)

David: In the preplacement report the cottage personnel indicated
that David was very much involved in homosexual activity, although
there was a decline in this behavior prior to his placement in the group

as compared to his initial period at the Village. The staff, however, still suspected that there was sufficient activity in this respect to warrant considering it a problem.

In the follow-up inquiries the cottage staff felt that there had been "no sexual activity observed or even hinted at." The cottage life supervisor said that David was now able to handle this problem by removing himself from the group in the cottage and concentrating on private activities such as reading. Another factor seemed to be the boy's physical growth, which had made him one of the larger boys in his cottage and therefore able to resist the advances of the larger boys.

Julius: Prior to the time he entered the group, Julius, a very small and weak boy, was removed from his cottage and placed in another with younger boys because he was "sadistically and viciously" forced by other boys to submit sexually to them. Following the change in cottages, and prior to his joining the therapy group, the new cottage personnel felt that Julius had still been involved in sexual activity.

In the follow-up study, the cottage personnel reported definite decline in this, and that the boy's close relationship to the cottage father seemed to help. However, his new-found strengths, which were attributed to his group participation, brought him into disagreement with the cottage father, and he finally fell into disfavor with the latter, which led to his removal from that cottage. In the current cottage, there were no reports of any sex activity. This the institution considered a significant improvement in this boy's adjustment. In addition, since joining the group, Julius changed from a "mousy, frightened, silent boy to a considerably more outgoing, more communicative, and more self-confident individual"; his caseworker described him as "much more alive."

Randy: Although there were no reports from the cottage in which Randy had lived of any sexual activity before the boy joined the therapy group, the school reported that there was a suspicion of his participating in sexual play. Teachers felt that this had to do with Randy's "passive adjustment" and feminine mannerisms. Although there was no proof of homosexuality, the school staff felt uneasy about the situation with Randy.

Both the cottage and school later reported that Randy's mannerisms had changed and his mode of behavior had become definitely more masculine. They ruled out any suspicion of current sexual acting out, either as a passive or active participant.

Steve: In the preplacement interviews, the cottage personnel indicated that Steve had been actively involved sexually with other boys. He was considered a passive, compliant boy who invited sexual activity.

In the follow-up interview, the cottage staff stated that there had been a decrease in this. The cottage life supervisor received reports that Steve's sex activity had decreased markedly, and at times it was felt that it may have been discontinued altogether. However, Steve frequently went home for week ends (in preparation for his discharge), and the cottage parents reported an upsurge in sexual activity on his returns. This was considered by the clinical staff to be a direct result of his pathological relation with his mother. The clinic personnel were attempting to evolve a plan that would reduce the number of home visits until a more appropriate arrangement could be made for his adjustment to the community. (It was our opinion that without continued intensive treatment, we could anticipate that Steve might relapse into homosexual activity on his return to the city).

Umberto: There were no reports from either school or cottage in the group preassignment data of this boy that indicated sex as a problem. His adjustment in this regard continued to be the same. Neither school nor cottage reported any difficulties in this area.

Fritz: Group preplacement reports from the milieu personnel made no mention of any difficulty regarding sexual activity. During follow-up, personnel again reported that there was no problem in this area with this boy.

The intellectual attitudes and the deeper intrapsychic urges have not been worked through in this group, which met for only twenty-seven sessions. These problems received considerably more attention in the group that met for seventy-five sessions and are fully reported in Part Two of this book.

4

Parents: Guilt and Rage

NEXT TO SEX in the hegemony of subjects causing severe tensions in our boys were their parents. The source of these disturbances was manifold: guilt for causing parents distress and disappointment; hostility for the treatment received at their hands; anger and rage at the parents' consent to send them to an institution; and guilt for harboring these negative feelings. This vortex of conflicting and anxiety-generating emotions and fantasies was dealt with by the boys with complete denial of the blamefulness of parents and severe blame and hatred of themselves. In all instances, as will be demonstrated by the protocol reports, the boys defended their parents. This behavior we considered to be reaction formations to their antagonisms in some, and infantile atonement in others. To diminish guilt and the resultant anxiety, the boys clung to the idea that their parents were justified in their treatment of them.

We recognized in these maneuvers also the ingredients of identification and self-image. For were the boys to admit to the inadequacies and errors of their parents, painful narcissistic injury would result: It would debase them in their own estimation and threaten the identification threads with their parents, as well as their own identities. For this the ego in every one of our boys was too weak, and although we recognized that working through attitudes and feelings toward parents was important, steps toward it had to be taken with great caution to prevent resentment and alienating the boys from us. As it is, this seemed to be an area in which our therapists made the most errors, because, to our knowledge, they had not adequately resolved their attitudes toward their own parents. The therapists, therefore, had to be guided by the supervisor against the tendency to point up blame of parents as part of their own countertransference syndromes.

It was the poet-philosopher Goethe who said: "Everyone has to understand his parents and forgive them." The life span of our groups was too short to help our boys attain such a degree of maturity, but we have made some inroads toward helping them to *understand* their parents. The forgiveness factor is an automatic result of an emotional separation and independence that would have taken a great deal of time to develop, so that we were able to make only slight inroads in this direction. If we understand the term "forgiveness" as it was meant by Goethe—not in its intellectual and moral connotations, but rather in its emotional significance—the achievement of such emotional freedom is the ultimate in maturity for anyone, and few, if any, ever really attain it in life. Such freedom can at best be gained only to a limited degree.

As an illustration of the process of working through a child-parent emotional syndrome and its effect upon the total personality integration, a rather extended summary of a case follows. Note should be taken of the fact that in this case, as in a number of others, we separated the presenting problems into "foci" or "nuclei." We then selected sample situations from the protocols of the groups to indicate how these foci were or might have been resolved or affected through the group interviews. Only one such study of many, which follows, is included in this volume.

Background History

PRESENTING PROBLEMS

Neal, a small, sturdy, Negro Protestant boy of 14.4 years of age was admitted to Children's Village as an "incorrigible." Adults found him an alert, bright, and friendly youngster, who communicated quite easily. Neal had been living in a foster home before he was committed. His difficulties became marked about nine months before, when he ran away to an uncle. During this period there was also an exacerbation of his problems in school, where he was in difficulties with each of his teachers because of poor conduct. He had also truanted, and the foster mother reported some stealing episodes.

FAMILY BACKGROUND

Neal was the second of three out-of-wedlock children by the same putative father. At the time of his mother's third pregnancy during her early teens, she was committed to an institution for defectives. Her IQ was 68. While she was there, her mother cared for the three youngsters. However, Neal claimed that his uncle took care of him until the latter went into the army, at which time the maternal grandmother assumed care. Neal's mother was paroled from the institution to her mother when Neal was five years old. She remained with her mother for three months and then left with a man and was currently reported to be living in a large midwestern city with another man and a number of additional children.

Neal seemed to have lived with his grandmother until the age of nine years, at which time she was hospitalized and the children were placed in an institution. Neal saw his mother for the first time since her disappearance at his grandmother's funeral, when he was ten years old. It was on this occasion that he learned that she was not his older sister, as he had been led to believe, but was actually his mother.

About a year later, Neal, his brother who was a year older than he, and his sister, a year younger, were placed in the same foster home. The sister was removed soon after because of difficulties in getting along with one of the children in the new family, and she went to live with her maternal uncle and his wife. The brother was also removed after about a year and a half, and sent to Children's Village because of his truanting, stealing, and general misbehavior. Neal is said to have felt deeply both these separations. He was apparently the only one of the three children who conformed and got along with the foster parents and their children.

The foster mother was restrictive and controlling and at times very punitive. She resorted to calling in neighbors to expose Neal's deficiencies, and asking them to chastise and punish him. Consequently, Neal had a reputation in the neighborhood of being an "incorrigible ingrate." The foster mother repeatedly admonished him to be "grateful" to her for the privilege of having such a "good home" since he was "nothing more than a castaway." In addition, she would blame him for her "heart attacks," which frightened the boy and made him very guilty. This feeling was intensified by the fact that he nursed the belief, implanted by his uncle, that his grandmother had died because of him. Getting older and chafing under the treatment he was receiving at the foster home, Neal began to steal and run away.

The foster father was described as a warm but firm person. Neal later told his caseworker that the foster father used to administer frequent whippings at his wife's behest, but that the man was not hostile toward him. Neal had always had difficulty in learning to read, write, do arithmetic, and spell. At fourteen years of age, he entered a vocational high school, since he was declared incapable of doing academic work. This was an additional area of conflict between himself and his foster mother, who had put a lot of pressure on him for high grades.

CLINICAL FINDINGS

The psychological test indicated that Neal suffered from feelings of depression and "obsessional preoccupation with his early roots and family origins." The report stated: "He tends to keep searching in his fantasy for the good, heroically statured parents, to feel removed and apart from the current parental surrogates (foster parents) who do not seem to measure up to his fantasy ideals. His unsatisfied dependency and frustrated adult-identification wishes keep him constantly on the move. With the onset of adolescence, it seems that his masculine-identification wishes are now particularly troublesome to him. He feels that he is being treated like a baby, and wants very much to develop the strength and assurance of a man. He is prone to release his tension on his overprotective frustrating environment, as well as to act out his fantasies through impulsive motor behavior, for instance, running away. *Diagnosis:* "Emotional disturbance of adolescence with obsessional preoccupations and compulsive acting out, precipitated by unsatisfied masculine-identification needs and long-standing feelings of insecurity. . . ."

At the remand home, Neal complained to the caseworker about his being "cooped up in the house" with his foster parents. He stated: "The only thing I could do as much as I wanted was to watch television," and complained about not being allowed to participate in the Boy Scouts, the Y.M.C.A., and other groups, as the foster mother feared "he would be in the wrong company." He stated that while he liked his foster father, he was not able to feel free with him for fear that the latter might betray him to the foster mother. At the remand home, Neal was found to be friendly, well liked by both staff and youngsters, responsive to supervision, cooperative in his chores, clean and neat in personal habits, but restless.

In the initial psychiatric interview at the Village the diagnosis of "passive-aggressive personality disorder" was suggested. The psychiatrist commented that the boy "reacts with a degree of detachment which is quite pathological." In academic work Neal appeared to have made a good adjustment. In the shop it was noted that he was "eager to work on automobiles but was generally quite clumsy and in a rather provocative way needs to ask many questions of the teacher." In the residence cottage he was eager to please the adults, but somehow managed in these attempts to annoy them. For example, when he offered to prepare coffee, he would spill it on the floor before serving it. It became apparent that while on the surface he was compliant and submissive, the underlying hostility precipitated clumsy behavior which provoked adults.

In three intelligence tests Neal was found to range between 80 and 96 IQ. However, a Wechsler-Bellevue Test at the remand home gave him an IQ of 115, though his reading level was 4.5 and arithmetic 6.4 at the age of 14.2.

CASEWORK TREATMENT

Neal was in treatment at the Village with one male caseworker for ten months. For a brief time he was seen twice a week, which was then reduced to once a week for administrative reasons. The caseworker was impressed with the boy's efforts at presenting himself as a "good boy." It was also apparent that Neal was attempting, albeit intellectually, to arrive at a clearer understanding of his problems. He saw himself as "the baddest kid ever in a foster home," and felt that people were "too nice" to him. He said that he did not want to get too close to anyone, because he was (in effect) afraid of being rejected.

The boy trusted his caseworker and had established a relationship with him to the extent that he would talk about his fears concerning a growing interest in sexual matters, and his conviction that he was a "terrible person inside." He had stated that he was frightened by his sexual attraction toward girls, feeling that upon closer contact he would be too stimulated and not be able to contain himself.

In addition, it appeared that part of his difficulties stemmed from the fact that the maternal grandmother, who had taken care of him, died of a heart attack. At the funeral, his uncle accused Neal of being the cause of her death because of his "disobedience." Matters were further complicated and guilt reinforced when the foster mother, who used somatic symptoms as a weapon of control over the children, also developed a heart condition and blamed them for it.

After ten months at the Village, there appeared to be "some improvement" in the boy's self-concept and greater self-acceptance. At this time he was transferred to another caseworker.

The new worker, also a man, began by seeing Neal twice a week, but soon he, too, was compelled to reduce it to once-a-week sessions. This worker found Neal to be "manipulative" and was impressed with his "superficial conformity and underlying anger." The worker was impressed with the theme which seemed to underlie Neal's productions about his relatives, which was that he was angry because "nobody was giving" to him (affection and things). He elaborated his fantasy of wishing to visit his natural mother. Since his mother was someone with whom he was said to have had no actual contact, this intent was understood by the caseworker as being in all probability a displacement of his concern about his guilt and anger toward the maternal grandmother, or toward whomever had taken care of him in his childhood. These feelings were never worked through.

Based on his conference with the caseworker, the following comments were made by the psychiatrist at about this time.

> What is obvious about this boy at this time is that his disturbance is not one of reality-testing, specifically. There is no real difficulty with reality. What seems to be in the foreground is the marked degree of isolation this boy is able to keep up while maintaining (seemingly) relatively good interpersonal relations, but of an entirely passive and very superficial quality. There is no overt antisocial acting out; instead, the quality of his relations with others is rather passive and compliant, but one which, in effect, gets him everything he wants. It achieves his immediate goals, but does not touch in any way his deeper pathology. He uses staff around him, generally, to further his own ends by pleasing them in this passive, compliant fashion, and is in that way able to keep the focus off himself. His inner personal relations, if examined superficially, seem to be good; his general progress around the Village is also good. If, however, this is examined in the light of recognition that he has not been able to accept or do anything with his basic need to manipulate and his basic compliance through which he does this, it is seen a little differently.
>
> I believe his general improvement has been quite good although of an entirely functional nature. His repressive powers apparently have been strengthened here and his social activities are much more adept and much less clumsy than they were. Nevertheless he remains very much isolated, operates strictly in terms of his own narcissistic needs, has no real feelings that are available to him, and overall lacks insight into this.
>
> Up to now we have not made a diagnosis on him, but I think now we can probably diagnose him as a *schizoid personality*. He does not fit the picture of the autistic, withdrawn eccentric that is the classical schizoid personality, but his withdrawal is certainly complete, although on the surface it appears not to be present. His eccentricities are certainly present at depth and, although on the surface he does not seem odd, he operates on strictly a self-oriented level. We have no real knowledge of his fantasy life because he has never been able to say or in any way to discuss it. I suspect, however, that it is quite rich, that it is substituted for his deeper relations with other people, and that his distance from people and the lack of depth in his feelings about himself are based on the withdrawal that is not completely obvious.
>
> The treatment procedure recommended is that the therapeutic contacts be characterized by attempts at broadening this boy's acquaintance with himself and help him qualify for himself such feelings as he does have. . . ."

In the two months following the conference reported above, the focus of casework treatment was around Neal's feelings about the possibility of living with the family of his married maternal uncle. During the following three months, Neal related dreams, some of which indicated preoccupation with whether he was acceptable to a woman; another revealed feelings of helplessness with respect to his aggressions toward his uncle. In another dream fragment there was the fantasy that "I am in a sword fight and the sword gets stuck in my throat." Neal also brought into treatment his pain when his uncle told him during Easter vacation that when he left Children's Village he could not come to live with the uncle, but would have to enlist in the army instead. It was at this point that Neal was placed in an analytic therapy group, about nine months after transfer to his second worker. He was described as a well developed, athletic-looking boy who managed his peer relationships, although sometimes "buying friendships, and though depriving himself of things, he did not get the returns he expected." With adults he was still compliant and ingratiating. It was clear that he was a victim of deep feelings of deprivation, depression, and hopelessness which prevented him from achieving academically.

The caseworker found that in the one-to-one relationship he could not reach the underlying hostility, which was recognized as being very intense and held in repression. It was felt that the element of universalization in the group situation would reduce the boy's guilt feelings and that the catalytic effect and the support from fellow patients would permit his bringing his hostility out into the open. Neal was considered as having excellent potential for deriving insight from group therapy sessions. Thus, after about two years of individual casework treatment, Neal was placed in a para-analytic therapy group.

Neal's nuclear problem can be considered to be a striving for identity, in the wider sense of the concept, and the resulting self-alienation. The secondary and derivative foci toward which therapy needed to be directed were:

1] preoccupation with the search for his mother
   a. early parental rejection
   b. guilt for original desertion by mother, and later, death of the grandmother
2] isolation
   a. fear of rejection
   b. poor self-image
   c. projection of hostility
3] passive-aggressive defenses
   a. facade of compliance
   b. impulsive acting out
4] fear of sexual development
   a. lack of male identification
5] school adjustment

Toward Therapeutic Resolution

PROBLEM   FOCUS   I.
SEARCH FOR A MOTHER

SESSION ONE

During the early part of this session, Neal was among the young-sters who were most vocal in denying they had any problems, and in criticizing the therapist's attempts to tie up any problems with their families. A few moments later, Neal again attacked the therapist, for trying to "blame the family for everything."

Later in the session, and stimulated by Joseph, who criticized Neal's mother for not keeping him with her, Neal said that he did not know who his mother or father were, and told the group that his mother "had" him and two siblings and "some kids someplace else and some more kids someplace else, and she is now in C———." He said he never sees her and never has heard from her; but he wanted to see her, so that he could tell her off. He kept repeating, "If I could get hold of her, I would choke her."

SESSION TWO

Again Neal ventilated his feelings about not having seen his mother, and said he had a right to be angry, because "I am up here and have no mother." After Frank spoke of his mother's drunkenness and his learning to protect himself from her attacks, Neal again talked of his mother and her neglect of him.

SESSION NINE

Neal began this session by saying he wanted to know what "forgiveness meant." The boys inquired why he was asking this ques-tion. Enjoying being the center of attention, Neal smiled and said that his caseworker had told him to ask about it "here." He went on to say that he knew he was always afraid to ask for things for himself, because he was afraid that people would say no to him. A lot of times he wanted to do things, but was stopped by his fear that people would not like him. If he gave into the impulse, he would have to keep asking people to forgive him. He explained that he was talking about this because recently he had received a letter from his mother. She had written to him from C———, where she seemed to have settled. She talked about seeing him, but he knew "inside" of him that this was never going to happen. He felt that he could never really forgive her for what she had done to him. Alfred commented: "Maybe you care more than you think, because you are carrying her letter around." James asked: "What else can you do but forgive parents?" The therapist remarked that sometimes boys may not be able to do so, and feel uncomfortable "inside" for that reason.

In answer to a question from the therapist, Neal repeated the story of his mother's abandoning him and asked: "Why can't I accept that she won't come back? Sometimes I think that it might be better if I didn't even hear from her; but I worry about her when I don't get her letters." Frank questioned what this had to do with forgiveness. Earl pointed out that Neal was trying to say that there was a connection between what was happening to him now, and the fact that his mother was away from him. Neal answered that that was exactly what he was trying to tell the group, that he was always looking for people to like him, and therefore always looking for forgiveness from people for what he did. He wanted to talk about it "here" because he knew that he had this longing to be with his mother. On the other hand, he knew that she would never really be with him. The therapist commented that what he was saying, was that he still had not really worked it out, and that he wanted to talk about it so that he could understand it. At the end of this session, Neal commented that he felt "easier" after the group talks.

SESSION TEN

After Frank had related to the group his experiences during a recent home visit when his mother was drunk and chased him out when he arrived, Neal asked why Frank's mother did not stop drinking. "Why doesn't she do something about it?" he asked. Then, as if in answer to himself, added, "But look at my mother. She may not drink, but she does things which are just as bad." When James commented that it was hard to understand why parents do what they do, but one still has to forgive them, Neal said that he was "working on forgiving all the time." *He had forgiven himself for being what he was like; now he had to forgive his parents.*

SESSION FOURTEEN

After a period of casual talk by the boys at the beginning of the session, the therapist asked what the boys wanted to talk about. Neal began by saying he had a problem he would like to have solved with which he had been wrestling for some time. When the group turned its attention to him, he said, half-smiling and haltingly, "I don't know if I should go find my mother and see her." He began his story by saying he did not know his mother until he was quite grown, and then went on to narrate the important incidents of his life as the group sat spellbound.

He said he had been told that his mother was his sister. It was not until his grandmother, who had brought him up, was taken ill, that he learned that his "sister" was really his mother. She had left home and "had babies in a couple of places." He and his brother were left in foster homes while his grandmother was in the hospital. His uncle always accused him of being responsible for his grandmother's death. Following the foster homes, he ended up in various institutions and finally at the Village. But all the time, he had had this longing to see his mother.

She wrote to him and often said she was anxious to know what he was like. For the most part, he felt that he would like to go and see her, and that if she were not really interested in him, he would become very angry, and "hit her or do something to her, even choke her." On the other hand, he felt that she did not know him. "Why should she like me? Why should she be interested in me, and why should I be interested in her?" This is the thing that constantly bothered him, he said. What should he do? Referring to his own situation, Frank told Neal that Neal had to accept that his mother "will never really be a mother" to him. Neal had "perfect permission" not to think of her and not to want her to be a mother to him, because she had not acted like one. Earl disagreed and said that no matter what mothers do, "they are still your mother," and added that Neal should still have "some kind of faith and trust" that somewhere, somehow, when he did see her, things would get better. There were comments by the other boys, to which Neal responded by elaborating still further his feelings of frustration and anger at himself for being caught in this emotional web toward his mother. "She never really tells me anything about herself in her letters. She never really once let me know what she is like. She is always asking what I am doing."

After more discussion by different boys referring to their own situations, the therapist attempted to tie up Neal's search for the mother and feelings of being responsible (guilty) for the loss. Neal said that this is what people always tell him. He recounted how when his grandmother died, his uncle had told him her death was his fault, because of his misbehavior. He did not quite believe it, as he had said before, and he has now come to feel that it was not his fault that his mother went away, but that she was "like this before I was even born." He added, "Sometimes I think the best idea is to fall in love with somebody and get married and raise your own family." James thought that maybe *he would be looking for the love he never got,* that maybe he would try to get from his marriage the love he could not get from his mother. The therapist commented here that there was agreement by the group, that it did not mean that Neal was looking for a mother, per se, but, rather, as the boys expressed it, it would be perfectly natural for him to want to establish a home that would be secure and stable, and give him love.

The therapist raised the question of how any boy in Neal's position might feel and act. After other boys had reacted to this query, Neal said that sometimes he got so mad that he did not know what to do. The more he knew that it was not his fault and he did not have to hang on to something that might never materialize, the better off he was going to be. The therapist attempted to elicit his clinging to guilt feelings further. Alfred responded with, "Sometimes the world makes you feel that you are to blame, so there is no way out of it." Neal agreed with this, and repeated that his uncle "keeps telling me I'm to blame for my grandmother's death." All of the boys were emphatic in their comments that Neal was not to blame and should not carry the brunt of it.

SESSION SIXTEEN

Neal was absent the previous week. He opened this session by complaining that the group had not finished answering his question, and that maybe one of the reasons he had not come last time was that "we don't come to any conclusions here." The group did not respond to this and instead continued with their facetious talk. During a pause, Neal said again, "What about it? Should I see my mother or shouldn't I?" When no one responded, the therapist asked him what he had got out of the last discussion. He answered, resentfully, that nobody told him yes or no, but that the group had talked about how he felt when his mother left him, and how he "carried something around inside" of him.

After several of the boys had reminded Neal of some of their previous comments, he went on to say that he knew his mother was "not really a very nice person," but yet he had the longing "inside" of him to want to see her. "Remember when I said they told me I was to blame for my gradnmother?" Silence fell over the group as he went on to say, "Maybe that still bothers me a little." He did not know whether it was true, but he thought about it a great deal of the time. The therapist asked how he connected the two matters he had brought up. Neal: "Do you think there is a connection?" He remembered feeling "bad inside" when his uncle would tell him he was to blame for his grandmother's death. On the one hand he felt that he really did not do anything to her, and he knew from what people told him that she died of an illness which had nothing to do with him. "Yet I have *that* feeling," he said. He then blurted out: "Maybe that's why I think my mother is away from me." Earl commented that he had been told that children feel very badly when their parents leave or do things to them, and they blame themselves, and maybe that was what Neal was going through now. At this, there was visible anxiety on the faces of the boys in the group, and one of them, as a reaction, began to talk loosely, but Neal interrupted and told him to "stop the nonsense."

When the group tried again to veer away from the subject, Neal interjected that they were not answering his question. "Should I see my mother?" he persisted. "What good is all this talking, if we don't come to any conclusions?" The therapist wondered what conclusions he expected, and Joseph thought that Neal "would not get an answer here; anyhow, *you'll have to make up your own mind.*"

SESSION SEVENTEEN

Neal spoke about his Easter vacation, during which he had visited his married uncle. He felt badly that during his vacation his (older) brother had made no attempt to contact him and added, "if that's the way he wants it, it's okay with me."

Someone had brought up the matter of movies. During a discussion of the film, "The Ten Commandments," Neal described the movie rather vividly and with a great deal of affect. (The therapist noted Neal's identification because of his being illegitimate.) He emphasized the finding of Moses in the bulrushes, of the strength Moses possessed in withstanding physical punishment, and being able to invoke the plagues and devastation on the Egyptians.

After this discussion, Neal turned to the group and said, "You know what I did on Easter vacation? *I told my uncle that I didn't feel guilty anymore* about my grandmother's death. I told him that I had been feeling it a long time, and that's why I never could be friendly with him, for I felt scared of him." Neal went on, smiling as he spoke. He felt "proud" of himself and "relieved inside." He related that his uncle had told him that he actually had never meant it, and wanted Neal to live with him after he got out of the Village. Neal said he knew that his uncle was having financial difficulties and that he was not able to take care of him. It was for this reason that his uncle wanted him to stay at the Village until he was eighteen years old. The therapist commented: "Neal sounds as if he feels good inside, being able to talk about something which had made him so unhappy all this time."

Later, when Frank spoke of his own situation and the fact that he found his mother again drunk when he visited her during Easter, Neal asked, "Why were you so upset? You knew what was going to happen!" Frank was visibly agitated during this session and mentioned at one point that he wanted to do "something" but did not know what. Neal (scoldingly): "It isn't your fault. Like me." Then to the therapist: "Do you think that's what's bothering him?" Therapist: "Well, Frank, like you, will have to say, 'this is it, and what am I going to do about it?'" Frank responded that there was really nothing he could do: "I will just have to accept it and work out something for myself as long as I don't hurt myself."

Neal came to the clinic a few minutes early to tell the therapist that he would not attend this session. He felt that he had "gotten as much as I can"; that he now understood his difficulties and did not feel he could gain from it further, and added, "or do anything for the others in the group."

Neal came to this session nonetheless, and began by saying he had not planned on coming but changed his mind, adding that this was the last time, however. Several boys asked him why, and he answered that he had "gotten as much out of it as I can. I know what my problems are and I know how to handle them, so I don't see any sense of continuing in the group." (Neal kept his eyes averted from the therapist as he was making this statement.) He went on to say that his dropping out had nothing to do with the "fellows" or the therapist. He said, "I know now that I don't have to feel bad about my uncle, and that this had a lot to do with the reason why I was getting into trouble. Now I understand it and I feel I don't have to come back anymore."

During a further discussion of this, Neal went on to say that he would see his social worker a few times and maybe he could get out of the Village; that was what he wanted. He felt that *he had reached the point where he had got some idea as to where and when he was going.*

Neal did not attend the last six sessions of the group. Because freedom from parasitic, symbotic, and anaclitic relations with parents are a function of the individual's total personality, the steps toward the resolution of other problem foci in the group by this patient are detailed in the following pages.

PROBLEM FOCUS 2.
ISOLATION

The therapist challenged Neal's comment to the effect that the only way one could get out of the Village was by "being good" (pretending to be), and added that there were times when he probably wanted to blow his top. Neal responded by saying, "Sometimes I feel like walking, walking, walking." However, he quickly added that the only reason he was at the Village was "because I have no place to go." A few minutes later, he raised the question, "Why stick all of us so-called bad boys in one barrel, and how do you expect us to get any better?" However, a moment later, he added, "They are keeping us from getting into more trouble."

SESSION TWO

At the beginning of this session, some of the boys expressed their reluctance about revealing themselves through questioning whether there were Dictaphones hidden in the room. Soon after, Neal asked the therapist, "What are we doing here? What are we supposed to say?" A number of the boys expressed resentment toward social workers, and questioned whether the social workers could be trusted. During this discussion, Neal was ripping the buttons off his shirt, and later tore at his shirt saying, "I only trust myself."

SESSION THREE

Neal said that he had spoken with his caseworker about what had happened at the preceding group session. "People do not listen to me, that's the reason I don't listen to other people," he said. For example, once when he asked a teacher for a pencil she did not give it to him until a half hour later. He concluded by saying, "Maybe if people would listen to me, things would be easier." Other boys agreed with him.

Later, when in response to a question the therapist explained the aim of the group in terms of the boys helping one another, Neal indicated that he did not understand it. The therapist further clarified that while he would be there to help them, it was they themselves who together would be working on their own problems. Joseph raised the question as to how they could help one another, if they were "unadjusted." The therapist asked for the meaning of the term "unadjusted." Neal said it meant "being bad in school and doing wrong things."

SESSION FIVE

Once again there were complaints from the boys about adults not keeping their word, and "bullshitting" them. Neal, giving an example, said that the boys had been told they would be taken to Times Square on New Year's Eve "if we behaved ourselves." Joseph turned to the therapist and said that he felt talking was "no good, because outside of this room they [adults] don't act or talk like you, they're different." Neal joined in the general agreement with this, and said that he felt that this was one of the reasons that talking was no good at all, unless "the outside of this room changes." He added, "Maybe we can trust you. Maybe we can talk to you, but what good does it do if outside of this room they don't treat us like equals."

This led to a discussion of equality for boys and adults, and Neal gave an example of how at his cottage the boys were not permitted to walk through the front door, although the cottage parents and their children did so. Further examples of inequality and injustice were narrated.

During a later discussion of "off-the-wall cats" (compliant boys), the therapist commented that these were people who were "just trying to get along." Neal said, "Well, maybe they are doing it for other reasons, too," and said that, "Maybe they are doing it for love." He added, "Maybe they want love more than anything else in the world and are willing to give up anything." The therapist agreed with this and suggested that sometimes people keep coming back, even though they are hit and pushed around, because they are looking for love, as Neal had said. Neal was one among the boys who agreed with the therapist's comment.

SESSION SIX

At the end of this session, when Earl raised the question of love and affection for his mother, the therapist spoke about boys not wanting to share their mothers with anybody else. Neal said that he thought he could share somebody he loved, so long as he got his equal share. "The question always seems to come down to whether or not there will be equality in sharing," he said. Near the end of the session, he was among the boys who said, "We didn't like the group in the beginning, but now we're finding it interesting and want to come more than once a week."

SESSION SEVEN

Neal again commented that the group should meet twice a week, and that he now looked forward to the group meetings. He added that he was not giving the boys "any kind of line," but that he felt better after coming, and that, "If we met twice a week, I would feel even better." Several of the boys were in agreement on this.

SESSION EIGHT

Neal phoned before the session, letting the therapist know that he would be five or ten minutes late, because he was involved in some work which he was obliged to finish. However, the group was a few minutes late in starting, so that Neal was present from the beginning. The discussion started with a request from Joseph to change the time of the group meeting. The boys rejected this, preferring to keep the current arrangements. Neal then went on to say that he had been enjoying the group sessions, and that they had been very helpful to him. Most of the boys verbalized that the group had been helpful to them, too.

Joseph initiated a discussion about a boy in his cottage who was soiling himself, and who was "dirty, smelly, and disgusting." The entire cottage group was indignant about the boy's habits, and were scaring him to make him stop soiling himself. The therapist expressed his understanding of their revulsion and appreciation of the boys' efforts. When someone remarked that boys who could not control their bowels were "crazy," the therapist commented that they, the members of the group, were not always in full control of themselves, either. The only boy who seemed willing to accept and discuss this statement was Neal. He said that he had been one of a group of boys from his cottage who had discussed this problem with the cottage life supervisor and the cottage father. They had talked about how difficult it was for the boy in question to control his bowel movements. (Neal first said, "pooping in his pants," but quickly picked up the therapist's term, "bowel movement.") The therapist explained that perhaps the boy could not control himself because he was worried or upset. Earl added that maybe the boy was scared. "This seemed to hit Neal like a light," the therapist commented in his report. Neal picked this up and thought out loud. He said that he had never thought about it before, but "because you are scared, that it could come out this way." The therapist reported, "Neal continued to think for the group, by tying up the idea that if one is scared or if one has some ideas that one does not understand, one can express them in this, or other different ways."

The therapist suggested that perhaps they could think of situations in which fears get in the way of controls. Neal quickly said that he used to wet his bed, until he was thirteen years old. He remembered that he would wet himself only at night, and that he really did not feel the urine coming out. He had no idea that he was urinating. He referred to this as an example of not being able to control oneself all the time. (The therapist commented in the protocol: "The idea of the mind and body being connected seemed to become very much part of Neal's thinking, and seemed to be echoed by the group.") After further discussion, which included the therapist's telling about soldiers' soiling themselves on the battlefield, Neal said that he could now understand what the boy in his cottage was going through. Greater acceptance of the boy in the entire group seemed to prevail. All agreed that it was understandable, even though it was still "disgusting."

The discussion then turned to whether fright had anything to do with boys not washing themselves. Neal said that probably this was a similar situation; maybe the boys felt the water would harm them. When

Alfred rejected this concept by introducing a reality element, Neal said in explanation, "They can't see, because something is blocking them, and when they get it [their fears] out, they will be able to see it [recognize the fear]." Neal looked very pleased with himself as he was saying this. There was further discussion centering around this topic, and Earl added that "maybe Neal is right, but it is a hard thing to accept."

SESSION TEN

Because of the evident change of attitude on the boys' part toward the therapist as an adult, it was suggested to him that he expand these feelings to apply to other adults and to the institutional staff in particular. The therapist therefore took the occasion to raise the question at the next session of the boys' repeated declaration that they did not trust adults, and asked why they felt that way. Earl thought that maybe it was because the adults in the community betrayed them. Neal added: "When once you get your fingers burned, you were careful the next time you got too close to the fire." The therapist explained that because the boys did not trust adults, and since they thought they were being punished by being sent to the Village, everything that adults did, even if it is good, would be considered and felt as acts against them. There was a thoughtful silence following this statement. The therapist then asked the boys what conditions they could think of that would make a social worker deny a boy a home visit. Neal made the following significant remark: "Everybody changes constantly, but instead, they may hold on to something which may never come true. Sometimes it is hard to face facts that are unpleasant."

SESSION TWELVE

At Neal's instigation, the group moved into a discussion around the athletic coaches who, while "freer with the boys with their hands," commanded respect and positive feelings from them. Several commented favorably about this, saying in effect that there were definite limits and they knew that if they transgressed these limits, they would be punished. This they considered fair. Neal said, "It is when you cannot understand [the intention of] adults, that it bothers you when you get punished." There was further discussion concerning the comfort they derived from the coaches, who had definite rules and whose behavior one could predict. A bit later, when the therapist attempted to elicit feelings about other adults at the Village, Neal said that, with all their faults, he would still prefer his cottage parents to others. All agreed that each one of them probably would have a different attitude or concept of what a cottage parent should be like because of their own (the boys') "personalities." The therapist picked this up to elaborate, and Neal added the comment, "This is what we have been talking about for some time: the outside [the larger city community] is not as easy as we think it is."

SESSION SIXTEEN
On the way up to the therapy room, Neal walked next to the therapist more closely than ever before. He told the therapist that he had been busy the week before. (Neal had failed to attend that session.) The therapist said that he regretted his absence. Upon entering the room, Neal took the chair in which the therapist usually sat. The therapist hesitated slightly before sitting down in another chair, pretending to look for cigarettes and matches. During this brief interval, Neal got up and moved over one seat.

SESSION SEVENTEEN
In this session, Neal had again taken the therapist's seat. The therapist went over to the other end of the table where there was a vacant chair and sat down. Neal initiated the discussion, and went on to talk about the baseball tryouts.

SESSION NINETEEN
Neal had again missed a session. The therapist happened to be coming from another building, one in which Neal was working (for pay) at the PX, and the two walked together to the building in which the group met. Upon arrival, Neal once more took the therapist's former seat. The therapist took the opposite chair. Neal again opened the session. He declared that he had not planned on coming, had changed his mind, but this was the last session he would attend.

PROBLEM FOCUS 3.
PASSIVE-AGGRESSIVE DEFENSES

SESSION ONE
At the very beginning of this session, the therapist noted in his report that Neal was one of the boys who were most vocal in denying they had any problems, and in criticizing the therapist's attempt to relate the boys' difficulties to their families. Neal said that the only problem he had was to "get out of here" (the Village); that everything was all-right and he was being "good." He said that the only way a boy could "really get out of here is by being [pretending to be] good."

SESSION TWO
During a discussion of resentment toward social workers, Neal was noted ripping the buttons off his shirt. He later tore at his shirt, and

said, "I only trust myself." He looked pleased when Karl described Neal's temper and when Karl related that Neal had at one time attempted to choke him when he was angry. Neal appeared to like this, and said that he did have a "big temper," but he was "holding it down now." A few minutes later when Frank graphically described how he had smacked his sister in the face, Neal was among the youngsters who displayed excitement and seemed pleased by Frank's recital. For some time he continued to crush savagely the plastic tray he was holding. He declared he was at the Village because he was angry, but had learned to "hide" his anger. He made no response when James remarked, "If you are not angry, this is wrong, too." Toward the end of the session, Neal commented that he was going to "get out of here soon by holding myself in and not getting into trouble."

SESSION THREE

At one point, Frank became quite upset and banged on the table, and later he shouted at the therapist that he did not like him—he never had, and never would. Neal stared in amazement at Frank and at the therapist, and became insistent that the therapist "should not put up with Frank's behavior." He later commented that he did not always get angry at the person he was talking to, but "nobody could talk to me like this." He added after a while that he did not understand what the group was doing, and that "We are going round and round, and Frank is making noises and I can't concentrate." He became more restless and began to rip at the cast on his injured hand.

A little while later, Frank again said he was angry, and said to the therapist: "Fuck you. This is what I think of you and everybody else." Neal became very disturbed and restless at this, and added that he could not get any help in the group when they "used such language."

SESSION FOUR

Neal came to this session about a half-hour late. The therapist reported that Neal stormed in, saying he was decorating his cottage for Christmas, to which he had been eagerly looking forward, when he was suddenly told he was supposed to be at the group. He asked if the therapist would mind if he left. The therapist did not respond, but the boys suggested that he sit down and have a cigarette, which he did. He then requested a Kleenex. The therapist gave him one. Frank told Neal that he should not be hanging Christmas things when he had "problems," and later added, "This is the place to talk about it." Neal asked again if he could leave. The therapist mentioned that the group had just been talking about his leaving, and he personally would prefer him to stay. Karl commented that "Nobody can force you to do anything," and that Neal's "continuing to sit" showed that he would be staying. Neal stayed through the session.

SESSION FIVE

During a discussion of "phoniness" and "double-talking" on the part of adults, Joseph introduced the subject of "off-the-wall cats," the compliant boys who would do anything the cottage parents wanted them to do. Neal, who brought a small dog with him said, "These kids are always making trouble for others." He later commented, "The off-the-wall cats won't say anything, but go along with whatever the cottage parents say."

During the discussion as to why boys might be compliant, Neal later suggested that perhaps they were looking for love and would give up anything to get it. The therapist contributed the thought that perhaps the compliant youngsters were unhappy because of their own low self-concept. This led the group to talk of how, after a period of conformity, a boy sometimes "blows up." James associated to this by saying that he might have been exaggerating how nice everything would be at home if he returned, and added that staying away from home sometimes during difficult periods helped him "until things calmed down." Neal stated that this was the reason why he used to "truant and stay away from the house." He wanted to avoid unpleasant situations.

At the close of this session, Neal picked up his puppy, placed it in a soft armchair, and said he was teaching the dog to bite, so that the dog could protect him. He then added that he did not want a dog that is "too friendly." One of the boys commented that maybe he wanted to keep the dog for himself, so that no one would take him away.

SESSION SIX

Joseph began this session by noting that Neal had been in the detention cottage because he had broken some windows in his cottage and had started a fire on the lawn. Seemingly enjoying being the center of attention, Neal explained that he had been picking up papers outside of his cottage as a punishment[1] for talking back to the cottage father. He felt that this was an unjust punishment, but thought that he was not going to make "a big fuss about nothing." While he was out on the lawn, he explained, his anger seemed to mount higher and higher, to the point where he could not control it, and he threw a match on one of the piles of paper that he had raked up. The fire spread to the other piles of paper before he was able to put it out. Without prodding, Neal went on to

---

1. This form of punishment has been eliminated since.

examine why he had done it. He said that he really had no intention of starting a fire, that he was "angry" and "saw red," and before he knew what was happening, the fire had spread.

He felt better after it, because he knew that "sometimes you have to blow your top. Maybe the next time I won't do it this way." At one point during the discussion of his feelings, Neal declared: "I knew that if I could have talked to someone, I would have felt better; but there was no one around to talk to." (The incident occurred on a week end.) The therapist commented that perhaps Neal was saying that if he could have understood why he was doing what he was doing, he could have controlled himself better. He would not have had to act out, and therefore would have been happier.

Neal seemed pleased at the attention he was getting and commented that he had been "bottled up for a long time, and just couldn't keep it down, because of what was happening in our cottage." He thought maybe talking about things would help, but nobody was available.

SESSION SEVEN

When James brought up his fear of retaliation from adults, Alfred commented that "sometimes you feel overpowered by adults." Neal agreed, and said, "This is where I always begin to get angry. People make me do things which I don't see why I should do, and when I'm forced to do something and have to do it, that's when I get angry." Shortly thereafter, Frank became restless, and James commented that Frank was worried about not hearing from his mother. Neal agreed that when "people are not around you and you have not heard from them, you begin to worry."

By this time we had noted the prevalence of the "doom motif" and the self-fulfilling prophecy trend in our boys, and we suggested to the therapist that these be discussed directly with them at the proper juncture. Accordingly, the therapist wondered why they always anticipated that something bad was going to happen rather than something good. At this, Frank became even more upset, and the therapist, attempting to help him with it, said that if Frank could talk about and understand what was troubling him, perhaps he could control himself; then he would not have to disturb the group. Neal readily agreed, saying that this was the way he felt it happened when he started the fire the previous week. He knew he was angry at the cottage father, but he was also just angry at being at the Village, and not having his mother. Everything "piled up inside of me and I really did not feel good even after I set the fire. I was angry at myself for letting go. That is why I went on and broke the windows." The therapist added that when Neal came to understand why and at whom he was angry, he would not have to go to the lengths he did.

SESSION ELEVEN

At the beginning of the session, the boys expressed some resentment, but also some understanding, with respect to the fact that it had not been possible to make up the session canceled the previous week because of a legal holiday. The therapist said that perhaps he should not have promised to make up the session when he was not entirely sure he could keep his promise. Neal said that he understood that sometimes one wanted to do things for people, but circumstances interfered. He went on to speak about his relationship with his brother (eleven months his senior). He explained that his brother borrowed a great deal of money from him, and at times Neal became angry, because the brother did not reciprocate by giving him money when Neal was home on a week end. On the other hand, Neal said he understood that, living in the city, his brother had many more opportunities to spend money than he might have, and that his brother could not, therefore, give Neal money. He thought that sometimes he should have been angry at his brother, but then he changed his mind and came to the above conclusion he had described.

There was some back-and-forth discussion about the demands from parents that resulted from giving things to their children. There was also expression of anger at mothers, with Earl adding that while "sometimes parents make it difficult, in the long run it is easier to go along with them." Neal thought that this was one of his problems: always going along with people and caring what they thought of him and not thinking more of himself. This always got him into trouble. He would not comment on this further, however, when the therapist and some of the boys tried to encourage him to talk more on the subject.

SESSION TWELVE

During a group discussion of horror films on TV, Neal seemed most fascinated by the science-fiction type creatures from outer space. After Alfred had explained many of the mechanisms involved in producing these fantastic pictures, the therapist commented that it was sometimes disillusioning to find out the "reality." James commented that it was like talking about things in the group: when you understand them, they did not frighten you as much. Neal agreed with this and acknowledged that often when he felt angry or was "getting angrier inside," he would not allow himself to recognize the fact that he was angry.

SESSION NINETEEN

Neal had started this session by saying that he knew what his problems were and did not see any sense in continuing in the group. When Joseph came in somewhat late, and a great deal of discussion ensued about his having run away, the reasons for it, and his feelings during "the run," the therapist had the opportunity to suggest that even "outside there would be difficult situations, but there one could not run away, and what then?" Alfred responded by saying that one "finds some kind of answer." Neal, on the other hand, said that he had not run, although he "wanted to a lot of times." But he knew that one had to "fight it out." At the end of this session, Earl sort of summarized the discussion and the common feeling by commenting that when there was trouble, "we're better off when we find a different way of handling it that doesn't get us into more trouble."

PROBLEM FOCUS 4.
FEAR OF SEXUAL DEVELOPMENT
SESSION SIX

Neal initiated the discussion by mentioning that "the man" in the detention cottage told him that it was not very good if boys "play around with themselves," because they are draining all their energies and it could interfere with their sexual life after they grow up. Some of the boys expressed doubt that masturbation was harmful, and felt that masturbation was universal among boys. Neal remarked that there were a lot of things he did not understand, and wondered about. His foster parents had talked to the girls about sex, but nobody had talked about it to him. Most of his information he "just picked up." Joseph said he thought people were afraid to talk about sex with boys because the boys would then "do these things." Neal agreed, and added that that was why his sister was told the facts of life and he was not, because with her "it would show." Frank added the comment that "talking about it did not necessarily lead to doing it." Neal picked this up and said, "Just because we talk about it in the group doesn't mean we feel sexy or have to do things, but it makes you feel comfortable inside."[2]

Evidences of Improvement

After Neal had absented himself from several of the last group sessions, a conference was held in which the caseworker, the group therapist, and the group therapy consultant participated. The caseworker reported that Neal discussed with him substantially the same topics that

2. This was our first analytic group, consisting of preselected boys with neurotic traits, and we did not attempt to work through with them their preoccupations with sex since the group met only twenty-five times. The subject was, therefore, dropped here, but was thoroughly discussed in our "demonstration groups" reported later on.

had been considered by the group. He talked about his relationship with his uncle and his feelings about his mother and brought out a great deal of feeling about them, as he had done in the group. As a result he began to understand his pent-up guilts and anger. Neal was becoming generally more assertive, and was no longer guarded or afraid of relationships as he had been before joining the group. He complained that his uncle, by suggesting that Neal remain at the Village until he was eighteen years old, showed that he did not want him. Because Neal gained so much from the group it was planned that the group therapist would attempt to encourage his continued participation in individual interviews. However, this plan could not be carried out due to time limitations. Neal did not attend sessions twenty to twenty-five, when the group terminated.

Two months after Neal quit the group, he was involved with several boys working at the PX in appropriating some funds to which they had access, but he voluntarily reported to his caseworker his participation in this escapade. As punishment, the administration put Neal "on restriction," and as a result he ran away.[3] Seven days later he was returned to the Village from the home of his uncle and aunt.

When seen by a woman psychiatrist several days after his return, Neal was bitter over the fact that despite voluntarily acknowledging his guilt, he was punished. He asserted that he had voluntarily confessed partly for himself, because of his own feelings, but even more so because he would not feel right if the other boys were to be punished for something in which he had also participated, since they would not have revealed his part in it. Neal complained that he had been punished in the past for offenses he had not committed, as well as for transgressions to which he had admitted. He threatened to get into further trouble as retaliation for the most recent "injustice." The psychiatrist manifested her concern about him. Neal seemed impressed with the fact that she cared about him and commented, "Why couldn't I have had a mother who feels like that? Do you know about my mother?" As the matter was discussed he commented: "I suppose you, too, think that I should forgive her."

At another point he said, "If I ever let out the feelings inside of me, it will be worse than running. I don't know what would happen!" The psychiatrist summarized her interview as follows:

> The current pressures on this boy activate, and are associated with, all of the damaging events of his life. He shows clearly the residuals of severe early deprivation and seething rage that he should have been so deprived. The situation which gives him tar-

3. These events were attributed by the caseworker to the cottage parents' impending departure from the Village, which represented to Neal abandonment by still another set of parents.

gets for his current resentment—which to him parallel earlier experiences—threatens to explode the rage which has been bottled up, and for which he has had no immediate target. He shows both a desire and a fear to trust that some friendliness does exist, as well as some capacity to see the possibility of striving to achieve something for himself if he can survive until that becomes possible. He now has some awareness of the futility of seeking infantile satisfactions that he had missed, and is planning some possible and real satisfactions if he can be tided over this crucial period.

The caseworker found that at the termination of group therapy, Neal showed marked reduction of guilt feelings regarding his grandmother's death and an increase in his self-esteem. Neal was now able to develop a strong, positive transference to the caseworker, by which he was incorporating the image of the worker as a protective and accepting father.

Neal reported a decrease in masturbation and a lifting of depression on awakening in the morning. He said, "I don't have to break things or pick on myself as much." He told the caseworker that he stayed away from the therapy group because he was afraid to continue revelations of his feelings and thoughts which might make the other boys laugh at him. His guilt about remaining away from the group was so strong that he did not feel entitled to attend the party at the last session, because, as he put it, "I abandoned the group."

The cottage parents reported that Neal was no longer "accidentally" destructive. His so-called "clumsiness" had disappeared. Although the cottage residents, as a group, were temporarily disorganized due to the impending departure of the cottage parents, Neal was one of the few who behaved "properly" and influenced the others to control themselves. He complained to the caseworker that "the cottage parents are jumping up and running off like all the others." As indicated, this event may explain Neal's participating in the theft of money after months of unblemished conduct and complete reliability.

In an interview after Neal had discontinued attending the therapy group, the caseworker suggested that he talk into the Dictaphone about his problems. At points the caseworker asked him leading questions. Neal's monologue and his answers to these questions are recorded verbatim in the following:

> So far as I, Neal K. knows, my name is Neal K.; don't know the rest. Don't know my father; know my mother's known as ————. Now as I know her, her name is ————. I have been in institutions for a very long time now. I have been with foster parents. Evidently my mother doesn't particularly care for me nor anybody in my family. She is a very problemed woman. In her days all she believed in was having a good time. She went out and probably

got all intoxicated; probably just went all over the streets doing nothing. She met a man; she had a kid; she had more kids, and that's why my life has always been in institutions now. My family's been all broken up.

My uncle supported me ever since I was knee-high. He took care of me, he had to go into the service and my grandmother took care of me. My grandmother died and my mother still didn't show up. Every once in a while I get a phony old letter saying "How are you doing? I want you back." I didn't know my mother was such a good lady from what I know. But I don't see how she could do such a thing—just have kids and just leave. Maybe she had problems when she was young. I don't know if I can forgive her or not.

I have never had a chance to love anybody. I won't accept love and I won't give out love because I am afraid people will do the same thing that my mother did. The only way I can get a friend is by buying one and giving them stuff, and still they play me for a sucker. This is all I can do to get a friend.

I am learning to have self-control over arguments and fights and things like that. I have always kept things in my mind and in my heart that I would never tell people that makes me the way I am now. I am afraid of the truth. I am afraid of what people may think when I tell them about my parents—just afraid in general.

I have a lot of friends. Some of my friends are leaving now from the Village and I don't know what to do, so I have to make new friends. I know they won't be with me all of the time, but I just hate people just always jumping off and going.

I don't know if I will ever get married or not because I am afraid to just trust people. I don't know why I can't cry; something in me just won't let me cry. I have no feelings toward my mother, nor my so-called father. Well, I have feelings, to a certain extent, that hurt me, but I just won't face it. I walk around with a big front on my face to make people think that I am a good boy. The only way I can get friends. I am not that bad. I have let people know how bad I am and I still have friends. This is one thing that I have learned besides many others. If I do something wrong, people still like me no matter how bad I am. I always test people which I shouldn't do—just to see how they would react toward me. Now that I have taken my mask off, as I said before, I still have my friends, so I no longer need this mask for protection—to hide.

The reason I fight people is because—I can't think of anything now, I don't know why I fight people. I am afraid of love maybe. Whenever anybody gets too close to me I run out on them, because I have never had anybody to love me, and if they did, I probably didn't accept it. I don't know what love is that much.

I feel that if I get too attached to a person he is just going to leave. I know that I don't need people all my life but . . . no I don't . . . why . . . well, I need somebody, but I don't think I need somebody until I get married. When I get married I hope my kids don't have to live a life like I have lived, with their mother and father just running off on them.

I don't know if I will ever forgive my mother, but now as I am getting older I am going to try to make the best of myself. I don't even know my mother's address. Only as I get older I forget her. Don't need her anymore.

A lot of people have helped me since I was so small. The only way I can pay them back is by being a good boy; that is about it. Well, I am being a boy. I am going to be a good, good boy as well as a bad boy, but without taking off the mask. As long as people know that I have done wrong and they know that people can do wrong and they forgive them. Now the trouble is, how am I going to forgive my own mother for something she's done?

She has about . . . let's see, about . . . five in B———, probably about six in C———, two dead—about the others, I don't know. If I ever get to see my mother I don't know what I am going to do. I feel like busting her in her face, because she did me wrong. I know that I am not the only kid without a mother or father, so maybe I shouldn't feel this way, but the trouble is I can't go on making people think I am so good when they know themselves I am not really that good.

I have been in the group discussions and heard other kids talk about their parents and I have understood some of their problems. The trouble is that I won't face my own and be realistic like they are.

The reason I ran away from the group [was] because I was afraid to face certain things I had in my mind and in my heart—sort of being a coward. No. I didn't think they would laugh. Maybe that is one reason I won't cry. If I do cry, they will laugh—so what? There are things that I am afraid to say because they just hurt me and I hate to bring up the same thing over and over again. I like to just forget about them. No, it is not all the same thing. I just made myself suffer for a lot of things that I probably made on myself or just didn't forget about. I kept a grudge. I learned most of these problems of mine and I try to face them out myself and with my social worker. When I leave here I don't know what is going to happen but I am going to try to make the best.

Eight months after Neal had left the therapy group his caseworker reported that he was continuing to utilize individual therapy, to work through hostile feelings, and to strive for greater self-esteem and further diminution of guilt.

During the six months of Neal's stay in the group, his achievement in reading advanced from 6.4 to 7.5 and in arithmetic he progressed from 5.7 to 6.3.

A year after he discontinued group therapy, his caseworker reported increasingly successful academic work, and that Neal was doing well on an off-campus part-time job. He had assumed the role of a big brother to, and had become supportive of, some of the younger boys in his cottage. Neal was now friendly with his physical education coach, a Negro, who also served as a teacher in a nearby community. This friendship extended to include the coach's wife and their three young children. Neal still occasionally expressed a desire to search out his mother "just to see her once." However, he no longer appeared to nurse his rage against her.

Follow-Up Study

Neal was discharged from the Village sixteen months after termination of group therapy. Neal's behavior during the four months prior to his discharge was described as typical of an average adolescent, without traces of the effects of the severe childhood deprivations and trauma to which he had been exposed. His reaction to girls of his own age was one of comfort, and he confided to the caseworker that he was well received at social gatherings in a nearby community and that he now recognized he had to "catch up" on current customs and "lingo" in which he was backward.

During the four months before his discharge, Neal made arrangements for renting a room in the home of the coach who befriended him, instead of returning to New York. As his involvement with this family intensified, Neal placed increasingly less emphasis on his relationship with his ambivalent aunt and uncle.

The same female psychiatrist who had interviewed Neal previously saw him again three months prior to his discharge and reported considerable improvement in the boy. She stated that he "manifested considerable spontaneity and humor," and she commented that he had become a youngster who "wanted support while working things out for himself."

He was now tall, sturdy, and very attractive. He continued to be self-supporting after discharge, working as a clerk in a large department store near his new home. His adjustment in the first eight months after discharge was described as "excellent." His close and happy relationship with his new "family" continued, and he was a "big brother" to the three children, all under five years of age. He had girl friends in his community, and one girl was becoming "special" for him. He joined an evening high school. The family with whom he lived planned to move to

Europe to study in a year, and they encouraged Neal to save money for his passage so that he could go along with them. The caseworker had the opportunity to observe Neal at a dance. None of the traits associated with a passive-aggressive personality, which he had been diagnosed to be, were in evidence. He appeared genuinely secure, not threatened or sullen as he had been before treatment, and was not fazed by the errors in dancing by some of the members in his party. The caseworker's reaction was summarized thus: "Neal is a boy who has successfully worked through most of his anger and guilt so that he is now capable of warm and spontaneous relationships and of a large degree of self-direction and fairly mature behavior. He no longer has a need for contact with his caseworker. . . . "

Two years after termination of the group, follow-up reports indicated that Neal had sustained the gains made in treatment. He finished high school at night, working full time in the same department store. He went with the coach's in-laws to live in a southern state, planning to go on to college there.

INTERPRETATION

While on the surface it may have appeared at the beginning that Neal's nuclear problem was intense yearning for his mother, ambivalent anger toward her, generalized and tenuously controlled rage, and overpowering guilts that resulted from this emotional vortex, his current difficulties were rather an outcome from inadequate self-identity and from self-alienation, which by his own testimony alienated him from people and other significant things in his world. Because of his meager relationships with significant people in his childhood, he became alienated from object relations and therefore from himself. The two persons with whom he had some relation—his grandmother and his uncle—had abandoned him at critical ages in his life, each by a different route. His alienation had strongly affected his individual casework treatment because it made it impossible for him to allow himself to develop a relationship with the caseworkers (one of whom also abandoned him); thus no positive transference relation could have emerged. A group, where transference was diluted and relationships favored, was indicated for this patient. Having found some degree of self-identity through the group, he was then able to relate better to the caseworker and utilize the experience constructively in therapy. Also, having found self-identity, his ego grew strong enough to permit entry into consciousness the debilitating feelings which he attempted to hold in repression, though unsuccessfully. The group was of critical value in this process.

The salutary outcome in Neal's case, however, was greatly aided by a favorable primary personality structure, and by secondary contributing conditions. One glance at this attractive, bright-eyed, and well set up youngster would convince one that he could bear up under burdens that might crush the less favorably endowed. However, his sustaining founts stemmed from the healthy identification with his grandmother and uncle with which fortune had presented him. Although he felt deeply his mother's abandonment, the sustaining support and consistent relationship with, and love from, the grandmother laid the foundations for ego strengths to bear up under the stress. The grandmother and uncle laid a foundation for relatedness in the boy that helped sustain him. The identification with these significant persons in his life who represented parental figures gave him a degree of identity which was lacking in most of the boys in our groups. It was essentially the need to re-establish identity on a sound footing that made it so necessary for Neal to resolve his guilt about his grandmother's death, which disturbed him so intensely because of the uncle's careless remarks. Because this uncle had again rejected him when the boy was ready to be discharged from the institution, one can speculate that having no ties or consistent relationships and guidance, Neal might have receded to acting out and to increasing delinquency. It is to the fortuitous relation and attachment to the former instructor's family who succored him that credit must be laid for the boy's complete rehabilitation. As we shall see elsewhere in this volume, boys who are fortunate enough to have, upon their return, constructive transitional ties have made their way back to life, while the others could make only marginal adjustments or have succumbed to the contending stress of their inner turmoil and outer pressures.

5

The Emergence of Para-Analytic Psychotherapy and the Inversion Technique

OBJECTIVE PROCEDURES for determining motivations and delineating the character of the delinquent present pitfalls that often mislead the investigator. Personal interviews and printed questionnaires (even those that conceal the pivotal items) uncover conscious ideas, awarenesses, and understandings. These devices and direct investigations employing the words *why* and *what* most frequently tap stored-up cognitive attitudes, ideas, and rationalized values that reflect environmental influences and personal distortions. The responses obtained by objective devices reveal in part the areas of which the individual is aware; but the unconscious and irrational springs from which impulses and urges flow remain hidden.

We would have been seriously misled had we taken the pronouncements of the boys at face value and as truly representing their essential personalities. It would have been equally misleading to draw conclusions from existing theories of personality and psychopathology even when based upon overt behavior and reactions. To get to the essence of the delinquent personality, enter into *his inner life*, and explore his unconscious so as to understand what was transpiring within him and what propelled him toward his particular way of life, a new approach and new methods had to be devised. We were aware from the outset of the difficulties that would face us. The defensiveness of adolescents was known to us from previous work with ordinary patients in urban clinics. We also knew how highly defensive and deceptive "delinquents" could be. We were also convinced that in this project, as in all other efforts to truly uncover and understand sources of motivations, the individual had to be placed in a *condition* in which he would reveal himself without being aware that he was doing so. Classical psychoanalysis is such a technique par excellence; however, other investigatory tools in personality research require similar approaches for *entering into* the hitherto strongly defended and repressed feelings, memories, and ideas.

This we attempted to do in our groups, and we feel we were richly rewarded in our effort. So as not to interfere with and possibly vitiate an effective ongoing treatment, our policy has been not to accept boys who made good use of individual casework available to them at the institution. The salutary catalytic effect of groups was amply demonstrated with members of the institution's population, whose accessibility was slight or nonexistent. All the boys included in demonstration group C (the group discussion protocols of which are reproduced in Part Two), for example, did poorly in casework treatment, and all have sustained impressive gains in the group.

The mechanisms of mutual identification, catalysis, and mutual interstimulation that are always present in groups, and especially in therapy groups, impel self-revelation both verbally and, even more importantly, by nonverbal means. These served us as cues and determined our conduct in the group interviews and in the differential dealing with individuals. Our boys were impelled (as are all patients) to reveal their inner selves as they were stirred by what they themselves had said and by the revelations and reactions of fellow group members and the therapist's conduct and statements. The consistently satisfying relationships with peers and the therapist dissolved defenses and begot attitudes that served the ends of introspection and self-confrontation. The totality of this state on the part of the patients we term the *analytic condition*.

Goals and Difficulties

As the interviews proceeded, the protocols became increasingly more revealing of the real nature of our boys and of substratum tensions that activated their asocial and antisocial acts. The communicants were thus stripped of defensive toughness and of deceptive mildness, as in the case of Neal, for example. The boys revealed themselves for what they essentially were, and it became clear that our work had to be directed toward two distinct goals, intimately interrelated: the behavioral and clinical polarities. In the first, our task was to alter immediate behavior, and in the second, to effect intrapsychic change so that improvements could be sustained beyond the institutional life. This polar relationship is somewhat different than in the treatment of pure psychoneurotics, where behavior reveals intrapsychic processes. In our boys, the characterological acting-out façade *veiled* their unconscious tensions, which fact is made palpable in the protocols.

Ordinarily, in the treatment of psychoneurotic patients, behavioral improvement flows from altered feelings and ego-libido realignment; minimal concern is, therefore, directed to conduct and ideas per se. With our patients, however, it was their acts that brought "punishment" on them, a fact of which they had been made palpably aware, and they, therefore, continued to contemplate these acts and not causal or concomitant feelings. One of the important characteristics of the boys' value system and psychic organizations was that, by their own professions, at least, their behavior was ego and superego syntonic. As we proceeded with our group discussions, it became clear at the beginning it would be necessary to go along with them in this respect and concentrate on anecdotal and behavioral content. However, it was equally certain that the boastfulness and bravado were only tenuous means for self-deception, and a façade. The boys were operating largely on a system of denial and rationalizations, and their childish defensive self-justification mechanism was projection. According to them, it was the world that was wrong, cruel, and unjust, and they were innocent, mistreated, and misunderstood victims of adults' ignorance and cruelty.

However, despite the seeming self-acceptance and syntonicity of these ideas and the antisocial behavior, we began to suspect from their facial expressions and occasional remarks that behind the boys' armor of aggression and toughness were great reservoirs of guilt and anxiety which they desperately sought to conceal from themselves and others. Once this was established in our minds, we came to appreciate how delicate our task was to be. We recognized that the usual practices for *uncovering* unconscious conflicts, suitable for psychoneurotics, and the instrumentality of *confrontation*, used with patients with character disorders, could not be used in their pure forms with our boys. In the absence of conflict, as in character disorders, confrontation generates minimal anxiety, but where the foundations of behavior anomalies are repressed anxiety, as we guessed was the case with our boys, such confrontation would result in increased stress that would cause them to turn against us. On the other hand, it was essential that they come to a point in ego strength and maturity where they could examine their conduct, values, and attitudes in the light of social norms, which they had finally to accept.

Only through the recognition of inner motives and by establishing communication between the ego and the unconscious could they overcome their interpersonal and self-alienation. However, because of our boys' heightened paranoid feelings, their injustice collecting, and the trigger-like defensive aggressiveness, it was essential that we avoid offending them if we were to overcome their resistances to self-confrontation. It also became clear, as already mentioned, that the boys operated from the basis of the primary process and magic as revealed in immature reality-testing patterns, infantile feelings of omnipotence, and an inordinate variety and degree of superstitions (which are recorded in the protocols appearing later in this volume). These were among the intrapsychic states contributing to the basic immaturity and alienation in our boys, and resulting in the social and interpersonal maladjustment with which we had to deal. However, as long as the boys denied anxieties as part of their pattern of defiance, among other things, our ultimate aim—maturing personality—could not be achieved. On the other hand, to unleash anxiety before the boys' egos were strengthened would threaten them too much and could have caused physical or psychological withdrawal from the therapeutic arena of the group (which actually occurred in one of our groups due to clumsiness on the part of one of the therapists). Maturity could emerge only when anxieties had been gradually and sensitively worked through. This therapeutic climax was reached in a small way in Group C, which had a longer existence (seventy-five sessions).

Establishing Rapport

The first step was to establish rapport between therapist and patients to a point where the latter would feel unqualified confidence and security in their being accepted unreservedly. By their own declarations, they needed to *trust and be trusted*. In our supervisory conferences we never failed to stress that it was essential in the treatment of asocial youth to differentiate between the *act* and the *condition* of the actor. We can be of therapeutic help to a person only when we accept his condition. Though the act is not necessarily accepted, it can come under open scrutiny only when the patient feels *accepted as a person*. In the initial stages of treatment—and this is especially true of children and adolescents—patients feel accepted when their conduct goes uncriticized and unchallenged, and thus anxiety and guilt are not aroused.

We believed, therefore, that our therapists had to be prepared to face a period of chaos and turmoil, especially in the unselected "delinquency-saturated" groups (C and D), and we were not in error. These two groups did prove to be more obstreperous by far, and acted out resistances in a direct and challenging manner, as the protocols clearly show. Later, as the boys began to affirm in words and attitudes confidence and trust in the therapists, evaluation by the boys of their own behavior and its consequences and, later, exploration of feelings, backgrounds, and motives became possible, but always following the cues and clues given by the group members. Such clues were replete when the boys reached the *analytic condition* and conversations, actions, and reactions grew introspective, unhampered by fear and caution. Feeling unrestricted and unthreatened, they acted upon now-undisguised impulses and cravings and allowed themselves to regress individually and as a group to early fixations and strivings. These manifestations were identified and discussed with the therapists during the supervision conferences, and their hegemony was evaluated. Out of this emerged procedures for dealing with, elaborating, and relating such manifestations to reality and the condition of each patient.

The general plan was *1]* to permit even the most bizarre acting out, which automatically led to the boys' unrestricted verbalization of past acts and relations; *2]* to guide them at carefully determined appropriate times to reflect on these; and *3]* to introduce new perceptions and values in relation to the material produced; *the ultimate aim of this process being the establishment of inner controls.* Throughout, only specific events and reactions, rather than principles or generalities, were considered as the boys presented them; first accepting them for a long time as cathartic discharge and later by confrontation and ratiocination. In the early stages feelings and anxieties were bared without elaboration, but as the interviews progressed and a therapeutic climate emerged, we sought through questions and suggestions to direct the boys toward examination of the suitability of feelings and acts and their effectiveness in specific situations, pointing up choices in the modus of dealing with environment and people. This procedure can be effective only when the pressures of hostility and guilt have been reduced; at first the practical and pragmatic aspects are put forward, while the moral and ethical desiderata are held in abeyance or are underplayed. When this plan is followed, patients are gradually freed of anxieties and, therefore, of defensiveness. As will be seen in the protocols, once this process was set in motion, the boys on their own momentum, helped one another to "understand" conduct and to evaluate its efficacy. As the emotional impedimenta were cleared, our work took on at times an educative or re-educative character, which ultimately led to considerations of the moral structure of society and its advantages.

It was our aim in the clinical area to provide our youngsters with an unthreatening climate in which they could and would ventilate feelings without fear of disapproval, criticism, or punishment. This ultimately led to regressive free association, to re-experiencing vicariously affect-laden events in their pasts and to revealing anxieties which they had defensively denied and had instead reacted to by acting out. The objectives were of a reconstructive nature, through diminishing narcissistic components by facilitating relatedness and responsibility and by promoting development from the infantile oral-anal phases into the genital phase (essential for mature responsibility and self-control).

To promote this unfolding in the psychosocial development of the adolescent personality required fine balancing of therapeutic elements in the functions of the therapist, for overemphasis on one element to the neglect of others would not only have reduced effectiveness, but might have lost the boys to us. The immediate had to precede the subtler intrapsychic reconstructive efforts. Much time was, therefore, given over to the boys' regressive occupations, such as testing the therapist, to acclimatization to the group, and to "griping" against the institution, the staff, and people generally. Only when the emotional decks were thus cleared could an entry be made.

The Objective: Self-Control

As the interviews in the various groups unfolded, it became increasingly evident that the immediate sources of the boys' difficulties in their environment were impulsivity and lack of controls, characteristic of the immature personality. Self-control then became the ultimate objective of our effort to reclaiming these unsocial, impulse-ridden, delinquent, acting-out boys. But just as working through guilt and anxiety opened the gates to maturity, so was maturity a prerequisite for self-control. As long as the boys attained pathognomic self and social pseudo identity through general negativism and destructive acts, there was slight possibility that they would be able to control their impulses. These controls could be derived only from corrective identifications, the internalization of the therapist's ego and superego; the release of ego energies bound up in hostility, guilt, and anxiety; new awareness of personal worth; sloughing off of feelings and expectations of doom; and finally, acquiring conscious awareness of the need for and of the power to exercise control. The point was reached in the boys' development where they became aware of, and were willing to recognize, the temptations and the provocations that their homes and communities provided for asocial and antisocial acts; yet, at the same time there arose in their minds doubts as to their ability to ward off such threats in a manner more consistent with their newly evolved concepts and more benign expectations from life. That they were able to differentiate between earlier unsavory conduct and new standards and values is attested to by a telling incident, one of many such. Once when the boys had returned from the city after a prolonged holiday visit, they fell to boastfully reminiscing at the group sessions of former delinquent performances. After a while, one boy summarized the group's attitude by the statement that they were talking of "fond memories of the past." A further demonstration of maturity occurred near the end of the group's life, when the boys on their own verbalized their inner conditions and the conditions in their milieu that would militate against success in their efforts to alter their life patterns for the better.

It was at this point that we introduced the concept of the *onto-archaic mind*. This term represents the idea that people respond to stimuli in a manner that they have been conditioned to in the past; because of this conditioning, they continue to respond as they had been conditioned even when the old reactions no longer suit a current situation and when consequences are injurious. Because of the time at which this concept was introduced the boys in our demonstration group were quick to comprehend its significance.[1] As will be seen in the group protocols, they quickly applied the idea to their own behavior and recognized that despite hurtful results to themselves, they at times still reacted in their customary manner. They came to recognize that their actions stemmed from archaic or habitual patterns. We found this concept extremely useful in effecting change in behavior, but it would not have been fruitful before feelings had been worked through and a degree of maturity was achieved. As the boys continued to narrate problem-generating conduct, the therapist was now able to indicate that they were acting according to dictates from onto-archaic minds instead of employing newly acquired norms. This was a very simple and logical application of a principle with which the boys never failed to be impressed, and which served as a frame of reference for behavior even after they had left the institution, as some of the boys' correspondence included in this volume shows (see Chapter 19).

As this concept became integrated into the boys' mental equipment, they seemed to grow somewhat hopeless concerning their ability to live by it and to alter their attitudes and behavior. To counteract this, we repeatedly sounded an optimistic note. We frequently explained that they were not unique in this. Everyone, everywhere, passes through a period of such struggle in his emergence into the estate of adulthood; each has to gradually give up early narcissisms, aggressions, selfishness, stubbornness, and pugnacity of childhood in order to "grow up." We indicated that there was a protracted inner struggle ahead of them between the deeply entrenched onto-archaic mind that dominated them and the new norms they had acquired. Also, as they continued to live by the dictates of the new norms, new conditionings would be established by *repetition*, rendering the new norms a permanent part of their lives and conduct. The actual manner in which this unquestionably effective concept was used in the rehabilitation of our boys is recorded in the protocols of our demonstration groups in some detail (see also the letter from Michael, pp. 732-733).

1. We have never reached this point of development in the groups that met for only one school year, however.

We have seen that alienation is a problem of the ego. Instead of just controlling and regulating instincts, the ego should become involved also in their operation. The delinquent's ego energies are at the service of impulse (id) instead of being utilized to suppress, repress, control, and direct instinctual infantile pleasure urges and impulses. In the delinquent life pattern, the ego permits rages against normal external controls and frustrations and unleashes retaliatory drives and autarchic (infantile) fantasies. With adolescents generally, and delinquents in particular, it is necessary to make these operations conscious by direct means, which characterized our work as "para-analytic" rather than strictly "psychoanalytic." We discovered that working through solely neurotic elements and anxiety did not serve the therapeutic needs of our boys (which fact holds true of all adolescents). We had to help the boys evolve a *modus operandi* or *tools for living* for their new life aims. But we knew that direct, moralistic urging or punitive measures could not be effective for generating or inculcating these. We had to first break down the defensive armor against narcissistic injury and overwhelming anxiety and *enter into the personalities* of our boys before we could even attempt to take the first steps in their behavioral and psychosocial rehabilitation.

Reconstruction as an Aim and as a Process

What each of our boys needed was reconstruction of a seriously impaired ego-functioning and the establishment of some degree of communication between the unconscious and the ego. In the first instance, the ego had to be strengthened and its energies (which were drained by its dealing with latent anxiety, hostility, and self-pity) released and made available for inner growth and for constructive social uses.[2] In the second instance, we had to free the individual of his alienative urges and censors so that noxious impulses and fantasies could be made conscious and thus available for evaluation and control to the emerging, healthier ego. We agreed with Dr. Flescher's formulation of this process as it operates in the delinquent personality, but not entirely so where neurotics are concernd. Dr. Flescher says: ". . . Ego strength [is] the capacity to *acknowledge* on the conscious level the instinctual and emotional drives, and—in the face of an unsuitable reality situation—*the ability to endure frustration without resorting to repression and with-*

2. See S. R. Slavson, *A Textbook of Analytic Group Psychotherapy* (New   York: International Universities Press, 1964), Chapter VIII.

out deteriorating interpersonal and group contact by succumbing to these drives."[3]

Because of the impaired ego formation in the boys we were dealing with, mere strengthening of the ego was not enough. It was also essential that we give these energies self-fulfilling and socially constructive direction. If misdirected, ego strength might become a menace, as is also the case with a superior intellect. As will be made clear in the protocols, our principle of onto-archaic mind versus new norms and values helped us greatly in implanting the directional awareness in our boys. The direct dealing with the *modus operandi* and the *modus vivendi* and with forging tools for living and dealing with actuality was a means of establishing direction for ego-functioning which paralleled its strengthening. The practical procedure we employed is amply demonstrated in the protocols.

Short cuts are seldom available to the psychotherapist—or to anyone, for that matter—who aims to alter emotionally charged or otherwise compelling needs, attitudes, and conduct in another. Psychotherapy is a slow and arduous task of reconstruction and re-education that requires great patience, the ultimate in attunement to the manifest and covert processes and feelings in patients, and sensitivity and keen tact in dealing with them. Psychotherapy based on short cuts and directness is doomed to failure and frequently proves extremely harmful. Reproach and punishment, criticism, and persecution, which are universally resorted to in institutions for the correction of delinquents and criminals, not only fail to correct, but rather give the offender a justification for his past and current antisocial destructive acts and feelings. When so treated, he grows more convinced that the adult world (represented by the institutional staff) is his enemy, and this only serves to further mobilize hostilities and destructiveness.

Rehabilitation starts at the point when the delinquent youngster discovers a benign adult who understands his desperate struggle and who has a genuine interest in helping him. To help the delinquent reach this point is no simple task. The delinquent does not trust any adult. Adults are his mortal enemies, and his desperate clinging to this conviction presents great impediments to altering it. He does not wish to give up attitudes by which he has lived most of his life. Besides, there *is* a realistic base to his views and feelings, for adults *did* hurt him and *did* mutilate his spirit.

The initial approach, therefore, has to be one in which these uncompromising feelings and convictions are weakened to a point where they

3. Joachim Flescher, *Mental Health and Prevention of Neurosis* (New York: Liveright Publishing Corp., 1951), p. 346 (italics his).

are overcome. In the residential situation this can be achieved with less difficulty than in the ordinary living milieu, because the essential order and natural disciplines that arise from peer-group living and participation can be incorporated and conditioned in the day-to-day living process without arousing rebellion as intense as it does in the home. It has been amply demonstrated that the needs of adolescent delinquents can be met in a good residential setting and that the youths can gradually be won over to the pervading mores.[4] The setting designed for restitutive and corrective relations and experiences can be flexibly employed the better to meet individual needs than is possible in the ordinary family and community. A re-educative milieu, properly managed, offers opportunities for social experimentation with less risk than do the explosive situations in family and neighborhood.

It is a rigid law in psychotherapy that the approach to the patient must first be made at the level at which he comes to us, so as to give him a feeling that he is accepted for what he is and that no criticism or disapproval is implied in the therapist's attitude. In the case of our boys, we had anticipated that they would be infantile, impulsive, angry, and suspicious, and we were prepared to accept the manifestations of these emotions in action. In the observational groups, for which members were chosen according to already established criteria, acting out was minimal, because the criteria employed in choosing patients for these groups—neurotic anxiety and the search for relief from inner conflicts that caused their discomfort—obviated the urge for severe acting out. But in the case of the "delinquency-saturated," unselected, demonstration groups, acting out reached rather high intensity. This was especially so in the group in which the boys were sexually disturbed and in which we found ourselves with a number of active, more or less confirmed, homosexuals (group D).

Having been accepted with their infantile acting out, and having received oral gratifications (food, cigarettes, freedom in talking) and dependency, the boys became convinced that the therapist could be "trusted."[5] This discovery and their change in feelings altered their ego functionings. Whereas in the past much of their ego energies had been consumed in dealing with paranoid-like vigilance, hostility, and guilt, they were now freed of these enough to make more ego energies available for intrapsychic growth and for dealing with external reality; hence, almost uniform improvement in conduct, in school achievement,

4. See Slavson, *Re-Educating the Delinquent through Group and Community Participation* (New York: Harper and Brothers, 1954; Collier Books, 1961).

5. The reader will recall that we attempted to withhold food from the boys in the para-analytic groups on theoretic grounds, but reversed our stand when their insistence convinced us of the importance to them of "being fed."

in attitudes, and dramatic improvement in bearing and appearance began to show.

The first, and what we considered a most important, step in therapy was to arouse a feeling of *trust* toward the therapist, as already indicated. Surprisingly, we found it comparatively easy to achieve. The contrast in the treatment they received from us with that to which they were accustomed, currently and in the past, was striking enough for the boys, after an initial period of suspicion, to believe the genuineness and sincerity of the therapists' attitudes and understanding. As we shall find in the protocols, this transformation occurred in a number of steps. At first the distrust was conveyed openly, then by wariness, concealment, and uncommunicativeness. The boys openly questioned the therapists' reliability and integrity; they then accused them of "spying" and reporting on them to the authorities; finally, they became convinced of the therapists' honesty and genuineness of interest in them. This, too, they verbalized rather freely later on.

It was our conviction that once our boys verbally communicated their distrust of the therapists the ice was broken, for it demonstrated their dawning capacity to feel free to reveal feelings without fear. We looked upon their aggression as a step in reducing alienation and as increased relatedness, and therefore accepted their attacks without rancor. This attitude convinced the boys of acceptance more readily than words could have. The manner of dealing with open and disguised aggression by therapists was the subject of frequent and prolonged discussions in our supervisory conferences.

Initiating the Inversion Process

Having succeeded in demonstrating our reliability and interest, and being assured of the boys' trust in us, we were now ready to "enter into their personalities," a step to which reference has already been made on a number of occasions. The ability to recognize the point at which this could be done stemmed from our experience with the observation groups as we studied the successions in the content of the boys' productions in the interviews and their free conversations. The sequence was more or less uniform. At first, the boys griped, blaming and finding fault with others and with their environment and gossiping about staff and cottage fellows. This stage was followed by boasting about the severity and frequency of their antisocial acts. Both were interspersed with superficial chit-chat about occurrences in the institution, the academic school, and events they heard of on the radio or saw on television.

All in all, their interchanges consisted of trivia and had as their basic

characteristic preoccupation with matters outside of the boys themselves, *in exterio,* as it were. Such superficial talk in out-patient adolescent group guidance in urban clinics is beneficial in cases of behavior
disorders and some types of mild character disorders. But having discovered in our boys underlying suppressed anxiety and severe guilt feelings (as well as other neurotic tensions), we were convinced that therapy
with them would have to address itself to levels deeper than chit-chat
about current events and people. It was necessary to reach their
bound-up anxieties and their compensatory fantasies, if we were to
succeed in rehabilitating them.

Adolescents are notoriously resistive to revealing themselves to
adults, and antisocial adolescents are particularly so. Also, as already
noted, in their increased paranoid-like states, any maneuver to examine
feelings, attitudes, or conduct was readily distorted by them as containing criticism or disapproval. However, it was essential that we find
a way to *invert* our boys' habitual psychic gaze from outward to in-
ward. Following the therapeutic law of taking the lead from patients,
we suggested to the therapists that when conditions become propitious
they at first pick up for discussion and elaboration subjects which *did
not involve the boys personally* or events in their lives, but rather topics
that might stir their intellectual curiosities. The therapists were warned
against addressing themselves during this period directly to the feelings
or thoughts of the boys, as this might be interpreted as criticism, attack, or an effort at exposing them.

We were unable to determine at this point whether the boys' persistent chit-chat and talk about trivial events represented resistance,
flight into reality, or whether it reflected intellectual and cultural
impoverishment and diffuse hostility characteristic of their families and
neighborhoods. However, we did not feel it important at this point
to determine the reason in advance, for whatever it might have been,
leading the boys on to more significant productions without arousing
suspicion or resentment, if possible, would be all to the good. Our aim
was to slowly redirect their characteristic projective pattern toward
examining their own feelings, attitudes, and conduct.

This is the cardinal principle of the *inversion technique.*

We hypothesized that once a significant emotion was touched off
by a seemingly intellectual inquiry, the boys' anxieties would propel
them into unraveling feelings. A dynamic concatenation process in
the human unconscious automatically occurs and, continuing as a chain
reaction, leads to associated and articulated thoughts, memories, and
feelings. This process is usually inhibited by superego censors or is cut
off by ego-defensive resistances. It is then the subtle task of the therapist
to find means to counteract these censors and dissolve the resistances.

Points at which the inversion process was initiated, as reflected in the protocols, were thoroughly and repeatedly discussed during the supervisory conferences with the group therapists. These discussions prepared them to recognize opportunities and to deal with them appropriately. The therapists were repeatedly warned against prematurely invading *threat areas*, especially involving nuclear problems of individuals. This cautiousness may have well been the major reason for the effectiveness of this technique.[6]

Only sensitive strategies during the early periods in treatment (when the paranoid-like responses were still in dominance and ego and superego defenses intense) made it possible for the inversion process to take root. Inversion cannot be forced, taught, or inculcated. For example, applying techniques from his casework training, one of our therapists repeatedly employed the phrase, "let's figure out," "if you figure this out," or "we are here to figure things out." With the help of the therapist, the group members did "figure out" the "reasons" for some of their unsuitable actions and even feelings, but only *understanding* was derived, and that of temporary endurance; their feeling tone remained unaffected.[7] The intellectual "understanding" they acquired was not incorporated into their psyches. They were, perhaps, temporarily enlightened, but their emotions and conditionings did not change, nor were their autarchic, sado-masochistic, alienating, and self-destructive urges. To achieve or effect the latter requires the *reliving* of past feelings and release of bound-up anxiety, thereby opening the channels to the unconscious and preconscious. Even under the best conditions, some of these maximal aims can be achieved only to a limited degree with adolescents, and even less so with the type of youngster we were faced with. However, some headway, despite all limitations, had to be made in these directions before relatively permanent reconstruction of personality could be hoped for; each had to enter the forbidden precincts of his psyche, *invert* his gaze, rather than dissipate it in unfocused directions or by blaming others. Inversion results from profoundly stirring inner emotional experience; it cannot be achieved by didactic learnings, by intellectualizations, or by discipline and punishment. The spark that activates the deeper layers of consciousness has to be touched off. Once this is done, the flames can easily be fed, but the first step demands great sensitivity and subtlety and, above all, dedication.

The protocols of the demonstration group show clearly how the

6. The capacity to plan and anticipate developments in therapeutic interviews is gained from extensive practice by perceptive therapists, who may not require the close supervision which this pilot project made necessary.

7. It was this therapist's groups that we found necessary to terminate in midstream because of the uncontrolled acting out by the boys which he inadvertently evoked by his directness.

dynamic of inversion was introduced by activating curiosity in a scientific phenomenon during the height of resistive acting out (see session 16, pp. 333-339), and how we kept it alive in later sessions. Once the stirring inner processes were set afoot, dramatic revelations of dreams, memories, fears, anxieties, hostilities, fantasies, guilts, and other feelings came in rapid succession, and are recorded in the boys' own words.

But there came the time when the light of reason and understanding also had to be thrown upon the jumble of revelations—such as clarifying the relation of cause and effect, distortion and projection, and sharpening awareness of the sources of conduct and its intent. New and more suitable instruments for dealing with situations, too, had to be adduced through group discussions and, when necessary, advocated. Each step was planned and steps appropriate to the evolving personalities of the patients outlined as revealed in their attitudes, conduct, and discussions. Basic feelings had been worked through, and ideas evoked or suggested for discussion, in accordance with sound tenets of learning: namely, readiness, relevance, and repetition—the three R's of a meaningful education.

As will be seen from the protocols, all ideas and "interpretations" that were offered before the boys were ready for them evoked no response, or the response was a negative one. The same fate awaited therapists' remarks that were not relevant to the latent content of the current preoccupations of the boys and their communications. It was in this area, as well, that considerable vigilance had to be exercised. Not only do therapists frequently respond to the obvious denotation and the "logic" of the dialogue (manifest content), but they are often misled by subjective countertransferential reactions of their own to ongoing affect-laden proceedings. Their own feelings as to what is important frequently divert them from a cathected subject that may pervade the group or occupy an individual. In all therapy, what is psychologically significant may be at variance with what seems logical. Only too frequently therapists, instead of perceptively following psychologically relevant directions, pursue logical syllogisms, to the detriment of the therapeutic intent. The protocols also reveal how important repetition is in the therapeutic and re-educational processes, more so even than in learning, for re-education involves psychological and neuronic *reconditioning*. The onto-archaic mind has to be replaced by new responses and attitudes.

Dealing with Resistance and the "Doom Motif"

The resistance to self-revelation which is always encountered in psychotherapy is multiplied many times in adolescents and was still further magnified in the members of our groups. It required utmost caution and skill to prevent it from becoming completely insoluble. We thought we had made progress in breaking through this rigid defensiveness when one boy declared tersely, "Nobody likes to see [admit] their own faults," because the remark by itself was evidence that he, as also others in the group, had become aware of their own defensive feelings. The very fact that the statement was made indicated diminution of resistance and of the fear of self-confrontation. We accomplished this by acceptance in the early sessions, with studied detachment toward the most bizarre behavior. A great deal of time and tact were devoted to engendering in the boys' minds an image of the therapists as accepting, understanding, and nonjudgmental; having a genuine interest in them *as persons;* and at the same time not allowing the therapists to become abettors of the boys' anarchic infantilisms and impulsivity, for this would have encouraged regressive trends. The maneuvers to achieve this have consumed many hours of supervisory discussions which flowed from the boys' and therapists' statements and the group protocols.

As we succeeded in overcoming resistances and dissolving other impediments to self-revelation, another manifestation of the so-called "delinquent" personality came to the fore in later group discussions. This was the "doom motif" in the boys' unconscious. This discovery was a clue of paramount importance to our work. The doom motif, prevalent among the boys in all our groups, was the obsession that they were doomed to a life of catastrophe, defeat, and failure, eventual imprisonment, and similar dire misfortunes. The boys felt they were trapped, with no avenues of escape available. The doom motif repeatedly appeared in their conversations and in dreams. In one case, for example, a boy (in analytic group A) narrated a dream in which he was being ground between the gears of two huge wheels. After a group discussion of the evil prospects ahead of the participants, one boy summarized it thus: "Everybody talks about help, but there really is no help!" The unanimous and ready agreement with the statement on the part of the other boys made it clear that all were weighted down by feelings of impending disaster and black destinies, and all were victims of hopelessness. In fact, in a number of boys the doom motif reached a point of superstition, so that a cottage mother's angry prediction that a boy would get into difficulties soon after leaving the Village became an abiding obsession.

Forebodings of doom, superstitions, and magic, generally, were other matters with which we had to deal. It seemed to us that the expectation of doom (unconscious need for punishment) was in part an extension of the boys' parents' punitive and denigrating attitudes toward them; however, as therapy proceeded, we found that it might also have been the result of awakening feelings of guilt for past behavior, feelings against which the boys had violently defended themselves before by projection, denial, and rationalization. The doom motif was among the many "cues" with which the boys spontaneously provided us, indicating channels along which to direct group interviews.

Revealing Underlying Feelings

As the interviews unfolded, following for the most part the spontaneous cues given us, we were compelled to revise our original concepts as to the meaning of the boys' behavior and their values. As they reached the *analytic condition* or mood, the boys' past conduct and pronouncements no longer appeared to be ego syntonic but rather counterphobic and defensive. The analytic mood was stirred by the therapist's interpretations, psychoanalytic concepts and dynamics, and the boys' own growing, extremely eager efforts at understanding their emerging guilts and anxieties. These were made particularly evident in their dreams. Feelings that had been deeply buried and defended were now revealed to the light of day.[8] This part of the interviews as seen in the protocols is perhaps the most impressive and meaningful in the rather numerous sociological, ethical, and psychological subjects the boys discussed.

For many months such feelings had not been revealed, and they came through first in dreams recounted entirely spontaneously. At no time had the boys been asked to remember or to bring in dreams. The dreams seemed to be set off by the progressively more stirring self-explorations in the groups. As the unconscious became involved (or touched off) in the interviews, dreams were automatically recalled and their significance recognized. Their content included anxiety, punishment, hostility, wish-fulfillment, sex and incest, patricide, and dreams with Oedipal content.[9]

Our demonstration group (group C), the complete record of which is reproduced elsewhere in this volume, was particularly productive of

8. We have suggested that psychopaths are potentially subject to devastating anxiety which they have so thoroughly repressed at so early an age that it becomes unavailable to the ego and to traditional psychotherapy. See Slavson, "Counter-Indications of Group Psychotherapy for Patients with Psychopathic Personalities," Chapter 5 in *The Practice of Group Therapy*, S. R. Slav- son, ed. (New York: International Universities Press, 1947), pp. 95–106.

9. Support for this and all other theoretic formulations, deductions, and observations will be found in the group protocols from which they have been derived, as well as from protocols from other groups not included in this volume.

dreams. This was due, in part, to the skills the therapist had acquired in utilizing and making them meaningful to the boys; but the more likely reasons might have been that this group met for almost two years (seventy-five sessions), as against the one school year for the observation groups (twenty-five to forty sessions), and that we had acquired a body of knowledge about our adolescents from the preceding observation groups. The longer period of "working through" in group C unquestionably influenced the catharsis, and deeper levels of the unconscious were touched off as a result.

Another set of underlying feelings which were not discernible at first but were laid bare as the group interviews progressed consisted of guilt, defeat, and stigma. To a large extent these feelings had been engendered by the boys' sequestration from family, friends, and their natural communities. This, we felt, was also one of the reasons they came to the defense of their rather cruel and neglectful parents, repeatedly asserting that they "deserved the beatings" they had received at parents' hands. A few of the boys went to the length of asserting that had they not been beaten they would have "gotten in trouble," apparently refusing to recognize how much in trouble they actually were. Some, during such discussions, would insist that "no matter what your mother does to you, she is still your mother"; while others defended the right of parents to do with children whatever they wished, "because they feed you and support you."

Every criminotic and delinquent act involves a covert masochistic as well as a sadistic intent, but in the case of our boys the masochistic wishes were rather blatant, and their voluntary abrogation of self-respect and individuality was striking. These revelations supplied us with further clues as to the direction therapy had to take. For one thing, we had to find means of arousing "self-respect," that is, engendering a healthy identity in our youngsters through raising their level of maturity, as far as the time allotted to us would permit, and give direction to their lives. Our protocols and studies of individual progress show the striking success we had in this regard in our demonstration group (C) and the impressive inroads that were made even in the shorter periods in the observation groups.

In verbal productions and in their dreams, the boys revealed fantasies of, and preoccupations with, intense violence, both that which they had committed against others and that which was committed against them. These preoccupations seemed to us at least in part counterphobic (denial of fears of attacks, of castration, feelings of inadequacy and impotence.) One could not help but feel that the recurrent bravado was a reaction to self-doubt which served to establish for the boys at least a minimal degree of self-identity. The boastfulness and grandiosity

with which real and often fantasied events of violence and seeming "courage" were recounted gave us ample foundation for these
conclusions.

The themes 'of violent and uncontrolled aggressions, gang fights, and
"rumbles" were boastfully and very frequently repeated. Pugnacity and
explosive violence seemed to characterize the essential attitude of our
boys as they responded to the slightest real and fancied provocation by
threatening of beatings within the school community and in the group
interviews. They seemed devoid of any other means of dealing with
narcissistic injury, since violence was their fetish. Refraining from fighting was actually inconceivable, a sure sign of cowardice, of being
"chicken," the worst possible appellation in these boys' estimation. These
false concepts of courage and personal excellence seemed to be deeply
ingrained in the value systems of the peer and adult cultures from which
our boys came. They had been indelibly imprinted by parents, siblings,
and other adults and peers in their environment and by the brutalizing
treatment to which they had been subjected. Because of the attitude of
"righteousness" with which the boys defended their life pattern, we
thought long and carefully before approaching this subject. To discuss it
peremptorily would have exposed us to the risk of alienating the boys
by conveying the feelings that our alliance lay with the social mores
and in opposition to their own.

Self-Exploration

When the propitious time to examine their attitudes arrived, we
openly declared that impulsivity was a characteristic of immaturity and
childishness. However, as the group protocols show, this subject was
not touched upon before we were assured that transference-counter-
transference relations between therapist and boys was solidly established
on a positive footing and that the boys' ego defenses would not be
threatened beyond their capacities at the time. It was only when we
felt that they could confront themselves with this theme without devastating anxiety that we decided to proceed. We pointed out that their
lives were governed by "a law of the jungle," suitable for other animals
but not for humans, that society could not have come into being and
continued to exist had these principles been predominant. This refrain
was repeated innumerable times in the course of the seventy-five sessions
of demonstration group C.

We found that in all our groups, the boys had awareness (if not fear)
of outer threats. These were all-consuming in their considerations for
the future and for life generally. In view of the boys' ingrained practice
to act out rather violently against their expectation to be attacked, we

decided that their social rehabilitation could be achieved only if these attitudes formed one of the major topics of our therapeutic effort. However, because of their pivotal significance and latent meaning, they had to be approached with great caution. We recognized that much of the boys' bravado was really a form of counterphobic defensiveness, which, in our view, stemmed from two sources: actual fear and anxiety on the one hand, and inner threats resulting from guilt that they had hitherto attempted to suppress and which now was emerging into the preconscious.

Since the outer threats were the more tangible, and a part of their recognizable experience, it was easier for the boys to reveal them in the discussions and for us to deal with them; the inner threats (guilt and "conscience") and the capacity to distinguish right from wrong were matters much more difficult for the boys to recognize. We realized that in order to change values and frames of reference both the outer and the inner pressures would have to go hand in hand, and identification with the therapist's maturity and superego would be the pivot in this reconstructive effort. Therefore the attitudes of the therapist, as well as the procedures used, in their innumerable ramifications were the subject of frequent and prolonged consideration in our supervisory conferences. We emphasized that reconditioning narcissistic and antisocial ego urges can be achieved only when the boys will accept the therapist as their corrective ego ideal, and will model themselves after him. What the boys needed was to experience a good family, with a father image as a suitable model. In fact, not occasionally the boys did spontaneously refer to the therapist as "our father."

While the boys were always ready to talk about the ever-lurking outer threats and dangers, it took a great deal of time, and great tact, to involve them in considering the other side of the coin. Their paranoid-like orientation to life had to receive special attention, and as already indicated, ratiocination alone would not be sufficient; the attitudes of the therapist and his support were the foundations for change in the boys' subjective reconstruction. We repeatedly emphasized to the therapists that what the boys needed most was to find an adult who honestly and genuinely understood and *respected* them. This would correct the negative intent the boys projected on all adults. When once the boys volunteered that "there are some grownups on the staff of the Village who don't want to hurt us," we were convinced that we had made telling progress toward our aim. Even before that statement was made, frequent assertions by the boys of their "trust" and "appreciation" of the therapists appeared in the interviews, but what was more important was the sloughing off of hostile feelings and deriving comfort from trusting and being trusted.

Emergence of Allotropic Feelings

However, unlike psychoneurotics, acting-out "delinquent" young-sters are not given readily to the mechanism of *transference in reverse* (displacing newly acquired benign feelings from therapists on parents and other persons in the environment).[10] We have, therefore, applied the flexibility of para-analytic therapy in the later stages of treatment and have planfully followed up cues and signals during group discussions to bring to awareness how unfounded in reality the boys' convictions against adults were, and pointed out their paratoxic distortions. As will be shown in the protocols we gave the boys technical terminology and explained to them in detail the dynamics of these terms, and the distortions on which their feelings and thinking were based. This ordinarily is impossible to achieve with the type of boy with whom we were dealing without a prolonged preliminary free group interchange, with its impact of one boy on another, and the challenges each offered to the others. Nor could these ideas find response if presented didactically or in lecture form. The ideas took root only because they had been introduced at points of relevance and lessened defensiveness, emotional flexibility, and a degree of maturity that resulted from working through some basic pathognomic feelings and attitudes. Premature effort in this direction would have fallen on deaf ears and carried with it a real possibility of antagonizing and alienating the group.

Having overcome initial suspicions, the boys' newly found confidence and trust in the therapists, the unmistakably warm feelings toward them, were expressed during the group discussions. These were conveyed directly by expressed interest in the therapists' personal lives, their marital status, the number of children they had, and their relationship with their children: whether the therapists talked to their children as they did to the group. Later, positive feelings took more obvious form. One boy mused: "If my father talked to me as you do to us, I would not be in trouble now." Another exclaimed: "Why can't my father explain things to me as you do?" However, our interest in our patients' attitudes extended beyond the transferential relations with the therapists. The aim was to alter feelings and attitudes toward *all* persons, and some evidence of this growth also became apparent. One episode that illustrates this follows.

Because of building alterations, our most "delinquency-saturated"

10. Slavson, *Analytic Group Psychotherapy* (New
York: Columbia University Press, 1950), p. 105.

group (D) was assigned to meet in a well-appointed executive conference room with brilliantly shining furniture. The boys scrupulously refrained from disturbing the meticulous order of the room; they protected the highly polished furniture, and on their own restored the room to perfect order after each session. In one of the sessions the matter of moving to a simpler room in the newly reconstructed building was broached by the boys. Various opinions were expressed. One said, "When I first came to this room I felt uneasy because I was afraid if anything happened in the room our group would be blamed for it." Another wondered what the staff thought about their using the room and where the Director of the Village sat during staff meetings. A third boy said that the reason they cleaned the room so thoroughly after the sessions was to "show the staff that we could use a room like this." A fourth stated: "At first it was like being in a place I didn't belong; but I don't feel that way now."

The therapist asked whether the discomfort in being in the room could stem from the fact that it was a "staff room." One of the group responded as follows: "I got you . . . we're comfortable now with you, so it wouldn't make any difference where we are." To this another added: "It [their former feeling] had to do with the staff being on one side and us kids being on the other, and never the twain shall meet."

During a discussion of how the boys always tried to provoke adults, one of the boys remarked: "We always liked you [the therapist]. We never tried to get you mad." While this statement did not mirror the facts in the case, nonetheless the boys seemed now able to distinguish between acting out and actual hostility. Thus, as the boys acquired some degree of identity by working through their feelings and attitudes and by their growing self- and social awareness, they have become less self- and socially alienated. They had grown increasingly in alliance with themselves (integrated) and with their milieu (related).

The Emergence of Insight

Emotional needs had been met by the friendly, comforting climate in the group and by the benign and warmhearted attitudes of the therapists, which led to greater maturity in the boys. However, it became clear that situational therapy alone would not be enough here, as it might be for small children and youngsters in latency, and therefore in the group sessions we planfully elaborated on feelings and events with pertinent psychological principles and explanations. As a result the boys soon came to distinguish between the "conscious mind" and the "unconscious mind" and, as the protocols reveal, later explained how these determined such of their behavior as stealing, truancy, running away, conflict with siblings, antagonism toward parents—and in more simple terms, displacement and transference phenomena—and the nature and types of defenses like denial, escape, and projection that they had been employing.

Upon the suggestion of the supervisor technical phrases and terms were supplied by the therapists, but only after relevant ideas were invoked by the boys themselves and fully clarified, not before. Subjects, and many times also explanations, had been derived by the boys themselves, frequently with astonishing native perspicacity. Because formulations were not presented in didactic or abstract form, but rather drawn from, and related to, the boys' own cogitations or feelings, they were of tangible significance and functioned as guides to life. We avoided any similarity to classroom procedures and unrelated, abstract theories. Only when we felt that the participants were ready and evinced interest did we proceed with a topic. In the protocols the descriptive phrase, "You could hear a pin drop as the therapist was explaining this," frequently appears. The Socratic method of question and answer was the predominant procedure employed, so that the boys would be challenged to think through, to explore, to seek explanations on their own, and thus gain insights through their own efforts. This not only facilitated insight, understanding, and assimilation of ideas; what is even more important, the procedure gave them a feeling of status, of participation, of achievement. Only in the final stages of a discussion, and only when it was deemed necessary, would the therapist enlarge on an idea, buttress conclusions by facts, supply confirming illustrations, and point up the relevance of the topic in hand to other of the boys' own life situations.

The protocols contain a plethora of instances of this, but it would be an error to assume that the proceedings in the group consisted of a heuristic carnival. Ideas were rather the superstructure overlaying the the discharge of a variety of feelings, negative and positive, overcoming resistances and defenses, and withstanding self-confrontation. Without such inner strength and flexibility, the content of the discussions would be not only useless as a therapeutic armamentarium, but would have threatened and disturbed our emotionally fragile young patients.

6

Phases in the Para-Analytic Process and the Roles of the Therapist

IT IS CLEAR from the preceding discussions that the major requirement in the treatment of the type of boy we were dealing with was flexibility. We had to follow the unfolding of interests, perceptiveness, and receptiveness. We assumed from the very start that no one method could be suitable for our purpose, that we would have to vary our approaches from time to time, though maintaining our sights and goals. The second requirement which we were prepared to meet was that for a long period (if not throughout treatment) 1] the group interviews would have to be *reality oriented* (abstract ideas, theory, and values would have to flow from actualities in the lives of the boys); 2] that *clarity, fitness, and directness* of remarks and questions by therapists would be of the essence; and 3] that *confrontation* as well as *exploration* would be necessary; lastly, 4] the therapists would have to be throughout in *tacit alliance* with their patients rather than appearing to be on the side of the adults and their world. Alliance, however, did not mean approval of what was unacceptable; rather it was acceptance of the boys' condition, an understanding of the inner struggles that begot their special behavior.

From the earlier observation groups we were able to identify definite sequences in group interviews, which were later amplified and extended in the demonstration groups. The content of the group interviews, both in manifest and latent phases, followed the general lines of the personality unfoldment and increasing ego strengths of the participants. As personal security increased and the boys' self-images improved, communications grew more meaningful and more revealing, and out of their enhanced psychologic literacy came clearer understanding of people and of themselves. A rise in the general maturity level, self-identity, self-awareness, and better inner integration were followed by self-control and conscious efforts of varying degrees at social integration. The total outcome of these complex inner processes was a marked reduction of alienation.

An analysis of the various steps and phases of development as they appeared in the protocols of the group sessions seemed to suggest nine classifications discussed below. However, these phases were not always separate and distinct; they often operated concomitantly, fused with one another, or one appeared as another was tapering off.

RESISTANCE

Resistance took the form either of random motility, noisiness, inconsequential chit-chat, boastfulness, or talk about "top realities." The therapist's role in this phase was determined by the mood of the group, its accessibility, and the number and type of allies he was able to attract among the boys. Where there were one or more boys with status in the group, who wielded influence over the others, the task of overcoming the resistances and terminating the acting-out behavior was not so difficult as where no such aids were available. In our first group (group A), Neal (see pp. 62-90) was just such a helpful influence. In fact, he determined to a great extent the pace in the discussions and was largely responsible for the salutary results in that group. In the group of the highest delinquency saturation, with intense sexual disturbances (group D), which was conducted by the same therapist, there were no such effectively benign controls forthcoming from the group, and the resistance phase persisted for a much longer period.

Whatever procedure is adopted during this initial phase, the therapist must convey his acceptance of the patients' current state of being and of their behavior, and must bring the group under control through a positive transference toward himself. An illustration of the importance of this principle is the reaction of the boys to the therapist when they asked to be removed from group B (see pp. 131-135) because of the therapist's premature steps at interpretation and, especially, confrontation. Passivity should be the rule for the therapist in the early sessions before he can deal with resistance and acting out. The very shock of an adult's nonresponsiveness to rowdyism serves as a deterrent, since it raises the level of anxiety in the boys, even though the anxiety is not apparent.

In our demonstration group (group C) the most influential boy was a hardened delinquent. It was he who helped perpetuate the resistance period in this group, which extended for four months. The therapist seemed discouraged by the group's lack of movement and required repeated reassurance from the supervisor that the boys could not possibly continue in their mood interminably and that he would at an appropriate time be able to break through. This prediction proved true (see session 16, pp. 333-339).

PROJECTION AND DEFENSIVENESS

In the next phase the conversations were more focused, but the boys predominantly blamed others and exterior circumstances for their predicaments; professed their own innocence; griped against staff members, some teachers, and caseworkers; expressed suspicion of all adults, including the group therapists; and were in general defensive against recognizing or becoming aware of their own parts in causing the difficulties in which they found themselves.

To overcome this ingrained tendency was one of the critical tasks in our work. While it was essential that the therapists should not be marked as a defender of adults and their world, they nevertheless could not acquiesce to the massive blame and complaints. We have, therefore, considered this phase of the interviews as a period in which ventilation took place of accumulated rage harbored against all adults, their world, and everything it represented. Had the therapists become identified with this world in the slightest degree, their effectiveness would have ended. We considered that much that the boys had said during this period was also intended to test the therapists as to the side they were on. The therapists, therefore, had to concentrate on creating an image of themselves as persons different from everything the boys had expected them to be. They had to prove themselves in order to gain the boys' confidence and trust, or their effectiveness would have been completely negated and treatment bogged down. We urged the therapists to concentrate during this period on building an image of adults completely at variance from what had been imprinted in the boys' psyches in the past. Steps in that direction had already been taken through the manner in which resistance had been dealt with. The therapists' tolerant and understanding attitudes impressed the boys with the fact that the therapists were "different" from all other adults, and they verbalized this impression later on. While in this phase the image-building continued. Of even more significance was the fact that the boys were gradually becoming convinced that they could expect treatment from the therapists other than that which they customarily received from adults.

The therapists did not remain entirely passive in this image-building process. They uniformly displayed interest in what the boys were saying, but were always careful not to invade sensitive (threat) areas, such as relations with parents. When parents and their conduct were mentioned by the boys and the therapists responded (though they had been instructed not to do so), the reactions of the boys were uniformly violently resentful. We were equally careful not to react to a boy's reflections upon himself, for this, too, is a threat area, and in addition is often a boy's test of a therapist's attitude toward him.

When in the therapist's judgment a reaction to a boy's feelings and unhappiness was indicated, the therapist did so to convey his empathy, as is usually practiced in casework guidance and treatment. However, he could not support delinquent acts or hostile destructiveness. While pronouncements must be honest, one can be honest and still withhold remarks that may hurt or alienate patients. We reserved confrontation for a later stage in treatment when the defenses had been diminished and the positive transferences toward the therapist were secure.

DREAMS AND SEX

It will not be surprising that in these adolescent boys, dreams that led to discussions of sex preceded other psychological revelations. Even a brief view of the intrapsychic difficulties of our boys, as well as the age factor, would indicate the naturalness of this phenomenon. The intensity of sexual tensions at this chronological age and the anxieties and guilts bound up in them would tend to create strong preoccupation with sex. Not all the dreams were concerned with that subject, however, as the protocols make clear; anxiety and wish-fulfillment dreams also made their appearance. The inquiries as to the meaning and source of dreams, which *always* came from the boys in all our groups but one, led to the inquiry as to the cause and meaning of feelings and urges. These were explained to the boys with complete frankness, except for areas which we felt they were not yet ready to comprehend, or which might prove too disturbing at a particular stage in the emotional development of some boy or boys. Examples of these were homicidal and incestuous urges and homosexual wishes, though at later stages these matters, too, received attention.

Discussion of primary urges and associated feelings resulting from dreams quickened general curiosity and understanding of psychologic processes that led to "psychologic literacy." This was of major value in the growth of our boys.

Imparting sex information, which all the boys eagerly sought, was entirely on a factual level. As already reported, we used pictures and charts in textbooks as visual aids and answered all questions frankly.

Because this procedure is recorded extensively in the group protocols, it will only be mentioned here. Of great significance to the process of rehabilitation of delinquents are discussions of sex. The need for social regulation of sexual activity of the individual always came into purview, and all the questions were met head on; conclusions were drawn for the necessity of regulative instrumentalities in the orderly conduct of society and as biological survival devices.

In answering questions about sources and meaning of dreams, the boys were introduced to the concepts of repression, the unconscious, condensation, distortion, and anxiety and wish-fulfillment. In later sessions, the boys would, on their own, attempt to classify, analyze, and interpret their own and each others' dreams. Added to the therapeutic value of revealing and discussing dreams the boys brought in *voluntarily* from the start was their becoming psychologically aware and gaining understanding, which contributed to their emotional growth and insights.

RESCUE FANTASY

One of the universal infantile characteristics of the boys under our therapeutic care was the intensity of their oral fixation, which took the overt form of unfounded complaints against the food at the institution and of insistently demanding food and cigarettes at the group sessions. But more characteristically, this fixation, which resulted from prolonged deprivation during preverbal and preconceptual phases of development, was conveyed by less obvious mechanisms. Among these were unreasonable demands, injustice-collecting, dependencies (usually covered by a façade of bravado), complaining, and whining. The impression the boys produced at first was that of small children from whom the bottle was suddenly taken away. Their pouting facial expressions were reminiscent of frustrated small children. Later, their oral dependencies were shown by affluence of devotion to and gratitude toward the therapists, who had met their oral needs both materially and symbolically. When the boys' intellectual curiosity was aroused these infantile dependencies were shown through the eagerness of their desire *to be given*, in this instance, more information. It had the stamp of oral hunger.

Their dependency and infantile fears were particularly clear in the boys' communicated forebodings of doom and of being destroyed. Their anguished manner as they spoke of expectations of disaster conveyed their unspoken appeal to be rescued like small children. These rather husky adolescents, in their maturational backwardness, entertained rescue fantasies about their parents, especially their mothers. The potential rescuer in this instance was to be the therapist as a substitute parent.[1]

The rescue fantasies were met with verbal clarification and guidance, which helped bring forth the charismatic quality of the therapist. However, this was planfully accomplished in a manner that did not permanently tie the boys to the therapists or perpetuate or reinforce dependency. The manner in which this was done is illustrated in the protocols.

PSYCHOLOGICAL LITERACY

We made a special point of taking advantage of every opportunity to fire the boys' imaginations and curiosities by inquiries into reasons for facts and phenomena that preoccupied them. With external phenomena as a start, we led them by the inversion process to examine human motivations in general terms, and made efforts to impress them especially with the relation of cause and effect. Up to a point we allowed the boys' disorganized and undisciplined thinking and stray, unrelated statements to go unchallenged. As their curiosities were aroused, however, and they displayed genuine interest, the therapists would question the connections in their rather jumbled thinking and introduce (and later keep repeating) the relation of phenomena and behavior to determining causes.

Because of the climate of the institution, the boys' experiences with casework interviews, references to what the boys may have read, and particularly the emotional tensions under which they lived, it was inevitable that questions concerning themselves and their conduct would be forthcoming. Guided by the supervisory discussions, the therapists avoided being too direct, but later proceeded to make inroads into *self-confrontation* by carefully worded questions. After a period of this, the boys volunteered remarks concerning themselves, their feelings, and their attitudes.

Being able to speak of their hitherto defended feelings indicated an alteration in their ego-defense systems and increased ego strengths. These more favorable circumstances encouraged us to confront the boys from time to time with their attitudes and conduct, drawing specific conclusions and offering explanations. However, our emphasis was still upon general principles and systematic thinking. Such concepts as defenses, distortion, projection, displacement, hostility, fantasy, and onto-archaic

---

1. On occasion the boys did refer to the therapist as "father." During a particularly affect- and anxiety-laden discussion, a boy would impulsively say: "I wish you was my father. I wouldn't be in trouble," or, "Why didn't my father tell me these things?" or would exclaim about the therapist, "He *is* our father."

mind were introduced at points of the boys' psychologic readiness, and repeated references continued to be made to them by the therapist and the boys themselves in later sessions as the boys attempted to understand their own and each other's behavior and reactions. There is an abundance of illustration of this development in the protocol records. However, it must be recognized that premature imparting of information cannot but prove barren. It must be given at points of intellectual and emotional readiness, and information must be relevant to interest. The learning dynamic of repetition was employed at many points and in many connections in the interviews.

INVERSION

Analysis of dreams, frank discussions of sex and enlightenment on its various aspects, information the boys acquired about physiology and anatomy, their increased psychological literacy, and particularly their strengthened egos and decrease in defensiveness and denial could not but enhance self-awareness and readiness for self-confrontation, giving rise to the courage to turn the discussions on themselves. Some of the learnings and insights acquired through the group discussions had been from time to time spontaneously applied by some of the boys to themselves, and the therapists now took a hand at this—first cautiously, and later with more directness and greater frequency. The process of self-confrontation which was going on in a covert, partly unconscious way, was made conscious, and the boys—sometimes on their own, at other times through the suggestions of the therapist—finally entered the phase which we term *inversion*.

Inversion usually appears quite early in the treatment of psychoneurotic adult patients, but has to be fostered for a long time with all adolescents and is frequently never attained. It was at this period that the boys recognized their part in generating difficulties for themselves and others and were able to evaluate objectively not only themselves but even their parents. They now reached a point in their emotional development and ego strength at which to view their parents for what they were without feelings of guilt, narcissistic injury, or loss of identity. Having acquired a sounder identity of their own through identification with, and support from, the therapist and the group, their dependencies upon parents had been decreased and the boys could now examine not only themselves but also those from whom they had drawn for their self-images and identities in the past.

As a corollary to self-confrontation, the boys had now recognized that the blame for their "troubles" could not be laid entirely to others. This diminished the deeply ingrained pattern of projection, displacement, and distortion by which their hostilities fed and through which they kept alive their compensatory ego ideals and false identities. In this respect inversion was in direct opposition to phase two, that of projection and defensiveness. It was also during the height of the inversion period that self alienation was rapidly on the wane and self-integration began to make more rapid strides.

INTROSPECTION

During this period, introspection made its appearance among some of the more sensitive boys. A striking example of this was Louis's soliloquy, which appears on pp. 520-521. Like Louis, others, as well, came to the group in disturbed states with underlying anticipation of disaster and doom. Having come to regard reality more maturely and recognize their own deficiencies, the boys' anxieties and self-doubts increased. This phase is clearly shown in the protocols. With these we dealt directly. We did not allow such negative feelings to take deep root and become inured in the psyches of our boys. As the recordings reveal, the therapists, prompted by the supervisor, explained that these feelings of uncertainty stemmed from earlier dependencies and were part of the onto-archaic mind; that if the boys would examine themselves objectively they would find that they had done many things successfully and showed strength and determination in the past, even though some of the things they did were not according to Hoyle. In the case of some boys, direct encouragement was given by the therapists.

Gradually, the group interviews took on an entirely different character. Every one of the boys in the demonstration group (C) began to view himself in a more sanguine light. There was hope and determination for a constructive life apparent in speech and manner, and all set themselves to making definite plans for their future, when they would return to their homes and communities. They talked about school, jobs, marriage, and parenthood.

INSIGHT

Inherent to inversion is insight. The two dynamics operate concurrently, but differ in one important respect. Inversion may operate on the intellectual plane alone, without deeply affecting emotions, and it may not, therefore, serve as an instrumentality for personality reconstruction. To achieve the latter it is necessary that ratiocination not be employed as a resistance tool, and that the feelings of hate and love, depression and elation, guilt and righteousness be expressed and worked through in the context of the patients' current lives and memories. It is possible to misconstrue self-examination verbalizations as being of therapeutic effectiveness and to equate "understanding" with "insight." The former is purely an intellectual process that seldom affects attitudes, feelings, or behavior with any degree of permanence. Mere understanding is particularly ineffectual in patients such as our boys. We had to reach and bring to the surface feelings against which they defended themselves and, through the benevolent attitudes of the therapist and the group, counteract the ego defenses, thereby rendering the personality less rigid and less impervious to change.

Properly understood, insight includes emotional flexibility as well as intellectual understanding. In fact, emotional flexibility is its major ingredient. Insight can emerge only in the absence of defensive rigidity, protective denial, and self-deceptive self-image. Only when these conditions no longer exist can intellectual comprehensions and codified values take root dynamically and effectively. We found these formulations of extreme importance in reaching our final goal. Self-deception, rationalization, self-justification, and reversion to self-generated values and rejected social codes continued to reappear even in the advanced stages of therapy, and long after they seemed to us appropriate. These regressions to onto-archaic processes were a source of concern to us, for we felt, in a sense, the boys did not *incorporate* the improvements they displayed in and outside of the group. We have dealt with them as best we could, and we came to the conclusion that perhaps the length of the treatment was too brief to completely prevent regression in the future which can be viewed as "character resistances" to basic change. We could, therefore, envisage recurrences under stress of delinquent behavior in some of our boys. They had to live longer with their new personalities than we allowed them.

Just as the treatment of some patients with character disorders leaves *neurotic residue*, there seemed to remain in our boys *character residues* after the neurotic features had been worked through to a considerable degree. In the instance of the neurotic residue, we usually recommend further individual psychoanalytic psychotherapy or formal psychoanalysis, according to the needs of a specific patient. Character-disorder residues, on the other hand, require a corrective living situation extending for a long period of time in which the demands upon the individual do not activate his old patterns in the process of adjustment and survival. These conditions could have been supplied by a greatly extended period of para-analytic group treatment in the institution beyond the seventy-five sessions, but even then the institutional culture would have to buttress the effects of the group at all points.

However, postdischarge follow-up studies on the boys in our demonstration group show that they have achieved adequate ego strengths to cope with unfavorable life circumstances with varying degrees of success (see "Outcomes," pp. 726-738).

The therapists' major function during this advanced period in treatment was to recall to the boys the knowledge and the psychologic understandings they had acquired, and to indicate that they could not as yet relate them to the ongoing events in their lives, and to their thoughts and feelings. We were impressed with the ephemeral and allusive character of their recently acquired learnings and seeming understandings, but were heartened by the ease with which they perceived the relevance of the interpretations given them and their readiness to accept them. The boys' defensiveness and resistances, so glaringly manifested at the outset, were now demonstrably at a low ebb, and their egos obviously in communication with the unconscious. The establishment of such intrapsychic communication (psychic cybernetics) is the major triumph of all psychotherapy, including psychoanalysis.

CONTROL

Because the basic manifest difficulties for which our boys had been committed to the institution, and which brought them in conflict with society and the law, was impulsivity, we considered our ultimate objective the establishment of inner controls that would prevent recurrences of unreasonable aggression. All our boys had suffered at the hands of unempathic adults, parents, and parent surrogates who were unable to accept the vagaries of a child's growing powers. Thus our boys were denied the exercise of these powers, necessary for personality integration and psychologic maturity. Victims of the prevailing behavioristic tenets themselves, these adults imposed absolute and even tyrannical authority upon the children, rendering them incapable of judgment and, above all, self-control. Individuation, so essential for psychological maturity, was denied them, and as a result, they remained helpless in dealing with their tyrannical raw, instinctive impulses in the face of external stress and internal strains. Having no resources, they acted on (infantile) impulsiveness.

Added to these immaturing impositions was the accumulated resentment toward the adults who had frustrated their sprouting energies and autonomous wishes. The prolonged and accumulated resentment became structured into the attitudinal stances of our patients, and came to dominate their very life patterns. The intensity of hate and feelings of resentment for being rejected, and the self-image of worthlessness to which this gave rise, undermined the organization of the boys' egos and caused in them self-alienation and consequent social alienation.

It was obvious to us from the outset that the disciplinary approach engendered by a behavioristic philosophy of personality and of human behavior could not possibly be effective. It was equally clear that the defective ego and superego organization of our boys would not be corrected by continued frustration of instinct gratifications. A strong ego is not entirely forged, as is erroneously assumed, by outside discipline, control, and deprivation. Stubbornness and bitter hostile determination result in some instances from such experiences, and this is often mistaken for ego strength. Most of our boys were certainly stubborn, and blindly so, but far from having the strengths which they simulated. Ego strength is rather an outcome of appropriate instinctual gratifications and restraints progressively applied by benign adults during the formative years of the child.[2] Overgratification of instinctual urges also weakens character, as does excessive frustration; one misdirects the native energies from which the ego draws its powers, while the other starves them. Exposing our boys to the same regimen to which they had been subjected in the past would only re-emphasize their difficulties, which the entire climate of the Children's Village sought to eschew.

As is clear from the foregoing discussions, the entire plan of treatment was oriented in the direction of fulfilling instinctual urges and supplying essential emotional gratifications consistent with the boys' ages and their conditions. Psycho-organic growth made the emergence of insight possible, and the boys gained it through their own expansion and efforts. Anti-alienative perceptions of the self followed, and energies hitherto consumed in morbid fantasies and acts became available for growth and expansion. For each of the boys, the total outcome of this web of psychic activity was a more mature personality in which the psychic forces became balanced and integrated.

As these changes became apparent, control of impulses was made the *conscious* preoccupation of the group. As the group protocols show, this was at first instigated by the therapist, but welcomed by the boys. The discussions conceptualized what seemed to have become cumulatively latent in their minds. Their readiness for it was intense and dramatic. Having emerged from their self-alienative state, they saw salvation in these discussions. All the boys in the demonstration group (C), the only group where this stage was reached, proceeded on their own to make plans for more benign lives after leaving the institution. Each one freely described his impulsive responses, his susceptibility to temptations, and gang followership in the past; each formulated solutions for himself to evade the malignant pressures from his neighborhood and some also from their families.

The subject of *control* and the uncertainties relative to it formed the

2. S. R. Slavson, *Child Psychotherapy* (New York: Columbia University Press, 1950).

content of a large section of the interviews near the end of the group's life. On occasion, when a particularly unjust treatment or a strongly irritating and provoking situation was discussed, one of the boys would respond with anger and vicarious aggression. His threats to do violence would invariably be countered by the others with statements on the inappropriateness of such a reaction and recall to him the conclusions in past discussions where such responses had been found wanting. Where the boys failed to involve the principle of the onto-archaic mind's operation, the therapist was sure to remind them of it. It is thus that controls were "inculcated," but only on the background of a corrected psycho-organic reconditioning in each of the boys.

Superego Formation

Because of the predominantly acting-out character of our group members and the action content of their communications during the interviews, it was natural that we would address ourselves to their ego-functioning and its controls. However, the integrated personality and its wholesome adjustment to the condition of living in a social setting entails the guidance and the regulation of the superego. An inner principle for selecting from among the multitude of impacts and opportunities that confront one in the complex social matrix of modern society is essential for individual and social survival. Judgment and acceptability of things as good or bad, right or wrong, just or unjust, beautiful or ugly, desirable or repugnant are the functions of the superego, with which the ego must be in consonance if harmony and inner peace are to be the lot of the individual.

It was obvious that the superego development of our boys, with few exceptions, was faulty. Of the triad of the psychic forces of man—id, ego, and superego—the latter is *solely* a product of external influences and relations. The superego, unlike the other two, does not have its roots in instinct or in the soma. Its source, quality, and content are derived from introjected unconscious identifications and conscious values and prohibitions which are ultimately lodged in the unconscious. In this process parents are almost the sole agency. It is their values, their standards, their esthetic reactions that the child progressively incorporates, though not without a struggle, at various stages in his development. The immediate peer group and, later, the morality of the social climate of the community, nation, and world add to (and may even somewhat alter) the basic parental superego, and what may be called the *ethos* the superego evolves. However, in this process, as well, the individual responds unconsciously to external actualities on the basis of the *parent-derived or basic superego* and incorporates them in his final or ethos-superego.

Because of the treatment they had received at their hands, our boys intensely rejected and grew hostile to all adults and rejected their values. They continued in their unmodified infantile narcissism and counterfeit feelings of omnipotence. What was even more ominous from our point of view was that the superegos of the boys' parents were narcissistic and asocial, as was also the ethos-superego of their milieu. We knew that an identity without a socially adequate superego is spurious, and if we were able to effect a lasting recovery in our boys, establishment of an adequate superego was essential. The task we faced was to derive strategies whereby the rather lax and unformed superegos in our patients could be reconstructed.

The essential mechanism of superego correction lies in introjection of the superego of an acceptable adult or adults. We looked forward to the time when this would occur in our boys in relation to the therapists, and later, perhaps, in relation to other members of the clinic and other staff. It was necessary, however, to first break the ground and till the psychological soil by loosening defensiveness and diminishing the alienative states in the boys so that they would feel comfortable with some adult, which in our case was the therapist in the group.

As already indicated, moral standards cannot be taught directly without arousing resentment, nor could we employ at the age of our group members the restraints and prohibitions parents employ with small children and out of which a superego is derived. We had to rely on more subtle developments from which superego factors would emerge. The discussions initiated spontaneously by the boys themselves of the need and validity of social controls and laws was a step in that direction, for they indicated by this that they had become aware of these sufficiently to give them consideration. They were on the road toward acceptance. The therapists' taking the lead in considering the validity of certain acts and attitudes was another move toward the same goal. Another was the boys' own discovery of the harm they brought on themselves by their conduct. When these were brought to the boys' view there were evidences of feelings of guilt relative to their delinquencies and relationships. This was made particularly evident during the discussions of sex, when the boys, in a burst of idealism, almost unanimously decided to abstain until they were "married and have a family," a decision which was obviously unrealistic. Depth psychology has shown the concatenation between the Oedipus crisis, sex, and superego, which our boys seemed to corroborate in their spontaneous discussions.

Despite these evidences, which we considered stray and somewhat superficial, it was our suspicion that the boys would not come by wholesome superegos through these means. Superego development in their cases, as in everyone else's, would have to come through introjection of values from adults and the milieu in which therapy was to occur, as well as the values of the macroculture. We were particularly disheartened by the constant repetition of the resolve, even toward the end of the limited course of our group treatment, that they would not commit any acts in the future that would get them "in trouble." The criterion "not to get in trouble," rather than the recognition that an act is wrong because it inconveniences or injures someone or is contrary to the ethos, is obviously narcissistic and asocial in nature. While the superego is not devoid of narcissistic elements in its structure, its intent is allotropic, and this was not evident with our boys. Obviously either the brevity of the therapeutic relation or the total setting was not productive of the subtle conditions for the emergence of a more oceanic superego structure. We considered this inadequate superego reconstruction the weakest link in our work and anticipated unpleasant repercussions in the future.

The subject of "implanting" superego judgments and restraints occupied much of our attention during the supervisory conferences, for even the therapists repeatedly referred in the group discussions to the fact that the boys "got in trouble," and when plans were considered for the boys' return home, their future behavior was evaluated by the therapists with reference to "not getting in trouble again." It was our personal contention that such a criterion, if really followed, provides easy leeway for delinquent and criminotic acts—an act need not be eschewed as long as one is not discovered at it. It is interesting that the admonitions by the supervisor to balance these statements by pointing out the hurt or injury to others, as well, was never followed by the therapists, which was not the case in all other matters.

One could speculate on reasons for it, but perhaps it is best to let the matter rest.

Summary

The characteristics of the adolescents with whom we were dealing that required special attention were intensive sensitivity (paranoid-like reactions), feelings of being defective and inadequate, exacerbation of Oedipal hostility and guilt, pregenital sexuality, sexual tensions, hedonism (with underlying desperation), a feeling of doom, magical thinking, inadequately developed superego, restitutive wishes, injustice collection, orality, masochistic orientation, weak ego and overstrong defensiveness, feelings of helplessness and reactive aggression, exhibitionism, defective and fluid identity, atonement for unconscious guilt, herostratic mechanism (shifting blame from parental figure to society), self and social alienation.

The operational dynamics of the boys' egos were by and large characterized by impulsivity, defensiveness, denial, fluid identification, omnipotence fantasies, magical thinking, autarchy, self-hate, self-contempt, grandiosity, insecurity, dependence, mistrust, projection, distortion, rationalization, flight from reality, frustration intolerance, hatred and guilt toward parents.

The therapeutic strategies we employed at different periods of treatment were permissiveness, acceptance, guidance, alliance with the patients, flexibility, reality orientation, interpretation, didacticism, the readiness-relevance-repetition complex, catharsis, conceptualization (such as self-fulfilling prophecies), the principle of the onto-archaic mind, and so on.

7

The Therapist as Reality and Symbol

The Role of the Therapist

IT IS NOT SURPRISING that, in a psychotherapy that blends ego and psychoanalytic therapies with an eye to overcoming antisocial behavior, the therapist would have to walk a tightrope. Ours was not an ordinary situation in the realm of clinical psychological treatment. Our boys were not motivated, their deviant value systems were highly cathected, their ego ideals were defective, and they were highly suspicious and distrustful.

The constituency of our groups was abnormal, too. It did not conform with the requirements of group balance in terms of variegated individual ego-functioning and behavioral patterns. The required balance of instigators, neutralizers, and neuters that tends to prevent reinforcement of pathogenic acting out and synergic behavior was not fulfilled. Groups saturated with an antisocial and impulsive constituency, such as ours were, could understandably reinforce destructive behavior. In addition to the homogeneity of attitude and motive, another factor that seriously menaces successful conduct of such groups is the high level of suggestibility and emotional infectiousness, to which our boys were very much disposed. Their egos were weak and they possessed inordinately immature personalities, which made them suggestion-prone.

One element in favor of the therapeutic possibilities for the groups, however, was the homogeneity of their apparent or obvious problems: they had all been exposed to repressive treatment; they had been rejected; they were banished and deprived; they all had similar objects of hostility. These conditions, while intensifying the boys' emotivity and mutual induction, also heightened identification and emotional resonance, mutual catalysis, and vicarious catharsis. It is our guess that the extraordinarily progressive richness and depth of the content of the interviews (as shown in the protocols) were predominantly, though not entirely, due to these common conditions.

As a result of the psychologic climate permeating the groups in early stages, the therapist had to supply the missing links in the usual group therapeutic chain. In addition to his usual functions, in our groups he alone had to act as the neutralizer, without the buttressing aid that ordinarily comes from some patients in a group, and he alone had to hold up to the group ego ideals and superego values that are commonly maintained to varying degrees by neurotic and conflicted patients. The absence of the neutralizing influences that usually emanate from the group itself allowed our boys' hostility to be mobilized and intensified against the institution, the staff, and people generally. In well-balanced groups, open hostility, in general, and toward the therapist, in particular, is mitigated by some members who feel threatened by it and grow anxious when the parental figure, the therapist, is attacked. Only on rare occasions, and then only when therapy had considerably progressed, did such corrective reactions appear in our groups. Although some participated with underlying anxiety, all the members added fuel to the fires of hate, both because they were genuinely enraged and for prestige purposes, for no one would be "chicken" or "teacher's pet."

However, it must be noted that when the therapists were adequate for their tasks, direct, open aggression against them readily abated after the initial expression of hostilities. Once the boys recognized in the therapist unconditional acceptance of them *as persons*, hostilities flared up only occasionally. These comparatively benign attitudes stemmed to a great extent from the fact that by contrast to all other areas of their daily life, past and present, the boys derived a genuine feeling of comfort and acceptance in our groups. They frequently verbalized this fact and therefore could not make the therapists targets of anger and rage—which in itself had therapeutic value for the particular type of patient with which we were dealing.

A trap against which we repeatedly warned our therapists was conveying any semblance of disapproval of the boys' conduct, past or present, or appearing as advocates for, or defenders of, adults and their morals and values in and out of the institution. *At the same time it was of utmost importance that therapists did not approve of or ally themslves, by word or gesture, with the antisocial attitudes and acts of the boys.* We delayed the presentation of adult mores and the social necessities for law and control until the time when the boys' emotional maturation and intellectual readiness would make it appropriate and effective. The protocols amply demonstrate the success of this procedure.

One stratagem we employed to avoid becoming the "devil's advocate" was inherent in the structure of the group therapy project. The boys knew the caseworkers had been involved in evaluating them and their conduct and making decisions on privileges such as home visits and final discharge, but the group therapist participated in none of these deliberations. The boys repeatedly questioned the part the therapists played in such decisions and had to be as often reassured on this score. Only in one instance, when a special problem had to be decided upon with the clinical staff of an agency from a distant city, was one of our group therapists constrained to attend such a conference. When this fact was brought out in the supervision conference with the therapist, we decided that the boy involved be seen individually and his permission obtained. The boy readily consented. Had he refused, the therapist would not have participated in the conference.

Until they were certain that the group therapists were not "reporting" on them, the boys refused to reveal anything of an intimate nature. As a precaution we went to the lengths of actually withholding all matters revealed in the group sessions from the caseworkers for fear that they might be passed on to the boys by word, gesture, or attitude. This drastic procedure was adopted as an emergency measure. Since the director of the project was not on the campus, the necessary steps for the education of the professional and nonprofessional staffs could not be undertaken. To integrate group therapy in a milieu requires continuous day-by-day contact with the various staffs, in groups and individually. We had no facilities for this. Where the group therapy personnel are on the grounds daily, the separation we have imposed is unnecessary, in fact, would be counterindicated. The appropriate practice is that group therapists treat the members of their groups individually as well when this should be indicated. However, this would involve alteration in administrative structure and procedures, which we avoided.

Therapists who do the actual therapy in institutional residential treatment should not be involved in administrative decisions regarding the residents. Once patients of the type with which we were dealing learn that their therapists participate in deciding on punishments and even applying normal deprivations, their resentments and the negative transferential hostilities *become actual*. The therapeutic relation then may come to an end: The therapist becomes an enemy who can no longer be entrusted with confidences. It was the consensus of all the adults who were involved in the project that this confidentiality was at the very root of its effectiveness.

Our strongest weapon in gaining the confidence of the boys was our forthrightness and honesty in whatever we said or did. A statement on any matter, true and pertinent though it may have been, was withheld if it might have produced a negative effect *at the time*, until the boys reached a maturational and conceptual level when it could be employed beneficially. At all times, however, what the therapists did say had to be genuine and honest. It was a matter of omission as against commission (of a psychologic error), but we were aware that equivocation, vacillation, and prevarication would set off chain reactions of suspicion-insecurity-hositility-resistance. This we scrupulously avoided. Whenever an error was made in this area, the reactions of the boys took the form of either acting out, withdrawal, or absenteeism. In our setting absenteeism occurred infrequently. The boys were assigned to groups as part of their "programs," but we did not carry out the institutional rules and made attendance entirely voluntary. The infrequency of absence was the result of gratifications the boys derived from the group sessions and the therapists' tact and genuine loyalty to, and interest in, the members. Attitudes on the part of the therapists had been conveyed spontaneously and planfully in appropriate action, but more importantly, their feelings were reflected in their attitudes.

For a considerable time direct reference to the boys was eschewed so as to prevent narcissistic injury and the arousal of guilt and anxiety. On the few occasions when therapists insensitively overstepped bounds, their effectiveness was greatly diminished, or they failed in their work. In one instance, we had to change therapists in midstream and in another we were compelled to terminate a group prematurely. The inroads toward self-examination by the boys were made by first examining behavior in abstract and general terms or in terms of hypothetical persons. This stratagem prevented arousal of the boys' paranoid-like defensiveness until such time as, cued by their remarks and behavior, we felt safe in entering sensitive or "threat areas." In this regard, as in all others, we awaited the boys' readiness.

A Therapist in Error

The following are some illustrations of conduct by a therapist who, because of personality blockings, was unable to get into the therapeutic mood required in the emotional re-education of delinquent youngsters despite supervisory suggestions, warnings, and direct instructions. He finally had to be replaced by another therapist.

In the second session of observation group B, one of the most hostile and acting-out boys complained in a shrill, angry voice that he was being called "gangster" by everybody in the Village. The therapist countered by saying: "If you are not one, why are you in the Village?" The therapist notes in his protocol report that "At this his [the boy's] speech became garbled in his state of intense anxiety." The lack of basic understanding as to what his role needed to be is demonstrated by another remark recorded in the protocol of the same session. The therapist wrote: "I found myself acting as moderator to bring the group into an orderly discussion." This attitude continued for a number of sessions despite the fact that we attempted in our weekly supervisory conferences to explain the function of the therapist with adolescents generally, and with the type of adolescents we were treating in particular.

A rather inexcusably inappropriate statement was made by the therapist when in the fourth session a boy said that he had never wanted to hurt his mother, but she always got upset when he did "something wrong." The therapist challengingly countered that it seemed that the boy had done things that did hurt his mother. The boy grew extremely anxious, forced a guilty, self-conscious smile, dropped the subject, and proceeded to recount his delinquent activities before coming to the group—obviously to spite or to provoke the therapist.[1]

In the sixth session the therapist "suggested" to the boys that they place their coats on the ping-pong table instead of strewing them around on chairs and floor.

The seating order as described in the protocol was interesting in so far as it reflected the feelings the boys entertained toward the therapist. "On my left, an empty place," wrote the therapist. Then a listing of the boys who sat next to each other. When the boys were settled the therapist asked them whether they had any difficulty about getting "passes." (These passes, issued by staff on each occasion, were intended to account for the boys' whereabouts at any given time. Boys were required to have these on their persons. In keeping with our policy of "trusting" the boys, we did not examine or sign these passes as required before they were returned to the office after the sessions). Then again, "I suggested that we start our discussion. There was a moment's pause with the boys looking at each other or into space. Then one spoke up aggressively. . . ." Later in the same session, when in their enthusiasm three boys became excited and began to talk simultaneously, the therapist notes: "I suggested that they take turns."

At one point, the boys discussed a particularly embarrassing and in fact shocking question relating to incest with mothers. It was claimed (perhaps projectively) that a psychiatrist raised this question with one of the boys. The therapist, in his insensitivity, proceeded to explore why the boys were so upset about incest with their mothers, explaining that "it might seem strange if they were to be asked whether they liked pickles

---

1. This reaction can be understood also as a confessional maneuver to allay guilt, justify his mother, and/or placate the therapist.

for breakfast, but they would not feel upset. Why are they so upset about incest? The boys became very angry, banged on the table and demanded to know how the therapist would feel if he were asked such a question involving his mother." The record reads: "I answered that it would depend on how I felt about my mother. There was silence, then Ray quietly said that one might feel upset if there was truth in it. I said that was a very good point. Could he think of an example? Bill interrupted, saying he still thought it was disrespectful for anyone to ask such an outrageous question. Dick then said: 'They [staff members] did it to make you angry so that you would say things you didn't want to say.' I asked: 'Like what?' Dick flushed, shrugged his shoulders, and fell into silence."

When in the seventh session the boys, except for Hank, were late in coming, Hank asked the therapist where the others were. The therapist did not answer beyond *shrugging his shoulders*. The boy suggested that the therapist telephone to find out. The following is the record of what transpired: "I asked 'why.' He said, 'Just to remind them [the boys] and get them on the ball.' I remarked that I was not a policeman and it was their responsibility to get here on time. It was up to them, not to me." Later in the heat of a discussion at the same session, Hank asserted that he was not upset about the subject that was being discussed and did not need any help [therapy] for it. The therapist responded: "Then I wonder why you are here [in the Village]." Bill (a particularly cruel boy) entered the discussion at that point, attempting to recount how he had been in a number of "accidental" fights; the therapist replied by asking: "Do you really feel that all of the times that you had been brought to court were the results of accidents, or maybe you had done something and got what you deserved [punishment]?"

During another discussion, when Hank talked about a struggle with teachers, the therapist records the following: "I commented that Hank often talked of hating teachers, just as Bill often complained of cottage parents. I could grant that grownups were far from perfect and often made mistakes, but I wondered what was really behind all this. Was it the teachers, cottage parents, or something else?" The group fell silent and seemed abashed. I remarked that our time was almost up and I wanted to leave them with a thought: We often did things in the present because of our experiences in the past, and it would be helpful for them if they could understand this. I then told them that some time ago in another agency I worked with a young man who was in constant trouble with the police, claiming he hated all cops. I told them that this man's father was extremely hard on him, treating him very cruelly, and, as he was never able to do anything about it as a child, he grew up with a great deal of anger toward people who seemed to him to be like his father. When he learned to understand himself and how he really felt, he found that he could accept cops as people like himself and he didn't have to go through life fighting a senseless battle. Though the boys seemed to listen intensely, the group remained silent and did not respond."

It was obvious that the therapist, in addition to his general insensitiveness, had in the last example overextended himself by submitting ideas to the boys which they were not ready to understand or accept. When Bill, the most cruel, aggressive, and acting-out boy, finally came to admit in the eighth session that he "liked to boss other boys around," that he knew he could not take too much responsibility, and that he had to control his temper or he would get into even worse trouble than in the past, the therapist said that this was the first time Bill had admitted to having a problem and that it was not only the cottage parents who made mistakes. The following is recorded: "At this Bill became quite anxious, slurred his speech even more noticeably, and retreated by insisting that it was not that he had problems with wanting to 'push kids around,' but he was always in a situation when something got him into trouble. I planned to respond to this but was interrupted by Hank. . . ."

Despite our effort to help the therapist understand the inappropriateness of his functioning in the group and his attitudes, he continued in the same general vein so that in the eleventh session Hank suddenly interrupted and in an openly defiant tone said that he wanted to be out of the group. Immediately Paul spoke up, saying that he, too, wanted to quit. The therapist remarked to Hank that his attitude came from his "resistance," since he preferred to talk about things other than himself and his own "problems." Hank became violently angry and pounded his fist on the table as he stood up, shouting in an excited voice that he had no problems and that he knew what he should and should not do and that he did not need the group to help him in anything.

We note further in the protocol of that session that Bill, Hank, and Paul spontaneously began to speak at once, and the therapist records: "I suggested that they take turns." Apparently the climate in the group became too oppressive, particularly after the therapist said, "We look at policemen the way we look at our parents, since our parents are the first people in our lives who give us orders and teach us how to behave." Bill responded to this that it was a lot of "baloney," that his parents "were fine," and that he certainly did not feel his mother "was like a cop." Ray attempted to say something but his voice was drowned out in the shouting of the boys. A flurry of movement toward the sink and the lavatory now arose. "The boys all seemed tense and strained and there was more smoking than usual," reports the therapist. Fred, who probably was too diffident to verbalize his desire to quit the group, came up to the therapist on the way out at the end of the session and asked whether there would be "a meeting" the following week. When the therapist asked him in return why he inquired, Fred shrugged his shoulders and looked abashed. Later, we learned that Bill asked his caseworker to be removed from the group.

The resistance generated by the therapist was marked in the next session, when the boys remained completely silent. When asked by the therapist what they wished to discuss, Gerald, as representative of the group, said he had nothing "bad to talk about tonight." This resistance was further manifested in the thirteenth session when only Gerald sat next to the therapist and there were three empty chairs between him and his neighbor on the other side. No discussion of any kind occurred, so that the session was terminated soon after the group gathered. At the following session the boys brought up the question of food, making a demand of the therapist that they be given food, which was in line with their hostility due to the anxiety generated in the group. The therapist was removed at this point.

The Therapist Replaced

With the new therapist, the climate in the group and the content of the interviews radically changed. We are reproducing in some detail the protocol of the second session with the new therapist, the seventeenth for the group, not only to demonstrate the effect of an appropriate therapeutic "style," but also as an exposure of our boys' pathognomic unconscious content, their fantasies, their confusions, their feelings of inadequacy, their strivings for potency and status, their sexual and incest fantasies, their suggestibility and superstitions.

We note that the seating arrangements have changed: two of the boys sat close to the therapist, on either side of him. There was a comparatively relaxed atmosphere in the group and a free and easy interchange in a fairly orderly conversation.

The boys were seated close to each other, with Gerald and Fred flanking the therapist . . . Paul went to the washroom and on his return brought a cup of water, which he offered to anyone who wished to have a drink. Jerry brought out a box of candy and shared it with the group. . . . When the boys settled down Gerald talked about rats he had seen. A disagreement ensued among Bill, Fred, and Jerry as to unpleasantness in the appearance of these mammals. Jerry thought rats were not unpleasant animals. Bill described them as "slimy" and said that the very idea of touching them repulsed him, while Fred commented on rats as dangerous, particularly when cornered. Jerry said that when he was younger he used to go "rat-hunting" with a number of his friends and enjoyed it "tremendously."

Bill's statement that he "would rather face a lion any day than a rat," brought laughter from the boys, and some commented that they could believe it. He then narrated a story told by some adult on the campus which seemed to have great meaning for him. This man, with some others, had cornered a rat. In its attempt to escape, the rat jumped on the man, climbed to his chest, and "was trying to get to his throat." Bill described vividly how the man was almost paralyzed by "the feel of the rat's feet on his chest." As the story was graphically unfolded, the boys in the group remained icily quiet and visibly shaken. Bill added that, as he was telling the story, he could feel the rat on his own chest and as he was saying it, he started to brush his shirt with his hands. At that moment someone scraped his shoe against the floor; Bill jumped up in alarm, and all the others also jumped from their seats in apparent fear.

To allay the anxiety that overtook the group, the therapist said the boys' response was more or less normal, considering how vividly Bill described the situation. Jerry responded by saying that he always thought of rats as being "slimy beasts," and what bothered him most was their long, bare tails. Fred did not like their teeth. He had heard about rats attacking people around the neck. Gerald said that he did not like the feel of the animal. Bill agreed with Gerald and talked more about the fur being "slimy." He went on to narrate how a "bunch of fellows" in his cottage recently killed a rat. As Bill described the details his speech became "clouded" and it was difficult to understand him, not only because of its rapidity but also because he seemed to mumble rather than enunciate the words. Fred immediately began to speak in a manner similar to that of Bill. (This contagion appeared several times during the session.) Bill continued to describe how the boys, after killing the rat, had burned it. However, before doing this they cut the rat open and watched "the intestines flow out." Fred protested that the conversation was making him uneasy and that "everybody was going to have bad dreams about it" as a result.

Gerald said that once after killing a rat, he did dream about it later. This statement prompted all the others to talk about the types of dreams they had had. The conversation now became very lively, with Bill, Fred, Jerry, and Gerald being most intensely involved. Paul remained absolutely silent from this point on and went to the washroom several times. Bill was the first to narrate that after he had killed the rat, he dreamed that the rat's whole family was coming after him. Fred said that he had a recurring "something like a dream" (nightmare) in which he was fighting "a monster that has many arms with prize-fighting gloves on them" and that he was constantly trying to defeat the monster. He is knocked down by the monster and gets up, but is never able to defeat it. He described the monster as being tall, with a man's head but with many arms. Bill remembered a similar dream in which he had a fight with some big man in which his teeth "were knocked out." He remembered distinctly how his gums were bleeding and he was awakened by the feeling of blood pouring out of his mouth. As Bill was narrating this dream, an embarrassed light giggle spread over the group as though they perceived, though vaguely, the latent meaning of the dream. A few of the boys assented saying, "Yes, I know what you mean. I had one like that, too."

Fred now recalled a dream in which "thousands of crabs were biting" him all over his body and as he attempted to brush them off, more would appear. The only way that he could get rid of them was to run, but he could not shake them off and they continued to bite him. Jerry said that he always dreamed about falling and he sometimes woke up on the floor, but in the dream it felt as though he were falling through space "and there never seems to be an end to the fall and in my mind it is almost as if I was going to be crushed to death when I hit wherever I am falling."

After a brief pause Bill asked, "Why do we dream?" The question was echoed by Fred, who then said that he thought that "you dream because you want something." Ray had now entered the conversation for the first time and said that he thought that "sometimes a dream may tell you what is going to happen." In the midwestern city where he lived there was a superstition that when you dream about teeth, someone is going to die. His grandmother had such a dream and her son died soon after. Bill did not agree and said, "You know it's a funny thing—sometimes I even dream about places that don't make sense." The therapist asked what he meant, and Bill went on to say that he dreamed about being home, but while he was at home, he saw himself coming out of his cottage (at the Village) rather than from the house in which he "lived." The boys thought he was "crazy to dream about the Village" when he was home in his own abode. Bill said he would never tell anybody in the Village his dreams because people would think he was "crazy" or they would laugh at him. Fred agreed and said maybe one could tell a "buddy of yours but other kids would laugh at you." Gerald remarked that, if anybody heard the group talking, "they would think we were all crazy." There was common agreement with this.

The therapist stated that it was important to understand dreams because they can help one understand one's difficulties, and he gave an example: Sometimes people disguise things and change them around because they are either unpleasant or because the people think they should not be thinking about such things. But if we could really figure out the meaning of things around us, it would make us "feel better inside."

Bill thought that dreams should not "be figured out," and went on to say that "they were just another side of you and something not to be touched." Fred said that he had heard dreams "mean things, something about maybe they were wishes for things to happen, like for example dreaming about girls." The therapist asked him if he could explain what he meant. Fred went on to say that perhaps what the therapist was saying was that some of the dreams that they talked about had something to do with their thoughts, like he thinks about girls a great deal. There was widespread agreement among the group with what Fred had said. Jerry, Gerald, and Ray agreed that girls were "always pleasant to dream about." Bill wondered if anybody experienced a pleasant dream and was awakened just as he was "enjoying himself." The boys broke into laughter at this. Fred said that he always tried the next night to return to such dreams, but Jerry pointed out that this is never possible. Gerald told of a pleasant dream he was having once in which he was "beating up" some grownup, and as he was really giving him a good thrashing, he was awakened by his cottage father . . . The therapist remarked there are thoughts that people "keep inside, and worry about. This gets built up just as we talked about last week. If they don't talk about and figure out their meaning, they come out in dreams."

Bill agreed with the therapist and said, "Take sex, for example, nobody ever talks about it." "But we sure think about it," asserted Fred. This remark, as well, brought laughter from the group.[2] The therapist stated that it was perfectly natural for boys fifteen and sixteen years old to have feelings on the subject. This statement by the therapist caused the conversation to increase in momentum and rapidity. Bill, the largest and most aggressive boy, suddenly said: "I know you guys will not believe it, but I never had any sex." There were "ohs" and "ahs" in response. Bill then said, "Yes, I had never had it. I talk about it as though I did, but I don't think anybody should do it until they are married." Jerry admitted that he had sexual intercourse and said he was going to continue "doing it all the time." Fred: "I kind of think that maybe it is wrong, but once you've had it, you can't stop. It's like a drug." Gerald and Bill did not participate in this conversation. Ray agreed with Fred and said that it was important and that it was a "normal thing." Bill turned to Fred and asked: "Well, what about if the girl you was having sex with was somebody else's sister? What would you do then?" Fred said that he recognized this as a problem, but "everybody is somebody's

2. At the point in the discussion concerning sex the boys began to play with lighted matches, particularly Bill. and Gerald. All of them cut small holes in and puffed smoke into their boxes of cigarettes, thus making smoke rings.

sister." Jerry thought that the girls he had sex with wanted to have it, and it was not always he that was forcing it on them. Bill said: "I made my sister swear on a stack of bibles that she would never have sex until she got married." Gerald thought that "they should have sex before getting married, that maybe there should be some understanding." The therapist asked what he meant by that, but instead Fred said, "Gerald probably meant that there should be some kind of love feeling between people."

Bill agreed and said that was why he did not "do it." The therapist wondered whether what the boys were saying was that it was all right for them to have feelings now about sex, but that as they grew older they would be in a better position to do something about it in a way that was pleasant and love somebody. What they were talking about now was what other people do with their feelings. Fred said, "Why don't people talk about what to do?" "That's right," said Bill. His mother never told him about it. He had to find out for himself. Jerry had found out from his older brothers who talked about it. Fred said he "picked it up from the street and I had to teach myself what to do and how to do it." Ray added that no one ever broached the subject with him.

The therapist asked why they thought adults did not talk to them about sex. Gerald: "Because they were afraid we are going to go out and do something about it." Fred agreed, and said that it really was not until he got to the Village and one of the coaches sat him down and discussed sex with him that he got some clear idea as to what it was all about. He added, "They're [adults are] afraid." Therapist: "You mean they're afraid because if you learn about it, you're going to go and do it? Still here we are talking about it because we know that the more you talk about things, the more you learn, the happier you are inside and the better you can control yourself." Bill said with emphasis: "Yes, I agree with you. But they don't treat us like that." "Who are they?" the therapist asked. "All the adults." "That's right," said Jerry. "They always accuse us of things that we do are wrong but they do them and it is perfectly all right. For example, my mother never told me about it or if she told me about it, she said it was wrong and then she went and did it."

Bill: "That's one thing I don't like, is to think about them [parents] doing it. My mother better not have babies." Ray declared that some day he was going to be a father and he was "going to do it. What's so wrong about it?" Fred agreed with Bill and said, "I don't like to think about it [parents having intercourse] either." While Gerald agreed with Ray, he said, "What do you expect them [adults] to do?" Bill shrugged his shoulders and said, "Well, I just wish it was somebody about ninety-five getting married for the first time"; then he added, "I guess they do it, but I don't like to think about it." Jerry pointed out that it was "a very natural function and if they didn't do it we wouldn't be here in the first place." There was laughter at this and the boys arrived at a consensus that sometimes it was upsetting to think about parents having sexual intercourse. This was particularly so when the boys were younger and did not understand. They now recognized the fact that it was a normal function between two people who were married.

Jerry said that he didn't remember his (younger) brothers being born but assumed that he "must have been around" at the time. Bill said that he had no recollection at all of such events in his family. The others remained silent. Fred said, "It was funny that when I was younger I was angry at people when they called me 'Sonny,' and when grownups talked about sex or something of that kind I was always either pushed out or told 'Sonny, leave.' " This, too, made him mad. He believed that he got involved with girls sexually because he wanted to stop people from calling him "Sonny." Bill said that he had a precisely opposite experience. When he was four or five years old, he was curious about sex and indulged in sexual play with girls. It was when he grew older that he stopped. Ray said that he, too, "started early," and from what he could gather thought or guessed that everybody "does that." The therapist (rather naïvely) said that what the boys were saying was that "when kids find they have penises they are curious as to what to do with them, and wanted to know what the difference was between a girl and a boy. This is called 'experimentation' and was normal, but when nobody tells them anything about their feelings, boys begin to feel bad inside about what they are doing."

"Gee," exclaimed Bill, "this is a good session. Why didn't we talk about this before?" Bill's enthusiasm provoked laughter among the boys. Bill continued, "I'm not kidding. I really mean it. I've thought about these things but nobody ever talks about them." He now spoke about a couple of girls "waiting" for him, when he went home on visits, who called him "handsome." They all wanted to see him, but his interest was limited to dating. He "does not touch" them. Fred called Bill a "fool" and continued by wondering why girls who had sexual intercourse got blamed more than the boys. Jerry cryptically remarked: "They get blamed or get pregnant." Gerald volunteered the information that there was a way of stopping "that," and mentioned "a safety." Therapist: "You mean a condom?" Jerry: "Yes, that's what I meant." Bill averred that "this was against the Catholic religion," and Jerry said he was happy that he was a Protestant. . . .

The therapist raised the question of whether the boys indulged in sexual intercourse because they had an urge to do so or perhaps because they wanted to prove to themselves that they were grown, as in Fred's case and his being called "sonny," for example. Fred agreed and said: "Every time you go home on the week end if you don't come back telling that you had sexual intercourse with women, you are nobody." Bill agreed with him. In the cottage, he would never tell anybody that he did not have sexual intercourse, because no one would believe him and if they did, he would be "looked down on." He then said, "For example, when I was only eleven, I was 5 feet 9 inches. Now look at me. I'm a man and if I don't act like a man to the kids and people, then there's something wrong with me." Fred sympathized with Bill's situation: "Well, maybe that's what I felt like too when they called me sonny. I wanted to be big." The therapist asked whether he thought he wanted to be big "for himself" or "so that other people would consider you grown up?" And was this difference important? Not waiting for Fred to answer, Jerry volunteered: "It's just like when you walked into the cottage when you were new, you had to establish yourself—one, two, three—who you were, or else your stuff was stolen or you was pushed around." Gerald agreed with Jerry on this score and Ray added, "If you don't establish right away who you are, then that's it, your life is tormented. Mine was a different problem than Bill's, because I was smaller and everybody likes to pick on the smaller kids, so I had to find either somebody smaller than me, or punkish, and beat him up so that at least there was somebody I could be boss over."

The therapist asked the group in general whether they felt it was always necessary to prove themselves in a way that got them into trouble or was "against the rules." Fred said, "Maybe we did it this way because it was the one way of getting the other kids to look up to you. For example, if you started smoking early, you were a big shot." Therapist: "It must be hard to always have to live up to something which is really not yourself and makes you uncomfortable. Maybe if we talk about it and figure it out, you wouldn't have to spend so much time keeping this up." Bill reacted to this statement with the declaration that he felt that sometimes there was no other way of handling a situation. "You got to the point where you got mad and just sort of struck out at the nearest person," he said. Jerry agreed with Bill's statement. He said that many times he felt angry when his big brothers pushed him around and the only way he could handle it was to go outside and beat somebody up. He pointed to Ray and said, "Just like what he said, about picking out the guy who was the least—the most punkish—and then you felt better inside." Therapist: "Do you mean when, for example, your parents did something to you and you could not get back at them, you would go and do something outside that created trouble for you?" Fred said, "Yes, you can't go against your parents even if they're wrong. It's impossible to do anything." Bill: "Sometimes you can hurt yourself that way." Fred turned to him and said, "You're right, it's like when you do something and they punish you, and then they try to make up to you, like they want to give you money to go to the movies, you refuse because you want to show them that you're mad at them, and no matter how you feel you want to go to the movies, you won't give them an inch." Ray pointed out to Fred, "Then you're hurting yourself." "That's what I mean," said Fred.

Bill said that was exactly what happened a lot because he figured that "the more you get mad at adults, the less you are able to do for yourself. They always seem to have you going. No matter what you do, you get it in the end." He remembered "as a kid" feeling this even more and how he used to have a dog, a boxer. He used to train the dog to be vicious and it would keep people and dogs away. His dog would attack other dogs, and Bill felt that the dog was protecting him. He continued to free associate. He remembered once, as still a kid, putting ants in a bottle. He put black ants in one bottle and brown in another and would feed the brown ants and starve the black. He would then watch the black ants die of starvation, but before all of them were dead, he would let them out and see if they would eat the brown ants. "It's crazy! It's crazy!" he repeated. Fred said, "No, I don't think it was crazy." Bill continued: "I remember how I used to catch ants or flies in school and tear off the flies' wings to see what would happen to them and whether I could kill them with a pencil." Therapist: "You mean it was not crazy because this was sort of an outlet for something that Bill was feeling inside, and if we don't understand what we feel, we think that the things we do are crazy but really they are not?" Gerald: "That's right. I know what you mean," and he went on to say that "what may be crazy to somebody is not crazy for the guy who is doing something; the ant business may be all right for Bill, or he may feel like eating shoes at the time and eating shoes might look crazy to other people." Everyone laughed at this simile, and began to talk about eating shoes and how, if someone walked in on them doing it, he would consider them all crazy. One of the boys mentioned a teacher he knew "who ate wood, but he was not crazy."

When the boys got to talking about being "crazy," Ray gathered up all the paper that was removed from the cigarette packages, placed it in the ash tray and set fire to it. Bill said maybe Ray was crazy. The therapist added, "Maybe what we are talking about may make some people uncomfortable," and warned the boys about the danger involved in setting fires in the ash tray. Bill wanted to know then if the therapist owned a house. The therapist responded in the affirmative. Paul said he thought so because the therapist was taking such good care of the room. The therapist countered this by saying that it was their room and he wanted to make sure that it stayed in good shape.

Conversation then turned to the subject of "thoughts that were inside" them and that as these thoughts "come out," they would find that they were not so strange or horrible or bad and, in fact, that they could "handle" these thoughts, and maybe this was what they were doing and talking about.

With this, the session ended.

On the way out, Bill said, "We didn't talk about food again." Fred: "Well what about it?" The therapist suggested that they bring up the question of eating at the next session.

Despite the fact that the therapist pressed too hard toward conceptualization and "understanding" of motivations, which was altogether premature and much beyond the boys' comprehension at this stage, the dramatic change in the climate of the group and in the content of the interview was nevertheless in clear evidence. These changes were the result of the therapist's accepting attitude, as contrasted with the preceding therapist, his allowing the boys to follow the course of their own interests, his floating attention, and his ability to perceive what the boys intended to convey by their statements (latent content).

The wealth and variation of material produced at this session characterized it as one of "ground-breaking," which needed to be followed by many more for "tilling the soil," for planting the therapeutic seeds, and for exploring the many avenues that have been opened up.

8

Reactions of the Boys

THE BOYS' RESPONSES to both analytic and activity therapy groups were uniformly enthusiastic. Traces of positive feelings were invariably present, even during the periods of testing and acclimatization, but as the boys became convinced that no danger lurked for them in the groups and that the therapists were trustworthy and interested in their welfare, these feelings were made unmistakably apparent. Even during the trying initial periods of acting out and high level of resistivity, the groups, with their climate of informality and freedom to express anger and suspicions, seemed to serve as a haven from the comparatively stressful, conflictual, and to varying degrees threatening, environment in which the boys had lived in the past. In the groups they were free of demands, inevitably made upon them everywhere else, which in their state seemed loathsome and burdensome. The boys viewed their lot as particularly unhappy and the environment, especially that in the institution, planfully designed to make life difficult for them. The boys repeatedly made these convictions known in the early group discussions. Because of the freedom they provided and the absence of pressure and criticisim, the groups served as a respite from the boys' largely imaginary persecutions and genuine tensions.

Reactions to Groups

The relaxed atmosphere and the "hominess," in contrast to all other areas, undoubtedly contributed to the boys' positive feelings toward the groups. This was also a major reason for the exceptional productivity in the interviews in our groups at the Village, as contrasted with groups of adolescents in urban clinics. As a climate of ease and mutuality arose, the boys frequently remarked how comfortable and pleasant they felt "sitting around, drinking coffee, and talking." However, in time, the groups assumed meanings beyond feelings of comfort, for soon they were described as places where "you discuss your problems and get better so that you won't get in trouble again." In contrast to their earlier defensiveness and denial, the boys gradually began to perceive and state openly that they needed "help"; that is, *they now declared themselves as patients*, a prerequisite attitude for psychotherapy to be effective. Only one of the boys of the many to whom it was offered refused membership in a group. (This one boy who balked at joining an analytic group proved to be actively psychotic and was later committed to a mental hospital.)

In all of our groups the boys, after a time, asked for more frequent "meetings" than once a week and that the groups continue beyond the one school year. They frequently expressed regret when the sessions terminated after ninety minutes and would say, "Gee, I wish we could sit here all night and talk." When a session was cancelled because of a holiday, the boys always insisted that one be arranged for another day of the week to make up for it. The attendance was uniformly good in all our groups, analytic as well as activity. The very infrequent absences were accounted for by illness or by the overlapping of a cottage party or an occasional off-campus trip, though on a number of occasions, boys absented themselves even from such activities to attend "group discussions," which they seemed to prefer. After our experience with the first observation group that met in the afternoon (and thus coincided with many community activities that were both beneficial to the boys and required by the institutional program), our analytic groups met in the evening.

To concretize our "trust" in the boys, we did not require of them the usual "passes" (slips, designating the location to which a boy was assigned at any given time, required to be signed by the staff member in charge, then returned by the boys to the "custodial"—later "security" —office at the termination of each activity). The rules on passes were at the time rigidly imposed everywhere, but we instructed our group therapists to tell the boys that the therapists did not require the passes, nor did they ever sign them. However, the boys, on their own, returned their unsigned passes to the custodial officers (in the administration building) after the group sessions.

Reactions to Therapists

Of even greater significance were the deep feelings the boys demonstrated toward the therapists. Their affection for them grew unbounded. During an interview in our demonstration group, for example, one boy said that he wished the therapist was his father. Another quickly and spontaneously responded: "He *is* our father. He spends all his time to help us."

In a discussion of "accountability" (that is, knowledge by the custodial officers as to the whereabouts of each boy at any given time), raised at the inauguration of our study, we "guaranteed" that no boy would ever abscond from, or disappear on the way to and from, the groups, whether the sessions were held by day or evening. Not one boy ever ran away from any of our groups during all the years of this study, though the boys came and went to the sessions completely unsupervised and with passes unsigned. One of our boys in group B (in which therapists had to be changed in midstream) did run off on the night of a group session, but he had first returned to the cottage, and in the company of a fellow cottage resident, not a member of the group, made his way to the city. This escapade was planned in advance and had no relation to the free movement to and from the group session.

In the Boys' Own Words

The following excerpts from group protocols, culled at random, illustrate the boys' attitudes toward their groups.

During a discussion of sex (session ten), Donald said, "Gee, this is a good session. I'm not kidding. I really mean it. I've thought about these things but nobody ever talks to us about them."

In session twenty-four the boys discussed a member who would be leaving the Village soon. Richard asked: "Is there going to be another group next year? If I don't go home, will I be able to stay in the group?" Donald added enthusiastically, "we can talk straight here."

At the point of being discharged from the Village (session forty-four), Donald said that what he would miss most about the Village were the Thursday night discussions. (Four weeks after discharge to the city, he came to the Village to visit with the group, paying his own railroad fare.)

When Michael met the therapist on the campus (preceding session sixty-three), he asked the therapist if the meeting could be changed to Wednesday evening, since he would be leaving for an Easter home visit Thursday, the regular meeting day.

On leaving the Village at his discharge, Louis said (session fifty-six) that he would like to return to the Village for the "discussion group." A week later the therapist received a letter from Louis stating that he planned to come to a meeting as soon as he could possibly arrange it. In the one individual interview with the therapist held just prior to his leaving the Village, he said: "I'm glad I came to the discussions on Thursday nights, because you always seem to respect me and what I have to say and now I believe I've got something to say."

During a psychiatric examination, Jules told the psychiatrist that he felt the group discussion "helped me change."

At session forty-three Macy urged Louis to tell the group about a quarrel he had the previous evening and said, "Go ahead talk, Louis; in this room there are no secrets."

In session forty-six when the therapist was describing how a child gives in to every temptation but an adult should not, Leonard said: "I think that's what we learned here. There is a time and place for everything."

Through a clerk's error, no "passes" had been sent to the boys (session nine), but they had come on their own anyway. . . .

During the discussion of Louis's being discharged from the Village, he said: "The only reason I would like to remain at the Village is that I could come to the discussions on Thursday nights. I got a lot out of it. I don't know how to say [sentimental] things, but I am going to say it anyway—thanks [addressing the group and the therapist]."

A session in January had to be canceled because of the heavy snowstorm which made it impossible for the therapist to drive to the Village. During the week, every one of the boys, upon meeting him on the campus, inquired why there had been no "meeting." The following session was set for the afternoon instead of the evening, because of another heavy snowstorm, and some conversation ensued about it. Louis said: "It makes no difference when we meet, as long as we meet. I am glad that we can meet."

The week before Louis was to leave the Village, Macy said: "Louis, I'm kind of sorry you're going, though I wish I could join you. . . ." Others joined Macy with similar statements. Louis responded by saying, "Thanks, boys, thanks. I appreciate it a lot. Maybe I'll come up and visit you on Thursday nights. We can sit around and talk about old times."

Macy came a little late to session fifty-eight and said that he had to go skating with a group conducted by the chaplain, but he wanted to come to the group for as long as he could stay. He asked the therapist to tell him when it was ten minutes past seven (which gave Macy only a few minutes in the group). He seemed reluctant when the time came for him to leave. Jules said to him: "You really don't want to go. You want to stay." Macy smilingly said: "Yeah, I would like to stay, but I better go, because I promised him [the chaplain] I would go with him."

In the protocol of session seven of group D (the high-delinquency-saturation group) we read the following:

> The boys were speaking of Thanksgiving, which would fall on the day of the group session the following week. The boys asked whether they could meet on another day instead. Randy suggested Wednesday, but was reminded by the other boys that they would be leaving for their homes (by train) that evening. The group then decided on Tuesday, which seemed to be the only evening all could come, though some were not sure, since they would perhaps have to pack their belongings for the trip. It was left that they would inquire about this of their cottage parents and the time for the meeting was set conditionally. On Tuesday, Fritz was first to appear. He was all smiles and greeted the therapist in a very friendly fashion. He announced that the others were coming soon. He inspected the hot water which was being boiled for coffee. As he did so, he said: "I sure look forward to these evenings!"

Long before the above incident, namely in session two, Randy had threatened to leave the group. David said: "I think Randy is crazy for leaving the group as there is no other place at the Village where we can sit around and talk."

At session five, the boys were saying how relaxed and free they felt at the group meetings. "Gee, it's nice drinking coffee here," said Fritz. Randy agreed: "Yes, I feel that way, too . . . it sort of reminds me of home; just sitting around, being free." In session seven, Fritz said: "It's better than going to see my social worker. I don't mean that just because of the coffee; *it's better talking with other guys than to one person.*" Session nine fell on a holiday and, at the boys' request, it was set for another evening because they did not want to miss a session. During the discussion at session twelve, David said: "I was sorry about the other meetings being canceled [because of snowstorms]. Even when my cottage father told me that the group was not going to meet, I came over because I thought I saw a light in *our* room." He proceeded to say that he knew "nobody could travel in such weather, but I still felt badly that we couldn't get together." James inquired how the therapist was able to make the phone calls [from out of town] to cancel the meetings. The therapist explained that he had driven part of the way to the Village, but found that the snowstorm was becoming too heavy and called from a telephone booth on the road. The therapist states: "David seemed to sum up the feeling of the group when he said, 'Well, we are together again tonight and that's the most important thing.' " In session fifteen, David said: "We can get a lot of help by coming here."

During session ten of this group of massively delinquent boys, a dinner and dance were held in the gymnasium for the unit of which David, Fritz, and Jerry were members. Adolescent girls from a nearby town were invited for the dance, which was always a red-letter day for the boys at the Village. However, after having eaten dinner, the three boys appeared at the group session, dressed as they were in their "Sunday best," instead of staying at the coveted dance. (On a number of other occasions, the boys have missed cottage and other community functions, which they could have attended, to come to the group sessions.)

Preceding session twelve, the boys of this group heard rumors that the therapist had resigned from the staff of the Village. (The therapist failed to inform the boys of this fact, because the preceding week, when he had intended to do so, a heavy snowstorm prevented holding the session.) Ray said: "I hear that you have resigned. Mr. B. told me, but I didn't believe it, because you didn't mention anything to us. So when I got the pass this week, I told Mr. B. he was wrong." Umberto came in at this point and said that he, too, had heard the news. His cottage father had told him about it. (It should be noted that we had arranged for the therapist to continue with the group until the end of the school year, even though he had changed jobs.) Ray said: "When I heard about it, the first thing I thought of was the club meetings and I was disappointed that they were going to stop, but when I got the pass I was glad again." Later during the discussion the therapist had asked the group what their reactions were when they heard about his leaving. Randy said that he "worried," just as Ray did, about whether the "group meetings" would continue. Jerry asserted: "I was floored when my cottage father told me, but when the passes came I felt better again."

Evidences of Improvement

Brief summaries of the reports of various staff members on the boys in the groups, as part of the follow-up studies and as described on pp. 726-738, are presented here. These summaries deal with the boys other than those in group C. In Part Two of this volume, the progress of the latter is presented in expanded form, as it was described by staffs of the various departments during the periodic progress and integration evaluations. The names of the boys are arranged in alphabetical order.

ALBERT (Puerto Rican)—after twenty-two sessions. *Cottage Parent:* "He became more masculine and more involved interpersonally with peers and adults." Follow-up a year later revealed that Albert went on to college and was following his interest in the art aspect of film production.

BILL (Negro)—after twenty-three sessions. Bill made some small gains in understanding the paradox of his physical (extremely tall) versus his psychological stature. He still needed a great deal of therapy to undo the deep traumata in his early life. When discharged at this point, he became involved in an accident in a stolen car in which he killed three persons of one family.

DAVID (White)—after eighteen sessions. *Cottage Parent:* "There are no traces of any sexual activities, which had been a real problem in the past. He offers to help other boys who cannot write or read." *School:* David gained 1.2 years in reading skills (in five months). "Appears to be less moody, is working harder, and is much more cooperative." *Case-worker:* "He has not 'opened up' as yet." *Psychologist* (after twenty-eight sessions): "IQ has risen 15 points. He has better concentration; lessening of primitive promptings; began to renounce infantile strivings; is more realistic; intellectual efficiency increased; fantasy, which bordered on autistic, yielded to intellectual control . . . healthier involvements in the external world."

DICK (White)—after twenty-two sessions. *Researcher's Summary* (of all interviews with staff): "While Dick appears a little less fearful and a trifle more vigorous than when he first came to the Village, he is still extremely anxious and acts out via thefts and provocations. . . . The orality component still is very marked in this boy."

EARL (White)—after seventeen sessions. Earl was removed by his mother after seventeen sessions, although the boy wished to remain. The boy seemed at that point more comfortable in expressing aggressive feelings. *Caseworker:* "Group stimulated individual treatment."

FRANK (White)—after twenty-four sessions. *Cottage Parent:* "Frank, who refused to wear his glasses before, now wears them willingly for the first time." He was not involved in as many fights as in the past. *School:* Frank's relationships with his peers are much better. "He does not have a need to be beaten up as he did before." *Caseworker:* "Frank has grown more insightful, more open and freer. He now recognizes his difficulties with his mother. Before the group experience, Frank was very resistive." *Frank* (to administrative officer): "It was really the discussion club . . . that was the most important thing. Kids could really talk about their real problems to each other with those who understand them best, and it wasn't controlled by grownups."

FRED (White)—after eighteen sessions. *Cottage Parent:* "In spite of occasional rebelliousness, the boy now has much better control over himself." *School:* "Fred no longer bullies younger boys, is more relaxed and more comfortable." *Caseworker:* "Fred was discharged from Children's Village. He was offered after-care appointments but did not continue because of distance and long train travel. He asked for, and was given, the name of a mental hygiene clinic in his own community. Fred could now talk about home problems he has had in the past. He no longer denies them; talks more freely."

FRITZ (White)—after sixteen sessions. *Cottage Parent:* "Fritz has no close friends; he does not relate to either cottage parents or peer group. In the past seven months he has not been involved in any acting out, which was formerly very severe. *School:* "Fritz seems to be 'marking time'; he makes little effort to work except on subjects he likes." *Caseworker:* "More communicative, but resists talking of significant material." *Psychologist:* (after twenty-eight sessions): "Oral sadistic impulses and fear have somewhat diminished. Narcissistic features have also diminished. He is better related to self and others; is exercising better control over his excitement and fears."

GERALD (White)—after twenty-two sessions. *Cottage Parent* stated in his report to the directors: "Gerald improved markedly . . . previously an immature, angry child now became a law-abiding, civilized person with a soft, tender quality. He gained understanding into his own operations." *School:* "Gerald now needs lesser outer controls." Reading advanced approximately one year. *Caseworker:* "Boy appears more mature; is showing typical adolescent revolt (not pathological)." *Psychiatrist:* "Prognosis good for long term goals . . . He presented [in the interview] clearly the nature of his problems."

HANK (White)—After adequate observation at twelve sessions, removed as unsuitable. He was found to be a full-blown psychopath whose behavior was slowing down the group. He tended to be ego-expansive and his talk created anxiety in the boys. After discharge, he stabbed a boy during a quarrel over a girl and was recommitted to a "training school."

JAKE (White)—after twenty-four sessions. *School:* Reading went up from 7.4 to 9.5 (in seven months). *Caseworker:* "Boy loosened up, especially in ability to feel hostile and aggressive and to verbalize. Ego-strengthening is most evident." *Group Therapist:* Very positive transference to therapist. "I wish my father was like you," was his statement in a group session.

JAMES (White)—after twenty-three sessions. Gain of three years and three months in school while in group for about seven months. James stated to his caseworker about the group: "I can talk with people up there [at the group] and get moral support." The caseworker felt that "James was now able to express his vitriolic feelings, which he had suppressed, understand them, and has gained some control over them."

JERRY (White)—after sixteen sessions. *Cottage Parent:* "Sexual activity seems lessened. He is responding to the structure of the cottage and is growing closer to the cottage father." *School:* "Jerry's relationship to his peers is much better now. The class seems to accept him more. His schoolwork still lags and he has difficulty in following abstract thoughts (IQ 85)." *Caseworker:* "Less fearful in interviews." *Psychologist:* (after twenty-eight sessions): "IQ jumped 10 points to 95. The boy's excessive fantasy world has diminished. He has a clearer time perspective; marked improvement in all focal problems; better involvement with people; and firmer appreciation of reality. The suicidal trend is not so great."

JOSEPH (White)—after sixteen sessions. *Caseworker:* "Joseph was able to sustain himself well after discharge from Children's Village in spite of unfavorable family environment. When he left Children's Village, Joseph said, 'I need maybe even an analyst.' Absences from group due to participation in sports team."

JULIUS (White)—after eleven sessions. *Cottage Parent:* "Julius was moved into a different cottage and is now able to resist sexual advances by other boys of which he had been a helpless victim. He now appears better able to interact with cottage father." *School:* "Julius improved 2.1 years in his reading skills (in five months). His academic work improved greatly. He seems more alive now." *Caseworker:* "Julius is much more verbal and freer since he has been in the group." *Psychologist* (after twenty-eight sessions): IQ dropped by six points to 94; dependency needs less apparent; "seems to have gained distance from his major problems without solving them and has become more alienated from himself and others." (*Note:* This boy was diagnosed as "constitutionally inferior" but actually made impressive improvements in appearance and social adjustment).

KARL (White)—after four sessions. Discharged from Village after session four.

PAUL (White)—after twenty-five sessions. *Cottage Parent:* "The boy is not as rebellious, is attempting to conform. When he wants something, he will ask for it in a decent way now." *School:* "The boy has hardly changed personally, but seems a little surer of himself. He is still extremely sensitive when corrected. "He advanced academically a full year. *Caseworker:* "Paul can now verbalize his anger toward his father and mother, which he denied before." *Psychiatrist:* ". . . limited improvement. His improvement in behavior has been at the cost of constriction in his personality."

NEAL (Negro)—after twenty sessions. Worked through his basic problem in the group in twenty sessions. Dropped out voluntarily. Continued at Children's Village for a year with distinction. Worked on the same job for three years after discharge and attended evening high school preparatory for college. Has girl friend. Adjusted well in all areas. (See full study pp. 62-90.)

RANDY (White)—after seventeen sessions. *Cottage Parent:* "Randy is no longer a baby. He is more mature and more responsible. He provokes punishment less." *School:* Randy advanced three years in reading skills (in five months). "Randy is much more of a boy now. He works very hard and is trying to help others to learn. No hint of former sexual acting out." *Caseworker:* Randy still finds it difficult to communicate with (female) caseworker, but does talk more. *Psychologist:* (after twenty-eight sessions): "Adolescent turmoil increased; increase in sexual promptings and anxiety; some suggestion of voyeuristic tendencies; fantasy life is under "tighter" intellectual control."

RAY (White)—after eighteen sessions. *Cottage Parent:* "Ray is more masculine and assertive. His sexual problems seem to have disappeared. *School:* Ray advanced approximately two years in reading skill. "He is more cooperative, more responsive, and is now trying hard in his schoolwork. He can do well in a regular school." *Caseworker:* Still uncommunicative in interviews. *Psychologist:* (after twenty-eight sessions): "Oral-sadistic fears and impulses have diminished. Lost some of his 'hard' narcissistic features; moved toward more healthful identity. This personality expansion is 'terrifying' to him *at this point.*"

ROGER (White)—after twenty-two sessions. *Cottage Parent:* Cottage father ill. Could not be interviewed. *School:* Academic progress equivalent to one full year. *Caseworker:* Boy is doing well in all areas; was helpful to cottage mother during cottage father's illness. *Community Center:* Boy was elected as representative to Children's Youth Council.

STEVE (White)—after fourteen sessions. *Cottage Parent:* "Sexual acting out has decreased." He is now well liked by cottage parents. *School:* "Steve's relationships with peers is much better, but he is more antagonistic toward teachers; his work continues to be slow; his skill in handwork has improved." *Caseworker:* "Resists talking about anything significant." *Psychologist:* (after twenty-eight sessions): "IQ gain of six points; the 'Oedipal furor' has disappeared; less inner turmoil and anxiety; less apprehensive; still maintains a wish to be nurtured; boy assumed 'flight into health' stance."

UMBERTO (Negro)—after eighteen sessions. *Cottage Parent:* "One can now hold a conversation with Umberto. He is using humor to discharge anger instead of moping as in the past." *School:* Umberto gained two years in reading skills (in five months) but sustained a drop in other "major subjects"; he is less moody, "no longer in a shell." *Psychologist:* "Umberto has resolved some of his paranoid attitudes toward women but has given up hope of ever relating to men and has become more vindictive toward men. Expansion of effective experience has accompanied these changes, as well as a tendency to view himself more realistically."

Table I shows the incidence of improvement in terms of degree. The table includes all of the thirty-four boys that had been involved in the project. Whether the improvement was significant or partial was determined by the number of times the designation was applied to the boy by staff members interviewed. Adjustment at school and in cottage were given greater weight than school achievement. Psychological and psychiatric opinions were given greater weight than those of cottage parents.

TABLE I

Incidence of Improvement in Para-Analytic Groups*

			GROUP		
	A	*B*	*C***	*D***	*Totals*
Significant improvement	6	2	6	4	18
Partial improvement		5	1	4	10
No improvement					
Dropped out†	1		3		4
Closed††		1			1
Placed late	1				1
Totals	8	8	10	8	34

   * Members of groups A and B had been chosen on the basis of established criteria of suitability for analytic group therapy. Groups C and D consisted of boys accepted more or less at random, and were designated as "delinquency-saturated" groups. Group D is the group that contained a number of seriously disturbed boys in the area of sex, with a high incidence of homosexuality. Groups A and B were observation groups and group C the demonstration group. Groups A, B, and D met for a period of approximately a school year, while group C extended through two school years, about twenty-one months or seventy-five sessions.
  ** Groups still in operation at the time of writing.
  † Dropped out: discharged from Village; refused to come to group; one boy ran away.
 †† Found unsuitable for group therapy.

A Case of Failure

The following is the case of a boy in our first experimental or observation group (group A) whose basic problem could not be resolved or significantly affected despite the fact that he had shown favorable behavioral and interpersonal improvement in the institutional milieu.

Frank suffered from an anxiety neurosis that required prolonged psychoanalytical individual treatment where he could develop a transference neurosis with a (male) analyst or psychotherapist. As we have shown elsewhere, a psychoneurotic who requires this type of transitory neurosis as part of his therapy cannot be reached by group therapy, even though his general ego-functioning can be temporarily improved.

BACKGROUND

Frank, fourteen-and-a-half years old, was committed to residential treatment because of neglect and because of a charge of continued truancy, petty larceny both in and outside his home, and unmanageable, disruptive behavior at school. He had received brief treatment in a community clinic, which seemed to quiet him down to some degree, but the recurrence of his behavior and its violence made it necessary to commit him to a county hospital for observation. A social study of the family and the findings of the hospital staff resulted in a recommendation that he be removed from home and placed in a treatment setting.

Frank was the third of three children. At the time of commitment both his older sister, twenty-six, and older brother, twenty-four, were married and out of the home. The family consisted of father, mother, and Frank. The father, a railroad man on a transcontinental route, was absent from home for weeks at a time, and since his trips were frequent he spent very little time with his son. He was described as an easygoing, ineffectual, quiet man who exercised little control over his family. The mother, on the other hand, was authoritarian, tyrannical, promiscuous, and a chronic alcoholic. Frank had witnessed at least one episode of sexual intercourse between his mother and one of her paramours. During one of the prolonged absences of her husband the mother "settled down" with one of her "boy friends" in a more or less permanent relationship. Upon his return, the husband gave her a choice between himself and the other man. She decided to return to her husband.

One of the persons who had had an influence on Frank's early life was his maternal grandmother, who had been very protective of Frank and favored him greatly. She had been in charge of the home while the mother was at work, but this arrangement no longer prevailed, Frank being committed when the grandmother had died.

Frank was an unplanned child, and his mother had been extremely upset when she discovered her pregnancy. She had attempted to abort, and later claimed that her drinking bouts began at the time of his birth. One of the significant events in Frank's life was his brother's marriage when Frank was eleven years old. This brother and Frank had shared a room, and after the brother's departure from home Frank developed a fear of the dark which persisted for several months and necessitated that a light be kept on in his room. During an interview in the community clinic, after describing the beatings he received from his parents, he stated that the brother had protected him against the mother's cruelties. But at the termination of the interview, when he was leaving the room, he turned back and said, "I don't like my brother John best; I like my dog Trixie best."

Frank's adjustment in the Village was described as "decisively poor." The noisy, uncooperative, pugnacious behavior which he had manifested in school before coming to the Village reappeared. He was described as being "provocative, manipulating, scornful, contemptuous, and condescending." He was "cynical, pedantic, pseudo-intellectual, with grandiose attitudes, and aroused universal antagonism among his cottage mates." Toward adults he was "sarcastic, critical, and demanding, and provoked punitiveness from them in return." His female caseworker made every effort to establish a relationship with the boy; she even saw him daily at first because of his extreme separation anxiety. But the outcome after a year's effort was disappointing. "While there was some superficial understanding," wrote the caseworker, "there was very little basic change in Frank over the period of a year of individual casework treatment."

BEHAVIOR IN THE GROUP

Frank, now fifteen and a half years old, was placed in an analytic therapy group which met for a period of six months. This was the first group in our project to test the response to group therapy of court-committed boys in residential treatment. During the first six sessions of the group there were the usual gripes against the institution, the staff, and adults in general. Frank, among others, expressed suspicion that the group was being watched and the conversations recorded. He was the most aggressive and the most disturbing member in the group. During the third session he screamed at the therapist: "I don't like you, I never would and never will like you!" At another time he threw an ash tray into the therapist's lap. His all-out efforts to create disturbances were resented by the other boys, who suggested that he be dismissed from the group. However, Frank's behavior was accepted with tolerance by the therapist, a fact that surprised the other boys greatly. After the third session, Frank asked to stay with the therapist for a while and revealed that he was very upset because his mother had been drinking heavily again and was very ill. It must be noted that when the mother drank she remained in a stupor for days on end, lying about sloppily on a couch, screaming vituperations at anyone who approached her.

When Frank came for his fourth session, he took a seat next to the therapist. When one of the boys mentioned sexual urges toward women, Frank suggested that "we leave sex out of this for awhile." This session, like the preceding ones, was characterized by a great deal of restlessness and complaints against adults' taking advantage of the boys.

During a discussion in the seventh session, Frank revealed that he had recently been bothered by the thought that something was going to happen to his brother. He dreamed about his brother getting hurt. He had had this dream twice before, and once his brother actually did get hurt. As he was saying this, Frank became very anxious and restless and walked aimlessly around the room. When this distractibility was called to his attention by the therapist, Frank said, "I am angry because they won't let me call my brother," and continued his roaming around. This type of behavior was characteristic of Frank and was in striking contrast to that of the other boys. They also had resisted treatment for a long period, but they expressed their resistance verbally. Frank, however, was given to much greater anxiety than were the others, and was the only boy who acted it out motorically.

Frank's complaints about his mother reappeared frequently during the group discussions. In the eleventh session, when the boys talked about stealing and homosexual activity, Frank remained silent. At another session he spoke of his acting up in the gymnasium because he felt "kind of miserable inside." He said he had had to do it even though he knew he was doing wrong. He claimed that one of the coaches had slapped him, but he seemed to accept this punishment with equanimity. He said, "You know where you stand [when one is punished], and that is okay with me if I cross the line."

A degree of calm became noticeable in Frank as the group sessions proceeded, but in the thirteenth session, Frank became very upset and attacked two of the more passive boys. His restlessness increased even more when the group started talking openly about their parents. His distractibility and disruptiveness mounted and he moved up and down the room. At one point he drew his cigarette lighter from his pocket and threw it out of the window. It landed on the slanting roof, and Frank attempted to crawl out through the dormer window. Because of the danger involved this was prevented by the therapist, who promised that after the session he would help Frank retrieve the lighter. Frank quieted down, but when the other boys began to speak, he vehemently pounded on the table with the blade of his knife. Concerned that the knife might ricochet and hurt someone, the therapist suggested that Frank be careful. But Frank ignored this, screaming that the Village was a jail and that he was in it for punishment. He repeated that he hated the therapist, used abusive language toward him, and carved the letters *f-u-c-k* into the polished top of the table. This startled and upset the other boys. The therapist attempted to encourage Frank to talk about what was bothering him, pointing out that this behavior must stem from some inner turmoil. Frank burst out that he felt like running away and proceeded to narrate how he had received a letter from his mother with a newspaper clipping about an unmarried girl who had become pregnant and that he was angry because this was a girl he could have "gotten into." The girl, recently released from an institution, was the daughter of a woman who had accused Frank's sister of being a whore.

When the group left, Frank remained to retrieve the lighter, and the therapist took this opportunity to talk to him. Frank began by referring to the mother's letter but proceeded at once to discuss his fears about his brother. The brother had not come to visit him and he was afraid that the brother was angry with him.

In the next session the therapist found Frank to be much quieter. During the early part Frank commented that he didn't like his haircut and added that the therapist, too, needed a haircut. Neal was discussing his mother, whom he had hardly known and who had abandoned him when he was a small child. Neal said among other things, that he would beat her if he ever saw her. Frank said he didn't think a boy should ever do anything to his mother. When asked why by the therapist, he said, "After all, my mother was drunk all the time and it is just something I have to live with. I used to knock the shit out of her, but that didn't do any good." When the boys questioned him, he corrected himself smilingly, "Maybe I didn't really hit her, but I wanted to at times." He proceeded to say that sometimes he thought it might be better not to have a mother around; he had one and she had not done him any good. He could not understand the attitude toward mothers because his mother drank and did not give him anything, "so why should there be anything in return?"

As the discussion progressed the therapist commented that sometimes people cling to feelings of guilt. Frank was the first to agree with this statement and elaborated that he always felt unhappy when he saw his mother drunk and that at times she accused him of doing things that "made her that way." At other times he felt guilty because his family worried about him because of his behavior.

It should be noted that Frank invariably chose a seat next to the therapist.

At the fifteenth session the conversation among the boys led Frank to confess that he had stolen money from a boy in his cottage. He claimed that he did it in retaliation for the theft of some objects from his personal locker. On the basis of previous discussions as to why people steal, one of the boys explored with Frank other reasons for his stealing, but Frank repeated that it was a retaliatory act. The effort on the part of other boys and the therapist to explore the meaning of his act did not prove fruitful.

At one point of emotional tension generated by the discussion, Frank said, "I know that I was mixed up and maybe I am getting unmixed, but it takes a long time, and it is hard to stay away from your family." When the therapist responded that the aim of the institution was to help the boys with these problems, Frank, for the first time, spoke favorably of it. He said, "Some people in the Village are all right and maybe they want to help us, but it is still a long way from home." He then turned to the therapist and said, "Do you remember when I tried to give you some money to hold? That was the money I stole. You did not report me, but somebody heard me asking you for the money and that is how I got caught." After a brief silence he added, "Changing takes a long time and sometimes moves too slow."

At the close of this session, as at many of the others, Frank lingered on after the group had left, but when he saw that another boy wished to talk to the therapist, too, he left the room.

The theme of the next session was parents, and the boys' relationships with them. Frank said resentfully, "Kids shouldn't feel that way about things." He stalked up and down the room and again proceeded to open the window. He conveyed his great yearning to go home during the holiday vacation that was coming. He revealed that during the previous week he had lain awake at night, unable to fall asleep; he had roamed around the cottage, occasionally meeting the watchman on his tour. When asked by another boy why he couldn't sleep, Frank answered curtly, "It's obvious: home." Another boy asked Frank why he didn't talk about it because, "when you talk you don't feel so tense." Again Frank burst forth with preoccupations about his mother being drunk, especially since the father would not be home now for a long time. He said that he felt guilty about his mother and recalled that she always blamed him for her drinking. She never drank when the other children were born; she took to drink after his birth, she said. "I always think about it, and when I think about it I feel rotten inside," he declared. Several of the boys expressed sympathy with him and one of them suggested: "You know that it isn't true." Silence fell upon the group. When the group left Frank remained behind to tell the therapist that he would stay with his brother on his visit home if he found his mother drunk.

The next session was held after the Christmas visit home. Frank came in particularly disturbed and immediately went to the window. The therapist warned him about leaning out. He challenged the therapist by asking: "What are you going to do about it?" The therapist told him

that he would send him out of the room. Frank sat down at the table
with the other boys, and during the discussion he talked about his
brother for a minute and then about a spider he had brought in a tin
can. The spider's name was Herman. At first Frank threatened to release Herman so he could sting the other boys, explaining that Herman
was poisonous. After a while he said that Herman was getting on his
nerves and that he would burn him. He lit a match and threw it into the
can, but the fire quickly went out. Frank then stuffed paper into the can
and set it on fire.

Recognizing Frank's agitation, the therapist asked him to tell the
group about his holiday vacation. At first he refused to talk about it and
the therapist asked him, "Do you mean your mother was drunk again
when you got home?" Frank exclaimed piteously: "I couldn't even get
into my mother's apartment because she was out [in a stupor] on the
couch again, plastered, so I went down to my brother's house and spent
the week end there." He then proceeded to describe how he had gone
back and forth between the brother's and the mother's apartments, but
she remained in a continuous stupor during the three days he was home.
Further discussion about mothers ensued as a result of Frank's narration,
which was terminated by his saying: "I will just have to accept it and
work out something for myself as long as it does not hurt me." After
this, he grew less agitated but was apparently unable to continue talking.
When the session ended he asked the therapist's permission to sit for a
while in the waiting room downstairs, apparently to collect himself,
before returning to his cottage.

For a number of sessions the boys' discussion had turned to girls and
women, with some members of the staff being mentioned as possible
sexual objects. When a boy jokingly spoke of a social worker with large
breasts, another said, "She always seems to be walking around stretching
her arms so that people can measure her to see how much she's got."
Frank identified her as his social worker and said, "I could measure her
anytime." Soon after this Frank declared that if his brother beat him up
he would accept it "because it is in the family." One of the boys changed
the subject. Frank agreed with still another who wanted to return to the
discussion of women and said, "Let's talk about women; it's a more
interesting subject." At one point the therapist remarked on the naturalness of sexual urges in adolescent boys. Frank misinterpreted his statement with the following remark: "You mean you really want us to go
home and feel them [girls] up and do things to them?" When the group's
laughter had subsided, Frank said: "I'll go around telling everybody that
you told me it was all right for me to do it." Again there was an outburst
of laughter. When the therapist questioned Frank if he really thought
that this was what the therapist had meant, Frank said, "I was only

kidding." Frank did not remain with the therapist at the end of this session.

In the next session an interesting episode occurred. Frank, who was a member of the ROTC, brought his boots and some shoe polish and proceeded to shine the boots in preparation for inspection. He asked the therapist if he could shine his shoes as well. The therapist asked him why he wanted to do it, and Frank's response was that he had some polish left. The therapist said that his shoes were new and did not really need a shine but thanked him for the offer. This incident is rather significant in terms of Frank's nuclear problem.

The next session, the twenty-third, Frank brought with him a book of pictures of nude men and women and loaned it to another boy who wanted to look through it. The matter of sex was brought up again, along with the fact that living in an entirely masculine environment caused some of the boys to be preoccupied with sex. Frank said, "Well, you know what to do about it," and made a motion with his hand indicating masturbation. When the discussion turned to heterosexual intercourse, the therapist explained the function of marriage as a means of satisfying the sex urge and ended saying that he was aware that boys always wonder about these matters and the feelings involved and that they sought means of doing something about it. Again, Frank said that he knew what to do and indicated by his hand the act of masturbation.

One of the boys volunteered that his father had once caught him masturbating and was very angry with him. Frank suggested that the father may have thought that it was something wrong and harmful to the boy. This remark was probably the result of a discussion in which the therapist had conveyed to the boys that masturbation, of which the boys were very much afraid, was harmless if indulged in moderately. When one of the boys introduced the subject of the cottage parents checking up on the residents of the cottages during the night, Frank said, "You know, there are a lot of queers around." The discussion seemed to have met some need in Frank, for he spontaneously said, "Well, we talked today."

In a supervisory discussion of the episode in which Frank offered to shine the therapist's shoes, it was suggested that the therapist's refusal be aired with Frank. The therapist therefore found an opportunity to ask Frank what he thought about the incident. The boy's response to this was that he tried to find ways of getting the therapist angry. One of the boys, Albert, remarked that Frank had made himself angry instead, since he had been rebuffed by the therapist. At this point Frank lost his temper with the boy. The therapist intervened by saying that Frank was really angry with the therapist rather than with Albert. He further stated that Frank was trying to show the therapist that he liked him and instead the therapist had pushed him away. "Like you?" exclaimed Frank, "Enough to kill you!" However, the statement sounded more like "I like you very much" than one of hostility. Frank again left with the rest of the group.

At the twenty-fourth session Frank once more appeared very disturbed and described a conflict he had had with his cotttage mother because of her slight to a Negro resident. During this recital Frank touched one of his arms and said that he was getting "boils" again and that it was the cottage mother who was "giving them" to him. The therapist stated that the boils might be caused by his own mother rather than the cottage mother. This sparked Frank's exclamation that he knew his mother was drunk again and "it is driving me nuts!" He had received a letter from her and from the manner of her writing he was sure that she was in a drunken state, and there was no one to take care of her because his father was away again. "If she would only stop for awhile!" he screamed. "If I was only home to take care of her!" He added that if he returned home he would have to stay with his brother, who would take care of him. His brother would never hit him. As the discussion progressed, Frank remarked that he really didn't need his mother any more, he was just concerned about her because there was nobody around to take care of her.

At the next session, the twenty-fifth and last for this experimental group, Frank was in a euphoric state. He chatted with people on the stairs and effusively greeted one of the group members who had been away for a few weeks because he participated in the varsity ball games. As the group was discussing these games, Frank jumped up and began to juggle ash trays. The therapist suggested that he put them down and that his behavior seemed to show that there was something bothering him. Frank said that he was going to throw an ash tray at the therapist, and he looped it into the therapist's lap. The group was startled by this, and some of the boys reprimanded him for doing "such a crazy thing." Frank said, "I told him [therapist] I was going to do it. You dared me to." He then rose from his seat and moved to another close to the therapist. The therapist suggested that Frank was upset about something and that talking about it would make him feel better. While group members expressed indignation at his behavior, the therapist repeated that Frank probably had acted the way he did because something was disturbing him.

Later, the boys were discussing termination. One of them, a newcomer, asked about having candy and ice cream. The therapist asked what they sounded like when they asked for candy and ice cream. "Babies," said Frank; "we are babies when we want candy." He then proceeded to nag the therapist to swap wrist-watch bands. "I want that band; I want your wrist-watch band; I want your wrist-watch band." The therapist told Frank that he could not have his band, since it was a gift, and several members of the group told Frank to "shut up," but he continued. The therapist asked Frank what it was he was trying to tell the group by his behavior. Instead of answering, Frank said, "I will count to thirty, and at that time I am going to take that band from you." A self-conscious hush settled over the group. One of the boys broke the silence, telling Frank that he better not try anything on the therapist. Nonetheless, Frank began to count, and the therapist turned to Jake, asking why he wanted to protect him. Jake said that no one should throw things at the therapist since he "didn't do anything to anybody." The therapist asked what he thought Frank should do about his conduct. At this point Frank stopped counting, smiled, broke into laughter and said, "Fooled everybody. I wasn't going to do anything to Mr. S."

Having broken through Frank's anxiety, the therapist again asked what was upsetting him. Frank said, "I am in trouble again." His grandfather had died and he had gone home on a week-end pass. At his uncle's home he persuaded his small cousin to sell him a wrist watch for a couple of dollars. The wrist watch was worth much more, and he was sure that when his uncle found out there would be trouble. He knew that his cousin had gotten it from his uncle as a present and, therefore, he wanted it. Jake said, "But this is no reason for going around throwing ash trays at people." Frank agreed and said he just did not know what to do with himself. He had gotten into trouble with his cottage parents the day before and a few days earlier. He struck his hand against the table in a manner that obviously hurt him. The boys minimized the importance of the events and tried to console Frank.

Later, when some of the boys asked the therapist for help in getting discharged from the Village, Frank said that he wanted to be around his sister because "she is nice to me and takes care of me." James said: "When Frank grows up and meets some girls, he will not always be talking about his sister. There will be other people." Frank grew livid with rage, grabbed James's shirt at the neck, and threateningly shouted, "Buddy don't ever say that again!" Questioned by the therapist, Frank responded, "I have no such ideas about my sisters and it is a dirty thing to say." James broke in and said that he had had nothing like that in mind at all and elaborated that, as Frank grew up, he would get married and would be thinking about his wife and family and "everything else." Frank, however, remained crestfallen and dejectedly murmured: "I just can't stand it any more. It is not the watch that is bothering me; it is what happened on the week end." He grew very quiet, his face became very tense, and he said: "It is my brother. When I went home for the week end I told my brother that I got smacked by the cottage father and he said he'd take care of the cottage father for me." But when later the brother and Frank were at the cottage, the brother said to him, "Straighten up!" Frank said: "My brother didn't give me a chance. He just told me to straighten up, and he didn't listen to my side of the story." Frank again violently banged his hand against the table, screaming, "My brother betrayed me!" Questioned by the therapist, he asserted that his brother was "the one person I could trust, the one person I could turn to. Now I have no one to turn to," and proceeded to blame himself for everything that occurred in his life. When the therapist said, "You blame yourself for everything that happened and maybe when something like this happens you get yourself in trouble at school, throw ash trays at people, hoping that someone will eventually hit you. This seems to be what you are doing to yourself now because of what your brother said."

The boys attempted to persuade Frank that his brother might have meant well. The therapist added, "Perhaps your brother in his ignorant way tried to help you." Frank burst out in intense rage, screaming, "Don't say that about my brother! He is the smartest man in the world!" The therapist explained he had used the word in a different sense than it sounded. He meant to say that his brother did not have all the facts. Jake now began to quiet Frank down.

Frank grew more cheerful toward the end of the session. As the boys were leaving, Frank was with Charles, the most recent arrival and toward whom Frank had been very antagonistic at first. They went out together, talking about Charles's brother, who once beat him severely, but whom he now loved because he felt that his brother was interested in him.

PROGRESS REPORTS

After twenty-five sessions the cottage parents described Frank as more direct, less evasive, and less manipulative in dealing with them. He was less provocative with his cottage mates and was capable of acquiring and sustaining friendships. While six months before he had been described by his cottage parents as the "lowest of the low," they now spoke of him favorably and thought that he had carved out for himself a "niche in the cottage group." He frequently took responsibility for the conduct of the whole cottage and even for the cottage parents' children.

Similarly, the school reported that he caused "much less trouble than in the past" and that he was willing to wear glasses to correct his unilateral strabismus, something which he had vehemently resisted before. He was still distractible and finished his tasks only with considerable difficulty. He continued to provoke other boys occasionally, but this had been greatly reduced in frequency, intensity, and duration.

The female caseworker who saw Frank during and at the termination of group treatment (not the same whose report was quoted) stated:

> Frank is now freer and more open in his expression of anger toward his mother and is able to accept the fact that she neglected him. While in the past he denied this, he now recognizes more objectively his mother's personality and problems as separate from his own. His verbalizations and attitudes reflect more trust of adults than prior to group therapy. He is now able to speak in a more factual way of "being wanted" at home and to say that he was "not too unhappy" at the Village. He recognizes Children's Village, not as a punitive agent, but as an instrument for help with some of his problems at home. The group acted as a catalyst for individual therapy.

The caseworker's findings were confirmed independently by the group therapist, who found evidence in Frank's productions in the group that Frank now recognized that his acting out was a result of inner turmoil rather than being due to purely external circumstances. He permitted himself positive feelings for the therapist and recognized himself as being "mixed-up" and having an unfounded mistrust of adults.

A memo from a top administrative staff member who spoke to Frank before his discharge from the Village a year after termination of group therapy stated:

> I think you will be pleased to know that before Frank left I asked him what he thought counted most in his stay at the Village. Somewhat hesitatingly he stated: "My cottage parents and Mr. G. (the Protestant chaplain)." We explored with him what was important to him about his association with these staff members, but he was quite unclear on the subject. After we shook hands, I said, "Good luck," and as he was walking out of my office he turned back and added, "It was really the discussion club with Mr. S. that was the most important thing." Frank then explained this by adding that the "kids could really talk about their real problems to each other with those who understood them best, and it wasn't adult-dominated."

DISCUSSION

There is ample evidence of the parents' neglect of Frank and of serious prenatal and postnatal rejections. The mother tried to abort him. After he was born, the mother considered him very ugly, and refused to believe that he was a normal-looking baby. She seemed incapable of tender feelings toward him, blamed him for her alcoholism, beat him, and finally placed him in an institution. Despite all this rejection, Frank was strongly tied to his mother. She was the focus of his libidinal strivings, and she created a void in him which only she could fill. At the same time, he felt himself responsible for her rejection of him and saw himself as unworthy of her love. This contributed to his weak ego organization and his incapacity to mobilize resources to meet the demands of his life. His distractibility derived from this, as well as from his deep inner yearning for love, and from the tensions generated by unfulfilled needs, which he vicariously satisfied by petty stealing from his mother.

Equally clear is his lack of identification with and support from his father. Because of the father's long absences from home, Frank was unable to achieve the identification that would permit internalization of the masculine traits of his father and his ego strengths, whatever they were.

Only one person seemed to play a constructive role in Frank's life, his brother, who was seen by the boy (in actuality or in fantasy) as one whom he "likes." Even this, however, he denied by asserting the stronger feelings toward his dog. An important factor in this relationship may be the fact that Frank and his brother shared a room. It is not known whether or not they shared the same bed. The boy's reactions to his brother, his continued reference to and dependency upon him, would point to a homoerotic or homosexual tie. The circumstances of this patient's life favored such a development from every point of view. The castration by, and masochistic submission to, his mother, the lack of opportunity for identification with his father, the mother's preference for her daughter, and the physical proximity of the brother at times of affect hunger, all would favor such an eventuality.

This hypothesis is supported by Frank's adjustment to life. His provocativeness with peers, which led to rejection and physical punishment, was a continuation of his masochistic submissiveness to a (sexually) castrating mother. His placating and devious approach to adults as strong persons can be understood as sexual submission, and his aggressiveness and attack upon the group therapist can be seen as a defense against his homoerotic feelings toward him. (Frank usually stayed after the sessions so as to have at least a brief time alone with the therapist, and his offer to shine the therapist's shoes can be construed as his assuming the submissive, catering [female] role in relation to a strong [mature] male.) His intense restlessness during the sessions, evidenced by frequent and impulsive standing up and walking around the room (the only boy in our analytic groups who did this), lighting matches, burning paper, scorching the table, carving on it, throwing things out of the window and perilously leaning out of it (symbolizing an attempt at suicide), all point to a homoerotic panic which gradually subsided.

That Frank came to terms with himself to some extent is evidenced by the report of the caseworker. "There is even more telling confirmation of this in his behavior and relatedness in school, the community, and casework. These changes can be attributed to the help he received from the group in overcoming his guilt and emerging from the tragic sense of life that was his." This was achieved by universalization and reduction of guilt, objectification, and reality testing. It was also sponsored by ventilation of feelings, discharge of hostility, and by being accepted. There were improved feelings of self-worth and an improved self-image. Group therapy thus affected ego strength and personality integration both structurally and behaviorally. There was in evidence an emerging and reliable self-identity. What was to be established in this case were the libidinal modifications effected by group therapy.

Here we need to view the problem both from its nonsexual and sexual aspects. The centripetal flow of the primitive libido brings expansion and growth of the personality in numerous directions, but only if there are appropriate stimuli and opportunities in the environment. The capacity of the child to utilize opportunities for growth is derived from the support he receives from key persons in his life. They can either enhance his growth, restrict it, or block it off. When not too crippling damage has been inflicted upon the growth urge in these primary circumstances, it can later be reawakened by stimuli from extrafamilial sources, such as school, friends, and other individuals and groups. But if the restrictive and crippling forces in the home have been of great intensity, the personality becomes impoverished, and compensatory and defensive adaptations and behavior patterns arise. One of the forms this took in Frank, for example, was stealing.

The comments of the various staff members pointed to unmistakable improvement in this boy's social adjustment and capacity for relating to other people, but at the time of his leaving the institution, we noted that this improvement was only partial and might not be sustained under the inordinately stressful circumstances of his life at home. This prophecy was based upon our recognition that Frank was acting out a "transference neurosis" developed in the group. This transference neurosis stemmed from his homoerotic (or homosexual) tie to the older brother, displaced (transferred) upon the therapist. A transference neurosis cannot be worked through in group therapy; its resolution requires an extensive libidinal transference upon an individual therapist.

Our prognostication unfortunately came true. Shortly after Frank left the institution, he experienced a traumatic event which added to his distress and ego strain. His father took him along on a cross-country trip, and upon arrival at their destination, introduced his son to his common-law wife and asked Frank to live with them as a member of this duplicate family unit. Frank instead returned to New York and obtained a job in a chair factory where his brother was employed. He stayed on that job for several weeks, after which he tried to enlist in the navy, but was rejected because of his defective eyesight. He then returned west, where he worked on a part-time basis in an amusement park and lived with friends of his father; we do not know whether this was the woman involved or whether it was a family of the father's acquaintance. While there, he met a girl and decided to marry her. He was at this time between seventeen and eighteen years old. Not having any funds, he returned to New York with the intention of earning and saving a sufficient sum of money so that he could go back and marry the girl.

Unsuccessful at obtaining the kind of job that he wished and that would pay him enough, he broke into an office building, stole some money, and later passed a bad check, apparently on a blank acquired during his illegal entry into the office building. When he learned that he was being sought by the police, he started west, hitchhiking and stealing on his way. He was apprehended and returned to New York, where he was sentenced to a four-year prison term on a charge of unlawful entry. All this transpired within one year of his discharge from the Village.

9

Reactions of Staff and Parents

Institutional Staff

IT WAS OUR EXPRESSED POLICY to involve staff to a minimum, other than those few that participated in the project, so as not to disturb the ongoing life and activities of the institution or cause alteration in its daily routines and program. We also decided that the project should be carried on with as little prominence as possible, both on and off the campus, so as not to arouse opposition or resistance to the study on the part of individual staff members (or the departments) who might feel threatened by the introduction of a new procedure. We felt that the less attention the project received during its study phase, the better it would be to achieve the objectives of our undertaking.

This seemingly anomalous position was taken partially because our work was planned to be only a "test," and we were therefore not ready, nor did we consider it advisable, to involve in it the two hundred staff members. The main reason for it, however, was the fact that the necessary personnel and machinery to integrate the project into the life of the institution was not available. At that time there was no one permanently assigned to interpret our work even to the clinical staff, or integrate it into the clinical practice, let alone the large numbers of nonclinical personnel. To introduce new procedures involving so fundamental a departure from traditional operation as our work was requires intensive and continuous educational and interpretational effort. The director of the project visited the campus only rarely for professional or administrative conferences. The supervision of group therapists and the analysis of records and the other studies were carried on off-campus.

We therefore kept in the background both personally and professionally after three initial sessions with the clinical staff, at which time the study was presented to them. No meetings were held with any other professional or lay personnel. The exception to this was the presence of a few of the professionally trained cottage life supervisors (not cottage parents) at the "integration" (treatment) conference on boys under their supervision. These conferences to review the careers of the boys in and outside of the groups were at first held twice during the school year. The participants in the conference were the caseworker, casework supervisor, group therapist, cottage life supervisor of the unit whence the boys came, the director of the project (who also served as the group therapy supervisor), and occasionally a psychologist. After two years, we found these conferences both cumbersome and inefficient, and replaced them by individual interviews with the same personnel (plus cottage parents) by the research associate, who then compiled the information obtained for the study.

Instead of directly asking the general staff to react to the presence of group therapy in their midst, thus making them self-conscious, we asked the administrative staff to record any reports, opinions, and gossip about the therapy groups as well as stray statements by the boys about their group experience. We regularly consulted individual "child care supervisors" (who are also referred to as "cottage life supervisors") as to their impressions and the information they might have garnered relative to the attitudes of staff to the project, as well as the progress of individual boys. These men, who lived on the grounds, knew intimately the adjustment and problems of each boy and the feelings of the cottage and other staff members concerning him.

The consensus was that the therapy groups in no way dislocated or strained the routines of the institution. When overlap arose in the scheduling of the groups and other after-school free-time activities, we shifted the time of group sessions to evening hours.

Some dissatisfaction was voiced by a few of the cottage parents because they were not consulted about, or involved in, the selection of "their" boys for groups. Ordinarily this would have been done, except for the reasons already stated for involving staff to the minimum. When group therapy becomes an integral clinical practice in an institution, cottage parents should definitely be consulted either directly or through the cottage life supervisors as to the choice of the membership in groups.

Only one cottage mother persistently criticized the group to the boys who resided in her cottage and spitefully attributed every misbehavior or act of disobedience to their belonging to the group. She would on occasion threaten to withhold permission to attend the group as punishment. Four of our boys in demonstration group C resided in her cottage, and on many occasions she was the subject of group discussions which appear in the protocols later on. She was a very rigid disciplinarian with a repressive, authoritarian character and obviously extremely possessive of her charges, particularly of one of the youngsters, whom she favored. She openly attributed every act of assertiveness, initiative, or insubordination to "that discussion group." When the situation became untenable, we called it to the attention of the cottage life supervisor, who remedied it by a tactful interview with the woman.

However, as the protocols reveal, the attitude of this cottage mother was not entirely unprofitable to the group. The discussions of her behavior and the boys' reactions to them and to her as a person and as a wife to the cottage father had a maturing effect upon them. Instead of becoming inured in resentment, which is ordinarily the case in such instances (with consequent reactive acting out), the discussions at the group sessions, and the resulting clarifications, brought to the unconscious of some, and the awareness of others, the similarity of her conduct to their own mothers' behavior. This helped in working through feelings toward the latter. In a telling way this repressive and possessive woman helped the boys to work out transferential Oedipal involvements with her and indirectly with their natural mothers. However, in the case of the boy with whom she, a childless woman, was intensely emotionally (and perhaps also unconsciously incestuously) involved, the group discussions proved of pivotal effect. She served as the proxy in his resolution of his intense incestuous feelings and dependencies upon his mother.

The catalytic role the therapist played in this process will become clear from the protocols. His explorations and confrontations activated the group to uncover and face their feelings. Quite on their own, they recognized their dependence upon the opinions of others, the absurdity of their needs under the circumstances, and the inevitability of the cottage mother's reactions, since she could not help being what she was. This understanding and awareness took more than a year in emerging, but had a telling maturing effect.

Casework Staff

The casework staff, of whom there were more than a score, were of mixed feelings. Of those who were involved in the project, most were enthusiastic and, as could be expected, others kept themselves aloof or felt threatened. Since boys of only a specified age belonged to groups, only a small number of the caseworkers were directly involved; the majority, having no relation to the project, remained passive or indifferent. Only two appeared to be antagonistic and tended to sabotage our work. The consensus was that their antagonism represented a facet of their personality problems, rather than a specific attitude toward group therapy.

In the years during which the groups were conducted, there naturally occurred a considerable turnover of caseworkers and psychiatrists. All of the latter, without a single exception, who were variously involved, approved of and supported the project on the basis of its good effect on the boys.

Parents

As part of our investigation, groups of mothers of boys residing at the Village were included in the project to ascertain their availability for guidance as a measure in delinquency prevention. Mothers of boys who lived in geographic proximity in New York City were chosen. The aim was to bring to the women's awareness the part families can play in conditioning attitudes and behavior in children, to help the mothers recognize some of the reasons for their children's socially deviant conduct and personality problems, and to prepare them for dealing with their sons in suitable ways when the latter returned home, thus preventing recidivism.

Accordingly, two particularly suitable female caseworkers selected from the clinical staff at the Village organized and led, under supervision of the director of the project, four "discussion groups" for mothers of boys in residence at the Village. While initially the work with the mothers' group was to be patterned after the child-centered group guidance of parents in urban child guidance clinics,[1] we stood ready to alter our approach to meet the needs of these women. In choosing mothers for the groups, the clinical staff, who had known the mothers of boys under their guidance, were consulted as to which they considered suitable candidates for the "discussion groups" according to established criteria. Membership in these groups included mothers of boys in the general population of the Village, not merely from any specific age "units" or only of boys in the therapy groups. The criteria were nonclinical, namely, we sought mothers   *1]* who were sufficiently intelligent to be able to understand ordinary concepts of child-parent relations;   *2]* whose defensiveness was not so rigid that they would be unable to accept or apply these concepts; and   *3]* who evinced interest in their sons to the extent that they visited them at the Village with some regularity or had otherwise expressed concern to the caseworkers. Mothers who appeared to reject their boys to a degree of neglect as measured by these criteria

1. Slavson, *Child-Centered Group Guidance of Parents*
(New York: International Universities Press, 1958).

were not accepted, as were those women who were neurotically involved with their sons or were manifestly psychotic.

The memo to the clinical staff relative to this undertaking read in part:

> The aim of the groups will be to *sensitize* the mothers to the needs of children without arousing guilt or anxiety. Our approach involves the creating of a climate that allows the parents to talk about, and become aware of, corrective practices re child rearing. The leader, through proven techniques, will evoke and lead discussions of behavior and experiences of both children and parents that will enable the latter to examine their own conduct and attitudes.
>
> This procedure proved effective with parents of children in urban guidance clinics. The experimental aim of our project will be to test this method with parents of delinquent (acting-out) children in residential treatment.

Selection: Counterindications

1] Neurotic mothers where the child is part of the neurotic syndrome—such as incestuous or homicidal urges.
2] Mothers who have invested in the child intense negative identifications, for example, those who identify their sons with a brother, father, or husband whom they hate.
3] Mothers of atypical children, for example, mental or organic defectives or psychotics.
4] Mothers who are themselves mentally retarded or who have a severe language barrier.
5] Mothers who are already involved in an effective casework relationship.

Selection: Indications

1] Mothers of boys on after care as well as in residence at the Village other than those described above.
2] Borderline or latent schizophrenic mothers will be selectively accepted, for we found them to respond to reality-oriented treatment such as these groups provide.

Groupings

Groups will be formed of mothers who are as far as possible educationally, socially, and psychologically on par, and will consist of mothers regardless of nationality, religion, or color as long as their points of reference to human relationship and human values are similar.

Mothers will be grouped according to geographic proximity in order to facilitate travel and thus prevent resistances on that score.

Conferences with individual caseworkers were held with the director of the project and the prospective group leader to select women for the groups. Caseworkers' written referral statements were discussed, and candidates were rejected or accepted with reference to the outlined criteria. Consideration was given to the social complexion of the group—that is, racial and cultural factors—so that the composition of groups would be a cross section of the metropolitan community from which the boys came. Thus, as far as they were available, white, Negro, and Puerto Rican mothers were placed in the same groups.

The group leaders visited nearly all the parents in their homes to explain the aim of the groups to them and to "size up" their suitability. A few, who could not be so contacted (usually because they were employed), were invited to the city office for the first interview at a time convenient to them. We sought in the individual interviews to ascertain the realistic situation of these deprived, poverty-stricken, and usually overburdened and predominantly depressed and harrassed women. A number of them could not attend groups because they were gainfully employed; others had small babies and had to arrange—and usually could not do so—for suitable baby sitters; a few were afraid to travel by themselves and had to be accompanied by their husbands; one (Leonard's mother, see p. 197), who traveled an unconscionably long distance, had to bring her small, mentally and physically retarded youngster with her because she could not arrange for anyone to take charge of the child; some found the fare too great a drain on their financial resources. All of these and many other problems had to be resolved.

Quarters for the meetings were obtained, usually gratis, from neighborhood centers, specifically from the Y.W.C.A. Some groups met at the New York office of the Children's Village when its location proved central. In these instances some of the women had to travel rather long distances and were subjected to complications in travel facilities.

We made available to the women during the sessions, candy, nuts, and cigarettes, and coffee and cake were served after the discussions. This was intended to give the sessions a social as well as an educational character and put the women at ease.

Repeated letters, telephone calls, and home visits were used as means to activate the women's attendance at the sessions, which were held on alternate weeks for a period of ninety minutes. The following description of one of the groups will perhaps convey the nature of the response on the part of our boys' parents.

Six mothers of the eight selected for this particular group attended the meetings at one time or another, with the maximum number at any one time being three. Two never turned up, though they faithfully promised to come when seen by the group leader.

The fourth session was attended by only one mother, though all eight women received reminders before each session. Following this session all the mothers were contacted either by phone or by letter, informing them that the next session would be the last before the summer recess. However, no one responded.

Early in the fall, the mothers who had attended at least one meeting the preceding spring were called on the telephone—or, those who had no telephones, were sent letters—to arrange for the first session. Three of the six remaining women responded that they would not be able to continue in the group because of various commitments either in jobs or at home. One had meanwhile become a client in a family agency. Another had no telephone and did not respond to several letters. The same two who ignored the invitations in the spring did not respond again.

To re-establish the group, the leader visited the homes of another panel of preselected women and interviewed them. Seven mothers were visited. Of these, two were not at home, even though they had been notified in advance of the time of the visit. Five were interviewed. Of these, one was rejected on the basis of new developments in the family situation, and one decided that she would not be able to attend because of her own and her husband's chronic illnesses. Three agreed to join the group and were found acceptable. More mothers were sought out to complete the group.

One of the difficulties encountered in visiting the homes of our boys was locating apartments in the ramshackle buildings where they lived. Rarely were their names on the bells in the halls, and those available were either out of order or the women would not answer the ring. It was, therefore, necessary for the group leader to make inquiries of superintendents in their cellars or of neighbors, often knocking on all the doors in the dilapidated buildings until the correct apartment could be found.

Of a total of ten mothers who were interviewed and who promised to attend, only one turned up. An urgent letter was then dispatched which brought the attendance to two. These two had not attended any previous sessions. We therefore decided to disband the group, which was the fate also of the other three groups after similar discouraging experiences.

Table II reflects the efforts made to involve the mothers in one of the groups.

The mothers' indifference toward the boys in our care; their rigid clinging to the correctness of punitive treatment and, in many instances, outright brutality they had meted out to their offspring; their unbending conviction as to the essentiality of authoritarian and dictatorial management of, and disregard for, children's individuality and self-respect—these attitudes were undoubtedly the major if not the sole cause of their offsprings' waywardness. Only rarely were we able to elicit some empathy with a child's struggles in his movement from childhood to maturity and his confusions and his needs. Even when a few of the mothers were aroused to some slight degree of sympathy and understanding, these feelings were ephemeral. Vacillating attitudes were easily resolved in the direction of their accustomed reactions and prototype punitiveness at the slightest misbehavior on the part of their children. In their resistivity or lack of comprehension, the few women who did attend the meetings devoted the time mostly to chit-chat and endless repetitions of the same commonplaces and gossip. The leaders' efforts at touching off a more comprehensive or wider interest or to convey an understanding

TABLE II

Schedule of Contacts: Mothers' Group No. 1

Member	Letters	Telephone Calls	Interviews	Meetings Attended
1	7	1	Home visit	None
2	7	No phone	Home visit	3
3	1	2	Home visit	None
4	3	No phone	None*	None
5	4	3	Home visit	2
6	5	No phone	Home visit	1
7	3	3	2 Home visits**	1
8	4	No phone	Home visits***	None
9	3	5	Office visit	3
10	4	No phone	None†	None
11	5	No phone	None†	None
12	3	No phone	Home visit	None
13	4	No phone	Home visit††	None
14	7	6	Office visit	1
15	5	No phone	Home visit	None
16	5	No phone	Home visit	None

* No response. Later rejected on basis of new evaluation of home situation by boy's caseworker.
** First visit mother not able to hold interview due to sudden death in family.
*** Not at home.
† Working mother. No home visit possible. No response to invitation for office visit.
†† Rejected after home visit. Woman too disturbed and too hostile for a group.

of needs and motives in behavior in children and in themselves proved fruitless.

These anomalous reactions of the women in our groups were not exceptional or unique, however. In a project for delinquency prevention with girls in a metropolitan city, which the present writer directed, four years of efforts at organizing mothers' groups met with failure. In order to eliminate the factor of personality of the leader and her style of leadership as a possible cause for our seeming failure, we assigned several leaders of different temperaments, and even races. The disappointing results were the same in all cases. In our Children's Village test, too, we employed two different leaders.

The reactions we have experienced in the two projects with mothers is confirmed by the findings of the Cambridge-Somerville Youth Study with parents of predelinquent and delinquent boys. The report of that project states in part:

> . . . In the first year, only one mother appeared for the first meeting and no subsequent meetings could be arranged. In the second year only one returned for another try. Despite their avowals of cooperation, letters and phone calls failed to induce the parents to become involved in the program.

In that study, fathers were found even more intransigent. Their responses "ranged from irate refusal to have anything to do with the investigators [social workers]," including such warnings as "stay away from my kid or else," to avoidance tactics, making home visits impossible.

This universal indifference on the part of parents of predelinquent and delinquent young people is no surprise. For were these parents more interested in their children, most of the children would not be where they are.

PART TWO

THE DEMONSTRATION
GROUP: *Protocols, Comments,*
and Individual Progress Reports

The Demonstration Group:
Case Histories

AS WE HAVE INDICATED, the group protocols are the essence of this publication, delineating as they do the actual process by which the aims outlined in preceding chapters have emerged and come to fruition. The records of the sessions, which follow this chapter, are interspersed with brief comments and interpretations of what transpired at the sessions (as a continuum) and the changes in the group as a whole are pointed up. At regular junctures are interspersed reports of changes in each boy's personality and his behavior as reported by staff members in the various departments of the Village—cottage life, academic school, recreation, and physical education—and caseworkers, psychologists, psychiatrists, and (occasionally) the group therapist.

The present chapter deals with the background social and clinical histories of the seven boys who remained in the group through most of its existence, preceding their placement in the demonstration group (group C), which, as indicated, was an unselected, "delinquency saturated" group. For the sake of space economy the anamneses of the boys who remained in the group only briefly are omitted. Thus anamneses and follow-up progress reports of Jameson, Kurt, and Jonathan, who were discharged or otherwise left the village, are omitted.

Donald

Background Material

PRESENTING PROBLEM

Donald, a well-built, white, Roman Catholic boy, fifteen years of age, was committed to Children's Village on a delinquency petition after he participated in stealing a car with another boy. Two years earlier he had been arraigned for throwing a "cherry bomb" into a school play yard. About a year after this incident, he was apprehended breaking into a cigarette-vending machine in a burned-out store. He presented serious difficulties in school for many years and was attending a special school for maladjusted children when he was brought to court. At this school too he was found difficult and, in addition, truanted very frequently. He claimed that he did this because he disliked the school, where he said he was attacked by "Negro gangs." The school authorities, on the other hand, reported that he had consistently physically attacked and abused younger boys at the school. Donald was inordinately impulsive and quick-tempered and was considered to be "a boy capable of putting his foot through a window" at the slightest provocation.

FAMILY BACKGROUND

Donald's father served in a menial capacity. He was described as a hostile and unreasonable person who vociferously complained of the fact that attending the court proceedings when Donald was tried caused him to lose time from his work. He placed the entire responsibility for his son's difficulties on the neighborhood and community influences. The mother did not appear at the court hearing, nor did she accompany the boy for the initial interview required by the Children's Village before placement of boys in the institution. She was described as a rather "infantile woman, an habitual drunkard, who was alternately extremely sexually seductive and indifferent toward Donald." She would go off on drinking bouts alone in various saloons and come home "dead drunk," refusing to go to bed with her husband. She would then wake Donald, send him off to sleep with his father, taking Donald's bed. In the process of waking him she would seductively handle his body. On many occasions she would telephone and have Donald fetch her home, because she was too intoxicated to travel by herself. This would at times occur at two and three o'clock in the morning. At other times, he would have to support her home during the day in the view of neighbors, which made him suffer great discomfort and shame. The mother was generally a flirtatious, seductive woman and attempted to flirt with the male caseworker who first interviewed her at the Village.[1]

One of Donald's brothers was living at home after breaking with his

---

1. The information relative to the mother's conduct and her provocation and seductiveness toward Donald was not available at the time of intake or when assignment to a therapy group was being considered. This information was garnered mostly from Donald's statements during the group interviews.

wife, while another, though in the ninth grade at school, never learned to read or write. He, too, was involved in an auto theft. This brother, Danny, served as Donald's ego ideal. Donald would do favors for Danny and would lend him money, and the like, but Danny always refused to do Donald any favors in return. Once Donald had a girl friend for two months, but broke up with her because Danny separated from his girl friend. There were also two sisters in the family.

The first time the parents had any contact with the caseworker was nine months after Donald was admitted to the Village. They refused to be involved in any way before that time. Despite this neglect, the mother tried to give the impression that Donald was her favorite child. She averred that he was "always good around the house doing housework; in fact, did it better than a woman could."

Donald was a premature baby, born during the seventh month of pregnancy. Donald had pneumonia at the age of two weeks and was hospitalized for twenty-one days. At the age of thirteen, he was struck by a car and remained in a hospital for five days. No discernible effects resulted from this accident.

CLINICAL FINDINGS

In the psychological study about a year before placement at the Village the psychologist stated that, despite a tough exterior, Donald was a frightened, tense child, who reacted to new situations in a passive manner. He acted out antisocial impulses against his environment because "his rational controls were inadequate and his ego strengths easily dissipated." The report stated in part: "While he feels no strong relatedness to any adults, he is least related to males in whom he perceives nothing of significance, an attitude that he has adopted as part of his own self-concept. Females, too, have a minimal meaning for him. He cannot really conceive the images of maleness and femaleness as one would expect from a fourteen-year-old boy." His IQ was found to be 99 (verbal, 86; performance, 112). He was practically a nonreader, reading at the 1.3 grade level.

During the intake interview at the Village, the psychiatrist noted that Donald was "extremely restless and blocked." At one point he was unable to recall the names of his siblings and said in a panicky voice: "I'm confused. I can't think. . . . I am nervous. If my mother was here I wouldn't be nervous." The psychiatrist concluded that "this boy seems to have only the most elementary idea of family life, or what to expect from adults, either men or women, and only the crudest and most childish understanding of his environment. He clings rather desperately to a mother who seems quite indifferent to him. He defended his mother's lack of concern for him at the same time that he described it; for example, his mother never appeared in court with him because she had to stay home with the other children. She could not accompany him to the Village for the intake interview because she was sleepy and did not want to get up so early. She had been out late the night before. His father does not really distinguish this boy from his other sons." Diagnosis: passive-aggressive personality.

The psychological examination administered about a month after placement at the Village referred to the boy's "reactivity to a phallic mother. He is impulsive but not destructive. His hostility toward her is expressed through passivity, for he is hopeful of making a *rapprochement* with this rejecting woman." The psychologist felt that the boy was capable of moving to "a proper masculine identification."

In the psychiatric interview held six weeks after Donald's arrival at the Village, Donald presented a rather handsome appearance, with evidence of considerable attention to grooming and dress. However, throughout this interview he was quite angry and frequently tearful— to such an extent that he choked and was unable to talk. He showed elements of infantile and regressive behavior. He would roll himself up in his chair, turn his head away and down, and hide his face in his hands. Frequently he bit his nails and a callous on the palm of his hand. He was reluctant to talk to the examiner or to answer questions. On one occasion during the interview he said in a very mature way, "I would appreciate your seeing me another time." When questioned about his family or his mother in particular, he would respond with, "I'm confused now and can't think but will talk to you another time."

Donald mentioned several recent incidents in which he had had great difficulty in controlling his impulse to strike out. There had been one occasion when a boy called his mother "a stiff." Donald did not really know exactly what that meant, but he struck out at the boy, "flattened him and then kicked him in the guts and face." He said he was unable to control himself. Speaking of his family, Donald showed real confusion. He stated that he had seven brothers, then enumerated four, including among these himself, as though he were discussing himself as a brother and a separate entity. He stated that there were two older brothers, giving as the age of one of them the same age as his mother's. He spoke of this "eldest" brother, age forty, first as his father's brother and therefore his own brother, then as an uncle, then as his brother again, and then differentiated this uncle entirely from another brother whom he said he had who was also forty years old. In desperation he finally said, "I could prove this to you if only I had my wallet and could show you a picture of all of them." He continued to be extremely confused and angry, with tears streaming down his face. His speech was filled with "hip" expressions such as "this was a real cool thing, man."

Donald seemed to have no adequate sense of right or wrong, feeling that whatever he wanted he could take because, by his wanting it, it belonged to him. There was a certain rebellious quality about his need to insist that what he wanted was right. During much of this interview he showed considerable preoccupation with going home for the forthcoming holiday, insisting that if he were not allowed to see his mother, which was essential to him, he would certainly run away. He volunteered, in addition, that if anyone "says anything about my mother again, I'll kill them," and, as an afterthought, added that he would kill anyone who spoke against his father, as well. This was the only time Donald mentioned his father in the interview. Donald stated that he liked his cottage father very much but insisted in no uncertain terms that he hated his cottage mother, who was "nagging" him all the time. The psychiatrist pointed out that while Donald seemed to have received very little interest, affection, or attention from his mother, he was "completely incapable of expressing any negative feelings toward her." He would not speak of his father, but he left the impression that he was quite frustrated and disappointed in him, and viewed him as weak.

The psychiatrist stated: "The least stress seems to result in a breakdown of the boy's defenses, and this is an ominous sign. The infantile and regressive qualities, as well as other evidences present, seem to indicate that the boy is capable of a better level of functioning. The evidences of regression along with the impairment in the thought processes alluded to above may indicate that a psychotic process is beginning. However, it is possible that the stresses of coming here, separation from the mother, and the deprivation and rejection he feels in the cottage resulted in a strain under which a transient episode of regression is occurring. Most of the picture seems to point to a severe character disorder or, more specifically, a personality trait disturbance in a nature of a passive-aggressive type of personality. However, the picture is not clear and a definitive diagnosis at this time is deferred."

When Donald was again seen by the same psychiatrist a month later, he was mildly distraught, and his appearance was relatively disheveled as compared to the first interview. His hair was uncombed, his shirt hanging out from his trousers, and his fly partly open. However, he was better able to relate to the examiner and did so more appropriately and warmly. He was quite anxious, however, and was fidgety, with some compulsive, repetitive movements, such as fingering the top of the desk and moving the zipper of his jacket up and down. There were signs of depression centered around his fears that his mother would disappoint him again and not send him the fare for his forthcoming week end home.

He requested permission to telephone her two or three times during the interview. He seemed to view his stay at the Village as intervals between week-end visits home.

When brought into a discussion of his family he continued in his confusion about his siblings. At first he mentioned that he had eight brothers and then enumerated only seven, one of which was himself and two of whom were the forty-year-old men who were apparently uncles. When the attempt was made to straighten this out, he did not respond with aggression and anger as he had previously. Instead he was able to conclude quite correctly that he was the middle child and that the older men were really his father's brothers, his uncles. The psychiatrist stated: "This boy is apparently not too bright and is sufficiently anxious so that his thinking might be interfered with, but not to the point where we can say a thinking disorder exists. It still is apparent that the boy's chief difficulty lies in his relationship with his mother, who has always lied and distorted reality, so that he cannot depend on her, or believe what she tells him. The ominous aspect of this is that under stress the boy seems to regress and to show transient episodes that resemble psychosis. At the present time, his defenses seem to be more intact and one cannot say that the boy is psychotic.

"Diagnosis: Personality trait disturbance, mixed-type, with some antisocial and with passive-aggressive features. Projective mechanisms are used, as is the defense of denial. Neurotic traits seem to be superimposed, with presence of anxiety and of mild depression. The predominant underlying pathology, however, seems to be characterological in nature with a relatively weak ego structure."

Interviewing Donald again four months later,[2] the same psychiatrist noted: "The boy's defenses seem to have been strengthened. The prominent features discernible at this time are an increase in the control of aggression and lessened depression. The previous diagnosis is confirmed. It is interesting to note in connection with the departure of the boy's (female) social worker, that instead of the regression that may have been anticipated, we have a reaction formation with a rise of negativism toward the therapist to whom he had earlier established a warm, giving relationship in which he was able to communicate his feelings easily."

Another psychological examination just prior to the start of group therapy (thirteen months after placement), repeated that "the dominant element in the clinical picture is a pervasive, free-floating anxiety. Donald experiences primitive, explosive affects, against which he attempts to

2. The frequency of the psychiatric examinations in this case was advisable due to the unclarity of the diagnosis and the discomfort, bordering on fear, on the part of the staff in relation to Donald.

defend himself through a variety of mechanisms—repression, suppression, and constriction. In spite of this, he has good resilience and is able to re-establish controls. He experiences much guilt over sexual impulses, and is fearful of the consequences, should he act on them. In this respect, and in some others as well, Donald differs from the delinquent syndrome and character disorder. He can be considered as essentially neurotic. Reality-testing, concerning the reality which his limited cognitive sense permits him to get in contact with, is good. Although Donald's fantasy life is very active, there are no autistic or psychotic features, and healthy elements predominate." The report also mentioned Donald's eagerness for inter-personal involvement, and his tendency to spoil relationships by becoming overdependent and demanding. The paternal figure was perceived as inadequate and evasive.

In an examination held at the same time (at the start of group therapy), the psychiatrist noted that the boy showed a "bored and laconic attitude, with a mixture of sullen hostility, yet with underlying suggestion of depression." He also noted "babyish, infantile smiling and laughter." There were evidences of improvement, but it was suggested that these were tenuous and transient. Donald's thinking often seemed illogical, inconsistent, and contradictory. The prognosis was "guarded, because of poorly integrated defenses, and inadequate controls over poorly understood aggressive impulses."

SOCIAL ADJUSTMENT

At the time of referral for group therapy, Donald was found to be generally greedy and voracious at meals in his cottage, affecting a blustering manner, and touching staff members at every opportunity, despite their clear indications that this was distasteful to them. It was said that there was "a wild quality" in this boy. He was described by the cottage father as a "loud-mouthed, lazy boy who must be individually supervised closely and goaded to do any sort of job at all." Contrary to rules, Donald's relatives repeatedly came to visit him, filling two cars and making a "picnic of it." Once she started visiting, the mother came frequently. The rules were that visitors had to come to the cottage parents, but Donald's family and friends ignored them, and gave food and money directly to the boy instead of to the cottage parents, as required. Repeated warnings were of no avail. Because the parents were openly defiant of regulations, it was necessary for the cottage parents to impose firm limitations on them, after the need for this had been explained to Donald. Despite the fact that Donald's family—parents, brothers, aunts, uncles, and friends—visited more frequently than did the relatives and friends of any other boy in his cottage, he was the only one who would wait on the road for his visitors to appear.

Donald usually spent his time in the cottage talking, teasing, wrestling, and participating in big muscle activities. He was unpopular with the boys and with his cottage parents.

The school personnel described Donald as a "daydreamer, with a short attention span." While he got along well with school staff, he kept himself at a distance from them. The report noted that just prior to the initiation of group therapy he was reading below the third-grade level (at the age of sixteen years) and was considered as needing a "great deal of structure and individual attention." He was a boy who could "easily be led into trouble even by a smaller boy."

During the first seven months at the Village he was seen by a rather warm, attractive, and talented female caseworker. She found him "extremely immature; like a very young child of three or four, who did not recognize the consequences of his actions." She noted that Donald always seemed to have "one foot out of the door of the Village." His usual anxiety was greatly increased by his separation from home and it was her impression that he was a borderline schizophrenic. At one point during his early stay in the Village, Donald turned on a gas oven and walked away. He returned to light it later, causing an explosion in which he received a badly burned arm and fingers.

Donald was "spontaneous in the interviews, related well and willing to explore his behavior in some of his dealings." He acknowledged to her some of his feelings of inadequacy, of being easily led by older, bigger boys, and, in a childish fashion looked to her for "magical solutions." The caseworker believed that the primary reason for his reaching out to her was a quest for relief from anxiety engendered by his separation from his mother. Donald developed negative feelings toward his worker, however, when he learned that she was leaving. (The worker became pregnant and was discontinuing her professional work.) This reaction on Donald's part was later characterized by the psychiatrist as a reaction formation, and as a sign of strength rather than weakness. Sometime later Donald was assigned to a male caseworker, with whom he continued until he was discharged from the Village.

This caseworker had a different professional orientation in his relations to Donald. He faced the boy with the "realities" of himself and his family and assumed a somewhat peremptory and direct approach to the boy. It was this caseworker who referred Donald to a therapy group. Soon after Donald's placement in the group he severely beat up one of his cottage mates, who required hospitalization and several stitches on his lip.

TREATMENT CONSIDERATIONS

Donald's personality and the clinical information on him presented us with a dilemma, for no definite treatment plan or any outcome from psychotherapy could be envisaged in his case. We accepted him for group treatment, however, first, because of our policy of not selecting patients for this particular group and, second, because we were intrigued by the complexity of the boy's psyche and wished to test the effectiveness of para-analytic group therapy with a patient as disturbed or "sick" as he seemed to be.

We suspected that Donald was not psychotic. His might have been a case of induced schizophrenia[3] or, more likely, anxiety hysteria.

Louis

Background Material

PRESENTING PROBLEM

Louis, a small, Negro, Roman Catholic boy, age 14.5, was committed to Children's Village by Domestic Relations Court. About a year earlier he had been apprehended running out of a luncheonette, where he had grabbed $16 from a cash register. There was the suggestion that this theft was instigated by three other boys, who used Louis as their tool. They later threatened to shoot him if he revealed their names. Three months later, while still on probation, he was caught, in the company of another boy, removing money from the drawer of a till in a public library that was left unattended. Louis was a member of a "fighting gang" in his neighborhood which had frequent "rumbles" (wars) with other gangs characterized by extreme violence and the use of dangerous weapons, which he later described in the group sessions. From the age of seven Louis had been known to a family agency in his community, where he was described as "an unhappy, tense child who had difficulty in getting along with children at school." When fighting, he would bite his opponents.

FAMILY BACKGROUND

Louis's mother, a Protestant Negro woman, was born in the South, the middle of five children whose parents died when the children were very young. She was reared by an aunt, with whom she got along

3. S. R. Slavson, *A Textbook of Analytic Group Psychotherapy* (New York: International Universities Press, 1964), pp. 513–517.

rather well. At the age of twenty-eight, she married a Roman Catholic Hawaiian. Louis was born ten years later. The mother was described by the Village caseworker as a calm, intelligent woman who felt chronically ill, and martyred. She had only a passing concern about her son, who, she said, was easily led. Since her husband was away at sea for long periods during Louis's early childhood, mother and son were alone a great deal. When Louis was seven years old, his mother sought psychological help for him because he "seemed too quiet and unhappy." At nine years of age, Louis was referred to a child-guidance clinic by the school staff, because he "was tense and unhappy and did not participate in play with other children."

There was very little communication among the members of Louis's family. The mother and the father had almost an impersonal relationship with each other, and the mother communicated little with the boy as well. She considered herself superior to the father and excluded him from the family relationship, assuming the controlling and directing role in it. The father discussed this freely with the caseworker at the Village and seemed resigned to it. As a result, he could not contribute to Louis's development even to the limited extent that his short periods ashore might have permitted. Despite all this, the mother had an image of herself as all-giving and all-protective; she had overgratified the boy, never setting limits to his behavior, and at the same time maintained an emotional distance from him.

Part of the difficulty was that she was a light-colored Negro and Louis was dark brown. Her rejection of Louis's physique determined to a large degree her emotional attitudes toward him, and her overgratification and overprotection seemed to be a reaction formation to these attitudes. Her rejection of the family led to her absenting herself from home at every opportunity. She accomplished this by working on jobs and making frequent trips to various members of her family, particularly to a city far away to visit a sister to whom she seemed strongly attached.

Louis's father had come to the United States at the age of sixteen. After a year he joined the navy, and later retired as a petty officer with a moderate pension. The probation officer assigned to Louis described the father as less aggressive than his wife and ineffectual in coping with his son's behavior. His wife accused her husband of overindulging Louis. The father defended himself by explaining that he had a heart ailment and was, therefore, unable to cope with the boy or "do things" with him.

When Louis was four years old, a twelve-year-old girl, a cousin, came to live with the family. She lived with the family until she was married. According to the parents, the two children got along well.

Louis believed that the girl was his real sister. There was also a sister younger than Louis.

CLINICAL FINDINGS

In the clinical study done at a temporary shelter prior to placement, Louis was found to be a "very immature boy who did not use his good intellectual abilities in coping with everyday situations." He achieved a full-scale IQ of 91 (verbal, 85; performance, 100). The psychologist pointed to the fact that Louis had difficulty in interpersonal relationships and "falls apart when environmental pressures become too great." He was described as "negativistic, insecure, hostile, aggressive, and suspicious. He tends to avoid dealing with emotional problems and postpones coming to grips with them. He constantly looks for structure, support, and environmental cues." In the psychiatric examination, Louis was found to be "depressed, guarded, and anxious." Diagnosis: passive-aggressive personality, passive-aggressive type.

During the intake interview at the Village, Louis admitted to the psychiatrist that his mother has "given up, since beatings didn't do no good because that only made me madder and madder. I would stay out late, and things like that." He added, "My father says he don't care; it's all the same to him whatever happens to me." Later, Louis told the psychiatrist, "I'm the black sheep, the only one wrong in the family." Although he talked about a career in electronic engineering, Louis exhibited a deeply ingrained fixated wishy-washyness about himself. The psychiatrist noted: "his expression also reflected his deep, severe instability. He varied and wavered from being friendly and smiling to moody, bored, indifferent vacant looks and yawning. He slouched in his chair in a play of contempt and disrespect." While Louis seemed to have taken over some of his mother's and father's attitudes, that is, his giving up on himself, and, in part, not caring what happened to him any longer, he did respond when the psychiatrist confronted him in an almost playful way with the unlikelihood of his ever changing. Then Louis's eyes welled up. "It seemed he did care what happened to him," remarked the psychiatrist.

The first psychological test report at the Village referred to Louis's disappointment with the father, who was adequate as a maternal, over-protective person in the dependency period of the boy's early childhood, but who could not serve as a model when he wished to be more assertive in dealing with an aggressive world. According to the tests, the mother was perceived by Louis as an overprotective person in the early stages of his childhood. The tests also pointed to the boy's great need for masculine identification.

In a psychiatric examination approximately five weeks after placement in the Village, Louis was found to be timid, frightened, guarded, and suspicious. The boy's behavior suggested that he expected imminent attack from the psychiatrist. He was described as a small, thin, somewhat underdeveloped boy who seemed to make himself appear even smaller "by folding up upon himself in his chair." Through most of the hour there were tears in his eyes, but he had relatively good control over them. At one point in the interview he looked around the room, carefully staring at the pictures on the wall as though he were expecting to see something like a tape recorder. He asked about the walls, wondering why there were holes in the wallboards. He asked if this had anything to do with sound and seemed reassured when he was told that this cut down on the sound transmission from one room to the next. He explained that he was on his guard about psychiatrists because they were "trying to look for something and find out things." He openly admitted that he did not like the examiner because he did not like the way he talked and he looked too stern. Later, he seemed more comfortable and relaxed; this occurred after something positive had happened in the interview, and Louis showed evidence of a growing positive feeling for the psychiatrist, with genuine interest in what was happening. The psychiatrist stated, "There is a kind of thinking he manifests which can best be described as evidence of characterological psychopathy. He seemed to show either an unwillingness or an inability or both to act on his own to distinguish between right and wrong. Though he knew that certain things were wrong, he felt that what he wanted he should have, so he would simply take it in spite of the consequences."

Louis told the psychiatrist that very little happened between his father and himself except when his father became angry at Louis's behavior and punished him by hitting him with a belt or his hand. At other times, the father would become so angry that he completely dismissed the boy, telling him he wanted nothing to do with him. This troubled and angered Louis to such an extent that he left the house on such occasions and did something just to get the attention from his father that he felt he would not otherwise have. "The neurotic conflict in this sense seems most particularly related to the father, but what may be present in the relation to the mother is not as apparent because of the boy's great difficulty in formulating his relationship with her. The mother also makes him angry sometimes but the worse thing she can do to punish him is to make him stay at home when he wants to go out. He often successfully sneaks out when she is doing something in the back of the house. This only makes her angry and she sometimes hits him. Somehow Louis is aware of the lack of ability of all of the members of this family to communicate with each other except through some kind of aggressive or mildly violent act." Diagnosis: personality-trait disturbance, passive-aggressive type, with neurotic conflicts which lead to acting out.

The psychiatric examination four months prior to the initiation of group therapy noted that although Louis had been at the Village about a year, he entered the interview in a state approaching panic, and the most careful attempts to allay his apprehension were only partially and momentarily successful. He sat hunched over in his chair as if he were trying to squeeze himself into the smallest possible space to avoid being a target for possible aggression. When questioned about his life at the Village, he showed increased apprehension, giving very common responses, such as that the cottage parents are "very strict about chores." In contrast, he talked more freely about his family and his life at home. On week ends at home he would go out only to the movies with his mother. He spent time at home because he did not want to "waste" any of his time doing anything except being home. Louis told the psychiatrist that he had an uncle in the army and a brother-in-law in the air corps but that Louis himself hoped to go into service as a sailor. The psychiatrist noted that Louis had not been able to relate to any male staff member in a significant manner. He stated: "When Louis reached early adolescence and began to relate more to peers, he became involved in delinquencies. [He lived in a very high delinquency area and it is not too surprising that he should equate delinquent acts with masculinity.] Louis gave the impression now that his rather mild attempts at assertiveness and at becoming one of the gang resulted in such catastrophic retaliations that he felt the only safe thing was to retreat to a passive, childish docility. He appeared to feel really safe only when he was at home, where both parents could see that he was being good and there were no disturbing outside influences. His experiences at the Village seemed to be reinforcing this regressive behavior; that is, he was at first very acceptable to the cottage mother. However, as he began to relate to his contemporaries, he became involved in some of their misbehavior and the approval was withdrawn. At the Village he could not withdraw from contact with his peers and retreat as he could at home." Diagnosis: passive-aggressive personality, passive-aggressive type, with neurotic reaction.

In a group therapy preassignment psychological examination at this time, he achieved a full-scale IQ of 100 (verbal, 106; performance, 93).

> He displayed excellent ability for concentration and rote memory. There were many intimations of his intellectual potential being in the superior range. The clinical picture presents much complexity and a number of paradoxical elements. There is in Louis much emotional turbulence within and a great deal of

fluctuation in his ego integrity as well as in his mood swings. His active but inappropriate fantasy life includes near-bizarre elements and he has thoughts which he does not know how to integrate and which he experiences as ego-alien. Superficially, he gives at first the impression of being stereotyped, disinvolved, and somewhat *schizoid*. The projective material indicates a marked schizoid trend, withdrawal with avoidance of interpersonal relations. There is no real break from reality, but in his angry withdrawal he is apt to be vindictive and retaliatory.

Anxiety and depression are experienced in relation to both parental figures (anxiety which speaks against a diagnosis of psychopathy). Louis feels lack of support and emptiness from the environment. His mother, it seems, only talks to him but does not really care for him. He may have experienced intense fright in relation to an overpossessive, domineering, controlling mother and his pattern of withdrawal was perhaps determined by such a maternal relationship. Hostility and sexual promptings are fused, without any distinction between them. Hostility, oppositional trends, destructiveness are related to frustrated dependency needs. Oral frustrations have been so intense that the aggression felt toward the mother is quite unacceptable and is projected, leading to a definitely paranoid orientation. With this paranoid sensitivity, he feels intensely lonely, very fearful, and also victimized, the latter providing justification for hostility, acting out, and oppositional attitude. Acting out is a function of his paranoid ideation and this strong defense appears as very difficult to break. In his intense mood swings, he escapes from a painful state characterized by depression, loneliness, paranoid suspicions into elated oppositional acting out. He is generally not sure of his reactions toward others and is alternatively fighting and withdrawing. Under stress, he assumes a paranoid position and his recriminations, angry accusations of others, tend toward the delusional.

In summary, the data reveal a loosely integrated character structure without real strength and without a clear-cut healthy control system. It is difficult to identify the case diagnostically for there is a variety of defense systems. He defends against his destructive tendencies with projection and paranoia. Another defensive mode is withdrawal, with passivity, inertia, and indifference. In addition, an abundance of free-floating anxiety and depressive affects are generated whenever he is psychologically in the presence of maternal or paternal figures. A diagnostic speculation which best fits the data is *borderline schizophrenia with paranoid and antisocial features*, emotional instability including anxiety and depression. In its complexity, this diagnostic inventory presents psychotic as well as neurotic elements, with also oppositional trends and acting-out tendencies usually pertaining to character disorders. Considering the lack of sound ego resources,

the prognosis is quite guarded. Louis is likely to be most difficult to reach because of the paranoid cycle in which he is
involved.

SOCIAL ADJUSTMENT

Prior to Louis's coming to the Village, the school reported
attendance and conduct good and that he was "always well dressed."
He was described as "lazy and indifferent." Work in all subjects was
poor. He kept leaving his books behind but had a supply of expensive
notebooks which he hardly ever used. Louis was considered to be
potentially at least of average intelligence. He was reading at 9.5 grade
level.

In the Village, preceding placement in group therapy, Louis was
described as passive, superficially conforming, but with intense underlying hostility that broke through in occasional negativism. He tended
to be a follower of the more aggressive boys as a means of bolstering
his strength. He was referred to the group primarily because he was
very resistive to, and achieving little in, individual casework treatment.
Louis entered an ongoing group at its twelfth session.

Relative to his adjustment at the Village prior to entering group
therapy, the cottage father described Louis as very neglectful in his
grooming and personal care. He had gotten into serious conflict with
the cottage mother over his disobedience and sloppy personal habits,
but some improvement had been noted. Louis incited arguments with
other boys by his "childish actions and playful nonsense." At such times
he would run to staff members and "turn on the tears." He was at times
defiant of the cottage staff in the presence of other boys, with the
obvious intent of impressing them, and was always in the company of
the more aggressive and destructive elements in the cottage population.
Staff members considered him "a little crybaby reaching out for a
pacifier." During the early months of placement he was involved in a
great deal of sexual activity with other boys, but this did not continue.
School staff described him as a follower and one who became easily discouraged when faced with a task with which he was not entirely
familiar or which he found difficult. He avoided direct contact with
peers and boasted of antisocial acts. He tended to incite disorder in
the classroom, though at the same time he seemed to want to establish
friendly relations with teachers. One of his characteristics was that he
did not seem to take himself seriously and seemed as though he was
unaware of the reactions on the part of other people. His reading was
at 10.4 level, and arithmetic at 5.9 grade. Although Louis went in for
athletics, he would "knock" himself. He played football, but called him-

self "the Hunchback of Notre Dame" or "Quarterback for Nobodies." He was an unusually good ping-pong player, the best in his cottage; when he lost a game he was crushed and stopped playing. His teacher noted that Louis seemed particularly sensitive about being a Negro.

TREATMENT CONSIDERATIONS

According to another system of clinical categories, Louis could be diagnosed as having a character disorder with neurotic traits. The character deviations stemmed from faulty sources of identifications—an absent and weak father and a rejecting mother—which prevented him from developing an inner identity, out of which flow security and direction. To compensate for the lack of such a psychoscope, he sought to find directional guides in peers, who instigated his initial acts of delinquency, through which he had found a self-image and an identity. Because of his mother's attitudes, his father's long absences, and the latter's personality inadequacies, and as a defense against his incest anxieties, Louis had grown up alienated from himself and, by the herostratic mechanism of the human personality, also from society. Therefore, the pattern of his life was one in which he gained fulfillment by socially deviant and criminotic acts, which are unfolded in their stark viciousness in the group interviews.

Louis's self- and social alienative personality structure led him to self-defeat in all areas of life, and since his family climate did not nurture progressive personality growth and unfoldment, he remained infantile and frightened.

The mother's inconsistent treatment of the boy, her provocativeness, and the father's absences during critical periods in Louis's psychosexual development failed to repress his Oedipal strivings toward his mother, and as a result he remained a victim of infantile impulsiveness and the tyranny of his primitive urges. These he acted out in rather violent forms, which he disclosed in considerable detail during the group interviews (see particularly pp. 306-307 and 340-341 of the protocols).

Thus, the façade of a behavioral character disorder hid an underlying neurotic constellation and an immaturity in which nonidentity and alienation played a pivotal role. The task of therapy in this case was, on the one hand, to bare the neurotic anxiety which was not apparent and work it through and, on the other, to expose the patient to integrative, maturing experiences, which, under the circumstances, would consist of relationships in which freedom, respect, and corrective identifications would be the chief ingredients. These conditions can best be met by a group, not only because groups are generally indicated for adolescents, but also because of the difficulty this boy would have in evolving a positive transference to an adult due to the defects in his primary relations. This prognosis was borne out in the reports of the psychologist in this case (see p. 596). Another significant indication for group treatment for this patient was the fact that his neurotic core could not be reached before the character defenses had been cleared away, and this can seldom be accomplished in individual psychotherapy.

Note: Louis joined the group at its twelfth session.

Leonard

Background Material

PRESENTING PROBLEM

Leonard, a slight, pale, white, Protestant boy was admitted to Children's Village at the age of 14.4 years. He had been arraigned on a neglect petition through the school authorities about three years before. Both he and his younger brother had been consistently absent many days from school. At that time, when he was eleven years old, his arithmetic grade level was 2.4 and reading level 0.9. He was placed in a special health class, because he was subject to many hypochondriacal symptoms. Leonard's family was under the care and supervision of a social-service agency.

Together with his brother, Leonard was first brought to the court's attention when he was thirteen years old. In addition to his massive truancy, the complaining officer described the home as "filthy and neglected." School authorities believed that his mother (who was later a member of one of our mothers' groups and seemed to be psychotic) kept him home for unnecessarily long periods after his frequent "illnesses." Leonard was at the time in a sixth-grade "opportunity class" for slow learners. The mother attributed the family's difficulties to the disturbed relationship between herself and her husband, from whom she had been recently divorced; she was completely unable to recognize her own part in Leonard's school difficulties. Despite the fact that she was unwilling to have him removed from the home, the court recommended placement in an institution, largely because of the mother's inadequacies.

FAMILY BACKGROUND

Leonard's mother, the youngest of three children in a Protestant family, married out of her religion when she was about twenty-five years old. Prior to her marriage she had been employed as a houseworker. She was described as an inordinately "disorganized person, unkempt and smelly," and neglectful of her home, which was "filthy." After her first arraignment in court she was referred to a family agency, and was found "inadequate, incapable of performing parental functions, and unreachable." The suggestion was made that she might be paranoid-schizophrenic. While Leonard was at the Village, she wrote a number of letters to him warning him that his father would kill him. She leaned on Leonard for support and proudly reported that, when she was ill, Leonard at the age of eight would prepare the meals for the entire family, including her husband.

The intake caseworker at the Village noted that the mother had a symbiotic relationship with the boy and that she needed to deny whatever problems he may have presented, since they reflected her own. She also said, "My son is like an arm; if we take away an arm, there will be pain and a lot of fighting to get it back." The mother was extremely threatened by any signs of Leonard's growing independence, maturity, and masculinity. For example, she prevented his obtaining a part-time job in a neighborhood grocery store. After his being placed at the Village, she still continued to keep him occupied with household chores on his infrequent week ends at home and discouraged his attempts to go out of the house. Leonard was repeatedly told that his father was "no good," and that he had run away and deserted the family and was the cause of all their troubles. Leonard was constantly admonished not to be like his father, and urged by his mother to stay close to her.

Leonard's father, about the same age as his wife, had been for many years an unskilled worker, but more recently was employed as a shipping clerk. The Children's Village caseworker described him as a mild, passive man. Leonard told the court psychiatrist that his father hit him all the time for no apparent reason and that he was glad when his father left the home. Leonard's mother claimed that her husband was jealous of her attention to the children, particularly of Leonard, even when he was still a baby. Leonard was eighteen months old when his father returned from the army. She attributed her husband's jealousy to the fact that he was an abandoned and neglected child.

The mother obtained a legal separation from her husband when Leonard was about eleven years old. The father subsequently obtained a divorce from her and soon after remarried. The father stated that he attempted to visit Leonard, but was prevented by his former wife. The boy was placed in Children's Village without the father's knowledge; he learned of it only when the Department of Welfare approached him about payment for the boy's care. Leonard's one sibling, a brother three years his junior, was epileptic and was found to have a "chronic brain syndrome with convulsive disorder and behavioral reaction." He suffered from gastro-intestinal ulcers. He attended CRMD classes in school. A psychiatric study made of the boy at the time of his first appearance in court indicated that some of his difficulties were related to extreme conformity to an overcontrolling, oversolicitous mother. No problems were reported in the relation between the two children.

Leonard's development was reported by the mother to have been "normal." The mother claimed that the boy's dental difficulties (at the time of placement he had relatively few teeth) were due to lack of calcium in the diet and attributed this fact to her husband's insistence that she economize and refrain from buying milk. She further claimed that when the father returned from the army, Leonard reacted to his presence with rage and temper tantrums. The mother lived with her husband's parents during his period of military service, but she raised the child as a Protestant, though she did not attend church or give the boy any religious instruction.

CLINICAL FINDINGS

The initial clinical study (done at the first court arraignment) described Leonard "as a somewhat chubby, round-faced boy. There was some evidence of chronic inflammation of his throat, but this did not appear to be serious. More serious was the boy's overly intense reaction to his illness, with what in an adult would be regarded as hypochondriacal concern. His intelligence was average-to-above-average potential, but his fragmentary schooling resulted in an arithmetic grade of 2.4 and a reading grade of 0.9. Thus the IQ of 85 is minimal. Potentiality is much higher and the retardation in basic school subjects could be overcome. The projective tests indicate a very healthy personality which is, however, beginning to react to the maternal overcontrol by emerging submissive feminine traits and overdependency traits."

A court psychiatric examination three years later indicated that Leonard was anxious and worried about the possibility of placement. The examiner noted that the boy looked old because of his toothlessness and that he related in "a submissive and clinging manner." Leonard was protective of his mother and the home situation and described his relationship with her as good. He said that she was strict with him and made him "mind." He admitted being very attached to her. He liked his father, but his father was always "picking on me." He said he was happy when his father left the home three years before. The psychiatrist concluded: "Leonard is a very passive, dependent, submissive child. He has a good deal of guilt feeling concerning the loss of his father."

Diagnosis: adjustment reaction of childhood in a youngster evidencing passive, dependent trends.

The psychological examination administered at this time (at fourteen years of age) yielded an IQ of 98. He read at 1.9 (eight-year level). He was found to be an anxious boy who exerted considerable energy toward keeping unaccepted impulses under control. There were indications of good ability to perform in social situations and alertness to the environment, as well as marked constriction and much depression. The projective material further pointed up a good deal of confusion around his sexual identification because of the absence of the father in the home.

The psychiatric intake study at Children's Village referred to the boy's bland, emotionally flat expression and voice. "He is hunched, pale, and toothless, like an aged man. . . . It is probable that adults would have to struggle not to let loose a feeling of disgust and impatience for which he is only too suitable a victim." His self-protective attitude included denial that his mother had any difficulties. "This boy is so unused to, and so afraid of freedom or revealing feelings, that he could not or would not admit feeling angry at anything. There is little fight left in him. This passivity is evidently his main strength." While "aggression" was noted, the psychiatrist commented that it was rigidly kept from emerging. He suggested that there was a schizoid element in the boy which explained some of his inadequacy. Diagnosis: inadequate personality.

A few months after admission Leonard was examined by another psychiatrist, this time a woman. His high-pitched, rather inflectionless voice was noted again, as well as his extremely limited vocabulary and unclear speech. He was once more extremely defensive of his mother and hostile toward his father, whom he did not want to see despite the father's many attempts to visit him. Leonard spoke of a man who had a pet shop near his home and of his plans to work for this man when he was older. The psychiatrist stated: "He expresses protective feelings toward his mother and ambitions to earn things for her, which usually signals Oedipal strivings. His relationship with his mother is complicated by his tendency to identify with her as well as to defend and protect her. Today, he shows a much more adequate personality and is far from being limp. There are indications that this boy may have reached a higher development level and then regressed somewhat." Diagnosis: passive-aggressive personality with neurotic traits.

The report of a psychiatric interview with the same female psychiatrist eight months later states that Leonard had been fitted with dentures, that he had gained weight, and was now "a surprisingly attractive looking youngster." It was found that Leonard had accepted some of the male staff at the Village as "good father figures" with whom he identified. However, since the "bad father" continued to be the source of much of the mother's complaints and these "good fathers" were not related to his mother, their value was limited. "They are not of really significant help in resolving the boy's conflicts in his relationship with his mother." The psychiatrist found no schizoid elements and felt that it was significant that Leonard's comments about the boys in his cottage were made in good-natured and tolerant manner and were apparently reality based. Diagnosis: passive-aggressive personality with neurotic reactions.

In the psychological examination four months later and just prior to the beginning of group therapy, Leonard found it difficult to give "firm answers," and his protocols were filled with expressions such as "something like that or something else." The male psychologist noted that he seemed to be constantly doubting himself. He obtained a full-scale IQ of 81. "Leonard is capable of correct appraisal through reality-testing, but does not exert himself much in this direction. Rather, he relies on fantasy living, daydreams, and ruminations, which are not abnormal content-wise and mostly of a compensatory nature. Under normal circumstances, Leonard's outstanding characteristic is inertia. He feels depressed, inhibited, and inadequate and prefers to remain inactive. Under stress, he is not able to tolerate much anxiety and is capable of a degree of acting out. The immature, impulsive behavior is accompanied by explosive affect. There are present evidences of maternal and other emotional deprivations extended over a long period of time. The paternal figure is perceived as very inadequate in providing a sound basis for masculine identification. At present, sexual identification is for the most part ambivalent. Leonard has gone through the various stages of psychosexual development with barely passing marks, so to speak. For the most part he is so involved in his security operations that he is liable to be diffuse and overgeneralizing in his perception of the outside world. He can best be characterized by a pervasive immaturity (extreme dependency and need to cling) with passive-aggressive handling of such needs."

Leonard was assigned to an experienced male caseworker whom he saw on a weekly basis for the first ten months. As the relationship continued, Leonard was found to be rather communicative. The caseworker commented that "Leonard had at one stage in his life perceived the father in a positive light, but because of the mother's attitude and his relation with her, he accepted her statements counter the father and is now acting out his feelings. He does have a masculine identification, however, and sees himself as fulfilling the father role in the family when he returns home." When this caseworker left the Village, Leonard was immediately assigned to another male caseworker and was again seen in weekly sessions. The new caseworker's comment was: "It is suspected that Leonard's chatter in a whiny voice throughout the interviews enables him to maintain control and prevent the worker from asking any painful questions of him." Leonard had begun to recognize his jealousy toward his younger sibling, however. The caseworker learned from the cottage parents that the boy had made a good deal of progress in his relationship with the cottage parents and peers; he had grown more assertive and communicative. The expressions of hate toward his father had gradually subsided, and he was able to say that he "feels sorry for him." The worker further commented that Leonard was still unable to reveal the rage he felt toward his mother.

SOCIAL ADJUSTMENT

Leonard began by being very quiet and isolative. The boys in the cottage perceived his fears and weakness and used them to full measure. They bullied and exploited him by making him do their chores and run errands for them. He was withdrawn from the cottage parents as well and usually presented a comic picture by wearing clothes too large for him, with several belts around his trousers. He spoke in a whining voice and his speech was unclear.

Leonard was doing remedial work in reading. His average at the time of entering group therapy was 2.8. While he was still an overly quiet youngster in the classroom, he seemed much less frightened of class recitations, had become more relaxed with the teacher, and asked for help more freely. The teacher referred to the fact that "Leonard tends to allow himself to be exploited by others and, when there is some one needed to run an errand or do a dirty job, Leonard's name seems to be suggested first."

TREATMENT CONSIDERATIONS

Leonard could be categorized as having a schizoid character, its origin being in hereditary traits, but greatly intensified by the disturbed home climate and the growth-retarding forces that operated in it. There are indications that the father was either schizoid or latent schizophrenic, while the mother was definitely a borderline schizophrenic. The parents, serving as models of identification, further promoted the pathology. The intense symbiotic relation with the mother enhanced the identification, and the overmature responsibilities imposed by her on the boy strained his ego resources. The content of his defenses, therefore, took on a reality denial nature. Characteristic of such patients is a defective body image, the results of which in the case of the mother are described by the probation officer and were evident in Leonard by the manner of his dress and grooming.

Leonard's self-doubt, depression, and inertia, a part of his partially constitutional ego debility and sociogenic defective self-image, generated in him a baleful identity and a resultant alienation. Although the original referral statement does not report it, it became known later in the group interviews that the boy had stolen in neighborhood stores.

In treating a boy of this nature, the therapist can anticipate only limited results due to the limitations of ego potentials. The hereditary endowments in Leonard's case delimit the results that can be achieved, but it is evident that, freed from the emotional shackles of the symbiotic relation with his mother and physical removal from her as an identification model and a controlling factor in his life, considerable growth could be effected. Treatment would have to address itself toward character change and reality-testing. Leonard later proved to be highly perceptive and intuitive, as schizoid persons often are.

Jules

Background Material

PRESENTING PROBLEM

Jules, a slim, white, Catholic boy of French background, 14.4 years old, was committed by court order after having been treated in a psychiatric clinic in his home community for two years. Jules had been stealing from his home and in school, was academically retarded, and was a "serious behavior problem in school." He frequently ran away from home and truanted from school. Jules was described in the referral statement as "extremely hyperactive, chronically restless in class, generally belligerent"; he stayed out late at night, and was "beyond the control of his adopted parents." In addition to weekly sessions with a caseworker of the clinic, he was receiving medication that had "a quieting effect" on him.

FAMILY BACKGROUND

Jules was one of five children of a first-generation French teenage couple. Their marriage was dissolved immediately after the birth of the last child. When Jules was about three years old, the mother, who had neglected her children, deserted them. There was the suspicion that the natural father, who was unavailable for an interview, was mentally defective. No information was available as to who took care of Jules between the ages of three and four-and-a-half years. At that age he was placed in· a temporary foster home, where, it was stated, he received "minimal care." For a year-and-a-half Jules associated with other homeless boys of a "dead end" character in his neighborhood. Jules bitterly complained when his sister, two years his junior, was placed in a permanent foster home before he was. At six years of age, he was adopted by a childless, middle-class French couple, his present parents. Jules continued to ask for his sister and often repeated his wish for one. He "even dictated a letter to the state Department of Social Welfare, asking that they send him a sister." Shortly thereafter, the parents adopted a girl, two years younger than Jules, whom he readily accepted as his sister.

The adoptive mother displayed "considerable concern about, and warmth toward, the two children, but seemed unable to constructively control Jules." She was rigid in her high demands upon him and entertained unrealistic expectations for him, setting up restrictions, threatening and warning him, almost provoking him to disobey her. Her consuming anxiety to maintain her "good name" in the small community in which the family lived dominated her relationship with Jules. The adoptive mother was extremely fearful that he might "do something to besmirch the name of the family." She felt that, since the name was not his by right of birth, he had to be particularly careful of it, as well as grateful for bearing it. The mother was chronically anxious, controlling, and indifferent to the boy's growth needs, having no conception of what child-rearing involved.

The father, a simple man, was a weak, passive, inadequate person, despite his huge size. He was overwhelmed by his wife's pressures and anxieties and looked to her for leadership and support. It was claimed that he had never punished Jules and left the discipline of both children to her. It is important to note that Jules discussed this in the group, saying that his behavior indicated he wanted his father to set limits for him as a sign that his parents cared about him. Both parents evidenced considerable guilt about Jules's behavior, which increased their hostility toward him. Their irritation was further enhanced by Jules's frequent assertion that he wished to go out and look for his natural parents.

CLINICAL FINDINGS

In the clinical study before placement the psychological tests yielded an IQ of 90 (performance 106; verbal 77). Responses to the projective tests indicated Jules's unwillingness or inability to share his feelings, and his reported emotional outbursts resembled the temper tantrums of a much smaller child. The psychologist stated, however, that the boy's emotional life was characterized "much more by dullness and cautiousness than explosiveness."

The psychiatrist who examined Jules upon placement in the Village described him as extremely defensive and relying on projection upon others to explain his difficulties. The boy described himself as having no interest in life and as being impatient with schoolwork, since he had decided on being a mechanic. He repeatedly returned to the theme, "I'm going to fail anyway" and displayed little confidence in himself. He appeared to be very hopeless. The psychiatrist stated: "His problems consist of a conflict between 'accept me as I am [inferior]' and 'I need and want to do better.'" Diagnosis: passive-aggressive personality with learning defects.

The psychological test administered to Jules upon his arrival at the Village revealed that he had to handle situations in a rigid and orderly fashion, by specific rules and regulations. The rules seemed to have been set by the mother—not as interactions in an emotionally meaningful way, but to give evidence of achievement, that is, "we must look good and proper at all costs." The father figure appeared to have played a background role but seemed to have supplied a degree of masculine orientation to the boy. Jules perceived the world as "fighting and angry, where it is best not to get too involved with anyone too long." It was felt, however, that Jules had sufficient strength available for integration and was capable of reversing the ongoing negative characterological process.

Because Jules ran away from the Village three times in six weeks and presented other difficulties, another psychiatric examination was held two months after his arrival. The psychiatrist found Jules alternately hostile and belligerent and ingratiating, with a façade of toughness. He expressed open hatred toward the Village, threatening to run away again, and spoke warmly of his adoptive parents. He described the father's punishing him by striking him on his buttocks with his open hand as Jules lay on the floor or stood rigidly receiving this punishment—which Jules felt he deserved. Some impairment of judgment was also noted. The main theme of the interview was the boy's "desperate desire to return home." Diagnosis: personality-trait disturbance, passive-aggressive type, based on neurotic conflicts toward parental figures.

At the re-examination just prior to the beginning of group therapy, ten months after Jules's arrival at the Village, the psychologist found that the projective material revealed "constriction with definite avoidance patterns motivated by fright." The report stated in part: "This is a boy who is unwilling to exert energy toward accomplishments of any kind. When reluctantly involved in a significant relationship, he can easily be intimidated; he is suggestible; he experiences deeply anxious feelings which lead to explosive behavior when his fright becomes overwhelming. He will rush about to hide his fright and to avoid facing his inadequacies, being particularly unwilling to admit sexual promptings. He would rather feel castrated and impotent than experience guilt over erotic impulses, and he compensates by emphasizing superficial signs of manliness." The psychiatrist characterized Jules as a "professional orphan." Diagnosis: passive-aggressive personality disorder, manifested by superficial compliancy and pouting, procrastination, running away, and acting out.

The caseworker described Jules as fluctuating between denial of problems and display of utter dependence, seeking to be rescued from his unhappy circumstances, and producing no significant material in the interviews but a conviction that he will fail in his adjustment in the Village and that he will be rejected by the staff and dismissed by the administration.

SOCIAL ADJUSTMENT

Jules's adjustment at the Village prior to admission to group therapy was "most precarious." He ran away on several occasions; was extremely hyperactive and easily became involved in fights with boys; was impulsive and would "do one wrong deed after another." His adjustment to his peers in the cottage was largely one of avoidance, but he also related to them by bribing them with the sweets and other goods which he received abundantly from home. He was particularly defiant. and argumentative with the cottage mother, and when scolded or admonished he would run away from the Village or disappear somewhere on the grounds for prolonged periods. In one instance he remained in hiding in an abandoned building a whole day and could not be located by the staff. The school reported that, while Jules had initially been a fearful boy, he was able later to show "a little better effort at containing himself." He could function best in "a controlled and structured situation in the classroom." When the controls were lifted, Jules became very hyperactive, restless, and tended to wander away from his work. He displayed no independence of any sort and had no initiative whatever. He seemed content to do his work on the periphery, not challenging anyone, thus preventing being challenged. His relationships with peers were distant, and they, on their part, seemed to leave him alone. At the point of entering the group, Jules's school status was reading—fifth grade; arithmetic—sixth grade; average—6.4, at the age of 15.1 years (that is, three years' retardation).

His personal appearance was uniformly sloppy. He seemed unkempt and disheveled and his clothes were far from being clean or cared for.

TREATMENT CONSIDERATIONS

On theoretical grounds alone, it would seem that this boy's difficulties arose from seeking, through deviant behavior, to gain the attention of the adults involved with him. This attention, even though of a negative nature, engendered in him an awareness of self. Jules's earliest formative years were replete with tension, instability, and destructive associations and therefore did not favor personality integration and an awareneess of his own being. His identifications were fluctuating and unstable so that his life had no direction, and his behavior, therefore, scattered. The disparity between his performance IQ (106) and his verbal IQ (77) indicates a blocking of the reflective process which might lead to his becoming aware of his familial dilemma. This is particularly significant, since he was found to perform adequately in school during psychotherapy. Jules apparently sustained a serious shock by his separation from his sister which served further to damage his self-identity. This injury was somewhat allayed by the adoptive parents' supplying him with a substitute sister, but the damage had already been done. Jules's frequent running away from home and later from the Village obviously had as an aim the finding of either his parents or his sister; this supports the identity-pursuit hypothesis.

Jules's self-alienation was made apparent by his unkempt appearance, his isolation tendency, his distrust of and inability to relate to people, and his conviction of being a failure. The therapy in this case would have to be geared toward breaking through his self-encapsulation and establishing healthy interaction channels between himself and others. If these relationships proved not to be so traumatic as those he had experienced in the past, they would establish a psychic bridge between himself and other persons, namely, help him to acquire object relations and generate an awareness of self and an identity that would support him in his general development and the strengthening of his ego. What this boy needed most, initially, was the security of stable relationships and unconditioned acceptance and status.

It could be expected that Jules would not do well in an individual therapy situation because the transferential complex would duplicate his past relationships, and that a group, where these relationships are diluted and are therefore less threatening, would be more suitable.

Generally speaking, the therapeutic effort would have to be directed toward character change, for there was no evidence of psychoneurotic content or symptomatology beyond his expectations of failing and of being rejected by everyone.

Our own guiding diagnosis was character disorder with neurotic traits.

Michael

Background Material

PRESENTING PROBLEM

Michael, a pleasant-looking, friendly, Negro, Protestant boy, aged fourteen, was committed to Children's Village after having been apprehended on a number of occasions for participating in neighborhood vandalism, stealing clothing from a department store, participating in shoplifting under the leadership of more aggressive boys, shining shoes without a permit, "malicious mischief" in the community, and being involved in the theft of a Cadillac car, in which he played a follower's role.

FAMILY BACKGROUND

Michael's mother, one of seven children in a farming family in Georgia, ran away in her early teens to marry a man much older than herself. She became frightened of this man and ran from him to live with an aunt in another southern state, where she had sexual relations with many men. She stated that she "could not be bothered with getting married" because she "would end up killing them [the men]." She said she had attacked and almost killed her former husband when she found him with another woman. She felt that now she could really leave her "boy friends" when they decided to go with other women. Therefore, she made it a practice to have a great many transient relationships, always anticipating that the men would leave her. She was sixteen at the time Michael was born, and gave him the name of the man with whom she was living at the time, though she believed the actual father was another man, a former penitentiary inmate. A more recent liaison was jailed for knifing another man during a fight.

Michael had five younger siblings—all born out of wedlock. The mother was unable to tell which of three of her men was the father of her last child. When Michael was nine years old his mother moved with the children to New York State, where she had been receiving public assistance. Michael's mother was described as immature, disturbed, with "intense hostility toward men." She was excessively critical of Michael, often telling him that "you'll never amount to anything. You're just no good." Michael recalled an incident when he was six years old. His mother told him to shift some heavy furniture around the apartment. She left, expecting him to do the job alone. When she returned, she chastised him severely because he had not done "a good job." Michael's concept of his mother was that of a severe critic, one who was invariably right. (In this regard, it is interesting to note that in the group discussions, Michael came to realize that his shoplifting was an attempt to prove to his mother that he could be "good at something.") The mother was "relieved" when Michael was removed from the home, declaring, "he worried me to death."

CLINICAL FINDINGS

Michael was in the sixth grade (two years under grade) at the time of placement, with an academic average of 80.

A psychological test administered by the court two months before placement at the Village yielded a full-scale IQ of 88 (verbal 99; performance 78). Michael's reading level was 6.1 at the age of fourteen years. While he was potentially of average intelligence, Michael lacked drive or motivation. He was found to be in good contact with reality and devoid of neurotic symptoms. The projective data indicated strong oral needs, mistrust of people, a tendency toward impulsivity, little anxiety, and only slight aggressive tendencies. Little evidence of guilt was present. The psychiatric examination held at the same time yielded no evidence of serious psychiatric disturbance. Diagnosis: adolescent behavior disorder, in an immature, suggestible boy of borderline intelligence.

A month following placement, the psychologist at the Village reported "an underlying schizophrenic process in a boy whose world has been confusion from the outset and who has made his adjustment accordingly." The psychologist stated that his reactivity was phobic, and compulsive defenses were very much in operation, without which there would be massive, uncontrollable impulsivity with potential destructiveness. There also appeared to be an obsessional quality in the boy's process of mastering anxiety. The cottage staff reported inordinate interest in, and anxiety about, food, and anger when food was not up to his requirements.

In school Michael "ran hot and cold" toward teachers. Though he would give the impression that he was "a good boy" and worked hard, he would become disruptive when he thought he was not being watched. He followed the more nonconforming boys and often looked sullen.

The psychiatrist's statement at this time indicated that denial was one of the boy's major defenses. He was impressed with the boy's need to deny any wrongdoing on the part of his mother, or that there was sex involved in the birth of his siblings. He wished to believe that a stork brought the babies to his mother. He was certain that his mother had had no boy friend for the past four years, and, when faced with the fact of his youngest brother's age (one year), he burst into tears. Later in the interview he upbraided the psychiatrist for making him cry, since others who interviewed him did not do so. This mechanism of denial pervaded all of the boy's thinking and feeling. However, he readily admitted to his own wrongdoings, recognized their antisocial nature, and displayed a degree of contriteness.

Diagnosis established was "personality-trait disturbance, with passive dependence predominant. Neurotic conflicts center around the absence of a father, the unresolved sexual strivings toward the mother, the multiple unexplained siblings, and the confusion in sexual identification. Anxiety is present, as well as potential depression."

At the start of group therapy six months later, an examination by another psychologist resulted in a full-scale IQ of 93 (verbal 94; performance 93). A significant drop in functioning was evident, and this, in conjunction with other findings, suggested the presence of a thinking disorder. The projective material suggested much more pathology than direct observations of behavior or clinical impression during an interview would indicate. "There is a tremendously active fantasy life filled with sadistic and sexual preoccupations. The boy uses sexuality to stimulate him out of withdrawal and depression. There is a considerable lack of differentiation between sexes: Homosexuality and heterosexuality are practically equivalent for him. The very disturbed fantasy life and the psychotic potential are related to his ambivalence toward the mother. Although he identifies with her and entertains magical ideation about her powers of attraction, he also deeply resents her, and wishes to destroy her by sexual attack. This pronounced pattern of ambivalence characterizes his emotional life, and limits greatly his ability to relate to others in a meaningful way. Since he does not get involved with anyone, he drifts easily into a variety of situations, maintaining an easygoing façade, seeking pleasures rather indiscriminately. In other words, he handles the underlying schizophrenic disorganization in a psychopathic style. His defensive isolation enables him to maintain control, and thereby the dangerous ideational content is neutralized and kept at a distance. There is much striving to conform, and, in spite of extensive underlying pathology, he manifests great resourcefulness in maintaining boundaries within his personality."

In a psychiatric interview a few weeks after initiation of group therapy by the same psychiatrist, Michael was found to be able to talk more realistically about his mother, and again no evidence of schizophrenia was found. The psychiatrist stated that "Michael seems to feel that the examiner accused him of having unnatural relations with his mother," and in his anger did not look at him directly. The diagnosis continued to be "passive personality-trait disturbance, passive-aggressive personality, passive dependent type."

Michael was assigned to a female caseworker four months after his arrival at the Village. At first, he related in a dependent way, seeking approval. In the interviews, he put his mother on a pedestal, but "did not know what he would want in a father, since he never really knew one." The caseworker noted as well that denial was Michael's overriding mechanism. He was seen once a week for three months, until the initiation of group therapy, when, in accordance with the policy established, the sessions were reduced to once a month. However, shortly thereafter, Michael requested a special appointment, evidencing anxiety at the separation. The cottage parents reported that Michael displayed more irritability and a slight depression at the discontinuance of weekly casework sessions. It was accordingly decided at an interdepartmental conference to resume the old plan. As Michael continued with group therapy, he began to communicate to his caseworker more freely. He said, among other things, that when he grew up, he wanted to have lots of money *but would not get married*. Otherwise, the content of his communications continued to be on a superficial level.

SOCIAL ADJUSTMENT

As long as he was left alone, Michael initially made a good adjustment in his cottage, but when the cottage parents attempted to involve him in the group he became difficult. Michael avoided contact with boys or staff, but would compete with the former who were friendly with the adults and attempt to displace them. When excited, Michael had a tendency to stammer and blink his eyes. He was very argumentative and persistent when aroused and, in a childish way, would repeat the same question over and over again. He did good work in school and maintained good, though distant, relations with boys and teachers, but he worked best when alone, requiring only minimal supervision. Michael was active in sports, particularly track, and easily proved himself the fastest runner at the Village—but only when clocked running alone. In competitions, he invariably failed: His pants would fall down; he would trip, or slacken his pace on the last lap, and then berate himself for the "accidents." He usually concluded that he was "not good enough to win, anyhow."

TREATMENT CONSIDERATIONS

The confused clinical picture Michael presented and the resulting variation in diagnostic conclusions can be attributed to the contrast in his basic structure and observable behavior. If Michael were schizophrenic, it would not be the result of constitutional inadequacy, but rather of the condition of his life; that is, it would not be *true* but rather *induced* schizophrenia. The inconsistencies with which his life was replete, his conflicting feelings of dependency and rage toward his mother, the confused relations among the members of his family, and the absence of a consistent male-identification object—all served to confuse him. This confusion was beyond his childish mind either to comprehend or to make any sense of, so that he had to resort for his security to denial. This, coupled with the understandable weak ego, resulted in a psychogenic schizophrenic-like defensive system which was not in conformity with his organic structure.

A major part of this system was occupied with his defense against his incestuous strivings toward his mother—witness Michael's fantasy that by his exploration of the mother's promiscuity, the psychiatrist accused him of having "unnatural relations" with the mother; and his denial of her having relations with any man by wishing to believe that a stork brought his siblings. He burst into tears when these beliefs were assailed by the psychiatrist. Confirmation for this hypothesis is to be found in his stealing as a means of showing his mother that he was "good at something" and in his need to fail in athletics, where he could easily have succeeded, for to succeed would constitute success also in his deeply repressed strivings, which were unacceptable to his superego. The fear of success, coupled with his understandably poor self-image derived from his family relations and his basically feminine identifications, robbed him of a secure identity, and alienated him from himself.

The sum total of the various noxious influences that operated in this boy's life have resulted in massive immaturity and characteristic timidity, so that he was enabled to commit his antisocial acts only in the company of one or more other boys, in the role of follower. Michael was not a "loner." He was dependent on others, which indicated a need and a capacity for relatedness, a favorable precondition for psychotherapy, even though he tended to be somewhat isolative in the cottage. His insistence on restoring weekly interviews with the female caseworker was not motivated by a desire for treatment but by a need for a dependent relationship.

The therapy for this boy would have to be directed toward changing his self-image, establishing a favorable identity, relieving some of his guilt feelings, and improving his capacity for reality testing so that denial would not need to be his operational life pattern. To the extent that these aims could be achieved, his self-defeating alienative trends would decrease. All this could be achieved in group treatment; however, because of the weakness of his ego, care would have to be taken not to overload, and in his case possibly overwhelm, his ego and cause a psychic break.

The incest motif, which is universal among men, was somewhat stronger in this patient than ordinarily among boys of his age because there was no father figure to defend him against Oedipal strivings at critical periods in his development and, therefore, he had inadequate repressions. However, in this situation the mother was not seductive, as is frequently found among delinquent boys. The mother's detachment prevented serious overstimulation, and this could make repression, though delayed, possible if the ego were strengthened and the boy's capacity for other object relations improved.

Macy

Background Material

PRESENTING PROBLEM

Macy, a friendly, well-built, white, Protestant boy of Czech parentage, aged 14.9 years, was committed to the Village as an incorrigible child by a children's court on a petition of the mother. Placement had been recommended by the family agency caseworker, who had worked with him for fourteen months prior to commitment. The mother complained about his mood swings; when agitated, he would shout and use abusive language. He was constantly touching, hitting, or pinching someone. He stayed out at night until twelve or one o'clock. At other times he would be "sweet," willing to accept responsibility and good to his father and mother. In a fight two years before his commitment, Macy suffered a badly fractured nose, and his speech was indistinct as a result. Eight months prior to commitment, he was suspended from school because of his "provocativeness and defiance." It was noted, however, that Macy had adjusted well at summer camp. The caseworker described Macy as "extremely immature, unable to separate himself from his disturbed environment or face responsibility for the difficulties which he had been causing." Intense sibling rivalry with his younger sister was also reported; he frequently talked about it to his caseworker.

Macy slouched as he walked, with a stooped posture and bowed head, and he looked furtively when he talked to adults. He had somewhat flattened facies with eyes held open wide, mouth drooping, and a broad, flattened nose. Along with his passivity and slowness in response, his appearance contributed to an impression of intellectual dullness. This was not actually the case, however.

FAMILY BACKGROUND

Macy was the sixth of seven children—three boys and four girls. Three of the siblings were married. His father, a small man of Czech background, was fifteen years the mother's senior. Because of a serious ailment he no longer worked, but stayed at home. Macy's difficulties became more pronounced when he was thirteen years old. It was claimed that at that time his former good relationship with his father changed to one of bitter hostility. The father was described as strict, rigid, rather irrational, generally angry, and weak; he beat the boy severely. The father's own dependency needs rendered him unable to exercise leadership or restraining authority in his family. He was isolated and felt outside the family circle. (The father died about six months before Macy was discharged from the Village about two years later.)

The mother, a tall, heavy woman, had had several "nervous breakdowns." She was unable to remain in the house for any length of time and was afraid of being alone. She appeared "highly narcissistic and immature with hysterical traits." It was suggested that she might be psychotic. She engulfed her children, not letting them separate from herself. Ambivalent and inconsistent in her feelings toward them, she either overindulged or rejected them, especially when they "misbehaved." All her children seemed to have poor judgment regarding acceptable limits to behavior.

Her own sexual confusion was reflected in a strong and compelling relationship she had for many years with another woman, which actually served to physically separate her from her family and her husband. She used her "illnesses" to dominate the family; for example, if someone rebelled or took an independent stand against her, she would get "sick," or warn of an impending attack, or complain about previous ones, thus making the children feel responsible for her illness.

Macy's eldest sister, twelve years his senior, was married and living outside the home. Macy spent much time in her home, and she was said to have carried much of the responsibility for him.

The family had a long history of conflict with the authorities. Macy's older brother, four years his senior, had been charged with disorderly conduct three years earlier. Following a probation department investigation, he was adjudged a youthful offender; sentence was suspended. The court investigation revealed that the children lacked supervision and the relationships in the home were "poor." Several years prior to this event, a neighbor filed a complaint with the city agency concerned with the protection of children to the effect that the children in Macy's family were not adequately supervised and were neglected. An investigation was made but no action taken.

Another sister, three years older than Macy, was brought to court, by the mother, about a year-and-a-half earlier, on a petition that the girl was a "juvenile delinquent, ungovernable, and failed to obey the lawful and reasonable demands of her parents." She was an habitual truant from school, and on one occasion absconded from home. Shortly after filing the petition, the mother requested that it be withdrawn, and the case was "closed." The official reports indicate that this girl was "probably retarded": She could neither read nor write, and was "not mentally aware of situations" around her. Another brother, five years younger than Macy, was said to be a preferred child. Until the social agency intervened, Macy shared the bed with this brother, who was enuretic. The parents' marriage had been unsatisfactory for many years. The father and mother quarreled and shouted at one another, involving all the children in their conflicts.

Macy's early development was relatively normal. Abrupt weaning from the breast at five months of age brought on strong reactions for two to three days, after which the child accepted the bottle. The bottle too was withdrawn abruptly at fifteen months. Macy, like all his siblings, had temper tantrums for many years. However, while the others stopped having these tantrums about the age of six, Macy's outbursts grew more severe until the age of nine years.

CLINICAL FINDINGS

In psychological tests given in his native city two months prior to admission to the Village, Macy achieved a "minimal" IQ of 88, with indications that he was capable of functioning at least on an average level. There were indications of serious conflict with, and ambivalent feelings toward, the father. Guilt and expectations of punishment were also revealed. Macy was described as an "immature adolescent with little overt anxiety, who acted out his conflicts." The psychiatrist who examined Macy at the time also found him "immature, defensive, and unstable." Diagnosis: passive-aggressive personality.

In the tests administered shortly after admission to the Village the psychologist noted that: "The focus of this boy's problem is the father, of whom Macy is terribly frightened." Despite the fact that the father was viewed as an inadequate object of identification, he was so frightening to the boy that as a result he came to feel sexually inadequate and did not differentiate on the psychological tests between girls and boys. He related to women more easily than to men.

In the psychiatric interview held about the same time, he was diagnosed as having a "personality-trait disturbance, passive-aggressive type, with dependent features and neurotic conflicts in relation to a disturbed parent-child relationship." The psychiatrist stated that "there have been too many older sisters who have attempted to mother and control him, which he has resented. In addition, his place as a younger son was usurped by a brother who was born shortly after Macy. There are also evidences of guilt and remorse, and a concept of himself as bad." The psychiatrist also stated that Macy "attempts to utilize denial as to his part in his difficulties, but does not use this defense adequately and the depressive effect of it is quite prominent. . . . He seems to have some fears about controlling his aggressive impulses . . . should the situation [at the Village] duplicate the situation from which he came."

At the time of initiation of group therapy (at 15.2 years, approximately six months after placement), Macy was retested by another psychologist, who found that in Macy, "the amount of health, as evidenced in the test material, definitely outweighs the pathology" and that "his positive resources are not being utilized to advantage." His "primary asset is an awareness and sensitivity to social demands. His inclination is to be compliant, ingratiating, self-contained, and passive. However, he could not tolerate these promptings and, instead, denied and reversed his behavior; that is, he became aggressive and belligerent. He feels strongly the need to assert himself, but does not know how." All of the projective material pointed to a struggle with the problem of adjustment to environment behind a façade of bravado and indifference, and an undifferentiated perception of the masculine role, which was considered as the focus of his disturbance. The test revealed that Macy's "self-image remains nebulous. His doubts about his identification are accompanied by confusion, dysphoria, strong feelings of inadequacy and helplessness against which he reacts by overaggressive and destructive behavior. . . . the maternal figure is perceived as quite disturbing, rejecting, and punitive and he experiences his oral demands as dirty, excessive, and shameful. . . . vigor and activity are associated with female figures. . . . socially acceptable behavior [is] essentially feminine. . . . His ego-alien oral demandingness is projected [on others], leading to the unconscious notion that others are as parasitic and destructive as he is, thus justifying . . . his acting out." In view of the fact that Macy's ego defenses were so ego-syntonic, the diagnosis suggested was "character disorder." Macy achieved a score of 93 in the psychometric test.

The psychiatric interview held at the same time noted a great deal of hostility toward the mother. It was felt, however, that all that Macy was conscious of was his extreme dependence upon her, and that his single and main purpose in life, at that point, was to return to his mother and home. Macy did not recognize himself as having any problems and the examiner did not consider him a suitable subject for psychotherapy. The boy said that he had nothing to say to the social worker and that what she said to him did not have much significance. He minimized the difficulties at home. His overriding desire was to return home to his mother. Diagnosis remained the same.

Macy was seen on a regular weekly basis in casework treatment prior to entry into group therapy. The caseworker stated that Macy consistently utilized projection and denial in dealing with his underlying feelings of inadequacy. He was, however, able to verbalize that he felt rejected by his parents, talked of his hostility toward his father, and discussed his sudden outbursts and his physical abuse of people.

SOCIAL ADJUSTMENT

For the first few months the cottage father reported that Macy had frequent crying spells, and was homesick. He needed a good deal of attention from the cottage staff to help him over this trying period, after which he seemed to get along well with the staff and his peers, and functioned well in most areas. The child-care supervisor reported that Macy had "some ability to relate to the cottage parents and seemed to be identifying with them quite a bit. He was a little closer to the cottage mother than to the cottage father. He has never been a problem and always goes along quietly with what is required of him and accepted limits." Macy was inclined to tease other boys. On one occasion, he took the crutches away from a boy who had an injured leg and ran off with them. In general he was a follower and would become, on occasion, involved in some others' misdeeds. Macy was a verbal boy, not particularly interested in athletics. He was a "kibitzer" around the cottage. Macy impressed the supervisor as being an essentially passive youngster who was concerned about the approval of him by the cottage parents. The cottage parents reported that, when he returned from a Christmas holiday home visit, he looked "very sad." After a talk with the cottage father he recovered his composure and seemed happy.

The teacher described Macy as bright and a good student. While younger than some of the other boys, he invested a great deal of effort and showed a lot of interest, and succeeded in doing well. He got along with fellow students, and "though not afraid to use his hands, he is not aggressive." Toward the teacher (who was a firm, but very friendly, person) Macy displayed no hesitation in asking questions about the schoolwork or even about the teacher's personal life. Macy often looked tired, as if he had not had enough sleep and often was observed day-dreaming.

TREATMENT CONSIDERATIONS

In a real sense this boy defied definition in a strictly clinical diagnosis beyond the fact that he had a serious character disorder. The diagnosis of "passive-aggressive" personality suggested did not strictly apply here, for, judging by his behavior, he was far from being passive. Neither could he be said to be neurotic, psychopathic, or psychotic. If one were constrained to formulate a diagnosis, the closest formulation would be extremely infantile character. His attachment to his mother, the very strong sibling rivalry with a five years' younger brother, his playful teasing of people and touching them, the infantile conceptions of his role in reality, as in school, his compliance to and discomfort with adults, his crying spells—all produced the impression of extreme immaturity and appealing childishness to which the childless cottage mother responded by making him her favorite. This relationship (with the cottage mother) extended his infancy and, as we shall see later, also served as a maturing influence in this boy's life.

Therapy for Macy had to be directed toward personality maturation through identification with a mature, self-controlled, strong adult and boys more mature than himself; by confronting him with tasks and situations that would mobilize and extend his ego forces; helping him discover interests and direct them toward achievement, thus improving his self-image and self-awareness; and by altering his role of infantile submissiveness to assertiveness and equalitarian relatedness.

This boy could best be reached by a corrective milieu in which a therapy group could play an appropriate part.

Note: Macy joined the group at its twelfth session.

Richard

Background Material

PRESENTING PROBLEM

Richard, a tall, white, Catholic boy, aged 13.3 years, was committed to Children's Village on recommendation by a psychiatrist at a general hospital. He had been sent to the hospital for observation a year earlier because of extremely disturbing behavior at school and frequent running away from home. Richard had a younger sister and a baby brother. He complained of severe headaches, which were said to be related to pressure from a plate in his skull reportedly placed there after he sustained a fracture at the age of four and a half years.[4] Whereas Richard had been receiving report cards with high marks before, at the time of referral to the Village he was doing poorly in his schoolwork, was disruptive and uncooperative in the classroom, and would walk out of the room and wander around in the halls. He stole other boys' lunches, lied, and frequently truanted. At the time of his admission to the Village, he was repeating the seventh grade.

FAMILY BACKGROUND

Richard's mother was the eldest of seven siblings, all girls. She was deeply tied to her mother and moved her family so as to be near her, though the move was greatly disadvantageous both financially and in terms of living space. The psychiatrist at the hospital described Richard's mother as "a woman oriented to a world of women who viewed men as usurpers, from whom she must expect mistreatment. Her masochistic needs are satisfied in her marital relationship, and the accompanying anger she feels at her inability to leave an alcoholic husband is displaced on her son. Anticipating like behavior from him, as a male, she rejected him. She considers both her husband and Richard as 'completely unmanageable.' Her comment was, 'I can't do anything with him.' She claimed that her husband beat her when he drank."

The mother repeatedly compared Richard adversely with his sister. Often, in the presence of the children she would say, "if only he could be like her [her daughter]." Richard was afraid of his mother, and frequently allied himself with his father against her. Thus, the family was divided into two camps: father and son versus mother and the girl. Richard's sister terrorized him, particularly since she was well aware that "telling mama" would result in his being punished. She was permitted to take his things, even abuse them, and where she was concerned he was not allowed to defend himself or protect his belongings.

It was not clear how this arose, but the fiction of Richard's having a steel plate (which was not dispelled until hospitalization many years later) was used by the mother as justification for her overprotection of the boy and, especially, for restricting his activities. This attitude was viewed clinically as a reaction formation to her hostility toward him. In an interview at the Village with both parents, she proved to be the dominant person, displaying severe anger toward Richard.

Richard's father, an alcoholic, worked nights as a utility man and

4. Repeated medical examinations later proved that no such plate was present in Richard's head.

delivered bread to stores during part of the day. It was noted by the hospital staff that father and son had almost a peer relationship. When Richard was small, the father was either at work or sleeping when the boy wished to play with him. But when he was only twelve years old, the father would take Richard to neighborhood bars, bragging that his boy could "drink as much beer and liquor as any man." He taught Richard tricks for avoiding paying for drinks, which he himself employed. The father enjoyed taking Richard for car rides, and when they got on a highway would drive 80 miles an hour in a 45-mile zone. When Richard became frightened or grew anxious, the father would ridicule him for being "yellow." When Richard was somewhat older, and contrary to the vehicle laws, the father made the boy take the wheel and encouraged him to drive at high speeds. This practice also continued while Richard visited his home on week ends from the Village.

Richard's early development was reportedly normal. When he was four and a half years old, however, he fell 35 feet from a rooftop and was hospitalized for a year. Electroencephalograms and neurological examinations over the years revealed no resulting abnormalities. Upon his return from the hospital the mother found him uncontrollable. He became very aggressive toward his sister. The mother had to resort to many restrictions on his normal activities, she said, because they would "dislodge the [nonexistent] plate." During the intake interview at the Village the mother, who dominated the session, displayed her rage and repeatedly expressed her expectation that Richard would become a "delinquent."

CLINICAL FINDINGS

The report of the clinical study at the hospital described Richard as a boy who had suffered "severe maternal rejection." On his runaways he frequently went to his maternal grandmother, and on one occasion he ran up a rooftop and threatened to jump off. He presented a severe management problem in the psychiatric ward. He used obscene language, and a pocketknife was found on him, which he knew was against regulations. He was very impulsive and grew extremely irritated when he had to wait for anything; he was abusive toward other patients, particularly one younger girl. He was "overactive, aggressive, and negativistic in the presence of other children." The diagnosis was "adjustment reaction of adolescence." The tests revealed no organicity. It was also noted that Richard had little capacity for relationships. The full-scale IQ was 111 (verbal 100; performance 121). The psychologist stated, "The behavior and reality orientation is such that his judgment is definitely impaired by his impulsive tendencies." However, the projective material was not suggestive of an acting-out person. The summary of the Rorschach test noted: ". . . Acting-out behavior is more a response to specific threatening situations rather than a generalized mode of response. His basic orientation seems to be of a passive, feminine nature with a good deal of ambivalence about accepting the sexual role of the male, an intense castration anxiety having its origin in an unresolved Oedipal conflict." The mother was perceived as "threatening, rejecting, and non-nurturing."

At the initial psychiatric intake interview at the Village, Richard gave the impression of being "stupid, dull, and inarticulate," despite the evidence of high average intelligence in the tests. The psychiatrist stated in part: "The boy is suffering from unusually severe apprehensiveness and anxiety that something bad is going to happen whenever he enters something new or when he is learning." The psychiatrist noted that Richard could not identify his major problem, namely his mother's rejection of him. The boy would prefer to take the assigned position of an inferior, defective cripple, retaining the hold she has over him, that is, one of disapproval, rejection, and hatred. His apprehensiveness was more of an infantile, free-floating tension of a child whose feelings are constantly being made uncomfortable, without the mental content usually ascribed to the verbal or neurotic levels of development." Diagnosis: personality-trait disturbance.

An examination by another psychiatrist a month after placement pointed out the "tough quality of Richard's voice." This psychiatrist found no evidence of discomfort, anxiety, or depression, nor any hostility directed toward the examiner. The boy tended to minimize personal difficulties and expressed feelings of warmth and closeness to his father. There were unconscious sexual overtones in his discussion of his mother. It was speculated that the boy missed his father, who worked during the night and slept much of the day. Richard freely admitted difficulties in getting along with his younger sister and revealed fear of his aggressive impulses, of losing control and hurting her. The boy had "many strengths and a fairly well-integrated personality." Diagnosis: neurotic trait disturbance in which neurotic elements were most prominent.

A psychological test administered at this time described Richard as a remarkably hostile, destructive youngster who was trying desperately to control impulsive acting out. "He is fearful of anticipated retaliation, be it physical punishment and/or rejection. The sado-masochistic ele-easy ability to move into a female orientation, that is, give up masculine strivings for safety and for the sake of not having to worry about the ment is quickly tied in with the strong latent homosexual problems and control over the destructive impulses." It was noted that Richard needed a quick discharge of energy which often resulted in impairment of his judgment. He was seen on a weekly basis in casework. After the initial period of intense separation anxiety, he seemed to settle down and verbalized well. The caseworker felt he was more available to treatment than most boys.

Prior to the beginning of group therapy, eight months after his arrival at the Village, Richard was again seen by the psychologist. He achieved a full-scale IQ of 115 (verbal 104; performance 124). "Intellectual constriction appeared to be related to fears of rejection and fears of frustration. The overprotective attitude of the maternal figure has enhanced dependency needs. Richard attempts to ward off frustrations by maintaining an attitude of withdrawal, which engenders in him considerable hostility and resentment. While the hostility remains internalized, his fear of it creates much anxiety, leading to somatization and conversion symptoms, a defensive pattern that provides him considerable relief and satisfaction. Richard is aware of secondary gains and it is likely that he would exploit any real ailment he might have. Sexual impulses are quickly inhibited and arouse much guilt and depression. His blockings are related to his attachment to his mother. His fairly accurate conception of sexual intercourse is an attempt at mastering his anxiety. Considering the main conflict areas, defensive pattern, and the presence of anxiety, the neurotic aspects prevail."

The psychiatric interview held at the same time (before assignment to group therapy) again noted that clinically the boy manifested many ego strengths and no evidence of hostility. "Part of the boy's satisfactory adjustment to his peers has been related to his compliance and in his tendency to avoid fighting. He shows fear of his aggressive impulses, of being hurt as well as hurting. His compensatory move to identify with a weak father by wishing to become a delivery man is also a strategy in relation to his mother, in an attempt to appease her and satisfy her so she will no longer be hostile or rejecting toward him." Diagnosis: neurotic trait disturbance with passive-aggressive and passive dependent features.

SOCIAL ADJUSTMENT

At the Village, prior to entry into group therapy, Richard was described as "an average youngster, perhaps a bit dull and slow and easily influenced by other boys," and easily led into disturbing behavior by them. His meager associations were limited to the more delinquent, acting-out cottage mates. The cottage father described Richard as a "nervous talker who always went beyond the subject discussed and drifted from one thing to another. He rode sick call to avoid chores." Richard was described as a very frightened child with little self-confidence. The cottage father had to assist him to learn how to play ball.

At the point of entering the group, Richard's reading was at the 8.3 level, arithmetic at 7.5, social studies at 6.0, and science at 9.2.

The teachers reported Richard to be a rapid learner but also a "quick forgetter." They felt he "needed to be able to assert himself more and to stand on his own feet." Richard was accepted by his peers at school, but was considered a weak boy. He required close supervision in shop work. In his academic class, he was found to be "a very impulsive boy unable to contain himself when he knew an answer to a question and talked out of turn, not allowing other boys who were called upon to answer."

TREATMENT CONSIDERATIONS

On the surface, Richard appeared to have a rather serious behavior disorder; indeed, so difficult was his conduct that observation in the psychiatric ward of a hospital was made necessary. However, his deviant behavior was an outcome of both character and neurotic sources. On the side of character we had here a boy with a weak ego organization due to *1]* identification with a weak, delinquent, and overindulgent father who depended on the boy for support against an irrational, domineering mother; *2]* the anxiety over the violent quarrels and frequent physical fights between his parents; *3]* his guilts for allying himself with the father against the mother; and *4]* the unfavorable comparisons the mother made between himself and his sister.

These life situations had engendered an adaptive need for preventing attack upon himself, or to keep it to a minimum, and this he attempted to achieve by placation and ingratiation and a denial of normal aggressiveness for a boy, which prevented the emergence of a self-identity and caused self-alienation. Moreover, the adjustment necessitated inhibitions and frustrations, behind which the normal aggressive needs accumulated, breaking through the ego controls in impulsive, disguised hostile reactions. These served to discharge tensions, as well as to bring on a self-awareness, which mechanistically is akin to a self-identity.

On the side of neurosis, his identification with his sister (desire to be like his sister) had stamped his personality and set him apart from the norm in boys of his own age, and his self-image was a defective one, which added further to the quantum of his anxieties. His sexual orientation was confused, for this boy had not lived through the normal Oedipal period and had not related to his parents as a couple. He felt about them as two distinct, unrelated individuals, and the father's treatment of, and his relation to, the boy generated considerable homosexual anxiety.

The boy's acting out at school and, later, in the hospital ward was part of his impulse uncontrollability. It served to establish a (temporary) homeostasis by discharging the tensions that were being built up in him. This conduct also served as a retaliatory measure against his mother and gave him an identity. The conversion symptoms amounted to a true neurotic mechanism of introjecting his anger as well as a means to compel the mother to give him his due of attention.

Treatment for Richard would require at first a completely uninhibited discharge of anxieties through suitable motoric and lingual channels, a change in his self-image, corrective identifications with an adult as a father substitute, and a masculine milieu in which he could feel uninhibited and unafraid to function in a male role. At the same time he would need to verbalize freely his suppressed anger against his parents and sister, recognize and accept the reality of his life setting, and learn to deal with it more adequately so that the members of his family group would react to his maturity more suitably. The ultimate outcome of these various intrapsychic changes, the dissolution of his deep-seated dependencies, and his, hopefully, altered family relations, would be a wholesome self-identity and self-alliance to take the place of his current self-alienation.

Protocols and Comments: Sessions 1–15

UNLIKE OUR FIRST TWO "ANALYTIC" (OBSERVATION) GROUPS, the group (C) whose sessions are recorded here did not consist of patients rigidly selected to accord with any specific criteria. These boys represented a fair sampling or cross section of the population at the school. We were unable to recognize serious psychoneuroses in any of the boys. The selection was made from a small number of candidates, with few rejections. In this regard as well this group differed from the others, for in the previous groups approximately one out of four were found suitable, while in this instance three out of four were included. Boys with intellectual deficiencies and those doing well in their relationships with caseworkers were not accepted. We rather concentrated on youngsters who for a variety of reasons were resistive to any psychotherapeutic approach or were otherwise unable to establish a relation with an adult.

All but one of the boys had at least a nodding acquaintance with the group therapist, and a number of them knew him through at least one interview on admission to the school, for he had been for some years the "intake supervisor" of the institution. In this capacity he was required to see the boys and their parents once prior to commitment. This encounter usually was a brief one, and in the case of the boys in question took place at least a year before the initiation of the group. It can therefore be assumed that the memory of that encounter was blurred in the boys' minds, and attitudes, if there had been any, had vanished. Nonetheless, note must be taken of the fact that however slight their memories of him, their initial responses to the group must have been in some respects different from what they would have been in the absence of even this brief contact. This fact is made apparent in the very first session.

The protocol of each session is followed by a very brief comment to point up some salient features of the interview in terms of the movement of the group only. Limitation of space did not permit interpretations of an individual boy's productions. Progress of the boys is summarized in periodic reports interspersed in the records, however.

The group met at 7 P.M., soon after supper and the cottage chores following it. Meals were served at the cottages and the residents were responsible for tidying up and washing dishes. This gave rise on many occasions to friction and resentment both among the boys and with the adults in charge—a husband and wife known as "cottage parents," who were present five days a week, and a single male "relief cottage father" on the other two days.

In preparation for the first session, the therapist and the present writer, who acted as supervisor, had discussed possibilities for initiating the group interview. Three possibilities were arrived at: *1]* to ask the boys what they would like to talk about;   *2]* to explain the process of psychotherapy as being free association and catharsis that would lead to their understanding of their difficulties and how to correct them; and *3]* to face them directly with the fact that they were placed in the Children's Village because of their behavior and the difficulties they had created for themselves and others. It was suggested to the therapist that he employ the one of the three approaches with which he would feel most comfortable. In view of the realism contained in the last plan and the fact that the boys were aware of the therapist's having information about them, the third was adopted as the most suitable procedure.

Session One

Jules was first to arrive. He came fifteen minutes ahead of the set time and found the therapist in the lobby of the cottage in which the group was scheduled to meet. He greeted the therapist and remarked about having to wait for the other group members. He then inquired whether it was all right for him to smoke. The therapist stated that it was quite all right if he so desired. A few minutes later he inquired whether he could go to the bathroom. The therapist was still in the lobby when the others arrived, five minutes ahead of the scheduled time. Donald, who headed the procession, was unknown to the therapist, who introduced himself to the boy and asked his name. This he was given, but Jonathan, who immediately followed Donald, said, "It's O.K. Mr. Ellery, we all know you." However, the therapist did not know Kurt, and therefore introduced himself to the boy. Jameson had not arrived yet.

On seeing the television set in the lobby which was supplied to the staff members residing in the cottage, Donald asked the therapist: "Do you have any objection to my playing it?" "No," replied the latter, and Donald turned it on. Jonathan and Jules joined him at the set.

Meanwhile the therapist entered the adjoining meeting room and at the stroke of seven re-entered the lobby and commented, "Maybe we ought to get started." By now all the boys had arrived. Donald rose and turned off the TV set, and all the boys present trooped into the meeting room and seated themselves at the oblong table. Leonard, the most timid of the boys, sat at the therapist's right. The therapist remarked in his report that though the boys entered the room "in a businesslike manner," there was "an air of solemnity about the procession."

The therapist started the session by saying that the boys probably knew something about the intention of the group, but he would like to tell them something about it so that all would have the same information. They all knew that each of them had been placed at the Children's Village because of difficulties they had had in school, with parents, and in their neighborhoods. He knew that all of them had had unpleasant experiences with people, that perhaps the conditions under which they lived were not "too good" and each had gotten into trouble because something "pushed them into it." "We have found from experience," said the therapist, "that very often feelings accumulate that get in our way and make for more trouble, and our experience has shown that when we talk about these feelings, such as feelings about people and ourselves, it helps." The boys were then told that the group was there for the purpose of helping them in this way, that by talking they could get over some of the feelings that had accumulated in them and which made them do the things they did in the past. In this group they could talk about anything they wished and everybody might discuss it. The boys were then reassured that whatever they talked about "stays right here. In other words, it is going to be held by me in strictest confidence. In the same way you should not talk to anybody about what the other boys say here."

The statement was met by hushed silence. Not a word was uttered by the boys. Jonathan and Donald looked at each other. Jonathan smiled embarrassedly, his face turning red. Kurt, with head on hand, stared at the table. Jules locked his hands over the top of his head and stared blankly at the opposite wall. He kept this pose for quite some time. Michael began to stir as if to say something, but apparently seemed to think better of it and said nothing, though he looked as if he were ready "to spring."

Suddenly Jameson burst into the room. Jameson, a tall boy for his age, appeared to have a chip on his shoulder and explosively announced,

"I don't want to stay here!" No one except the therapist looked in his direction. Jameson looked at the therapist challengingly and again announced that he did not want to stay and nobody could make him. The therapist calmly declared that he did not have to stay, but he might like to sit down and find out "what this is all about." In a very gruff voice, Jameson declared: "Nothing doing." The therapist again quietly commented that, if he would like to stay, "on our part we would like to have" him. Jameson again refused and asked, "Can I leave?" Therapist: "That's up to you, Jameson." He again indicated that Jameson didn't have to stay, but the Club Department had thought that he might like to join the group; Jameson interrupted: "You mean I don't have to stay?" "No, you don't," said the therapist. Thereupon the boy walked out. (After the session the "Custodial Department" was informed of the boy's absence so that his whereabouts could be accounted for.)

With Jameson's departure the silence continued. The boys still said nothing. Each remained in his position unchanged. Donald started to rise from his seat, but immediately sat down again. The silence persisted. Sensing the boys' discomfort, the therapist asked whether anyone would like to begin, even to complain about something.

Donald, looking down at the table, said: "If I'm going to discuss my problems I'm going to talk it over only with my social worker. My problems are my personal business. I'm not going to talk in front of these other boys." Stark silence again ensued, but Michael, Jonathan, and Richard looked in the direction of the therapist as if to see how he was going to react to this challenge. Then Richard said: "I feel the same way, too." Again silence. After a few minutes the therapist asked: "How do you other boys feel about this?" Michael immediately responded to this with the question: "Do you keep notes?" The therapist told him: "I do keep notes, because I want to remember the things we talk about, but they are only for my own use." Michael: "You mean you're not going to tell my social worker about me?" Therapist: "As I told you already, what we talk about here is confidential, and I will not be telling it to the social workers." Michael: "Man, that ain't going to help me any. All I want to do is get home. What's the point of me talking my problems out here if I do the same thing with my social worker? How is she going to know when I got my problems worked out?" Richard again affirmed, "I agree," and said nothing more.

Michael continued to the effect that he wanted to know whether if he talked his problems out "here" he would be able to get home sooner. Jonathan immediately picked this up. "Yeah, if we talk our problems out here does that mean you can get us home sooner?" Michael wanted a very specific answer to the question: "Do you have power to get me home sooner by talking to my supervisor?" The therapist specifically declared: "I do not have anything to do with anybody's going home. I have no power to decide when any boy here should go home." Michael then quickly interposed, "But if we work out our problems, does that mean we can go home?" Donald took the initiative at this point, declaring that he had been talking to his social worker until he was "blue in the face" but that had not gotten him home. His social worker kept telling him that "when I work out my problems I get home. But I don't get home! I don't know when I'm going to work out my problems."

Richard picked this up and said, "When I go see my social worker, as soon as I start to talk about my problems, he starts to talk about something else." He illustrated this by an example, as when he went to tell his social worker that he wanted to go home; his social worker suddenly asked him: "How do you get along with your mother?" Donald: "You know the same thing happens to me. As soon as I tell my social worker it's time to go home he keeps saying 'Do you really feel ready to go?' I try to tell him I'm ready, but he really isn't interested in the answer." Jonathan spoke up. "I got something of the same problem. I go to my social worker to get help for myself. I know I got problems and I tell my social worker I got problems; but she is not interested in my problems. For instance, she keeps telling me that I'm at Children's Village because my brother has a bad influence on me. When I try to tell her this isn't so, she says to me: 'Your mother overprotects you.'" Looking at Donald for confirmation, he said: "But this is stupid. I'm at the Village because I'm the one who got into trouble. I have the problems. My mother isn't at the Village."

Now Richard spoke up: "I know guys that go to Industry [a state correctional school]. They stay there six months. I come to the Village, which is supposed to be a better place, and they keep me here a long time." He then went into a long harangue about how his social worker had contacted the B——— agency that had sent him here but the agency kept putting his social worker off.

Donald said: "Yeah, I don't need my social worker to tell me why I'm at the Village. I know why I'm at the Village. I was a little wise kid. I used to give my mother a hard time. I used to stay out late and I always thought that because I was a little kid they couldn't do nothing to you. Before I knew it, I was in front of the judge and he sent me here. Okay, I'm not blaming the judge, but it's time I got out of here." Leonard, Jules, and Kurt said nothing during this lengthy exchange.

The boys continued along these lines for a considerable time, Richard becoming more active. He described one incident after another in which his social worker kept putting him off. Once when Richard told his social worker about a fight at his cottage, his social worker insisted on asking him how he got along with his mother. Soon a period of silence set in, the boys turning their eyes upon the therapist, with the exception of Jules, who kept staring into the distance with his hands still locked over his head. The therapist asked why this misunderstanding? Several of the group members who spoke up complained that their social workers "do not trust" them. Donald said: "I asked my social worker to let me go home for three months. I want to prove that I can get along all right. He won't let me." Jonathan: "I ran away because my social worker don't listen. All I want to do is show people that I'm not the same kid that came here, but they don't listen to me." Richard said: "If I go home, I wouldn't run around with the same kids I got in trouble with the last time, but my social worker doesn't believe me." He then described how his social worker set a date for his discharge, only to forget about it the next time Richard saw him. Donald added: "Yeah, my social worker gave me three different dates and I'm still not home. My social worker tells me that if I get home I'm going to get right into trouble again." Michael: "Yeah, I know my problem. I don't have to talk about it. All I want to do is to get out and go straight. I'll bet my social worker any amount of money I can go straight, but I don't know how to tell him that I'm going to go straight. He keeps saying it's not going to be so." There was now an aggrieved expression on every face. Even Jules, who had been staring impassively, now began to show resentment. Leonard drummed with his fingers on the table and said, "Yeah, this is the same old story; it always happens."

The therapist asked the group as a whole: "Do you feel that you are not trusted?" Jonathan seemed to brush a nonexistent speck on the table away and said in a very low voice, almost as if he were talking to himself: "I don't know if that's it." Donald turned to him and asked: "Do you know what else it might be?" In response, Jonathan merely shrugged his shoulders. Michael addressed the therapist: "Maybe you can get me out of here by telling my social worker that I come to the group and I discuss my problems"; he was quickly interrupted in this by Jonathan, who said "A guy always gets blamed in this place," and then described how he had been accused by a supervisor of having given a cottage parent a nervous breakdown.

All the boys focused their eyes on Jonathan. He now became the center of attention as he described how once, when he was in the shower singing, he was told by his cottage father to stop. When he continued, the cottage father beat him as he was naked in the shower with soap in his eyes. He could not defend himself. He made a move to hit the cottage father, however, but checked himself. There was a big scene of which Jonathan gave only sketchy details. Soon the cottage father was no longer working there. It was after this incident that the supervisor had told Jonathan that he had given the cottage father a "nervous breakdown." Leonard stepped in at this point, saying: "Yes, that always happens around here. One night a boy next to me was sleeping quietly and the boy next to him was fooling around. The cottage parents [he did not differentiate] ran up and began to hit the first boy that was handy; it was not the boy that was fooling around."

Richard seemed to sum it up for the group as he said, "They're too free with their hands; they hit you even before you get a chance to explain." Leonard leaned over toward the therapist and said: "That's just what happens," and as if in confidence: "You don't get a chance to tell your story." Following this, numerous incidents of injustice were recounted, with Jonathan taking the lead. He kept referring to one incident after another where he was the one to always get blamed instead of somebody else. The therapist commented that getting blamed all the time could surely leave one with "a load to carry." Jonathan: "You're not kidding. I don't care if they hit me if I really do something wrong, but I'm not going to get hit when I don't do anything."

At this point, Donald began to play with a wire coil that happened to be in the ash tray on the table. He watched the therapist for a reaction as he pulled the coil out. Jonathan looked at what Donald had done and he, too, looked at the therapist. There was an expression of expectancy on both boys' faces, as though they looked forward to a reaction. When nothing happened, Donald placed the wire back in the ash tray. Following this he got up, stood by his chair looking at the therapist, and after a moment of hesitation asked: "Is it O.K. to take a drink?" Therapist: "Sure, Donald." The boy went over to the sink in the room and took a drink.

Jonathan now launched into a complaint that he never got any mail, that his mail was read and kept from him. Once his mother had written that his aunt had died and that she wanted him to come home. By the time the letter was turned over to him, the aunt was already buried. Richard picked this up and said that something like that had happened to him, too. "My mother was supposed to come up one week end, but there was something wrong with her fingers, they swelled up. Nobody bothered to tell me. Later I learned that my mother was in the hospital." He then added, "By the time a story gets to you, almost anything can happen." Michael: "Well, how do you think I feel? I live in B——— [a distant city]. I can only go home once in a while. How do you think I feel not having any visitors?" Jonathan: "I live in R——— and I don't have any visitors either and I sure miss seeing my family." Jonathan concluded this by saying: "The Village should try to see to it that every boy gets home more often to see his family. How can he get help if he doesn't see his family?" He said he tried to talk to his social worker, but his social worker told him that those were the rules. He then launched into a vituperative attack on the cottage father (whom he had been accused of giving a nervous breakdown), saying, "This guy was a dirty rat, he always made up rules." When Jonathan asked him, "Why the rules?" he would say, "The rules come from on top and we got to follow them." Jonathan didn't mind rules, he said, but "I do mind those kind of rules." Michael: "Maybe we ought to have some say about the things that happen."

After another period of silence the therapist commented that from what the boys were saying it seemed that one of the things they didn't like was the fact that they found it hard to have their say, to give their side of the story. Richard immediately picked it up and said, "Yeah, that's about it." Leonard, again leaning over confidentially, said, "It always happens." Donald was activated by this to say, "My social worker tells me that I don't know enough," and added: "But I've learned a lot at the Village. When I came here I couldn't read, and boy, I can read now!" Jonathan: "I used to be bad in math but I'm learning something in math." Richard: "I know more math now than when I came here. Here they have small classes. When I went to school at home I used to be with forty boys and those forty boys weren't going to wait for me to catch up."

Michael picked this up and started a diatribe about the academic school at the Village, namely, that the teachers weren't interested, and this immediately turned the tide from whatever positive assertions the boys had begun to voice. Michael, for example, said that the teachers didn't teach; they were only interested in themselves. Richard said he had a teacher in math who used to stand around telling the boys how to cheat the bookies, and then turned to the therapist, declaring: "Imagine teaching us at the Village how to cheat bookies! I didn't come here for this." Donald now changed his orientation. He, too, was negative. "There's too much math. They concentrate too much on it and the math they teach isn't good enough. All they teach is 9 and 6 makes 15." He learned that years ago. The therapist refrained from pointing up the boys' ambivalences, their movement from negative to positive and now back again to negative, reserving this for a future date.

Jonathan suddenly asked what time it was. Showing him his watch, the therapist said it was 8:15. Jonathan asked how long the group would meet. He was told that generally the groups met for as long as necessary, but that "we break up about 8:30." Jonathan: "That's okay." A number of boys began talking all at once. Jonathan put his hand on his forehead as if to rub it and said: "Staying here I get so mixed up. I get so many ideas in my head. Maybe that's why I run away a lot of times." None of the boys picked this up; it got lost in the torrent of verbiage. Michael said, "But I still don't want to be at the Village," and went on to ask whether the therapist was sure he was not going to talk about what the boys revealed in the group. The therapist reiterated that whatever was said would be held in the strictest confidence. Michael responded: "But I know my problem." Jonathan, looking at him with a trace of disgust on his face, said: *"But that ain't the same thing as working your problem out.* That's what we're here for, to work our problems out." Donald backed up Jonathan, saying, "Yeah, you got to work out your problems, not just know them." The therapist affirmed this by saying, "Maybe it is different working out your problems, not just knowing them." Jonathan nodded his head in assent. Donald appeared very annoyed with Michael.

At 8:30 the therapist said it was time to quit, and the boys could continue the next week. Jonathan, looking at Donald, said, "This wasn't too bad." Donald nodded in agreement.

As the therapist was leaving the building, the boys appeared to be waiting for him. Michael asked him: "Will you give us a ride back to the cottages?" The therapist said he did not have his car, it was parked elsewhere. Michael said: "If you ever want your car fixed for you, you just bring it over to the auto shop. I work there, and I'll fix it for you." This led to a conversation on the walk back about the auto shop and what the boys learned there.

COMMENT

As expected, the boys showed some diffidence in speaking and a distrust toward the therapist and one another in this session. It was also expected that there would be considerable time consumed in this and later sessions with "griping," against the staff and others. The diatribes against caseworkers and cottage parents can be understood in terms of the boys' generalized hostile orientation toward others, but it also stemmed from their dependencies on an oral level. By implications the boys told us that they were not being catered to or protected (fed). This was soon revealed when they transferred the focus of their conversation to their families and their need to see their parents more frequently.

This nostalgic theme will appear from time to time but will vanish as the boys become more self-dependent and more emotionally mature. The first clue to the boys' justifiable and basic need, which we also observed in our previous groups, was the impelling desire "to be trusted," a recurring theme in interviews with delinquent adolescent boys and probably also with adult criminals. However, we need to understand the concept of trust used in this relation as being "accepted" and "having status," that is, not to be treated as small children. In another sense this means that they were striving to be treated as mature persons, which, in our opinion, is the core of treatment in the great majority of delinquents, as we shall see later in this material. We were given a more direct clue to this when Michael said that perhaps the boys should participate in the planning and conduct of the school.

This theme, as well as the urge for maturity and status, was the primary basic principle upon which we focused throughout the life of the group. There were other elements of minor importance that came to the fore in this interview, such as testing whether the therapist is a repressive and inhibiting person as were all other adults. Such testing appeared in many connections but was most blatant at the point where Donald uncoiled the wire, and both he and Jonathan watched the therapist's reaction. Another minor manifestation lay in the ambivalence in the boys' attitude toward school and the institution. It must be noted that in this and other interviews the complaints against the staff were greatly exaggerated, and much that was being said was fantasy. This fact is made clear as the interviews progress; later the boys accept the very same staff members with considerable equanimity, and sometimes even react to them with positive feelings.

Already at this session we noted some evidences of a positive transference emerging toward the therapist as revealed in the walk from the session and Michael's offer to repair the therapist's car.

Session Two

ABSENT: Kurt, Jules, Jameson [1]

The second session was held in the small lounge on the top floor of the cottage that housed the clinic, because repairs were being made at the other location. In this room comfortable lounge chairs had been arranged in a circle around a low coffee table. The boys expressed a unanimous preference for this room as a permanent meeting place. The therapist promised to discuss this as a possibility with the Club Department.

As the boys seated themselves, Michael and Donald began to giggle. They looked at each other in a sort of embarrassed way as they did so. Donald took a lighter from his pocket and handled it. This intensified the giggling on Michael's part. Donald at first sat down in a seat next to the therapist, but within a few minutes moved over to

1. Although the boys were required by the administration to attend assigned activities by the system of "passes," attendance at our groups was made voluntary by us, contrary to regulations.

Michael. Following this brief episode of giggling, silence set in in the group. Jonathan rubbed his bowed head as he stared at the floor. Richard sat looking as if he expected something to happen any moment. Leonard stared at the opposite wall. (Leonard did not utter one word during the entire session.)

As the silence continued, the therapist asked who would like to start "the ball rolling." This remark served to bring on further giggling by Donald and Michael. It seemed as though their behavior was part of a plot to prevent conversation. Soon the giggling subsided and again there was silence. Richard, however, had something of an embarrassed expression on his face. The therapist commented that perhaps the silence meant that the boys were finding it uncomfortable to begin talking. Michael slumped over in his seat and put one leg across the arm of his chair. Soon Richard took the initiative by calling out the therapist's name and in a very serious tone said he wanted to ask him something. He inquired whether it was true what his social worker had said—but then he did not give the content of the statement before he, too, sank into silence. The therapist asked: "What did your social worker say?" Richard then said that his social worker had told him that if he did not talk in the group he would be "kicked out of the group." Donald suddenly came to life and declared, "That's what my social worker told me too." (Donald and Richard had the same worker.) Richard continued by saying that when the aim of the group was explained to him, namely, "getting to know your problems," his caseworker added that "this is the group where you are supposed to talk." If he would not talk his worker would know about it and he would not be allowed to stay in the group.[2]

All the boys now turned their gaze in the direction of the therapist, awaiting his reply. The therapist's reply was definite. He began with the explanation that it can be uncomfortable to talk, especially in the presence of other boys, and *if* (this word was underlined by the tone of his voice) this is what they had been told then he could understand that it must make it even·more uncomfortable for them, not only when they talked but even when they did not talk. He then assured them that, as they were free to talk about anything they wished in this group, by the same token they did not have to talk about anything if they so desired. Michael at once picked it up and asked: "You mean we can talk about anything?" The therapist said yes emphatically. Michael immediately said, "Okay, then get me out of this place!" This negated

2. This may have been a fantasy. However, it is quite probable that this particular caseworker might have made a point of this and may have said it to the boys. The therapist therefore had to refute the statement very emphatically.

what he had been told the previous session, that the therapist was power-less to do so. But Michael pursued by asking, "Did you find any way you can get me out of this place?" He was given essentially the same answer he had received the preceding week, but before the therapist could finish his statement, Michael interrupted to protest: "But I know my problems! I don't want to be here!" The other boys seemed to pay no attention to Michael. In fact, at this point Donald threw him a look of annoyance, but at the same time said: "We all know our problems. We don't have to stay here." Jameson continued in the same vein: "Yeah, my social worker won't let me leave even though I know my problems." Here Michael, under great pressure, as if he were trying to get in ahead of the other boys, reiterated that he was "going to get out of this place" even though his worker did not want to let him go. The therapist, looking at Michael, said: "I'm trying to understand what you mean when you say you know your problems." The boy looked at the thera-pist as if he did not understand the question and repeated: "I know my problems." When the therapist indicated that he wanted "to make sure we are talking the same language," Michael definitively said, "I know all of my problems and I'm ready to go."

The therapist decided to concretize for Michael (and at the same time for the others), and pointing to his head said, "You mean you know it up here, and by saying you know your problems you mean, one: I got this problem; two, I got this problem; three, I got this problem." Michael: "Yeah, that's what I mean." Donald and Richard nodded in agreement. Therapist: "But is this the same as overcoming your prob-lems?" The boys looked puzzled. They seemed not to understand. A concrete illustration was then given them. "Sometimes a guy knows that he does something and maybe sometimes he doesn't want to know it or he doesn't want to do it. But even though he can say in his head, 'I don't want to do it,' something in his feelings pushes him to do it." A wave of understanding passed over Richard's face; he was nodding in assent, but said nothing. After a moment's silence, the therapist con-tinued: "When that happens it's true you know your problems, but you haven't overcome them. Which is more important?" Donald imme-diately responded: "To overcome it, of course." He said this as if it were the most natural thing in the world. The other boys to a man, except Leonard, chorused, "To know it." Richard picked this up and said: "I remember when I used to go into the Five-and-Dime. I used to go in and I wanted to buy something. I wasn't even thinking of stealing anything, but when I saw nobody was looking, all of a sudden I would find my pockets full of stuff. I didn't even know what was happening, but then I would find myself running down a street with a man chasing me." He went on to describe at great length how this had happened to him in a number of stores such as groceries, fruiterers, and the like. Each time he invariably seemed to get caught.

On the therapist's right sat Jonathan, and he was heard to murmur: "Same with me and cars." However, Richard was still the center of the stage; all the boys were now looking at him, absorbed in his stories, except for Jonathan. He was not looking at Richard. He sat with his head bowed low and seemed to be lost in thought.

When Richard had finished detailing his escapades, silence continued for awhile. The therapist asked Richard, as he had been saying that he did not mean to steal but found himself doing it, what caused this to happen? Richard looked surprised, as if he had never thought of it, and said: "I don't know. I just did it." The boys burst into laughter. Michael blandly repeated he hoped his social worker could get him to go home. He wouldn't have any problems when he went home. He had everything he could want at home so how could he have problems? Donald turned on him and said, "If you're such a big shot and you got everything at home what made you steal?" There was another burst of laughter at this, and Michael slumped further into his seat, putting his hand over his face. Donald now took over.

His story was vague in outline. It had to do with being a "smart-aleck kid playing hooky," not wanting to go to school. He spoke of himself as a "jerk." (It was unclear whether he called himself a jerk for not going to school, or for getting himself caught playing hooky.) Jonathan joined the conversation, saying, "I didn't go to school because of my girl friend." He paused, then continued: "My girl friend was going to another school. I wanted to go to her school but they wouldn't let me. They said I didn't belong in that district, so I played hooky." Before he knew it, he said, he started hanging around with "the wrong kind of boys," and they talked him into doing things such as taking rides in stolen cars. Donald, in a manner of the "all-knowing," said, "you were misled by them."

Richard now re-entered the discussion, saying that he hated his school because he "was always getting blamed." Again Jonathan was overheard saying in a low voice: "Just like happens here." Richard continued describing how the principal of the school always had it in for him. On a number of occasions boys used to call up the school and say there was a bomb planted in the school. At this Michael jumped up and exclaimed: "What?" Richard, as an aside, explained to him it was a bomb, a packaged bomb planted in the school. The boys laughed, but Leonard kept his glum, straight face. Richard continued. He was blamed for planting the bomb or, more accurately, for calling up the school and telling them there was a bomb when there was no such thing. The reason he was blamed was because he was absent, and "they" figured that the absent boy was the one who had been calling up and telling stories about bombs. Michael, Donald, and Jonathan took turns voicing how terribly unjust this was.

There was now silence, with the boys looking quite aggrieved that this should have happened to Richard. The therapist commented, "Were you the only boy that was absent from school?" Richard said, "No, a lot of boys used to play hooky" and went on to say that he had been creating a lot of "trouble" in school before. He was very sassy to the principal; he would talk back to his teachers. Many times he used to devise ways of playing hooky: He would wait until his parents left the house and then he would come back, sit in the house, and watch television. He would get caught and his father would give him a "real beating," so then he found other ways of staying out of school, such as not coming home and instead playing with boys in the streets.

Being blamed unjustly set off Jonathan to complaining about similar experiences at the Village, and this in turn stimulated a general griping session on the part of the boys, with Michael playing a leading role. However, no specific incidents were cited. It was just general griping. Jonathan's complaint was that because he came from a far-off city, his parents could not visit him. Michael, now looking very serious, said: "They [staff] don't give you enough time even if they [parents] come and visit you. They can only stay with you for two hours." The conversation now turned to mothers' visits and the distortions and delay of telephone messages boys received from home. Richard described an episode when his mother called to tell him that she could not come to visit him because her fingers were swollen. When he got the message, he was told that his mother was in a hospital with an asthma attack. Jonathan, Donald, Richard, and Michael joined with similar complaints.

The therapist asked the boys how they felt at such times. Donald said, "I feel bad." Richard, pointing to Donald, said, "Just like he says, you feel bad." Therapist: "Do you mean by bad that you worry?" Donald: "Yeah." The boys now began to use the word *worry* rather frequently, and Richard, as spokesman, insisted: "How should a guy feel but worried when he can't get his mother to talk to him on the phone? They won't let him near the phone when his mother calls." Jonathan: "I worry because I'm always afraid that something is happening to my mother. When she writes that she's going to call and I don't get a call from her, I worry." Michael, continuing to look even more serious than before, joined in: "You don't know if something happened or not." It seemed that this subject activated a great deal of anxiety in the group, and Donald changed the subject by introducing complaints against the Village and how one got blamed for things. However, as he continued he mentioned how one got "blamed on the outside, too" for doing things. In general, the tenor of his stories was that adults were very unfair.

The conversation became desultory, with many digressions, during which Jonathan again talked in general terms about how unfair staff members were. Donald and Michael came back to the matter of not getting phone calls, talking about it in a rather intellectual way. There was no anger in their voices. Now that the tension and anger had subsided, the therapist commented on the fact that the boys talked about their being very worried when they did not receive phone calls. Donald related himself to this rather immediately in the following manner. He again described himself as a smart-alecky kid, who would stand before the judge when he was "picked up" and pretend to cry. The judge would tell him to go home and be a good boy, then he would go home and tell all the boys how he "fooled the judge." He described in a somewhat involved way how the last time he was caught playing hooky his mother had caught him. The truant officer came to his house and took him to court. His mother and father were called and the probation officer, in the presence of Donald, interviewed them. He interrogated them as to whether they knew that he was playing hooky. Donald said, "My father could have covered for me if he wanted to." As he said this, he stopped himself, then said that his father had replied, "I don't know." His mother, however, had admitted that she knew he was playing hooky. A few minutes later Donald commented, in passing, that his mother could have lied for him, too, if she had wanted to. Then, almost to correct himself, he added: "But they had to tell the truth and I was sent away. Man, I'm glad I was sent away. If I stayed home I just would have gotten into trouble another way."

As Donald was telling his story, his shoulders were tensing up and his eyes were blinking, as if he had a tic. His face was beginning to flush red. Leonard sat looking fixedly at Donald, scratching his cheek. Donald was again telling the boys that it was "lucky" he got "sent away." After all, he could have gotten into much worse trouble by being out; but there was a very definite undertone of anger at his parents for not covering for him, as well as resentment for being sent from home. When an anxious silence ensued, the therapist commented: "Maybe you were glad when you were finally sent away, but it is also possible that another piece of you wasn't so glad. *You could have the two feelings.*" Donald: "Yeah," in a tentative tone as if he were thinking it over, but was not sure. Again his eyes began to blink as he said, "I probably would have gotten into all sorts of crazy troubles outside."

Richard interrupted to tell his story. He said that since he was a kid he used to have headaches. One day his parents took him to the hospital and the next thing he knew he found himself in a ward, with screened windows. "You couldn't get out. I wanted to get out and I picked up a chair and began to throw it against the window. Big men came and dragged me into the ward with grown-up men and told me to behave. I told them to stick the place up their ass. Then they gave me a needle." Richard dramatically described how he "went under" (as a result of the sedation). The boys were all ears, and Richard described how when they brought him oatmeal on the ward, he used to go to the bathroom and try to throw it down the toilet bowl but was stopped by the nurse. The nurse asked him: "What are you trying to do?" Richard said to her: "You mean I'm supposed to eat this stuff?" The nurse told him if he didn't they would put him away, they would fix him, he'd go to a place he didn't like. Donald interjected: "You mean you went to that place because you had a cold?" Richard said, "No, because I had a headache." He continued with stories of his headaches, how they used to "bother" him and a doctor used to tell him: "You must never play football. You can play baseball but no football." His mother used to tell him that, too. Richard indicated he did not like being told this. He never found out what the headaches were all about. The boys in the group listening sat silent now as Richard looked down, his face red. Therapist: "Did you feel something was wrong with your head?" Richard looked up, grinned, looked down again, and quietly said: "Yes." [3]

Before the therapist could explore this further Jonathan began to describe his symptoms and how he had gone to the dispensary at the Village because of a persistent cough. He had pneumonia, but they did nothing for him. Finally he had to be sent home to a hospital to be operated on.[4] Before that he was in the hospital at the Village. They kept him in bed for three days and did not even take his tem-

---

3. It seemed that when Richard was about four years old he fell out of a window and was taken to a hospital, where he remained for a number of days. The mother reported that the boy had fractured his skull and a steel plate was inserted in his head. Until about a year before, both mother and son were convinced that he bore such a plate. When the facts were checked with the hospital which had referred Richard to the Village it was found that Richard had been thoroughly examined there, including an EEG and X-rays. No evidence of any skull plate was found. The EEG was negative.

Richard was examined also by a doctor in a medical group, and the doctor there had told the mother, in response to her question, that the steel plate in the boy's skull was securely in place and she had nothing to worry about. The referring hospital at that time checked on the story and confirmed that the doctor did actually tell this to the mother. When the doctors at the hospital tried to tell the mother and boy that there was no such plate in Richard's skull, they met with a great deal of resistance. Even when they showed the X-rays, Richard and his mother clung to their original idea. However, when the mother was seen before Richard's commitment she was no longer insisting that there was a metal plate in her son's skull.

4. There was suspicion of cancer, and the boy had undergone an exploratory operation.

perature. When he asked the nurse why he was being kept in the hospital, the nurse said: "It's punishment because you don't eat your food."

Since the time for termination of the session had arrived, this could not be investigated further.

COMMENT

In this session again the oral dependencies of the boys and their level of oral development is revealed by their nostalgic discussion of their homes. This feeling, however, became modified in their minds when some of the boys began to explore the reasons for their sequestration from their homes and for their being away. An important development here which carried with it some risks was the therapist's attempt to interpret the difference between "understanding" and "working through" a problem. This distinction may have been introduced too early. However, Jonathan had given us the cue for this in the preceding session when he said to Michael, it "ain't the same thing as working your problem out." The therapist, therefore, thought perhaps the boys were ready for the differentiation of the two concepts.

Another cue which we took from the boys to work on in further interviews was their need to understand and accept causality in life's phenomena (including the causality of their own behavior), as indicated in Richard's narration of his stealing escapades, which seemed to him quite irrational and unreasonable. This theme—the relation of cause and effect—we exploited later for the benefit of the boys' maturity.

Still another cue for a theme to be worked through with the same intent was the projective patterns by which these boys operated. We have noted how they heaped blame upon the staff of the Village, the school, and the community as a whole. This projective tendency we had to convert into *inversion*. The manner by which this was done will appear in later discussions. The boys spent a great deal of time in griping against the school, largely as a defense against continuing to talk about their homes and parents, which generated *inner threats*, as differentiated from the *outer threats* with which they were able to deal with less anxiety. We see this occurring in session two as the boys began to talk about their mothers and Donald escaped by changing the topic to the Children's Village. There was a twinkle of insight occurring during the discussion when Donald made the point that he got blamed for doing some of the things that he did on the "outside" as well as at the Village.

An effort was made by the therapist to activate insight (to hidden motivations) when he said that Donald may have been glad for being sent away and especially when he made the point that "You could have the two [oppositional] feelings." It was our feeling that this group moved somewhat too fast and we could expect reactions to it.

We made a note of another cue to be discussed in subsequent sessions, namely, the *hidden motivations* for stealing which puzzled Richard, since there seemed to be no need for it from the material point of view. As will be seen, some extremely interesting and rather profound discussions around this topic arose at different points in the interviews.

An error was made by the therapist when he asked Richard the question: "Did you feel something was wrong with your head?" Such a question may be very threatening and disturbing to a boy who already had some suspicions of being insane.

Session Three

ABSENT: Kurt and Jameson

The boys had some difficulty getting started. They sat rather quietly, and, when some minutes had passed, Michael, Richard, and Jonathan began to giggle. Jonathan said: "Here we go again. We always wait for the first one to start." Michael turned to Jules and said, "You ought to start today because you weren't here last week." Jules said, "I have nothing to say." Donald: "How come? We all have to say something here. Since you weren't here it is only fair that you start." All the boys looked in Jules's direction, most of them giggling, except for Leonard, who sat quietly throughout the session not saying a word. Jules said nothing and looked rather uncomfortable. His face appeared to flush. Richard took the initiative, turned toward the therapist and asked whether he was writing reports on the boys. Almost simultaneously, Donald pointed at Michael and said: "Maybe you shouldn't bother to talk today. All you ever talk about is how to get out of here." Michael did not respond to this, looking rather blasé. The question that caught on was the one Richard asked about writing reports. The therapist told Richard that he did not write reports, but he did keep notes on what the group talked about. Richard wanted reassurance. He asked: "You mean you don't put reports in our records every week?" He was told that that was the case. He then said, "That's good, because I don't want my social worker to find out what we are talking about."

At this point, Jonathan, speaking to the therapist by name, said: "You know, this is a crazy sort of place. I'm trying to go home in November for Thanksgiving instead of December. The reason I want this is because when I go home for Christmas it is not the way it used to be with my father being dead. Christmas is just like any other day to me.

My brother is in prison. When I come home I don't have much to do; but this year my brother is getting out of prison in November. My girl friend is going to move away in November and I want to see her before she moves. That's why I want to go home in November." He then wondered whether he could go home for four days in November and five days in December. This would make nine days, which he would be entitled to in December, since he lived far away. Michael immediately said: "No, it will cost the Village too much money. They won't let you break it up like that." Jonathan cast his gaze downward and said, "I guess they won't."

Silence again set in and was broken by Jonathan. He reiterated that it just wasn't the same way any more going home for Christmas, now that his father was dead. The therapist asked him what he meant, and Jonathan stated that since his father died his mother had been "on welfare." She felt very sad but she walked around always with a smile. She pretended that she was having a lot of fun, but he knew that she was not, and since he knew that his mother was suffering he didn't feel too good about it. Also, when he went home there was an uncle in the house who always sat around playing cards. Last year when he went home for Christmas, he went to a movie. That was the way he spent his Christmas. Michael, slouching in his chair, looking up at the ceiling seemingly lost in thought, reacted to this by saying, "Christmas is just the same as any other day for me."

Jonathan continued to say that last Christmas, after the movie, he and a couple of friends picked up some girls. They went riding and then "had some fun." The therapist asked what he meant by "having fun," Jonathan smiled and as all the boys began to giggle, said: "It ain't what you might think. We just had a good time. Before we picked them up the girls weren't having such a hot time themselves. They didn't have anything to do Christmas night so we got together and we all went out."

All of a sudden he changed the subject. He began to talk about a psychiatrist he had seen and how upset he was as a result. Turning to the therapist he asked in a rhetorical sort of way: "You know what this psychiatrist asked me? He asked me if I ever had intercourse with my mother. I got so angry, my face was red. I wanted to punch him, but I tried to control myself. That stupid jerk saw what happened and he said to me, 'Control yourself now, or you'll have to leave.' " He had said to the psychiatrist: "How would you feel if I asked you if you sleep with your mother? You would be angry, too!" Jonathan then turned to the group and reported that the psychiatrist had asked him to leave. He continued that he had recently seen a psychologist for a test, but she was different. "She's nice to talk to." Donald stepped in and said: "Yeah, I like taking those psychological tests. I saw her, too. She is not like that stupid psychiatrist." There was a sexual connotation in the tone of Donald's voice. Jonathan interrupted to say: "The psychiatrist not only asked me about my mother. He asked me if I went to bed with my sister." Donald exclaimed: "What a stupid bastard he is!"

During this interchange Michael had taken out his cigarette lighter, lit it, and, looking directly at the flame, had sung in a low voice, "Happy birthday to me, happy birthday to me." Now he seemed to come out of his lethargy and gazed at the ceiling. All of a sudden he said to Jonathan: "Hey, you said your brother was in prison. What prison is he in?" Jonathan said he was at Coxsackie. "Where's that?" asked Michael. "Coxsackie, New York." Jonathan appeared unwilling to talk about his brother. The boys seemed to sense this and let it drop.

During a brief silence Jameson stalked in (about ten minutes after the session had started) and brusquely announced that he quit, looking very defiantly at the therapist. The latter invited him to have a seat so that he could find out what this was all about. Jameson announced with finality that he didn't want to sit down and did not want to receive passes any more to attend the group. He then turned on his heel and stalked out of the room.[5] During this outburst, Donald had said to Jameson that he did not have to come, but that he was acting like a "stupid dope." After Jameson left, the boys sat around giggling again when Richard said, referring to the Village, "This is a stupid place." He described how a certain staff member—he decidedly would not mention names—sat around with the boys and told them about all the underworld figures he knew. He felt this was a "stupid thing" for a staff member to do. Jonathan seemed to know the staff member because he said: "Yeah, he tells us how to bet on the horses and make a killing, but he doesn't know what he's talking about. There's a guy in Education [school] who always talks about sex with us—how he goes out with all kinds of women." Richard and Michael appeared to know the staff member. They confirmed it, with Michael saying, "That's all he talks about."

All of a sudden Richard asked the group, "Did you hear about Dale Totten, who was sent back to his mother?" A discussion ensued about the injustice of this. Why couldn't *they* be sent back to their mothers? The discussion was held largely among Donald, Richard, and Jonathan. Suddenly Donald said: "I know my problem. I'm ready to go home." Then as an afterthought, addressing the group and himself, he said, *"But I know, I ain't got it worked out yet."* Jonathan turned smilingly to Donald. Richard kept insisting that the best way to get out of here

5. The boy's manner made us suspect that he was psychotic. This was later confirmed clinically, and his progressively agitated state made commitment to a mental hospital necessary. He was dropped from the group after this session.

was to pretend you were crazy the way Dale did, then they'd let you *go home to your mother.* Jonathan said, "Maybe that's what we ought to do."

Donald at this point stated a general question to everybody, "What's the big idea about the newspapers calling us mentally disturbed?" He said he had read in the newspapers about juvenile delinquency and juvenile delinquents were referred to as mentally disturbed. The therapist asked Donald what he thought this meant and Donald said, "mentally disturbed," pointing to his head. Richard cut in: "It means we ought to be in Bellevue Hospital if we are crazy." The therapist asked Richard directly whether he felt he was at the Village because he was crazy, but Richard did not answer. *All the boys remained silent.* The therapist then said to the group: "I know that you are not at the Village because you are crazy. You do have problems, but this is very different than being crazy." The silence continued and the therapist became aware that the boys were not ready to follow this line of investigation. The atmosphere was sterile, and he dropped the subject for the present.

Another gripe period ensued led by Richard, and during it Donald turned to Jules and said: "You haven't said anything all night. Why don't you open your mouth?" Jules said: "I got nothing to talk about." Jonathan: "What do you mean you got nothing to talk about? You got problems the way we got problems." Jules: "If I got problems I talk to my social worker." Richard: "You can talk to your social worker about your problems, but you should talk about them here, too." Still looking at Jules, he turned his hand and, pointing his thumb in the direction of the therapist, said: "Didn't you hear Mr. Ellery say that whatever we talk about stays in this room? It's between him and us. He's not going to tell your social worker what you talk about." Then as an afterthought added, "He better not." (Jules had been very absorbed in the discussion, especially when Jonathan was discussing the psychiatrist.) Jules was now leaning over in his chair, moving his tongue around in a circle in his open mouth.

Richard, following the trend of the conversation, turned to the therapist and said: "Hey, Mr. Ellery, do you know why the other guy I got into trouble with was not sent to the Village? They only sent me." Therapist: "That's a good question. How come they sent you to the Village?" Richard said spontaneously: "Because of my behavior!" He then began to talk about how he and this other boy used to "play hooky." His friend was still out and he was "here." Jonathan to Richard: "Why did the court send you here?" Richard: "The court didn't send me here." Everybody looked puzzled. Therapist: "Who did send you here?" Richard made a fast move to drop the subject by beginning to talk about a cottage mother who did not "dish out" meals properly. He described how the cottage mother did not like boys to talk about automobiles.

When Richard talked about automobiles, the cottage mother slapped him in the head and told him he should not be talking about them. His cottage father used to be a speed racer. Richard then said, "If she doesn't like people to talk about automobiles, why did she marry a guy who used to race them?" He then went on to describe how his cottage father always talked about how powerful his car was. Richard once asked the latter how many miles he got to a gallon on his car, and the cottage mother said to him: "Mind your own business!" This continued for a while, and then Richard began to move back to describing the boy who was not apprehended. "He is still going around free." On his last home visit, Richard saw him, and that's how he knew the boy was "outside."

The therapist considered it necessary that Richard be freed of his confusions and projections in this matter and said: "I am trying to understand it. Do you mean that you were just picked up out of the blue and placed here?" Richard said: "Oh no, my mother and father said I got to come here." He then described in rather vague terms how he had been a victim of a deception by his mother and father. They had brought him up here for an interview; then he went home, and later his father told him he got a letter from Children's Village saying he was to bring Richard here. He said that a caseworker at the court had told him that there were cows and horses here and he could stay only four months if he so desired, but once he got here, "I found out you can't even have a home visit before you're here three months." One of the reasons he was bothered about being at the Village was that, in case his father died, his mother would be all alone or, if his mother died, then his father would be alone. There wouldn't be anybody to take care of either if the other should die. He also added, "My father has heart trouble." He went on to say that the doctor had told his father that he had a touch of cancer, and if he continued smoking he was going to die. Before he arrived he used to think about this all the time and that was why he did not want to come up because he was worried as to what would happen to his parents; he added that his mother, too, had "heart trouble."

Jonathan: "Just like my family. My whole family has heart trouble." The therapist asked Richard what made him think that his parents would die. Richard: "Maybe I used to think about it because I didn't want to admit that I didn't want to come to the Village, so I used to say I don't want to come here because I'm afraid something is going to happen to my father or mother." Jonathan picked this up: "I think about it too sometimes. You know I don't have a father and if my mother dies I'm going to have to be here for another five years." He could go home to his sister but the Village wouldn't believe that his sister could take care of him.

As this discussion touching upon sensitive areas in the boys' lives was going on, a procession developed to the washroom. It was started by Jonathan, and when he returned Donald went out. Richard followed him when he returned.

In Richard's absence, Jonathan started a story about the Lady of Fatima miracle. A child who saw a vision of the Virgin at Lourdes was given a letter by the Virgin. This child is now a grown woman and still living. In 1960, this letter was supposed to be opened. In the letter there might be a date announcing when the world would end. Michael quickly jumped up from his slouching position and asked the therapist whether he thought that if the world was coming to an end the Village would let the boys go home. Richard, who had returned, said in all seriousness: "They better let us go home." If the world came to an end he wanted to be home with his parents. Jonathan said, if the world did come to an end, he wanted to be near his father's grave, and Richard went into a long, involved story about whose grave he wanted to be near. It was not clear whether it was the grave of his mother's or his father's parents. He announced that there was a certain rosary they could wear, and by fingering the rosary and saying their prayers they could stop the world from coming to an end. Jonathan had entered the discussion, but he spoke in a very low voice which only Richard seemed able to hear, and Richard was explaining to Jonathan about the rosary. Jonathan commented that when the world came to an end some people would go to heaven and some would go to hell, but he dropped this subject and quickly turned to Donald to ask about the rosaries.

Somehow discussion was dying out. *The boys looked weary.* Donald seemed to cap its demise when he started to ask the boys what each would do or what activities they would join after leaving the session.

COMMENT

This session was characterized by a discussion of *top realities* and skirting or escaping from involving deeper emotions. There was also considerable fatigue displayed by the boys, which can be attributed to consumption of energy in the suppression of feelings and the effort to confine themselves to commonplaces.

Again, of course, the theme of dependence on their families and nostalgia toward the home and mothers comes through. Richard's effort to speak about juvenile delinquency as equated with mental disturbance (insanity) was quickly scotched by the boys through general silence, a silence brought on by anxiety. The resistance, however, had been aided by the therapist's asking Richard whether he felt he was at the Village because he was crazy (which was the wrong thing to do at this early stage).

Griping made its appearance again as part of the resistance.

It will become clear later why Richard spoke of the death of his parents, for in later sessions he expressed rather openly a wish for their death. However, here he disguised it as *concern* about their death.

Nonetheless, the group entered upon anxiety-producing topics such as death, the world coming to an end, and various threats and calamities. In this session, too, it was our feeling that the boys had moved too fast and reactions had to set in.

Session Four

This session was characterized by a noticeably strained atmosphere. The therapist felt massive resistance throughout, a resistance thick enough to "cut with a knife." This was manifested by repeated steering away from any meaningful discussion and inordinately long periods of silence. The resistance may have emanated from the inner threat that the topics touched upon in the preceding sessions represented, and the resultant anxiety.

The boys came to the session somewhat late. Jonathan was first to arrive. Donald followed, but then told Jonathan that he had forgot to "check out" through the custodian and, telling the therapist that he would be back in a few minutes, left the room. On the way out, Donald encountered Richard, who was just on the verge of coming in, and told him where he was going. Richard said that he, too, did not check out and Donald invited him to go along with him. Richard and Donald came back within five minutes. Kurt came in and immediately asked to talk with the therapist. He said he wanted to quit the group. The therapist told him that he had nothing to do with assignment of boys to groups and referred him to the Club Department. Kurt looked rather puzzled, but did not pursue the subject. He took a chair and sat down quietly. Leonard and Jonathan came in together, both saying "hello" to the therapist, and took seats. Jonathan, who generally sat at the opposite end of the room from the therapist, now took a seat, only one chair away from him. After a few minutes of waiting, Richard and Donald came in and the therapist asked who would like to begin that evening. Michael had not yet arrived. He came about twenty minutes after the session began.

The therapist's comment was met with a massive silence. Donald looked in the direction of Richard. Richard smiled and slouched in his chair. The silence continued for four to five minutes. Donald broke the silence by saying: "Wait until that guy gets here, then we will have something to talk about." This remark brought laughter from all the boys. They seemed to know whom Donald was referring to. Addressing the group, Richard said, "When he comes in, he'll say 'I quit.'" Donald: "If he does, I'll throw him down the stairs."

The therapist then realized that the boys were referring to Jameson. Silence followed. Leonard now began to squirm in his chair and Donald was blowing smoke rings. Following a minute or two of this, Richard spoke up and said, "Jameson just doesn't want to discuss his problems." He added, *"Some boys just don't like to discuss their problems."* He said nothing more and no one picked this up. When asked by the therapist if he could tell more about what he meant Richard only repeated his statement and it was again followed by silence. The therapist then said: "Sometimes many people try hard to avoid their problems. This doesn't mean that they can succeed in doing it, but they do try." Jonathan at once picked this up and said that he always thought about his problems though he tried not to. He said: "Sometimes I think about them all day." Looking quite worried he fell silent. His head was bowed and he kept rubbing his forehead.

There was *an air of restlessness among the boys.* Even Leonard, who generally sat very quietly, appeared to be crossing and recrossing one leg over another. As the silence continued, the therapist asked Jonathan if he could tell more about what it was that he thought about. Jonathan did not respond to this, but Richard said that he had found out that he was going home for Christmas. Jonathan appeared to be almost grateful for the change in subject and commented that he was going home in November instead of Christmas. He talked about remaining at Children's Village during Christmas, since he would be going home for Thanksgiving in November. He wanted to know from the boys what it was like on Christmas in the Village when one was the only boy remaining in the cottage. Donald told him that sometimes "they [cottage parents] take you to dinner or you go to a movie or ice cream parlor."

At this point Michael walked into the room, which set Donald, Kurt, and Jonathan to giggling. Michael looked somewhat disheveled, wearing a knit cap that extended over his ears. In general he presented quite a comical appearance. The giggling increased until finally Jonathan resumed his conversation, saying that one time when he was not allowed to go home he ran away. Jules corrected this: "You ran away a couple of times." Jonathan did not respond to this; he continued by saying that he had run away to Manhattan, but almost in the same breath said that the reason he ran away was because he was very homesick and also he wanted to see his girl in R———, where he lived. Richard smiled at this but did not say anything. When Jonathan did not continue, the therapist asked about the seeming contradiction. Jonathan responded by saying that he went to Manhattan because he "wanted to have fun first" before

going to R————. He not only went to R———— to see his girl, but he
also saw his probation officer, who had promised him that he would leave
the Village in September. He had not gotten word from him, so it was in
September that he took off. Then he added that at other times he ran for
no reason at all. The therapist commented that sometimes people do
things that may appear to be without reason, but there is always a reason
for everything.

Michael pulled a cigar out of his shirt pocket. This served as a signal
for general hilarity on the part of the boys. Donald commented that
Michael was going to "stink up" the place with his cigar. Michael went
through exaggerated motions of lighting his cigar and visibly relaxing
in imitation of a gentleman of leisure. After this byplay and laughter,
Richard introduced a discussion about the food in his cottage. He complained that there wasn't enough of it that was good food. This was
picked up by Donald, who proceeded along the same lines.

After this talk continued for a while the therapist asked why the
complete shift in the conversation. None responded to this effort at
interpretation of the resistance. Turning to the therapist Michael announced that this was his birthday and he wanted the boys to sing happy
birthday to him. Nobody responded to this, and Michael in a semi-
comical manner began to plead with the boys to sing happy birthday to
him. Receiving no response he finally told the boys that when he gave
the signal, they were to start singing. He counted 1, 2, 3, and raised his
hand as if to lead the group, but nobody responded. Donald asked
Michael how old he was. Michael told him that he was sixteen, and with
this the matter was dropped.

Richard again began complaining about his cottage. Jonathan complained about having to wake up too early; he hated to get up early and
cited an incident that occurred one morning. He was having "a beautiful
dream" and his cottage father slapped him on the "behind" and woke
him up. All the boys looked in Jonathan's direction as if desiring to hear
more about this, but no more was forthcoming. The therapist asked if he
could tell more about the "beautiful dream," but Michael became active
again by taking out another cigar from his shirt pocket and offering it
to Richard. The attention of the boys now became focused on this.
When Richard reached out to take the cigar, Michael withdrew it.
Donald said, "Give me the cigar." Michael: "I will not, I am only
teasing." Michael got up, went over to Jules and, leaning over, whispered
in his ear. The content was not overheard, but nothing transpired
as a result, and Michael returned to his seat. *There was a great deal of
moving about in the room and shifting in the chairs.* Donald got up and
leaned against the table at the far end of the room. The therapist remarked that the boys seemed restless about something. Did they want to

talk about it? This was completely ignored and the boys seemed not to have heard it.

Donald went to the bathroom and when he came back Richard went out. When he returned, a discussion arose between Michael and Richard about Jameson's not returning to the group, Richard commenting that "Jameson always does this. He acts like a big baby."

Jonathan immediately got involved with complaints about his cottage parents, but soon shifted this to a declaration that he now no longer tried to run away. He had more "will power" now than he had when he first came. When asked by the therapist what he meant, Jonathan said that he never thought that he could have stayed at the Village this long without running away. Richard said to him, "You are different now." After this fleeting interlude, *the restlessness became quite marked.* The therapist tried to universalize the discussion by asking if others had any experiences similar to Jonathan's. Jonathan said that everybody in the room had run away in the past except Michael and Leonard. *The restlessness had now increased to a point where continuing a discussion seemed impossible.* Michael and Richard went to the bathroom. The therapist commented again that the boys seemed to be having trouble "getting together tonight." Maybe there was something bothering them.

Michael turned to him and asked: "Do we have to come to the group?" The therapist temporized by inquiring what he meant. Michael said, "Give me just a yes or no answer." The therapist told Michael that he was trying to understand what he was asking: Is he saying he doesn't want to come? Michael: "I don't want to come here if I can't see my social worker. My social worker told me she would see me only once a month. I haven't gotten a pass [to see her] yet." (The therapist had been informed and knew that Michael had seen his social worker recently, because he had made a request through his cottage father to see her and ask her about withdrawing from the group.) Michael continued by saying that there was no point talking about his "problems" in the group if he could not talk about them also with his social worker. Jonathan, Jules, and Leonard all indicated that they felt similarly. The therapist said that there must have been some misunderstanding. He was certain that arrangements could be made for them to see their social workers more frequently. With this, there was a visible decrease in tension. The restlessness subsided and there arose a hubbub in the group, the content of which the therapist could not detail.

When this subsided, Leonard seemed to take the lead in the discussion for the first time. He said that he was going home every month instead of every other month as in the past. Michael, looking now considerably more relaxed, asked Leonard what he meant by that: "How come?" Leonard explained that since his mother was ill and he'd been very worried about her he was allowed to go home every month. Richard: "How can you go home every month when I can't go home every month?" Michael appeared to be interested in what Leonard had said and inquired: "What's the matter?" Leonard answered this in vague terms, saying, "My mother has an infection in her foot and she is going to go into the hospital." At this point, a few minutes before the termination of the session, Richard and Donald rose. Donald said he had to go back to the cottage to see a certain program on television, and the two boys left the room. The rest looked very eagerly at Leonard, wanting to hear the rest of his story, but Leonard appeared not to be interested in continuing. Being uncertain, the therapist asked Leonard whether his mother was already in the hospital. Leonard said that his mother was going to enter a hospital. He did not know what was going to happen to her but he worried about it. Michael picked this up and said, "Well, what is it that you are so worried about?" Leonard did not say anything in response. He lowered his head, and it was obvious that he had talked about as much as he was going to at this session.

Since it was 8:30, the session ended at this point.

Michael lingered and asked the therapist again about seeing his social worker. He was told that he would be seen by his social worker more often; being in the group did not mean that he was not to see her and that there must have been a misunderstanding. Michael said: "Okay, Mr. Ellery. See you next week."

COMMENT

The resistance to the therapist had come from the anxiety generated in the preceding sessions. While none of these boys, with the exception of Leonard, could be considered on the surface as psychoneurotic, it became obvious to us (as was also the case in our other groups) that underlying the acting out of the boys was massive anxiety. This anxiety, when provoked, constituted an inner threat which they sought to prevent from manifesting itself. The therapist did well to assert himself when the boys became overly restless and he asked Jonathan to tell the group what he was thinking about. This prevented diffusion in the group. Though Jonathan did not answer, he proceeded to talk resistively about a commonplace in reference to his holiday.

Following our suggestion at the supervisory conference after the preceding session, the therapist pushed forward the concept of cause and effect when he very subtly commented that sometimes people do things that appear without reason but there is always a reason for everything. However, he was very careful not to enter into an extensive disquisition;

rather he added "a straw to the pile" started in the previous session. However, when later the therapist, erroneously, attempted to interpret resistance by asking the group why there was a shift in the conversation, there was no response. This stratagem cannot be used so early in treatment. A direct reaction to the therapist's effort at dealing with resistance was acted out by Michael; also, when the therapist asked Jonathan to elaborate on his "beautiful dream," Michael pulled out a cigar and offered it to Richard,[6] thus diverting attention from what was transpiring. Soon after, the therapist noticed that "there was a great deal of moving about in the room."

The resistance took a very direct form when the boys insisted that they did not wish to come to the group unless they could see their social workers, a reversal of their earlier attitudes when they attacked the caseworkers. These attacks were resumed in later sessions when the boys were acclimated to the group and had found security in it. (None of the boys in the group had been productive in their interviews, according to the social workers.)

NOTE

Since they had been nonproductive anyway, it was the intention that contacts with caseworkers be held down to a minimum, so that the effect of the group could be better judged. However, as revealed in session three, the boys seemed unready to forgo the security they derived from the attachment to an adult. Especially was this the case since the group therapist had told them that he would not take part in determining the length of their stay at the institution, which was paramount in the boys' minds. Apparently the deprivation of seeing caseworkers proved a source of resistance in the group therapeutic process; we decided to clarify this for the boys. Accordingly, at the suggestion of the supervisor, a special meeting was called by the group therapist for the purpose of doing so. It was a ten-minute meeting. The following boys attended: Richard, Donald, Michael, Jonathan, and Jules. Leonard did not attend nor did Kurt. Kurt was seen individually by the therapist the following day on this matter.

The boys were told that the therapist had discussed the situation with the Club Department and was advised that there had been a misunderstanding between their caseworkers and the department. Being in the

6. There is the possibility that the cigar represented symbolically a penis, thus suggesting fellatio in which some of the boys indulged, and the others knew about it intimately. Note the giggling and hilarity on the part of the boys when Michael first takes a cigar from his pocket.

254 The Demonstration Group

group did not mean they are not to have contact with their caseworkers, and, therefore, they would be seen by them on a regularly scheduled basis.

The response to this appeared to be a positive one, although, as Donald indicated, they were not entirely sure that what was said would be so. He asked: "How come my caseworker told me he would see me only once a month? Here it is already over a month and I wasn't called." Richard seconded this. The therapist reiterated what had been said, stating in very definite terms that they were going to be seen by their workers. Michael became the spokesman of the group. Donald wanted to know who had raised the question of more frequent interviews. Jonathan and Jules pointed to Michael. Michael did not seem to take the credit. In fact, he seemed rather subdued but satisfied that he could now see his caseworker more frequently.

The therapist asked the boys whether they thought that he was not allowing them to see their worker. Richard said, "I think we all understand that you have nothing to do with it." Donald nodded his head in agreement. As the short meeting was breaking up, Richard turned to the therapist and said, "Thanks a lot, Mr. Ellery." Michael mumbled his thanks.

As planned in the supervision conferences, the caseworkers had been advised that they were to send passes to the boys before the week was up and when they saw them to tell them that there had been some misunderstanding with the Club Department and that they would be seeing the boys on a regular basis. The workers were also advised that a "scatter system" should be set up so that there would not be a massive call on the boys. Thus the boys would not suspect that it was their behavior in the group that brought results and that they had succeeded in exerting pressure on the staff. A schedule was worked out so that all the boys would be seen before the next group session.

Session Five

ABSENT: Kurt

Donald, Michael, and Jules arrived on time. While the group sat around for five minutes waiting for other boys to arrive, Donald raised the question of whether the group could have coffee during the sessions. He volunteered to bring a jar of instant coffee. The therapist informed him that following Michael's request at a previous session, the therapist had discussed it with the Club Department and was told that they were going to look into the possibility of providing coffee. Donald raised the question of obtaining an electric stove and again offered to bring coffee when one became available. Leonard and Jonathan came in at this point, about five minutes late, and Donald asked them whether they would like to have coffee at the meetings. They assented.

Jonathan had a portable radio that he was playing, but as soon as the discussion began he turned it off. Again, there was the initial silence, with the boys looking at one another as if to see who would start. The therapist said he would like to review briefly what the purpose of the group was. He told the boys that in this discussion group the purpose was to talk about problems and to help one another in "figuring them out" and finding ways of overcoming them.

Donald immediately responded by saying he wondered whether it was possible for a social worker to be at the meetings. When the therapist asked if he could elaborate on the idea, he said, "Maybe every week a different social worker should come to the meeting." Since no one followed this through, the therapist asked Donald the purpose of this. He said that he did not know whether his social worker believed him that he was really talking about his problems in the group. Jonathan seconded Donald on this saying, "Yeah, how do we know?" Donald again stated that he did not know that his social worker really knew what the group talked about. He went on to question how he was ever going to get out (of the Village), since in his experience his social worker really did not believe that he was talking about anything in the group. Jonathan said: "How do you know the social workers will even come? They don't work at night and they are not going to give up their free time to come to listen to us." The therapist expressed interest in their feelings that their social workers did not believe them and were not interested in them.

Donald: "What's the point of talking to my social worker, or even talking here? We [the group] talk about the same thing every week I know my problems. When I get out I'm not going to get into any more trouble. That's what's important, isn't it? Just knowing your problems?" The therapist wondered whether the boys remembered a previous discussion about this, namely, about knowing problems. Donald: "Yeah, I remember and I remember we talked about the difference between knowing and working out problems." However, he continued by saying that what was important was that the boys only have to know their problems. Jonathan added: "As long as you know your problem, you will never get into trouble again." Leonard disagreed. "But it's not the same thing," he insisted. The therapist felt that the boys were more ready to differentiate between knowing a problem and working it out than they had been in session one, and therefore proceeded to elaborate on it. He gave an example of how one can know his problem and yet go on repeating the same mistakes. Donald insisted that this was not true of him. He went into a long explanation of how he came to Children's Village.

He had been at a "600 school" (for difficult children), where the teachers used to search him. On a number of occasions he was beaten, not because he did anything wrong but because they assumed he had. As a result he played hooky and finally wound up in Detention House. The problem as Donald saw it was that his father did not really know Donald was being taken to court. His father had "influence." He knew the probation officer and, had his father known about it, had his mother told his father originally, his father could have talked to the probation officer and maybe Donald would not have had to go to Detention House. He was beaten by a staff member named Chuck for seemingly no reason at all. He said nobody could make him go to the 600 school because it was such "a rotten place." Everybody, from the boys to the teachers, used to pick on him. There were Negro and Puerto Rican boys in his class, and he could not get along with them because they had gangs and "if you were white they attacked you." He then went into a lengthy explanation of the 600 school, that it was something like a prison, the doors kept locked. Everything he did was checked. They went through his pockets, and when they found more than a dollar on him he had to answer a lot of questions. Therefore, what was more natural than playing hooky from such a school?

The therapist commented that it sounded as though he was pretty unhappy in the 600 school, but how come he had to go to a 600 school? Donald evaded the question and proceeded to describe the principal of the school as "an old bastard." He didn't like boys. "He used to hit me on the ass, leaving welts, just because I played hooky a couple of times." And he launched into a long narrative about how he was involved with everybody in the neighborhood who was known to the courts. He himself was not actually involved in stealing, but, when money was stolen, "they" invariably, in picking up the boy who had stolen the money, found Donald with the other boy. For instance, he had a friend who stole money from a blind newsstand dealer, and when the police came to pick up the boy, they found Donald with him. So Donald was implicated. On another occasion a boy had run away from home, and Donald had made arrangements for the boy to sleep on the roof of his house. While Donald was describing this, Michael was sitting in deep thought. Jonathan looked as though he were asleep. He was extremely quiet—something unusual for Jonathan.

At this point Richard came into the room. He was a little out of breath and declared that he was late because he was with a group of boys who went with a staff member to a football game in a nearby town. On the way back the battery in the car failed and they were stuck on the highway. He said, "You can call my cottage, and they will tell you that is so." Therapist: "I don't have to call the cottage. I believe you." Richard seemed satisfied and launched into a long narration as to how the car broke down and how they were helped by the state police. After his prolonged narration, to which the group gave silent attention, a long silence ensued. Donald continued his conversation. He said, "You see, I knew my problem." The therapist responded by saying: "Now we both know what you did, but what we don't know is what made you have so much trouble." Donald: "What's the difference. I just know my problem." Jules spoke up at this point and with tongue-in-cheek said: "Sure you know your problem. Everybody but you is out of step." At this point Michael spoke up: "That's right, You don't have any problems. *It's just everybody else got problems.*" Donald was visibly annoyed by these remarks.

Richard was becoming noticeably restless. He stood up several times to arrange his trousers. Finally he said: "Hey, Mr. Ellery, you know what happened to me? My stupid social worker saw me for just a lousy ten minutes. He called me in and said to me, 'How are things going in the group?' I told him things are going okay. My social worker said: 'What do you mean they are just going okay? You've been in the group four weeks now and this is all you've got to say?'" Seeming very angry, Richard said: "I wasn't going to tell him anything about the group." Donald spoke up and said: "You see what I mean? Ten minutes, that's all the time they give you." A lengthy silence ensued.

Donald looked directly at the therapist and with intense anger on his face said, "There's no reason why we gotta talk about our problems." Therapist: "Do you feel angry with me?" Donald: "No, I don't feel angry with you." Richard: "How interested can your social worker be if he only sees you ten minutes? I didn't see the guy for a whole month and, after you told us that our social workers are going to be seeing us, he sees me for ten minutes." Did they feel that the group therapist had let them down? Richard was very explicit in denying that this was the case, and immediately launched into a tirade against the Village: how the social workers "never see you [for an interview] and when they see you they try to talk about things you don't want to talk about, and they are even trying to get you to talk about the group."

Donald got up and began to pace around the room like an enraged, caged animal. Michael, too, rose from his seat, walked over, and spread himself out on the couch. Richard ran out of the room, but came back almost immediately and said to Jules: "Hey, put on your radio, will you?" Jules appeared happy to oblige and turned it on. The song that was being played was one of Richard's favorites. When one of the boys tried to start a conversation, either Donald or Richard would stop him saying, "Shut up, let's listen to the music." Leonard looked visibly annoyed. It was obvious from his appearance that he wanted conversation to continue, but Richard prevented it. The music continued for some time and no word was uttered by anyone in the group. At one point Jules sang along with the radio. *Donald threw defiant, angry glances at the therapist* as if to see what he was going to do. Finally, the therapist raised the possibility that the boys were trying to say something through their behavior. "Could we try to consider this?" No response. After a long lapse the therapist asked: "Are you perhaps trying to say that you don't want the discussion group to go on?"

Here Leonard, the silent one, took the initiative and spoke up: "I want to be in this group and I want us to continue." Turning to Jules he said, "Why don't you turn that radio off?" Surprisingly, Jules turned the radio off at once. Michael said: "Yeah, we want to be in this group. We don't want to leave the group, *but let's talk about different things.* Every week we talk about the same thing." Donald, still enraged, ran out of the room but was back in a few seconds, mumbling, "Lousy social worker."

The therapist raised the question that one of the things they might want to consider was whether they viewed him—the therapist—as a social worker. Leonard immediately said yes. It was almost as if he meant to say no, because he immediately followed up and said, "You're not the same thing." Richard said, "Yeah, you're a social worker like all the other social workers and we want to talk to our real social workers," but then went on to qualify that there was no point to it. "They don't listen." Jules: "Look, if we're going to be in this group, let's talk about a lot of different things." Michael: "Maybe we ought to have a secretary to take down all the things we say. Then every week we can go over what we said the last week *so we don't have to talk about the same thing.*" Donald wanted to know how come the therapist did not take notes. Jules corrected him saying: "He must take notes." Donald said, "You never told me." Michael said: "Yes he did. He told all of us he takes notes." Michael was trying very hard to get a discussion going, but Richard and Donald constantly worked against it, with Richard again inviting Jules to turn on the radio. Michael asked Jules to keep the radio off. Richard went out, but Jules compromised by playing the radio very low.

Michael asked the therapist to list subjects for the group to talk about each week. The therapist commented that, since this was their group, they might have things they wanted to talk about, rather than those he would want them to discuss. Michael: "Can we talk about sex here?"

Therapist: "If you want to you can discuss sex." Donald quickly said smilingly: "Good, but there's nothing wrong with my sex life. When I get home I get plenty of it." Michael: "There's nothing wrong with my sex life either, so you got to find something else to talk about now." Michael then turned to the boys: "What else do you think you ought to talk about?"

Donald suddenly stood up and said he did not want to stay after 8:00 (instead of 8:30) because of some visitors and a party going on at his cottage, and he did not want to miss a favorite television program at 8:00. Leonard said: "Yeah, eight o'clock is a bad time." Michael suggested that the group meet at a different hour so that no one would miss the things that went on in the cottages. Michael and Richard said that at 8:00 they sometimes had parties or went to a movie.

From this the group moved into a discussion as to the time most convenient for all. The boys did not seem to be able to agree on a time and the therapist wondered about starting a half-hour earlier, that is, 6:30. Donald, Richard, and Jules said that would be fine with them; Michael, however, complained that he would have to eat "in a hurry" and he did not feel like running after eating. The boys reached a compromise saying that they would like to come at 6:45 and possibly end at 8:00 P.M. This was agreed on.

By this time, Richard had disappeared from the room. Donald stood at the door as if ready to go, but Michael was getting the boys back to a discussion, saying, "Since this our own group, let's elect a secretary who will take down what we say." Jules: "I don't want to be secretary." The other boys, going around the room one by one, said pretty much the same thing. Richard and Donald had left by this time, but Richard came back and asked Michael what he had missed. Michael told him "nothing much." At this point the discussion revolved around the activities in the cottages and how it would be better if the boys could come a little earlier next week. While this was going on Leonard was telling the boys that maybe they ought to get together before they come here and discuss what they were to talk about. He said to Michael, whom he saw as somewhat of a leader, "There are a lot of things we got on our mind that we could talk about here." Richard: "Why don't you shut up and mind your own business?"

Jonathan, who had not said anything throughout the session, now indicated that he didn't care what happened here in the group. The week end he had been looking forward to in November (Thanksgiving) was "not there any more." He was told he couldn't go home. As a result he said he was going to run away; he'd had enough of the Village. Anyway, even if he were allowed to go home, he would run away. Jules tried to draw Jonathan out as to what had happened. Jonathan said, "I'm not going to talk about it, so don't ask me any questions." The session ended on this note.

COMMENT

The resistance of the group continued, though the therapist had attempted to break through it when he restated the aim of the group. Donald and others blocked him by asking whether caseworkers could be present at the group discussions and entered into a tirade against the schools and the community. Michael attacked Donald's projective mechanism when he said: "You don't have any problems. It's just everybody else got problems." This moved in the direction of one of the principal aims of our therapy. However, one cannot be certain as to Michael's insight in making the statement.

A confirmation of our original assumption that the boys' request to see their caseworkers more often was only a resistance maneuver against the group was their harangue against caseworkers at this session.

The freedom of acting out provided by the group gave the boys not only release, but also a feeling of status and acceptance which later was expressed in their initiating a choice of a subject for discussion and the suggestion that a secretary be elected. The latter was prefaced by the proponent, Michael: "Since this is our group. . . ." However, they used status to buttress their resistance when they insisted that they would talk on different subjects at each session rather than "the same subject," the same subject being their problems, tensions, and anxieties. And when Leonard suggested that "there are a lot of things we have got on our minds that we could talk about here," Richard (and probably the other boys) began to feel inner threat and told Leonard, "Why don't you shut up and mind your own business!"

Session Six

ABSENT: Kurt

Richard came earlier than the scheduled time. He found the therapist in the room, and said, "Gee, I'm the first boy here." Shortly thereafter Jonathan arrived. Jonathan literally drooped. He looked very depressed, head bowed low and as though he carried the burdens of the world on his shoulders. He sat down in his usual chair, slumped over, as Richard and the therapist discussed various coats and the suede one Richard was wearing, which had been given to him as a present. Jonathan cut in to say that he had just learned that his two sisters were sick. One had rheumatic fever, but "nobody knows what's wrong with the other." His girl friend was paralyzed and could not move her hands or legs. An aunt in New York and another aunt in R——— had just died. (It sounded like a Greek tragedy.) Richard, however, did not pay attention to Jonathan and continued to talk as if Jonathan were not present. The therapist expressed interest in what Jonathan had said, but the latter did not continue with his plaint.

Soon the other boys came into the room. There was some exchange among them as to where they were going later in the evening, who was going to the gym and who going back to the cottages. After this, a long silence. Donald brought his portable radio with him and was playing it quite loudly. The therapist expressed an interest in it, and Donald went into a long dissertation about how the radio worked, how one could attach a special antenna and earphones, the kinds of batteries required, and so on. When the boys began to talk, Donald turned off the radio, but on occasion would turn it on and hold it very close to his ear so that others could not hear the sound. Michael turning to Leonard said, "Why don't you start talking tonight?" Leonard, who was usually very quiet, thought a moment and then said, "Okay, I got something to say." Turning to the therapist he declared that he went to his social worker, asking for an extended home visit, since he would be going home on Thanksgiving week end. He asked his social worker whether he could get a few more days so instead of being home for two days he could be home for four or five. His social worker told him that he did not think this would be possible. Leonard said with a smile, "I knew all along that I couldn't get it, but I asked the question anyway." When asked how he felt about it, Leonard said: "I wasn't too disappointed. I knew they would say no. Nobody else gets it." The therapist wondered whether he felt the same way on other occasions when he got no for an answer. Leonard immediately responded by saying: "I used to do this in school. Every time I used to ask the teacher a question like could I go to the bathroom or could I leave the room, I would always expect her to say no. Once in awhile they fooled me; they would say yes."

Michael, who was slumped over in his chair, closed his eyes and acted as though he were asleep. Jonathan said: "It's like with me. They always said no to me," and immediately proceeded to complain. He was very vague and Michael suddenly raised his head and asked: "Well, who you talkin' about, man?" Jonathan said that he was talking about his probation officer, who didn't like him and "has it in" for him. It was his probation officer who was really keeping him here. His probation officer was back in R——— collecting a salary and "doesn't give a damn" whether Jonathan stayed here the rest of his life. The therapist wondered what it was that made his probation officer not like him. Jonathan:

"I don't know. My probation officer is always telling me about his own sons and that's all that ever seems to interest him. He doesn't care about any other boys." Donald spoke up and said: "Just like a lot of people. They let you stay here, but *they don't care about you.*" Jonathan supported Donald's comment that people just "let you stay here, not giving a hoot whether you leave or don't. They keep you in school but don't teach you anything." He went on in the same vein. Donald turned to Michael, who still had his eyes closed, and whispered something to him. Michael answered him in kind. Both boys became restless. The therapist commented that maybe the group could talk about people who did not care about them.

Richard at once began to talk about his bad experiences in school: He was "left back," teachers used to hit him, in short, everybody in school seemed to "have it in" for him. Donald immediately spoke up saying: "I had a lot of trouble in school, too. I was the lousiest reader in class." Richard: "So was I." Leonard: "I didn't even know the alphabet." A discussion now ensued among Michael, Leonard, and Richard about how teachers today were too young; they did not teach enough. In the old days it was different. Schools, in general, didn't teach. Richard continued along these lines, turning to the school at Children's Village where "they don't teach you either." All the teacher did was stand around and talk about how he bet on the numbers and things like that. The therapist commented that, on the one hand they were talking about how unhappy a place school was—Donald interposed "there is nothing unhappier"—and yet they were also bringing up a problem of not being able to read. Richard said, "I remember when I was first starting school the teacher would call on me and make me read in front of the class and I couldn't, so then I would always try to get out of it."

The therapist asked Richard directly what it felt like to stand in front of a class and not be able to read. Richard: "I was very embarrassed." Donald said: "When I went to school out of the Village I used to have 31, 30 boys in the class and I couldn't keep up with them. The teacher wasn't going to give you any special attention." He went on to narrate that here at the Village it was different. When he first came he didn't know how to read at all. Now he could read at the fifth-grade level. Leonard spoke up and said, "That's pretty good." Michael: "Well, here at the Village they give you a little more attention than they do in the schools outside."

Richard: "I remember when I used to try to read. I used to begin to stutter and then I couldn't say a word. I used to jump from one paragraph to another picking out only the words I knew and the teacher used to make fun of me and then I didn't want to go to school, so I played hooky." Richard moved away from the subject and began to talk about how at the Village they didn't help much in learning how to read either, though he did make a little progress. He now changed the subject again and spoke about the psychiatrist whom he had seen recently and who had dared Richard to run away by saying, "Why don't you run away if you don't like it here?" Richard had said to him: "I'll think it over. I might do just that." Jonathan spoke up, describing the psychiatrist as a "dumb bastard," because he had asked Jonathan about wanting to sleep with his mother.[7] Jonathan described how he grabbed hold of the doctor and began to pound at him. Donald asked incredulously: "You really hit him?" Jonathan said, "I did." (Jonathan had told this story in session three, although then he said that he just sat angrily, *wanting* to hit the psychiatrist.)

Michael returned to talking about school experiences, of not wanting to go to school, of not being able to read. Jonathan reaffirmed that he now could read "pretty good." In fact he'd got books at home that he read every so often.

In an effort to lend some significance to the discussion, the therapist expressed interest in the fact that Richard would stutter when he was asked to read before the class. Did they know what caused the stuttering? Leonard said, "When you are very nervous you stutter." Donald: "When you are embarrassed and nervous and feel like running, you begin to stutter." Jules, who was quiet up to this point and was reclining on the couch, said: "Yeah, I remember once in a while that used to happen to me. I used to get tongue-tied. I didn't know what to say when I had to read." The therapist agreed with the boys that when one is "nervous" and tense, especially when one is unable to read, to appear in front of a class can be embarrassing. Stuttering can be produced that way. Donald asked: "Did that ever happen to you, Mr. Ellery?" Therapist: "I remember when I started school and had to read in front of the class. I did feel very nervous and I often did feel kind of embarrassed." Donald nodded as if in sympathy with the therapist's problem.

The therapist asked the boys, "Was it everybody in the class that couldn't read?" Richard: "No, there were just a few of us. We just fooled around. We weren't interested." Michael: "I used to walk around the classroom." Jonathan: "I was always thinking about girls. I went to a school and there was a girl sitting next to me. I was always looking at her instead of looking at the book." He told how he used to steal books from the library. Donald said that he, too, used to steal books and one day a "man from the library" came to his home and told his mother, but his mother chased the man out of the house, shouting: "Leave my son alone. Stop picking on him!" The boys laughed at this. Donald

7. This is obviously a distortion, part of the boy's hostility syndrome toward adults.

warmed up to the subject as he described how his mother "chased the man with a broom in her hand."

When the hilarity died down Richard embellished on how terrible his school was. "The principal would leave you back because he didn't like you. If you didn't shine your shoes right they would leave you back." The therapist asked Richard whether he was "left back" because his shoes weren't shined or because he had trouble in reading, but Richard continued describing how the principal had chased a boy. The boy jumped over the fence but didn't quite make it, and one of the spikes caught him in the calf of the leg. Richard then proceeded to say that when he was "left back" he didn't like it because he was with boys younger than his age. The therapist commented that he could understand Richard's not liking to be in a class with younger boys, and then said to the group: "Here we have raised a very interesting point and maybe there is something we could begin to figure out." They have said that it wasn't the whole class that didn't know how to read, just certain boys. It is very hard for anyone to learn to read, but what makes it harder for some boys than for others? Donald immediately picked this up and said: "I remember when I was in class, I was always looking out the window. My mind used to wander. I couldn't concentrate." Michael: "Yeah, I found it hard to concentrate. I was always looking at something other than my textbook."

Richard in the meantime was talking to no one in particular about how he did not get a clean textbook. The school was holding back books from the boys and that was the reason that he couldn't learn to read. While Richard was still talking, Leonard was telling Michael that "reading is a pretty tough thing and you got to concentrate all the while or you can't learn to read." Jonathan spoke up and said, "I know what my trouble was, I was concentrating on my biology teacher." This caught everybody's interest, but Jules, Donald, and Michael soon went over to the electric plate and began to set up cups for distribution of coffee. The three distributed coffee to the rest of the boys and the therapist and set out a plate of crackers. Donald went over to the therapist to ask him how much sugar and cream he wanted in his coffee.

The boys being very much interested, Jonathan continued to tell them about the twenty-one-year-old female biology teacher he had had. All he would do was look at her "tits." He didn't care about doing biology. The boys laughed at this. Richard took the floor and began to talk about about how at the age of twelve, when he was at camp, a girl attempted to seduce him, and how a counselor beat him because the girl told the counselor that Richard tried to rape her. Jonathan was not to be put off, however, so he started a side discussion with Leonard. The therapist could not overhear what Jonathan was saying, but it had something to do with sex. Richard, in a voice loud and clear, was describing the sex orgies that took place at camp, with him just an innocent bystander. Coffee was by now distributed and all the boys sat down listening to Richard's story.

Richard was now back with the counselor who had beaten him because a girl had accused him of trying to rape her. He said: "I was twelve. I didn't even know what sex was." The therapist asked: "At the age of twelve, you never knew about it or thought about it?" Donald, boastfully. "Boy, when I was eight years old I had sexual intercourse with a sixteen-year-old girl." This diverted the group's attention to Donald and he took full advantage of it. He described a sixteen-year-old girl who was prostituting with boys in the neighborhood. One day a a friend of his had told him about this girl. He went to a place near the waterfront and there was this girl "with her tits hanging out. I open up my zipper and my dick was hanging out." He went over to the girl and he said, "Hey, your tits are hanging out." She said to him, "So what, your dick is hanging out." The boys responded to this narration with general hilarity. When it quieted down Donald continued: "I took the girl into a truck and screwed her. I was pretty anxious. I never did it before. This was my first time and I was finding out all about it. I didn't even know where the pussy was." Leonard looked very embarrassed. He blushed.

Richard interrupted Donald: "Hey, listen to this," and went on to tell about a girl he knew who was taking money from a lot of men and "she would let them do anything they wanted to her." He used to like this girl but after he found out about her, he wouldn't even go with her any more. This girl once told him that her brother had screwed her in the shower. Richard made a face of disgust and said: "You know her brother is in C—— Hospital now. He's a crazy guy." He went on to describe the girl's father, who used to "drink booze." Her younger brother, not the one in the hospital, also used to drink. The father used to give it to him. Richard continued for quite some time describing how the police had once come to the girl's house and caught six men who were in the apartment with her. He described how once he had peeked through the door and saw this girl running around practically naked. She was wearing only a towel and there were men in the apartment. At one point the therapist asked what had made this girl do all these things. Richard said, "I guess she just liked money." Leonard and Michael added, "Yeah, she did it all for money, and really liked it."

As the group were finishing their coffee, Donald became very busy. He went to the washroom, brought back a paper towel, and began cleaning up the floor where a few drops of coffee had spilled. He winked at the therapist when he caught his eye as if to say, "Look at the good job

I'm doing." Jonathan in the meantime was trying to take the floor away from Richard by saying that he once was "jumped" by a girl who knocked him to the floor and tried to "rape" him. He then asked: "Can a girl get sent up for rape?" The boys broke into laughter at this. He then began to boast about the many adventures he had had. He had had intercourse with eight girls, he claimed.

When this talk had died down, the therapist commented that the group could continue talking next week. It was now 8:20 and they had agreed in the preceding session to break up at 8:00 P.M. As the group descended the stairs, Donald hung back and turned to the therapist: "Mr. Ellery, are you a social worker?" "Yes." He looked at the therapist awhile and then said: "You know I got a social worker. I don't think I'm progressing with him, but we really had a good talk tonight."

COMMENT

The boys still offered resistance, but now felt free enough to narrate their misbehavior in the past, admit to it, and talk about their real and probably also fantasied sexual escapades. This might also have been a testing maneuver of the therapist, but its significance lay in the fact that they felt comfortable and secure with him, which laid the basis for more significant self-revelations, and hence self-confrontations, in the future.

Session Seven

ABSENT: Kurt, who was discharged from the Village.

Jonathan was first to arrive. He said that he had been running; it was a long distance, and he was out of breath. He sat down and remained silent. The other boys filed in. As soon as Michael had taken a seat he said: "I don't think Richard is going to be here tonight. He quit just like Jameson did." Donald confirmed it, saying that Richard probably would not come. Michael looked at Donald as if to say, "You said enough, don't say any more." Suddenly Richard walked into the room. Jules, who was lounging on the couch, said, "Yeah, we know, you quit." Both boys burst into laughter, and Donald said, "Go ahead, say it, you quit." Richard smiled and said, "Aw shut up, who's asking you?" and took a seat. Nothing more was said about this.

While this was going on Jonathan was already beginning to describe his adventures on a runaway, and once Richard sat down everybody in the room turned their attention to Jonathan. Jonathan talked for about eight minutes of his experiences in running away with several boys from the Village, describing how he slept on a roof, how one night he got drunk, and woke up in a strange room. The first person he saw was his friend's sister. His friend was still not apprehended. Seeing the girl, Jonathan jumped up and ran out of the room. The boys laughed at this and Richard asked, "Why did you run?" Jonathan: "Because I was sleeping in the same room with Leroy's sister. I didn't want her to see me. She was still asleep." He then described how he and the other two boys stole from a bakery truck that was parked, and how one day when he was standing in a hallway "making a girl, a cop came into the hall" and asked: "Why don't you get yourself an apartment?" The boys laughed at this. Jonathan then went on to tell that Leroy's sister liked him. One day Leroy caught his sister "fooling around with a boy and beat her bloody." Jonathan became "very, very mad" and jumped on Leroy, but then Leroy said: "Get off me, you dope. Don't you know what my sister did?" He asked Leroy what happened and the latter explained that his sister had hit him, kicked him "in the balls." That's why he was beating her up. Jonathan explained that then it was okay with him.

Richard interrupted to tell about how cops on a number of occasions chased him over rooftops, and Jules interjected a question as to why he was being chased. Richard did not answer but continued to relate that he had a certain cousin who was beaten up by the police. Jonathan gave details on how he was beaten by the police on one occasion because they thought he had narcotics on him. He was searched, and when they did not find any narcotics, they beat him further to make him tell them where he had hidden them.

While this was going on Michael found a magazine in the room and began to leaf through it. Every so often he would divert his attention from the magazine to ask either Richard or Jonathan, who were competing for the audience, to clarify certain points about the exploits they were describing. Donald looked very restless. He got up, walked out of the room, and then returned. He became very much interested in the water which was boiling for coffee near his chair. He periodically turned the thermostat on the hot plate. He concentrated his attention also on the coffee, the crackers, the sugar, and other things.

For some time Jonathan and Richard appeared to be holding a private conversation as the attention of the others was focused upon them, completely ignoring the therapist. Nonetheless, Jonathan and Richard tended to look at him as they described their exploits. Michael, too, when he lifted his eyes from the magazine, looked toward the therapist, as though curious what his reaction was.

Jonathan appeared to be "stealing the show" from Richard and was holding the boys entranced with his descriptions of exploits while "on the run" from the Village, of sleeping in a variety of places, scrounging for food, and the contacts he had made in the city. The therapist asked how he felt while "on the run." Jonathan answered: "It feels the greatest! It's freedom!" Richard seconded this, saying, "Boy, if you can get out of the Village it feels grand." Jonathan now brought the discussion again back to describing Leroy's sister; she used curse words, and although Jonathan used to like her, he no longer did, because she cursed so much. He then said that was why he did not mind too much when Leroy was beating her.

Richard said that he knew a lot of words in French. In fact his mother was French and when she didn't want him to know something she talked in French. He once had a friend who taught him a lot of French curse words. Jules (who was of French extraction) asked Richard something in French and what it meant. "I never heard it," said Richard. Jonathan said: "I'm French. I know a lot of words in French," but Jonathan could not answer Jules's question either. Michael said something in French, and Jonathan said, "That means penis." The boys all laughed as Donald looked in the direction of the therapist. Richard went on to describe how somebody in his family had taught him the word for "eating" in French, but it was really the word for "shit." He didn't know it, so he came home one day and, wanting to impress his mother, asked her for food in the French he was taught. What he got was a resounding slap on the head. His mother was furious at him. Richard immediately switched to another subject, talking about an uncle of his who had once beaten a man, "hanging him up on the wall" and slapping him. He then went on to talk of a sister of this uncle's who used to "rat" on him all the time and how the uncle got into trouble with the police. Jonathan immediately said that he knew a fellow who got into trouble because his sister "ratted" on him.

Knowing that Richard had a rather severe problem with his sister, who had always been presented to him by his mother as being far more intelligent than he, a better student, and so on, the therapist raised the question as to whether Richard found in his experience that sisters report on one. Richard literally leaped out of his seat in his eagerness to tell of his troubles with his sister. "My sister is a dirty bum." Leonard got up from his seat and took the chair next to the therapist and said quietly: "I got trouble with my brother, too." Richard went on to tell of several situations where his sister was the favorite. For instance, Richard would stay up late watching television, his sister sitting near him. His father would come over and say to Richard, "Get to bed." Richard would say to his father, "What about her?" The father would say, "Mind your own goddamned business; just get to bed!" Michael, almost under his breath, commented: "That's what happens when you got sisters. They get you into trouble." Richard, however, was not going to give Michael a chance. He described several incidents in which his sister, knowing that he stayed away from school and such, reported it to his parents.

Jules was initiating a side conversation with Donald (who was now busy serving coffee to everybody and asking the therapist how much cream and sugar he would like in his coffee) commenting that he had eight (sic!) brothers.[8] Michael was helping Donald in the preparation and serving of the coffee. Jonathan said that he got along fine with his sister; sometimes his sister gave him money. The therapist turned to Leonard, who was sitting next to him, saying that he wanted to say something about him and his brother. Leonard said: "I taught my brother to mind his own business. I once wanted to beat him up. Now he knows that my business is my business and his business is his business. I don't bother him and he don't bother me." Richard and Jonathan were comparing notes concerning their respective sisters, with Jonathan being very protective of his, and Richard telling Jonathan of how his eleven-year-old sister was going out with a boy. He had seen this boy for only two hours and when he got home he was going "to beat this boy's ass" if he didn't like him. Michael turned to Richard and asked: "How old is this boy?" Richard said, "He's either thirteen or fourteen." He said he had to know a boy who went with his sister and to make sure he was a nice guy; otherwise, the boy had better watch out!

The boys now became very restless. Donald and Michael were moving about serving coffee, and Richard again monopolized the discussion, narrating incidents of violence. He told of someone he knew who had gone to Harlem and gotten an ice pick in his back. Jonathan told of taking a chain and putting it around a boy's throat who tried to fool around with his sister, and almost killing him. Since Richard's voice was much louder than Jonathan's he seemed to be commanding more attention.

Richard continued at some length about the gangs, the beatings in Harlem, the friends he knew that were beaten up, and so forth. Jonathan invited Richard to come around to his block in the city where he lived and see what went on there: the muggings, picking pockets, blackjack-ings, and so on. Donald now began to describe a fight he had with a boy in his cottage and how severely he had beaten him up. Richard stopped talking long enough to ask Donald what had happened, and Donald said that the boy had kicked him "in the balls." Michael began to laugh at this, and Donald angrily turned on him and asked: "What's so funny?"

Gradually the discussion shifted to acting out. Richard described

8. The anamnesis records only four boys in the family.

putting on a white sheet one night and going over to the bed of a boy whom he knew as "very stupid," waking him, and whispering that he came to take him to heaven in a death carriage awaiting outside. He mimicked the boy, who had begun to weep and call for his mother. There was absolute silence as the boys listened to this story. Richard then described a television program he saw that had to do with ghosts, people being frightened, miracles happening, and so on. When Richard finished, Jonathan stepped in and described how he and a friend had gone through a cemetery and put red paint on a tombstone. The friend in passing by the tombstone brushed his hand against it and became frightened, thinking the red was blood. Leonard said that one night in his cottage he and two other boys had scared the daylights out of a boy by dressing up like ghosts. With relish and glee he described how the boy, running in fright, had fallen down a whole flight of stairs. Leonard, who sat next to the therapist, turned toward him as if he were telling him the story in private. Richard now told of a boy he knew, with whom he had gone on a trip to Bear Mountain, and who had covered his eyes while passing a cemetery, pointing up his right hand, because when you passed a cemetery and did that the dead people would go to heaven. Richard had asked him why he covered his eyes, and the boy said, "I'm not going to look at no cemetery."

Donald rose and began straightening up the room and announced he was not going to be the only one to clean up tonight. The others had better help him. No one responded and Donald went about cleaning up the floor, on which some water had been spilled. Leonard picked up the therapist's empty paper coffee cup and put it away. *The conversation turned back to beatings*, with Richard again taking the initiative. Jonathan described how he used to steal cars and smash them up. Around his block boys play "chicken." Two boys get in separate cars at opposite ends of the block and race toward one another. The one who puts his foot on the brake first is chicken. Donald burst out laughing and said, "I used to steal cars, too," and began to describe gangs he knew who "picked up" cars and sold them across state lines.

The therapist, feeling that the nature of the conversation might be intended as a test of him, remained quiet throughout.

Jonathan went over to Jules, who was still lounging on the couch, to tell him of some experience he had, but because he whispered it the therapist could not hear what was said. Donald came over to the therapist and said that he was given a pair of good shoes by some of the "club ladies" (volunteers). They were real heavy but he didn't like the style. He would have liked to have *given them to the therapist* and would bring them the next day. He asked the size of the shoe the therapist wore and was told. Donald examined the therapist's shoes by touching them;

as he did so he described his shoes in detail. The therapist asked their width, and Donald said he thought they were size C; this was much too narrow. Donald seemed very disappointed, saying they were "beautiful shoes." He didn't want to give them to his father because they would not fit him, and he didn't want to wear them *himself*: He didn't like the way they looked, they were too heavy. He thought that the therapist might like to wear them.

The conversation turned to going home the next week for Thanksgiving. They would be leaving on Wednesday, and the therapist commented that there would be no meeting of the group, since it met on that day. Jonathan said, "I'm not going to be here, either." Richard: "You mean you're running away?" Jonathan: "No, I changed my mind. I'm not going to run away. Mr. D. is going to take me off the hill for a trip."

As the group was leaving, Richard and Donald stayed behind to help clean up. The others walked out of the room rather slowly, and when the therapist came down he found Donald waiting for him. Pointing to the therapist's office, he asked: "Is that your office?" "Yes, it is." "Can I see it?" The therapist invited him to come in. He looked around, saw a pipe on the desk, and asked whether the therapist smoked a pipe. He did. He then examined the pipe, wanted to know what kind of tobacco the therapist smoked, and was shown the brand. Donald then said that he, too, smoked a pipe and added: "*I wish you were my social worker. I can't stand the one I got.*" The therapist told Donald that he did not see any boys individually. Donald said he knew that.

Richard, who must have been standing outside the door, came in and said he wondered if the therapist had anything to do with allowing him to make a phone call (home). The therapist told Richard that he had nothing to do with that. Richard said that at the time when he began going to the group he had asked his social worker about making a phone call. His social worker had told him that, since he was now going to the group, whenever he wanted to make a phone call he was to ask the therapist. The therapist repeated his statement about not being involved in phone calls. In the meantime, Donald had noticed the therapist's eyeglass case on the desk. He examined it and said, "*I'm going to make you another one* out of leather and I'm going to stitch it." He took a yellow pad and a pencil that were lying on the desk, traced an outline of the eyeglass case, and repeated that he was going to make a case in the shop.

Richard left, and Donald repeated the story of the fight he had had, displaying a bite on his hand. He said he didn't want to hit the boy, but the boy was goading him on and kicked him "in the balls." The therapist commented that he was sure he had his reasons for fighting.

Donald said: "Yeah, I was going to talk about it tonight but somehow I didn't get to it. Well, Mr. Ellery, I guess I'll be seeing you in two weeks since we won't meet next week. I'll be home"—and he left.

COMMENT

This session demonstrated a continuation of the boys' resistance. Their conversations consisted of inconsequential incidents, but were important as displays of power and potency for some of them.

The themes were violence, incestuous trends toward their sisters, fear of death, and superstitions (magic). These were conglomerated in their unconscious. We shall deal with the place of violence in their lives and their fears of death in later sessions; discussion of incestuous attitudes toward sisters will be omitted as too threatening. However, with their growing psychosexual maturity these feelings should be adequately repressed.[9]

Note need be taken of the growing positive transference toward the therapist: he was served coffee, one boy wished to present him with shoes, another to make an eyeglass case for him, and another wished the therapist were the boy's caseworker (father). The slow pace with which the boys left the meeting room might have meant that they felt guilty toward the therapist, or were themselves dissatisfied with the content of the interview. They could not assert now, as one boy did at another session, "We had a good talk tonight." However, it was better to allow the boys to experience this frustration than to draw them out. Frustration at this point eventually leads to more rapid and more sound emotional maturity.

Session Eight

All the boys came on time, Michael and Richard last. Michael explained that he had had to run all the way because he didn't want to be late. Leonard took a seat remote from the other boys, who were not in their usual places. Jonathan took a seat on the couch with Jules. Michael sat in the chair that the therapist ordinarily occupied. Jonathan at once initiated a conversation by inquiring from the therapist where he could take his brother after his five years in prison. The therapist did not respond to this at once, but seeing Jonathan waiting for an answer, said that there were any number of places he could take his brother. Jonathan quickly said, "Yeah, I know, but where I want to take

9. This topic was openly brought out in the second year of therapy.

him he'll get in trouble again." Asked what he meant, Jonathan replied that there was a certain street in R——— where one could get a lot of girls whom he described as V-girls. But since his brother was on parole, he would get into trouble.

Michael asked how long the brother would be on parole, and Jonathan said that it would be a number of years. Jonathan then asked the therapist directly: If his brother asked about the girl who had accused him unjustly of raping her, would the therapist advise him to tell him where she was? The therapist asked Jonathan if he felt some sort of responsibility for his brother. Jonathan said he did. After all, his brother was the best friend he had. Then he concluded that he did not think he would tell his brother where the girl was because he would beat her up and get himself into prison again.

Richard entered the discussion, telling about a number of girls he had known who could get fellows into trouble because they often claimed things happened to them when they really did not. As soon as Richard said this, Michael became restless, playing with and examining his fingernails. Donald looked disgusted. Jonathan turned the discussion to some of the incidents around his neighborhood, with special emphasis on the gangs. (Jonathan's manner of talking was quite different from the last group session. His voice was now stronger. He no longer talked in a monotone, and did not appear to be mumbling to himself as in the past. His head was not bowed or resting on his hand.)

As Jonathan was describing to the boys some of the incidents that occurred in his neighborhood, Richard said, "I didn't have such a good week end home." His aunt had to be taken to a hospital, and given oxygen and blood plasma. He steered clear of the therapist's effort at exploring his feelings in this matter and instead talked about his visit to the hospital with his parents, as a result of which he did not get a chance to do a number of things he had planned. However, he was not going to tell anybody what he was going to do. The boys in the group had been on week ends for Thanksgiving except Jonathan and Michael, and the therapist inquired as to what their week ends had been like. Donald said he had a nice week end; in fact he had come home (to Children's Village) drunk. Jonathan asked him what he had been drinking but Donald, looking in the direction of the therapist, said it was none of Jonathan's business. No one said anything about this. There appeared to be a lot of moving about at this point, reflecting considerable restlessness.

The conversation became diffuse and difficult to follow. Jonathan talked about a couple of boys he knew that had gotten drunk. Richard was not listening to him and began to talk about an uncle of his who drank and then quickly switched to talking about a television program he had seen. Donald, with an uncomfortable smile, looked visibly annoyed with Leonard, who withdrew from the group. Donald angrily asked the therapist point blank whether he had attended any conferences on the boys as yet. Jonathan responded to this, saying: "He doesn't go to your conferences." This the therapist confirmed. Recognizing the resistance of the boys, the therapist said: "I notice that whenever you talk about yourselves, something begins to happen. You begin to move around or change the subject. I can understand that perhaps you are uncomfortable about it and yet I really wonder if you realize the value of talking, what purpose it serves."

The boys stopped acting restless and their attention turned to the therapist. He continued: "Let me give you an example of what the value of talking is." He then told of two men walking down the street when both spot a dollar lying on the sidewalk. "Both run, but one of them picks it up and puts it in his pocket. The other suddenly sees red. He clenches his fists, grits his teeth, and becomes so angry that he attacks the man who picked up the dollar. What happens then? The man who is being beaten yells, a policeman comes, and the man who was doing the beating is taken to jail. He loses one, two, or three weeks of work, and he then does not have enough money to support himself or his family. Now it looks like the whole fight started because of the dollar, but is this really so? The man who got so angry could just as easily have said to himself, 'Well, next time maybe I'll be faster and it isn't worth getting into trouble for this.' He goes off to work, makes wages, takes it home, has enough to live on. But what made the man see red when he did not pick up the dollar. This was related to deep feelings of anger, frustration, shame, wanting to get even—feelings that maybe the man carried within him all his life, and these feelings have gotten worse. Even when he sits in a chair he does not feel comfortable; he is restless, he squirms. It has been found from working with hundreds of people that one of the ways to overcome and work out and not continue to be bothered by these feelings that push you into trouble is to talk about them. To get to know them, and maybe in getting to know them, they won't have to take such a toll of you. You don't have to be so afraid of them. It's like when you were a little boy, you heard footsteps, you were frightened, you turn on the light and, there, it was only your parents. You wonder what you were so frightened about. It is the same way with our feelings."

During this speech the therapist received the complete attention of the group except for Donald, who seemed uncomfortable and squirmed in his seat, and Michael, who was staring at the ceiling as if he were trying to remove himself. Jules leaned over, looking intently at the speaker, his mouth open, his head nodding in agreement. The therapist went on to describe other situations that might bother the boys, reminding them how they had talked a few weeks before about sex and that this was another thing that bothered all boys everywhere. Coming out of his reverie, Michael commented that once he was awakened by footsteps at night and found that somebody had a key to his apartment. This brought laughter from the group. However, the laughter was short-lived and the boys became silent again. The therapist continued by telling them that sometimes a fellow just sits in a chair but even just sitting bothers him. He finds himself restless and nervous. Donald nodded his head in assent. The therapist included himself in the discussion and told the boys that a number of years ago he used to find himself very restless and didn't know what was bothering him. He was tense, his stomach didn't feel right, but he discovered that by going to somebody and talking about these things he was helped a great deal. Different people can handle this in different ways. They surely have all known women who, when they get tense, nervous, and angry, scream to get it out of their systems. They have not learned how to talk about what bothers them.

Leonard immediately said, "That's happened to me." Asked what he meant, he said: "I used to get very restless. I can't sit in a chair." When the therapist tried to explore this with Leonard, the attention of the group was drawn away by Michael, who was setting a piece of paper on fire with a match and putting it in the ash tray to burn out. This act made the boys even more restless. Donald at once applied himself to preparing coffee for the group. Richard stood up, placed himself at the center of the floor, and began to tell the boys about what he planned to do next time he went home. This was in no way related to what had been discussed. The therapist said very directly to the boys that it appeared that what he said stirred up something in each one of them. "Look what's happening," Jules quickly said. "You sure got Michael, look at him!" Donald stated that he got restless very often, but when the therapist tried to explore this, Donald quickly shut off the discussion.

There was now bedlam in the room, a great deal of commotion and random activity. Michael went out to the washroom and soon came back; Donald was distributing coffee, and Michael took over this job. But interestingly there was a shift in the seating arrangement. As each boy picked up some crackers and was waiting for his paper cup of coffee to be brought to him, he sat down closer to the therapist. It reached the point where he thought that some boys would literally sit on his lap. Leonard rose from his chair at the end of the room, moved over to be near the therapist, but took a seat on the arm of a leather chair which was farthest removed from the therapist. He started a conversation with Jules which had something to do with what was just said. The therapist asked Leonard if he wanted to talk about it to the group as a whole, but he became very embarrassed as Jules motioned to him not to say anything.

Donald yelled out to Michael, "Don't forget to make a cup of coffee for Mr. Ellery!" and then began to talk about his having come to the Village drunk after his week end. He had been drinking vodka, gin, rye, and other things. Jonathan interrupted to describe the liquor cabinet at his home, with stocks of practically every conceivable kind of liquor. Donald, however, pressed on, saying that he was very much afraid to return to the Village. He did not want people here to see him drunk. Jonathan again attempted to take the conversation away from Donald. This time he talked about a night watchman "who bothers the boys at night." His shoes squeak and this wakes up the boys at 2:00 and 3:00 A.M. Everyone became interested in this. Jules, resentfully: "Yeah, they are constantly watching us." The therapist asked what he meant by "constantly" being watched. This gave rise to a group discussion the tenor of which was that "wherever you go, there is somebody looking at you. They always have to know where you are and what you are doing." Jules said, "The people think they're so smart and we have to prove that we're smarter than they are." He described a cottage father who was always trying to outfox him. He was always trying to see where he was, as if to guard against his running away. When Jules became aware of this he hid himself where no one could find him just to prove that he could be smarter.

The therapist asked: "What do you think would happen if there were no night watchmen?" Jonathan immediately picked this up and said, "Probably none of us would run." Michael: "Come on, you know some of them would run." Jules: "Well, some boys will always run, but most of us wouldn't. They don't have to watch us like a hawk." The therapist commented that from what the boys were saying he got the feeling that they were constantly involved in a battle of outsmarting adults. Jules immediately said: "That's true. It never happened to me when I was home, but here at the Village I always find ways of showing the people that I'm just as smart as they are." Donald: "I don't do that. I just mind my own business." Therapist to Donald: "What happens when people don't let you mind your own business?" Donald: "Then I get very mad and have nothing to do with them." Richard was now describing his experiences at the Village and at home, how he would find ways to outsmart the truant officer and the staff in his cottage. His cottage parents were always ready to believe the worst and not give him a chance, so he might just as well do things because they wouldn't believe him anyway.

Although the boys remained seated, the group was becoming restless, with a lot of shuffling of feet. Donald returned to talk about his drinking escapades again and how he was afraid to come back to the Village. His fears were realized because, when a supervisor had found that he had liquor on his breath, he gave him a "bawling out"; he was treated like a small child. Everyone in the group now joined the discussion about drinking. Even Leonard claimed that on occasion he had taken whiskey. Therapist: "You know, I kind of wonder. What is the jazz you get from drinking?" Donald immediately said: "You know that is the kind of question Dr. ——— asked me when he found out I was drinking. He said to me, 'Why do you drink?' and I told him, 'To be happy.' He said, 'What's the matter, aren't you happy at home, you have to drink?'" The therapist smiled at Donald and said, "Okay, are you saying that I am like Dr. ———?" Donald said, "No, that's not what I mean," and dropped the subject. Therapist (to all the boys): "Look, here is why I asked the question. I remember when I was your age, on one or two occasions when a buddy would come from the army, I would have a couple of drinks. It feels good for a while but then there's that little extra drink that just makes you sick." All of the boys nodded their heads. Leonard laughed aloud: "Yeah, I know." The therapist attempted to describe graphically coming home drunk, going to bed, closing one's eyes, and all of a sudden how the room spins.

Jonathan, Richard, and Donald were talking to each other, confirming that this is exactly what happened. Therapist: "Okay, this is what happens. You get sick as a dog so where is the jazz?" Donald: "I drink because things feel better when I got liquor inside me." Jonathan: "Yeah, you feel you haven't got a problem in the world. You're walking real nice with liquor inside you." Leonard: "It's just a habit. Once you drink, you can't stop." Therapist: "But there's a reason for this habit. When you smoke a cigarette there is something in the cigarette that acts to make it habit-forming." Using the word *physiology*, he said that there was a drug in cigarettes that created a habit, but liquor isn't like that. Richard said he knew people who wouldn't even eat food; they would rather drink. Therapist: "How come a person would pass up food to take liquor?" Richard: "I guess they just got to be like that. Maybe without liquor they don't feel they can ever do anything. I know when I grow up I'm going to drink all the time. I won't be able to stop." The therapist attempted to pursue this further, but Richard withdrew and the therapist dropped the subject.

The group was breaking up now. Michael raised the possibility of changing the meeting time from a quarter to seven back to seven because he couldn't finish his chores in time. The group discussed this, the leaders being Jonathan and Donald, with the other boys quietly going along. Leonard finally said that he did not care as to the time. At this the boys agreed to change the time back to seven o'clock.

COMMENT

Donald's need to be well thought of by the therapist (positive transference) was reflected in his embarrassment when Jonathan questioned him about his drinking (he looked at the therapist). The other boys showed the same need by their obvious anxiety.

We had for some time been aware that the boys did not have any understanding of what therapy was or the reasons why they had been committed to the Village (beyond punishment). We had discussed it during our supervision conferences and decided that whenever an opportunity presented itself the need of inner change and the process by which this change can be effected should be brought to the boys' attention. The therapist did this in this session, though somewhat clumsily. The fact that the therapist included himself, thus reducing the gulf between himself and the boys, was helpful, but the boys on the whole were not ready for it and resisted continuing along the lines of self-analysis (inner threat).

One of the aims we set ourselves and which we repeatedly discussed at the supervisory conferences was to evoke in the boys some degree of "psychologic literacy"—the understanding of causation and purpose in the human psyche. The therapist aims to do this in relation to drink and the need for drink, but obviously the attempt was made too soon.

Session Nine

Donald and Jonathan were first to arrive, about five minutes early. Donald brought a container of powdered coffee and one of milk, saying that he had finally brought the coffee he had promised he would. He went on to explain that he obtained the coffee and milk from his cottage. This instant coffee was better than what the group was using and he would like the boys to try it. He then leaned toward the therapist and brushed off the trouser leg of his pants, saying, "You got dirt on your pants." Turning to Jonathan, Donald said he was not sure he would be getting his week end because of what happened "last time." He explained: "I fucked myself up this time coming back late and drunk. I shouldn't have come back drunk." He went on to explain (to Jonathan) that tonight in New York his mother was supposed to see his caseworker, who would discuss with his mother his going home for the Christmas week end.

By this time all the other boys except Richard came in. Jonathan said Richard would not come this evening. When Michael asked, "How do you know?" Jonathan did not respond. Richard came in a few seconds later.

Donald announced to the boys that he had brought coffee. This served as a signal for Michael to walk toward the hot plate to see whether the water was boiling. In the meantime, Donald continued by saying that he sure hoped he would go home for Christmas. Richard said that he was expecting to go and didn't know why all the boys shouldn't be going home. A discussion at this point ensued, led off by Michael, about how many days "out-of-town" boys[10] got. Jonathan maintained that they get seven days at home; Michael reminded him that it was actually nine. Jonathan insisted that the two extra days were for traveling. "You can't really spend them at home," he said. Jules said that even though he really was an out-of-town boy he didn't get nine days in a row because he lived in C———. Michael: "Well, that isn't too far away. You don't need two days to travel there." Jules: "I know. You can get home in about an hour."

Jonathan narrated how cottage parents could prevent boys from going home on week ends if they really wanted to, but did not imply that they would do this. If he had to stay at the Village he knew the cottage he would like to be at. "It's the cottage Leonard is in. I like those people." He wiggled his eyebrows to indicate the double meaning of this statement. Leonard seemed to recognize it and began to laugh. Jonathan continued: "That's a good cottage to be in. I could get along fine with the cottage mother and with the third person there." The boys laughed at this. The therapist was puzzled and asked Jonathan whom he meant by a third person. Jonathan replied: "The cottage parents' daughter." A discussion ensued, led by Jonathan, about the good-looking cottage mother and her daughter. Finally he self-consciously murmured: "I wouldn't mind," and dropped the subject while Leonard was still laughing.

Donald asked Jonathan how he liked his new cottage parents. Jonathan said that they "don't know the ropes" yet. The cottage father never asked him to do anything directly but worked through the cottage mother, so Jonathan was having trouble with her. He did not amplify this and there was silence for a while. Finally, Jonathan said in a lower tone: "I don't give a shit what they do or don't do. They seem all mixed

10. Boys from distant cities, other than New York City.

up about what they want the boys to do. I mind my own business and they leave me alone." All of a sudden Michael again asked Jonathan whether he was sure that he had seven or nine days vacation. Jonathan replied that he would get seven: "They do give two extra days for traveling, but you can't consider this part of the vacation." Donald walked over to Michael, gave him the can of coffee he had brought, and told Michael to make a cup of it so that Mr. Ellery could try it out. In the meantime Richard started to talk about a new boy who was admitted to Children's Village. He learned that this boy had once robbed a large jewelry store in New York. Another boy who participated in the robbery was sent home because he pretended in court that he was crazy. He also had a lawyer who talked the judge into sending the boy home. Jonathan wondered how this was possible. Why did they send the boy home if he acted as if he were crazy? Richard said he didn't know, but thought that there was something unfair about it.

Jonathan changed the subject. He said that when he went home there were certain girls he was going to look up and was going to have a good time with them. As he was saying this, he looked slyly at the therapist. Richard, too, gazed at the therapist and began to laugh. Jonathan was now speaking in a low voice, something of a monotone, about what he was going to do at home. His speech was indistinct and it was very difficult to hear him. Simultaneously Richard was holding forth on how he would like to spend all his time just having "one big ball," and wishing he could fall asleep now and wake up when he was ready to go home. The therapist commented that days can pass pretty slowly when you're waiting for a week end. Richard: "That's right, every day seems like a week." Michael: "Yeah, I would like to fall asleep tomorrow morning, wake up or be awakened by somebody, and be told that it was time to get ready to start going home." Donald's response to this was that he didn't care, he didn't have to fall asleep; he could wait.

Michael was now beginning to distribute the coffee. Donald went over to help him, took a cup of the coffee to the therapist, and asked him to taste it, saying that the therapist could get this same kind of coffee for the group next week. The therapist asked him what brand it was and Donald named it. Michael spoke up: "Yeah, that's good coffee." Leonard: "My mother used to use this coffee and I liked it when I had it at home." The therapist promised to buy the coffee. Sparked by Donald, a discussion arose as to the possibility of obtaining a percolator. Donald offered to bring one next week. Leonard told him that if he could not get a percolator, maybe Leonard could bring the one from his cottage.

There was a lot of moving about at this point, with Jonathan and Richard holding a private conversation. Jules had gone out for a while and returned. During the interval Leonard seemed to seize the opportunity and said to the boys in a loud voice that he had a good deal of work in the cottage. The boys quieted down and asked him what he meant. Leonard said he cleaned the cottage parents' room, waxed the floors, and did some light dusting; he received $5 a month for it. This combined with his allowance gave him quite a bit of money to spend. Donald: "That's not bad." Leonard said that when his mother came up she gave him some money, too, so he always had money in his pocket. Jules wished he could get a "deal" like that so that he could have more money to spend on cigarettes and maybe buy himself some clothes.

Again a commotion arose in the group as the boys began to move around with considerable alacrity. Jules went back and forth to serve coffee to the boys who had yet not received theirs. Jonathan and Richard were again involved in conversation which the therapist could not overhear. Jonathan said something about girls he knew in the neighborhood to whom he was going to be introduced by his brother when the latter came out of prison.

At this point Leonard turned to the therapist and said: "I want to tell you something that happened the other day. There are two boys in my cottage who are smaller and younger than me and they are always picking on me. I try not to pay any attention to them but finally I just lost my temper. I got mad because they are always calling me names. Once in a while when the cottage parents aren't looking, one of them pokes me in the back. I didn't want to hurt them, I know they're smaller and I know they got problems, but I couldn't take it any more." He then described how in losing his temper he picked up one of the boys and threw him against a cabinet which fell over. The contents of the cabinet spilled all over the floor and his cottage parents made him stay up until midnight cleaning up the floor. The other boys were permitted to go upstairs and go to bed at the usual time while he had to stay behind and clean the floor. He described how angry he was about this and about the boys' picking on him. (It appeared that Leonard, in his shyness, was taking advantage of the group's present distractability to ventilate his feelings to the therapist without being overheard.) The therapist commented that he could easily understand his feeling angry about it. Leonard: "I usually like to mind my own business, but these boys wouldn't let me mind my business. They had to keep picking on me."

Richard, who had overheard the last remark, asked Leonard, "What happened?" All the boys seemed to quiet down and turn their attention to Leonard. Donald repeated, "Yeah, what happened to you?" Leonard looked at the therapist in surprise. He had not anticipated anyone overhearing the conversation. Richard insisted on knowing what happened, and Leonard kept looking at the therapist as if he did not know what to do or say. He gestured with his hand to the therapist as if giving him permission to tell the boys what he had just said. Therapist: "You want me to tell them what happened?" Leonard: "Yes, please." When the therapist finished, Jonathan reacted by saying boastfully: "Nobody picks on me in my cottage! They used to, because they thought I was smaller than them, but I stood up and fought back and even though I didn't always win they learned that they're not to pick on me." He launched into another harangue about his brother coming out of prison, saying that the girl whom his brother had "made pregnant" was married and that her husband had died. He implied that the girl married a policeman, and by way of a eulogy said, "He was a good cop." Donald burst out laughing at Jonathan's putting the emphasis on the word "was." Jonathan suddenly said: "I wish I was Jewish. If I was Jewish I would be at Hawthorne instead of Children's Village." At Hawthorne, at least they have girls. He knew a couple of the girls at Hawthorne. In fact he used to see one of them when he was "on the run"; he described her as a real mean-looking girl, but she was loads of fun. Donald and Michael snickered at this.

Richard wished that when he went home he could stay "a long time." Jonathan: "Why don't you just not come back?" Richard: "Oh, I want to come back, but I wish they would give me more days at home." Donald: "You ought to be glad you're not in some other institutions that never let you go home. Here, they let you go home once in a while." Richard: "Yeah, that's what one of the teachers was telling us, but that's a lot of jazz. This teacher was telling us how there's an institution in Chicago where you can't even go home once a year." Jules said that if they didn't let him go home he would make sure that he got out of the Village.

At this point Jonathan turned to Donald and began to involve him in some discussion about drinking. However, Donald didn't appear to be too interested. He appeared to be more interested in what Richard was saying. Richard was standing up, telling the boys about a certain bar he had gone to with his father. While his father was seated at a table at the rear of the bar, the bartender gave Richard a glass of beer. Richard took the glass of beer to his father's table and began to drink it. The father asked him, "Where did you get the beer?" Richard said, "The bartender gave it to me." The father then drank Richard's beer, gave Richard the empty glass, and said, "Let's see you get another glass of beer from the bartender." Richard took the empty glass to the bartender and told him, "Fill it up," and the bartender did. He then described how his father went over to the bar and bought the bartender drinks until he was drunk. Leonard laughed as Richard really warmed up to the subject. He described how his father got the bartender drunk just to prove to Richard that he could get anybody drunk. (*Note:* In Richard's case record, the father is described as a delinquent and as having encouraged the boy in his delinquent behavior.) Richard now boasted of an uncle who could "drink anybody under the table." At this point Jonathan turned to Donald and got him involved in a discussion about drinking. Although the therapist sat next to Donald and Jonathan, he could not overhear their conversation, since Richard was still standing up and haranguing the group. All the therapist could hear was Donald telling Jonathan something about the bars he frequented, the girls he had picked up. There seemed to be a contest between the two, carried on in low voices, as to which frequented more bars. Every so often Jonathan would cast his eyes in the direction of the therapist to see how he reacted to their conversation.

Richard began reporting on a trip to a department store in a nearby town with his cottage mother and a few other boys. One of the boys was passing remarks about a woman shopper. Richard did not want to be associated with him as he felt ashamed of his companion. On the drive over, the cottage mother told the boys to make sure that they did not have "glue on their fingers" (meaning that they should not steal). Richard continued to narrate his experience at the age of four of falling out of a window, of having been taken to the hospital with his head completely bandaged, his leg broken and in a cast. He demonstrated to the boys the position in which he was lying in the hospital while in traction. The peculiar quality of his recital was his detached, matter-of-fact manner, almost as if he were an observer rather than the victim. Richard then leaned over and invited the therapist to look at his forehead, to see how the right side of his forehead protruded. The left side of his forehead was depressed. While Richard was making his speech, Michael was lying on the couch, his eyes covered by his forearms.

Richard now told of being bitten by a dog, giving gory details, describing blood rushing out of his leg, covering the ground, while the dog hung on to his thigh. He had to have ten stitches. He then said that when he came home from the hospital he would go into the bathroom and pull off the tape just to look at the stitches. Every so often the stitches would pop. Jonathan and Donald stopped to listen to this latest detail from Richard but soon returned to their own conversation. Richard now launched into a description of how when he was younger his mother would get angry and hit him on the head. His father in a rage warned her not to hit Richard on the head because of his condition. However, when he used to get angry he, too, would hit him on the head, then his mother would become annoyed and yell at the father. When he was a "kid" he was never allowed by his mother to play stickball; he couldn't play football, and he couldn't run around. When he went out of the house, his mother was always worried about what would happen to him. After this Richard quieted down and took his seat.

Quite a commotion began in the room. Jules had run out again but soon came back. Michael turned on the couch toward the wall. The therapist asked Richard how he felt when he was not allowed to play freely. Richard's face suddenly grew red. He said, "I felt just like a rotten damn." Leonard immediately stepped in and said: "Yeah, that's what I was trying to say before when I was telling you about my cottage. When your parents don't let you do things like this, they make you feel like a big baby." Richard: "I didn't feel like a big baby, but I felt like I was glued to the house. I didn't like the idea of my mother always worrying about what's going to happen to you and they always go around watching you. You feel like a little boy." Jules got up and began to collect the empty paper cups. Michael proceeded to clean up the room. Richard started to talk about an uncle he did not like. This uncle had a daughter whom Richard was dating. His uncle used to encourage him to kiss the girl, but Richard refused to do it. When he was in the hospital, the uncle used to come and visit him, and would sit on his bed. Richard, knowing that he was there, would pretend to be asleep. Then Richard changed the subject by turning to Donald, who was still involved in conversation with Jonathan, to tell Donald to bring milk next time in a carton, for ordinary milk was better than evaporated milk (which the therapist supplied).

COMMENT

The theme of dependence upon the mother is emphasized. However, the concept of "home" was substituted and the topic was less personalized and affect-laden. Movement toward the therapist and the group made its appearance. Donald, for example, brought food for the group and brushed off some dust from the therapist's pants. Distractibility was lessened, even though the content of the session was still of negligible therapeutic value.

Donald's lack of interest in discussing drinking with Jonathan was an important step in his development, for this was one of his claims to strength and importance; however, when he monopolized the group discussion later, he boasted about it and involved his father in his narration. Here we become aware of another therapeutic aim: the need to substitute a healthier ego ideal for that of the father and the hard-drinking uncle. This would become one of the functions of the therapist.

Richard acted in this session as a typical *monopolizer*, and he was permitted to do so partly because he played into the other boys' resistance and partly because the content of his narration struck a resonance in their own wishes and experiences. These were, among others, striving for potency, latent homoeroticism, and sibling rivalry.

Note need be taken of Leonard's slowly growing self-assurance, obviously by identification with the other boys, and his capacity to relate to the therapist. This is a good example of "vicarious therapy."

Session Ten

ABSENT: Jules[11]

Richard was first to arrive. He was followed shortly after by Donald and then Michael. Richard came in puffing and was jabbering with Michael about some fight. Donald picked this up and said that there was going to be a fight outside and he was going to be there. Richard seemed to forget about the fight and said, "I got a lot of problems at home I would like to talk about tonight." He went on to tell that he saw his mother fighting with his drunken father, who was beating her up. It seemed that his mother had thrown a spoon at his father at the dinner table over some minor disagreement and the father had gone out, got drunk, and come back home and beat up his wife.

By this time all the other boys were entering the room. Donald seemed to have something on his mind. He turned to the therapist and told him that there was a fight going on downstairs, and would he mind if he went down to watch it? The therapist said to Donald that it was up to him and Donald began to leave the room. Michael, however, said, "How do you know Mr. Ellery wants you to go downstairs?" Donald said, "Well he didn't say I couldn't go," and ran out.

Richard sat somewhat slumped over in his chair, his face tense. He appeared very disturbed, cracking his knuckles. Jonathan had overheard the last part of Richard's earlier description of the fight downstairs. Michael became involved in a discussion of it. From what Jonathan said, it seemed that a staff member had already arrived on the scene and was breaking up the fight between some boys. Donald returned to the room and got into a conversation as to who beat up whom and what kind of fight it was. Jonathan demonstrated it by shadow punches. Donald commented that a boy had his head "stomped."

While this was going on, Richard was still sitting, not really listening. He was visibly very tense and upset. He started by saying that his caseworker had called him in and told him about his father and mother fighting, his father beating up his mother, and now Richard wasn't even

---

11. It was later learned that there was a change of cottage parents this day and Jules had been given his pass early in the morning (instead of the evening) so that he had forgotten about the group meeting.

sure whether he could go home. He said he wanted to go home because he had to do something about this situation. Even if he got "beaten bloody" he was going to warn his father to lay off his mother, and if his father didn't listen, he would beat him up. Michael: "Maybe you can't go home because they are afraid if you go home you are liable to stab your father." During Richard's recital Jonathan was trying to involve Donald in a further discussion of the fight, but Donald, who was sitting at the opposite end of the room, was not listening. Jonathan kept looking around the room and whenever he caught the eye of one of the boys, such as Michael, who was really listening to Richard, he would start to talk to him about the fight. This did not deter Richard, however. *Leonard, who did not say anything, was very keenly interested in what Richard was saying.*

Richard was now describing how his father in a drunken state on one occasion kicked his mother and knocked her to the floor. Donald asked: "When did this happen?" Richard said it happened "on Thanksgiving." Donald: "Thanksgiving? Why didn't you say anything before this? Did you see it?" Richard: "No, I didn't see it but my social worker from E——— General Hospital got in touch with my social worker here at the Village and told him about my mother and father fighting. He called me in and told me it might not be such a good idea to go home for Christmas." Now, Richard said, he did not know what was going on at home. All he knew was that his father was beating his mother. He called up his sister the other day and she acted as if she did not know anything. This made him only more suspicious because she did not seem to want to tell him what was going on. He didn't know what to do. He would like to go home and "straighten things out." Then he said: "But when I leave home and come back to the Village they are going to fight again. I can't stop them, being here all the time. Maybe I ought to warn my father. I may even have to kick the shit out of him."

Jonathan had succeeded in attracting the attention of Donald and Michael and involving them in a discussion about the fight downstairs. Richard sat seemingly lost in thought while the boys were discussing the fight. When this conversation seemed to die down, the therapist commented to Richard that he seemed to be in a pretty rough spot. He said: "Yeah, I am. I don't know what to do. I've got to stop my father from beating my mother. I don't know how, but by God, I'm going to stop it even if I get killed." Michael turned to Richard and repeated: "Then they surely won't let you go home. You're liable to stab your father." Nothing further was said at this point.

Donald turned to the therapist and asked: "Mr. Ellery, do you read reports on us?" The therapist said that, before the boys came to the group, he had read something about their backgrounds. Donald, as if to test him, said, "Okay, would you tell the boys something personal about me?" He followed this up by asking, "Do you know why I'm here?" The therapist commented that he knew something about his having to come to the Village. Donald: "Okay, who sent me here?" Therapist: "The court." Donald: "You're right. Well can you tell all the boys more personal things about me?" Therapist: "I don't feel it is right for me to tell everybody what I know about you personally." Donald winked at the therapist and said okay. Jonathan now distracted Donald, who started a conversation with him about going home for the Christmas holiday and having a couple of drinks together.

Richard launched again into the recital of the fights between his parents. Jonathan interrupted him, saying, "My mother and father never fought but L.'s parents always used to fight." (L. had been "on the run" from the Village for some time.) Jonathan then described how L.'s father used to beat his mother, knocking her on the floor and kicking her in the ribs. No one in the group appeared to be particularly interested in this story.

Richard returned to bewailing his parents' fighting: "I only wish they wouldn't fight, that I could stop them. I get so mad at my father, I feel like throwing him down a flight of stairs." He then said whenever there was any kind of argument at home, his father immediately went to a bar and got drunk. When he came home his mother would say to his father, "There you go again, getting loaded." The father would say to her: "Who the hell is asking you? When you go to Bingo games I don't say anything. You don't have any right to tell me when to drink and when not to drink." Richard sat back and seemed very "nervous." He kept putting one leg over the other. The therapist said, "Richard, are you feeling there is something you must do about the situation that is going on between your parents?" He said: "Yes, that's why I'm talking. I don't know what to do. If only I could stop my father from drinking, but I don't know how." Therapist: "Do you feel it is possible for you to stop your father from drinking?" Michael stepped in and said: "Richard, you know you can't stop your old man from drinking booze. It's a habit with him." Jonathan: "Yeah, there is something wrong with his brain if he's got to drink all the time. He can't control it anymore." Michael added: "Yeah, the only thing that is ever going to stop your father from drinking is when he dies." Richard: "Then I wish he would kick the fucking bucket already. Maybe we could have some peace at home."

Michael went to the end of the room and began to make coffee, Donald joining him. Donald soon returned and took a seat next to Jonathan, and the two became involved in a discussion about girls in town, which had something to do with L. and his girl friends. (It was interesting to watch Donald trying to listen to Richard at the same time that Jonathan was talking to him.) Finally, at one point when Richard said that his father was just a "stupid slob," Donald said to Jonathan, pointing to Richard, "Shh, let's listen to him." Jonathan kept quiet for just about two seconds and once again was talking into Donald's ear, absorbing Donald's interest.

Richard turned to recalling memories. When he was younger, his father used to come home drunk and his mother would send Richard to sleep with his father because she didn't want to sleep with him. He told the boys that one night when his father came home drunk his mother said to him, "Go sleep with your father and keep an eye on him." Richard got into bed with his father. In the middle of the night his father woke up and thought it was his wife and began to beat him. Richard, with face flushed, dramatized how he began to scream, "Leave me alone; leave me alone; it's Richard!" Then he said: "There were nights I used to go to sleep and was afraid to close my eyes. I knew I was going to have terrible dreams. One night I was screaming because I had a horrible dream. My mother came over and shook me and then had to slap me to wake me up from the dream." Throughout this recital, Richard stood up. He now sat down, looking at the therapist as if expecting some remark from him. The therapist commented: "It must have been terrible for you, Richard." Richard: "Yeah, all the nights I used to try to fall asleep, but I couldn't. I was so afraid that there would be a fight." He then said: "You know what I felt, Mr. Ellery? I used to feel panic all the time at home." He went on to say that his mother was always upset because his father used money for drink which they should have used for food. Michael: "How much money does your father give your mother?" Richard: "I don't know," but then, "Oh, about $40 a week. I think it's something like a month. Something like that a month." Michael: "Then how the hell do you get food at home?" Richard: "That's the problem. My mother is always in debt. She never has enough money." Here Richard looked directly at the therapist and said: "Mr. Ellery, you're a man. I thought maybe you could tell me what to do at home."

Jonathan was still whispering into Donald's ear. The therapist asked Richard: "How long have your parents been fighting?" Richard: "Ever since I was four years old, when I fell out of the window." He then went on to say that since that time his mother and father had argued, blaming one another for his having fallen out of the window. The mother told the father that if he had only been at home Richard would not have fallen out, and his father would yell back at the mother: "You should have been in the house and, if you had been in the house, Richard wouldn't have fallen out of the window." Therapist: "You mean your parents are still arguing about who should have been in the house when you fell out of the window and this is all they argue about?" Richard: "Yes, every time something happens either my father or my mother throw it up to one another about my falling out of the window. Maybe if I hadn't fallen out of the window, they wouldn't be arguing." Therapist: "You mean that all this time you've been feeling that your parents arguments are your fault?" Richard: "Yeah, that's what I mean." Michael: "But that ain't right, you were a little boy. What did that have to do with it?" Richard: "I don't know, but that's the feeling I get." Michael egged Richard on to describe again what had happened, and Richard went into details as to how he had leaned up against a metal rod and had fallen out. Michael: "Well, where was your father when this happened?" Richard: "My father was downstairs and he saw me coming out the window." Michael: "So what happened then?" Richard: "My father ran to catch me. He stuck his arms out and broke my fall. He busted his two arms trying to break my fall." Michael: "In other words, your father saved your life?" Richard: "Yeah, he did save my life." A visible change came over Richard. His face lost it flush. He seemed almost relaxed. His body grew less tense.

Leonard: "I got an aunt and uncle who always fight like that. They are always yelling and blaming one another over their kids and the kids feel it is their fault because their parents keep yelling about them." Donald said to Richard: "Richard, why don't you stop talking about all this. Look, you are only working yourself up. The best thing you can do is try to forget. Otherwise you're going to be a nervous wreck. I once had a fight with my father and I tried to hit him back. Boy, he gave me a slap. I jumped under the bed and I never raised my hand to my father again." At this there was laughter in the room.

A custodian walked into the room and said he would like to turn on the light that illuminated the roadway below. As he was leaving Donald invited him to have a cup of coffee. The custodian declined. After he left there was a lot of commotion involving a great deal of walking around in the room. Michael called out to the therapist: "How about giving the boys a Christmas present by taking us downtown to a movie some night?" Richard was now standing, which was usual for him when he talked to the group, but he was no longer tense, and continued with his narration of the fall, how he been laid up in the hospital and had many stitches. He sparked Donald to describe how his fingers were nearly cut off once and required many stitches. Richard related an incident of a boy who had fallen on a barbed-wire fence and cut his forearm open, with the skin hanging and blood running all around. A prolonged conversation ensued between Donald and Richard about blood, stitches, which hospital was better, and so on.

At the conclusion of it, Donald took a seat next to the therapist and said: "There is something I've been meaning to talk about with you, but I can't remember what it is. Did you ever have that happen to you, that something is on the tip of your mind and you just can't think of it?" Therapist: "Yes, that's happened to me." Meanwhile Richard was describing to Leonard and Michael his various operations. Jonathan was trying to interrupt by telling the boys about fights he had had in his old neighborhood, but nobody in particular was listening to him, and Donald was claiming the therapist's exclusive attention. In a low voice so nobody else would hear him, Donald said he now remembered the problem he meant to ask about and with which he would like to have help. He had a girl friend back in the city with whom he was corresponding and whom he saw on a number of occasions when he was on home visits. The last visit he did not see her. It was almost as if he had stood her up and then found out that the girl was very angry with him. He was upset because he was not sure whether the girl liked him or not. What he wanted to know was whether when he went home for Christmas he should see this girl? "I want to find out if she still likes me," he said. The therapist asked: "How *can* you find out whether she likes you or not?" Donald: "Yes, you are right. Maybe the only way I can find out is by seeing her." Then he raised another problem, almost as if he were testing the therapist's responses. He said: "My social worker always tells me not to go with friends I used to go with before I came up here, but when I get out it is hard to make new friends. Besides, how can you give up friends you were practically born with?" The therapist commented that of course it was very hard. Donald seemed satisfied with this answer, but then exclaimed: "Oh yes, now I know what I want to tell you! You know when I was younger there used to be a bum around my block. He was kind of middle aged. He was a quiet guy. He did not bother anybody and whenever I would have some money I would give him a nickel or dime to get himself some coffee. I did not want him to go hungry. When my father would see me with this bum, whose name was Charlie, he would yell at me and would say I was bad because I gave him money. One day this bum was sitting on the sidewalk and a bunch of niggers came over and began to beat him. I got a stick and went after the niggers, and I got beaten up."

Donald described how he had had to hide his wounds from his parents and had attended to them himself by putting band-aids on them. "It hurt to be beaten, but I felt good trying to help this guy. Once I got another buddy of mine to take this bum to the Salvation Army and we got him clothes and a good meal and the Salvation Army even got him a job. Now he is working and wears nice clothes and he is not a bum any more." His eyes began to glow and he smiled as he said: "You know, I feel good because of that. It feels good to help somebody." The therapist: "That was a nice thing to do." Donald: "Yes, I always think about that. It makes me feel better inside many times."

While the conversation between Donald and the therapist was going on, Richard was telling Jonathan and Michael about a boy who was returned to the Village after he was discharged. This boy was something of a "fairy," according to Richard, and he went through motions imitating the boy in question. A discussion now ensued among Michael, Jonathan, and Richard about various boys who "peddle their ass around" the Village and how they have "to buy protection" from stronger boys so that they don't get "screwed" all the time. Leonard was sitting a distance away from the discussants and did not participate, nor did any one attempt to involve him.

The session was breaking up, and the therapist commented that there would not be any meeting the next week because most of the boys would be on home visits. The next meeting would be held the following week. Donald interjected that he "wished we could sit around longer today." Michael: "Yes we ought to sit around until about nine o'clock." As the group was leaving, Donald came over and said: "I may be going home in February. I may go to a boy's residence in the city." Then: "Don't worry, I'll come back to see you Mr. Ellery. I think most of us are glad we did not quit this discussion group. If we had quit we would not have had any place where we could talk about our problems. When I come back to my cottage after we meet Thursday nights, I feel a lot better."

COMMENT

Richard's extensive and free recital about his parents was a continuation of his positive transference feelings toward the therapist. The warm relation and confidence in the latter permitted him to recognize his negative feelings, even his death wishes, toward his father, for now he was accepting the therapist as a positive paternal object cathexis. We have discussed the attitudes necessary on the part of the boys to deal with this problem. The parents of these boys were completely unresponsive to treatment or guidance. It was, therefore, necessary for the boys to be prepared to bear the full burden of their families' disharmony.

We decided to attempt to accomplish this in the course of treatment by guiding them to accept the inevitability of the situation and by building up their ego strengths so as to become objective toward their parents. Whether we succeeded in this, later events will show.

The first step in this direction was taken in this session when the group, sparked by the therapist, countered Richard's feelings of guilt for his parents' fights, for it is partially guilt that ties the child to his parents. Another step in this direction was taken when the boys told

Richard that he must accept the fact of his father's drinking as something about which he couldn't do anything. It was up to his father.

Richard's need for his father's love was dramatically demonstrated when he relaxed as he spoke about his father saving his life. This ambivalence in all the boys was one of the foci toward which our therapy would have to address itself.

Donald's disclosure of having attacked his father generated anxiety in all the boys and a period of abreactive restlessness set in. This was followed by vicarious indulgence in violence and mutilation, a characteristic of adolescents' feelings of impotence, castration, and defective body image.

Up to this point even the significant material in the interviews concerned other persons or relations with others. The first step toward self-awareness made its weak appearance when Donald, in his intimate talk with the therapist, tried to understand his feelings toward his friends. This self-awareness led to his recall of his benevolent relation with "the bum," and elative pleasure from his beneficence.

In this session for the first time the subject of homosexuality was introduced; it was to be elaborated by the boys in later interviews.

The relief and status derived by the group was becoming conscious and verbalized by them. Thus, the transference upon the therapist was converted toward the group. This paralleled natural families, where the attitudes toward parents are converted into, or displaced upon, siblings and the home.

Session Eleven[12]

This session was held after the boys had returned from their home visits for Christmas. Richard and Jonathan were the first to arrive. Richard entered into a lengthy narration with Jonathan about a fight he had just witnessed at the gymnasium. Jonathan listened in a somewhat detached manner. Jonathan had a very droopy and depressed appearance. He had returned from a home visit in R——— just a few hours earlier.

Richard turned to the therapist and reported that he had found "things were okay at home." His father was not fighting with his mother. Actually, it was the reverse. His mother was picking on his father, but his father was "keeping his mouth shut." Also, Richard's father was not drinking much now. When Richard got home his father brought out a bottle of whiskey and invited him to have a few drinks with him. His father told him it was "okay to drink, but don't do too

12. When absences are not shown, it is to be taken that
    there was full attendance at the particular session.

much of it." The therapist commented that somehow Richard had discovered a reversal of the situation he had expected. Richard repeated that his mother "picked on" his father, the latter saying nothing. His feeling was that the family problem was settled and he was relieved. He turned once more to Jonathan and now began to describe his drinking, visiting relatives with his father, and the relatives' offering him drinks, too. Although he had had quite a bit to drink, he did not get drunk, he said.

It was now about fifteen minutes after the time set for the session and no other boy had arrived. It was obvious that the change in the day from Thursday (which was New Year's Eve) to Wednesday caused some confusion in scheduling. The therapist consulted the two boys present and they suggested that the others might not have received their passes. The therapist called to check on this and found that passes had been handed to the boys but apparently they had not noticed that they were for Wednesday instead of Thursday. At 7:25 all the boys turned up.

Donald was the only one to comment on the fact that he had not remembered the change in the date. After this remark silence descended upon the group. Jonathan, seeming to be lost in reverie, made desultory comments about girls he had seen on his home visit, and then proceeded to describe a girl he had met on the train to the Village. He had told her that he was twenty-one years old, worked in Dobbs Ferry, and earned $200 a week. When the girl asked him to take her out, he told her that for a reason he could not tell her he was busy at night and did not have the time to take out girls. The boys were listening in a half-hearted way. The group as a whole seemed in a mild state of depression. Donald commented about having been home and averred half-heartedly that he'd had "a good time." Richard again mentioned his drinking sprees in the homes of various relatives, including his grandmother and an uncle, but aside from these comments no real sharing or interchange took place. All seemed tired.

Donald took over the job of preparing coffee, with Michael and Jules assisting him. Otherwise there was quiet in the room. After a time the therapist said, smilingly and facetiously: "Everybody looks kind of pooped tonight." Michael smiled nervously in the direction of the therapist, but no one made any comment. Jonathan then described the many different kinds of drinks he had had while at home, something about twenty-one brands. Richard joined in, with the two competing as to which had had more drinks without getting drunk. Donald introduced a conversation about other boys in his cottage who had gone on home visits, with the group listening for a while when Richard talked about a friend of his who also had been on a home visit. Soon the subject petered out. Donald suddenly asked the therapist if the group could stay late.

Therapist: "Until what time?" Donald: "Till nine o'clock. I don't have anything else to do. We would like to stay here." Jonathan immediately said no. Donald, angrily to Jonathan: "What do you mean no?" Jonathan: "You ain't running this group. We stay here until the regular time." None of the others entered the discussion and Donald did not pursue it.

Richard turned to Michael and asked him when he would be going home again. Michael grew very irritable (perhaps because he had not gone home for Christmas; he did not tell the boys, but Jonathan had mentioned the fact earlier when Michael was not in the room). His response was an angry, "Why do you want to know?" Richard persisted, "I just want to know how long you're here." Michael again: "Why do you want to know?" Richard: "Okay, forget it; forget that I asked you." After Richard said this, Michael said that he had been at the Village about nine months and that the next time he would be going home would be Easter. "Does that satisfy you?" he asked. Richard: "That's all I wanted to know."

Since no further conversation arose at this point, the therapist said that the Club Department informed him there were going to be two new boys added to the group (to replace the two who had been removed). He mentioned their names, Louis and Macy. Jonathan's immediate reaction was: "Oh, shit. I'm not going to come here any more." Jules, who was reclining on the couch, said, "I don't know why the hell they need new boys here, there are too many of us here already." (There were six boys in the group at this point.) No one else picked this up, however, and silence ensued. After several minutes Donald broke in, saying that he didn't like the idea. Jonathan immediately spoke up: "I don't like the idea of that Louis coming into the group. He always talks too much." Michael: "Yeah, he's got a big mouth and he's always shooting it off." The group now grew noticeably restless. Donald ran out to the bathroom; Michael walked over to the coffee pot; Jules closed his eyes as he lay flat on his back on the couch. Richard went over to sit on the couch and leaned over Jules's legs. He placed his elbow on Jules's inner thigh and began to snap the fingers of his right hand as if he were beating time to some imaginary music. This continued for a while. Jules finally said to Richard: "Why don't you stop it. I can't stand it." Richard got up and took the seat he had been occupying.

A great deal of commotion arose as the coffee was being distributed. Whereas in preceding sessions, Donald served the therapist a cup of coffee, he did not do so now. Finally, Leonard got up, asked the therapist if he would like some coffee, and brought him a cup. When Donald saw this, he told Leonard to make sure to bring the sugar as well. Michael turned to the therapist and asked whether he had selected the new boys.

He was told that the therapist had not; the boys were selected by the Club Department. Donald said, "Does that mean that as each one of us leaves, another boy would come in?" The therapist told him that, although it would be up to the Club Department to decide, this was probably what would happen. Another silence ensued for a while and was soon replaced by private conversations between Jules and Donald and Richard and Jonathan which the therapist could not hear. Finally the therapist commented that he gathered that the boys did not like the idea of new boys coming to the group. Jonathan: "I don't give a shit. I'm not going to be here that long anyway." Donald yelled to Jonathan: "Yeah, you're going to be another guy who is going to yell 'I quit!'" Michael turned to the therapist and said, "Can I leave earlier tonight?" Asked what was the matter, he said he had to see a basketball game and immediately said he wanted to leave at once. The therapist told Michael that although he was not compelled to stay and he could go, maybe there was something bothering him, and perhaps he would like to talk about it. Michael said there was nothing bothering him; there was a good basketball game going on in the gym now and he wanted to see it. With this, he put his coat on and left. There was no comment from anyone.

Again there was a lot of back-and-forth movement, as Jules got up, walked over to Donald, and started a conversation. Jonathan was now discussing drinking with Richard. Leonard joined them and listened in, and later said something about his knowing a gang in his neighborhood that always hung out in bars. He did not specifically say that he himself went with this gang. Jonathan pulled a small box out of his pocket and showed it to Leonard. Jonathan smirked at this, and quickly put it back in his pocket. (From what the therapist could see, it looked like a box containing contraceptives, but he could not be certain.)

When there was some semblance of quiet, the therapist tried to get the boys' feelings about new members entering the group. He raised the question as to what it felt like when a new boy came to their cottages. This seemed to arouse some response. Donald said, "It feels crummy." Richard: "Yeah, it's crummy because you got to break a new boy in and everybody suffers while you do it." Therapist then asked what he meant by this, and Richard continued: "Well, we know the ropes and we got things going pretty well. When a new boy comes in, the cottage parents got to spend their time showing the new boy what to do." As soon as Richard said this, loud shuffling of feet ensued. Donald began to walk around from one chair to another, but then sat down at the far end of the room. As he did so, he said, "You know, it's a funny thing, I used to steal and rob, run away, and the only thing they ever sent me up here for was playing hooky." Richard: "Yeah, that's the same thing that happened to me. All the times I wasn't caught and the thing I do get caught for is a crummy thing like playing hooky." Jonathan described a number of friends he had who ended up in "prison." He pulled out of his pocket what appeared to be a news item from a R——— newspaper and read it aloud. It reported that a youngster (who was a friend of Jonathan's) had been picked up for stealing, was placed on probation, and then picked up again for breaking his probation and sent to a reformatory. The group's full attention turned to this.

Jonathan then began to tell the boys that when he was home his brother was home from prison and together they sat watching a television film called "The Big House," which was about a prison. He went into a long detailed discourse of the movie, about a "snitcher" who got someone in "trouble," and who was killed when he went over the prison wall. Donald commented that he would like to "tear the snitcher's head off." The group's attention was glued on Jonathan's depiction of the movie, and he appeared to enjoy being the center. In a clear, stentorian voice he described how a knife was passed among the prisoners at the dining table and placed against the back of a "screw" (prison guard); as he and his brother sat watching the movie his brother told him that he would tell Jonathan everything that was "bullshit" in the movie, since he had been in prison. While Jonathan was detailing the story, Richard every so often asked a question. Donald and Jules kept telling him to shut up, but Richard would be quiet for a few moments and then again speak up. Everyone was irritated by him, and Jonathan was growing visibly angry. Finally Richard turned to the therapist and said, "I like to get these fellows mad at me"; turning from the therapist, he asked another question. Jonathan said that if he didn't shut up, there would be a fight. Richard did not respond; he just sat back in his seat as Jonathan continued with his story.

As soon as Jonathan had finished, Richard went on to describe a television movie he had seen. The boys initially appeared to be cool. But Richard was doing his best to embellish his story about a prison, about dope addicts, and such, and soon attracted the attention of all the boys. As usual Richard was standing up as he talked and re-enacted the addicts' "taking their needles," and the like. Jonathan interrupted to say that his brother told him that there were two kinds of guys in prison, addicts and "queers," but then amended this by saying there were some guys that were neither, "like my brother." The discussion about prisons had continued for some time when Donald said to Jonathan: "You trying to make prison sound good, aren't you? Boy, I hope I never land up there." Jonathan in self-defense said, "No, I'm not trying to make it sound good." Donald: "You damn well are trying to make it sound like it is a great thing. Only creeps end up in prison and I don't want to land up there." After this interruption Richard continued with his story of the television program, and when he finished the session ended.

As the therapist was leaving, Donald came up to him to ask if he had any small change. Donald had to make a phone call. The therapist pulled out of his pocket a $5 bill and a nickel, which was all he had. He offered the nickel to Donald. Donald took the nickel and said he'd get a nickel from someone else and thanked therapist for the "loan." He then said, "Let me just feel the five-dollar bill." When he was given it, he crumpled it in his hands, smoothed it out, and returned it.

COMMENT

In this session rather severe regression was manifested, obviously due to the rejection from home and the renewed sequestration from their customary environment, friends, and relatives. These frustrations are displaced on the therapist, as when Donald did not serve the therapist coffee as he always had in the past, and on the new members (siblings). The regression process even reached the level of homosexuality when Richard vicariously acted out masturbation with Jules.

The therapist, sensing the boys' hostility displaced on to himself, should have delayed the announcement of the addition of new boys, which at this point only served to intensify their hostility toward him and increased resistance to his efforts at exploration of feelings.

Ordinarily, a therapist could have faced the group with their behavior and explained the reasons for their feelings, but this would have been risky, in fact inadvisable, due to the emotional state of the boys and the as yet incomplete transference attitudes toward him.

Session Twelve

(Louis and Macy joined the group for the first time.) Initially, Jonathan and the therapist were alone for about five minutes before the time set for the session. Jonathan reported on the achievement tests he was taking at school. He was finding the tests rather easy and expected to "pass." He had discussed with Mr. F. going back to school after leaving Children's Village and working at the same time. In the course of this conversation the therapist commented that working and going to school was not always easy. Jonathan realized it, but though he was offered a full-time job, he would still like to finish high school. Mr. F. had agreed to help him with this plan. He would try his best to carry the load of working and attending school, and since he would be getting out of school at 3:30, he would have time to work on a part-time job. At this point other boys filed in and Jonathan stopped talking.

As Michael came in he overheard the last of Jonathan's conversation and asked him what he was talking about. Jonathan repeated what he had said to the therapist. Michael kept confusing Jonathan's statements, repeating: "You mean you are going to go to school only for five minutes?" Jonathan began to show slow signs of frustration, trying repeatedly to explain to Michael what he meant. Jonathan finally said, "Oh, just forget it." Richard and Louis had not yet arrived at this point. Michael informed the therapist that these boys would be late because they had to go to confession.

Michael looked around the room and said, "Well, who is going to begin tonight?" Leonard: "I'd like to begin. I got something to say." Leonard declared that he was due to get a "special week-end pass" home, but it was canceled because one of the boys in his cottage had run away and the cottage parents as punishment canceled all passes for boys who were scheduled to go home. Michael immediately said: "Are you sure about that? That don't sound right." Leonard insisted that it was so. Jonathan: "What a crazy system. No reason why you should suffer because another boy runs away." Jules spoke up and said: "Yeah, what does this have to do with you? If another boy runs away why should they take away your week end?" Leonard with a very calm, almost blasé mien, said, "I don't know; this is what they told me." Leonard then proceeded to describe how he had asked his cottage father about it and he'd said, "This is the way the thing is."

Footsteps were heard outside the room and Jules commented, "Here comes Richard." Louis, Macy, and Richard came into the room about five minutes late. The therapist introduced himself to Louis and Macy and said, "I guess you know the other boys in the room." They said that they did. Macy shook hands with the therapist, and Louis said, "Yes sir, my name is Louis K." Jules to Louis: "You don't have to say 'sir' to Mr. Ellery. Just Mr. Ellery is good enough." Macy took the seat at the farthest end of the room, on the couch next to Jonathan. At first Louis sat down in a chair next to the therapist, but after a few minutes moved directly across the room to another chair.

For at least a full hour Louis kept staring directly at the therapist. He would at times turn away, but soon resumed his stare, apparently watching the therapist's reactions. Jonathan did not waste any time in getting Macy into a discussion about girls. Macy had not become involved, and Jonathan was doing all the talking. His talk had to do with girls where he lived and the many dates he had with them.

Soon quiet set in. It was interrupted by Leonard, who narrated that he had spoken with his social worker about the canceled pass, but the latter had told him he would have to discuss it with the cottage parents. Leonard said, "I guess I just can't go home on my week end." The therapist asked Leonard, "How do you feel about it?" Leonard thought a moment and said, "I think I feel pretty mad." Therapist: "I don't blame you, but from the way you're talking you certainly don't sound mad." Leonard: "Sometimes when I get mad and I can't do anything about it, I just try to forget that I'm mad, because there is no point in being mad." Jonathan yelled out from the other end of the room: "So what? You can still be mad." Michael: "I would be mad if something like this happened to me." Louis now spoke up and said, "Yeah, Leonard, a lot of guys would be mad if they lost their week end like you did, but . . ." and shrugging his shoulder said, "that's the way the ball bounces around here." Donald laughed at this and then got up and started preparing coffee. Michael joined him for a few minutes, but soon stopped, leaving Donald to work over the coffee.

Jonathan suddenly exclaimed: "Aw shit! I forgot something. I meant to bring a pencil and paper to write a letter." Richard: "Who are you going to write to?" Jonathan: "I'm going to write to a couple of gals who always write me, but I haven't written to them in a long time. After all, that's the only mail I get." Richard: "You mean you don't get any mail from anybody at home?" Jonathan: "Once in awhile I get mail, but I don't get very much of it." *Jules and Michael produced comic books and began to read them.* There was quiet in the room as the therapist said to Jonathan: "What's it like when you don't get mail from home?" Jonathan immediately said: "A lot of times I just sit around and worry. I get very moody. I'm always thinking that there is something wrong with my mother and my sisters and there is, too. They are pretty sick people." He went on to describe that his mother couldn't walk too well; she was a sick woman; she had trouble with her legs; and so forth. Leonard said, "I get mail, but when I don't get mail I worry too; that's why I like to get my week ends." Louis: "I don't worry about that too much, because my mother comes to visit me. I write regularly to her, and when I don't write then she really comes up to see what's happening." Michael turning to Louis said, "So that's the way you get her up, huh?" Louis did not say anything.

Again silence. The silence persisted for several minutes. Jules and Michael continued with the comic books. Some of the other boys began to look somewhat sleepy. Finally the therapist said: "You know, fellows, something interesting is happening here. We begin to talk about mail from home, how you feel about it, and all of a sudden dead silence descends on everybody." Michael laughed nervously. Louis quickly picked this up and said, "Even though I see my mother a lot of times, I still want to go home, and if I was Leonard I'd be pretty mad about not

being able to go home." Leonard: "Who said I'm not mad? I'm mad."
This time there was affect in his voice. Jonathan said, "Many times they
don't want to let me go home because when I come back from home,
I'm kind of moody." No one responded to this, however, and the therapist asked Jonathan if he could explain this a little more. Jonathan: "Well,
I feel kind of sad about having to come back to the Village." Richard:
"Yeah, well who wouldn't feel sad about having to come back to the
Village?" Louis advanced this sentiment a step further: "It's not only
coming back to Children's Village but, sometimes things happen at home
and you come back kind of moody. Sometimes you go home and your
parents are sick and you are worried about them and when you come
back people expect you to feel gay, happy to be back." Richard: "Yeah,
ain't that the craziest thing? When you come back and you are not
jumping around, your cottage parents think you don't like them."
Jonathan: "Sometimes when I come back, the next day I just don't feel
like getting out of bed. I feel like sleeping rather than getting up and
going out."

Jonathan then told how the supervisor came into the cottage in the
morning, waking the boys up, and Richard described how this supervisor had "a very ugly bulldog and when the boys eat in the cottage
the bulldog is around. All you have to do is look at the bulldog and you
vomit." This statement was met with general hilarity. The boys continued to discuss their reactions to "this ugly bulldog," Leonard saying sometimes he felt like picking up a shoe and throwing it at him,
but he was afraid the dog would bite him. Jonathan: "That's why I
sometimes run away, because people expect me to feel happy when *I
don't feel happy inside.*" Michael said, "I never run away." Jonathan:
"How long you been here?" Michael: "I've been here about ten months."
Louis: "You been here ten months and you never ran away?" Michael:
"No." Leonard: "I never ran away, either." Richard: "I ran away about
two times, but there's no point to it. They catch you and they bring
you back." Macy: "I think I ran away once, but I try to stick it out."
The therapist said: "That's interesting. What makes some boys run and
other boys stick it out?" Louis at once said: "That's a very good question, Mr. Ellery. Why don't the boys who don't run away talk about
it." Michael: "Well, some guys figure that there is no point in running
away. You just have to be here a longer time." Louis: "Is that the only
reason? Sometimes they don't make you stay longer because you ran
away." At this point Jules, who had had a spinning top in his hand,
was winding the cord around it and threw it to the floor. This seemed
to distract the boys. Donald grabbed the top and threw it on the floor,
attempting to spin it with the cord. His hand slipped and Richard yelled

out: "Hey, watch out, Mr. Ellery's sitting there. Don't hurt him." With this Donald and Jules went out to the anteroom to play with the top.

Meanwhile, Richard began to tell the boys that if he ran away he would go all the way to the West Coast where his uncle lived and nobody would ever be able to catch him. Leonard said he had a girl friend who lived in France, and if he ran away he would try to get to France. Louis thought he would go down south, while Macy was telling Jonathan that if he ran away, he knew a lot of boys on the outside who would "protect" him, give him food, a place to sleep, and all that. This went on for quite some time, with Leonard now expanding his boundaries to Japan, and Jules soon became part of the discussion by saying he would go all the way up to the Maine woods if he were to run away. Donald busied himself with serving coffee. *Louis got up and brought a cup of coffee to the therapist.*

After the fantasying as to where each would escape had run its course, the therapist jokingly interjected: "By now you fellows are all over the map. Leonard was in France, Richard on the West Coast, but I kind of wonder what keeps you here. There are no walls or fences to stop you from taking off." Richard at once said, "I wouldn't do it because I know my mother would worry sick over me." Louis: "Yeah, the same for me, my mother would be worried sick about my running away." Donald chimed in: "My mother would worry but I would still go to Michigan. I got a buddy in Michigan and I would live with him." Jules: "Yeah, but how would your parents feel?" Then speaking about himself, he said, "I wouldn't want my mother to get sick worrying about me." Richard: "Yeah, I'd love to get out of this place. There are too many rules and regulations—people always telling you what to do; but I don't want to worry my mother." Then turning to the therapist: "Mr. Ellery, if you were a boy here would you run away?" Therapist: "I wonder if you are asking me if I know what it feels like to be a boy at Children's Village, to be told by adults what to do, to not be able to take off any time you want to." Jules was nodding his head as the therapist spoke and then said, "Well, do you know, Mr. Ellery?" Michael spoke up and said, "I think he knows what it is like for us." Louis: "You know this place is boring; it bores the hell out of you!" He then added: "You know what's so boring about this place? It's stereotyped."

The boys all turned toward Louis as if they had never heard the word before, and Louis went on to explain: "Every morning you get up, it's the same faces, the same room, the same routine. You're always doing the same thing." Richard: "I get sick and tired of looking at Jonathan's face." Jonathan sat up in his seat and said to Richard, "You better watch it; there's going to be a fight." The boys in the room burst out laughing and the tension eased. Richard continued on the theme. He said, "This is the only place in the world where I feel bored." Therapist, turning to Richard: "You mean in the whole wide world? This is the only place that you get the feeling of being bored?" Leonard interrupted: "I used to be bored in school, too, not only at the Village. "Jonathan: "I was never bored in school; school never bothered me."

Macy, who was sitting next to Jonathan, turned to him and said: "That's funny, it bored everybody else. How come school didn't bore you?" Jonathan: "I didn't feel bored, I just felt mad," and he took over the conversation. When he went to school he was never really happy. He wasn't happy because everybody, instead of calling him by his name, Jonathan, used to make mistakes and call him by the name of Sam. Michael asked who Sam was. Jonathan said: "He's my brother, don't you remember, stupid? My brother had a lousy reputation in school. He used to have fights with teachers, get kicked out; he wouldn't take shit from anybody. When I came to school I tried to mind my own business, but people wouldn't let me." He continued that whenever he did anything "out of the way" they would never "bawl him out" for what he did; they always would say to him he was just like his brother. "Even when I used to walk down the street, people who knew my brother used to say there is that P——— kid. They didn't mean me, they meant there goes the brother of that guy Sam, who is locked up."

He stopped and gazed at the floor. There was complete silence in the room. The therapist said, "Jonathan, it sounds as though you had a pretty terrible load to carry." He said: "Yeah, that's what I meant to say. I was always carrying my brother's reputation. Nobody was ever interested in me. As soon as I would come into a new class the teacher already had it in for me. If I talked to somebody next to me the teacher would yell out, 'Don't behave like your brother!' I used to be so fucking mad I always felt like running away from school. After a while I got bored; I couldn't sit in class and concentrate." Leonard broke in: "Yeah, I couldn't concentrate either in class. I was always looking out of the window. I was always thinking about something else. For instance, like my girl." Jonathan: "That's what I used to do, I was always thinking about girls, what I would do with them."

Macy spoke up and said, "You know something like that always happens to me." He then mentioned a teacher at the Village who was always telling boys they were a bunch of "dirty thieves." This female teacher, who was an elderly person, was always ready to pounce on a boy, according to Macy's description. If he got up and walked near her desk she would accuse him of wanting to get into her pocketbook. Louis said: "Yeah, I know that girl. She's just like my aunt. She's got degenerative brain disease." Macy: "Shit, if they're going to keep calling me a thief, they won't believe me if I don't steal." Jonathan turned to Macy and said: "I used to feel that way, too. After a while I found myself always trying to protect my brother. I felt like I was the only guy he had in the world who was nice to him and didn't say bad things about him." It was now 8:30, and Jules asked: "Can we go now?" This served as a signal for Michael to get up and start to leave. Jonathan made no effort to go, but Macy got up and said to Jonathan: "Come on let's go. We'll be late." Jonathan got up and left with Macy, Louis following.

Although Michael began to leave, he came back to take some of the left-over coffee back to the cottage with him. Donald remained behind. Donald said that he didn't feel like leaving today. "Remember, I didn't want that guy Louis in this group? He's not such a bad guy. He's loads of laughs." He then said that the substitute auto shop teacher had loaned him a key to the car and Donald had been driving the car around the grounds of the Village by himself. Michael didn't believe him, and Donald went into a long explanation of how he started the car, shifted, and so on, attempting to convince Michael. The latter was attempting to pour hot coffee into a wax carton but the carton began to leak. Donald said to him, "Wax carton is no good for hot coffee." Michael asked the therapist if he had a bottle. The therapist told him there was one in his office, and Donald said he would go down with the therapist to get it. This they did. Michael filled the bottle with the coffee, put it into a paper bag, and left, thanking the therapist for the bottle.

COMMENT

The hostility of the preceding session abated. The boys have again become acclimatized to the new surroundings and a state of obsolescence has set in with respect to their homes. They still revealed dependence on their mothers, but soon launched into introspective analysis of feelings and reactions to sequestration from their habitat, failure to receive mail, unhappiness "inside," moodiness upon return from home visits, and the like. This movement from projection upon others to self-awareness is a significant development for acting-out boys such as these were and held good promise for *inversion*.

The boys revealed a great deal of unsuspected anxiety and inner tensions which treatment had to take into consideration and which would later become one of its foci. Note should be taken of the increased frequency of silences. These were caused by the fear of inner threats and were defensive in nature. They are a form of flight reactions. The therapist dealt with them skillfully by helping the boys to break through them, not only by what he said, but also by the relaxed, uninvolved manner in which he said it.

Note need be taken of Leonard's verbal participation in this session, indicating increased security and assertiveness, and Louis's dramatic act in serving coffee to the therapist after his intensive study of the latter. Louis is a very "tough customer" and extremely bright and intuitive.

The boys now address themselves more directly to the therapist, using his name. This occurs more frequently as the sessions progress, indicating growing positive transference feelings toward him and acceptance of him.

Session Thirteen

Michael was first to arrive, coming in about five minutes early. He immediately sat down next to the therapist and commented on the nice appearance of the therapist's jacket and inquired where it was bought. Being told, he said he would like to get one just like it. He liked sport jackets because one could wear them with different pants. Gradually the boys began to come into the room and were present by seven o'clock, the time set for the session.

There was silence for a very brief period when Donald, slouching in his chair, opened the discussion by saying in a very low voice: "I got a lot of troubles." He was barely audible, but soon raised his voice and said that he wanted to go home for his parents' wedding anniversary, which would take place in February. However, he didn't think he would be able to do so. The party was scheduled for a Sunday night, and even if he did get a week-end pass, he would have to return to the Village before the event took place. For a while he remained thoughtfully quiet, when Michael spoke up and said, "Can't your parents change the time so that they could have the anniversary party the night you are home?" Donald didn't say anything at once. Still slouching in his seat, he finally said that his parents could not do that, because they could not find a catering hall for Saturday night. There were too many bookings for that night. Besides, they wanted to get a music band and so far they hadn't been able to find one available for that Saturday night. Saturday night was the busiest night in the week for such things. Jonathan to Donald: "What are you going to do?" Donald: "I don't know. Maybe I just won't come back." Jonathan: "If it was me, I'd just as well stay home [for the party] and then come back." Michael: "Why would you stay home now? I thought you were going home in February." Jonathan did not respond to this. Suddenly the boys began to move around the room, while Richard sat reading a comic book, seemingly oblivious to what was going on or to the discussion. Donald toyed with the coffee pot.

Jules changed seats, and Macy engaged Jonathan in some discussion which was drowned out by the general melee.

After a while the therapist commented to Donald that he seemed to be unsure as to what to do and wondered whether it was really impossible for his parents to change the date of the party. Louis, overhearing this comment, said, "I still don't know why that should be so hard." Donald: "All I can tell you is that I talked about it with my mother and she told me how hard it is to get a hall for Saturday night." Richard looked up from his comic book: "Can't you talk with anybody here about switching the night that you are home?" Donald: "Maybe I'll do it, but I don't think they'll go along with it. You know, rules and regulations all the time." Jonathan: "If it was me I wouldn't give a shit about the rules and regulations. I would stay home if my parents were going to have a party." Macy to Jonathan: "You'd probably spend all your fucking time drinking." Jonathan agreed, and a discussion now ensued between Jonathan and Macy about what they would drink if they were at home.

Donald shouted to Richard, who was sitting closest to the door: "Hey, Richard, shut the door will you? I want to talk." Richard did not stir nor did he look up from his comic book. Donald shouted again: "I told you shut that God damned door!" Again Richard did not answer. Leonard, who was sitting next to Richard, got up and shut the door, which was ajar because the last boy in had not closed it properly. Donald said in the direction of Richard: "You're a lazy bastard. I'll get even with you." He continued the discussion with Jonathan on drinking and said, "Mr. Ellery, did you ever get drunk?" The therapist told Donald that he had got drunk twice, and went on to explain that he was "sick like a dog." Donald immediately picked this up and said: "Yeah, that's just what happens to me. When I do a lot of drinking I get so sick I puke and vomit all over the place." Leaning forward in his chair he said, "Can you tell me why when a person drinks liquor they get so sick?" Louis, who had said little up to this point, chimed in: "How come you feel like a wet dog after you've been drinking?"

The therapist went into some details as to the effect of alcohol both on the digestion and the brain, pointing out that "the lobes of the brain where all the thinking takes place get the signals haywire and mixed when there is alcohol in the body." Richard got up and left the room. Jules said, "Yeah, I read about that in a biology book, about the part of the brain that tells you what to do, how to move." Donald told Jules to be quiet, "Let's hear what Mr. Ellery has to say." The therapist continued describing how a person lost the sense of balance and nausea developed because the stomach was trying to get rid of the liquor; it couldn't hold it. He then went into some explanation of the fact that in most automobile accidents it had been found that 75 per cent of the drivers had been drinking liquor and as a result, when they should have moved their right hand, they moved their left hand. Louis interposed: "Yeah, I know. Your reflexes get all screwed up."

All the boys now became interested in the subject, and Louis took over. He said that once he had been a passenger in a car driven by a man who had been drinking, and he described the accident that ensued. Jonathan: "That's stupid. You shouldn't drive when you're drinking. I never drive when I'm drinking." Donald: "You can really get killed drinking that shit." The boys giggled at this, which seemed to break the tension that was mounting as a result of the discussion. When the laughter died down, Jonathan turned to the therapist and said: "You know, you got a beautiful car, Mr. Ellery. I really like the way your car looks. About a year ago I was planning on stealing your car." The boys again laughed. Richard now came back and on hearing the tail-end of this statement said, "What car?" Jonathan: "Mr. Ellery's car. I love Chevvies. They're good cars." Therapist (to Jonathan): "What stopped you?" Jonathan: "I figured I'd get into a lot of trouble so what I did was I walked down to H———, I took a car in H———, drove it to Y———, and abandoned it there. Then I got a hitch back to the Village." Michael turned to him and said, "You're bullshitting." Jonathan ignored Michael. Michael then said to him: "You could have stolen Mr. Ellery's car. He's got a lot of insurance on it."

Louis said: "Man, you ought to see what goes on around my fuckin' block. You park a car around there, you come down and that car ain't going to be there." For the next fifteen to twenty minutes, Louis talked about the gangs in his neighborhood. It was unclear from his description exactly what gang he belonged to, but he named some well-known gangs, described their fights and rumbles, skirmishes and attacks —how he used to "move" against other boys in company of his gang with bricks in his pockets; how they once "jumped" a boy and stomped him until he bled. The boy who was stomped was lucky, he said, that there was a hospital in the vicinity where he was taken by the police, otherwise he would have died. The entire group's attention was glued upon Louis, except for Leonard, who sat quietly looking at the wall across, his attention appearing to be on the periphery of Louis recitation.

At points of his narration, Louis grew manic in his elation: His eyes blazed and his mouth was wide open as he described riding on the subway in company with a gang, and how a boy in the train who was a member of a rival gang was stabbed with a bayonet by one of the members in Louis's gang. Louis nearly foamed at the mouth with relish as he recounted how blood spurted out of the back of this boy. This was greeted with laughter from most of boys in the group. Donald had been serving coffee to the boys rather quietly and was attempting to heat more water, but the electric coil failed. While listening to Louis's story he was also trying to fix the hot plate and succeeded in doing it.

After the excitement caused by Louis's narration, the group was beginning to break up into little cliques to discuss the gangs in their neighborhood and the gang members they each knew. Louis, in spite of the fact that boys were now no longer according him their undivided attention, was standing up in the middle of the room continuing to describe how his gang attacked other gangs with bayonets and radio antennas ripped from parked cars, and how they slashed the faces of boys. He explained that the usual cause for these attacks was belonging to other gangs. He described how, when riding on the subway with a gang, after a fight where they had beaten a boy with a chain, the police came up to him. He demonstrated in dramatic fashion how he curled up in the seat and gave the impression of being "just a poor, innocent little boy." Finally, Louis sat down, but discussions continued in small cliques. Macy was talking with Jonathan; Donald joined Leonard, who appeared to be demonstrating with his foot (his fantasy of) how he used to stomp boys. Richard remained somewhat out of these discussions. Jules, too, remained quiet. Louis, excitedly, now went over to Jonathan and Macy and entered into conversation with them.

After a period of this, the therapist decided to "pick" on Louis. In the midst of the turmoil, he asked Louis how he felt when he was involved in these fights. Louis again stood up and said loudly, "Man, I felt damn good." When the boys heard this they stopped talking and burst into a peal of laughter. Louis said: "I don't give a shit about guys getting beat up. I had a real jazz of a time with my gang." Richard turning to the therapist said, "The only reason most guys join gangs is that they have to." Michael who sat slouching in his chair, almost as if he were asleep, overhearing what Richard said, turned to the therapist and said: "Yeah, that happens a lot of times, where you can't walk down a block without somebody coming over to you and asking you what gang you belong to. Every morning you leave the house and they ask you: 'You going to join a gang or not? You're going to get the shit kicked out of you.' After a while you just join a gang for protection." This statement put a stop to the clique discussions and all participated in agreeing that most of the boys in the group had belonged to gangs at one time or another just "for protection."

The therapist told the boys that he certainly could understand it; that maybe they did feel they had to belong to a gang to be protected, but he had another question. Not every boy in the neighborhood belonged to a gang. Was it really so impossible not to be a part of a gang if you really didn't want to? Louis reacted to this by saying: "Sure, it is. Most of the boys who were in the gangs with me were in the gang because they were very unhappy at home. Many times these boys used to come home from school and there was their mother and father just cursing and beating on one another, yelling and screaming; so what are these guys going to do? They go down to the street; they look for fun. What's the only kind of fun you can find in the streets? The only fun I could find was being with a gang." Louis was struggling to keep a general tone to his statement, as though it did not apply to him. Louis continued: "A lot of boys find that in a gang they get things they don't get in the home." Donald asked: "What do you mean?" Louis: "Well, as I said before, you get fun. You got buddies that can run around."

At this, silence fell on the group. The therapist commented that Louis seemed to be saying something interesting. What did the other boys think? Richard: "I had the same experience as Louis. I remember all the boys I knew in gangs even though I never really belonged to any big gangs. Most of those guys just didn't like being at home." Donald added: "A lot of the gangs I knew, their problem was that they were always looking for colored boys to beat up and the colored boys were always looking for white boys to beat up." Michael: "Yeah, that's the way a lot of gangs in my neighborhood are. If you was colored there were certain blocks you couldn't walk on." Louis (who *was* Negro): "I knew certain blocks that I'd get my head handed to me, so I stayed away from them." Richard said in something of a resigned fatalistic tone: "That's the way it is. You know it's sort of handed down from one year to another, white gangs and colored gangs." The therapist interjected his puzzlement about why boys fight other boys supposedly because of color. Richard said this was the way it had to be. When the therapist pressed for an explanation, Louis said, "That's just the way it goes; it happens every year like that." The therapist said to Louis: "We were talking before about boys joining gangs because of how they feel at home." Being more specific he asked how they felt about their parents and did it have anything to do with boys picking on other boys and using color as an excuse? Louis said: "That's an idea. I never thought that way." Donald: "Nah, I don't think so. I think it is just the way it happens. There are white gangs and there are colored gangs." Jonathan: "Yeah, white gangs and colored gangs. Why can't there be mixed gangs? Why do guys pick on other boys if they don't like their color?" Leonard: "Maybe it's just an excuse." No one followed through on Leonard's suggestion. Jules stood up at this point and said: "It's 8:30. It's time we started going." The group trooped out.

COMMENT

The growing positive transference toward the therapist was reflected in Michael's admiration of the therapist's coat and his desire to possess one like it and in Louis's confidence in the therapist as shown by his revealing his gang activities. It was Louis who scrutinized the therapist closely at the beginning and apparently decided that he was trustworthy. Jonathan had no hesitancy in confessing his intention to steal the therapist's car and of actually stealing another. But of greater significance was that now almost for the first time the boys included the therapist in their conversation for a long period and repeatedly addressed themselves directly to him.

The discussion of drinking gave the therapist an opportunity to extend the group's psychologic literacy by relating a physiological state to behavior. This was well-timed and obviously relevant, for the boys were avid to pursue the subject. Here the theme of cause and effect was advanced which will gradually become a central topic of the group interviews as it related to themselves.

Louis, who was always preoccupied with violence and sadistic acts, launched into a narration that made all the boys guilty, and again the projective defenses were mobilized: they were *forced* to join gangs, they said.

During the supervisory sessions we suggested that one strategy to combat the deeply ingrained projective pattern (blaming others) in our boys was to point out that not everyone behaved as they did. What was the difference? The therapist appropriately raised the question here and the first step in *inversion* was made at this point, though it was still diluted by the idea that parents are at fault.

Note that Louis, the most violent and the "toughest" boy in the group, is first to recognize the relation of the climate in the home to delinquency.

NOTE

Following the thirteenth session we decided to omit food and coffee at the sessions. This was done in an effort to prevent the commotion usually created by the preparation and distribution of coffee and the oral-regressive effect of eating, with the consequent diminution of anxiety in the boys. This we thought worked against more meaningful interviews. Also we felt that possibly the supplying of food diminished the emergence of hostile feelings toward the therapist. With these considerations in view, we decided to make the electric plate unusable by disconnecting one end of the coil so that no electricity would flow through it.

During the entire session that followed (session fourteen) Donald busied himself trying to repair the heating element in the electric plate and was oblivious of the discussion that was going on around him.

After prolonged manipulation and testing, he discovered the difficulty and repaired it, prepared the coffee, getting it ready a few minutes before the session ended.

Session Fourteen

In this session again Louis and Richard competed for the attention of the group by describing the various cartoons they had seen on TV. First Louis stood up, describing Popeye and his eating spinach. Then Richard stood up and elaborated on it. After some minutes quiet descended. After a while Richard, using his index finger as if it were the barrel of a pistol, started shooting at the boys, making appropriate sounds. Jonathan said to Richard: "The way you are acting means you don't belong in this kind of group." Louis laughed at this and said: "He's been at the Village too long. That's the trouble. After you've been at the Village too long you go crazy. The Village makes you crazy." The therapist asked Louis what he meant by this, but Jonathan answered instead. He said: "There are a lot of maniacs running loose in this place. One thing this Village got more than anything else is a bunch of sex maniacs." Richard: "You're not kidding. I know a couple of guys in my class who are sex fiends," and he described a young female teacher who had been the object of molestation on the part of a number of boys. Louis elaborated, describing how boys walk up to her, put their hands on her "butt," and walk away as if nothing had happened. While Louis was in the midst of this, a commotion ensued. Donald got up and left the room, returning shortly thereafter to work on the heating element again. Jules began aimlessly walking around, and Michael started a conversation with Jonathan. The therapist said: "Boys, somebody has raised the question of sex and all of a sudden there is a lot of moving around in the room. Maybe we ought to try to figure out what all this means." Jonathan turning from Michael said: "I noticed that, too. This happened before. When you talk sex, everybody starts acting like crazy."

Richard cut in and proceeded to describe another teacher, an elderly woman, who on a number of occasions was "goosed" by boys in her class. A thunder of laughter met the statement, but it had the effect of quieting down the boys. Jonathan thought that anybody who would goose an old lady must be a sex maniac. Louis said in his neighborhood a couple of elderly ladies had been "jumped on" by boys, but he himself would "never do something like that." Richard: "I got a teacher who's always telling us about all the girls he screws and some of the boys in the class get a hard-on." Louis, going through a masturbatory motion with his hand, though he did not touch his genitals, said, "Yeah, he gets everybody to do this." The therapist asked Louis what he meant and Louis said, "To masturbate, beat your meat." Jonathan: "Yeah, this same teacher told us that if we beat the meat we're going to go crazy."

Macy spoke up and said: "A lot of boys go crazy if they masturbate. It affects their brain." Macy turned to the therapist: "Don't you know a lot of boys that went crazy from jerking off?" The latter responded to this by saying very directly to Macy, since the other boys were now listening, that he did not know of any boy who ever went crazy from "jerking off," but maybe they ought to talk about this since it seemed to be on their minds. From this developed the discussion, largely led by Jonathan, as to why boys masturbated. He said he never knew any boy who didn't masturbate, and he looked at the therapist for confirmation. This the therapist gave, saying that in the process of growing up boys do go through a phase in which one way to relieve their sexual feelings is to masturbate. Jonathan was still skeptical as to whether "you still do not go crazy." Louis said, "Well if you don't go crazy maybe you do make yourself kind of tired and wear yourself out a bit."

Michael confirmed what Louis had said, commenting that he knew "some guys in his cottage" who walked around looking dead all day because "they play with themselves at night so much." Macy: "Everybody in this room masturbates at one time or another, but nobody looks that tired." There was laughter at this and the therapist commented that perhaps we ought to consider what it is like for boys being at the Village away from girls, with only boys. Jonathan picked this up: "That's why a lot of guys in this place are so 'hommy' [homosexual]; they go around trying to have sex with other boys." Macy: "I never did it. I wouldn't let anybody have sex with me." Michael got up and walked over to the couch and tried to spread himself out, but Jules, who was sitting on it, wouldn't let him. A prolonged discussion ensued as to who was sleeping with whom in the cottages, with Louis speaking in most deprecatory terms of a few boys in his cottage who were always trying to "pluke" (have sex with) other boys. This conversation lasted for a considerable time. Richard, Louis, Jonathan, and Leonard, who joined in toward the end, were most involved in the discussion.

The therapist suggested that the group try to figure out what made boys have sex with other boys. A general murmur passed through the room to the effect that nobody knew. The therapist then described the natural temptation for boys who live together to act that way. Jonathan did not know what the word *tempted* meant, and said, "You mean they feel kind of itchy to do it?" The therapist said, "Yes, that's another way of putting it." Jonathan: "Well I never feel itchy to do it." Louis: "Not me either." The therapist raised the question whether the boys thought that feeling tempted to do something was the same as really doing it.

Jonathan, peremptorily: "Yes it is. There's no difference." Macy: "Sometimes I'm tempted to beat up a guy but I don't do it." Louis got up from his seat and began to walk around the room. Richard said to Louis: "Why don't you sit down? Stop walking around so much, you're making me nervous," and went on to say that sometimes he was tempted to "squeeze a girl's ass," but he stopped himself from doing it. There was silence for awhile and the therapist commented that having a feeling was not the same as acting on the feeling, and gave an example of the difference between feeling like hitting somebody and doing it. It's perfectly okay to have a feeling. It can't be helped. It's natural.

Macy said: "That reminds me, the other day I was sitting in the cottage. I was all alone. I had a feeling I just wanted to bust up the fucking cottage." Richard: "That happened to me in auto shop. I was sitting there and all of a sudden I wanted to start fucking around in the auto shop and tearing things up." Louis: "In my cottage whatever boys feel they do. If they feel like fucking another boy they go ahead and do it and nothing stops them." Leonard said quietly: *"That's because they can't control their feelings."* Not a word was heard from Jules, who sat on the couch staring somewhat blankly at the opposite wall. Michael was slouched over in his chair as if he were not involved. He eventually got up, walked over to Donald, and worked with Donald on fixing the hot plate.

Macy revived the discussion. He said that sometimes he sat somewhere and got so "tense and bothered" that he wanted to do "something," but he did not know exactly what he wanted. Turning to the therapist Jonathan said: "That's happened to me too. I get very nervous like when I come home from the Village or I come to the Village from home and sometimes I'm sitting around not doing anything. I get very nervous." Richard said, looking at the therapist: "Mr. Ellery, is there a reason why things like that happen?" The therapist: "There is a reason, and maybe you boys would like to try to figure the reason out." The boys did not know what to say. The therapist asked whether they ever had the experience of looking at something or somebody and began to be bothered, and yet they didn't know why they were bothered. Louis: "That happens a lot of times." Macy: "Yeah, like walking into a room. You see a red chair and all of a sudden you don't like the chair. Sometimes you meet a girl and you like her and yet you don't like other girls. Why does that happen?" The therapist: "Did you ever hear that your brain is divided into two parts? One part that you think with, that you remember with. Then there is another part that holds memories you don't even know about, memories of things that happened to you a long time ago—memories of things that people, like your parents, may have done to you and this part always affects the other part of the brain that you think with and are aware of." Richard: "I know; what do they call that? Isn't that what they call the subconscious mind?" As soon as Richard said this, Louis became fidgety. He got up, wandered over to Jules, who was sitting in the couch, and announced to the boys he was going to sleep. Nobody paid attention to him.

Macy said: "Maybe that's why sometimes I'm in a room and I don't think much about anything and then I find I'm getting a hard-on." Richard yelled: "Then you must be thinking about sex!" Jonathan corrected it by saying, "Maybe you don't even know you are thinking about sex." Macy appeared as if he were *trying to digest the idea* and then said, "Maybe." Michael walked over to the wastepaper basket, put it on the table, and used it as if it were a basketball hoop by pitching into it crumpled paper cups. He invited Jonathan to join him in the game. Jonathan did join him, but played half-heartedly; he appeared interested, but also wanted to continue the discussion. Although the therapist was tempted to raise the question of why Michael was trying to divert attention from the discussion, he refrained from doing it in view of Michael's pathology (schizophrenia). After a short while, Jules rose, took up his coat, and said that he was leaving. Donald reminded Jules that he had not had his coffee yet. Jules said that he didn't want any and left.

Richard and Macy moved to take seats next to the therapist and Leonard followed suit. Richard said that he had heard that sometimes people have dreams because of "that subconscious mind." Macy didn't believe this and Richard told Macy to ask the therapist, who confirmed Richard's assertion. Jonathan came over to the group and said that whenever he thought about his girl friend as he was lying in bed, he later dreamed about her. Richard asserted that many times dreams come true and went on to quote many instances, without being specific, of people he knew who dreamed about things and they came true. Richard claimed that he had a relative who dreamed about finding money and the next day, sure enough, he found some money. Jonathan said: "You mean when you dream the dream is going to come true?" The therapist said that it usually is a coincidence. Richard: "Sometimes when I go to bed I'm not even thinking of sex and I have a sex dream. Why does that happen?" Since it was 8:30 the therapist said to Richard that because this was a good question how would he feel about bringing it up the following week? Richard said: "Sure I'll bring it up next week. We can talk about it."

As the therapist was leaving, he found that he could not get his car off the ice on the parking space. Donald must have remained in the vicinity because he came over and helped push the car. This done, he asked if the therapist would drive him to his cottage. His cottage was within about 200 yards of the parking space. The therapist agreed to do it. When Donald got into the car he asked all sorts of questions about it: how much it cost, was it bought new, how much the insurance was, and so forth. The peculiar aspect of this conversation was that Donald asked at least three times the name of the make of the car. Even though he was told each time, he seemed to forget, and a few moments later repeated the question.

COMMENT

The boys, having been intrigued by the subjects of dreams and sex, introduced these on their own. This was both an infantile and counterphobic maneuver. Just as the small child does, our very immature boys have to find their way to knowledge through narcissistic channels: they have to become curious about themselves before they can turn toward the world around them. In their state of genital primacy and with their guilt and anxiety relative to it, the subject becomes paramount. The counterphobic aspect of it arises from their guilt about their antisocial acting out, in this instance homosexual acts. A frank acceptance of it and uninhibited discussion allays these inner threats and relaxes the participants by relieving tensions; but what is more important, advances in emotional maturity and personality integration are made thereby.

Despite their intense interest in the subject, the boys parried and attempted to block it by various diversional strategies: moving about; shuffling of feet; talking about teachers and girls; and so on. But realizing the prevalent and intense interest, the therapist held them to it with good results. One of the superstitions—psychosis resulting from masturbation—is laid low, which is very helpful in reducing fears and anxieties prevalent among boys of their cultural milieu.

Of first-rate therapeutic value is the *differentiation between impulse and act* that was made here, as was Leonard's formulation about feelings and their control, as well as the introspective awareness of and curiosity about where feelings stem from. This gave the therapist an opening to introduce the idea of the conscious and unconscious "mind," which as we shall see later was to play a major role in the improvement of these boys. The totality of the discussion advanced psychologic literacy immeasurably.

Note need be made of the abreactions of some of the boys to the anxiety aroused by the discussion, the physical movement of three of the boys toward the therapist, Donald's seeking him out after the session, and his intense interest in the car (as part of the therapist).

It was now blatantly evident that sex is paramount in the boys' preoccupations, but we decided to delay pursuing it until the catharsis in this area would be more fully achieved. We felt that there was much more the boys had to reveal *to* themselves, and giving them "sex education" (which we did later) at this point would have terminated the discharge of pathognomic feelings and fantasies. However, since a therapist must always keep ahead of his patients, we spent many hours in our supervision conferences in preparing to deal with this subject in what seemed to us appropriate steps and in drawing on the principles of *natural* (biological) *morality*, which will become clear in later interviews.

Session Fifteen

ABSENT: Jonathan

Since we had decided to cease providing coffee, the electric plate was removed and the boys were to be told that it was broken. As the session began, Donald in a rather offhand manner asked the therapist what had happened to the hot plate. He was told that it was broken. He inquired where it was and was told that it had been removed to the repair shop. The maintenance personnel were not sure, however, whether it could be mended. Donald said that had he known he would have brought his own hot plate, which he kept in the shop. No more was said about it nor was any mention made of coffee. Throughout this session there was no show of fidgety or restless behavior. Louis and Jules read comic books during most of the session. Michael read what appeared to be a small pornographic booklet that was given to him by Richard. He was stretched out on the couch during most of the session reading the small pamphlet. It was very obvious that he had an erection as he did so.

The session began with Richard's saying to the therapist: "You said last week you were going to tell us why people dream." The boys' gaze turned on the therapist who, referring to the previous week's discussion, repeated that people have two parts to their mind, the conscious and what we call the subconscious mind, and that in the subconscious mind are stored the memories of whatever has happened to us which we cannot always remember. Richard interrupted: "In the conscious mind is everything you can remember, right?" The therapist agreed. Richard: "When you see a light bulb it is really your brain that is seeing the light, not your eyes, right?" The therapist affirmed this and Richard proceeded to tell a current joke: "A little boy comes to his mother and says, 'Mommy, can I go to the movies?' The mother responds: 'No, you can't. Go back and read your Braille.' "

None of the boys laughed at this. Richard: "Don't you get it?" Donald: "That doesn't even sound like a joke." Richard explained, "Because the boy is blind and he's asking his mother if he can go to the movies."

Jules, looking up from his comic book: "So what's so funny?" Richard said, "You guys are stupid," and proceeded to explain what Braille was —how one runs his fingers across a page that has raised dots instead of letters and thus reads "with his fingers." Macy said that he had once seen a book of Braille. Richard returned to the subject at hand and asked, "When you sleep, you dream of things you wasn't even thinking about before you went to sleep?" Macy: "That means maybe you think you wasn't thinking about it. Isn't that right, Mr. Ellery?" The therapist explained that when one sleeps the part of the mind that one is not aware of during the day begins to come out and images are made which are the dreams. They are memories that one does not want to think about or wants to forget.

The therapist also stated that sometimes dreams are frightening and are really symbols, that is, things represent something in one's mind and one cannot always take a dream at face value. One has to understand what the dream means. Macy: "Is that something like wet dreams?" Richard: "Yeah, I get wet dreams once in awhile. I wake up after I have a wet dream and my underwear is all wet with scum. But I have wet dreams even though when I went to bed I wasn't thinking about sex. How can that be?"

The therapist went into a rather lengthy explanation of this, describing how boys growing up begin to have "sex feelings." Sometimes they did not know what to do about these feelings because, unlike lower animals, they could not just go out and have intercourse and have children. "When you are young," said the therapist, "you can't support children and yet you still feel like having intercourse. When you don't have the opportunity for this you feel tension, a nervousness in the body. The way the body gets rid of this nervousness and tension is by having wet dreams." Following questioning by Macy and Donald, the therapist explained how sperm or "scum" (the two terms were used alternately) is "manufactured in the balls or testicles," and the body has to discharge it. Richard now described how when he awoke from a "wet dream," he felt wide awake. Leonard: "You mean you don't feel nervous any more?" Richard: "I don't know, I just feel wide awake." Louis: "That's why some boys beat the meat sometimes (referring to masturbation). They get rid of nervousness that way."

Donald picked this up and said: "I get rid of it another way. I got a couple of girls and when I go home I just lay them down, get on top of them and that's the end of it." From this ensued rather lengthy narratives by Donald, Richard, and Louis, with Michael chiming in, of the fornication they engaged in. At this point Louis raised his eyes from his comic book and took over the conversation. He described in very vivid detail the girls he had known, virgins and non-virgins, and how he got them to have intercourse by putting "Spanish fly" in their soda or their coffee. Louis's language as he talked about the subject was shockingly obscene. For example, as Louis addressed the group, standing up and bouncing up and down, he said: "I get the broad on the ground and get on top of her and cream all over her. The girls beg me to fuck them after the Spanish fly, but I play cool and say, 'I got a lot of time, Baby.'" He talked as if he were an outrageous Don Juan and, with a total lack of restraint and complete impassivity, had had all the sexual experiences that could possibly be encompassed within a lifetime. Donald and Richard now got into a recital of the different girls they had "screwed" in the balconies of movie houses. Donald described in vivid detail how he would strip a girl in the theater, lay her down in the back aisle of the balcony, and "jump on top of her." Jules rose, left the room, and was gone for about five minutes. When he got back Richard said: "I know what you were doing. You were probably beating on it." This brought laughter from the boys as Jules's face turned as red as a beet.

Donald's description of his exploits was now beginning to take on a different quality. He described how after he "screwed" a girl he told her to "get out of here." The therapist held Donald to this, commenting that what he was saying "showed he had some feelings about it." Donald said: "When I screw a girl, just before I'm going to get on top of her I don't know what to say. I feel all tongue-tied. After I do it, I don't like her." The therapist encouraged him to describe further how he felt and he said: "I don't know. I kind of feel maybe she's dirty." The therapist commented, *Is it possible you feel guilty?* Donald thought about this for a while and said, "I don't know." Richard: "Well if you don't feel guilty you feel afraid. When I get laid I'm always afraid that the girl may get knocked up. I may have to support her kid if I give her one." Michael put down the book he was reading and, still stretched out on the couch, appeared to be listening to what was being said.

Louis, Richard, and Donald were again describing their sexual exploits. The therapist commented that "somehow we had started to talk about how you feel about doing this, and now we are moving away from it." Michael: "They are trying to change the subject." Donald said he had a lot of friends, whom he spoke of rather admiringly, who did only one thing in life: "They go around fucking girls." Richard described all the boys he knew that "fuck girls," and that that was what he wanted to do, too. He turned to the therapist and said, "There's nothing wrong with going around fucking girls all your life." Therapist: "Well, that's one way of living." He proceeded to say that it had been found that in most cases boys who spent their lives like this felt very worried and afraid, and generally did not even enjoy sex, though they talked about it a great deal. At this point Richard said: "I met a boy who screwed his sister and his sister is in a mental hospital now. The boy even bragged about screwing his sister."

There was general agreement that this was "the worst thing a guy could do, screw his sister." Richard: "Why should a guy be afraid of sex?" No one ventured an answer and the therapist volunteered: "Boys can be very bewildered by sex feelings, not knowing what to do about it. Also, many boys at an early age are taught that sex is a dirty thing." He described how sometimes a boy was caught masturbating by a parent and was hit or threatened. Richard said that this never happened to him. Donald added that it never happened to him either, but Richard returned to talking about the boy "who screwed his sister," with Michael saying, "That's the craziest thing a guy could do."

The therapist raised the question at this point of the possibility of not "screwing your sister" but thinking about it. Donald's reaction to this was immediate and definite. He said, "I never had any such thought in my mind." Richard: "Me neither. Who would ever think of things like that?" Louis: "There must be something wrong with a guy for thinking about things like that." The therapist elucidated to the boys the fact that all human beings as they grow up, both boys and girls, become aware of differences in their bodies. A boy realizes that he has a penis and his sister does not have one, and he gets curious about this. This happens to everybody regardless of where they live, and it is part of growing up. The boys followed this with absorbed attention, and the therapist utilized their interest to ask if they had ever heard of the "Oedipus complex." Donald asked, "What's that?" The therapist explained that every boy and girl, as they grow up, has a desire in the "subconscious mind" to sleep with the father or mother. A girl wants to sleep with the father, a boy with the mother. They are not always aware of it, but aware of it or not, this is a natural part of growing up. Michael: "I never thought of things like that." Donald: "Me neither. That's stupid." Richard then said, "I used to sleep with my mother when I was a little boy, but I did that only because I was afraid of lightning."

This statement set off a discussion among Leonard, Richard, Donald, and Macy about how, as little children, when they became frightened, they ran to their mothers' beds. Donald said he felt safer because he knew there was his mother who would protect him, as when there was a storm outside and he would hear thunder and imagine he was going to get struck by lightning. He followed this through by saying: "A couple of years ago I came home and went into the bathroom. There was my mother taking a shower. I saw her naked but I just walked out. I didn't get any ideas in my head. Sometimes my mother comes over and asks me to zip up her dress in the back. I do it, but I don't think of screwing her." Macy: "Even if you did think about it, it doesn't mean you are *going to die.*" Donald responded by saying: "I just don't think of it. *Even if I do get a thought like that in my head, I get it out of my head so fucking fast I don't even know I had it.*" Suddenly he asked for a cigarette from the boys in the room. Nobody would give him one and he became very angry. He walked up to each boy separately demanding a cigarette. The therapist commented that he must be feeling kind of tense now. Perhaps he felt that if he had something in his mouth it would make him feel better, would soothe his tension. Louis picked this up and said, "I bet *he would like to have a tit in his mouth* right now."

Richard quickly stepped in and said: "I remember something that happened to me when I was about five years old. I think I used to pee in bed and when I'd wake up in the morning I'd hide the sheets. One night I woke up and my pajamas were wet. My mother found the pajamas even though I hid them and she thought that I was playing with myself and she told me I was going to grow up to be a crook if I play with myself. She told my father and my father told my mother that it isn't possible that a boy of five could be playing with himself." His mother beat him "unmercifully" so that he would not play with himself again. Immediately following this, Richard told of how, when he was a little older, his mother used to give him money to pay bills, such as the electric bill. He had to go "to the gas and electric place," and he used to keep part of the money and then come back and tell his mother that he lost it. This used to lead to a lot of fights between him and his mother, and his father used to get in on these fights. Macy: "You were sore as hell weren't you?" Richard: "Naw, I wasn't sore at my mother. I just wanted to get even with her." From this, Richard went on to describe how he used to play hooky, run around with the gangs in his neighborhood, and so forth.

Louis said, "It's time to go fellows." The boys rose and began to leave. On the way out, Richard continued to describe to Donald the fights and the stealing in which he used to get involved in his neighborhood.

COMMENT

The striking development in this session was *1]* the involvement of the boys in psychological understanding as they at once continued the discussion of dreams on their own and, *2]* how easily they now accepted and responded to the forbidden incest urges without excessive anxiety and anger, which are so common in the average person, adolescent or adult. Donald's almost direct revelation of the repression of his incestuous wishes was quite dramatic for an adolescent so early in the course of treatment. Equally interesting were Louis's recognition of the relation of anxiety and oral regression ("tit in his mouth") and Macy's vague perception of the relation between the ideas of incest and death.

The therapist's increased activity was noteworthy both in interpreting resistance and exploring the boys' unconscious and repressed guilt-provoking feelings and urges.

However, the rather surprising productions in this session stemmed from feelings that still remained in the unconscious. It was necessary for therapeutic effectiveness that their meanings be recognized and enter the realm of the ego. We emphasized this repeatedly in our supervision discussion and pointed out that the process would be a difficult one. It was certainly risky to continue in the same channels, for it might "scare off" the boys and increase their resistance; or they might quit the group. The approach to self-understanding had to be made by less threatening paths, rationalistic and conceptualistic. Intellectual curiosity generally had to be first aroused before true inversion could be achieved. This is the essential fact of para-analytic therapy, and we therefore decided to lie in wait until the boys presented such an opportunity.

12

First
Intermediate Progress Reports

IN THIS CHAPTER are recorded progress reports obtained from various staff members after approximately fifteen sessions of group C. The interviews with the personnel were held at different intervals for the different boys, according to the severity of their problems, since we were bent upon preventing any serious damage to the boys themselves and disturbance to the institution's community. The reader will, therefore, find no uniformity in the spacing of the reports. It is recommended that the case histories in Chapter 10 be reviewed before reading the progress reports in this and subsequent chapters.

Donald

After Fifteen Sessions

In the cottage, Donald appeared as "a shadowy figure, often moody and depressed." The cottage life supervisor reported that at several case conferences on Donald, staff members requested a neurological study of him to determine whether there was an organic base for the boy's behavior. At times, Donald looked as if he were "drifting around in another world." He was extremely forgetful and seemed to be concerned about the fact that he often discovered himself talking loudly and rapidly, yet, in his own words, "saying nothing." He seemed in dread of losing his temper and within the preceding two months had begun to question the validity of his delinquent attitudes, which he had taken for granted in the past, and to some extent also the attitudes of members of his family. He had been asking his cottage father what made it wrong to strike a boy that one disliked, as if the idea that there might be something wrong with such a course of action had never occurred to him before. His family continued to break the institutional regulations in the presence of the boy and at times even involved him in their delinquent acts, creating considerable problems for the cottage personnel, as well as for Donald.

The teachers had not noticed any change in Donald's conduct. There was some improvement in his manual skills, but none in his academic work (reading average was still 2.3, arithmetic 3.4). There was slight improvement in attitude and compliance to rules, according to his classroom teacher. The remedial reading teacher reported that as soon as Donald learned to read a word he almost immediately forgot it; there were times when he could read a whole paragraph correctly, but when the teacher asked him to reread it for practice, the boy could not recognize even one word of what he had just finished reading.

In casework interviews, Donald began to talk about his family situation and to recognize to a small degree that the burden of change was on himself because when he went on home visits, his mother allowed him to go out with boys whom she knew had a "history of trouble," instead of prohibiting these associations. The mother did not even reveal to the father what he had done. Donald asked the caseworker to talk to his mother about this, feeling that he himself could not change her ways. Donald had in every other respect resisted any effort at establishing communication with him.

We must confess that the inroads made toward reality-testing by this boy, as slight as they were, greatly surprised us. His coming to question his mother's reactions in so short a time and his awareness of her attitudes and his own responsibility for protecting himself against unsuitable friends were evidences of progress which we did not anticipate in so brief a period.

It would seem that our hypothesis of a possible anxiety hysteria in this patient had found some confirmation in his "drifting around in another world" and in the sudden blockings to remembering or recognizing words and sentences which he had read only moments before. Donald's preconscious incestuous involvement with his mother was not known to us at the time, but this mechanism of instantaneous obsolescence could be understood as a defense against holding any information, for it might ultimately lead to becoming aware of his forbidden feelings. Therapy should, therefore, lead to weakening superego censors and making available released energies in the service to the ego. This release Donald could not receive from individual treatment alone in the institutional setting. His incapacity to relate, his distrust of adults, and his extreme defensiveness against unconscious prohibited strivings could not be reached without the catalytic effect of other boys and the permissiveness of a peer group. The first step in detaching himself from his mother was made when he criticized her indifference toward his associating with antisocial friends. It was along this path that the boy's redemption lay.

Louis

After Eight Sessions

In the integration conference held on Louis after he had been in the group for eight sessions, the caseworker reported that she had accidentally revealed to the boy that his sister was a foster sister, not realizing that Louis had been unaware of this fact. This information proved very traumatic for him. Louis raised many questions about whether he was really the foster child, and not his sister. The caseworker further stated that in her interviews Louis continued to be "noncommunicative, withdrawn, and generally resistant."

There was a marked contrast in Louis's conduct in individual and in group therapy. In the group, he was spontaneous and was one of the most verbal youngsters. He had on occasions dominated the group with descriptions of his perverse sexual experiences, using profanity and obscenities to an extreme degree. The question was raised whether Louis was psychopathic, though there were indications against this conclusion. It was recommended that he continue in the group, and that a re-evaluation of his case be made in three months.

In all other areas, there seemed to be little change from previously cited reports.

Very little change could be expected in this brief period of treatment. However, we felt that Louis utilized the group situation beneficially. In his narrations of violence and abuses he had been discharging much of his accumulated anxiety which in the past he released in acts. The verbal discharge reduced his tensions, which in the past were canalized into antisocial, vengeful conduct. He was discovering that rage and hate need not be acted out; they can also be "talked out," and this he was able to do for the first time in the group without fear of retribution.

The permissiveness of the therapist and the group spelled acceptance and therefore "respect" for his personality and for his rights as an individual. These conditions are essential for growing maturity.

Louis's sexual acting out in the community and the perversions in which he was actively engaged while at the Village denote a pregenital phase in psychosexual development; and his narcissistic self-indulgence was a form of ego-centeredness characteristic of pregenital and pre-Oedipal development. The direction therapy needed to follow here was toward general maturity of personality so that the infantile characteristics and strivings would be sloughed off.

Leonard

After Fifteen Sessions

Cottage parents reported that Leonard was now speaking quite clearly and coherently and engaging them, as well as the boys, in conversation. He had begun to write letters home and his writing ability improved considerably. He no longer allowed himself to be bullied and "pushed around" by other boys: he defended himself adequately when anyone attempted to hit him. The boys learned that they could not push him around. Leonard, though at this time helpful to the other youngsters in the cottage, no longer permitted them to exploit him as they had in the past. The cottage mother noted that "three or four weeks after the 'discussion group' began, Leonard began to adjust more appropriately." He no longer wore several belts on his pants and began to wear clothes that fit him, and the boys had stopped teasing him about his false teeth. Leonard still seemed sensitive when teased and he once said, "They think I'm a jackass, but I'll show them I'm not." On another occasion he told the cottage parents: "I like the discussion group. I am able to discuss things about myself that I never was able to talk about before." Leonard spoke to his cottage parents and the other boys about his father, whom he viewed in a more favorable light than before.

Leonard's teacher reported that while he was still somewhat withdrawn, he had begun to express himself more freely and was a little more assertive than previously. His grooming continued to improve. However, severe difficulties in academic work continued.

The caseworker also noted an increase in assertiveness and was impressed with Leonard's more mature manner. He used to be "extremely passive and would speak in a whiny voice. More recently, he has been able to verbalize complaints about the Village, which he did not allow himself to do before," wrote the caseworker.

In a psychiatric examination at this time, the psychiatrist noted the boy's friendly greeting and his taking the initiative in introducing topics for conversation. Unlike the previous interviews, he volunteered considerable information. The psychiatrist stated: "Leonard talked about the group therapy project, enumerating the participants and volunteering the opinion that he was surprised to hear other kids talk about their problems and he compared theirs with his. Leonard is showing more anxiety and restlessness now than in the last examination. In part, this anxiety seems to have been mobilized by the group sessions and in part by his acceptance of his social worker. Both of these factors threaten the stability of the defenses he had erected to fend off any recognition of a negative component in his relationship with his mother. These factors may in time make it possible for him to approach his core problem. His defenses have been working pretty successfully and his reality situation has reinforced these defenses. His mother's very real need for him at home tends to reinforce his resistances."

Leonard seldom spoke at the group sessions, but it was obvious that he listened very carefully and thoughtfully. His reality-orientated and, at times, deeply philosophic pronouncements based on the group discussions gave the lie to his apparent passivity and detachment. He was a participant-observer. His participation was verbally passive; but it became clear later that he was very much involved intellectually and emotionally.

As is usually the case with withdrawn patients in groups, Leonard's initial progress was rapid and, in a telling sense, dramatic, in the first brief period of treatment. He made considerable strides in improving his self-identity and in his movement toward ego integration as opposed to his original alienation.

Jules

After Fifteen Sessions

The cottage parents reported that Jules was slightly more relaxed and more poised, although essentially still an isolated youngster. He had begun to show more interest in his surroundings and in the occurrences in the cottage. He would sit with the other boys on occasion and appeared interested in the conversations. Occasionally, he would walk over to observe their activities. Perhaps the most significant change was in his relationship with the cottage mother. He no longer argued with her and did not run off when admonished as he had done some months back. He stopped threatening to run away from the Village, which he had constantly done before.

His teacher reported that Jules still had to be urged to study, because he still did not exert effort on his own in the classroom. If pressed too much, he would sulk or put his head on the desk and go to sleep. The teacher stated: "He is not motivated and negates all attempts to lead him into learning."

In his infrequent casework interviews, Jules was very fearful of becoming involved with the caseworker. He talked of going home and little else. The foster parents continued seeing the caseworker at their local child guidance clinic and it was felt that little could be accomplished with them. This was also the impression of the intake supervisor at the Village, who had interviewed them at the time Jules was admitted. The mother was a rigid woman, the father meek and passive. Both were uneducated and unintelligent, simple folk with unrealistic expectations of this boy, in which he constantly frustrated them. Both felt guilty for their failures with Jules and angry with him.

However, it seemed that the expected "loosening up" of the rigid defensiveness on the part of this boy was slowly occurring and his self-encapsulation was diminishing since he had joined the group, though at a very slow pace.

Michael

After Fifteen Sessions

In the cottage Michael was described as still largely an isolate, moving from group to group and avoiding emotional involvements or identifying with anyone. His general adjustment continued to be inoffensive. He had become more communicative with his cottage parents, would ask them questions and discuss the cottage program. He was less argumentative and less persistent in making his points, or in asking the same questions over and over again as he had in the past. There was some suspicion that Michael might have been instigating the fights that occasionally broke out in the cottage without getting into the frays himself. During the preceding six weeks, he had written to his mother less frequently, but was worried because she had not been writing to him as often as before. He was afraid she "had a boy friend." Michael was described as a restless boy and tended particularly to avoid the cottage mother.

Michael continued to show improvement in school, maintaining a serious attitude toward academic work, and was helpful in the classroom, volunteering to do chores and helping the new boys.

When examined by the same psychiatrist as before, he was found to be "cheerful, casual and at times inappropriately smiling with a degree of silliness. Infantile features were in evidence, with paranoid tendencies, possibly sociopathic traits and some suggestion of an impairment in the thinking processes." However, the psychiatrist felt that the boy was not "overtly psychotic." It was recommended that another psychiatric examination be arranged in two months.

Five weeks later, a (integration) conference was held with the group therapy and casework personnel participating to evaluate the course of treatment and, if necessary, to change the treatment plan.

The caseworker characterized Michael when he first came to the Village as "a suspicious, resistive, testing-out youngster who, although talking about the incidents that led to his placement in the Village, tended to minimize and deny his own role in it. More recently, however, he has become somewhat more realistic about his home situation." He recognized that he could not depend on his mother for his welfare once he returned home. At the start of group therapy Michael had verbalized resistance to his going to the sessions since he discovered that it would not help him "get out of the Village any sooner." As time went on there was a marked decrease in these complaints, but the casework interviews continued to be on a superficial level consisting of narrations of current events. At this point, Michael was making plans as to what he would do when he returned home. He expressed concern about a sister who had run away and appeared to be living somewhere with a "boy friend." Michael rarely showed overt anxiety, even when he talked about his mother's male friends.

The same teacher who had reported on Michael previously stated: "Michael is now less sneaky and his interests are now real rather than being a façade as before. While he is more conforming, he no longer does so to get on my good side. He now conforms out of his desire to do so and a genuinely good relationship."

The group therapist reported that when Michael first came to the group he raised many questions which he pursued "with tremendous persistence." For example, he repeatedly asked whether his coming to the group would mean that he could leave the Village sooner and whether the therapist could "go to conferences" and get him out of the Village. When this was handled realistically with him he dropped the subject.

Michael was not very verbal and "his personality was very tenuous";

nonetheless he had "something to offer to the group." In his own way, he helped others to hold to reality. On a number of occasions Michael brought "down to earth" a boy who was given to flights of fantasy by questioning these fantasies. When another boy claimed that he was sent to the Village only because he truanted "once in a while," Michael was the first to question this, forcing the boy to admit that he truanted a great deal.

Michael never came late to the group sessions and he never left before they were over. Although at times he appeared withdrawn and closed his eyes, from his remarks the therapist was aware that Michael was "taking everything in," though he was throughout more of a listener than a talker.

In the group Michael presented a rather pleasant façade, always greeting the therapist and the other boys who were present when he came in. On one or two occasions he remarked about the clothes the therapist wore. Recently he had joined the other youngsters in discussing dreams, narrating some of his own, and had attempted to instigate other boys to start the "discussions," although he never initiated one. Michael once stated that he knew the Village had "done something" for him. He realized that "getting in trouble does not pay," that when he left the Village he would live a life that would no longer get him "into trouble with the law."

It was noted that following Michael's membership in the group the various staff members had become aware that he was probably schizophrenic and that treatment would have to follow supportive rather than exploratory, uncovering, psychoanalytic lines. It was also emphasized that the boy came from a neighborhood culture where criminalism was normal and much of the referral problem had to be viewed in that light. It was also recognized that Michael needed to picture his mother defensively as a wonderful person, though unconsciously he may have had an urge to destroy her. The primary need was seen to be to strengthen the boy's ego and help him evolve more operational defenses. It was felt that this could be effectively achieved in group therapy.

His acting out and discussions in the group, his being accepted as part of the group, and his unsocial behavior being tolerated without arousal in him of guilt and anxiety loosened up the boy's pathognomic defenses and tended to open his true personality to view. This brought in its wake the exposure of the real nature of the boy, so that the psychiatrist and other members of the staff, who hitherto had overlooked it, recognized the degree of the boy's illness.

We see considerable movement along the lines envisaged in the referral discussion: Michael had moved, though slowly, in the direction of object relations; he had moved away from his mother (decreased correspondence) and became more realistic concerning her (accepted the fact that she might have "men friends" and that he could not count on her when he returned home). He recognized his part in getting sent to the Village, accepted the fact of his sister's delinquency, and explored plans for himself after his discharge from the Village. All these changes came as a result of strengthened ego and a better self-identity. The boy could be said to be moving toward a more benign self-alliance (as contrasted to his former self-alienation).

Macy

After Fifteen Sessions

The cottage reports indicated that Macy was a cooperative, compliant, relatively passive boy, continually striving to win the approval of both cottage parents, and particularly the cottage mother. He went along quietly with what was required of him and accepted limits.

The teacher noted that Macy was accepted as part of the group and was "very much one of the boys." He observed that while typically Macy did not pick on any of the other boys, he had picked on one boy when the teacher was not watching him. (This boy had a reputation for engaging in homosexual activities in a passive role. He also compulsively talked about his mother.) Macy's schoolwork continued to be good. However, the teacher had noted a change in Macy in the preceding month or two. He occasionally dozed off in class and often came to school looking physically tired. However, he was always alert when something of interest was going on in the class. In summary, Macy seemed much less "peppy" than formerly, although his academic work continued to be good.

Macy continued to see his caseworker once a week through this period (later changed to alternate weeks) and was found to be essentially a very compliant, dependent boy, evading talk about anything of significance, but repeatedly demanding to go home to mother. He would keep looking at the door rather than the caseworker. More recently, however, he had begun to display hostility toward the caseworker, becoming aggressive in demanding that he be allowed to telephone home. When the caseworker attempted to explore his need to talk to his parents, Macy would become very angry and threatened not to talk at the interviews.

Macy said that he wanted to be a lawyer, although he was also thinking of going into the armed services. His favorite activity appeared to be wrestling. (Macy had recently injured his back while wrestling.) He was the favorite of the cottage mother and presented no management problem. The cottage mother "appeared to go out of her way to give him her attention."

At a recent interview Macy had related a dream, which he had never done before. (Obviously the change was a result of the group discussions.) In the dream he saw a tall, vague, unidentifiable man. Macy could not quite make out who this man was. There were also a number of "cops in blue uniforms wearing red bands around their arms." He saw himself fighting with the man, trying to "shoot it out" with him, but the man would not die. Finally Macy ran away. No attempt was made to discuss or interpret the dream by the caseworker, nor did Macy say anything further about it.

Already some feeble steps in the direction of maturation had been taken by Macy. He was able to attack another boy surreptitiously in school. (It is of interest that the chosen target was one who was characterologically similar to himself.) His tendency to doze off and be less "peppy" at school might have a number of meanings, but it was possible that his childish eagerness had abated and he was less involved in *everything* that went on around him. He was more *selective*, for he continued to be alert whenever something of interest was transpiring. Also his need to teach and tease boys had been redirected to an interest in wrestling. He had become aggressive with, and demanding of, the caseworker, as contrasted to his former extreme compliance. The vague, undefinable *man* in the dream can be understood as being his own emerging masculinity with which he was struggling (to continue in his infantilism), but "it" would not die.

Richard

After Fifteen Sessions

The cottage father reported that Richard had improved in a number of areas. He walked with a more vigorous pace, instead of ambling as in the past, and his "nervous conversations" had diminished. Though participating more, he was still a "fringe member of the group," and gullible. Richard still had to be urged to groom himself, though there was a noticeable progress in this area as well. When conversations arose he attempted to monopolize the stage, made a bid for recognition, and sought to impress adults and peers, but he was "much more relaxed than ever before." Richard no longer used illness as a bid for attention and was going to the infirmary much less frequently.

Richard's teacher as well noted changes in the boy since he had begun attending the therapy group. He was no longer so eager to answer all questions and on occasion actually fell asleep in class. His eagerness about school had decreased to the extent that he once failed to turn in a book report for four weeks, but did so finally under pressure. The teacher had gained the impression that the excessive interest in school in the past was more of a "pretense" and that Richard had become "more open and direct." His relation with the teacher was "cooler and more distant, seemingly as a result of a decreased need to placate and be ingratiating." He acted more independently.

The caseworker was impressed with the marked change in the boy. Whereas previously he would present himself as a rather happy-go-lucky youngster with no problems, he now appeared to be rather depressed when he saw her. This she related to his home and family situation, which was "going from bad to worse." Richard continually talked about his family and what went on in his home. His mother had recently said to him: "Why don't you go back to the pigs where you belong?" However, the caseworker viewed his productions as a sign of growth, since before entering the group Richard had never revealed anything about his parents. In contrast, he now described with a great show of emotion the fights between his mother and father. This was especially true when he returned from home visits, which provoked a great deal of anxiety in him. The parents usually failed to visit Richard at the Village for three week ends after his home visits and he interpreted this as meaning that he must have "done something wrong" when he was at home. In recent weeks Richard reported that he had received some attention from his mother at the expense of his siblings. This resulted in increased rivalry between him and his sister, who had always been preferred. (The mother, it should be noted, was seen by a caseworker at the hospital in her community.)

At a joint (integration) conference on the boy, it was felt that individual treatment was essential to Richard at this point. He was very anxious and seemed to allay a good deal of his anxiety in the group, but the individual therapist could help the boy work through his depressions by discharging his feelings about his family situation. The depression was considered, at least in part, a reaction to the guilt feelings he had toward his family. The individual sessions could be used to work through his guilt. Richard was now able to recognize the disturbances in his family and appeared willing to consider his life situation with some measure of reality. It also appeared that he was passing through the Oedipal phase in his development and now perceived his parents as a couple rather than as individuals and, therefore, was now in intense rivalry with his father.

Another conference was suggested to re-evaluate the situation in three to four months and determine whether or not the therapy group might have intensified the Oedipal anxiety. It was conjectured that possibly Richard's monologue in the group sessions respecting sexual intercourse with mothers might have sparked a great deal of anxiety in him. If this were true he might have to be removed from the group. Continued evaluation of Richard's response to both individual and group therapy was recommended.

As anticipated, Richard was the most loquacious boy in the group and his lengthy recitals were frequently accompanied by physical movement or by his standing up as words flowed from his mouth in great profusion. He was the only boy who would rise as he spoke, except for one other who rose only when he became very excited. Richard's general relaxation was partly due to the fact that he had thrown off his tensions by his unhampered communications and acting out in the group, but more so by the fact that for the first time in his life he was fully and unconditionally accepted by an adult and a group where, because of his brightness and loquaciousness, he enjoyed a superior status. This reduced his compelling need to stand out at school, since now he enjoyed a new and satisfying image of himself which gave him greater security to be "himself," instead of playing a role and pretending.

His newly found identity was reflected in his total behavior as reported by the cottage parents and by the schoolteachers, but this was made even more palpable by his growing interest in his grooming and appearance. Of important note is the fact that the mother now no longer downgraded him in relation to his sister and even defended him against her, which she had never done before. This development can be understood as the mother's perceiving the unhabitual strength in Richard, his more mature conduct, and the self-respect he emanated, which in turn induced respect for her son in her.

13

Protocols and Comments: Sessions 16-33

Session Sixteen: The Breakthrough

THE BOYS REMAINED rather quiet for a considerable time. No one seemed willing to venture into a discussion. Richard and Michael looked at one another and briefly giggled embarrassedly. Louis stretched himself out on the couch and was staring up at the ceiling. After a period of silence, Richard took the initiative and, calling out each boy's name, asked him if he had anything to say. Each responded by saying no. Richard: "Too bad." He then pulled a piece of paper out of his pocket, folded it, made a slit, put it to his lips, and by blowing through it produced a shrill sound. He invited all the boys in the room to do likewise. Michael was the first to follow suit. Richard announced that he would go around the room calling each one, and as each was called, he was to make a noise. Michael made the loudest noise. Leonard, however, did not use paper, he made a moaning sound with his lips. Jonathan did likewise. Louis made a squeaking sound. Richard started the second round, and when it came to Michael's turn, he again made a rather loud screeching sound through his paper whistle.

The therapist turned to Michael and said: "That's a very interesting noise. It sounds like the noise when an airplane breaks the sound barrier." Michael turned to the therapist and with obvious interest declared: "I heard of planes that break sound barriers. How does that work?" Richard at once entered the discussion by describing for Michael how when a plane reaches a certain speed, it makes a booming noise. Michael did not seem satisfied with the explanation and, turning to the therapist, asked how the sound was produced. The therapist demonstrated with gestures that, when an object moves, the air creates resistance, and when a plane reaches a certain speed the resistance is so great that it was almost as if the airplane had to break through a wall of air. In "breaking through" the air, the plane sets up "tremendous vibrations" which are heard as a "boom." (As the therapist was making this explanation, all the boys became quiet and attentive.) Jules: "Isn't it true that sometimes things will burn up when they go through the air?"

The therapist explained that this occurred because of friction that was set up by air resistance, at the same time recalling to the boys that one rubs his hands together to make them warm or when one uses sandpaper heat can be felt through the sandpaper. Special metals have to be made for airplanes so that they will not "burn up" when they are subjected to the heat. The therapist mentioned that some boys might have seen a shooting star. Donald said that he had never seen one, but Richard said: "Oh, I've seen them a lot of times. When you look up at the sky at night, you see something flying through the sky and it's all lit up." Louis wanted to know what makes a shooting star. The therapist explained the origin and nature of meteorites and how they are illuminated through the heat generated by friction in the air. Louis wanted to know how long it would take to travel to a star. Donald interrupted him and asked whether the earth was a "star." The therapist explained the difference between a planet and a star, and stated that the sun was a star from which the earth derived its heat. The stars we see are really so many suns. Louis said he had heard that it would take a long time to reach a star. The therapist speculated that it would take about a million years to reach the nearest star in an airplane if it could be done.

Jules averred that "we could never live that long so probably we could not get to a star." Louis: "Maybe some day they will develop an airplane that could go so fast, it wouldn't take long to get to a star." Since the boys appeared very interested in the subject, the therapist introduced the concept of the speed of light, 186,000 miles a second, and added that some stars are so far away that though we could see their light we could not be sure whether the stars still existed. This seemed to puzzle the boys, but Donald quickly picked up the discussion and asked many questions about how this could possibly happen. The therapist explained that if a star were many trillions of miles away the light we saw as a star may have left the star a thousand to a million years ago, so we could not be sure by the time we saw it whether that particular star is still in existence. Michael exclaimed: "Hey, that's interesting. You mean we look at a star, that star might not really be there any more?" The therapist confirmed this. Donald: "I guess that means that if we turned on the light in the room somebody standing millions of miles away and looking at our room would not see it for a couple of hours."

Jules asked: "Is it true that scientists do not believe in God?" Therapist: "Some scientists do and some scientists do not." Louis: "I heard that the sun is very, very hot. How hot is the sun?" Therapist: "The center of the sun is about two million degrees." Louis: "Man, that's hot! We probably couldn't go to the sun. We would melt if we got near it." Donald: "The airplane would melt before you got anywhere near the sun." Louis asked at this point whether there was any place on earth where it was as hot as the sun. The therapist told Louis that on earth there was no such spot, but that scientists were trying to duplicate it in laboratories in developing such things as atom bombs.

Michael picked this up and began to tell the boys that if there were another war there were going to be atom bombs, cobalt bombs, and hydrogen bombs dropping all over the "fucking place." Donald said that if there were a war, he would leave the Village and try to get back to his family. Louis: "You'll be fucking lucky if you get to see anybody again." Donald became restless at this point and, taking hold of his genitals, said: "I better get back to my family. They ain't going to keep me at Children's Village if they drop atom bombs around here." Michael wanted to know whether there was any kind of shelter one could go to should atom bombs fall, while Richard declared he had heard that "they are making fallout shelters where people can go and hide." Michael: "I don't know what good that's going to do. What bothers me is that without even asking us . . . I don't like the idea of people deciding what they are going to do with my life."

There now arose a free group interchange about some ways of preventing war. Louis, taking the lead in this, described how if he could have his way he would send a couple of planes to Russia, would sneak through the radar, and would drop "a couple of hydrogen bombs." In that way Russia would never be able to attack us. Donald: "You would never get away with it. You're thinking is stupid-like." A few minutes later, though, Donald said, "Maybe we ought to bomb the hell out of them and then they can't get to us." Michael said to Donald: "I'm glad you're not the leader of this country; if you was, there wouldn't be anybody alive here." Macy: "I don't think there's going to be a war. Russia is afraid of us, and we're afraid of Russia. The only reason we're afraid of each other is because Russia and we got the atom and hydrogen bombs and nobody wants to get killed." Jules: "Yeah, nobody wants to get killed but sometimes people make some stupid mistakes and you get killed whether you want to or not." Louis: "Maybe what they ought to do is have a big arena and let everybody in the arena and fight it out man to man with their fists instead of using guns and bombs." Jonathan: "Why do they even have to fight? They can sit down and talk things over. It's like a lot of guys around here, they're always looking for trouble. If they used their mouth instead of their fists they wouldn't get into so much trouble."

Donald, still holding his hands on his genitals, was becoming quite agitated. He said: "Let's stop this stupid discussion. *I don't like the idea of dying.*" Therapist to Donald: "This seems to worry you." Donald, with obvious anxiety, said, "Nobody likes to die; there's nothing strange about it." In a casual, offhand manner the therapist said that, of course, it was quite normal not to want to die, but sometimes even though people did not have any immediate reason for thinking about dying they still worried about it, as some people worry about having an illness. Even though a doctor assured them that there was nothing wrong with them, they still worried. Richard at once said: "That happened to me many times. I used to think I was sick and my mother would take me to the doctor and the doctor would say there was nothing wrong with me and still it didn't stop me from worrying." Donald, interrupting Richard: "Many times when I lie in bed at night after I have had a date and had a good time, I lie in bed and think about what a good time I had. All of a sudden I get kind of worried. I begin to worry about if I'll always be having a good time or if I'm going to die before I can have any more good times." He continued by describing how when he fell asleep he had dreams that he was falling through space.

Louis abruptly rose from his reclining position on the couch and said: "Man you got dreams like that? I get those dreams all the time. I dream that I'm running and that I fall over a cliff and I keep falling, falling, falling and, boom, I wake up. Boy, they're scary." Leonard: "I sleep in a bunk and sometimes I dream I'm falling. I wake up and I'm on the floor." Jonathan, turning to the therapist: "Mr. Ellery, what makes dreams?" (It will be recalled that in the preceding session when the group discussed dreams, Jonathan was absent.) The therapist began to recount for Jonathan how in last week's discussion "the two parts of the mind" were described, but Richard interrupted him and recounted to Jonathan how there was a conscious and subconscious part of the mind. Macy, stepping in, stated that the group then spoke about the "subconscious mind having memories that you can't remember any more."

Jonathan responded: "I've been having the same dream for years," and went on to narrate his recurring dream in which he saw himself and his family being consumed by fire, and added: "That's why I can't stand fire. I hate to even look at it." He said that one night he was sleeping and having this dream. All of a sudden, about two o'clock in the morning, he was awakened by footsteps. He looked out the window and there he saw his cottage father leave the cottage, go over to the garbage can outside, and start a fire in it. He kept staring at the man, who stood there looking at the fire. The man then lifted his head and kept looking up at the sky. There was a "crazy look" on his face. Jonathan thought his cottage father was "really crazy," because this was a crazy thing to do at two o'clock in the morning. Jonathan said: "Maybe I have that dream because, when I was young, a lady upstairs in my house was burned up in a fire. I still remember her legs, they were all black; her flesh was burned."

Jonathan fell silent. Richard asked whether there was a book called "something like *Interpretation of Dreams*," and what that meant. The therapist confirmed the existence of such a book and explained about dreams as symbols, clarifying the term "symbol." From the general nodding of the heads, it was apparent that the boys understood it. The therapist proceeded by saying that dreams do not always mean what they appear to, even though some dreams can be awfully frightening. Jules said he used to have a dream when he was a little boy about worms crawling over his head, but he hadn't had the dream any more. Michael: "Is it true that some people don't dream at all?" The therapist explained that people dream, but they often do not remember dreams, because they don't want to. Donald said that he hadn't dreamed in years.

Jonathan started the boys on a discussion about what went on in his cottage, how his cottage was actually "run" by the boys and the cottage father had to "beg" them to turn off the television set and go to bed. Donald became very active in this discussion, describing his cottage, where there used to be cottage parents who were "afraid" of the boys. The discussion now gravitated to commissions of cottage parents, how stupid they were, and how boys "get away with things." This continued for a while. Since this conversation seemed to be leading nowhere, the therapist commented that a little while ago the boys were talking about dreams and the subject was suddenly changed. "Why?" Donald's response to this was immediate. He said: "I don't want to talk about dreams. They're stupid things." As soon as he said this, however, he told of a dream in which he was away from the Village, living with his parents, and then he would wake up and be back at the Village and hated it. Macy: "I used to have a dream like that a lot of times. I dreamed that I ran away from the Village and when I came home my mother and father said to me, 'You don't have to go back to the Village, because you're discharged from the Village.' But then I'd be awakened and I was still at the Village and I was so fucking mad!" Michael: "Why do you dream dreams like this?" The therapist said that sometimes dreams serve the purpose of fulfilling a wish "that you may not be aware of." Donald: "That's funny, when I used to have those dreams I used to feel that I was going to stay at the Village and not run away. Maybe I really did want to run away and was dreaming about it." Michael: "I used to have dreams that I had a lot of money in my fist and was clutching my fist and when I woke up at night my fist was still clutched, but I didn't have any money in it."

Jules put on his jacket at this point, left the room, and did not return. It was about 8:25 P.M. (He left five minutes early on two other occasions.) Macy was describing how he used to dream about owning a bicycle because he never had a bicycle and he wanted one very badly. His parents didn't have enough money to buy him one. He would also dream of riding the bicycle and falling, hurting himself. Jonathan became active in steering the discussion away from dreams and onto cottage parents again, describing how boys in his cottage had worked out a system whereby they evaded chores they were assigned to by the cottage parents. This continued until 8:30, when the session ended.

As the therapist was leaving, Richard came up to him and began to talk about "something that had happened" to him. He prefaced this by saying, "I wanted to tell you something but I can't remember," and then remarked, "I'll bet there is a reason for not remembering." The therapist agreed to this. Richard then told of an episode that occurred when he went home for a visit. As he was getting off the train his foot began to hurt. He wasn't sure whether his mother would be home when he got there. He walked to the telephone booth, and all the way over his foot kept hurting. He then called his mother and found his mother was home. She told him that she was looking forward to seeing him. Richard then said: "When I left the telephone booth—the funny thing was—there was no more pain in my leg. Isn't that funny? I'll bet my leg hurt because I was so worried about coming home."

The therapist agreed. After this Richard ran off to join Donald, who was standing at the foot of the stairs waiting for him.

COMMENT

It could be expected that a phalanx of group resistance would appear after the threats from the unconscious were set in action at the last session, and the therapist did well when he perceptively grasped the opportunity of introducing the discussion of airplanes and followed it up with elucidations of natural phenomena, such as breaking through the sound barrier, melting of metal by friction, shooting stars, interplanetary distances, and such, which would be nonthreatening and of interest to adolescent boys. Because of the prevalent social climate and newspaper items, this led to a consideration of war, atomic weapons, fallout, and as an inevitable consequence, death.

All this represented external threats, but Donald translated it into his fear of death and his cogitations about it after he had a "good time"— he had to be punished for enjoying himself. This may stem from guilt feelings or from unconscious memories of the punishment by his parents that a child incurs for being playful. In either case, enjoyment begets anxiety. Jonathan revealed the same condition in himself as a result of his emotional resonance with Donald.

The suggestion of self-awareness (inversion) was introduced by Donald again when he speculated that while he consciously thought that he did not want to run away, his dream indicated to him that in his unconscious he really did wish it.

A real reversal of roles occurred when the boys now spoke of the cottage parents as being under the domination of the boys. This "switch" is characteristic of early childhood when the offspring attempts to reverse roles and do for the mother what she has hitherto done for the child. It may signal for boys a change in self-image and the diminution of dependency feelings (improved self-identity).

The episode of Richard's conversion pain in his leg (because of his uncertainty as to his mother's welcome) and his interpretation was not only remarkable, but indicated that he had gained real insight through the various discussions in the group. This was also demonstrated by his remark that his forgetting must have a "reason." Thus in this boy, at least, the important principle essential for the inversion process and the recognition of the relation of cause and effect had begun to penetrate.

We considered this session as the *breakthrough* in the treatment, and the remark by Donald as to his fear of death was of critical importance in launching the boys toward the gradualness in therapeutic unraveling of their problems. This session is a sort of midpoint between the early resistive top realities in which they indulged before and the productions overladen with anxiety of the later sessions.

The boys' interest in dreams has to be understood only partially as a canalization of their unconscious. It has to be viewed at this juncture rather as an intellectual curiosity about a phenomenon, though one of intimate concern. This assumption is important here, for should the therapist plunge headlong into the latent content of dreams he would generate insoluble resistances and the boys might turn away from him and disrupt the group. It would be necessary to feel the states of emotional readiness sensitively and especially those of the ego defenses of the "leading" members before deeper interpretations were attempted.

As it was, the therapist took a very serious risk when he brought out incestuous Oedipal feelings in session fifteen. Although he got away with it on that occasion, such risks should be taken with great caution. The therapist must have felt secure in the transference situation. The control (or supervisor) frequently cannot judge the mood and readiness of a group and he needs to rely to some extent on the judgment of the therapist to "feel" the group climate and act upon it.

Session Seventeen

ABSENT: Jonathan and Michael. Both boys had run away.

Jonathan ran away two days after the last group session. That evening he appeared to be very upset because most of the boys in his cottage were going home on visits, and a number of them kept teasing him because he was held back. As this provocation continued, he became increasingly agitated and later disappeared.

At the start of the session Richard and Donald reported that Michael would not be coming. Michael had told them that he did not feel like coming today. (Later the therapist learned that Michael had run away with a number of other boys from his cottage in protest because they had some difficulty with a cottage staff member. Michael had been "picked up" in a village about seven miles distant and brought back.)

There appeared to be considerable commotion in the group about distribution of cigarettes that were provided for the boys by the Club Department at all sessions. In the past there had been little ado about it, but Donald in this instance picked up the package of cigarettes and was distributing them to the other boys in the group. Richard claimed that he did not get his share. Donald defiantly said, "Tough shit." Richard replied to Donald: "Fuck you, you bastard. Give me the cigarettes I want." Donald: "You can kiss my ass. You don't like it? I'll meet you after we end tonight and we'll have it out." Louis encouragingly: "Why wait until after the session. Why don't you just do it right now?" Jules to Louis: "You are the fuckinest instigator I ever saw." Donald angrily to Louis: "Yeah, you fuckin' little instigator, what do you want to do, see blood?" Louis responded to this by saying, "I was born an instigator." Richard told Louis to go "take a flying shit" for himself. Louis repeated teasingly: "Yeah man, I'm a born instigator!"

Nothing further was said. The therapist turned to Louis and asked him what he meant by what he had just said. Louis: "Just like I said. Man, I'm a born instigator." He then went into a very lengthy description of a number of fights he had instigated. Sitting in his chair, which happened to be next to that of the therapist, he rocked back and forth as he was saying: "You guys ain't seen the cats they got around my way. Boy, you can get a fight going there as soon as you whistle. I remember one kid who never used to want to fight. I talked him into fighting with a guy I knew would beat the living shit out of him. That fuckin' cat got such a licking! They got him on the floor; they were stomping all over him. They nearly busted his stupid head!" There was a smile of satisfaction on Louis's face as he was describing this scene. Louis continued to the boys: "I like to watch a fight once in a while. See two guys go at it and then draw blood. Man, that's really living when you see something like that! I don't go for this petty shit of guys just using their mouths on one another."

Donald to Louis: "If you ever got me into a fight, I would make sure I would turn you into a bloody mess. You stupid little bastard, what the hell you doing going around pushing boys into fights? You must be crazy to get a kick out of something like that." Louis: "What do you mean, I'm crazy? If you're going to live in this fuckin' world you got to realize this fuckin' world is a fuckin' jungle and you gotta learn how to live in a jungle." Macy: "Yeah, the Village is like a jungle. All guys ever do around here is fight."[1] The therapist wondered what got fights going. Donald said that when he got into a fight he just began to "pound." When he got into a fight, at some point he did not even feel punches on him any more. He knew that a fist was hitting him in the head, but he just could not feel it. He described his head as being "numb." Leonard spoke up and said that this happened to him, too. He said, "When I get into a fight I just begin to swing wild." (This is pure fantasy.) He went through the motions with his arms how he swung wild. He continued: "I take a beating sometimes but I make sure that the other guy gets a beating too." Donald did not let Leonard finish. He returned to describing how when he got into a fight he just charged, his hands swinging. For a moment silence settled upon the group and the therapist asked Donald if he could describe a little more what he felt during a fight. Was he saying he didn't know what happened? Donald said: "Yeah, something like that. Like I said before, somebody can punch me in the nose but my nose won't even feel it. I can even get kicked in the belly, but I'm not going to feel that kick." Jules got up and left the room, probably going to the washroom. He returned in a few minutes.

Louis began to talk, blocking Donald. He narrated that around his way he'd seen "so many fuckin' fights." "It's the way of life around my way," he said. No one seemed to be listening to him. Donald and Richard had struck up a conversation between themselves. Louis continued, saying that if anybody picked on him at the Village "they're going to get their ribs busted." If he couldn't get them at the Village, he'll wait until they went home; he'd get them then. The therapist asked Louis how he felt when he was in a fight. Louis said: "I don't feel anything. It's a most natural thing in the world. Shit, when you're in a fight you're going to get in as many punches as you can before the other guy has a chance to touch you."

1. Like most of the other vituperations against the institution, which were fiction or exaggerations, this too was fantasy. A striking change in this regard makes its appearance in later sessions.

Richard had now picked up a magazine that had been in the room. He was leafing through it. Macy demanded the magazine after Richard was finished with it. Louis walked over to Richard and asked him for the magazine, and Richard gave it to him. Louis looked at the cartoons in it and described them to the boys, who did not respond. It appeared as if they were not interested and were not paying attention to him. (This may have been due to the fact that the boys' powers of abstraction and sophistication were inadequate to grasp what he was telling them.) Louis seemed to recognize the boys' indifference and stopped describing the cartoons to them, but continued quietly leafing through the magazine.

The therapist asked: "What gets these fights going? Isn't there some other way to settle things except by a fight?" This was met with silence. Donald said, "If I had known we were not going to have the hot plate for the coffee, I would have brought my own hot plate from the auto shop," and added that there probably would have been no point in bringing a hot plate because there was no coffee. Donald looked quite agitated now. He said: "I like to have coffee. When we used to come here, it was nice to be able to sit, wait for the hot water to boil; you had something to look forward to. Now there's nothing to look forward to. I just don't like sitting around." The therapist asked Donald directly if he could tell a little more about this feeling he was trying to describe, sitting around and not having coffee. Donald said: "It's like sitting around with nothing to do. I was never able to sit around and do nothing."

Macy immediately picked this up and said, "That's like me, when I just sit around and I ain't got anything to do, I always feel like doing something, so I got to do something with my hands." Donald: "Yeah, that's right. If not with my hands, then I like to have something to eat." The therapist asked Donald if he knew what it was he was now describing. Donald: "Yeah, I know what that is. That's the thing they call tension." Macy picked this up and said, "That's nervousness, ain't it, Mr. Ellery?" The therapist agreed, and went on to comment that there are many people who, when they feel tense, have to have something in their mouth in order to feel better. For the same reason some people who felt tense stamped their feet on the ground, moved their hands, or ran out to the bathroom.

Because the boys seemed interested, the therapist described how there were many stout people who grew that way only because they always had to eat. This made them feel better when they were tense, and went back to their experiences at the time when they were infants. One of the first things a baby wants to do is eat. He wants to be breast-fed. It gives the infant a good feeling; it relaxes the tension. Donald said he heard that breast feeding was much better than feeding a baby by bottle, because a baby liked to be breast-fed. Louis to Donald: "You just want a big fat tit in your mouth." Donald looked at Louis and said: "What's so fuckin' funny? Keep your stupid mouth shut!" He then went into a lengthy description of a friend of his who used to have a twitch of the head, demonstrating it as he talked. He had watched his friend so long that once he got a twitch himself. Once they went into a diner to eat. There were policemen there and, noticing the twitch of his head, they questioned Donald about his smoking marijuana. Macy said that he knew guys who "did this" with the eyes (blinking rapidly with his eyes). Questions were directed toward the therapist by Richard and Macy as they described various symptoms, asking if these were expressions of tension. Richard wanted to know whether thumb-twiddling showed tension.

Donald told that he always felt better when he had some booze in him. He described "a couple of parties" he went to where there were a couple of nice "chicks" around and he wanted to "make time" with them. As soon as he got a "couple of drinks under his belt" he found himself feeling good inside and he was able to walk over, ask them for a dance, start kissing them, and while dancing even rub against them. He continued: Once a bartender asked him if he was old enough to be served and Donald pretended that he had identification to prove that he was. The bartender didn't even bother to examine his identification. He was now back to discussing what happened at parties, how he generally came "a little tight" and, "Boy I really make out!" On one occasion a fellow tried to cut in on him when he was dancing with a girl. Donald warned him to get away. The fellow wouldn't listen and before Donald knew it he had "smacked" this fellow. The boy was on the ground and Donald was stomping on him. His friends at the party had said to him, "Boy, you sure took care of that cat!" Richard cut in and described how when he went to parties he always made sure he had a couple of drinks because then he could "grab hold" of a girl and "feel her ass." She wouldn't say anything but he felt damn good when he grabbed her ass. Donald said: "Yeah, I know what you're talking about. I can have a hard-on when I'm dancing with a girl, but that don't bother her."

The therapist asked Donald whether he felt the same way when he was sober, when he didn't have a drink. Donald thought for a minute and said: "Yeah, I feel the same way. I don't give a shit." Macy said: "When you're sober you feel more self-conscious; you can't do things like this when you're sober," but his words seemed to fall on deaf ears, because Donald was now back to describing what a "big shot" he was at parties and the boys were very attentive. However, Louis got up, put on his coat, said that he had to go back to the cottage, and left the room (about fifteen minutes early). (It seemed to the therapist that Louis left because he failed to get attention from the boys.)

During a pause in Donald's monologue, the therapist interjected the possibility that when he drank it made him feel big, which he may not have felt otherwise. Donald added: "Well, I sure feel different when I get drunk. It's good. I feel happy. I don't think about anything. All I know is I'm on top of the world." The therapist commented that a few minutes ago somebody had used the term *self-conscious*. Richard quickly asked what the therapist meant by that. Therapist: "Self-conscious means that you're worried about the kind of impression you're making on other people. You worry about what other people think about you, about how you look, and so on." Donald and Macy nodded, saying, "Yeah, yeah; when you're sober you're always thinking about those things, but not when you got a couple of drinks in you."

The therapist asked Donald about the feeling of "self-consciousness," but Donald did not respond. The therapist then tried to be more specific and said, "Tonight we were sitting around talking about fights, getting into fights, tension, and being self-conscious, and maybe there is a connection in all of this." Macy: "I don't know, I don't think so. I drink just because it's good. In the summertime I drink a lot of beer." Donald: "When you drink a lot of beer you always got to run to the bathroom to take a piss." Macy: "I don't mind taking a piss. Beer is good, it quenches your thirst. I drink soda but that don't quench my thirst like beer does." Macy continued by saying that when he drank he didn't have a worry in the world. He didn't think about anything except how happy he felt. Donald said: "Yeah, you just feel good. You feel good and happy."

Richard now entered the conversation and asked Donald if he knew of a certain bar in their neighborhood. A discussion arose between Donald and Richard about which bar Richard had in mind. Then Donald told Richard he knew the name of the bar. Once this was established, Richard launched into a story about himself and his friends going to the bar. They lined up and each bought all the others drinks. Donald said that when he went on home visits and had extra money, he could throw away a five-dollar bill just by buying drinks for "other guys." "It's the best way I know to spend that lousy five-dollar bill," he said. Macy reintroduced the concept of self-consciousness by saying to Donald: "I bet you never feel self-conscious when you got a drink." Donald: "What the hell you think I just been telling you about? How can you feel—what do you call it, conscious—if you feel so good?"

Donald then turned to Richard and again discussed the bar they both knew.

It was 8:30 and the session ended.

COMMENT

Louis, more than any one of the other boys, made us aware that they all lived by the "law of the jungle," a subject of lengthy conversation in our supervisory conferences. This life pattern obviously resulted from the absence of sublimational channels and from experiences in their environment and culture which served to arrest their development on a level of primitivism. We did not feel we could work this through indirectly and had decided that when the opportunity presented itself we would formulate for them the reason for social ethos and its survival function. We had decided to root the discussion in biology and "natural morality," that is, describing controls of impulse and appetite as essential for survival. We saw how useful this forethought was, for Louis now spoke of the jungle pattern quite openly. The therapist did well not to "open up" the subject at this point, considering the regressive mood in which the group was. We had to wait until more was said on the subject by the boys themselves and thus became readied and inclined to understand and accept what we would tell them.

The regression and anxiety with which this session was characterized stemmed, of course, from the boys' visits to their homes. These were enhanced by the two runaways and by the absence of coffee. The regression took standard forms: orality (Louis: "You must want a tit in your mouth"; vicarious satisfaction by talking of drinking alcohol, and so forth); talking about fights—aggression; boastfulness of power, prowess, and spending money—insecurity. The last also had a homoerotic implication. Each exposed the strength of his powers and the size of his possessions, which in its psychoanalytic implications represented the size of the penis and potency. Note the boys, through the free-association process, spoke also of heterosexual acting out.

On a number of occasions the therapist explored accompanying (not always underlying) feelings as related to behavior and acts. This set an *attitude* toward such explorations and formed a basis for inversion later on.

The group had moved away from the consideration of the overintense intrapsychic and too threatening areas of the preceding two sessions, which was good. We would bring them forth when the boys were more ready for them.

Session Eighteen

ABSENT: Jonathan, who had run away and had not yet returned.

Michael and Jules were the first to arrive. On the way Jules was filling in Michael (who had been absent the preceding week) on the fact that "there was trouble with the cigarettes; the boys grabbed cigarettes." When Michael came into the room he said hello to the therapist and then went on to tell him that he'd "got an idea about the cigarettes." Every week one boy should be assigned to hold the cigarettes and distribute them. This week he was going to hold the cigarettes and he was going to give each boy an equal share, so that some boys "don't take more and leave other boys without any cigarettes at all." Michael then lapsed into a discussion with Jules about how many cigarettes each boy should have. They figured out that, since Jonathan would not be present, they would divide the cigarettes among seven boys. Jules said that seven into twenty meant that one boy was going to have one cigarette less. Michael and Jules continued the discussion for a while as to how they could divide equally twenty cigarettes among seven boys. The therapist finally resolved this dilemma by giving them one of his own cigarettes. Michael thanked him, saying: "Now it will be easy. Everybody will have his cigarettes equal-equal."

As the other boys started to file in, Michael informed them of his plan. There was no dissent, and he gave three cigarettes to each boy. After this Michael told the therapist in a low voice about his running away the previous week and that he did so because he had an argument with his cottage father. The argument arose from the fact that a pair of pants that he had sent to the laundry was not returned. The cottage father told Michael that he had never sent these pants and that he was just using this as an excuse for getting new pants. While Michael was narrating this, a discussion arose among Donald, Louis, Jules, and Macy as to the number of cigarettes each had, as if to reassure themselves that all had an equal share. Michael continued to talk to the therapist, still in a low voice. Leonard, however, did overhear, and asked some questions about the runaway. This cut Michael off and he said, "I ain't going to talk about it."

Donald immediately began to ask questions about the "hot plate for the coffee"; where was it, was it returned, and so on. The therapist told him that as yet he had not gotten it back. As far as he knew, it was still being repaired. Donald said that he was very upset. "I wish there was coffee. Shit, man, if I had known I would have brought that lousy hot plate from auto shop." Then almost as if to remind himself, he said: "I couldn't bring that one either. I heard that one is busted, too." Jules confirmed this. Michael was sandpapering a piece of cedar wood he had brought with him which had a French curve in it. Macy asked him what he was making. Michael: "I told a hundred people today already what I'm making. I'm not going to tell a hundred more." Louis, as though to tease him, asked: "What are you making?" Michael said, "I told you in the gym this morning, remember?" Louis thought a moment and said, "Oh, yeah, you did." Michael sat back as if he were expecting more questions, but no one questioned. Finally, he announced that he was going to take black tape and tape the handle. Donald: "It looks like you're making a knife." Michael: "Don't worry about that, I ain't going to make any knife."

Michael turned to the therapist and asked if he had received "any reports" as to when he would be going home. The therapist told him that he had not, and Donald said: "I know that in four months I am going to go home. Comes June I'll be out of here, legally or illegally." Michael: "Why do you want to go home in June? That's the beginning of the summer and that's when most boys get into trouble." Donald: "I ain't going to get into trouble. All I want to do is get out of here and get a job. I'm going to be a mechanic. I can get a couple of jobs. My father is going to get me a job. My uncle could get me a job and I know a couple of friends outside who can get me jobs." As Donald's monologue proceeded, a quality of uncertainty set in his voice, almost as if he were questioning each of his statements. The therapist picked this up, saying that although most boys talked about and looked forward to the day "they get out," as they got closer to it they sometimes began to get worried. Donald said: "Yeah, I know many guys don't even want to go when it is time to get out; but that ain't me. I really want to go and I'm going to go one way or another." Donald went on to describe how he was tempted on a number of occasions to run away but it would have done no good because running away might just have added to the time of his stay at the Village.

Michael: "I wish when you came to the Village you came with a [determinate] sentence. If you knew you got to stay two or three years, at least you know at the end of that time you go home. This way they are always giving you a different story as to when you get home." Macy: "But at least you didn't go to prison." Michael: "Damn right. This fuckin' place is a crazy place, but it ain't prison." Donald said that when he got out he would not be coming back again to visit any of his friends. Richard: "Me neither. They won't see me for another year." Donald changed his mind: "Maybe a couple of guys around here I would like to see and then I could come up and visit them." Louis: "But they don't let you visit for at least six months after you are out of here." Michael: "I never heard of that." Louis asked the therapist whether this was so, and the latter responded that he had never heard of this rule. Donald: "Yeah, that's a lot of bull. Maybe if they had sent me up here the first time I got in trouble I wouldn't have had all those fuckin' times getting into trouble at home then having to be sent to Youth House, then running away and all that. Shit, when I think back I was pretty lucky. I could be sitting right behind bars now. I was a real crazy kid."

Michael now joined in by saying he had gotten into trouble by stealing, shoplifting, "fooling around in school," and truanting, and that he did this only because he was having a real "jazz of a time." Donald:

"Yeah, that's why I did it. It was a jazz of a time. I thought it was a lot of fun getting away, not getting caught, going before the judge, pretending I was innocent and the judge sending me home. Finally I did it once too often. Before I knew it I was in Youth House. I was locked up and then I knew I didn't have a chance of getting out of it that time."

The therapist raised the question as to whether they got "into trouble" just because they were having a "jazz of a time," since all the boys he had ever known who got in trouble with the law, did so because of their feelings about what was happening between themselves and their parents. Donald defensively: "Nothing was happening between me and my parents! Everything was all right!" Michael: "Me neither." Macy: "Naw, I don't think there was anything happening between me and my parents. I was happy at home. I just had a good time getting into trouble." Louis yelled out: "What do you mean a good time?" Macy: "I don't know. I was a wise kid. I thought I could get away with things. I didn't think that what I did was so terrible, just stealing pennies here and there from parking meters once in awhile." The therapist commented that one of the reasons the group was having these discussions was to talk about feelings as to what happened at home with parents, since every boy that he had ever known in the Village had gotten "into trouble" because of his feelings about his parents at home.

Louis immediately took over the discussion. He said: "It may be true for some guys, but it ain't true for us. I know some guys come home, they open the door, and there's their mother smoking a reefer. There's their father walking around without any pants, so fuckin' drunk he can't even stand straight." As Louis was describing this the boys laughed very nervously, which served to feed Louis's loquaciousness. He went on: "I know some guys come home at night and there's their mother laying on the ground [floor], a man on top of her pumping away. The old man is standing there drinking his fuckin' booze; doesn't give a shit. The mother invites the boys in, says, 'Come on honey get your prick out and jump on me.' The guy says to his mother: 'No mom you get laid by that guy first. I'll stand on line and wait for mine next.'"

Louis continued in this vein, while the other boys were becoming extremely anxious. Their anxiety was evident in a sort of hysterical, giggling laughter. Jules had left the room to go to the bathroom. Macy was walking around the room nervously and Richard, though he was laughing, slumped down in his chair and closed his eyes, pretending to be asleep. The therapist turned to Louis and asked him if what he was describing had happened to him. The giggle turned into a burst of laughter from all the boys in the room. Richard said: "He fixed your wagon didn't he, Louis?" Michael: "Yeah, he's sounding on you." Louis: "Naw, that didn't happen to me; it happened to some guy I know who comes home and sees his mother with her cunt out. This guy gets a hard-on just looking at his mother's cunt." Donald: "Well, that didn't happen to any of us here. So what the hell are you talking about it for? When I go home my parents look after me. I ain't got any trouble with my parents." Macy: "Yeah, we get into trouble but we get into trouble because we don't listen to our parents, not because our parents do something!"

A pounding against the windows was suddenly heard. Donald got up, looked out, and said there was a hailstorm outside. The hail and rain were so dense that one could barely see through them. Donald asked the therapist what time it was and was told it was eight o'clock. He said: "I got to get back to the cottage. I'm not going to take a chance and break my ass getting back if this gets worse." With this he got up and, with Macy joining him, started to leave. Richard: "Wait for me. I'll go with you." Louis lay on the couch for a while and then got up and walked out of the room, leaving Michael and Leonard with the therapist, since Jules, who again had gone out to the bathroom, had not returned. Michael looked as though he was undecided whether to go or stay. He finally said: "Would you please drive Leonard and me back to the cottage? I'm afraid of this fuckin' weather." The therapist agreed and drove them to the cottage.

COMMENT

Michael's planning for the group and undertaking to administer his plan was one evidence of positive *transference to the group-as-a-whole*, which had been demonstrated also by other boys in the past when they undertook preparing and distributing coffee. The transference toward the group was also demonstrated by Donald's and Michael's change of attitude toward the Village. Instead of heaping vituperations, they saw it now as a benevolent agent.[2]

The discussion about going home brought into relief the fact with which we had been concerned in relation to our other groups as well. Somehow the idea was not convincingly conveyed to them that since the institution was not an instrument of punishment, there could not be determinate sentences, but rather there was a corrective intent for their psychic life and motivations. We had, therefore, decided some time ago that in the future when the boys become aware of their emotional

2. I have termed this mechanism as *transference in reverse*, namely, where the attitude toward the therapist is displaced upon the parent. In this case the group is *in locus* of the therapist and the Village is *in locus parentis*. See S. R. Slavson, *Analytic Group Psychotherapy* (New York: Columbia University Press, 1950), p. 105.

processes and their inappropriateness, we would straightforwardly tell them that they were patients requiring treatment. If necessary, we would also draw a parallel between the Village and a general hospital where patients go for specific therapy.

In a sense, movement in this direction was made by Donald and Michael, who confronted themselves with their transgressions and their "badness" when they described the intransigencies for which they were committed and by the therapist's raising the question of whether they committed all these acts because of a "jazz of a time." But when he tied this up with parents, he trod on dangerous ground (threat areas), and the result was just short of disastrous. The boys became very anxious and vehemently denied the applicability of it to themselves. This also led to Louis' shocking description of mothers and open incest—a counter-phobic reaction—and forced the boys, due to their mounting anxiety, to generalized motility and finally to leave the group a half-hour early.[3] Only the fact that the boys felt the therapist's genuine affection for and interest in them rescued the group from disintegration.

However, note must be taken that the boys were becoming more aware of their feelings and could confront themselves and accept the results of their deviant acts. They now "understood" that if they had not been sent to the Village they could not have stopped misbehaving and would have received more stringent punishment. All this spells maturity, decrease in untenable ego defenses, and inversion. However, the therapist's premature move in relation to parents offset this as far as this particular session was concerned.

NOTE

There was no session the following week, partly because of a heavy storm, but more so because we felt that the boys would benefit by the delay, during which the anxiety and anger evoked by the preceding session would be dissipated. The next session, too, was delayed a day and met in the afternoon instead of the evening because of a heavy blizzard that made movement on the campus in the dark too hazardous.

Donald absconded from the Village between the two sessions. The reason for it, it was later ascertained, was that because he had stayed away an extra day on his previous home visit without permission and neither he nor his father had informed the authorities, he was told by

3. There is a surprise in store for the reader later on when the boys, on their own, describe their parents in negative terms and express their anger and death wishes toward them. But to do this, they had to first work through many of their dependencies and defenses.

his caseworker that there would be no more week-end home visits for him. His caseworker also told Donald during the interview that his father was a delinquent, and Donald ran home to report it to the father, who later threatened to sue the Village. Donald returned after an absence of a few days, before the next session.

Session Nineteen

ABSENT: Jonathan, still AWOL; Jules, in hospital with a cold; Leonard, reason unknown.

The session began with Donald distributing cigarettes, saying that he wanted to make sure that "everybody gets their fair share." This took but a few minutes. Michael seemed upset by the fact that it was Donald who had charge of the cigarettes. (It will be recalled that, in the preceding session, Michael had done this job.) However, no conflict ensued because of it. Donald shared the cigarettes equally among all the boys.

Following this, as the boys were now seated, Donald began by stating that he ought to be getting out of the Village by June, and that he would be getting a job. Michael commented that he wished he knew when he was getting out. No one responded to this, and Donald made the statement that the only reason he was at the Village was because he truanted for four days. The therapist commented in a rather offhand manner and in a questioning tone: "You are at the Village only because of four days of truancy?" Donald smiled and said: "Yeah, only four days of truancy and then I was caught. But I also stole a car." He then described how he had gone to a parking lot, saw a car with a key in it, took the car, and drove it around the lot. He was apprehended by the police. He said he stole the car because all his other friends had cars and he wanted to see what it was like to drive one. He had "a lot of fun" while he was driving around, but now that he thought about it "it wasn't worth it." He had to come up to the Village, and one thing he learned was that for a few minutes of fun you can sure get into an awful lot of trouble.

The therapist commented that it sounded as though he had discovered something very important, that an indication of growing from childhood into manhood is the fact that you think things over *before* you do them for pleasure; you think about the consequences of what you do. Donald said: "That's right. I wouldn't do a thing like that again because now I know even though you can have pleasure for a while you can sure get into a lot of trouble." Richard seconded what Donald had said, commenting that he always thought it was a lot of fun to just take things and run and not get caught, but if he knew anything now, it was that it's a pretty hard job not getting caught and having to pay a price.

While this discussion was going on, a conversation was carried on privately between Louis and Michael, who were both lying on the settee, their heads close together, though their bodies were slanted away from each other. The therapist could not overhear what they said, but it was evident that Louis took the lead. It had something to do with going out with older girls. This conversation continued throughout the session, except at the few points noted.

As soon as Richard finished, Louis stopped talking to Michael and commented aloud that he wished that he had been "given a sentence." He couldn't stand the idea of coming to a place and never really knowing when he was going to be getting out. Macy said: "Yeah, I would rather have gone to a place, gotten a record, and been given a sentence and know that I would get out in a certain time. Like this, somebody tells me that I'll be getting out then, then somebody else tells me another time, and I'm never sure when I'm going to be getting out." The therapist said that it was generally prison where you get a definite sentence and wondered whether the boys were saying that they would have rather gone to prison, or had they been sent to Children's Village for another reason? Donald immediately picked this up and said: "Yeah, I know. We came to Children's Village because we are supposed to be rehabilitated. I learned some things at the Village. They taught me how to read when I couldn't read before, but I got friends on the outside who can't read at all. In fact, one friend works on construction. He can hardly read two words together, but he makes $160 a week and he doesn't have to read. All he has to do is use his hands." He went on to say that with his head he couldn't learn too much, but with his hands he could do practically anything, and if he could get a job using his hands, then he could make some money.

At this point a discussion arose, initiated by the therapist, as to how they felt on seeing fellows who could hardly read or write making money. The therapist recalled the time which was called the Depression, when to be a messenger for Western Union you had to be a high-school graduate or at least you had to know pretty well how to read. Louis seemed to know quite a bit about the Depression. He stopped talking to Michael and told the boys how people used to stand on line for free soup and other food. Richard grew very much interested in this and asked the therapist if he could confirm what Louis had said, which the therapist did. Richard: "Gee, maybe it's okay that the Village taught me how to read because at least I can get a job and tell the boss that I'm able to read something." Macy said that he felt two ways about this. His feelings on the one hand were that he wanted to have a record, because when you have a record it means you go to a place where you get a definite sentence and they let you out at the end of that time. On the other hand, he'd have to go to jobs with a record and have to tell people that he was an "ex-con."

Donald, Richard, and Macy began a discussion as to whether or not they got anything out of the Village. They described the Village as just a place where they were being confined, with Donald at times saying that he had learned how to control himself and that he didn't get into fights. He had learned how to keep out of trouble and when he "gets out" he would not get into trouble. The therapist commented on the contradictory feelings that were being expressed by the boys. Richard immediately said that what bothered him was that he had friends "on the outside" who had done a hell of a lot more stealing than he ever did; yet he was the one who got caught. The "other guys" did not get caught. In fact, when he went home, there was one guy who always said to him, "You better get away from me, you're a jinx; you get caught," and teased him by inviting him on stealing expeditions. Louis, still on the settee, again turned from his conversation with Michael and said: "Yeah, if you don't get caught you don't get sent to this place. There are a lot of cats around the neighborhood that never got caught and they ain't here, but I am."

The therapist reminded the boys that in the preceding sessions, somebody in the group (it was Donald, but his name was not mentioned) had said that maybe he was lucky getting caught, since otherwise he would have gone on stealing bigger things and then really got into trouble. The therapist recalled to the boys a story that appeared in the papers in a nearby town about a year before about a girl of sixteen who was arrested for shoplifting in a department store. She looked so innocent that the judge let her go. A week later she was arrested again for shoplifting. Again she was freed. She talked a good story and looked like a college girl. Then, a month later, the girl stole a car, drove it down a busy highway at eighty miles an hour, and crashed into another car, killing its occupant. All eyes were on the therapist. Since the boys' interest held, the therapist continued. Before this occurred, one night the girl was found by the police walking along a deserted parkway. The police brought her home and did not even tell her parents about it. Later it came out that the girl was involved in many other incidents, but she was smart enough not to get caught. All of this led to her stealing and later to a killing. The therapist ended by asking the group, "What do you think should have happened?" There was a spontaneous response: "They should have caught her the first time and done something." "What should have they done?" asked the therapist. Donald said: "That girl sounds like she needed help. They should have sent her for help."

Richard: "Yeah, letting her go didn't do her any good. They only gave her more chances to get into big trouble." Richard: "You know, this guy who always makes me feel, I don't know how, but the guy who talks to me about going stealing and then tells me I shouldn't be with him because I'm a jinx, he makes me feel stupid." The therapist asked Richard if he could explain this feeling further and he said, "He makes me feel crummy, like I'm a small kid." Therapist: "I know how you feel, but maybe the boy who tries to get you into trouble should feel small rather than you. You boys are now learning to do the things you want to do but will not get you into trouble instead of doing things just because somebody dares you or calls you chicken. I'm sure everybody here knows about somebody getting into trouble because they were called chicken, and they had to prove that they were big shots, and not chicken." Richard immediately said: "That happened to me. I was at a party one night when somebody dared me to put my fist through a window. Like a jerk I did. My thumb nearly came off; it was hanging by the flesh." He showed the therapist his hand where there was a scar near the thumb. He said, "I did it because I didn't want to look small and I took the dare." Macy said facetiously, "So you would have been a big shot without a thumb." Richard went on to narrate another incident that involved stealing from fruit stands because boys in the neighborhood had invited him, for had he not gone along he would have been called chicken. He said it was hard not to do things with guys that you grow up with all your life. Donald: "Yeah, I know what you are talking about, because the same thing happened to me. I stole a fuckin' car only because I wanted to show the other guys on the block that I can have a car too. So what happened? Here I am, and now all I can think about is when am I going to get out."

A cross discussion developed between Macy and Donald and Donald and Richard about the various guys on their blocks who got involved in stealing, and similar matters. This continued for some time. From what the therapist could hear of these conversations, there was a mixture of admiration for "those guys" but also a sense of relief that they were not with them. This was clearly expressed by Richard when at one point he mentioned someone by the name of John, who was going to land in Sing Sing because he was "such a stupid bastard that he's always willing to do real crazy things."

The time for terminating the session was at hand, but the boys appeared reluctant to leave. Donald ascribed it to the fact that he didn't want to go back to the gym, while Louis suggested: "Let's just sit around and talk tonight." Richard turned to the therapist and began to tell him about the snowstorm of a few days before, the lightning and the thunder, and then said, "Isn't it true that lightning really comes up from the ground, not down from the sky?" The therapist (surprised that Richard knew this odd fact) agreed with him. Macy wanted to know how it occurred. A discussion of the phenomenon followed, involving positive and negative electrical charges. Richard said that when one sees lightning and counts to eighteen, one will hear thunder. Macy said that lightning and thunder are two different things, but Donald disputed this and both boys turned to the therapist to settle the matter. A detailed explanation was given them as to the nature and speed of light and sound. Louis now talked about his having been told in some class at school that there was a lot of electricity in clouds. Macy said a man called Steinmetz studied this subject. The scientific discussion continued for some time before the group left.

COMMENT

The problems that arose in the sharing of cigarettes made it obvious that the boys were not mature enough as yet to deal with this social situation. The sibling rivalry, which took the form of suspiciousness and resentment toward the one who distributed cigarettes, was a result of orality, a stage from which these boys had apparently not as yet emerged. Since the boys were not ready to recognize this reaction as a problem and discuss it, the therapist's stepping in could have been perceived by the boys as criticism, which we thought we should avoid at this stage of the transference attitudes, reserving such confrontation for a later time. We therefore decided, as a first step, to *alter the situation* so that conflict would be avoided, or at least diminished. With this in view we suggested to the therapist that he place the cigarettes in an urn before the boys came in. The therapist emptied the package of cigarettes into it, making it possible for each boy to take his own share without feeling that he was being placed in an inferior status by "being given," thus reactivating associated hostile feelings. This solved the problem quite adequately. While at first this session may appear as one of resistance, actually it was of value insofar as it truly reveals the level of the boys' emotional development at the moment. Keeping in mind that these are acting-out boys, their awareness of the relation of impulse and act, of the pleasure urge and the indiscriminate acting on it, are of utmost importance in rehabilitation. There is no doubt that a growing sense of reality—act and consequence, and the value of pleasure as against the price one pays for it—were emerging. These awarenesses were still rudimentary and still in the realm of the intellect, but a beginning was being made.

The boys were also able realistically to evaluate the benefits they derived from their stay in the institution and compare themselves with their friends with objectivity. The reaction to being called "chicken," which create many problems for young people in our culture, was an important one, and we devised a procedure for exploiting it for the ends of therapy which will be recorded later on.

On the whole one gains the impression that the boys were strikingly more mature in their bearing as well as understanding. Donald's recognition that the girl about whom the therapist talked needed "help" was rather an achievement, for the boys would automatically apply this to themselves as they continued in their growth.

The point was emphasized during the supervisory discussion after this session that the emphasis upon merely avoiding "getting into trouble" might have the effect of increasing rather than diminishing delinquency. The narcissistic effort to "keep out of trouble" may permit much antisocial and criminal activity as long as one evades consequences. The principle of not being found out does not beget a social or moral code. We therefore suggested that it be supplemented by the phrase, "not annoying or hurting others." We planfully eschewed using the phrase, "breaking the law," for the boys might have projectively perceived the therapist as on the side of the law and, therefore, against them.

Session Twenty

ABSENT: Jonathan, still AWOL.

The therapist placed eighteen cigarettes into the urn which he had obtained. When the boys came in, they at once noticed it. Some of them commented on it, and each helped himself *to one cigarette.* There was no grabbing or any evidence of anxiety concerning the cigarettes.

After they were seated Donald produced a tea bag from his pocket and announced that he was planning to prepare tea. Since there was no electric stove available, he went to the washroom next door and let the hot water run for a considerable time. He soon returned with a cup of water in which the tea bag was immersed. He found the sugar, which the therapist had neglected to remove, and helped himself to a heaping teaspoonful of it, took a sip of the tea, and announced that it tasted wonderful. He then returned to his chair and sat down with an air of the "lord of the manor," the privileged person in the group.

Michael launched into a complaint about the fact that the hot plate was still not available and wanted to know what had happened to it. Donald reminded him that it was broken. Michael said he wished they would get it fixed "so we could have coffee." Richard: "Maybe we ought to bring the hot plate from the auto shop." Donald declared he was not sure they would be allowed to do it. Jules looked very annoyed as he said he would like his coffee at the group meetings. Donald, with an obvious provocative intent, smacked his lips, repeating that his tea tasted very good. With this, the discussion around coffee was dropped. The boys sat silently for about four minutes, when the therapist commented that there seemed to be some feeling about not having coffee tonight. There was no response and the silence continued for another two minutes or so. Donald, stretching himself out in his chair, propped his feet up on the low coffee table in the middle of the room on which the cigarette urn and ash trays were located and said: "It's time you guys acted like civilized people. Nobody is grabbing cigarettes tonight and that's the way it should be." This aroused a kind of self-conscious giggling from some of the boys, including Louis, Jules, and Michael.

Donald turned to Louis and said: "What are you laughing at? You're the bastard that started all the grabbing." Louis: "It wasn't me; don't bone on me." Donald: "You're full of shit. It was so you. You started grabbing cigarettes. We didn't grab before you started. You see when you don't grab nobody else grabs and that's the way it should be, like a bunch of civilized guys sitting around." The therapist detected a flutter of tenseness in the room and an undercurrent of suppressed giggling on the part of the boys. Leonard seemed embarrassed because he was laughing. All of a sudden Louis got out of his chair and almost defiantly took two cigarettes from the urn. As soon as he did this, Jules jumped up from the couch on which he was sitting and grabbed two cigarettes. Macy did likewise. Donald laughed and said, "I knew you stupid bastards would do that." Louis: "Shit, man, if we don't get ours somebody else is going to get it."

Now Richard jumped up and took some cigarettes. There were now three cigarettes left. A silence descended upon the group. The therapist commented that it seemed as if the boys did not trust one another. Richard said: "That's right. If we don't get our cigarettes, somebody else is going to take them from us." Louis immediately stepped in and said: "You got to understand the psychology of these things. You see, people got all different psychology. They know that if they don't take, somebody else is going to dish them out of it. That's why they don't trust each other." Macy seconded it: "That's right; it's like in the cottage. If we don't grab the food somebody is going to take our helping." Richard spoke up and confirmed what Macy had just said, namely, that in the cottage either you grabbed or you didn't get all that was coming to you. Louis brought the discussion back to boys around his block at home who could get other boys to do things for them by offering them cigarettes. He then said, looking at the group, "I don't trust these cats in the room," and went on to say that "if you turn your back somebody is going to grab the cigarettes from you."

The therapist commented that they were talking about not being able to trust one another, and wondered whether this distrust started there and then, or was a part of something that started before they came to the Village. He pointed out the fact that here they had been together (in the group) for twenty weeks, and yet it seemed they found it hard to trust one another. Jules: "That's right. We have been together for twenty weeks and still this goes on." Richard took the initiative at this point. He began by describing how his mother used to catch him smoking and would be very angry at him. She used to yell, and on a number of occasions hit him. What made it even worse was the fact that his sister used to "bone" on him. Whenever his sister saw him with a cigarette, sure enough she would run and tell his mother. His father saw him smoking on a number of occasions and offered him cigarettes, telling him: "Don't tell your mother that I gave you the cigarette or that you're smoking. Don't let her catch you." Richard tried not to let his mother catch him, but on one occasion he forgot that she was around. She caught him and he got hit. He wanted to tell his mother that his father had given him permission to smoke, but he felt he would be "boning" on his father. Finally he did tell his mother that his father had given him permission, and his mother got very angry with his father and there was a fight. Richard sat back quietly. There was quiet in the room.

The therapist asked Richard how he felt about it. He thought for a while, but did not answer. Michael said: "Parents shouldn't do that to boys. They should be together on things like this." With this, Richard began to speak again. He said that his "lousy sister" made things worse for him, because she would always "bone" on him to his mother. He then went back to discussing the fight his mother and father had about his smoking, and how the father had admitted to the fact that he had given permission to Richard to smoke. Following this, his mother agreed to let Richard smoke, but not on the street. If he had to smoke he should do so in the house. Richard then said that at a later point his mother seemed to have forgotten the fact that she had given him this permission, because when she found him smoking again, she got very angry and denied that she had ever permitted it. The therapist again tried to ask how he felt about all this and he said he wasn't sure. Donald to Richard: "You must have been in a pretty lousy spot." Richard agreed, and the therapist seconded it, saying that he could understand the kind of spot he was in and wondered whether Richard felt he had to smoke "on the sly." Richard thought for a while and said: "I couldn't stop smoking, so I was going to get a cigarette one way or another, but I didn't like the fights that used to happen, so I used to find ways not to be caught when I was smoking. Even my sister stopped boning on me."

On the heels of this, Richard launched a rather lengthy description of how when he was young his mother and father would go out and his mother would say to Richard: "You better stay at home and watch your sister and baby brother." On top of this, every hour on the hour his mother would call to make sure he was at home. He then described how he really did not stay at home, but once he figured out that his mother would call him every hour, he would run downstairs, stand around in the candy store with friends, and just before the time his mother was to call, run upstairs again and be there to answer the telephone. Once his mother came home unexpectedly and found him out of the house and gave him quite a beating. Richard justified the beating he received by saying that she was worried about him and wanted to make sure that he was all right. He then said that he was going to tell a story about some of the "crazy things" that happened to him when he was alone, which he had reported also to his parents. They must have been worried about him as a result. However, Louis cut him short. He looked at Richard and said, "You know what the trouble was?" Richard seemed puzzled at first, but then asked, "Tell me, what was the trouble?" Louis: "Your parents just didn't trust you; that's the problem." Instead of waiting for a response, Louis turned to the therapist and asked what time it was. Therapist: "A quarter to eight." Louis said, "I have an important letter to write and I've got to go back to the cottage." With this he rose, put on his jacket, and left the room.

Macy began to move around. (When Macy had come into the room he seemed to be limping and the therapist had asked him what the matter was. He said he sprained his back wrestling at the gym.) When he started to walk he told the therapist that his back hurt, and he shifted to another chair with a straight back. Jules had gone out to the washroom, but came back within a few minutes.

Richard launched into a story of how a number of years ago, while at home, he used to get mysterious phone calls. When he answered the phone somebody would laugh. Richard imitated the laughter; it was that of a drunkard. The person would hang up. This was repeated a number of times. Richard finally called the telephone company but they told him that they could not trace the call and suggested he call the police. This he did not want to do, but when he walked down the street, all of a sudden he would notice that somebody was following him. Whenever he turned around, a man would stop walking. Richard recognized the man as someone who lived in his apartment building a few floors down. One night he was at home and there was a ring. It was this man at the door. When Richard saw him, he said, "What do you want?" The man laughed and said, "Hello Ricky, I like you." Richard told the man to "get the hell out of here" or he would call the police. The man denied that he wanted anything from him. Richard called the man a liar and said: "You're the guy who was bothering me on the phone. I recognize your voice." The man laughed at this. Richard had told his parents about it and at first they did not believe him. But when he told them later, when all this recurred a few times, his father went to talk to the man.

It was obvious that Richard's narration was stirring up the boys. Jules, who had come back from the washroom, put on his coat and left the room. Donald slouched in his chair and, unzipping his jacket, buried his face in it. When Jules left, Michael got up, went over to the couch where Jules had been sitting, lay down, and covered the upper part of his body, including his face, with his lumberjacket.

At one point the therapist asked Richard if he could clarify what relation there was between what he was now narrating and what he was talking about before. Richard returned to saying that because of these things happening to him, his mother used to call him up on the phone when he was babysitting with his sister to make sure that he was all right. He then returned to his monologue, which continued for approximately twenty minutes, with a brief shift occurring when he mentioned that when he was little he used to be afraid of a lot of things. He used to sleep in a room where there was an open door. At night his father would come home and would hang his coat and hat over the door. When Richard would wake up at night, it looked to him like somebody was in the room and, dramatically, he described how he used to scream: "Hey, who are you? What are you?" But then he would remember that he ought not say anything, or he might be attacked by the specter.

Macy interrupted at this point and said: "I remember I used to be very afraid when I was a little kid, but I can't remember all the things I used to be afraid of. Oh yeah, I know. I used to be afraid of sleeping in the dark. I liked to sleep in the dark because I couldn't fall asleep with the light on, but once the light was turned off I used to be afraid." Richard turned to the therapist and asked whether he had ever heard of anything like this. The therapist answered Richard's question by saying he had. "Most children, while they are growing up, do have many fears about things." Donald bestirred himself, lifted his head out of his jacket, and said that he was going back to the cottage. It was now about 8:20 P.M. Richard asked whether the therapist was ever afraid of anything when he was a child. The therapist told him that he was. As soon as he said this Macy said: "I used to have a lot of weird dreams when I was a little boy. I can't remember most of those dreams now," and went on speaking in a vague way for a while, but Richard stepped in and asked whether the therapist had heard about a book that described why "these things" happen. The therapist said he had. Richard then asked why they happened. Since it was rather late the therapist asked Richard if he would bring the question up the next time the group met. Richard said he would. He thought there was a book in his cottage where he could look up information and maybe he could bring the book to the meeting next week.

The group was getting ready to leave. Michael rose from the couch and came over to tell the therapist that when he was a kid a lot of "scary things" used to happen to him. He mentioned not being able to sleep when he heard someone walking around. Richard, Leonard, Michael, and Macy grouped around the therapist and were competing with one another in a bubbling sort of way, telling him that next week they were going to talk about all the "scary things" that happened to them. Michael wanted to know whether any time in the therapist's life there had been things he was afraid of. The therapist reiterated that there were. Michael said, "Okay, let's talk about it next week." With this the boys left.

COMMENT

This was obviously a resistive session, which may be attributed to hostility aroused by the denial of coffee. Even the mature response to the placement of the cigarettes into a communal receptacle at first was later erased at Louis's provocation, and the rule of the jungle was again evoked both in act and word.

However, Richard's "openness" in criticizing his parents and the other boys' recall of earlier dreams and fears may have served to clear the channels for more therapeutically effective productions in the future. A step had been made in this direction at the end of the session when the boys decided to continue the discussion of dreams at the next meeting.

The clustering of the four boys around the therapist may be a reaction to their guilt arising from suppressed hostility toward him because of being orally deprived and an unconscious feeling that they did not perform at the session up to his expectations, as they perceived them to be.

NOTE

On the day preceding the next session, the receptionist told the therapist that Donald had left a message for him to the effect that he would bring a hot plate from the auto shop to the meeting the next day. Since we felt that it was crucial that the boys not have coffee and thus siphon off anxiety, and also because its preparation served to dissipate attention and induce regression to an oral level, it was decided that two things should be done. One was to disconnect the electrical outlets in the room. The other was to instruct the auto shop personnel not to turn over the hot plate to the boys. This could be done, however, only if the auto shop personnel would not let the boys know that these arrangements were made by the therapist.

The auto shop staff was contacted and it was discovered that the regular teacher was absent and the class taken over by a substitute. The help of the educational counselor (principal) was accordingly enlisted, and he arranged for the appropriate dealing with the situation. Should Donald request it, he would be told that the hot plate could not be removed from the auto shop, since it was staff property and not the school's.

At about four o'clock of the day of the session Donald rushed into the therapist's office. He told the therapist that the educational supervisor had told him that if the therapist called him approving it, he would give Donald the electric plate. Fortunately, the supervisor was not in his office. However, Donald noticed an old plate resting on a shelf in the room. It was broken and unusable, or so the therapist thought. However, when Donald plugged it in, it worked. Donald asked the therapist if he could bring it to the meeting room later in the evening. The therapist had no choice but to agree to it.

After Donald left, the therapist disconnected one of the wires in the hot plate and took it upstairs. Even though the outlets in the room had already been disconnected, there was still the possibility that the boys would repair them.

Session Twenty-One

ABSENT: Jonathan, AWOL; Macy, ill in infirmary.

Michael was first to arrive. He greeted the therapist rather warmly, took a seat, and remained silent. Leonard arrived shortly thereafter, then Jules. When Jules came in he said there was a very thick fog outside; it was very difficult for him to find his way walking through the fog. The therapist had brought a small quantity of coffee and sugar, since the boys had forewarned him that an electric plate would be brought in. Shortly thereafter Donald came into the room. The first thing he did was to go to the hot plate; however, Jules had already attempted to start the electric plate, found that it was not working, and discovered one of the wires disconnected. When Donald turned his attention to it, Jules informed him about the "broken" wire.

Donald's reaction was one of anger. He mumbled "son of a bitch" under his breath and then wanted to know who had broken the wire. Jules told him that it must have been somebody who had come into the room before the boys arrived. Donald said: "That's what happens when you leave the thing around like this. Some stupid kid must have broken the fucking wire." He then said in a voice full of both determination and agitation that he was going to fix that hot plate if it was "the last fucking thing" he did. In the meantime, the other three boys present at the time took the powdered coffee and empty cups, went into the washroom, and filled them with hot water from the tap. For the first half-hour this was the only activity of the boys, while Donald was growing increasingly agitated as he persisted in attempting to fix the electric plate. His attempts began to be dangerous. He discovered a wall outlet that the therapist had not seen, took the wire from the hot plate, took off the plug that seemed to be corroded, removed the insulation, and stuck the exposed wires into the wall outlet. Sparks shot out of the wall and Donald jumped clear. Jules, Michael, and the therapist warned Donald against putting exposed wires into the wall receptacle, but it was to no avail.

After this incident Donald sat down and began to toy with the hot plate, attempting to fix it. He said several times that he should have kept the hot plate with him; then nothing would have happened to it. He asked Michael to go to the auto shop and get a soldering iron. Michael said he wasn't going to make the long trip now, and suggested that Donald make coffee by getting hot water from the "bathroom." Donald refused.

While all of this was going on, there was no conversation but that about the coffee. The three boys from R cottage, namely, Richard, Macy, and Louis, had not yet come into the session. It was now about 7:20 P.M., that is, twenty minutes past time. The therapist decided to call the cottage and discovered that the associate (relief) cottage father who was in charge that night had forgotten to give the passes to the boys. In about ten minutes Louis and Richard came. (As noted, Macy was in the hospital.)

Just before this, and soon after the boys had their coffee, all conversation died down. Donald was still very busy trying to repair the hot plate. Michael spoke up and said, "I thought we were going to talk tonight." Leonard became embarrassed, and began, "I once had a dream and when I woke up I was in a sweat." However, Michael interrupted, saying: "There is one dream I remember I'll never forget. I was about four or five years old. Yeah, I mean it. I was four or five years old and I still remember that dream. It wasn't a dream, it was a nightmare." He dreamed that he was in bed. Surrounding his bed in the darkness were a number of devils with pointed heads and long tails. He said that maybe he saw these things because he saw a "bad picture" (film) or maybe because of things his mother had told him. The devils had red faces and white eyes and their teeth protruded. When he woke up, there were the devils still standing in the room looking down at him. He was frightened but didn't dare move or turn on the light, because had he turned on the light the devils might have jumped at him. "What a crazy, fucking thing that was!" he exclaimed. "I was scared. I was little. I couldn't even scream. My mouth couldn't even open the lips." After a short pause he spontaneously said, "When I saw those devils I thought it was *because I was bad.*"

He then asked the therapist directly what he thought of the dream. The therapist asked if Michael could tell some more about his thinking about his being bad. Michael said: "I don't know. When you are a little boy you can't be bad. Maybe I was bad. I don't know. My mother used to tell me something I don't remember." Then: "Isn't it true that before the age of twelve, you aren't responsible for what you do and your sins go on your mother. After you're twelve, you get the sins when you do something bad." Now Leonard interrupted Michael and said that he remembered having "very scary dreams" after seeing "bad" pictures on television and in the movies. It was at this point that Louis and Richard came in.

The moment Louis stepped into the room there was a change in the atmosphere. Richard made an announcement that he had received a pass for 7:30 (instead of 7:00), and displayed it to the therapist. Sure enough, someone had changed 7:00 to 7:30. Louis, in the meantime had gone over to Michael and began to involve the latter in a discussion. Louis had a wad of paper in his hand which he threw at Michael and Michael threw back.

Now shuffling of feet and moving around the room ensued. Jules, however, sat quietly and was attempting to carry on the conversation by describing how he used to have bad dreams, but only one nightmare. He said this in a very low voice, and when the therapist tried to ask Jules more about it, Louis boisterously yelled out to Donald: "What the hell are you doing over there." Donald told him that he was trying to fix the hot plate. Donald asked Louis for a pocketknife, which Louis gave him. Donald was at this point extremely agitated. He had the knife in his hand and was throwing it to the floor. (The therapist found it necessary to divide his attention between the discussion and seeing that nothing untoward happened to Donald.) The therapist asked Donald from a distance if something was bothering him. Donald forced a smile and said, "There ain't anything bothering me." Jules and Michael laughed at him and Michael said, "You are pissed off about something."

Donald put the hot plate down, got up and walked to the other end of the room. The electric hot plate was in a mess, it was completely dismantled. Almost every part of it had been removed, and the therapist realized that Donald could not possibly reassemble it. Donald, though he was sitting on the couch, looked as though he would hop. His face was flushed and he asked how much the hot plate cost. The therapist told him about $10. This made Donald even more agitated. The therapist said to Donald, "Do you feel responsible for breaking it?" Donald jumped up and said, "Yeah, I broke the fucking thing and I can't put it together again." His eyes were moist as he said, "I'll give your secretary the $10 when I see her." (The therapist wondered how Donald knew that the hot plate belonged to his secretary, but obviously Donald had learned this somewhere.) The therapist told Donald that he need not do that. This can happen to anybody. (But the therapist was unsure at the same time whether he should have relieved Donald's guilt for what he had done.)

The therapist asked Donald if he wanted to talk about how he felt about it. Donald said, "I got nothing to say." But then he added: "I feel bad. I didn't want to break it." (The therapist was rather surprised that Donald felt guilt about what he had done, because his reputation among staff members was that of a youngster who felt no guilt about anything he did.) The therapist said that he could appreciate how Donald felt, but as one grows up one begins to find that one does have feelings about the things one does. Donald looked and said, "I never thought it was so fucking hard to grow up." There was giggling at this from Jules, Leonard, and Michael. Donald seemed to quiet down. He went back to the other end of the room, resumed his seat, and said, "I'm going to fix this thing if it's the last thing I do."

Things quieted down; silence had descended on the group for a few minutes when Richard turned to the boys and said, "What were you talking about?" At the same time Louis invited Michael to a game of cards, and joined him on the couch. A game of poker started. Leonard filled in what the boys had been talking about and Richard said: "Oh yeah, that's what we were going to talk about this week. I remember Mr. Ellery saying that we could talk about it today." Richard then proceeded to describe how he had a lot of dreams, but without describing any one specific dream he asked the therapist, "What makes dreams happen?" Leonard reminded Richard that in the past they had talked about the subconscious mind, and Richard said to Leonard, "I asked Mr. Ellery, not you." Leonard: "So what? I can still tell you." Richard again was describing how he used to have a lot of "crazy dreams," especially after going to a movie, but then he changed this and asked specifically "What makes dreams?"

The therapist reminded him of the previous discussion about the subconscious part of the mind, that "when you went to sleep the subconscious mind began to make pictures of things you wanted, which we called wish-fulfillment dreams, and of how we felt about ourselves, and often when we dreamed it was a way in which our minds showed us some of the things we tried not to think about during the day." Richard: "How can you understand a dream? Is there a way of doing it?" Richard and the other boys who were now listening (Donald was still busy with the hot plate and Louis and Michael were playing cards) were introduced to the idea of "free association"; that when you describe a dream and then just talk about it, the first things that come to your mind very often tell you what the dream is trying to say. Richard seemed to relax and said, "You mean all I got to do is tell you a dream and say the first things that come to my mind and then maybe I can know what the dream was?" The therapist confirmed this, explaining how dreams are interpeted.

Richard now volunteered a dream he had of a big gorilla who was crushing him. Then, "Okay, now all I got to do is think of something about this dream." He began to hem, haw, and stammer. Leonard encouraged him: "Go on, think." Richard: "I remember going to my cousin with my mother. My mother gave me permission to smoke when I was fourteen, and I was smoking then. My cousin took me to a movie and. . . ." He stopped for a while, then continued, "Oh yeah, I saw a movie about a gorilla; that must have been why I was dreaming about a gorilla." Richard, turning to the therapist, said, *"It's hard to say the first thing that comes to your mind."*

Jules picked up his coat and said he was going back to the cottage and left the room. Quiet again descended as Richard was trying to think of another dream. All of a sudden, Michael spoke up. "Well, continue the conversation!" Leonard: "I thought you were playing cards." Michael: "I can play cards and listen at the same time." Then he added, "I like to talk about this." Richard: "Aw, shit, *I can't think of anything more tonight.*" It was now 8:30, and the group began to break up. Michael came over and said he wondered whether "we could talk about this again next week." The therapist said they could. Leonard: "I'll try to remember some more dreams I have and I'll tell the boys about them next week."

Louis would not let Michael leave the room. He grabbed Michael's hat and threw it around. Michael was yelling for the therapist to take the hat away from Louis, but Donald had come over to talk to the therapist so that the latter pretended he did not hear. Donald wanted to know what the therapist would tell his secretary. The therapist said that he would explain to her exactly what happened! "That you tried to fix it and that it broke." Donald: "Shit, do you have to tell her that?" Therapist: "What would you want me to tell her?" Donald: "Tell her it just broke. She don't have to know anything." The therapist explained to Donald that he did not think it would help if he were to make up a story. Maybe Donald would like to come along and see the secretary and tell her what happened. Maybe he would find that she understood. Donald: "No, no. I don't want to see her." The therapist then said that he always found it generally worse to make up a story than to tell the truth. Donald: "All right. Maybe you do the right thing by telling her what happened." This was said with little conviction. He then again wanted the therapist to make up a story how it "just happened" to drop while nobody was holding it. The therapist told him that he would not do this. Donald then said: "Okay, let's see what happens."

COMMENT

Although the intention of these comments is to bring into relief the group process, attention needs to be directed here first to Donald's preoccupation with food (coffee in this case) and his extreme feelings of deprivation when it is not forthcoming and, second, to the state of agitation and later fear in reference to his dismantling of the electric plate. Such reactions in their extent and intensity made us suspect pathology, possibly latent or borderline schizophrenia. If that were the case, it would have been advisable either to prevent the occurrences that caused the agitation or to have helped him to reassemble the stove, or the therapist might have undertaken the responsibility of getting it repaired so as to remove the anxiety from the boy.

In the past several sessions, the boys had turned to dreams as a topic for discussion on different levels. Dreams seemed to have challenged and intrigued them, but one must be vigilant to the fact that this might have been a resistance maneuver. Richard's stumbling over the word that would have identified the prototype of the gorilla in his dream (the father) and the anxiety induced by it when he later declared, "I can't think of anything more tonight," are psychoanalytically significant.

NOTE

On the day preceding the next group session Donald and Jules brought the repaired electric plate to the therapist's office. Donald claimed that he had put it together in the auto shop. (It is quite probable that the job, because of its complexity, had been done by a staff member.) Jules said that now the group could have coffee and that he would bring instant coffee to the session; he asked the therapist to supply milk and cookies. We decided, therefore, in the supervision conference to remove the pot in which the water for the coffee was heated. Should the boys inquire about it, the therapist was to say that he did not know where it was, that it was probably removed by someone. If necessary he should take part in looking for it.

Session Twenty-Two

ABSENT: Jonathan, AWOL; Macy, still in infirmary with injured back.

Louis was first to arrive, and was soon followed by Jules. They sat talking quietly about the supper they had just had in their cottages. About two minutes before 7:00, Michael came in and immediately asked the therapist whether he had brought coffee, milk, and crackers. The therapist said that he had made this request of the Club Department, but as yet had not heard from them. Michael, slightly disappointed, did not pursue the subject. On seeing the hot plate he asked where the pot was. The therapist told him that he had been looking for it and was not able to find it. Michael exclaimed: "Maybe somebody took it with them!" The therapist agreed that this might have happened. Leonard, Richard, and Donald came in together at this point. Donald immediately looked around the room for the hot plate and asked about the pot. The therapist repeated the explanation he had given Michael. Donald appeared very upset. He took a large jar of instant coffee from his pocket, saying he had bought it for the group, and expressed disappointment that the Club Department failed to supply crackers and milk. He declared that the pot must be around somewhere. Even though the therapist told him that he had looked for it, Donald said he would find it, asking the therapist where he had last seen it. The therapist and Donald went downstairs to the office of the former's secretary, where the pot had last been seen. A thorough search of her office and that of the therapist's was made, but the pot was not to be found. Donald was disappointed but seemed to be able to contain his feelings. Upon return to the meeting room, Donald said to Leonard, "Why don't you run over to the cottage and get the coffee pot, and bring back some milk and sugar." Leonard agreed to do this and left.

Richard had brought with him curtain rods which could be separated into two parts. He gave one of these to Donald, keeping the other for himself, and challenged Donald to a "duel." The two boys dueled for a while in the room, then left to continue it in the hall outside. The therapist had the impression that Richard deliberately tried to disrupt the session. Leonard was out of the room during this byplay, and Louis invited Michael to a game of cards, which they played sitting on the couch. Jules crouched near Louis and watched the game. Donald and Richard returned to the room still dueling.

Meanwhile Leonard returned with the supplies and a pot. Michael commented on the speed with which Leonard had returned, since the cottage was a considerable distance away. When Leonard returned, Michael left the card game and joined Donald in preparing the coffee for everyone. (The receptacle into which the electric plate was plugged had been overlooked when the others were disconnected.) Richard, looking glum, sat down in a chair. In the meantime Jules took Michael's place in the card game with Louis.

The preparation and passing of the coffee proceeded quietly. The boys were scattered in various spots around the room, rather than in the usual circle. Richard, almost in a monotone, was telling about his having seen the psychiatrist that day, referring to him as "a fucking bastard, a stupid prick who asks a lot of dumb questions." Donald walked over to the therapist and said, "When I didn't see that coffee pot I was so fucking angry." As he said this, he made a fist and shook it in the therapist's face. The therapist looked up at Donald with a slight smile. Donald opened his fist, and with the palm of his hand stroked the therapist's head saying: "I'm glad we finally got some coffee." He then returned to his seat.

Michael said to Richard, "What are you bullshitting about?" This served as a signal for Richard to announce to everyone in the room what had happened between him and the psychiatrist. Richard complained that Dr. F. had taped the conversation because he had seen him leave the room with tapes in his hands. (The doctor had probably dictated his interview with Richard after it took place. However, Richard thought there was a hidden microphone in the room.) The therapist explained to Richard the probable reason for the tapes. Richard: "I don't give a shit. I don't like Dr. F. dictating on me," and complained that the doctor had raised the question about the possibility of Richard's ever going home. Richard said that the doctor told him that if he did go home, he would only steal again and get into trouble because he was so upset all the time. Richard: "He is full of shit. He only works to get his money. He doesn't know anything." Michael seconded this.

Richard continued to complain that not only did he have to put up with Dr. F., but he'd got "a faggot" for a social worker, who was so "fucking stupid" he didn't know his "ass from his elbow." Richard: "Listen, this is what this faggot does. I'm in his office; all of a sudden he gets a telephone call. He spends about twenty minutes on the telephone talking with somebody about opera." Donald interrupted: "Yeah, he's always talking about opera to somebody on the telephone," and he mimicked the caseworker's voice. Richard continued by describing how the caseworker had told somebody on the telephone that he was going to throw a party for some opera star. Richard: "What the hell do I have to come to his office for to hear that shit? He doesn't want to see me; he just wants to talk on the telephone, and at the end of the week he gets paid." Michael stated that this was all social workers ever did. They were always talking on the telephone; they were always writing reports. Once in a while they saw you; but they really came to work just so they could get their money at the end of the week, and they were not interested in the boys. Richard continued at considerable length to express hostile feelings toward his caseworker, describing many instances when he had sent Richard passes to come to his office and then did not see him on time, always looking busy doing something else while Richard sat and waited. The therapist felt that Richard's vituperations against his caseworker were a smoke screen for something much deeper. This was confirmed.

Jules asked the therapist the time and was told it was about eight o'clock. Jules said he was going back to the cottage. Since Jules made a practice of leaving early, the therapist asked about it. Jules said that at eight o'clock on Thursday nights there was a television program he liked to watch, and with this he rather summarily left the room, a half hour before termination of the session. Donald took Jules's place playing cards with Louis.

These incidents allowed Richard to catch his breath. He described with very real anger how the caseworker talked about his parents. Mimicking the caseworker's allegedly effeminate voice, he said: "You are very depressed, and you are very depressed because you go home and see your parents. Maybe you shouldn't go home and then you won't be depressed." Richard then said: "How does he know I'm depressed? What a stupid prick! All he wants to do is sit and talk on the telephone, and when he gets off the telephone he tells me how depressed I am. Not letting me go home isn't going to stop me from being upset." He then launched into a tirade against the Village: The only reason he was up there was because the Village made money on keeping him there, and so forth. If he stayed there beyond the time he was supposed to, he was going to run away and he didn't give a damn. He was going to "get out of here legally or illegally," and if he got out illegally, he was going to the West Coast and nobody was ever going to find him.

Richard had stopped talking and there was quiet in the room. The therapist commented on Richard's "anger." The latter denied it, which brought forth laughter from Donald, Louis, and Michael and a smile of awareness from Richard himself. He then said that because he was at the Village, his mother was constantly worrying about him, and he always got upset because his mother worried about him. He didn't want her to worry. If he were to go home maybe she would stop worrying and then he wouldn't have to worry about his mother worrying about him. Michael spoke up, saying that he knew his mother was in the hospital and he wished he could go home because he was worried about her. If he thought that she was worrying about him, he would also want to go home to prevent her from doing it. Richard now changed the subject back to the Village and "stupid cottage parents," and so on.

The therapist stepped in at this point, calling Richard's attention to the fact that two weeks before he had said that even when he was at home his mother worried about him. Leonard turned to Richard and said: "That's right. You said it here." Richard fell silent and seemed to mull over this thought for a while, but then continued to affirm that if he were home his mother would stop worrying about him. The therapist asked if he blamed himself for his mother's worrying. Richard said he didn't know; he didn't think so. Michael: "What is she worried about? They are taking care of you here." Richard: "So what? She worries anyway." The therapist indicated that perhaps it was impossible for him to do anything that would stop his mother from worrying. This seemed to be a new and strange concept to Richard, because he said, "I thought my mother worries because of all the things I always used to do and I got into trouble and that's why I feel so crummy." Donald spoke up from his card game: "But you're not doing those things any more and your mother still worries." Richard ignored this and reverted to justifying his mother's worrying because he was at the Village and the Village would not let him go home. Richard was oblivious to his contradiction, for he stated that once he ran away he would go to the West Coast and no one would find him. The therapist brought the inconsistency to his attention, but Richard finally described in detail how if he ran away he would hide at the Village for "a couple of days." People would go to his home to check with his mother if he had gone home; then after three days of hiding, he would head for the West Coast. Leonard suggested to Richard that if he desisted from running, maybe time would not be added to his stay at the Village, and he then could go home "the way everybody else goes home." Richard would not listen to this. From the time Jules left at eight o'clock until the end of the session, Louis sat leaning back in his chair with a far-off gaze in his eyes and did not participate in the group's discussion.

The session ended at 8:30.

· C O M M E N T

This is obviously a resistive and in some respects a regressive session, as made obvious by the diversional tactic in obtaining coffee and the card-playing. The attack upon the psychiatrists and caseworkers is to be understood as displacement of hostility against and dependence upon mothers, as evidenced by Richard; it could also be displacement of resentment against the therapist as a depriving and frustrating person because he did not supply food. Donald's gesture of shaking a fist in the therapist's face would weight the evidence toward the latter. This session, as well as other incidents in the past and in subsequent sessions, leaves little doubt of the orality (and, hence, pregenitality) of the boys— a matter of which we took note and later dealt with.

We decided to allow this resistivity and acting out to continue, since we believed it served the purposes of catharsis and self-revelation (as well as our diagnostic aims), for we learned more of the basic and operational personalities of our boys through it. We also believed that by permitting it we were cementing the transference and altering the boys' image of all adults as punitive, depriving, and hostile.

Session Twenty-Three

ABSENT: Jonathan, discharged from Children's Village; Jules, in the infirmary with a fractured ankle.

Michael was first to arrive, about three minutes early. He nodded his greeting and sat down quietly. Louis arrived on time. Unlike at preceding sessions, when he had usually come in a hyperactive mood, raring to get involved in a conversation, he appeared rather quiet and sedate. Donald soon came in with a portable radio, which was playing very loudly. He immediately approached Louis, threw a deck of cards into his lap, and invited him to a game. At the same time he looked around the room to assure himself that the hot plate was there. Leonard came in a few seconds later with an aluminum pot. This had obviously been arranged in advance. Richard and Macy now came in.

Richard seemed very talkative. As soon as he arrived he began telling Donald and Louis about a fight he had witnessed. It was unclear as to who was fighting and who won. Richard had a stick in his hand, the top of which was painted red, and the bottom, gray. He said that he wanted to make it all red, suggesting that he would like to cover it with "the blood of some people."

Donald apparently intended to disrupt the session: He had brought the radio and invited Louis to a card game, and he continued to play the radio rather loudly. The therapist asked Donald to turn the radio to a certain station, since music which he liked was played on that station at that time. Donald tried to find the station. Louis told him that it was at the bottom of the dial. While doing this Donald also turned down the volume. He asked Richard where the coffee was. Richard pulled out from his jacket pocket a small jar of instant coffee. Donald asked whether anyone had brought milk. No one had. Donald asked Richard if he would go to the custodial office and get some, for he knew the custodians had canned milk. Richard ran off with alacrity.

In the meantime, Louis drew water from the washroom tap into the pot and placed it on the hot plate. Donald continued to play cards with Louis. Michael was helping Leonard. Macy was telling the therapist about his back injury and that he had been "laid up" in the infirmary. The two talked about it for a while. Macy said that he was injured while he was wrestling and attempted, with little success, to explain exactly what was wrong with his back. At one point he mentioned that he had a "ruptured disc." Donald, from his game, said he'd never heard of that, but he'd heard of a "slipped disc." Macy: "Yeah, maybe that's what it is." Macy and Donald got into a conversation about Donald's visit, with Macy saying that he had wanted to get out of the infirmary and return to the cottage, but the doctor would not let him. Donald said to Macy, "You're out now, so why don't you forget about it?" Macy didn't respond to this.

Turning to the therapist, Macy related that the doctor told him "to take it easy for a while"; that he would be allowed to play sports after his back was all healed, when he didn't feel any pain whatsoever while walking. While Macy was talking, Donald turned up the volume on his radio so that it was difficult to hear what Macy was saying. The therapist asked Donald if he would be good enough to turn the volume down. Donald did so, saying that he did not realize how loud the radio could really play.

Richard came running breathlessly with a container of milk. Now Richard, Macy, and Leonard were involved in preparing coffee, which they accomplished very quickly. Michael took responsibility for passing out coffee to the group. The mobility in the room ceased. The boys were seated and Donald and Louis continued to play cards, each boy sipping his coffee. Louis: "What do we talk about tonight?" There was silence, and Louis began to stir. He looked in the direction of the therapist, then around the room, and said, "This is a pretty good group and you're okay" (referring to the therapist). Nothing else was said. The therapist asked Louis what he meant. Louis stood up and declared: "We got freedom here. *We can do and talk about anything we want.* This ain't like the other places in the Village," and gesticulating with his arms he continued to say that when you went to school, "everybody tells you what you got to think and what you got to do. When I go to see my social worker, she always tells me what I got to talk about. That's why I never talk about anything with her." He mimicked her voice, which aroused laughter in the others. Louis then said, "At least here I know I can talk about anything or I don't even have to talk about anything and you [therapist] don't force us." Richard: "You're a social worker aren't you, Mr. Ellery?" The therapist said that he was. Richard: "You're a different kind of social worker. You're the first social worker I ever knew that didn't make boys do what you want them to do. You let them decide what they want to do." Donald: "Yeah, he's a good guy."

Louis sat down and remained rather quiet. He did not return to the card game. The therapist asked Louis whether he found that only social workers told him what to do. Louis responded by saying that when he went to school, "on the outside," he was in a class where you could never ask questions, because the teacher used to call you "stupid" for even asking a question. Macy: "How could you ever learn that way?" Louis, standing up: "That's right. You never do learn that way. If you can't ask questions then you don't get any answers and nobody does any talking in the class, so we used to fool around and then the teacher would get mad because we fooled around." Donald to Louis: "Pick up your hand and let's play cards." Louis sat down and returned to the game with Donald.

Michael now proceeded to make another batch of coffee. Macy said that he would like another cup when it was ready. Coffee was ready very soon, since Michael drew hot water in the bathroom, and it boiled much faster. Coffee was passed around.

Richard now began to describe his school experiences. When he went to school there were a bunch of boys in the class who were considered stupid. He was one of them. These boys always got into trouble because the teacher called them "stupid." The teacher was giving her time and attention to the boys in the class who could read and write well, so the "stupid ones" found themselves getting bored and would "horse around." Richard said he could not read well and felt that it was due to the fact that the teacher was always hurrying him. Just as soon as he finished one lesson, the teacher was ready to go on to another. He couldn't keep up with it. Donald now raised the volume on the radio. It was so loud that the therapist could hardly hear what Richard was saying. Again the therapist asked him if he would turn down the radio, which he did at once. The therapist asked him why he was turning it up. Was he trying to stop the discussion? Donald said he didn't mean it; his hand just slipped and touched the volume knob. He acted very apologetic, saying: "I'm sorry, Mr. Ellery. It won't happen again." The therapist asked Donald if there was anything bothering him tonight. He denied that there was, and said that "it is pretty nice here tonight, sitting around talking, listening to music, drinking coffee. There is nothing wrong tonight." Richard said, "He's just making a pest out of himself," to which Donald replied: "Shut your fucking mouth! I told you it was just an accident." Nothing further was said.

Louis picked up where Richard had left off by saying that his social worker told him that maybe one of the reasons he had trouble in school was because he was upset at home. He said that he read much better now, because the Village had helped him a lot in learning how to read. Richard agreed with Louis that the Village had taught him, too, how to read better. The therapist asked Louis what he thought about the social worker's opinion that he could not learn because of what went on at home. Louis strenuously attempted to evade the issue. He said things were quiet at home now and that he would be going home soon. There was a time when his mother was constantly telling him what to do, and he didn't like that. It used to upset him, but even then he could talk to her and stop her from "bossing" him. Now she no longer told him what to do. The therapist tried to bring him back to the subject, asking him what it was his mother used to tell him to do, but Louis would not discuss it.

Richard became quite restless. He began to giggle, which appeared inappropriate to what was being said. He then walked over to the window, opened it, crawled out, and sat on the fire escape for a few minutes. There was banter back and forth among Donald, Macy, and Richard while he sat on the fire escape. Richard would every so often stick his head into the room and seemed to enjoy the attention his behavior was arousing. After a while the therapist commented to Richard on one of the occasions when he stuck his head in that he wondered if there was something in what Louis was saying that was upsetting him. Richard denied it with almost complete lack of affect. Louis then joined Richard at the window. Michael went out to the bathroom for a while, and Macy picked up a magazine that he had brought with him and began to leaf through it. Leonard asked to have a look at the magazine. Macy gave it to him, asking him to hurry up and look through it because he, Macy, wanted to read it. Leonard leafed through it quickly and returned it.

Richard climbed back into the room and reported that it was beginning to rain. Then he tried to involve the therapist in a discussion of "how come it rains. What makes it rain?" Leonard seemed to know a great deal on the subject and said that rain came from clouds, and when clouds get cold they "drop the water." Richard corrected Leonard by saying, "Clouds don't get cold, they are cold all the time, they always have loads of water." Macy, too, became involved in the discussion by taking both sides of the argument, agreeing both with Leonard and with Richard. Finally Richard turned to the therapist and asked how the water got up into the clouds. The therapist described the process of evaporation and condensation in the air. Leonard, Macy, Richard, and Michael appeared very interested in this. The discussion was extended by the boys into an exploration of the formation of rain, hail, and snow.

Richard said he liked to sleep when it rained; he liked the sound of rain. Macy now began to talk about how he had an *"awful lot of trouble sleeping at night."* There were many nights when he hardly got any sleep. "Ask Richard; he'll tell you. In class sometimes I can't keep my head up. I'm so sleepy because I couldn't sleep at night." He had trouble sleeping because he lay in bed and thought. He thought about going home, about the things he did during the day, and such. Sometimes he was "very nervous at night" when he was trying to sleep. The harder he tried to fall asleep the less sleep he seemed to get. The therapist asked Macy if he could tell more about the things he thought about. In a very blasé manner, Macy said that he just thought about going home, about the things that happened during the day—like what happened in school, what happened at the gym, and what happened at the cottage. (There was no affect in the manner in which he described his cogitations.)

The therapist said that many times people could not sleep because the things they thought about were upsetting, and when one was upset it was hard for him to fall asleep. It was found that if one talks about these things, they were no longer as disturbing. Macy: "I'm not sure I'm upset. I don't feel very upset. I don't feel very nervous, but just lying in bed thinking about, for instance, playing ball at the gym, I start thinking about it and I find I'm not falling asleep. Sometimes I lie in bed and I· think about what I'm going to do when I get home, like going to a movie, meeting my friends on the street, and before I know it it can be one or two o'clock. I wake up, I go to school, and I'm very sleepy in school. I find ways to hide my face from the teacher in school so the teacher doesn't see I'm sleeping."

Richard was becoming restless and looked as if he were about to start "kidding around." Sure enough he did. He walked over to Louis to watch the card game. He then walked over to Donald, took his radio, and turned up the volume. The therapist asked Richard what the matter was and he said, "Nothing is the matter." Donald took the radio away from Richard and told him to go back to his seat, which Richard did. By this time Macy was diverted from whatever he was going to say. He was now leafing through the magazine that he had lent to Leonard. Since it was 8:30, the session was ended.

As the therapist was leaving, Donald came up to him, threw his arms around him, gave him a hug and said, "You're a good guy, Mr. Ellery," and ran down the stairs. As Louis was leaving, he said, "We ought to meet until nine o'clock instead of till half-past eight."

COMMENT

Our hunch that our "permissiveness" would eventually bring desired results was justified by the events in this session. The positive feelings toward the therapist were solidified, and the boys gave the reasons for it. Donald's acting on his impulse took this feeling a step further. Because of the security of this emotional hegemony, the therapist permitted himself to tell Donald directly to lower the volume on his radio on two different occasions, even though his acts were derived from sibling rivalry with the other boys who engaged the therapist's attention at the time. He also attempted to explore Richard's feelings.

The positive feelings toward the therapist were displaced upon the Village and the boys now perceived it as a benevolent agent, quite contrary to their earlier attitudes, thus counteracting their alienations.

Because of these various benevolent feelings, Richard inquired as to the cause of rain, something that he was not permitted to do by teachers in the schools in the city, and a discussion arose that led to the association with sleeplessness. This was interesting in the light of what occurred in session sixteen. There the fear of death and of dying grew out of an exploration of the phenomena of sound and airplanes; here, similarly, awareness of tension emerged from a discussion of the phenomenon of rain. This was in direct confirmation of the process of inversion; that is, where projection and curiosity under proper conditions and properly handled lead to introspection.

NOTE

Because the settee (couch) was used for lounging by boys, sometimes two at a time, we suggested at the supervision conference that it be dismantled, since it could not be removed. The therapist removed the mattress to another room and turned the base upside down. When Louis came he inquired why the settee was dismantled. The therapist told him the mattress had been taken out. Louis voiced disappointment that he would not be able to play cards now, but said nothing beyond that.

Before the boys entered the room the therapist plugged in the hot plate and placed on it a pot of water because in past sessions the excessive activity of filling the pot with water and heating it caused a great deal of commotion. The step was therefore taken to reduce the diversion. This seemed to be effective.

Session Twenty-Four

ABSENT: Jules, in the infirmary with a fractured ankle.

Louis and Richard were the first to arrive. When Louis entered the room he grabbed half of the cigarettes in the urn. The other half he gave to Richard, saying, "Let's not give anybody else any cigarettes." He later changed it to: "We'll give the boys their cigarettes as they come in." This Louis did as each boy entered the room.

Michael and Donald entered the room and Donald immediately looked to see whether the coffee pot and the hot plate were there. Satisfied that they were, he quietly sat down. Michael had brought with him a stack of comic books which he had picked up in the lower lobby before he came up. Each boy now selected a number of them and several became preoccupied with reading. Leonard had come in quietly and sat down.

There was serene quiet in the room as all the boys, except for Richard and Leonard, were reading. Macy soon appeared and he, too, sat down, helping himself to a comic book. Leonard, finding that the boys were reading and there was no conversation, began to read a comic book, too. (It looked like a passive-resistance campaign on the part of the boys, though easy availability of the books may have been a factor.) The group presented the appearance of a gathering of small children. The situation obviously required action on the part of the therapist and he approached Richard, who was not reading, although he had a book resting in his lap. The therapist turned to him and said: "By the way, Richard, remember we talked about reading that book on dreams? Have you had a chance to look at it yet?" Richard: "No I didn't. I don't have that book here. That book is home. I was thinking of reading the book when I go home on my next home visit." *Macy and Louis raised their eyes stealthily* from their books but instantaneously fell back to reading.

Richard continued: "I used to do a lot of dreaming. One dream I always remember is when I was a little boy, I was about five years old. This happened about a year after I fell on my head out of the window. I had dreams of big snakes chasing me; big pythons used to come after me and I used to run and I used to scream to my mother." He described how he would wake up, his feet clammy, his hands moist, and he would have headaches. Donald spoke up from his reading: "I remember dreams like that. Big fucking pythons used to come after me. I thought they were going to eat me." Richard took over the conversation from Donald and described snakes crawling "all over" him, trying to bite him, his fighting off the snakes, and how he used to be afraid to fall asleep. Following this brief interchange there was silence.

Now Richard took up his comic book and began to read, as did Donald. The room had the aspect of a reference room in a library. The therapist said, "Gee, I wonder what a dream like that means?" Richard turned and said: "I think I know what that means. Snakes are devils; there are devils chasing you." He said no more, but the therapist encouraged him to think further about it by saying, "Why should devils be chasing you in your dream?" Richard: "I don't know." Therapist: "You know that sounds like a dream someone told us here about devils." Michael immediately spoke up and said: "That was my dream. Devils mean you did something bad and they are chasing you." Richard: "Oh yeah, I remember now. I always figured that the reason the snakes were chasing me in the dream was because I must have done something bad and I was going to get punished. Shit, I must have done an awful lot of bad things when I was a kid."

A discussion arose among Donald, Richard, and Michael in which they *narrated to each other the "bad" things they did*, such as stealing, truanting, and the like. The conversation began to assume the quality of a bragging contest. In the midst of it, Donald got up to prepare coffee and was soon joined by Michael. The two boys filled (paper) cups with coffee and passed them around. Unlike the recent past, this proceeded rather quietly, with Michael interrupting boys at their reading to ask them how much sugar they wanted. However, the preoccupation with the coffee did end the discussion.

The therapist waited until coffee was distributed to the boys and Donald had brought a cup for him. Donald asked the therapist how it tasted and was told that it tasted good. All the boys were now back to reading the comic books. The therapist decided again to take the initiative and said that from the dreams that were just told, it seemed that at some time in their lives the boys must have heard people tell them that they were bad. Michael looked up from his reading, scanned the room, and said: "I remember my grandmother. She was always telling me I was bad. When I was a little boy that's all I used to hear from my grandmother." Richard turned to the therapist and asked, "How does that dream show it?" The therapist told Richard that in the dream he was being punished by the snakes and (bringing it to a somewhat different level) said: "Didn't you ever hear about boys who do things getting caught because they want to get punished? Sometimes they do it when they are awake and sometimes they get punished in their dreams." Richard: "You mean in your subconscious mind maybe you do things bad just so you get caught, but you don't really want to admit it to yourself, but you do admit it to yourself when you fall asleep and you can't control what you dream?" "That's pretty interesting, Richard," said Donald. Michael resumed talking about his grandmother. He said: "I don't remember my grandmother too good. I do remember she used to yell at me all the time and bawl me out. She's dead now so what fucking difference does it make?"

Richard: "I remember when my grandmother died," and went into a rather lengthy detailed history of his (maternal) grandmother's passing away. He had a very vague and hazy memory of it. He remembered his grandmother as being a very nice woman. "But my grandfather, my mother's father, was even nicer than her. He used to give me everything I wanted. You know, he used to talk with a foreign accent. He couldn't talk English too good." Richard then described how the grandfather would take him out, buy him hot dogs, French fries, and other things. He then proceeded to describe how when his grandfather had died, his mother was extremely upset. There used to be nights when she could not sleep, and other nights, when she did fall asleep, she would wake up screaming that she had seen a vision of her father. Richard used to be afraid because his mother would start running through the house. Although at the start he spoke of this with some affect, as he continued the affect gradually abated and he described things he and his grandfather used to do, such as fishing, eating out, going for walks. He added with feeling that he was very upset when his grandfather died, and then stopped short.

Donald looked extremely sad, more so than the therapist had ever seen him before and during the life of the group. The therapist asked Donald what the matter was. Donald: "Oh, nothing." "For nothing being the matter you sure look kind of sad," the therapist remarked. Donald got up and began to walk around his chair and finally said: "I remember an aunt, Marsha. I loved her and she loved me. She died a couple of years ago. There wasn't a thing in the world I wouldn't do for that woman. She used to look after me; she used to give me things I wanted and needed. I was so fucking upset after she died I didn't want to live." Richard: "Yeah, I used to think like that, too. I remember when I was a kid I used to say, shit, I don't want to live if my grandfather can't live. I used to be afraid to go to sleep. My grandfather died in his sleep. I thought maybe I would have a heart attack in my sleep, but then I used to think to myself if that's the way I got to go, that's the best way to go. You don't suffer; you don't have any pain."

Michael pulled out a deck of cards at this point, and began to shuffle them. Louis asked him to play cards, but Michael refused. However, this was enough to break into the discussion. Everyone except Richard went back to reading comic books. Donald had gone over to make some more coffee for himself, Michael, and Richard. Richard turned to the therapist and said: "Boy, when you were in New York today I should have been with you. I would never have come back to the Village. I would have run." (The background of this remark is that the therapist had been in New York earlier that day and came to the Village about one o'clock. Richard saw him driving up, had run over to the car, and asked the therapist where he had been.) In response to Richard's remark, the therapist said, "I would have trusted you, Richard." Richard turned saying, "Would you?" Donald said: "Sure he would. I wouldn't have run from Mr. Ellery. Shit, anybody who trusts me, I'm not going to run on them. If Mr. Ellery left $10 in the room tonight, I'd give it back to him. I wouldn't steal it because I know he trusts us." It was obvious that the discussion veered away from anything meaningful.

Louis, who joined in, talked about teachers at Children's Village, what "stupid asses" they were. Nobody seemed to pay any attention to him. Soon the boys returned to reading comic books. The therapist was tempted to raise the matter of the comic-book reading as a form of resistance, but he felt that this might only serve to intensify it. Instead he reverted to Richard's statement of being trusted. For a while the boys seemed uninterested, busily reading their comic books, but the therapist continued: "I'm sure every boy here had an experience with this." Donald responded: "One thing I know, anybody who ever trusts me I'm going to be okay with. That's why I loved my Aunt Marsha. She really loved me and trusted me and I never did anything wrong when I was with her."

Richard was activated by this and briefly talked about his grandfather, but changed the subject by engaging Donald in a discussion about his grandfather's taking him fishing and eating seafood. Soon Donald, Michael, and Richard were deep in a conversation about the various types of seafood they had eaten in Italian restaurants, with Donald asking the therapist if he had ever eaten "scungilli," and other things. Then Richard talked about his grandfather walking on the beach and digging into the sand with his heel looking for clams. He talked about the preparation of the clams and of eating them. Donald took over the discussion and talked about frying clams on clambakes he had attended. The therapist finally said, "By the way fellows, did anybody here ever have a clam dream?"

All the comic books in the room were lowered. Louis looked up and said: "A clam dream? What the hell is a clam dream?" Richard: "Yeah, Mr. Ellery, what do you mean by a clam dream?" Donald: "Never heard of a clam dream. That sounds crazy." The therapist said, "A clam dream is one where you are dreaming that walls are closing in on you." Donald: "Oh that kind of dream! Sure I had hundreds of those." Richard: "Yeah, when I was a kid I used to dream about walls closing in on me all the time." Louis: "Okay, Mr. Ellery, what does that dream mean?" The therapist wondered if the boys had any idea what the dream meant. No ideas were forthcoming. Richard: "Mr. Ellery, do you think you know what that dream means?" The therapist said to Richard that sometimes boys have that dream because, like the dream they had talked about before, it was a kind of punishment dream. Richard: "That sounds right. I remember once I was sitting in a chair and ripping the leather on it. My mother didn't want to give me something and I was sore and I wanted to get back at her so I took a pencil and kept sticking it into the chair. My mother then really got sore, and I told her that if she had given me what I wanted I wouldn't have ripped the chair." Donald laughed at this and said: "I was once riding with a boy on a bus and there was a sign in the bus saying, '$500 reward for information leading to arrest of anybody defacing property.' Me and that boy made an arrangement where I snitched on him; the boy was sent up for three months. I got $500. When the boy came out I shared the money with him—$250 apiece." He laughed at this, but there seemed to be a note of embarrassment in his laughter, almost as if he felt guilty.

Following this, Donald said: "I want to ask you something, Mr. Ellery. Maybe you know the answer. Why is it when I go to sleep I can't think of sex any more. I used to go to bed at night and if some of the boys would tell a dirty joke I would begin to get a hard-on and I'd start thinking of a naked girl and putting my prick into a naked girl. I can't think of that any more. When I start getting a hard-on, I think like I'm putting my prick in my mother and my hard goes down." The boy seemed completely oblivious of the significance of what he had said and the therapist thought it advisable not to pursue it at the moment. Donald continued: "A lot of times I used to go to bed at night and I used to beat the meat [masturbate]. After I creamed [ejaculated] I would fall asleep. Before I beat the meat I couldn't fall asleep." Richard: "A lot of boys wake up with yellow spots on their sheets." Michael laughingly said: "Hey, Richard, if you didn't look for them how would you know they were yellow spots?" This brought general laughter and Richard, Michael, Donald, and Macy began to talk at once.

Macy repeated his story of the preceding week, of how when he went to bed he could not sleep because he thought about playing ball the next day, about going home, and such. He then turned to the therapist: "Does that mean maybe I'm so nervous I can't sleep?" The therapist tried to relate to what Macy was asking and agreed with his supposition, but asked him to be more specific. This Macy did not do. At this point Michael and Donald almost simultaneously asked the therapist "how come boys have to beat the meat?" The therapist responded directly, reminding them of a previous discussion of how in growing up, nature was preparing them to be fathers, and they began to become aware of sexual feelings. Since they were as yet unable to establish sexual relations, tensions built up, and masturbation relieved these tensions. Donald went into a rather lengthy dissertation on how he used to enjoy "beating the meat." There used to be a teacher at the Village who used to walk around "shaking her ass." He would look at her and then would run into the cottage, go to the bathroom, and "beat his meat."

Richard stood up (which he often did when he spoke) and launched into a description of photographs that a teacher showed the boys. These showed him on a beach with a girl lying on top of him. There were other pictures of the girl in various poses with her legs spread, and the like. Richard demonstrated the poses. His demonstrations provoked laughter from the boys. He then described a boy in his classroom with a female teacher who used to sit behind the desk with her legs spread out. "You could look right under the desk and see her pussy," he said. "This boy once crawled on his hands and knees right under the desk and nearly got his nose caught in her pussy." Michael looked at Richard angrily and said: "Aw shut up. This is a serious discussion." Richard at once sat down and said nothing.

Michael turned to the therapist and asked: "Mr. Ellery, isn't it true you go crazy when you masturbate?" The therapist asked Michael where he had got this idea and he said that one of the teachers at the Village had told this to all the boys, that masturbating led to something happening "to the nervous system." The therapist went into a lengthy explanation of masturbation, emphasizing that of itself it does not cause harm to the nervous system, and one cannot go crazy from it. Masturbation in itself is normal at a certain point in life. Michael interrupted: "Well, that is the first time I ever had this kind of an explanation. I always thought you go crazy if you jerk off." Donald: "No, don't you remember about a month ago we were talking about it and Mr. Ellery said then that you don't go crazy from jerking off. If you did we would all be running around like real crazy asses here." This last remark was greeted with laughter. Louis spoke up in a (mock) angelic voice saying: "What is jerking off? I never heard of it." Michael laughed at him, and said, "You're so full of shit, it isn't even funny." Donald to Louis: "Go back to reading your comic book, you bullshit artist."

After this interruption, questions came thick and fast. Richard wanted to know why certain girls were virgins; they didn't want to "get laid." The therapist explained to Richard that very often girls—and he really meant women not young girls—were afraid of sex. They have a problem about this. Richard immediately took this over and said, "Yeah, I know, some girls are afraid of having a dick in them; they got real problems." Donald asked, "How come fellows are queers?" The therapist answered Donald's question by saying that boys often wondered about this, and that all people in the process of growing up could have feelings for both sexes, but part of growing up meant learning to control the feeling for a person of the same sex in order that eventually one could have sex with a member of the opposite sex *in order to produce children*, which was the function of sex. Sometimes, because of some unusual experiences, this control was not acquired. Many times when a boy found a problem in having sex with a girl, he began to worry about whether he would prove to be a "queer."

Donald immediately responded to this by saying: "Sometimes I got real problems when I try to screw a girl. It's not really when I screw her, but after I screw her. When I pull my dick out I feel kind of crummy. I don't know what to say to her. I don't even feel like holding her. I enjoyed having sex with her, rubbing her up and all that, but when I get off, I don't know, I don't know what to do." The boys were listening very intently to this. Turning to the therapist Donald then said: "Mr. Ellery, there is something I want to ask you that is very personal. Please don't get mad at me. I wanted to ask this for a long time." After a moment of hesitation, he said: "You remember when you got married and *you gave your wife a baby*, how did you feel? You know what I mean, when you creamed? How did you feel after you did it?" Therapist: "Are you asking me whether I felt dirty?" He said, "Yeah, that's right." "Are you asking me whether I felt rotten?" Donald: "That's right. Did you?" "No." Donald: "You didn't? You sure you didn't?" "No, I didn't, Don." Donald got up from his chair, took the seat right next to the therapist and in a lowered voice, holding the therapist's arm, said, "I got a real problem, Mr. Ellery, I don't know what to do." There was anguish in his face as he said: "I don't know why after I have sex with a girl I feel so rotten. I hate myself for having sex. Before I have sex I don't give a shit. I'm real hot and I don't care what I do. I go to a dance, I dance with the girl, I rub up against her tit, I feel her ass, and then when I get her good and hot and I cream inside her, I don't know what to say to her. Sometimes I feel like saying 'I love you' but I can't say it. What is it, Mr. Ellery, tell me." Richard came over to say something to the therapist but Donald dismissed him: "Leave Mr. Ellery alone. I'm talking to him."

Louis had by this time drawn the other boys off into a side discussion, except for Macy, who was listening very intently to what Donald was saying. The therapist said to Donald, "You know, Donald, you kind of told us tonight why you have this problem." "I did? What did I tell you?" "You don't remember, Don?" "No, why have I got this problem?" The therapist took a long chance with Donald, but since the problem was so close to the surface, he said, "You know Don, maybe you feel that way because after you've had sex it feels almost like you had sex with your mother." Donald looked at the therapist with surprise and exclaimed: "How did you know that?" The therapist reminded him of his having said this himself. Donald thought back for a moment and said, "Yes I did." Therapist: "You know Don, maybe that's how you feel, but these girls are *not* your mother." Donald: "I remember when I was about fourteen, I came home once with dirty pictures in my wallet. My mother happened to find it and saw the pictures. She yelled and screamed at me for carrying them around. I felt like shit; I didn't know what to say to her; *I felt so rotten for even thinking about it.*" He then went into a long dissertation again on how "shitty" he felt when he had sex with a girl, and wound this up by saying: "Many times I feel I shouldn't even have sex, but I want it, and I have it anyway."

Richard now came over and asked, "Mr. Ellery, when you wanted to know about sex, did you go to your parents?" The therapist said, "Most boys generally go to their fathers." Richard: "I couldn't go to my father and ask him about sex. I wanted to do it a lot of times but I know my father, he'd kill me if I asked him a question like that. He'd say to me, 'What the hell have you been up to?' " Donald: "You think your father is something. My parents would hang me up by the feet if I came and asked a question like that." He then turned to the therapist and said, "You think that's why I feel that way about sex?" "That might very well be, Don—from the way you told us how you feel about sex, the way your mother talked about it." He said, "That's right, she used to make me feel like a piece of shit for even thinking about it."

The time for the session had been overextended. Richard started to walk out, and this served as a signal for most of the boys to go. Donald was not ready to drop the discussion, however, saying that he would like to talk some more. Therapist: "How about next week?" "That's all right. We could talk about it next week if it's all right with you." The therapist assured him that it was. As the group was walking downstairs the therapist overheard Richard talking to Macy about his father, Richard saying that his father was the kind of guy who, if you came and asked him a question, always thought you were "up to something," so you didn't ask him any questions.

COMMENT

After a brief initial resistance and continued efforts at testing the therapist (Macy and Louis raised their eyes stealthily), the boys launched into the most significant group interview so far. The seeds for this were sown in the preceding sessions and now bore fruit. Their feelings of "badness" and need for punishment have come to the fore. The boys had become vaguely aware of these from previous discussions, but now they were conscious of them and confronted by them.

What was most striking about this discussion were the tender feelings conveyed by a few of the boys toward grandparents and an aunt. In fact, the tender feelings toward "Aunt Marsha" were brought out in direct relation to Donald's speaking of the therapist's "trusting" the boys. This is an example of "transference in reverse." Even more impressive was Donald's yearning for tenderness in sex. He was saddened by its absence, and the therapist dealt with it most skillfully, though perhaps overcourageously. Such an incursion into the unconscious (relating to incest urges) might have had disastrous outcomes. The therapist apparently "felt" that he could take this risk. He was right, for when he made the connection with Donald's feelings toward his mother, Donald spontaneously asked: "How did you know?" Apparently it was in his preconscious.

The decrease in former crudeness and the emergence of delicacy relative to sex is unmistakenly conveyed by the wording of Donald's question to the therapist. He refers to intercourse as when ". . . you gave your wife a baby." His awareness of his inability to be tender to a girl after intercourse was further evidence of his growing "finer" feelings; so was his statement: "I felt so rotten even thinking about it [intercourse]."

In this connection the boys' negative Oedipal feelings toward their fathers were bared when they talked of the latter's crude and nonunderstanding reactions to the boys' needs and confusions. This breaking away in such an objective manner from the ties toward parents precedes understanding (and later forgiving) them and the dissolution of ego (self-image) defenses. Such confrontations are paths toward maturity, which was, as we shall see later, our paramount aim.

For some time we had been discussing at the supervisory conferences the importance of leading the boys to view sex not only as pleasure but as having a biological aim and a social responsibility. Having been prepared for this, the therapist took this opportunity to plant a seed of these ideas when he included the phrase, "in order to produce children," in his statement. This would bear fruit in the future.

Session Twenty-Five

ABSENT: Michael, on home visit; Jules, still ill.

Richard and Louis arrived fifteen minutes early, because of the Easter school recess. Richard sat reading a comic book. Louis brought along a crossword puzzle that had been distributed to boys in the gymnasium. Louis's manner was very friendly as he involved the therapist in helping him. The therapist was surprised at the boy's ability with words for the rather advanced puzzle, since he was able to supply most of them by himself. Macy was the only boy to arrive late—about fifteen minutes —probably because he attended church services. Leonard and Donald came on time. When Donald came in, Richard said to him, "I thought you were going to church tonight." Donald: "I was supposed to go to church, but I'd rather come here." Richard: "You'll get in trouble." Donald: "I don't care. They can't make me go to church."

This was the first session at which Donald did not at once proceed to prepare coffee. He took a seat next to the therapist and said: "We said that we were going to talk about that thing again this week. Okay?" Without waiting for a reply, he continued: "Mr. Ellery, when you were younger and you wanted to screw a girl, how did you ask her?" The therapist asked Donald what he meant (obviously playing for time before answering the difficult question). Donald said: "You know, like when you want to take a girl and you want to fuck her. What do you say?" Louis interrupted to ask the therapist for a word for his crossword puzzle. Donald became very annoyed and said to Louis: "Don't start that shit tonight, will you? If you are not going to talk sit quiet." He then repeated the question to the therapist. The therapist said, "If I remember correctly the matter we raised last week was about the problem of feelings after a boy has intercourse." Donald: "You're right, but I want you to tell me. What do you say?" The therapist said that he was aware of what Donald was asking him, but wasn't he really saying that there was something that made him feel uncomfortable about this? The therapist continued that actually the words were not important, and often no words were necessary; it really depended on what you felt. (The therapist felt that Donald was trying to get him involved in a discussion of sex on several levels: *1]* curiosity about an adult's sex life; *2]* attempting to get a vicarious thrill out of these revelations; and *3]*, which may have been the important factor, his returning to the problem raised at the preceding session, namely, his feeling of disgust with sex.)

However, Donald responded to the element of feelings raised by the therapist. He asked, "You mean you can go out with a girl and have sex and you don't have to ask her?" and went on to say that when he went to a party, he and a "couple of fellows" took out girls after the party. They went to the park. The other fellows went behind trees, stood the girls up against trees and "have sex with them." He did it too and he liked it, but he didn't know what to say. He just started to "pump" on a girl and he felt kind of "shitty."

Louis looked up from his crossword puzzle and said: "What's so fucking hard about that? All you got to do is tell a girl to drop her drawers." Leonard laughed very uncomfortably at this and looked as if he wanted to dig a hole and bury himself, as it were, since the conversation seemed to embarrass him extremely. Donald reacted to Louis's statement with: "Maybe that's okay for you, but I can't go ask a girl to just drop her drawers." Macy, who had walked in the room a few minutes earlier and heard Donald's statement, said: "I can't either. After I screw a girl I don't even want to talk to her. I feel so fucking disgusted with her. There was one girl I screwed and it was a gang job. Then me and the fellows were talking and the girl was in the other room. The girl said something and I yelled out to her, 'Shut your mouth you stupid whore.' Next thing I knew the girl was crying and she ran out of the apartment."

Richard rose from his seat and went out to the fire escape and sat down there, claiming that the room was too warm. Therapist: "Is it the room or the discussion?" Richard turned to the therapist with his mouth open wide. Louis looked up at Richard and said, "He's got your number!" Richard said nothing but crawled back into the room, sat down in his chair, and asked the therapist: "You don't mind if I sit on the fire escape do you, Mr. Ellery?" Therapist: "Richard, I don't mind if you sit on the fire escape, but I kind of wonder if you want to sit on the fire escape because there is something about this discussion that bothers you." Again Richard did not respond.

Donald (to therapist): "You still didn't tell me what I'm supposed to say." "You know, Don, what you really want me to do it get you off the hook. We started to talk about something last week, and this is the important thing, and I know from what the boys have been saying here that having sex makes them feel guilty, and this is something most boys feel." Donald: "I got another question. Is it true that if you are fed by your mother's chest, you're liable to become a queer?" Without waiting for an answer, however, he got up and began to prepare coffee. Macy joined him and the two worked at brewing and distributing it. Richard picked up the question that Donald had posed: "Yeah, I wondered about that, too," but then quickly changed the subject and said: "You remember last week we were talking about the parents you go to to get sex information? I once went to my father and asked him how old I should be when I have sex. My father told me I should save it for when I get married; that I shouldn't have sex before I get married." Macy: "I don't know why, but most boys go to their father when they want to talk about sex. For me it's easier to go to my mother."

Louis now became quite active. He said: "I know all about sex. I don't have to ask my mother or father. Hey, Donald, were you breast-fed?" Donald: "No." Louis said that a lot of boys were breast-fed and a lot of boys were fed from the bottle. The boys who were breast-fed became sex maniacs, all they wanted to do was get a lot of "titty juice." Louis imitated with his mouth the sound of a child feeding at the breast, which brought forth laughter from the boys. Richard began a description of some of his sex adventures, but in very vague terms, and in the middle he stopped and asked the therapist: "When you have sex with a girl are you supposed to put in only the tip of your dick or the whole thing? I don't know, Mr. Ellery." Donald yelled out: "Put the whole fucking thing in, what are you saving it for?"

This served to encourage Louis to describe in vivid detail how he and a "couple of boys" had a "gang-bang" at a hotel in B————. There was this "elderly lady" lying on top of the bed and Louis was first. He "got in and pounded away on her," then the other boys got on her and started to "pound away." Louis demonstrated as he talked by rolling his body to show how the woman acted and her moaning and groaning. "Then all of a sudden there is a fucking noise in the room. In came this big bruiser, he was the husband, and he said, 'Who's fucking my wife?' Shit, all of us got our asses out of there and we hid in the hall and then I walked up to the door and I heard this guy get on top of his wife and begin to 'pound on her.' I looked through the keyhole and there he was. He had his dick in her. I must have made some noise because the guy jumped off and yelled out, 'who's out there?' That's when me and the boys all took off." The boys were now convulsed with laughter, with Richard laughing the loudest. Leonard had a pained smile on his face and was trying to bury himself in reading a comic book. When the laughter subsided, Donald came over to the therapist and asked: "You don't give a girl a baby every time you screw her, do you? If you screw her during the period you give her a baby, but if she is not bleeding she can't have a baby."

Suddenly Donald said: "What's the matter, Mr. Ellery? You don't look so good tonight. I've seen you look better on other nights." Therapist: "Don, you got something there and I'll tell you what I'm thinking." "What?" "You know Don, I've been sitting here and listening to all the screwing you fellows get involved in, and the more I hear it, the more something strikes me. What strikes me is the feeling that you are probably talking about all of this to hide the feelings of being afraid of it, a feeling of guilt—and every boy here feels guilty. Even Louis."

Louis spoke up: "Yeah I feel guilty. That don't stop me from screwing, but I still feel guilty." Donald: "Shut up, Louis. Let Mr. Ellery finish." "This is a very important part of your life," said the therapist, "and I can understand that you probably all have a lot of questions about it. There are many things you don't know, and in not knowing, perhaps many of you are a little afraid, but you hide this by bragging about all that you've done almost as if you were trying to work up a hard-on here tonight." Richard: "I thought that's what Donald was asking. He wants you to give him a hard-on." Donald to Richard: "You probably got a

bigger hard-on than I've got." Everyone was quiet now. Donald took the
initiative and said: "Okay, Mr. Ellery. Remember, I asked you about
girls bleeding. Why do they bleed and what happens if you have sex
with them when they bleed?" Macy seconded Donald's request: "I never
found out what makes a girl bleed. How come it happens only to girls
and not to boys?"

The therapist took this opportunity, for which he had been prepared
for some time in advance, to place sex in the context of biological life
and to extend its meaning for the boys. He started with the word
menstruation and explained its place in the development of the woman.
Sex, he said, is the means by which life continues. Without sex, without
nature preparing the bodies of boys and girls for sex, the human race
would die out. Menstruation was the result of nature's way to prepare
the body of a girl, when she reached the age of about twelve or thirteen
years, for her role—to bear children. The therapist described the
ovaries, the Fallopian tubes, and the passing down of the "egg" into the
uterus, and how the uterus develops a lining to feed the "egg" and later
the foetus via the placenta; then the process of fertilization, namely, the
uniting of the sperm with the "egg." When fertilization occurred, he
told them, the woman stopped having "periods," she did not menstruate.
There was intense absorption on the part of every boy as the therapist
described this process. At one point Louis, almost in wonderment, said,
"So that's what happens when a man scums into a woman!" Donald
corrected him: "The word is *sperm*," and then said to Louis: "Why don't
you keep your mouth shut? Mr. Ellery is trying to teach us something."

Richard asked: "Is that why some girls want to be virgins? They
don't want to have a baby?" The therapist agreed and said: "Girls see
sex as the way of having children. To have sex outside of marriage means
that they might have children outside of marriage and there wouldn't be
a husband around to take care of the child, to earn money, and it is pretty
rough for a girl to have a baby with nobody around to take care of
either her or the baby." Richard: "I don't blame them then. I wouldn't
want to have a baby and not have any money to take care of the baby."

The therapist now introduced the idea that there is a difference between having sex outside of marriage, as they were talking about it, and
having sex after marriage. Outside of marriage you always felt guilty
about what you did, whereas when you were married, you not only had
sex because you needed it but also sex meant more. When you loved
your wife, one of the ways of expressing love was through sex. In that
way you didn't feel rotten about what you are doing. Donald said:
"When I get married I'm not going to have sex with my wife every
night. I'm going to have sex with her only when I want to give her a

baby, and my wife and I are going to have to agree when we are going to have a baby." Richard: "That's okay for you, but when I get married I want to have sex every night." Donald: "I don't want my wife to think I'm a sex fiend. I'm going to be happy when I get married, but sometimes the thing I worry about is, is my wife liable to leave me? She's liable to take off and I'll be left all alone." (Although there was a possibility that Donald associated having sex with his wife as "dirty," and feared that she might leave him because of it, there may have been another theme present, namely, fear of being abandoned—the doom motif.)

Macy picked this up as he said: "I worry about that too sometimes, about getting married and maybe my wife will desert me. I'd hate to have that happen to me." The therapist said, "I know that boys sometimes have this feeling, that people are going to desert them, and this comes from somewhere, because you carry this feeling with you even before you are married." Donald (peevishly): "My wife is not going to desert me. I'll desert her!" Therapist to Donald: "Did you ever hear the story of the man on a job who thinks he is going to get fired, though he really isn't. He just *feels* he is going to get fired, so he runs to the boss and yells: 'You can't fire me, I quit!' " Macy: "That's what bothers me about me and some of the boys in my cottage. I've got some very good friends in the cottage, two of them, and we get along all right, but we are always fighting. Remember I told you about how I don't sleep at night? Well that's what I don't sleep about. I lie in bed and I think about this. For instance, we sit around talking, me and my friends, and before I know it, we are teasing one another. Then somebody says a word and that gets me mad and I feel like fighting. I don't know why this happens, do you Mr. Ellery?"

The therapist asked Macy if he could give him some details. Macy said he could not, but he considered it "a stupid thing. You're friendly with a guy and yet you are fighting with him. If somebody else ever says anything against me or my two friends then we fight them, so even though we fight with one another we still kind of protect one another."

Richard did not let Macy finish. He said: "Mr. Ellery, I know Macy's talking to you, but there is one more thing I just got to know tonight. Will you tell me about it?" Therapist: "What is it?" Richard: "Did you ever hear of things that girls put inside their cunt so they can't have a baby? What are those things?" Donald: "Oh they can put a pill inside." Richard: "Yeah I heard of that, but I know there is something else. It's a sort of round thing." The therapist supplied Richard with the word he was looking for: *diaphragm*. Richard wanted to know what it looked like. Using the top of a coffee jar the therapist demonstrated approximately its shape. Donald then wanted to know what it covers "inside the body." The therapist told him about the cervix which was the "opening to the womb." Macy wanted to know about what happens to the sperm then. The therapist explained how the sperm is prevented by the diaphragm from entering the womb and after a number of hours "it dies" and the diaphragm can be removed. In this manner the sperm is prevented from uniting with the "egg."

Having received this information, Richard and Donald withdrew to a corner of the room, apparently to continue to talk about it. They spoke rather quietly and the therapist could not overhear them. Macy soon returned to the problem with his two friends in his cottage, whom he named. Speaking directly to the therapist, Macy said that he knew that whenever he had a "good friend," he would always end up fighting with him. Louis was listening rather intently to what Macy was saying and told Macy, "Maybe you can't stand having good friends." Macy: "Is that possible, Mr. Ellery?" "Yes, that's possible." "I always thought about that. I don't see other boys who have good friends fighting with each other, but I'm always fighting with my friends. It's not really a fight. We just kind of tease one another. Sometimes we begin to hit each other on the head. You know, just kidding around, but after awhile we are not kidding any more."

Since the time was up, the therapist asked Macy if he would like to continue the discussion next time the group met. Macy: "Sure, maybe we can find out why I am like that, because then maybe if I find out I can get some sleep at night. I don't want to lie in bed all night thinking about it."

COMMENT

It appeared that the "delicacy" to which we referred was limited only in relation to the therapist's sex activity, not to the boys' own. They continued to use the common terms characteristic of their backgrounds and culture. We took note of the use of language and changes in it served as indices of the boys' maturity and personality integration. This development emerged later in a rather dramatic way.

In this session we exploited to the full the opportunity of placing sex in a context entirely alien to the boys' feelings and values, and they seemed to respond, though we knew that this was only in a superficial way, mostly to please the therapist. The deeper interpretation the therapist gave the boys of their underlying fears and guilts was both timely and appropriate. By this time defenses had lowered, because a prior threshold of recognition had been established. The response, therefore, was as immediate as it was significant.

The emphasis upon what we term *"natural* (biological) *morality"* (as differentiated from societal restraint) is more acceptable to adolescents because the very idea of social restraint mobilizes rebellion and resentment. This was another subject which was discussed lengthily and in detail during many hours with the therapist, with detailed suggestions as to the manner of presentation. The anatomical and physiological information presented to the boys took the social codes and controls out of adult arbitrariness and instead placed them into a nonhuman, mechanistic realm. As a result, they were less objectionable to the young.

The homoerotic element in the discussion was revealed in Richard's statement that Donald sought an erection through the conversation with the therapist and in Macy's description of his "teasing" relation with his "good friends."

This was the first time the boys have broached the subject of *doom*: their fears of their future wives' leaving them. This was a major preoccupation, though an unconscious one with our boys, to which we turned extended attention much later in the course of the treatment.

NOTE

Since the boys displayed so keen an interest in the subject of body functions, we suggested that the therapist bring diagrams of the human body and of male and female reproductive organs. Books were accordingly obtained from the nurse and Community Center staff that contained such illustrations. This was done in preparation for the following session should the boys again raise the same or similar questions. The therapist was to repeat the same information, but concretize it through diagrams and photos. However as will become clear from the following protocol, this opportunity did not arise. The group became interested in another meaningful topic and it would have been inappropriate to block it off.

Several days before the twenty-sixth session, a boy brought some liquor on his return from a home visit. Donald and four other of his cottage mates drank so much of it during the night that they were found in the morning in a state of stupor. Donald became violent and broke about twenty windows with his fists. It took three staff members to bring him under control. He was given cold showers, slapped, and so on, to bring him out of his condition. While in the stupor Donald shouted that he was going to "kill everybody," and that he hated the Village, and used vituperative expletives. Finally, as he was being put to bed, Donald told the cottage life supervisor that he was sorry for what happened and thanked him for his help.

Session Twenty-Six

ABSENT: Michael, on home visit.

When the therapist entered the room he found Richard, Louis, and Jules already there. They had come early. Jules had a cast on his right foot. He looked up with a smile as though anticipating the therapist's inquiry. The therapist greeted him. Jules was very warm in his response. The therapist inquired about his foot. Jules told him "it's healing all right" and that the cast would be coming off in another week. He said he fractured the ankle of his right foot, but felt "much better now." He could get around. The therapist said he was glad to see him back. While the therapist was talking with Jules, Macy, Leonard, and Donald entered the room. The boys took seats and grew silent. The therapist allowed the silence to continue for some time. Donald got up to get water from the washroom for the coffee, and he put it on the electric stove. The silence continued.

After about five minutes Louis spoke up, saying that when a boy named Morton returned to his cottage, "he's going to get the shit kicked out of him." Macy seconded this by saying, "The boys in the cottage warned Morton not to run away and warned him that if he runs away all the boys in the cottage will lose a trip." Since Morton did not heed the warning, several boys, including Macy and Louis, were going to "jack him up" (grab him and beat him up). Louis, shaking his fist, demonstrated how he was going to "beat on Morton's face." Richard, who lived in the same cottage, said that he was "sore as hell" at Morton, too, because now the boys would be denied the trip. The cottage parents had warned all the boys, he said, that if any boy ran away, the trip would be canceled. In response to a question Macy confirmed that this had actually happened, the boys had "lost trips before" because someone in the cottage ran away just before a scheduled trip.

Louis and Macy took turns in describing how they were going to "stomp" Morton and "break his ribs" for running away. Richard, on the other hand, did not speak of beatings. He was more concerned with how unfair the cottage parents were for not taking the other boys, who did not run away, on a trip. However, the anger appeared to be directed toward Morton, and none of it at the cottage parents, who were punishing the group as a means of control. From what the boys said, it would appear that the cottage parents were actually provoking runaways, because just before every trip they announced that should one of them run away, the trip would be called off.

The therapist suggested the possibility that Morton, by running away under these circumstances, was actually inviting a beating, that he wanted to be beaten, and asked whether if this were the case beating him up would do any good. (The therapist raised the question because he knew Morton to be masochistic.) This statement seemed to have no meaning to the boys, for Macy and Louis continued talking about "using their fists" on Morton. This topic ended and silence again set in. Louis and Macy looked very angry, but said no more. Louis broke the silence by repeating that he was going to get all the boys in the cottage to beat up Morton, and that would teach him a lesson. "He'll never run away again and mess things up for the others."

The therapist wondered whether using fists settled anything. Louis: "It sure does. He won't run away." Taking his cue from Macy, Louis said, "He won't run away again after I'm finished with him." The therapist wondered where "this business of using the fists was learned as a way of settling issues. There was no response to this for a while; then Louis said: "My father and mother used to jack me up. They'd grab ahold of me and while my mother held me, my father used to punch me in the face and then in the stomach." The faint smile that played on his face as he began to say this disappeared before he finished his statement. The therapist asked how he felt when this happened to him. Louis: "It did me a lot of good. I learned what I can't do. I didn't want to get my ass kicked in all the time by my parents." Macy: "My father would never beat me; he'd talk to me. But my mother, she used to grab ahold of me and bang me on the head." Jules: "My father knocked me out unconscious twice."

Richard started to describe how when he did "something bad" he knew that his mother would hit him, but he was never sure about his father. "My father used to let a lot of things slip by. He wouldn't hit me all the time. Then, sometimes I did some little things and then my father would get so goddamn mad, he'd just haul off and slam me with his fists. Then when I would begin to cry, he couldn't stand my crying, so then he'd start slapping me in the face, saying I was a sissy for crying. When my father used to hit me I used to cover my face. I didn't want my father to see the tears in my eyes; then I knew my father was going to beat me more. My father—he's a nice guy, but I never know when he's going to hit." Donald: "Yeah, it probably did you a lot of good. At least it taught you not to do bad things." Richard: "Yeah, it did me a lot of good. I would have gotten in trouble if I didn't get beatings."

The therapist asked whether getting beatings really saved anybody in this room from getting into trouble. The response seemed almost a unanimous chorus of yes. Only Leonard remained silent. The therapist assumed a slightly sarcastic tone when he said that the beatings did so much good that here everybody was at Children's Village now. Donald, pugnaciously: "What do you mean?" Richard: "Yeah, what do you mean? It did me a lot of good. I could have gotten into a lot of trouble if I didn't get beatings." Somewhat abstractedly, and detaching the discussions from the boys' own experiences, the therapist said that it had been found statistically that more boys "get into trouble" who have a history of beatings than those who were not beaten so much. "In fact," he said, "we have found that sometimes boys get into trouble as a way of getting even because of how they feel about these beatings." (Note that he said "beatings" and not "fathers.") Jules picked this up and said: "I didn't mind getting beatings. I didn't feel any way about it. I thought my father was doing me a favor by keeping me out of trouble."

Richard, however, reacted to the therapist's statement about boys getting into trouble as a reaction to getting beatings and asked the therapist how he knew about this. The latter told him that as part of his job he came to know a lot about what had happened to the boys at the Village, and one thing that was true of all of them was that there was almost always a history of getting beatings, and most of these boys acted the way they did because of how they felt about being beaten. Donald: "You did the intake on me, didn't you? Do you know anything about my background?" The therapist said that he did. Challengingly, Donald wanted the therapist to tell something about his background. The therapist said that he could not reveal this information in the presence of others. (It will be recalled that precisely the same situation occurred in session ten.) Donald: "I'm going to see if you really know anything about me. Do you know anything I ever did on the outside before I got to the Village?" Therapist: "Yes." Donald: "I give you permission to tell us one thing I did." Therapist: "I know that you were once found in a car that didn't belong to you." Donald, with a sheepish smile on his face: "That's right. Maybe someday, Mr. Ellery, you can *see me alone and explain to me what makes me do some of the crazy things I used to do* that got me here, not only got me here, but sometimes *I do crazy things when I'm already here.*" The therapist agreed, but indicated at the same time that this was exactly the purpose of the group, namely, to find out what got the boys into the difficulties that led to their being sent to the Village.

At this point Donald said to the therapist: "Mr. Ellery, if your son got into trouble wouldn't you kick the shit out of him? In fact, if one day you got a letter in the mail saying that your boy has got to come to Children's Village, I bet you would grab ahold of him and beat his butt. Ain't that so?" Richard immediately stepped in and said: "Yeah, what would you do if you saw your son getting into trouble? Wouldn't you feel like killing him?" The therapist calmly responded by saying that if he found his son was getting into trouble he would want to sit down and talk with him and find out what was bothering him. Donald (with a look of complete disbelief on his face): "You would sit down and talk with your boy?" Therapist: "I would." Donald: "Well, why would you want to talk with him?" Therapist: "I would want to find out that maybe there was something I was doing that was upsetting my son and maybe this was getting him into trouble. Maybe when I was coming home nights and my boy wanted me to talk to him, maybe I was kind of short-tempered with him and I wasn't really listening to what he was telling me. Maybe he was getting into trouble to get some attention from me." Donald: "I know a lot of boys that get into trouble to get attention from their parents." Macy: "Sure, there are lots of boys who do that but their parents don't know any better. Their parents aren't educated, so their kids get into trouble and then the parents got to come down to the police station and get their kids out of trouble. In he meantime, this is the way their kids get all the attention." Richard added: "Parents always think that by beating their kids they are helping them, but they ain't helping them. They are just making them sore."

Macy: "Mr. Ellery, why is it at the Village they never put brothers in the same cottage?" This gave the therapist an opportunity to introduce the boys to the concept of "sibling rivalry," explaining that "sometimes siblings, or brothers and sisters, will fight with one another to get attention from the parents, each one feeling that the other is getting more attention, and this continues even when the parents aren't around." Richard: "That's the story of me and my sister. When I was smaller my sister was always getting all the fuckin' attention. My sister really used to use this. You know what she would do? She used to watch me like a hawk. When she would see me doing something wrong, right away she would run and tell my mother and before I knew it, my mother was beating me up. I used to be so goddamn angry at my mother—and then my father, you should see what he used to do to me! I told you how he used to punch me out." Richard then proceeded to narrate how on occasion his father would be good to him by letting him drink whiskey. The therapist commented that Richard must be somewhat confused. At times his father beat him up for minor infractions and at other times he offered him whiskey to drink.

Louis was becoming increasingly agitated. He rose, left the room, and did not return. It was now about 8:10. Jules used the excuse that he had to go back to the cottage to do a chore he had left undone and went out. As soon as Jules and Louis left, Richard changed seats, taking one next to the therapist, and said: "There's something I never told anybody before, but it bothers me and it bothers me every time I go home for a week end. My father never knew how I injured my thumb." (He showed the therapist the thumb of his right hand. There were stitches at the base of it.) "About two years ago, me and a bunch of boys went into the Consolidated Edison Building. We broke in. We were fuckin' around and then we started to throw things around and I put my fist through a window. They had to take me to a hospital and stitch me up. When my father came to the hospital, I told him that I got this in the school yard on a broken Coca-Cola bottle. I've never really told my father what happened. When I go home for week ends, I want to tell my father but I'm afraid. He's liable to start beating on me."

Donald ran over and impetuously said to Richard: "Look, I've got to talk to Mr. Ellery, will you shut up for a minute, Richard?" Richard remained quiet. Donald asked the therapist, "Did you hear what happened to me the other night?" (He was referring to his intoxication.) The therapist told Donald that he had. Donald: "I'd like to tell you about it 'cause it's been on my mind." He then said that he had gone to bed that night and was awakened later in the evening by a "couple of boys" who had stolen several bottles of Canadian Club from a supervisor's apartment. He tried to go back to sleep, but the noise in the room prevented him from falling asleep, so he decided to stay up and had several drinks with the boys. The cottage parents, if they were around, seemed to pretend they did not hear them, because nobody came down to the dormitory when all this noise was going on. After a number of drinks, one of the boys began to laugh "hysterically." Donald was infected by the laughter and he, too, began to laugh "hysterically." One of the boys in the room put his fist through a window. Donald said: "This went to my head. I didn't know what I was doing and I started to put my fist through every fuckin' window I could grab ahold of. I went from one end to the other, just smashing my fist through the windows. I didn't know what got into me. Then Mr. B. and Mr. T. tried to revive me. I was mad at them. I was yelling and cursing the Village—a stinkin' place, how you always have to go to the gym, the rotten school—but after they kind of revived me I felt very sorry for what happened and I told them so."

Macy to Donald: "You could have killed yourself that way." Donald: "That's what worries me. I realize I did a very stupid thing. I don't know what got into me." The therapist pursued this thought, pointing out the consequences of drinking liquor and his real concern that Donald could have injured himself, explaining about the artery in the wrist and how he could have severed the artery with consequent paralysis of the arm or bleeding to death. Donald: "The rotten thing is that I wanted to go home and they were planning to let me go. Now, I'm sure they're going to think twice about it." Therapist: "You know, this sounds familiar. You told me a number of times that just when something nice is about to happen to you, you do something to kind of louse it up."

Donald: "I was thinking about the same thing, Mr. Ellery. Every time something is all set for me, something happens to me, and then I always worry about what is going to happen to me after I do it. I didn't want to drink the liquor. *I was going to control myself* but with all the noise in the room and everybody inviting me to take a drink I couldn't control myself, and now I know I fucked myself up pretty good. I guess I was pretty angry at the Village for not giving me a week end when I was supposed to have one." Therapist: "I can understand your being angry at the Village, but who did you really take your anger out on?" Donald immediately perceived the meaning of this. He quickly said: "I know. I took it out on myself. *I hurt myself. I didn't hurt anybody else.*"

Since it was now 8:30 the therapist said to Donald that this was an important subject and he should talk about it further. Perhaps he could do this at the next session. Donald agreed to do it.

As the therapist left the building, Richard, who had obviously waited for him, ran up behind him and said, "I want to tell you about this business about my father and my thumb." He then explained in detail how his thumb was "practically hanging," about the stitches, the injections "to kill the pain"; and, though this happened two years ago, he still couldn't tell his father about what happened, but it kept bothering him. The therapist asked Richard what it was that made it so hard for him to tell his father about it. Richard: "You got to know my father. If I tell him, then he'll smack me for holding out on him. After all it's two years ago since this happened. Then he'll scream to me, 'What else are you holding out on me?' and he'll slap me again. Maybe he won't, but I just can't go up to him and tell him about this, but it keeps bothering me." The therapist told Richard that he understood his struggle and maybe "next week we could get into this further, and find out what you could do about it." Richard: "Okay, that's a good idea." The therapist proceeded toward his car. Richard yelled out: "Take care of yourself going home tonight, Mr. Ellery. See you next week!"

COMMENT

This session could be characterized as one of awakening of the superego. Having introduced the "rule of the jungle" (mass beating of Morton), which was followed up by the therapist's exploration of the inefficacy of physical violence and the evocation by association of the punitive paternal image, the appearance of guilt was facilitated: in Donald, his car-stealing, his irrational behavior, and his drinking bout; in

Richard, his deceiving his father; and vicariously in the others present. For Louis and Jules the mirroring of fathers in the negative light was beyond their readiness, and they reacted to it by flight. As it was, the boys who participated had gone a long way in ridding themselves of the "family romance" and thus freeing themselves of its limiting ties. This theme was a continuation of the transitory and perfunctory bouts with the subject (family) in preceding sessions. Now it had finally been dealt with openly, which was an important step.

The therapist's wholesome and humanistic description of how he would deal with a wayward son touched off positive feelings toward him that further cemented the transference. Among the peripheral outcomes in this interview was Donald's increased self-awareness and his expressed desire to be helped to bring himself under control, the introduction of the idea of sibling rivalry, and the thoughts about violence, which would form a good part of future discussions.

One can only speculate whether the discussion in the preceding session propelled the boys into the phallic (genital) stage from oral and anal stages as was reflected in their attitudes toward food and the use of "foul" language. Entering the phallic phase may have generated new self-awareness and power, making it possible for the boys to view their fathers more realistically. As the dependencies were decreased, the defenses were also minimized and greater objectivity (ego) made its appearance. A new type of identity seemed to be emerging in some of the boys, as well as an awakening of the superego.

Session Twenty-Seven

The preceding week there had been no meeting because of a holiday. The boys all arrived at the same time and on time. Richard and Louis were the first to appear, but Donald, Michael, and Leonard were not far behind. Macy and Jules appeared a few seconds later. Donald brought his portable radio, which he kept going quietly almost throughout the session.

There were just a few moments of silence after the boys sat down in a circle, and then Richard launched into his story of what had happened to him one evening. He said he had "an epileptic fit." Gesturing with his arms and moving his legs he described how he had lapsed into a fit as he was lying in bed. He did not really remember what had happened and asked Louis to explain details. It developed that Louis slept next to Richard and he confirmed everything Richard had said, agreeing that it was an "epileptic fit." Richard took up the narration of how the boys in the dormitory held him down; one boy stuck something in his mouth so that he would not bite his tongue, and the others covered him with blankets. Richard claimed that his fit lasted about ten minutes. It was interesting to note that, in describing this episode, Richard appeared very calm and displayed no anxiety. The cottage parents were off the night of this episode and the "relief man" was not aware of what had occurred. (The following day the therapist checked this story with the nurse, who told him that Richard had been taken to a general hospital for examination and had another appointment two weeks later for an electroencephalogram. No adult witnessed what Richard had described to her, and she guided herself by what the boys had told her.)

Richard appeared to enjoy the attention he was receiving through his story. In response to the therapist's question Richard indicated that he was not worried about it at all. He saw no reason for worrying. Jules interrupted to say that sometimes adults worry about things that kids don't worry about. He gave as an example of this the time when he had a fractured ankle. He hadn't really worried about it. It didn't bother him too much; he got around. Richard, however, would not let Jules continue. He said that at about the age of five years he had had a seizure similar to the one he described but had never experienced one since, until just the other night. He firmly repeated that he himself had absolutely no memory of what had happened, being guided entirely by what the boys in his dormitory told him. Richard stopped talking. This seemed to break the spell. Donald and Michael rose and proceeded to prepare coffee. The two worked together quietly. The therapist, addressing Richard, said that medication was now available that could control these attacks. However, Richard was getting quite a kick out of the incident.

During Richard's recital, Louis had been a rather attentive listener. In fact, he appeared much more serious and much calmer than he had been in the preceding sessions. He now began to describe "accidents" that had occurred to a number of youngsters at the Village. One boy, for example, was hit by a car; another fell from a truck and was injured rather severely. He continued this for a considerable time. Donald, who had returned to his seat after distributing coffee to everyone, joined this discussion, describing a number of his cousins who had been hurt at one time or another. The therapist addressed himself rather directly to this by saying that it sounded as though sometimes people went out of their way to get hurt. Louis immediately understood the meaning of this remark and said, "That's the way some of the guys around here can get away from doing work, by getting hurt and lying in the hospital." Donald smiled and said, "I once did that, but I wasn't really hurt." The therapist asked Donald if he would like to tell the group more about what had happened, but he did not appear ready for this. Richard looked very knowing.

After a few minutes of silence, Jules said, "People can get sick when they want to sometimes." Donald: "What do you mean?" Jules: "I don't know. They just can get sick." He then told about a boy at the Village who, on occasion, in order to "get away with things" started getting sick. Jules: "The funny thing is he really does get sick. He looks sick." The therapist tried to get a discussion going of how this occurred. Noting that the boys were attentive, he briefly told them how children discovered that one of the ways of getting what they wanted was by being ill. Also, sometimes when children felt they did not get enough attention, they might resort to using illness as a means of getting it. Some grown-ups used illness for the same ends, as a "leftover" from their childhoods. The boys were very interested and attentive as the therapist spoke.

Richard was the first to comment. He said: "*Maybe that's why I always run down to the hospital. I remember as a kid I used to try to goof off at home, but my mother was always on my ass. She would never let me rest. When I didn't want to go to school, I sometimes would pretend I was sick and then she'd throw me out of the house.*" Donald: "I didn't goof off so much when I was a kid. I just would steal and rob." This sparked Richard to speak of a boy he knew who landed in Sing Sing because he used a gun in a robbery. This seemed to excite Louis, who at once joined in the conversation describing a "couple of guys" he knew who had used guns and robbed. One of these guys actually shot and wounded the proprietor of a store. Donald interrupted to say: "Shit, that's one thing I never did in my life. I never used a gun and I never will. Maybe if they hadn't sent me to Children's Village I'd finally have used a gun, but now that I'm at the Village I realize how pretty close I came to hurting some people."

Richard said that he, too, felt that way. He often thought of the times that he was tempted to get a gun and stage a "stick-up." Maybe if he hadn't been sent to the Village, this eventually would have happened. The therapist commented that the boys could now see some positive values resulting from their being at the Village; they seemed to feel different about some things than when they first came. *Richard, Louis, and Donald agreed that they did.* There was a general nodding of heads at this.

Silence ensued for a short while, and this time the therapist took the initiative. He said, addressing all the boys: "This business of shooting off guns, carrying guns, is kind of interesting. Do you know what gets people to do this?" There was a negative shaking of heads. The therapist then said that often people do such things when they do not admit to themselves that they are angry about things. This he tied up with an earlier discussion of psychosomatic illnesses (which was not recorded), such as heart disease and ulcers, caused by angry feelings that remained unexpressed and unrecognized. Very often a person who used a gun did so out of anger about things that had happened to him years before but which he might not be aware of, and although anger was a very natural thing for everybody, what was most important was being aware and knowing that you were angry. For if this was not the case, then anger would be expressed against yourself by getting sick or against others by explosive acts. "In the group we try to talk about our angry feelings so that explosions won't happen." Donald was most interested in the psychosomatic phenomena. He said, "That's what happens when the unconscious part of your brain is really controlling your body." Richard agreed, saying: "That's right, remember we once talked that way about having dreams. The unconscious part of you—boy, it sure gives you a rough time sometimes. One thing that always used to get me angry, but really angry, was my sister."

Now Richard again launched into a long, detailed tirade against his sister, who was always "snitching" on him, and told how his parents were always siding with the sister. Unlike in the past when he remained impassive as he talked, *now his face registered rage*, which grew in intensity as he proceeded with his complaints. His rage was reflected in his high-pitched voice and the rigidity of his body as well as in his face. The attention of all the boys was riveted on him. Louis sat by very quietly listening to what Richard was saying as the latter described incident after incident of his sister's provocations that led him to do something against her; then she would run to report him to the parents. He never "got a chance to answer." He was hit first, questioned later. He then turned to describing the situation at home now when he went on his periodic visits. When his sister tried the same thing, his father sided with him. (Later, however, he stated that even today, when he went home for a week end, the sister invariably attempted to provoke him into doing something for which the father still yelled at him, rather than at the sister who was the real culprit.) While Richard was talking, Louis spoke up: "I got a younger sister, too. She gives me a hard time like yours." Richard would not be interrupted. Donald now sailed in: "Hey, Dickie, when you're finished talking, I got something to say to Mr. Ellery." Richard did not listen to Donald either, and continued his harangue, narrating one incident after another.

When Richard stopped to catch his breath, the therapist said that he was getting a pretty raw deal, and asked why the parents let his sister get away with all this. Richard: "They don't. Now they protect me." (Obviously this was not the fact, for his feelings in the matter were unmistakably conveyed in his voice, which was colored by extreme anger, and in his face.) Donald jumped in at this point and said to Richard: "Look, you've talked enough. I got something I got to talk over with Mr. Ellery." Donald went over to Leonard and asked him if he would exchange seats with him, since Leonard was sitting next to the therapist and Donald had been sitting across the room. Leonard agreed and the two exchanged seats. Jules, in the meantime, had got up and announced that he was heading back to the cottage. It was now about eight o'clock. Louis walked over to Macy and Michael and got the two boys involved in a discussion. This did not appear to be one of his usual efforts at disrupting the current discussion; it was rather a continuation of it. Louis was describing his troubles with his sister at home and a mother who would never punish her. Michael, being an interested listener, made occasional comments which the therapist could not hear. It seemed like a constructive conversation among three boys conducted in a mature manner.

Donald, on the other hand, complained to the therapist about his brother. He set out by describing a little brother who always "tagged" after him when he was home and that he felt very angry about it. When he left the Village, he would buy presents for this little brother of his. He was going to take him out, for he owed him a lot. Donald continued in this vein for quite some time. Finally the therapist asked what it was that he owed this little brother, and why? Donald stopped to think for a moment and then said: "When I used to be home I used to want to go out with my friends. My little brother used to want to tag along. I didn't want him with me. In fact I used to be angry with him; then I'd feel stupid. Here I am a big boy feeling angry at a little boy! I'd feel rotten, like I was doing my brother dirty. I wanted to take him along and yet I didn't want to take him along. Now I'm up at the Village and I can't do things for him and I feel I hurt him."

Richard and Leonard, who were sitting near the therapist while the others had their private circle, were listening to Donald's plaint. Richard (to Donald): "You don't have to feel so bad." Donald: "I know. Up in my head I know I don't have to feel so bad, but that's why I'm talking about it, because I really do feel bad." He turned to the therapist and asked him if it was "natural" for a grown boy not to want his little brother around when he went out with his friends. The therapist said that it was entirely natural. Donald: "But my parents didn't act like it was natural. They used to tell me to take him along and then I'd have to say to my parents, 'I don't want to.'" Therapist: "What happened then?" Donald: "I'm not sure. They wouldn't yell at me but they kind of acted like I was doing something wrong. Sometimes they'd just give me the 'silent treatment' and not say anything to me. That's why I feel kind of mixed up now." There was a brief silence, and then Donald: "I don't like being angry at my parents." He dropped this subject as quickly as he raised it, as if it were "hot coal," and went back to repeating how he did not want his younger brother around, but on the other hand, felt responsible for him as his big brother. When he left, he said, he would take presents for this little boy.

Leonard had got up and started to walk out of the room, and this more or less served as a signal to end the session, but the boys seemed reluctant to leave. There was a lot of milling around. Donald and Michael were industriously cleaning up the room, making sure there were no coffee stains on any of the tables. The therapist walked out slowly with Richard. As soon as the therapist left, Michael ran and closed the door. He and Donald remained inside. Michael yelled: "Don't worry about us, Mr. Ellery. We want to do something. Please don't come in for a while. We'll call you." The therapist and Richard stood outside as the latter, now that he had the therapist alone away from Donald, was describing how he had gone out with a cousin of his and his uncle blamed him for getting the cousin "in trouble." Richard had been so angry he picked up a chair and attempted "to go after" the uncle. Richard was describing this in a very rapid, somewhat garbled fashion. Donald soon opened the door and invited the therapist to come in. He said: "But walk in slowly. Give us a chance to get out of the building and then look at the blackboard" (which was part of the furnishings in the room). Donald, Michael, and Richard scampered down the stairs. On the blackboard, the following was written in chalk:

> Mr. Ellery, this is a token from the boys. We appreciate everything that you have done for us. We enjoy having you for our group discussion leader. God Bless You.
> The Boys

COMMENT

Again we find a considerable drop in the intensity of the content in this session after the high pitch the weeks before. It was as though the boys could not bear up emotionally under the strain. Richard's narration of his seizure (if it was a seizure), set off Louis (as could be expected) into a harangue about violence and mutilations, which with the help of the therapist was turned into a valid therapeutic consideration of psychogenic illnesses. It is both interesting and significant that Richard, who was hypochondriacal, applied it to himself.

Several of the boys turned to discussing their relations with and reactions to siblings, a subject that was rarely touched on before and then perfunctorily. Having bared the behavior of their parents the week before, they now entered into a more meaningful exploration of this other area of their family lives. The cathartic value of this is quite obvious, for it naturally would lead to a more normal attitude and better relations as feelings are unloaded, and greater objectivity would be achieved as a result. Though this should occur later in therapy, it already has taken root in Donald's guilt arising from his rejection of his younger brother. However, the mention of his anger toward his parents caused him to retreat at once from this threat area. He still had a great deal to work through to face that part of himself.

No emotional profundity, beyond Richard's rage, was uncovered in this session. It had been a very useful one nonetheless, though only on the ego level. Much psychological literacy was acquired, such as use of illness as a secondary gain, sources of hypertension, the significance of guns as a reaction formation to a sense of weakness (a subject we had explored before in our supervisory conferences), and the recognition of the utility of conscious awareness as against the sway of the unconscious. It is thus that maturity is advanced, through para-analytic psychotherapy, and it is of *utmost* importance to adolescents, especially when character disorders are involved.

The positive transference toward the therapist was again displaced upon the institution. Thus the boys would be disposed to utilize the growth opportunities it offered, which they resisted and criticized before. When Donald spoke of using a gun he now did not say he "would get in trouble," but "may have hurt people" (allotropic direction). The concentration on "accidents" was counterphobic. Richard exhibited affects which were new in his development. The boys were freer in destroying "family romance" as they talked about siblings and parents; they were on their way toward separation from the family and thus greater personality maturity. Again Donald's superego asserted itself, now in relation to his little brother

In this and in several preceding sessions the therapist concentrated on extending the boys' *psychological literacy*. In this session it occurred much more directly. More important even than the content was the changed tone and psychological curiosity displayed in this session, which reflected the boys' expanding maturity.

Session Twenty-Eight

The session began with Donald asking the therapist whether he knew when the group would be discontinued (for the summer). Jules informed him that the "other clubs" ended in June and asked the therapist to confirm it. The latter indicated that although the other clubs terminated in June for the summer vacation, he would be notified by the Club Department when this group would end. Michael said, "Would you please ask the Club Department to let us go on all year?" Louis chimed in: "That's right, if the Club Department will let us come here all year, we'll come. This is a good group and I like coming." Macy nodded his head in agreement. The therapist asked the boys what they felt they were getting out of the group. Michael: "We talk a lot about a lot of interesting things. We don't talk about these things anywhere else." Donald: "It's nice to sit and talk. I never thought I would like it, but I like talking here." Louis said: "I feel like Don. Even though I fuck around sometimes, I learned a lot of interesting things, like how come we got into trouble and how come things bother us sometimes, and what makes them bother us."

While Donald was taking part in the conversation, he was simultaneously writing a letter. When he had finished writing, he asked the therapist for a stamp. Donald offered to pay for it, but had only a dollar bill, and the therapist told him: "It's all right. You can owe it to me." Donald then asked the therapist to mail the letter for him. "You can read the letter first if you're worried that there is something in it I shouldn't be sending out of the Village," he said, but the therapist told him that he "trusted" him. Donald placed the letter in the envelope and sealed it. "Thanks a lot, Mr. Ellery. I want you to know that there is nothing in this letter that I couldn't ordinarily send out, but I want it to get out tonight." The letter was addressed to a boy who had been at the Village and whose name the therapist knew.

This transaction ended the discussion recorded above. Michael said to Louis: "Maybe we ought to talk about Russia tonight and the possible war." Donald: "Yeah, they may start dropping bombs on us, especially after that airplane was caught over Russia." Louis: "Mr. Ellery, do you think there's going to be a war?" It seemed that the boys were anxious about it and the therapist spoke about it in specific terms. He told them that as far as he knew, it did not seem that there would be a war, because nobody could win it and there would be no point to it. Louis: "I hope you're right, because that's the way I want to feel." By this time Donald had walked over to the other end of the room and began to prepare coffee. Macy joined him in this. Macy asked the therapist if he would like a cup, and the therapist said yes.

The discussion continued between Michael and Louis. They recognized that there were "evil people on earth." There might be a war and the worst thing that could happen was that babies would get killed. Michael said: "It's terrible when babies get killed, but at least they can go to heaven. Nobody else can go to heaven." Louis challenged him on this and a discussion arose between the two as to whether adults can ever get to heaven, with Michael holding that only babies can, never adults. Louis averred that adults do have a chance if they're "good." Michael's response was, "Well there's no point talking about me, 'cause I'm bad and I ain't got a chance to get into heaven." The therapist noted that Michael had said the same thing in previous sessions, and addressing him said, "You must think of yourself as a very bad guy." Michael at first denied it, but then said: "Well I did a lot of bad things in my life." Jules: "That doesn't mean you have to be bad all your life, or that you're just going to get punished for what you did in the past." Michael could not accept this and defended his position on religious grounds. The therapist stated that all boys, at "a certain stage of growing up," feel that they are bad, because people told it to them when they were children. He drew a parallel from some girls who, though pretty, think that they are ugly-looking because as children they had been told that they were ugly. Even though they looked pretty to everyone else, they went on feeling the way they were told when they were children. This became part of "their mind." Here the therapist used the term "incorporation." Richard at once picked it up and asked what "incorporation" meant. The therapist gave him, and the other boys, a functional definition. "You take on what people think of you and you begin to think of yourself the way other people say you are." Jules's response to this was: "That's me. If people tell me I'm bad, I'm going to be bad. What's the good of being good?"

Michael, to prove his position, focused on the fact that he was sent to the Village because he was bad. He was being punished and that proved he was bad. Donald agreed that he, too, was here to be punished, otherwise "they would have let me go home long ago." He had learned his lesson, he said. The therapist responded to this by directly taking up with the boys the question whether the Village was for punishment. Is that all they really say in the Village? Was punishment all they got out of the Village? Louis said he could have gone to W———— and would have been out in eight months. The therapist agreed, but also pointed out that 75 per cent of the boys who go to W———— get into trouble again after they leave and wondered if there was something else they could get out of the Village. "For instance," he said, "here you are in this group. Is this punishment?" Don: "No, this isn't punishment. This is where we get help." Jules: "Yeah, we can talk here. It doesn't feel like somebody's pushing us here." The therapist commented that most of the boys who came here were poor in reading. Maybe nobody had improved in reading. To this there was an immediate reaction. Don: "What do you mean nobody's improved in reading? I can read two years better than when I came." Michael: "You should see me read! I'm a pretty good reader now." The therapist then reminded the boys that in the preceding sessions someone had said that if he hadn't been sent to the Village, he might have killed somebody.

This set off a discussion about zip guns and how they are made. Don initiated it by describing the zip guns he had made from cigarette lighters. Louis said he had a number of friends who carried zip guns on them, and from this he proceeded to question why boys needed to make or carry guns. Richard playfully poked Jules's shoulder. Louis to Richard: "Cut it out, will you! What are you trying to do, break it [the discussion] up?" Richard sat back and grew quiet. Louis then said, "Okay, Mr. Ellery, tell us why do boys make guns?" The therapist described how when you felt kind of weak and small, you had to build up a front, and you felt stronger when you had a gun. It made you feel bigger. This explanation, because of its importance at this point, and because the boys appeared interested, was extended for quite a while. Toward the end, the therapist told a short story by a French writer about a small child, kidnaped by gypsies, who had a smile carved into his face and went through life with a constant smile. Everybody thought he was very happy, but anyone who looked into his eyes could see sadness. "So, even when people carry guns, act big, or get drunk, you have to try to understand what gets them this way. Sometimes when people try to act big and push others around, it really shows that they don't feel so big inside." Macy responded to this by saying: "I bet that's why I'm so tempted to drink. When I got problems I don't want to think about them so I drink. Then I can't stop myself." Louis: "Mr. Ellery just told you why you do it."

Donald asked whether the therapist felt he, Donald, would be able "to make it outside." Therapist: "I think I trust you, Don." Donald: "I wish you were my social worker. My social worker doesn't trust me." Louis: "Yeah, how can we get you for a social worker?" Therapist: "It seems one of the important things to you fellows is to get people to trust you." Jules: "Every time I'm bad and I do something wrong, I know it's because somebody didn't trust me, and when they don't trust me I can't stop myself from getting into trouble." The therapist commented, "Maybe what was more important was not whether others trusted you, but how did you feel about trusting yourselves?" Michael's response to this was, "That's one thing I can't do." The therapist asked him what he meant, and he said: "Well it's like this. If I were in a room all night with a pretty girl, I might want to screw her, I might feel tempted. Like if there was a thousand dollars lying around on a table and it belonged to somebody I didn't know and I was alone I might be tempted to put it in my pocket." Louis added: "I might be tempted, too."

Richard suddenly turned to the therapist: "How would you feel, Mr. Ellery?" Therapist: "I think I'd be tempted too, but the difference between being a child and a grown-up is that when you're a child, you do things and don't give a damn about what happens. Most fellows would be tempted if they were alone with a girl all night, but when you grow up, you get concerned as to what might happen if you act on your temptation. Temptation is very natural, but before you act you kind of begin to wonder whether if you're going to do it, will it get you into trouble with others or with yourself and how you're going to feel about it." Donald: "In other words, *it's okay to be tempted, but it's another thing to act because you're tempted.* I want to ask you something personal, Mr. Ellery. Were you ever mad at your mother and father?" The therapist said that he was. Donald repeated: "You were." Therapist: "Yes Don, I was." Donald: "When I was a little boy, I must have been about eight years old, I used to see my mother and father fight. One night I saw my mother kick my father in the balls and he grabbed my mother and was going to choke her. I grabbed a knife and I warned my father that I'd kill him. As soon as I said it, I dropped the knife. I went to my room and I cried, and I hated myself." Donald then turned to the therapist and asked: "You know what I mean?"

Therapist: "Don, it can be pretty frightening for a kid to see his parents fight." Donald: "Right. What always used to go through my mind when I saw my parents fight was that maybe they would divorce one another and then they wouldn't have me around any more and I wouldn't have a father and a mother. My father used to start a lot of fights, but my mother wasn't always right. For instance, my father would come home; he'd give my mother the pay and she would say, 'You owe me another ten dollars.' My father would say: 'I spent the ten dollars. I worked hard; I had a couple of drinks with the boys.' My mother would call my father a 'son of a bitch.' I don't blame my father for having a couple of drinks. He works, he earns the money. He's got a right to a couple of drinks if he wants them. But I remember when my mother used to go to bars and she'd call me up (sometimes at three and four o'clock in the morning) and I'd have to go get her. I had to take money from the house, grab a cab, go get my mother, and bring her home. I didn't mind. I liked being with my mother. I felt I was kind of protecting my mother." Donald cast his eyes downward. They were wet.

Every boy sat motionless. The therapist, as well, was deeply moved by Donald's communication, but more so by his manner and his feelings. The therapist asked: "Don were those the only feelings you had?" Donald: "What do you mean, Mr. Ellery?" Therapist: "I bet you were ashamed, too." Donald lowered his eyes again and said: "I was so fuckin' ashamed I wanted to kill my mother. I used to have to bring her into the building and here were all the people standing around and I was ashamed to go in with her because I didn't want them to see the way my mother looked. One night I felt like murdering my mother but as soon as I thought about it, I went into my room, I locked the door, and laid down and cried and said, 'God forgive me.' I shouldn't have those thoughts."

Deeply moved, Donald rose and asked Michael if he wanted a cup of coffee. Jules had walked out of the room. It was now about ten after eight. The therapist commented to Donald, "I bet it was pretty hard not to have thoughts like that." Donald turned around at the coffee table, where he had been standing with his back to the therapist and said, "Did you ever feel like murdering your parents?" Therapist: "When I was a kid, I used to be angry enough to feel like killing them." Louis: "Sounds like all the times I used to see my mother drunk," but he did not continue. Donald: "I used to think that I was going to get punished. In fact, once I fell down and bloodied my nose and this happened about the time I thought those things and I always thought I got my nose bloody because of my thoughts." The therapist indicated that you couldn't help having such thoughts when you were angry and ashamed, and it didn't mean your parents were going to die because sometimes you might want them to, or feel like hurting them. Donald walked over to where the therapist sat and said: "I can remember now all the nights I wished my parents would die, then maybe I wouldn't have to listen to their fights. But they don't fight any more; they get along okay now. It was just when I was a kid that this happened." Michael: "I never wanted my parents to die." Macy: "What makes you so different? I don't want my parents to die, but I used to get pretty pissed off when they'd have fights and I was alone in the house."

Leonard's face was flushed a deep red, although he had not said a word throughout the session. He sat almost as if he were riveted to the chair. Michael stood up and said, "All right fellows, let's clean up." Donald: "I'll help you tonight." Michael and Donald cleaned up. The other boys said they were going back to the cottages. The therapist remained behind with the two boys. Donald came over and admired the shoes the therapist was wearing and wanted to know how much they cost. He then said: "I'm glad you were a kid, too, once, Mr. Ellery. You're a social worker now, aren't you?" The therapist said he was. Michael to Donald: "Knock it off; he's not going to be your social worker."

COMMENT

The significance of this session cannot escape the experienced psychotherapist. Now the group was a truly "working group." It was devoid of resistance and was characterized by psychological literacy, ease in self-confrontation, growing awareness of self and feelings (inversion), and guilt—all of which spell identity.

The recognition of the naturalness of temptation and the difference between temptation and acting on it is of pivotal importance in the rehabilitation of "acting-out" youth and constitutes a long stride toward ego integration and maturity.

Since language is an important key to personality, note need be taken of the increased frequency with which the therapist's name had been used by the boys in recent sessions and their including him in their discussions. The latter signifies the growing positive transference toward the adult, their trust in him, and the discovery that an adult can be of value as a guide and confidant. Such attitudes are later redirected toward other adults in the lives of patients by the mechanism of "transference in reverse."

Session Twenty-Nine

Before the session began, Richard told the therapist in a low voice that his transition conference[4] had been held recently, and wanted to know whether the therapist attended it. Donald overheard this and said to Richard, "How many times does he [therapist] have to tell you that he does not go to conferences?" Richard said that his caseworker told him that it was agreed at the conference that he was getting along "pretty well" at the Village. However, the coach reported that he did not get along too well in recreational activities. Richard clarified this, saying that what the coach said was that he did not participate enough in sports activities. Louis said to Richard, "You don't have to participate in sports if you don't want to." This ended this conversation.

The boys experienced difficulty in beginning the session. To some extent this could be attributed to the warmth and humidity of the room. There was a rather languorous feeling in the group and everybody looked somewhat sleepy. The therapist, too, found himself tempted to close his eyes and just drowse. After about five minutes of silence, during which the boys just sat around drowsily, the therapist commented that it was kind of quiet tonight; didn't anyone have anything he would like to talk about? No one stirred.

Michael asked whether it would be possible for the group to take a trip sometime during the summer either "to a show or roller skating or both." The consensus among the boys was that they would like to have

4. Predischarge conference of clinic and milieu staff.

a trip like that. The therapist said he would consult the Club Department about it. Michael asked to have also a picnic on the trip. Donald spoke up, saying that he was asking too much; he ought to be glad if the group just got a chance to go to a show and Michael should not make a "hog" out of himself.

Michael asked whether the therapist had checked with the Club Department as to when the group sessions would end. The therapist told him that he had discussed it and was told that although, in the past, groups had ended in June, this group would continue through July since the boys requested it. Michael nodded his head, smiling with satisfaction. Leonard, in a somewhat lazy fashion, repeated the last part of the sentence, to the effect that the group would be continuing in July but did not express an opinion one way or another. Louis, however, said that he would be here and was glad that they were continuing. Donald said: "Looks like I won't be here. I was told that I'm going to be leaving in June and there's a job waiting for me, so I guess I won't be with you boys." Then, with a smile: "When I get out of here, I'll come up and visit you." Louis countered this: "Maybe you won't have to bother. We'll come and visit you in Sing Sing." Richard broke into loud laughter and, turning to the therapist, asked: "What's the toughest prison to get out of?" Before the therapist could answer, Louis said, "Sing Sing." Richard thought it was Alcatraz and asked the therapist to confirm it, which he did.

A discussion now ensued among Richard, Louis, and Donald. Donald was preparing coffee for the group, which made it necessary for him to talk with his back turned to the group. He said that he had heard that they had man-eating sharks around Alcatraz, and that nobody ever escaped from there. Richard had heard that twelve guys once escaped but that they were never found, so maybe they were eaten by the sharks. Louis giggled at this: "I hope the sharks had indigestion." Leonard spoke up to say that he, too, had heard that Alcatraz was a tough prison to get out of, and somewhat perfunctorily Jules agreed. The only boys who did not contribute to the conversation were Macy and Michael. Michael was busy picking his nose.

There was a brief silence during which all looked rather lethargic. The therapist commented that "from the discussion, it appears that you boys are kind of concerned about prisons." Louis immediately got up, walked over to the window, and climbed onto the fire escape. He remained there a few seconds when Donald called him back, telling him: "Don't make an idiot out of yourself. Come back and sit like the rest of us." Richard: "I'm not worried about prison. I'm not going to land up there." Leonard (to Richard): "How can you be so sure?" Richard flushed. Louis now said: "That guy Willie Sutton, he was a pretty smart guy. In fact, he was a genius. He got out of so many prisons and they couldn't find him." Macy agreed that Willie Sutton was a genius. Louis looked to the therapist to confirm that he, too, thought that Willie Sutton was a genius. The therapist: "I don't quite see how Willie Sutton was such a genius. In his whole life he's been out of prison for only ten years. So how can he possibly be a genius?" Louis, looking as if he were trying to break off the discussion, said, "Okay, so he's a dope." Macy still persisted that Willie Sutton was a genius. Richard, Donald, and Michael got into a discussion as to who was the current outstanding criminal. They didn't seem to know. The therapist again raised the point that the group was very curious about criminals and prisons. This was met by a silence which lasted some seconds and which was finally broken by Donald.

Donald said to Richard: "Tell Mr. Ellery about that dream you had." Richard: "No, it was stupid." Donald: "So what; all dreams are stupid, but we talk about them. Go ahead, tell Mr. Ellery." Richard turned to the therapist and said: "The other night I dreamed that I went home and while I was home, in my dream, I met this boy. We went out together and we got caught stealing. Next thing I knew I dreamed I was in front of the judge and the judge sent me away to prison for five years." Michael immediately said: "You know dreams can come true sometimes." Richard: "I know. That's why I was so scared in the dream." The therapist asked him what he was scared of. Richard did not answer, and changed the subject by telling the therapist how he and "a couple of boys" in his cottage were planning to take a trip with the cottage father. He continued a short while, but realizing what he was doing, returned to his dream. He said, "By the way, what kind of dream was that?" Donald interrupted and said, "You haven't told Mr. Ellery the whole dream like you told me." Richard: "The rest of it was too stupid. I'm not going to tell it here." Donald: "Go ahead. Tell it. Other boys told dreams." Richard grew very uncomfortable. Jules rose, and though it was only 7:40, began to leave the room, saying to the therapist that he was going back to the cottage to finish working on a locker box. With this he left.

Donald continued badgering Richard: "Tell Mr. Ellery about the dream. Nobody is going to laugh." Richard kept shaking his head and said nothing. He then spoke up and asked: "Like I asked you, Mr. Ellery. What did that dream mean? What do you call that kind of a dream?" The therapist told Richard that since he did not know the rest of the dream, he could not be sure, but from what Richard had told him it sounded like he had what is called an anxiety dream. Macy wanted to know what that meant. The therapist explained anxiety in terms of feeling tense because you're afraid of something that is going to happen and you're not quite sure what. Macy picked it up and said, "You mean like waiting for something and you don't know when it's going to happen, right?" The therapist agreed, and then turning to Richard said, "Maybe you're not too sure about what's going to happen to you when you get out and what it's going to be like on the outside." Donald: "None of us are worried about that." Therapist: "It would be pretty natural to be kind of worried about what it's going to be like once you leave the Village—the kind of job you're going to get; about going to school; whether you'll be able to control yourselves on the outside." Macy: "I worry about what's going to happen when I go back to school. I haven't been in a regular school in a long time. I don't know if I'll be able to make it in a regular school. Shit, if teachers pick on me or if I can't do the work I might do the same thing I did before—play hooky—and then I'll be in trouble again." Richard was listening very attentively. Louis to Richard: "I'll bet you feel the same way." Richard: "Well, if I dreamed that, I guess I do feel that way. I'm not going to have the same friends when I get out. In fact when I go to my old neighborhood now, I don't see any of my old friends. It's going to mean making new friends and I'm not sure yet the kind of guys I'm going to meet and if I'm going to get into trouble again. I don't want to spend the rest of my life in prisons. I always had the feeling *it's something like fate*, something is going to happen." The therapist encouraged Richard to tell the group more about these feelings, but Richard did not seem ready to continue.

Following a brief silence, the therapist said, "Maybe what we're talking about is this feeling of what's going to happen to each of us and whether we can ever amount to much." Richard's eyes seemed to open wide, as if this had struck a chord. Leonard, sitting back in his chair, said offhandedly: "That's what we talked about before, isn't it? About the feeling of amounting to anything." The therapist agreed and reminded the boys that in preceding sessions they had talked about the feelings people can "carry around" when people don't have faith in us, especially when we're small and we're told by different people that we're not so good. Michael was now reclining on the couch where he had been sitting. He lifted one leg, placed it against the wall, and said: "That's what I remember used to happen to me. My mother always told me that when I grow up I won't be much. She always told me when I was a kid that I can't do anything right. Every time I tried to do something my mother would never say it was good. She'd always show me a better way of doing it, and then tell me if I was smarter, I would have known how to do it." He fell silent, but encouraged by the therapist, he said, "Let me think," and soon added: "Like when I was a kid I remember once my mother asked me to move a couch. I didn't move it right. I was supposed to put it a certain way against the wall. I can't remember everything. Oh, yeah, I was supposed to put it against the wall, and I didn't put it the way my mother wanted me to do it. Then she came over and pushed me away and told me, 'you never get anything right.' "

While Michael was talking Louis got up and went out on to the fire escape again. No one said anything, however. Michael continued. "There were a lot of other things that happened, but I can't remember now." Therapist: "Do you still believe what your mother said to you?" Michael: "I do. She was grown; I was a kid. She knew more about me than I did. I guess she was right. I still get the feeling that I'm going to get into trouble, that things can't come out right. Sometimes I tell myself I'm not going to get in trouble, but I really don't believe it. Oh yeah, I remember now. I remember how I used to steal. I was always with a bunch of guys and we'd go out and we'd steal and I was a pretty good crook."

With this, Michael stopped talking. There was dead silence in the room. The therapist said to Michael, "I guess you proved that you could do things after all." Slowly Michael raised himself from the couch, looked at the therapist with a grin, and said: "That's pretty good. I never thought of that. I know I proved to the guys I was with that I could steal. Nobody ever called me chicken. *Maybe I was also proving something to my mother.*"

As usual Richard got into the act and proceeded to talk about the times he stole because he was called chicken. He had learned that being called chicken "only gets you into trouble if you try to prove you're not." Donald: "Me, too. Don't think anybody's going to call me chicken and get me into trouble like they used to." Leonard spoke up: "That's the favorite way guys get other guys into trouble. All they got to do is to say chicken and boys take them up on it." Leonard then spoke about car races he had heard about. Two guys heading at one another in cars, playing "chicken." The therapist used this to repeat the thought that one of the signs of being grown up was not having to prove yourself by taking chances with one's own and other people's lives. In fact, one of the differences between a grown person and a baby was that when you grow up you realize that *you hurt not only yourself but you hurt other people as well*, and that this is good enough reason for not getting involved when guys yell chicken.

Richard, Donald, and Michael entered into a lively discussion of their adventures and escapades they had gotten into because someone yelled chicken at them, and they had to prove they weren't. Richard: "Look what happened to us. We proved we weren't chicken but now we're chickens at Children's Village, and I ain't going to be cooped up behind a cage the rest of my life because somebody calls me chicken."

Louis returned from the fire escape and eagerly joined the discussion, drawing Michael away and starting a conversation with him. Donald wanted to know whether when the therapist was younger he had ever gotten into a fight? The therapist told him on one occasion he had. It was with a friend because of loss of tempers, but "we shook hands after the fight." Louis spoke up and asked whether the therapist ever got into a "street rumble." The therapist said that he had not. Donald: "Not even once?" Therapist: "No. I didn't do it because I felt it was wrong. Also, I didn't want to hurt anybody and I didn't want to get hurt." Leonard, with a smile: "You must have used your head when you were a kid."

Time was up and Louis indicated that he was ready to go back to the cottage. After a brief silence the session ended.

As the group was leaving, Richard trailed behind the therapist and, just as they got outside the building, came up and said: "I want to tell you the rest of the dream. Maybe you can help me figure out why I had it." He dreamed that he was on the home visit, that he and his uncle and a gangster whom he had never seen before were driving in a brand new Cadillac. They came up to the Village and stopped at his cottage. Richard got out with a machine gun in his hand and shot down his cottage mother and a couple of the boys he didn't like. The uncle and the gangster sat in the car waiting for him. Richard looked very tense as he described this dream and said, "What do you think that means, Mr. Ellery?" Therapist: "Richard, when you feel angry, what do you do?" He said, "I keep it in." Therapist: "That's what I thought, Richard. Okay you keep it in. How do you think it comes out?" Richard: "You mean in the dream?" Therapist: "It sounds that way, doesn't it?" He said, "Yeah." The therapist assured Richard that this did not mean that he would ever do it just because he dreamed about it. Richard then said, "That's why it's good to talk about what you feel, right?" The therapist agreed. With this Richard said: "I'll be at the meeting next week, early, Mr. Ellery. I'll see you then."

COMMENT

The boys again found it difficult to get started after the self-revealing session of the previous week, but they were nowhere near as blocked as they had been in the past on similar occasions. The mention of Sing Sing (a state prison for adult criminals) in a conversational fashion set the boys off on a discussion of prisons and criminals. This could be a manifestation either of identification or a counterphobic maneuver. However, as the conversation proceeded it proved to be a part of the feeling of doom, a theme that preoccupied the boys, though it may have been latent. Tracing it to its origin as was done in the interview—carrying out the wish of the parents—is of utmost therapeutic efficacy for these acting-out boys.

The ensuing discussion about criminals proved too anxiety provoking, and Donald diverted it to a dream by Richard, but instead of providing a channel of escape, the dream led again to the theme of doom as an unconscious expectation of disaster. ("It's something like fate.")

Michael's recall of the origin of his feelings of defeat and failure to his childhood (when he was six years old) was in a sense a startling piece of recall catharsis; such is the acme of the analytic therapy process. Also, his recognition that his delinquencies were a way of disproving his mother's evaluation of him denoted an impressive level of insight and psychological literacy.

As already indicated, the question of the term "chicken" among contemporary youth, and especially among delinquents, and its being a source of dangerous and antisocial acting out had been under consideration by us in our supervision conferences. We anticipated that it would constitute in the future a major topic of therapy. The therapist was, therefore, prepared to explain the boy's response to the challenge it constituted and that it was a sign of a deep-rooted feeling of weakness and insecurity, that a person who was really sure of himself would not do anything foolish just by being challenged in this manner. In the present session the subject was only touched upon. Later it received full treatment. Note also that for the second time the concept of hurting others rather than just oneself, allotropy, was introduced.

Richard's phobic reaction to the killing episode in his dream was most significant. It revealed his homicidal preoccupations as being close to his consciousness and his fear that it could represent reality. The therapist correctly used the encounter with Richard after the session to dissipate his fears and to explain the source of his dream.

Note need be taken of the fact that once the discussion got started, it sustained itself on a high level of therapeutic communication and affect in contrast to the comparative resistivity and diffusion in earlier sessions. The defenses are down, self-confrontation is now easier, and the ego and the unconscious are in communication (intrapersonal communication).[5] However, a few of the boys had still not reached these levels, as witness Jules's and Louis's reactions to the mounting anxiety.

NOTE

In view of the fact that Jules persisted in leaving the group sessions before the set time of 8:30 P.M., and had left the preceding session twenty minutes earlier, we decided to deal with it, since it no longer was an incident or a trend: it had now become a pattern. At first we considered enlisting the cottage parents' cooperation. We planned to ask

5. Slavson. *A Textbook of Analytic Group Psychotherapy* (New York: In-   ternational Universities Press, 1964), pp. 261–264.

them to call Jules's attention whenever he returned early that he was scheduled to be still at the group. This could have been done, however, only if we were assured that they would not reveal to Jules that imposing of this regulation was instigated by the group therapist. Inquiry suggested that the cottage parents would unquestionably have shifted the responsibility upon the therapist. Therefore, we turned to the cottage life supervisor involved to deal with this matter. The supervisor indicated that there was no way of preventing these particular cottage parents from reflecting the situation upon the therapist, but that he would attempt to work it out with the cottage parents. Jules stayed through the next session and there was no indication that he was aware the therapist had had anything to do with whatever pressures were applied by the cottage parents.

It was also considered advisable in our supervision conference that Richard be told privately that the therapist had been thinking about his dream and came to the conclusion that though the dream he had narrated the previous week disturbed him, it actually meant that he was getting better because he was now able to dream about his feelings, which showed that his feelings were coming into awareness, and that this was the way feelings got worked out. Some day he would find that they no longer bothered him the way they did now. However, because Richard was with Michael when the next session ended and both boys joined the therapist as he walked to his auto, the therapist was unable to carry out this plan.

Session Thirty

The therapist came five minutes ahead of time. He had previously set up the chairs, put water for the coffee to boil, and placed the cigarettes in the urn. When he entered, Richard, Louis, Michael, and Leonard were already in the room. Within a few minutes Jules came. The therapist noticed that *all* the cigarettes had been removed. Michael turned to Louis and asked him for a cigarette. Louis gave Michael two cigarettes. Donald, looking quite angry, now came in. His first words were: "I better get my cigarettes tonight or somebody is going to suffer." There was no response, except for a smirk on Louis's face. Donald walked over to Louis and demanded cigarettes. Louis: "I don't have any. I only have two for myself." Donald, still very angry, turned away. It was obvious that his anger was not related to what had happened with the cigarettes. Anger was spread over his face even when he came in.

Donald sat down near the table where he usually prepared coffee, looking glum. After a brief period of silence, Michael asked the therapist whether he had discussed the trip with the Club Department. The therapist said he had and that they would try to arrange for a Radio City show and perhaps dinner. Michael smiled and asked when the trip would take place. The therapist said it would probably be set either for around the end of June or sometime in July. Donald asked the therapist to try to arrange the trip for June since he was leaving at the end of June. The therapist said he would relay this request to the Club Department. Macy thanked the therapist and said: "I'm glad you asked the Club Department for us, Mr. Ellery. There must be some awfully nice people in the Club Department if they're going to let us have the trip." Louis: "That goes for me too. If we all go together, we'll have a good time." Michael got out of his seat and offered to get a cup of coffee for the therapist. This served as a signal for Macy to bring the therapist crackers. Macy and Michael prepared and distributed the coffee very quietly and expeditiously. Donald did not participate, as he usually did, although he had given some directions to both Macy and Michael as to how much coffee and sugar to put into each cup.

Donald still looked enraged. He had a can opener in his hand and was poking the table with it. The therapist commented, "You look kind of upset, Don." Donald: "I'm not mad." Therapist: "That's funny. Do you know that you look mad?" Louis: "You sure do. What's pissing you off tonight?" Donald said nothing for a few seconds, then: "You guys are a bunch of fuckers. I'll fix your wagon. Next time I'll be the first boy here. I'll get all the cigarettes." No one said anything, but the therapist noticed that the boys looked somewhat sheepish, as if they were guilty about the division of cigarettes in which Donald was left out. The therapist said, "You know we've been together for quite some time now, yet it seems that there is still a problem about the cigarettes." Michael: "This is the first time it's happened in a long time, Mr. Ellery. When we started off, remember, the boys used to run up and grab cigarettes, and then we didn't do it any more. Now we're starting to do it again. That ain't the way we should act." Louis: "Like I always said, you want something, you got to be first." The therapist asked Louis about the need "to get there first," but Louis did not respond. The therapist reminded the boys that in a preceding session they had talked about trusting one another and said, "I wonder if there is anything in what we talked about that has to do with what has happened tonight." Michael: "I always get the feeling that if you try to trust somebody else they are going to grab things from you, so when I come up I take my cigarettes. I'm not going to wait for the other guys to take cigarettes and then I don't have any." Michael would not continue further. The therapist, however, pursued the topic: "Maybe you have reason to feel this way," but Michael only smiled sheepishly. Therapist: "I wonder what it feels like to you fellows when I trust you and don't stand watch over the cigarettes."

Practically every boy's face expressed embarrassment and guilt. The therapist was disconcerted with the effect his statement had had on the group and therefore did not continue. After a few minutes of silence, Michael said, "We always talk about people not trusting us, and yet you trust us and look what we did." Michael: "Maybe there ought to be another way of giving out the cigarettes." Michael immediately picked this up and said: "I got an idea, boys. Every week a different boy will be left in charge of giving out the cigarettes. Each one will take a turn; that way nobody is going to get dished out." Leonard: "That's okay with me; that's a good idea." Donald did not say anything. Louis: "If you other guys want it, I'll go along." Michael asked the therapist if it was all right with him. Therapist: "Fellows, this is your group and these are your cigarettes and you are free to decide how you want to handle it." Michael: "Then it's settled; right Jules?" Jules nodded, saying that he would go along with the plan.

This matter settled, Macy initiated a discussion as to which restaurant the group should choose on their trip. He wanted a specific Italian restaurant. Michael said he had had enough Italian food, maybe they ought to eat in a Chinese restaurant. Donald, still looking angry, finally spoke up: "Yeah, that's a good idea. Let's eat at a Chinese restaurant. We can order shrimp, egg rolls, things like that." The fact that Donald was suggesting a menu even before the group definitely decided on the restaurant brought some giggling. Leonard said he wanted to eat in a Chinese restaurant. Louis turned to the therapist and asked him what other types of restaurants there were. The therapist mentioned a few such as Indian, Japanese, Armenian. Louis wanted to know what one can eat in an Armenian restaurant. The therapist mentioned shish kebab and Richard took over. He told Louis what shish kebab was. The idea did not seem to appeal to the latter. No decision was made at this time about where to eat.

Now Donald rose from his seat and climbed out onto the fire escape. He found an arrow that had been shot into the roof of the cottage, removed it, and brought it into the room to show it to the boys. Then he returned to the fire escape. Louis and Richard joined him there. Richard soon came back and took a seat next to the therapist. He asked him whether it was true that rock is compressed sand. The therapist told him that it was just the opposite: Sand is rock that was worn away, "eroded." Jules immediately joined the conversation, which led to the question of how old the universe is, and how long man has been on the earth. Jules, noticing the commotion between Louis and Donald on the fire escape, said, "Those two jerks are going to kill themselves." The therapist called out to the boys on the fire escape: "How about joining us, fellows?" Donald and Louis at once came in. Louis: "Were you worried about us, Mr. Ellery?" Therapist: "I don't want to see you get hurt." The therapist wanted to raise with Donald the question of his need to get out onto the fire escape, but because of the ongoing discussion with the other boys, which now centered about evolution, he refrained from doing it. Louis immediately joined in.

Richard appeared to have a considerable knowledge of basic biology. Jules asked how it was that there were animals, men, and insects. When the therapist asked him to explain his question a little further, he wondered what determined whether "a growing thing" would be a man or an animal or a tree or an insect. This led into the subject of chromosomes. Jules appeared to know that man originally came from the sea, that there must have been a fish that was able to breathe air and that gradually evolved into something else.

Donald was impassively holding the arrow he had recovered from the roof. He brought it over to the therapist to show it to him. The therapist examined it. Donald pretended to have the bow and said: "If I had fifty pounds thrust on this arrow I could put it right through the wall. I bet I could even put it right through you, Mr. Ellery." This sparked Louis into a discussion of arrows and guns and he began to talk about jet fighter planes shooting at one another. Louis: "There are big fucking cannons. One shell and they can blow up half of New York." As soon as Louis said this the discussion ended. There was silence for a few moments. Then the therapist said: "It sounds as though you boys want to talk about shooting. If you want to, go right ahead." Louis sat up in his seat and said, "You really mean we can talk about it?" and he proceeded to do so, but instead of talking about shooting, he raised numerous questions about the various ranks in the army and navy.

Macy said that one of his teachers had told his class that he, the teacher, had been a spy during the last war. Richard: "Keep your mouth shut. The teacher told us not to talk about it." The therapist was now bombarded by a host of questions from Donald, Michael, Richard, and Leonard as to the differences among the various ranks of the army, the navy, and the marines. Fortunately the therapist knew the answers to most of the questions. What he did not know, Richard filled in. A dispute arose as to whether a "second louie" was a higher rank than a first. The therapist said that a first lieutenant was the higher rank. Macy and Louis disputed this, with Louis saying that a second lieutenant was higher, because second is higher than first. Richard settled this by saying in a rather dogmatic way, "a first lieutenant is a higher rank."

Louis: "Mr. Ellery, did you ever hear of the ship *Titanic?*" The therapist said that he had. Louis wanted the therapist to tell the boys about the *Titanic* and how it sank. For the rest of the evening the group sat around talking about the *Titanic* and the burning of the *Normandie*. Louis then asked: "Do you know of any other ships that sank? Tell us." Although the therapist knew that Louis was fascinated with the violent aspects of the events, he was at a loss as to how to explore it with him. In addition, the therapist felt that the boys would have resented the diversion, since, throughout the narration of the catastrophes and anguish, the boys had sat in absolute silence. Fascination was reflected from every boy's face. Donald, however, rose and said he was leaving (at 8:10 P.M.). The therapist turned to him and said that there was something bothering him. Donald: "No, nothing is bothering me. You're not mad at me are you, Mr. Ellery?" The therapist said that he was not mad, but maybe Donald was. Donald sat down and with a grin on his face said, "No, I'm not mad." A few seconds later he asked: "Is it okay if I leave now?" Therapist: "Don, maybe you ought to decide that." Louis to Donald: "Come on, why don't you sit down and tell us what's eating you." Donald: "I told you, nothing's eating me," and he then got up and left the room.

There now followed a very interesting and actually a rather enjoyable period as Macy started a discussion about the differences between West and East Germany. Macy questioned as to who were the leaders of West Germany and East Germany. Michael: "I'm glad I'm not in East Germany. When they catch a crook there they send him to Siberia. In this country they don't do that; they give you a chance to go to Children's Village." Louis wanted to know whether it was true that under Communism, when they caught a boy stealing they hanged him. The therapist told him that this was not so; that even in Russia they knew that when a boy stole, he did it because something bothered him. Macy said that he had seen on TV once what the Germans did in concentration camps. With real feeling, Macy, Louis, Leonard, and Jules got into a discussion of how Hitler was crazy for killing Jews. They never bothered him. Macy: "When I saw that thing on television, I couldn't eat. All those bodies just lying in big graves. How can somebody go so crazy and pick on people who didn't do anybody any harm? Did you hear what the Israelis did? They found this guy who killed six million Jews." Louis: "I'm glad, I hope they hang him up by his balls." Richard: "Hitler must have been crazy." Louis: "I'm glad I live in a country where that could never happen." Michael: "Why don't they tell us more about Communism? Maybe they got things that we could learn from." Louis: "Maybe they're afraid to tell us about communism. We might like it."

It was now about 8:35 and the group decided to end.

COMMENT

This was again a resistive session, probably because the boys feared to continue with the revelations of the preceding two sessions. The therapist did well not to press them, so that their defenses would not be threatened. However, what was significant was that the boys turned from talking about criminals and prisoners, as in the past, to *armed forces* personnel—a change in identification. Their interests in violence moved from personal to impersonal violence, such as sinking of steamers and liquidation of Jews.

Note the more mature and higher level of the content of the conversation as compared with the earlier sessions. The boys had definitely emerged from the pregenital into the phallic stage (interests in science, social problems, and the like). This progressive personality development was also shown by the use of superior language and their choice of words, as compared to earlier sessions.

The therapist's possession of relevant information greatly helped the continuation in this trend as well as his status as an identification model.

Session Thirty-One

Macy was the only tardy boy. He came about five minutes late. Michael took over the responsibility for distributing cigarettes. He handled the situation very quietly and there was no evidence of anxiety on the part of any member of the group on this account. His problem, since there were twenty cigarettes for seven boys, was how to divide them evenly. The therapist, therefore, contributed one, making the number divisible by seven.

Donald at once proceeded to prepare coffee. He spent at least ten minutes pouring the hot water into cups and distributing them. Louis meanwhile announced that he would have to leave early. His cottage mother told him that he had to finish his chore of cleaning. Should he fail in this, he would not be permitted to go on a week-end home visit. The therapist asked Louis if there were no other time in which he would be allowed to do his chore, but Louis insisted that he would have none. (Nonetheless, he did not leave until 8:30 with the other boys.)

After a few moments of seeming restlessness, which took the form of shuffling feet as in the early sessions and general lethargy, Richard began by asking how he could break the nail-biting habit. The therapist suggested that perhaps understanding why people bite nails could be useful. Macy, who had just walked in, said that nail-biting came from "nerves" and that, when he took an examination in school, he bit his nails. Louis said he knew a boy who used to take his shoes and socks off and bite his toenails. This brought on considerable laughter when Donald asked Jules if Donald could try on his shoes. Donald became the center of attention as he tried on Jules's shoes, which drew comments from Louis, such as: "Why don't you give Jules back his shoes? They're too small for you and you're going to break them." Richard said to Donald, "You're going to get corns on your feet from wearing shoes that don't fit you." Donald: "I know, I know. I'm not going to wear them out of here. I just want to see them, maybe I'll buy a pair like this." (Jules's shoes were a new pair and had very pointed toes.) Michael said to Donald: "You're acting like a jackass," at which Donald's face flushed with anger. He turned to Michael and exclaimed: "Mind your own business!" Michael said, "You think you can make me?" Donald did not respond. Following this interchange a short interval of silence ensued.

The therapist reminded the boys that they had begun to discuss nail-biting. No response. Louis settled back into his chair, assuming almost a prone position, and closed his eyes. The therapist asked: "What is going on tonight? Here we were talking about nail-biting, what causes nail-biting, and somebody had mentioned nervousness. Now there seems to be a lot of distraction. What is the matter?" The reaction to this was delayed for some time before Louis said, "We don't have much to talk about tonight." Michael did not leave this unchallenged. He said, "We always find things to talk about here." Richard picked this up and said to Leonard, "Didn't you once tell me that nail-biting shows that you're nervous?" Leonard: "That's right, I did." Again silence ensued and then Leonard said, "You know what 'nervous' is, don't you?" Macy: "Yeah. It's like when you're tight—you can't sit still—you're worried about something."

Donald left the room, supposedly to go to the washroom, but came back shortly. Now Louis got up and went to the washroom. He, too, returned within a few minutes. During this interval of about three minutes' duration, nothing was said. The therapist pursued: "I wondered if you fellows ever thought of nail-biting as a way of getting out anger." Louis, who had returned from the washroom: "Yeah, I know a cat in the Village who, when he gets angry, he takes a bite out of people." Richard laughed at this and said he knew somebody when he was in E——— Hospital who used to bite when he got angry. All the boys on the ward were afraid of him. One guy "socked him in the teeth and he didn't bite any more after that." Macy: "That's like when you're angry sometimes you eat a lot of food." Richard: "I used to do that when I used to get sore. I used to find myself putting stuff in my mouth."

Richard fell silent after this rather significant remark and the therapist asked him whether he had thought further on the matter. "Can you tell us the times when this would happen, Richard?" Richard said that he didn't remember and said nothing more. Again there was silence, which persisted for about two minutes. Finally, the therapist said to the boys: "You know, fellows, I get the feeling that maybe there is something that's happened that you might want to tell me about. Every time we start to talk about something, such as anger, nail-biting, and so on, I note that a big silence follows and I kind of wonder what this is all about." Jules now said: "Nothing has happened, Mr. Ellery. We'd tell you if it did." Donald: "I don't know of anything that's happened." Louis appeared interested. This was conveyed by a changed expression on his face. His rather bland quality was now replaced by an expression of interest, as if he were just awakened. However, the silence was not broken.

The therapist decided on a *tour de force:* "You know in the past sessions we were talking about the feeling of anger and what happens with it, especially when it's bottled up. For instance, did you boys know that sometimes when anger is bottled up you can feel kind of depressed? You know what I mean by depressed, this feeling of being blue and alone?" Macy: "Yeah, I know that feeling. I didn't have it, but I know guys who do have feelings like that. They sit quietly and they don't talk and they look kind of sad as if they are missing something." Richard: "Sometimes I kind of think to myself, what's the point of life? You're born; you live to about sixty years old, you never get to eternity—there is no such thing—and if you know you're going to die, what's the point of all this living?" Leonard immediately countered this: "That's not the way to look at it. You can't help dying, but while you're alive, you just got to live and make the best of things. Shit, if I thought only about dying I couldn't even enjoy anything, so I don't think about it." Richard: "You got a point there."

The therapist asked Richard if he would talk a bit more about this feeling and he said: "I don't know. I just think this way sometimes. If you could live forever, that's a different story. But to just live and kind of know that sometime you got to die—I don't know, it's just a funny feeling." Louis took over and got Donald and Michael involved in a discussion of killings, but instead of talking of individual murders as he had in the past, he talked of armies fighting one another.

Macy, being on the periphery said: "What do you guys think about what Khrushchev said about Eisenhower? Maybe there is going to be a war." Michael: "Yeah that guy is trying to blame Eisenhower for all the trouble in the world. He thinks he's a smart aleck." And after a moment he added: "If there's going to be a war I want to be home. Don't you worry about wars and dying, Mr. Ellery?" The therapist said: "I'm concerned, but I don't spend my time worrying about it." Jules: "Well, you would if you were in our shoes, because we're away from our families. If they start dropping atom bombs on us then we may die, and we won't be near our families when we die. At least you'll be home with your wife and kids." The therapist commented, "There seems to be a lot of concern with dying here. Maybe we ought to talk about it tonight."

However, instead of continuing with the subject he himself had introduced, Richard turned to describing how well he swam and bragged how long he could stay under water. Donald at once picked this idea up and asked the therapist to time him while he held his breath. He held it for about thirty-five seconds. This now became a game, with every boy in the room asking the therapist to time him while he held his breath. After the first round, they asked for a second chance. They were now competing with one another as to the length of time each could control his breathing. Instead of participating in this game, the therapist gave the boys his watch so that they could time themselves. Richard returned to the subject of swimming, but he soon introduced the subject of drowning and how if you were a lifeguard you could "save somebody" from drowning. Michael wanted to know what happened when one drowned. Louis told him the person got water in his lungs and sank and choked. Jules also joined in, describing various lifesaving methods. This he did very vividly, demonstrating by gestures as he was standing in front of the group. Donald then told about a friend of his who said to a boy, "I hope you drop dead." The next thing this boy fell off a pier and Donald jumped into the water and saved him. Donald described how he asked God to forgive his friend for wishing the boy dead.

Louis described another kind of death, death through sinking into quicksand. Jules asked the therapist what quicksand was, and the latter described it for him. However, in doing this, he also tried to bring the discussion back to what Donald had just said, namely, the belief that wishing somebody should die might make it happen. No response was forthcoming from the boys, and the therapist dropped the subject. Louis began to describe how he swam, and illustrated with his arms and hands how he struggled to stay above water. The therapist decided to try a different tack, and said, "You know this discussion reminds me of what we talked about a few weeks ago." Richard: "What do you mean?" Therapist: "You remember what we were talking about, the problem of 'keeping your head above water.' How you get along on the outside without drowning or getting snowed under with troubles?" Michael related to this immediately and spontaneously: "That's right, we were going to talk about that again. I thought about it, in fact, and I'm sure when I get back I'm not going to get into any more trouble." Macy said: "So am I, but I'm still not sure I'm not going to get into trouble in school. If any of the teachers give me a hard time, I'm not going to take it; I'm

428   *The Demonstration Group*

just going to play hooky. But I don't want to play hooky because I know that's going to cause trouble." Richard: "When boys leave the Village, some of them do good and some of them get in trouble. How come some of them have to get in more trouble after they had so much trouble and got into the Village?" Therapist: "Sometimes boys feel they are always going to head into trouble, and this feeling that they carry with them pushes them into it. It's like the thing you're afraid of you often bring about."

Donald: "Well, when I stole a car the guy didn't even press charges. He was a real nice guy." Therapist to Donald: "Was he really such a nice guy?" Donald: "What do you mean?" Michael: "Suppose you hurt somebody, would that guy have done you a favor by not getting you into trouble with the cops?" Referring to what the therapist had just said, Richard asked, "You mean like Bill when he got into trouble?" (Bill was a former inmate who, after discharge from the Village, stole an automobile with a companion, raced at ninety miles an hour when pursued by the police, and crashed into a station wagon, killing a man, his wife, and their child.) The therapist commented: "We could talk about Bill because we could learn something from what happened to him. What made him do what he did?" Macy: "I'll bet that Bill *wanted to get into trouble again and get sent away.*" Donald: "I feel sorry for him; he was a nice guy. I'm sorry he went and got himself all messed up again. He's not going to get out of E——— for a long time."

Richard: "He must have been angry at something to do something crazy like racing in a car." Louis tried to veer the discussion away by describing what "the guy in the station wagon who was hit" might have done. Richard reminded him that when somebody is coming at you at ninety miles an hour, you just can't be so smart. Donald said: "Bill should have stepped on the brake and stopped the car." Therapist: "Don, you can't stop a car at ninety miles an hour on a dime. But is that the important point? The question really is what happened that got Bill in trouble again. Somebody here has raised the possibility of Bill being pretty sore, pissed off at something." This got the group into a discussion about anger and "not working out" anger. For instance, Leonard said: "Bill always acted like he was a nice guy. He was friendly, always smiling, but I'll bet he was so sore at everybody that he used to hide it." He turned to the therapist for confirmation of this, which he received. It was now about 8:22 P.M., and Jules got up, left the room, and did not return.

The discussion continued. Donald said that he was convinced he would never get in trouble again. Richard to Donald: "You sound all right now, but don't be so damned sure. Look what happened to Bill." Almost by way of summation, Macy said: "Yeah, Bill wanted to get into trouble again and he wanted to get into trouble because he was angry, and I bet he didn't feel right about being outside. I'll bet he wanted to come back to a place like Children's Village." Though Louis expressed sympathy for Bill, he did not seem to idolize him. Louis: "I'll bet Bill should have stáyed here another year." Donald: "That wouldn't have done any good. What the hell is the difference, he was outside?" The therapist asked Louis: "What do you think would have happened in another year?" Louis: "Maybe he wouldn't have had *to get even with everybody. He could have talked about these feelings instead of acting* like he knew it all, and everything was going all right." Donald: "Maybe. But I'm not so sure it would have happened." Donald was now quite agitated. He wiggled in his chair as the therapist tried to hold him to what he had just said. Donald responded evasively by saying: "It's just too bad about Bill. I wish he didn't get into trouble, because now he's got something to regret for the rest of his life."

The hour was now past the regular time for ending, and Richard said that he was going back to the cottage. With this the evening ended. However, as the therapist was leaving the building, Donald, Michael, and Richard were with him. Donald said on the way out: "I was thinking about what we were just talking about and I don't know how I'm going to stay out of trouble when I leave Children's Village. Like when I'm with friends, I know there is going to be trouble, but I don't know what to do." Richard: "Me too. Like I'm going to be with friends, they may be new friends or they may be the friends I had before I came to the Village. If they want to get into trouble, I'm not sure I'm not going to get into trouble with them." Therapist: "Look, boys, this is something very important and we ought to talk about it next week." Michael, Richard, and Donald nodded their heads. Therapist: "If you fellows don't bring it up next week, I'm going to bring it up." Michael: "That's a good idea. In case we forget, you remind us." The three boys walked with the therapist to his car and wished him a good night.

COMMENT

This session can be characterized doubly: It was a display of extensive psychological literacy and even insight, on the one hand, and one of reality orientation on the other.

In the first category fall such remarks as the relation of nail-biting and "nervousness," anger and eating, Bill's auto accident as a result of his anger and unconscious desire for punishment, and the validity of talking through as against acting upon one's anger. In the second category fall the preoccupation with future adjustment to school and to friends, means of evading repetition of past misdeeds, and fear of future entanglements. These, by and large, point in the direction of mature planning derived from recognition of the boys' selves and their life settings, spelling maturity and increased capacity for reality testing. The boys no longer rely on parents and caseworkers; they evaluate and plan on directing their lives on their own, rather than falling back on others. (Richard, for example, sought help for his "nail-biting habit.")

As the boys projected themselves into the future and foresaw nothing but disaster, the therapist pointed out this expectation. This subject had been discussed, in anticipation of its development, in our supervision conferences, namely, the principle of "self-fulfilling prophecy." This important attitudinal pattern that invites difficulty and disaster was thoroughly elaborated on with the boys much later in the course of treatment with eminent results, as later recorded at the appropriate juncture.

Richard's pessimistic view of life evoked Leonard's profound existential precept that one who was afraid of death could not enjoy life; and the growth of allotropic feelings was indicated by Richard's remark that when one was a lifeguard he could "save somebody." For a boy like Richard, compared with his predominant egotropic attitudes of the past, this is real progress.

Note the therapist's more assertive role as he pressed the boys into a discussion, albeit one that was acceptable to them and to which they responded, and his subtlety in withdrawing from the group's regressive activity (holding breath) by turning his watch over to them rather than himself keeping time for their "game." The significance of this competitive game is a subject for interesting speculation.

Session Thirty-Two

Donald and Michael arrived about four minutes after the session began. Prior to their arrival, Jules had asked the therapist in a rather offhand manner what the penalty was for killing someone. The therapist asked Jules what he meant. Jules said he wanted to kill Mr. T., his cottage father. Mr. T., Jules said, was always beating "boys' asses" even though they had done nothing to deserve it. He "loses his temper and kicks the ass of the boy who happens to be nearby." Richard told Jules that they'll send him to G——— (mental hospital). Jules: "I won't kill the guy, I'm just kidding. But I once shot a boy." The therapist asked Jules about it and he said he shot a boy in a gang fight. As soon as Donald and Michael walked in, Jules stopped talking. Donald asked who had the cigarettes. Jules got up, took the cigarettes out of the bag that contained the jar of coffee, and distributed them among the boys. This procedure went rather quietly, without any comment.

Donald then turned to the therapist and said, "Thanks a lot, Mr. Ellery, for the report you made on me." The therapist asked: "What do you mean, Don?" Donald said, "Mr. W. [caseworker] told me that you reported that I'm doing very well in the group." (No such report was made to anyone.) Donald then said: "I'm glad you told Mr. W. how good I'm doing in the group. You're a real pal." The therapist asked him whether this was what Mr. W. had really told him and Donald quietly said: "Maybe I'm not supposed to tell you. Look, don't talk to Mr. W. about it, but Mr. W. told me that you had said that I participate in the discussion and that I'm doing well. From what Mr. W. said, I thought you came to a conference on me and told everybody at the conference about it."[6] The therapist told Donald that he had not attended any conferences on the boys. Richard to Donald: "Are you bullshitting?" Donald looked insulted and said: "No, I'm not bullshitting. That's the truth. The God honest truth. Ask Mr. W. yourself, if you don't believe me. Mr. W. said I'm ready to go home and I'm going home. I can't wait to get the fuck out of here."

Michael interrupted to ask again about the trip and when it would be held. The therapist repeated that it would be at the end of June or in the beginning of July. The date would be set by the Club Department.[7] Donald said: "Well I hope it is before I get out of here. Mr. W. was talking to me and he said I was ready to go home. He also said that maybe I should stay, but he felt that if I stay I might get into a lot of trouble." Then, screwing up his face, he said: "I'm not sure what he told me. It was something like that. I'm all mixed up right now." Louis was spread out on the couch and closed his eyes as Donald continued: "All I know is that I better get the hell out of here. I'm not going to get into trouble when I get out of here."

Macy interrupted and said: "Mr. Ellery, I want to ask you something. Why does a person always want to sleep?" The therapist was caught between Donald and Macy, who each talked on a different subject; he decided to pursue Macy's question. He therefore asked Macy what he meant. Macy proceeded to say that he found himself "always sleepy." When he was in class he always felt like shutting his eyes. He wondered whether it meant that he needed a tonic and that he was undernourished. In response to a question, Macy told the therapist that he had had a medical examination recently and the doctor did not find anything wrong. (In an earlier session, Macy had mentioned that most of his

---

6. It should be noted that this caseworker was one of the two who did not support our project, as part of their own rather serious personality problems.

7. This was a tactical error, since the boys should have been asked to set the date.

"troubles" in the city were in the classroom.) The therapist, therefore, asked Macy where he seemed to have most of his difficulties before he came to the Village. Macy said it was "in class." Therapist: "Now you're telling me that when you sit in class you always feel like sleeping. You can't keep your eyes open. Do you think there is anything in this?" Macy: "I don't know, I can't figure it out." The therapist said that falling asleep or the inclination to sleep could stem from being bored, which might come from being unhappy in a situation or not feeling comfortable in it. Macy: "I don't know what's bothering me in the class, but you're right, it's the same like it was when I was on the outside."

Richard seemed to become quite giddy at this point. He turned to Leonard and tried to provoke him to laughing. Leonard resisted it. Donald fetched water and began to prepare coffee, but returned to his seat as Michael joined him. The therapist commented that the boys were getting somewhat restless. "In fact, one of you is almost asleep" (referring to Louis, who was now lying on the couch). Louis opened his eyes and sat up. He looked extremely sad. He said: "I'm sorry, Mr. Ellery, my head is hurting me. I got into a fight and lost." Louis looked very pathetic, as though he were about to cry. Macy said to him: "I warned you to stay away from that guy. I told you there was going to be a fight." The therapist asked Louis if he could tell what happened. Louis just said, "I got into a fight and I took the worst beating." Therapist: "I'm sorry you got hurt. You can't win all of the fights; but what started the fight, Louis?" Louis, looking very depressed, lay down again without answering.

A period of silence now set in, but the restlessness had stopped. Donald: "I was home last week end and was with my friends. My friends wanted to go out and beat up some Spanish boys. I was going to join them but, at the last minute, something told me I would get in trouble. I kept telling myself, 'Don't, don't, you're going to get into trouble.' You know what I did, Mr. Ellery? I walked away. I went home. I felt much better because I knew if I went with those guys and got into a fight I would land up in trouble and I might not see the Village again. I might end up in jail." Donald sat staring at the therapist, who said to him, "Don, it sounds like you really used a lot of self-control." Donald: "I did. I did, but I'm not going to tell Mr. W. about it." "Why not, Don?" "If I tell him then he'll say I'm not ready to leave the Village and maybe I'll have to stay more at the Village and I want to get out of here." "Don, I know you're talking about Mr. W., but what are your feelings about leaving the Village?"

Donald stood up, moved around the room with his hands in his pockets, and said: "Like I told you. I want to get the hell out of here. I don't know if I'm going to get into trouble. I can't give you a guarantee. I can't give anybody a guarantee. All I know is I want to get out.

I want to be with my folks this summer. I don't want to spend the summer here at Children's Village." Therapist: "I hear what you're saying, Don, but this business of self-control after you get out bothers you doesn't it?" "Aw shit," said Donald, "it don't bother me." Richard broke into laughter and Donald turned on him: "What's so funny?" Richard: "It don't bother you? But look the way you're carrying on!" Donald at once turned to putter with the coffee and handing out cookies.

Leonard looked at the therapist as if to indicate that he was aware of Donald's embarrassment.

When the cookies and coffee had been distributed, the therapist commented very quietly, "You know, fellows, I was just about to bet ten dollars that somebody would get up and start doing something with the coffee." Macy: "How did you know?" Therapist: "I knew because we just started to talk about something important." Donald laughed at this, came over, and sat down next to the therapist, and said, "Are you saying I'm not ready to leave the Village?" Therapist: "Don, honestly, what is it you feel about leaving the Village?" Donald began to talk about going back to his friends with whom he grew up, how difficult it was to leave these friends, even though he knew that sometimes they got into "trouble." Macy joined in, discussing how when he left, he'd have to go back to the friends he knew. Richard confirmed this for himself, saying: "I'm not going to leave guys I grew up with. They are my friends." The conversation continued for a while as the three boys—Macy, Richard, and Donald—described their various friends, some of whom they mentioned by name.

Finally, the therapist said: "You know this has come up in past discussions—about having to go back to certain friends even though you have all said these friends get into trouble and when you are with them there is a good chance of your getting into trouble, too. I'm going to play a hunch with you. I'll bet that one of the reasons you go to these friends is because you feel that it is hard to make new friends, and not only that, but maybe *boys who don't get into trouble won't want you for friends.*" Following this statement there was a dead silence that lasted for several minutes. Richard then said: "You're too smart for us. I used to think about that. What would happen if I didn't go back to my old friends and would some of my new friends, if they found out I was in Children's Village, have anything to do with me?" Richard came over and sat down next to the therapist and said in a very low voice: "Mr. Ellery, you know when you go back you can't tell people where you were. They laugh at you, make fun of you, call you jailbird." The other boys seeing that Richard was monopolizing the therapist began to get that typical absent look in their eyes, as if they were trying to remove themselves from the discussion and seemed almost grateful that Richard was terminating it.

Richard continued, telling how he had to make up stories to people when he visited his home and they asked him where he had been. (He obviously was terribly ashamed of being at the Village.) The therapist said to Richard: "Maybe you would like to tell all of us about it. Maybe you'll find that other boys here have the same feelings." Richard looked embarrassed and shook his head. Donald: "Hey, Richard, talk up will you? We can't hear you." Richard, still looking embarrassed, smiled sheepishly. Finally he told the boys how he made up stories as to where he'd been living when people in the community asked him. Donald: "You think you do it? You should hear me knock that shit out. I tell people I'm in a military academy." Michael: "Yeah, I tell people I'm in the army. I don't like people to know I'm at the Village. I don't want anybody to think I'm a jailbird. People don't understand, sometimes." Donald: "I was called a jailbird. They treat me like I was a gangster or a crook. They even have little kids at the Village. I don't see why they have little kids at the Village. Those kids are too stupid to even know what happened. Why should they take them away from their parents?"

Leonard spoke up at this point and said, "I'm embarrassed sometimes." Now that Leonard had introduced this term, the therapist brought it into the open and said: "It sounds as though you are ashamed. What is it you are ashamed of?" There was no response. Therapist: "Fellows, you feel ashamed of having problems, problems you need help with?" Donald: "So what. But how do you get rid of these problems? How do you get out and know you are not going to get into trouble any more?" Therapist: "By being here and talking about the things that push you into trouble. This is what we are here for." Donald: "Well, why can't you just tell me what got me into trouble and then I won't get into trouble any more." The therapist tried to differentiate between being told and really knowing "in your guts" what got you into trouble. Michael: "I'll bet you don't know what got me to steal." The therapist looked directly at Michael and said, "You told me the other night." "What?" The therapist mentioned to him how he told him about stealing and how he needed to prove to his mother that "he could do something." Michael laughed: "I was hoping you would forget about that." Leonard: "If Mr. Ellery should forget these things, he couldn't help us anymore."

The boys again became restless. Donald exchanged places with Louis on the couch. Louis took a chair, saying his head hurt and he had to sit up. He said he had lumps on his head from the fight. Macy moved around the room. Therapist: "Boys, if I thought it would really help you to avoid this discussion, I would be the first one to avoid it, but you know I think we are onto something, and as much as you move around we've got to come back and talk about this." This statement ended the restlessness. Donald: "Like we were talking, Mr. Ellery. What's wrong with going back with these friends?" Therapist: "There is nothing particularly wrong, except I really wonder what pulls you back to friends you know are going to tempt you into trouble?" Donald: "I know my problem. I'm easily led." Michael: "That's right. Me too. I'm easily led." Therapist: "Naw, it's not that easy boys. There is something else, like for instance maybe going back to these friends has to do with the way you feel about yourselves. When you feel as though you are a crumb or a bum, you've got to find friends who are like that too." Donald immediately said: "That's what my mother always used to say to me. She used to say: 'Look out for those bums on the street corner. They are going to get you into trouble.' And you know what? I didn't look out, I went to them."

Richard began to smile nervously and said: "My mother always used to tell me, 'Look out, you are going to get into trouble; look out.' And what do you think happened? I got into trouble." Donald: "My mother and father, they don't trust me. I go downstairs, I come back, they say, 'Well, what happened?' as if I had robbed something. I didn't rob anything, I just went down to stand on the corner. My brother goes with friends but they don't do anything, they just sit around drinking sodas looking at one another. I used to go with my brother, but I'm sick and tired of looking at his face and the faces of his friends." Macy: "When I go around the block I know there are boys that don't get into trouble, but I figure it is going to take me a long time to know them, and now that you mention it, Mr. Ellery, I don't feel like going with them because then they may not like me."

Donald, who was sitting next to the therapist, placed his hand on the therapist's arm, as if to speak confidentially, but suddenly said in a voice for all the boys to hear: "Now that we're talking about it, I used to think about that. I know a lot of guys who don't get into trouble. I was kind of wondering how come I'm never near them. I'm always near the guy who's going to get me into trouble." There was silence and the therapist said, "It seems as though we are now talking about taking on feelings that parents and others in our family have about us, and how we live with these feelings, believing them about ourselves." Donald: "Well what do you expect to happen? When all your life all you hear is, 'Look out, look out, you're going to be a bum'?" (Donald said this, mimicking his mother's voice and manner.) Leonard said, "When I began to move around in my diapers, I was always told what I can do and what I can't do." Donald interrupted: "That's it. If you ever want a kid to get into trouble, just keep telling him what he can do and what he can't do, and show him you can't trust him. Then he'll grow up *believing he can't trust himself, either.*" Macy: "My mother always used to talk to me nice, but even though she was talking nice, she kind of let me know that she was watching me. I didn't want her to watch me. I didn't do anything I had to be watched for." Donald again said: "That's right, they are always watching you. They are always making you think you are going to get into trouble! So what's left to do but get into trouble because you don't know how to stay out of trouble."

Silence fell on the group. Donald got up and went to talk to Leonard. Michael immediately yelled out: "There you go, getting off the topic again," and gazed at the therapist as though seeking approval. The therapist winked at him (indicating that if he wanted to be his assistant it was acceptable). Michael followed this up: "Come on, let's get back. What about what happened?" Richard: "I remember once I had a tattoo. I was twelve years old and I made a tattoo on my hand. Then I crossed it out, but there was a mark. When I went upstairs my father saw it and, before I knew it, his hand was across my face. He beat the fucking shit out of me; said I had a tattoo of a naked girl. All I had tattooed on it was my initials." The therapist said to Richard that he had talked a lot about getting hit. How did he feel about it? Donald stepped in and said: "Hey, Dicky, you got hit more when you were at home than you ever got hit at the Village. You don't got no complaints against the Village. Shit, if they hadn't sent me to the Village I'd be a real mess now," but then, as if he were dealing with an inner conflict, added: "But that don't mean that I don't want to leave the Village."

Richard: "You bet your ass I got hit. I didn't care when my father hit me. But my mother! Boy she used to hit me! I couldn't stand my mother hitting me, but even worse, I couldn't stand her talking to me. You know what would happen, fellows? She would hit me and I'd be bawling, then she'd sit me down and she'd talk to me nice like, and tell me and explain to me why I got hit, and then I'd really bawl because I'd feel so bad for getting my mother angry so that she had to hit me." The therapist commented, "Richard, when you got hit you weren't even given the right to be angry." Michael: "Yeah, that's real funny. First you get the shit kicked out of you, then you get to be made to feel sorry for getting the shit kicked out of you, like it's all your fault." Richard looked up as if this were a novel idea to him and said: "Yeah, that's right. I got the shit kicked out of me and then my mother makes me cry, making me feel bad for getting hit." Louis got up and said: "My head hurts too much. I got to get back to the cottage." It was 8:30 now, and all left.

COMMENT

From the outset, hostility was registered against adults in the Village (Mr. T. and Mr. W.). These feelings in a sense also involved the therapist, who was a part of the staff, and made their appearance in a very mild form when Donald groundlessly quizzed the therapist on whether he was saying that Donald was not ready to leave the Village and Richard challengingly insisted that he would not quit his friends. There were other evidences implicit in the climate of this session along the same lines. In a sense, the therapist had indirectly provoked hostility toward himself by his increased activity in the previous few sessions, his insistence and his confrontations of the boys with their problems.

This is desirable, for the aims of psychotherapy can be achieved only when transferential hostile feelings are expressed toward the therapist as a parental figure. In the setting of an institution, unfortunately, the patients cannot allow themselves to do so to other staff members, partly because of fear, but in this case more so because the group therapist was the only completely permissive and "nonpunitive" person. He was the one who provided the only haven on the stormy sea of their lives.

For the first time one of the boys (Donald) reported the exercise of self-control against temptation by "friends" ("Where the id was, the ego must be"—Freud). Donald's statement brought to the fore newly emerging ambivalent feelings in the boys about their undesirable friends. The insight into the role of parents in conditioning the self-image is both significant and connotes a high level of psychological understanding. What is even more important was the freedom with which they spoke of their parents. This, of course, might serve to entrench in the boys their projective mode (blaming others, in this case, parents), but we dealt with it later in terms of their own self-reconstructive efforts. This was a stage the boys had to pass through.

Feelings of self-alienation came through in this session for the first time on a preconscious level, of which we took note. The general impression of the session was that the boys continued in their psychomaturational process and developing self-identities.

Note need be taken again of the changing role of the therapist. He was now direct, insistent, and "breaks through" the boys' resistances, which is the technique in para-analytic psychotherapy, since he was now secure in the transference.

Session Thirty-Three

Donald came in about eight minutes after the session had begun. Perhaps the heat in the room on this mid-June evening caused the rather quiet and lethargic beginning. Macy brought with him magazines from the lobby. He and Leonard were leafing through them. This quiescent occupation seemed to set the tone for the session. After a brief delay Louis invited Michael to a game of cards. Throughout most of the session, these two quietly played cards and seemed removed from the discussion. Macy had his left hand bandaged. When the therapist asked him at the beginning of the session what had happened, he said that he broke his hand in a fight. The therapist said he was sorry to see his hand hurt and asked if Macy was in pain. The boy said their was no pain. The therapist asked if "anything was solved by the fight." Richard answered instead: "Well, he learned he can break his hand." Macy merely smiled and there was no further discussion of this.

Richard asked the therapist if he knew when Richard would be discharged from the Village. When informed in the negative, Richard remained sitting quietly, seemingly lost in thought and then said: "I think I ought to be leaving sometime around January. My caseworker told me that if everything goes all right and if the conferences they hold on me are okay, I can go in January. I know I'm going to be going back to school because *I want to finish my education.*" There was a pause of about a half a minute, then Richard, speaking in a low voice, told the therapist: "When I was in school, like parochial school, they used to give me a rough time there. Those sisters, they don't take any crap from you." He proceeded to complain that he was given beatings by the sisters almost daily. Sometimes they wouldn't actually hit him, he said. They would threaten him with beatings if he didn't behave. Richard: "I didn't want to get hit there, so I behaved." Richard explained that he did not like parochial school and, when the family moved, changed to public school. In public school he didn't get hit. He enumerated one incident after another of his "fooling around." On a number of occasions, he was sent to the principal's office and would promise to behave, but when he got back to class he "fooled around" again.

It was during this narration by Richard that Donald walked into the room. He entered quietly and sat down, looking depressed. After a few seconds, he got up, sauntered over to the electric plate, looked at the boiling water, which the therapist had put on, went to the washroom, came back into the room, and made himself a cup of coffee. He did not prepare any coffee for the others as he usually did. Jules, seeing this, got up and proceeded to make coffee for the others and distribute it. While this was going on, Richard continued to speak in a somewhat low voice to the therapist, with Macy and Leonard still reading magazines. He was describing putting tacks on teachers' chairs, giggling in class, and getting the teachers "upset." The expression on Donald's face now changed from one of depression to surliness and anger.

Finally Richard fell silent, and silence permeated the room. Therapist:

"Richard, from what you've said, it sounds like you were doing all the wrong things, like fooling around in class, almost as a way of getting yourself hit." For some moments Richard did not answer and then asked: "What do you mean?" Therapist: "From what you're saying it sounds as though you were trying to get hit or punished." Richard: "I just was having a good time in class. It was a lot of fun to just kid around." Therapist: "Well, I remember last week you were all talking about being hit, and now this week again we're talking about the same thing, getting hit or getting punished, and you act up until it does happen." Richard: "Don't sound right for a guy to want to get hit. I never thought I did anything because I wanted to get hit." Leonard looked up from his magazine and said to Richard, "Maybe you liked it that way." Richard did not respond and silence again settled for a few moments.

Donald seemed agitated. His eyes were half-closed and his body very tense. The therapist decided to break into his state of agitation and said: "Don, what's the matter?" Donald's immediate response was: "Nothing, nothing is wrong. What makes you think something is the matter?" Therapist: "You look as if something is the matter." Half-turning in his seat Donald said: "My 'transition conference' was called off. My social worker told me that they are not going to hold the transition conference, and that, on June thirtieth, there is going to be a conference with the psychiatrist. Sons of bitches! I wanted to get out of this God damn place. Now they called off my transition conference. I don't know what's going to happen with Dr. J., but I'm going to get the hell out of this God damn place."

Silence followed this outburst. Therapist: "Don, you sound pretty upset." "God damn right I'm upset! I was looking forward to this transition conference. Sons of bitches are going to call it off on me. I'm going to get out! You can't hold me here! Why, I've been here long enough. I don't know what they are going to talk with Dr. J. about at this point." With this, Donald got up and proceeded to serve coffee to Jules, Leonard, and Richard, who asked for seconds. This took but a few minutes, after which Donald sat down, still looking agitated —though somewhat less so—and not saying anything. Therapist: "Don, I know you are upset about what happened, and I know you have a lot on your chest." Donald: "You're right, I do," but said nothing further.

Jules got up, walked over to the window, and climbed onto the fire escape. Seeing this, Donald joined him. The room was silent and extremely hot and stuffy. The therapist turned back to Richard, commenting, "We were talking about your getting hit." Richard: "I don't know what there is more to say about it." Therapist: "Maybe what more there is to say is what it is that made you want to get hit." Leonard briefly looked up from his magazine and said, "That's right; that's what we were talking about." Michael overhearing this, turned away from Louis, with whom he was playing cards, and said, "What was we talking about?" Leonard: "Listen to Richard." Richard said, "Why should I want to get hit?" Therapist: "Maybe you felt as though you deserved it." Richard: "Deserved it?" Therapist: "Yes, Richard, sometimes a boy carries around a feeling that he ought to get punished. That's another way of saying he feels guilty. You know what I mean?" Richard: "Yeah, I know what guilty means. It means like you feel you done something wrong and you should suffer for it."

As this point Jules climbed back into the room through the window with Donald following him. Donald was carrying his shoes in his hand and a smile on his face. As soon as he was in the room he announced, "Boy, I nearly fell off." Jules fell to describing how Donald was trying to climb the roof in his bare feet. Now Donald had the center of attention as all the boys looked toward him to hear what had happened. Donald went into an explanation, stating that he wanted to see if he could climb the roof. Extending his left hand he said, "Look at my hand." His hand was shaking visibly. "Shit, I was scared. I nearly fell off the God damn thing. I could have gotten killed."

After Donald finished, the therapist said to the boys, "I wonder what got Donald to climb the roof just now." Donald turned and said, "I just wanted to see if I could do it." Therapist: "Don, you know I've got another hunch." Donald: "What's your hunch?" Therapist: "Somehow I get the feeling that you were just trying to hurt yourself." Donald: "What? Hurt myself? I don't want to hurt myself. Why should I want to hurt myself?" Therapist: "I get that feeling from what happened to-night. You are upset about your transition conference. The next thing, you're climbing the roof, doing something dangerous where you can really get hurt. I don't think that it is just an accident that this hap-pened." At this Donald said: "I got to go to the bathroom," and began to leave the room. The therapist looked up at him, smiled, and said, "That's okay, Don; I'll be here when you get back." Donald smiled in the therapist's direction and as he was leaving mumbled something to the effect that he knew the therapist would be there.

The therapist felt it was important to keep the discussion going while Donald was out of the room and said aloud, "I wonder what got Don to climb the roof just now?" There was no answer. Leonard and Macy continued their thumbing through the magazines. The therapist said laconically, "Gee, I wonder if we can find the answer in a magazine?" Leonard lifted his eyes and grinned sheepishly. Macy acted as if he had not heard. The card game between Louis and Michael continued.

Jules asked the therapist: "What are you trying to say, Mr. Ellery?" Therapist: "What we're talking about tonight is this idea of hurting yourself. There are reasons why people try to hurt themselves. One of them is wanting to kind of punish themselves because they feel guilty about something. You do something wrong and you must get even with yourself." Leonard: "Like pinching yourself when you make a mistake." Donald now came into the room and sat down quietly. He was visibly less agitated than when he had first come in. The therapist continued: "You know, sometimes boys do wrong things like stealing, fooling around in class, not going to school as a way of getting punished." Richard: "You mean maybe something like what I did?" Not waiting for a reply, he continued: "That's funny, I had a dream the other night. I dreamt that they had my transition conference and I went home. I was riding a bicycle in a brand new neighborhood. My parents moved to a brand new neighborhood. The next thing I knew, I was on a motorcycle. I don't know what happened to the bicycle. I went down a block, took a turn, and just around the corner I was back in my old neighborhood and walking down the street. An old man tried to cross. I headed at him on my motorcycle. I tried to stop, but couldn't. Just as I was about to hit him, I woke up."

Jules's immediate exclamation was, "Wow!" Richard turned to the therapist and asked, "What does that mean?" Therapist: "Maybe we can figure that one out together. What were we talking about last week?" Richard: "About going home and staying out of trouble and not getting into fights." Therapist: "And Richard, what were you complaining about?" Richard: "I remember; I was saying I didn't know whether I could stay out on the streets and not get involved with my old friends again." Therapist: "Now let's look at the dream. This is what we call a fear or an anxiety dream. Even though when you get out of the Village you are in a brand new neighborhood, before you know it you're headed for your old neighborhood, and in the dream you're just about to hurt somebody." Richard: "Yeah, that's right. I guess that means I'm kind of scared."

Donald immediately interjected: "Listen to this. Remember we were talking about the times you can't sleep at night? Well, I've been kind of thinking. I know there were a couple of nights I couldn't sleep. You know why I couldn't sleep? Just as I am about to fall asleep, I see a picture in my head of my mother and father being carried out of the house in a coffin. I get so fuckin' scared I just jump out of bed." Richard's quick response to this was, "God, what a hell of a thing to dream!" Donald continued: "But I don't even dream this. I know it's not a dream. It just gets in my mind before I go to sleep, and then I try not to think about it, I wake up and say: 'God forgive me. God forgive me. Hail Mary.'" There was silence. Donald then asked, "Mr. Ellery, why do these things come into my head?" Therapist: "Do you have any idea?" Donald: "No, I don't even try to think about it." He then asked: "Do you have any idea, Mr. Ellery?" Therapist: "One of the things I know is that, as he is growing up—sometime or another, because of what happens between him and the people who raise him, like his parents—a boy can sometimes wish that his parents would die." Jules: "I never thought that!" Leonard: "Yeah, something like when you get hit by a parent and you are sore."

Donald picked this up: "That's right, when you're sore. But you really don't mean it when you're sore. It's just that you're hurt and you want them to die because they hurt you, but then you don't want to think about it. I remember once my kid brother was riding on a bike. Remember me telling you that my kid brother was a pest? He always wanted to do what I wanted to do; always wanted to go where I wanted to go. Well, he was riding on a bike in the street and something happened, I don't know, he said something to me that made me mad and I yelled out, 'I hope you get run over, you little bastard!' The next thing I knew, a car hit him while he was on the bike. I remember him lying in the street with blood coming out of his leg. I stood there crying. I went over to him and I wanted to pick him up and I couldn't pick him up. I just stood there looking at the blood coming out of his legs and I was crying and a policeman came over and said, 'Take it easy, sonny.' When the policeman said that, it made me feel better. He gave me a handkerchief and I dried my eyes. I blew my nose, and then I didn't feel so bad. I felt like I almost killed my brother." While Donald was talking, Michael and Louis stopped playing and put away the cards. Michael said: "Boy, what a story! I'm glad it never happened to me."

Donald said nothing more. The boys sat looking transfixed. The therapist broke into the silence: "Don, do you remember how you felt?" Donald: "I had that crummy feeling inside, like what happened was my fault." Therapist: "That's the feeling that's called guilt, as though you were the one who was responsible. One of the feelings peculiar to all humans is this feeling, left over from childhood, that when you wish something and if by chance it takes place, you are responsible, and it happened because you wished it, and when you feel responsible you want to get punished for thinking this way. In other words, when you grow up—and this has happened to all people—you grow up with the idea that what you wish may really happen." Donald: "That's why I get so scared. Maybe when I was a kid, I used to wish my parents to die, but I didn't want them to die, Mr. Ellery. I didn't want them to die. I was just sore." Michael: "I never remembered thinking anything like that." Richard stepped in and said: "In other words, if it just happened, then *that's what they call a coincidence*. It doesn't happen just because you think about it." Therapist: "That's right."

Now the group became distracted. While no one was moving about, the attention seemed to be turning away from the subject. Donald turned to Leonard; Macy joined them, and the three were talking about something which the therapist could not hear. The therapist said loudly, "Would you like to share it with the rest of us?" but there was no response. All the therapist could overhear was that the boys were talking about bicycle-riding. Jules had gotten up to leave the room and Macy yelled out, "Wait for me, I'm going with you." Since it was 8:30 P.M. the session ended.

COMMENT

The ability of the boys for self-confrontation was increasing. Richard's and the other boys' enumerations of their transgressions in school and the community no longer have the ring of boastfulness and self-maximation. They are now preliminaries to understanding themselves and the causation of their behavior. The therapist was prepared to meet their curiosity and needs in this respect and became active—explored and uncovered—so that behavior could become accessible to the examination of the ego and, therefore, to control in the future. This is the indicated procedure with acting-out adolescents and would be only partially effective with psychoneurotic patients and a supplementation to resolution of intrapsychic conflicts. That is why we addressed ourselves here mostly to the character (ego) rather than the libido (para-analytic versus psychoanalytic therapy).

The ease with which the boys now faced hostility and even death wishes toward parents revealed intimacy with, and acceptance of, prohibited feelings and thus facilitated catharsis. However, to reduce the guilt, the boys could have been told that death to a small child means only the removal of the offending person and not his demise. A small child has no concept of the true meaning of death. The idea of self-punishment and self-destruction is a new one to the boys and they have the opportunity to trace the sources of guilt and deviant reactive acts. This later became a major focus of the interviews. Psychological literacy is broadened in a number of directions in this interview.

When Michael denied ever having death wishes toward his parents, the therapist did not pursue the subject with him, because Michael's basic personality structure was schizophrenic. The therapist was repeatedly cautioned against depth therapy with this boy because of it.

14

Second
Intermediate Progress Reports

Donald

After Twenty Sessions[1]

In an evaluation of Donald's response to treatment, in which the caseworker, group therapist, the director of the project, and the cottage life supervisor participated, it was determined that Donald was not accessible to individual treatment. It was recognized that this boy was subject to intense latent anxieties and might be characterized as a "neurotic delinquent." A major difficulty in reaching him was the fact that he could not develop positive transference feelings toward the caseworker (partly because of the latter's authoritarian manner and critical approach) and a constructive attitude toward the Village. The latter was in part also due to his parents' conduct and because they had repeatedly threatened to invoke court action against the Village for his return home. Donald was aware of these maneuvers on the part of his parents. At one point Donald flatly refused to come to see the caseworker and no appointments had been arranged for him for some time.

Donald's relationship with his caseworker had steadily deteriorated, and at this point the caseworker was "giving up on the boy." Donald was extremely resistive to coming in for appointments. The caseworker felt that an important factor was that when Donald went home for

---

1. See p. 321, opening paragraph.

week-end visits, he "seemed to fall apart." He returned drunk following a Thanksgiving week end. The parents were "very negligent" in their care of him, according to the caseworker, and did not cooperate with the Village. The caseworker had actually told Donald that his family was responsible for and encouraged his delinquency. Donald was now very angry with the caseworker and would not share anything meaningful in his sessions with him.

The group therapist reported that Donald initially presented himself as a "hardened delinquent youngster." He was completely preoccupied in the early sessions with making coffee for the group. However, when the coffee-making apparatus was removed, Donald began to describe with great impetuosity and a neurotic kind of enthusiasm in an almost ceaseless fashion the various delinquencies in which he had been involved, such as stealing cars, truanting from school, and the like. He was aware that his family had protected him from being committed before and that this had allowed him to go on with more delinquencies. Donald then went on to describe sexual incidents with girls that bordered on the bizarre. He described having sexual intercourse with girls in the dark aisles of movie theater balconies. Throughout, there was marked use of obscenity. He further described his drinking bouts.

At approximately the fifteenth session some change was highlighted in Donald. He began to recognize through the group discussions that his drinking was a form of release from feelings of being extremely self-conscious. He said that when he was sober he could not even approach a girl and ask her for a dance. Becoming aware of the inappropriateness of his acts through the other boys' reactions and group discussions, Donald was able to recognize that perhaps he was fortunate that eventually he had been placed at the Village, because if he had been allowed to go on as he had and commit further delinquencies, he might have ended up "in prison."

In the beginning therapy sessions, Donald was violently outspoken against the Village in almost every area of his living experience there. He considered the restrictions as a continuous encroachment upon him as a person. However, recently he had verbalized anxiety about returning home, finding a job, anxiety about school, and such, as had other boys. Donald once admitted that he had got "something from his experience at the Village"; namely, his reading had improved. He now realized that many of the things he had done in the past were pleasure motivated and that he had to pay a "pretty stiff price for that pleasure." At one session, he said that as he grew up he could not always do things just for the pleasure of it.

In a psychiatric interview at approximately this time, the fourth since Donald had come to the Village, the psychiatrist commented on his improved behavior. "Donald seemed pleased," reported the examiner, "and said he was glad I noticed it. He said that he used to become excited too easily, which would get him into trouble. Now he was trying to prevent trouble, so he was controlling himself." The psychiatrist then described the boy's relaxed and easy manner and friendly attitudes toward him.

The project director indicated, however, that, though to a lesser degree, Donald still operated by evasiveness and still manipulated people, slithered out of threatening situations by such acts as preparing coffee, frequently going to the washroom, ingratiating himself with the therapist, and so on—all mechanisms of escape. In his opinion, this boy seemed devoid of motivation because of defective superego identification with his parents and was "probably a serious character disorder with very defective identifications." It was concluded that individual casework interviews would be terminated and Donald would be carried solely in the group. However, following the practice of the institution, he would be seen by the caseworker on an administrative basis in relation to the boy's routines, home visits, and other matters of that genre.

Louis

After Twenty-One Sessions

THE COTTAGE PARENTS REPORTED that though Louis's relationship with them was still "rather cool," he seemed to be more friendly than in the past. He had the reputation of consorting with the most delinquent boys in his cottage, but currently was choosing friends from among the quieter boys who were not pugnacious, troublesome, or defiant. He "can now be reasoned with," and though he still engaged in horseplay, he seemed to know when to call a halt. Marked decrease in the boy's participation in sexual activity in the cottage was also noted. "In the beginning," the cottage staff stated, "Louis was involved in a great deal of homosexual activity. He apparently abandoned this of late, is more self-directed and less under the influence of peers than before joining the 'discussion group.'" Louis now had the reputation among the boys as one "who would not permit being sexually molested. He used to pirate food from other boys, but this, too, has stopped." In general, the cottage staff felt that Louis "seems to be giving up his role as a follower and is trying to find a way to speak his mind and assert himself; yet he does not do this in an offensive way which in the past resulted in conflicts with adults or peers." His image of himself was still a poor one. Though Louis participated considerably in athletics, he seemed to have a need to be overly critical of his accomplishments and to downgrade himself.

The caseworker stated that Louis seemed less hostile in his infrequent interviews than previously, though still unwilling to discuss anything meaningful. He appeared much more relaxed and not as ready to fight at the least provocation. The mother refused to see the caseworker, and Louis was aware of this. Louis told his caseworker "one way to become friends with me is to become friends with my mother."

In the six months prior to this report, Louis's reading grade reached the 11.1 level and arithmetic 6.5 (as against 10.4 and 5.9, respectively). A major evidence of change in the boy was that he no longer broadcast his antisocial attitudes in the classroom, although at times he would still talk about "dope" and various vices in an attempt to impress the other boys. It was noted that Louis himself would grin as if he were becoming aware of the inappropriateness of his conduct.

In the wood and sculpture shops, Louis displayed considerable talent. His coordination had improved greatly and he could work independently and well, whereas at the beginning of the school year he made many errors, in spite of (or perhaps because of?) explicit instructions from teachers as to how to proceed. In the wood shop Louis's relationships with peers and adults were described as "excellent." However, when the time came to clean up, he would slack off and let other boys do his share of work. He was now seeking out the shop instructors and their praise. This development was in sharp contrast to his former attitude of ignoring all adults.

The maturing effects of the group had become more evident. The boy's improved self-concept and self-value reduced the degree of self-alienation: he sought out more constructive associations; he became less suggestible—a major problem before; he gave up homosexual activity as he grew more assured and stronger. What was rather important in these developments was that, as a result of his inner alliance, as opposed to his former self-alienation, his capacity for relatedness was enhanced, as manifested in his relations to the cottage parents, caseworkers, teachers, and peers. He had become able to assert himself without being offensive. This inner integration strengthened his ego so that he was, as a result, able to mobilize strengths for school achievement in the classroom, creativity in the shop, and control over his impulses and anger—all of which spell maturity.

Leonard

After Thirty-Three Sessions

The cottage parents described Leonard as still more responsive to adults than at the time of the previous report. He had become a friend of all the boys and they had made a practice of discussing their problems with him and asking his advice. He was characterized as "the social worker" for the boys in the cottage and considered an "elder statesman of his peer group." As such, he was not actually an integral or active part of the group itself. Although still essentially a compliant youngster, he seemed to be aware of this need of his. He recently joined a "work group" on a cleanup detail in the Village, earning $50 a month, and now took great pride and care in his appearance. Leonard perceived himself as a more mature person than in the past and tried to set a pattern of behavior for others in the cottage. On two occasions he was overheard advising two of the more delinquent boys who invited him to join them in a stealing escapade they had been planning not to go through with it. The episode did not come off.

The caseworker reported that Leonard said spontaneously that he liked the group discussions because he had a chance to learn that other boys had problems and what these problems were. He now demanded things for himself and was beginning to express angry feelings. Rather spontaneously, he discussed his father and said, "I used to hate him, but now I see him as a weakling and I guess he has his own problems." Leonard still did not discuss his relation with his mother, but the caseworker recognized the "maturing process going on in the boy, not only emotionally, but also physically. He now bears himself erect and there is a firmer quality in his voice."

In school, the improvement was primarily in behavior and attitudes. He now raised appropriate questions about the studies, in contrast to earlier in the school year when he was completely withdrawn and shy and spoke only in response to direct questions from the teacher. Leonard had begun to display a keener interest in academic work. In the shops, he continued to be "all thumbs," though on many occasions he sought help from the teachers. Leonard was punctual in doing assignments and seemed to be making a very real effort to keep notes; and he worked hard. His scores were: reading 3.0; arithmetic 3.1 (as compared to 2.2 and 3.0, respectively, six months before). The teachers could offer no explanation for this rather slow progress despite the remedial help he was receiving Neither could they explain the marked improvement in the boy's attitudes and behavior.

The psychological examination administered at this time pointed up no significant change in Leonard's IQ over the past year. The intellectual potential was again estimated as average. However, Leonard was presently more inclined to exercise intellectual control, and rational factors were significantly more in evidence than in the previous tests. "Along with the increased intellectual control," the psychologist stated, "Leonard experiences a decreased tendency and also a lesser need for closeness toward others. He has presently a deeper awareness of his inadequacy, of having been hurt and deprived. From the 'feeling of being nothing' he has shifted to the 'feeling of being bad.' The realization of his deficiencies is quite poignant and too crushing an experience for him, so that he now resorts to denial and also reversal of affects. It may be that his inadequacies have been too rapidly exposed, so that he now cannot tolerate this reality and reverts to being silly and going through major mood swings. There is no withdrawal from reality in a bizarre manner, but he is moving away from people on a realistic basis, refusing to get hurt any more. He feels threatened by intense interpersonal relationships and retreats to conventional, stereotyped ways of relating.

"There is still considerable inhibition in the sexual area, but less avoidance and ambivalence. Although Leonard experiences more guilt and more of a sense of inadequacy, he is also more eager for gratification. He is emotionally more alive and alert, and has more expectations. Many of the repressive mechanisms are gone and there is an increasing awareness of drives and impulses. The reawakening in the emotional sphere is accompanied by intense guilt and considerable uneasiness. In summary, a comparison between the current clinical picture and the one described earlier (directly before joining the group) indicates gains in terms of increased intellectual control, decreased impulsivity, and a revitalized emotional life. In spite of this gain in ego strength, he experiences stronger guilt feelings and a deeper sense of inadequacy."

The behavioral picture as gathered from the various sources reported above did not support some parts of the psychologist's interpretations. Nor were these alleged intrapsychic problems revealed by Leonard's dramatic physical change in appearance and bearing. What was evident, rather, was the enormous growth in the boy's capacity to relate to people —adults and peers—and his benign self-image and ego strengths. Contrary to the evidence in the psychological interpretation, Leonard was freed from his depressive schizoid introspection about his "badness" and "inadequacies" by discovering, as he stated to the psychiatrist, that other boys had "problems" similar to his own. This universalization set him up greatly in the area of guilt, self-blame, and feelings of being stigmatized. Had he felt what the psychological tests seem to have revealed, Leonard could not have taken the place among his peers as reported by the cottage and school staffs, nor attained the status in gainful employment which he did.

He was now on the road to attaining an identity apart from that of his mother and a growing sense of reality which, revealed in the group interviews, had taken a tangible and practical direction.

Jules

After Thirty-Three Sessions

Most noticeable improvement occurred in Jules's functioning in the cottage. He appeared now to be quite fond of his cottage mother, sought her out to talk with her and to get praise from her for his chores. The relationship with the cottage father seemed much the same as before, that is, a kind of "live and let live" existence. There was also some improvement in his relationship with peers. He no longer ingratiated himself by sharing his goods. Although practically the tallest boy in the cottage, he had the reputation of being weakest. Now he had begun to fight back, and was considered the third boy from the top in leadership. Whenever the two top boys were absent, Jules assumed leadership of the cottage group. His leadership was generally of a constructive nature, and he did not use his powers to undermine the cottage parents' status, as was more or less customary for other boys. When asked to do something, Jules was still negative at first, but on a second request always acceded. His initial resistance was considered as a strategy to focus adults' attention on himself. Jules was no longer depressed or moody and now frequently even smiled. In the past boys used to make fun of him because of the "grouchy look on his face." This was no longer in evidence.

The caseworker·reported that Jules remained relatively passive and uncommunicative. His tone of voice, his demands, always seemed to convey the idea: "I was gypped as a kid; therefore, the world owes me a living." However, the caseworker noted that something had happened just recently that was "somewhat startling for Jules." He requested that he be present at an interview the caseworker planned with his adoptive parents. At the conference he proceeded to tell his parents that he now knew where all his troubles started, namely, when his sister was "born," and that was why he began to steal. He learned about this in the group discussions, he said, and proceeded to tell his mother that she never gave him enough care and attention, and was always nagging him. The mother became extremely defensive and told the boy: "I'm always good to you. You shouldn't be this way, because I'll not always be with you. Some day I'm going to die." The father's attitude was characterized by the statement: "Look at what we've done for you and look how ungrateful you are."

The caseworker reported that the passive, bored look on Jules's face had disappeared. He had become more outgoing and more demanding during the interviews, got involved in discussions as to what he would like to achieve for himself. He saw himself as always being with his parents and, he said, he had no intention of getting married and raising a family. The caseworker noted that Jules appeared visibly more troubled and anxious and because of it was now seen by the caseworker on a weekly basis.

In school, Jules presented two different façades. He still appeared to lack interest, though he now tried to conform to classroom routines more than he had previously and was more self-contained and quieter than he used to be. However, he still did not voluntarily communicate with the teacher, nor did he interact much with his classmates. In the academic classes, such as social science and English, Jules was relatively relaxed. He no longer wore the sad and worried look on his face prevalent a year before and seemed much more responsible for routines. He worked on a ninth-grade level in these subjects. His average mark was 80 (equivalent to a B mark). Previously he had barely passed with a minimum requirement of 65. He was courteous toward adults and at times even overcompliant, whereas before he had always eyed adults suspiciously.

Another teacher, however, reported that Jules "picked on younger boys," got out of his seat without permission, and walked around almost as if he sought to be punished by the teacher. This particular teacher noted that Jules would initiate conversations about sex with the other boys. In the shops, which presented boys with highly structural situations, Jules, despite his excellent skills, did poor work and showed little interest in it. He was characterized by the shop teachers as being stubborn.

As compared with examinations of six months before, Jules had achieved more than a full year's advance in his scoring: reading, 8.6 as compared to 7.7; spelling, 7.1 as compared to 5.9; arithmetic, 7.3 as compared to 6.2.

The psychic integration in Jules was going forward but it was still occurring on a segmental basis; that is, he was growing in some areas, but still not in others. He had become freer in relationships and intra-psychically, but was still resentful of younger children as he was of his younger sister. He did well and related well in the school area, where he was interested and felt comfortable with most teachers, but acted out in the classroom of an unsympathetic and repressive teacher. He became more assertive with peers and related better to his cottage parents, but was still afraid of contemplating separation from his adoptive parents and afraid of the responsibility of marriage and raising a family of his own. These dichotomies are not unusual in the reconstructive process and are in accord with the segmental growth of soma and psyche of all children. What was now needed was more time and more freedom for Jules to fill in these gaps, so that his personality as a totality could even up in its development to the degree of its maximal potentialities.

Michael

After Thirty-Six Sessions

At the termination of the school year the following information was elicited on Michael. For about four months, the boy had gone through a rather stormy period with his new cottage parents. At that time he seemed to be rather negatively oriented and would "pick up on little things"; there always seemed to be some element of disquiet in the boy. He then seemed to settle down, became much friendlier, and though remaining somewhat of an isolate in his peer group, tended to get along with most of the people around him. There were no difficulties in his sleeping or eating habits, and he was not considered a management problem. After his last home visit a change was again noted in Michael. He became somewhat more withdrawn and more antagonistic toward adults and "was always ready to jump to wrong conclusions." When someone called his name, he was ready to conclude that he would be asked to do something he did not want to do, such as a chore. Yet he was not truly a management problem, except when the cottage parents attempted to involve him intensively with the group. There appeared to be "a very schizie quality about Michael." The reason the last home visit was so disturbing to Michael was that he had begun going out with a married woman, about nineteen years old, who had two children. Michael's mother had literally been forcing this relationship on him, and Michael appeared to be completely confused about this. Michael also felt at a loss with the new cottage parents. They were more demanding than the previous couple and he appeared to feel that there was too much pressure for him.

However, Michael did not become openly defiant. Rather, there was a kind of silent, smoldering antagonism in the boy. If approached and spoken to in a calm voice, Michael was reasonable. He appeared to need cool, individual attention that was really not available in the cottage and this, it was felt, might be another reason the boy was withdrawing more from the group, refraining from talking with the cottage parents, and was often found by himself, sitting and thumbing through a magazine or toying with objects in his hand, such as dominoes.

The caseworker, who had seen Michael once a month, was aware of the problem with the cottage parents, and because of it she now saw him once a week and felt that the boy was working out rather well with the cottage parents. He was growing less antagonistic toward them than he had been at first. He verbalized his recognition that although he sometimes looked for a fight, he knew that the cottage parents were really trying to help him and maybe there was something that he was doing that led to trouble. He could talk about his part in making trouble in the cottage, saying that he knew that when other boys "horsed around" he would laugh at their antics. Maybe the cottage parents resented his laughing when the boys were making trouble for them.

Michael now appeared realistic as to what he could expect when he went home. He said he knew his mother could not do much for him and that he would be pretty much on his own, so he would have to find something that he could do. As a result, he was thinking about the possibility of returning to school, and maybe learning a trade when he went home. The caseworker did not know about the girl friend with the two children that Michael was reported to have been seeing when he went home.

The caseworker pointed out that Michael was still essentially a withdrawn, nonverbal youngster and still usually wore an expression of sullenness. (It should be noted that in the therapy group this was not the case. On the contrary, there was often an expression of interest in what was being said.) She felt that there was little communication between herself and the boy, that essentially he remained mostly nonverbal. She thought that Michael was "still rather schizoid."

In school, on the other hand, he continued to make progress and was described as "all student and definitely a hard worker." A few months previous to this report, Michael had asked for and been given the assignment of delivering newspapers to staff members. The staff commented on the boy's punctuality and his good manners and noted that this development coincided with what was observed in the classroom. He was now making a real effort to control himself and seemed to literally think over what was being asked of him, almost as if he were trying to decide on the justification for getting angry. He was deriving a great deal of pleasure from praise for his conduct and work in the classroom and began to seek out the teacher to show his work to him and receive praise. His tests put him close to the eighth-grade level. Teachers noted that by the end of the school term (coinciding with this report) Michael was assuming positive leadership in the class. He had allied himself with the teacher rather than against him, or isolating himself from him as in the past, and maintained a serious attitude toward the academic work. He was helpful in the classroom, volunteering to do such chores as cleaning up the room and straightening out the chairs at the end of the period. He also helped new boys who came into the class by lending them his notes and showing them the work, as well as in other ways. Michael was now able to get along with the boys who were bigger than he and in the last few months had avoided getting into any sort of difficulties.

Michael maintained his progress, despite two disturbing events: the change of cottage parents, which must have been a very disturbing experience for him, and the involvement at the age of fifteen-and-a-half years, with a married young woman with two children, especially since this was instigated by his own mother.

Macy

After Thirty-Three Sessions

Macy continued to be a "model child" in the cottage, closely attached to the doting cottage mother. He had not expressed any hostility or displayed rebellion in any form. However, more recently there had been some suspicion that he acted out when the regular cottage parents were absent and the associate cottage father was in charge. While Macy did not seem to be directly involved in many of the skirmishes reported, there were grounds for suspicion that he was responsible for stirring them up.

The teacher reported that Macy was becoming less conforming and more assertive in class. The teacher speculated that the lessened conformity might account for his lowered reading and arithmetic scores. (Reading score dropped from 8.3 to 8.1; arithmetic, 8.4 to 7.2.) Despite this, Macy read close to his age level (the ninth grade). The school principal stated that the major change in Macy during the school year had been his transition from a very quiet, withdrawn, and conforming boy, discharging social amenities in relation to his peers, to a youngster beginning to show rebellion. When Macy did not like an assignment he now would say so, though he did not actually challenge teachers. He became much more restless. Recently he had asked for more difficult school assignments, and the teachers speculated that his restlessness might have been due to his need for more academic stimulation.

The caseworker reported that there had occurred a major change in Macy: he had become extremely argumentative. The arguments always had to do with demands for week-end trips home. When the caseworker raised any question about the family, he would tell the caseworker, "mind your own business," whereas previously the boy would just sit with a smile on his face and try to look pleasant. He claimed that the cottage mother was attempting to get him discharged. When the caseworker tried to discuss how he felt about this, he became abusive, telling the caseworker, "mind your own business" and "who the hell are you to ask questions?" The caseworker reported that this was quite a change, for in the past the boy had been very quiet and pleasant and said absolutely nothing about himself or the home situation. Macy had recently indicated an awareness that he was very dependent on his mother and that going home meant living with her, having to "listen to her" (obey her) and do exactly what she wanted. This immediately brought forth hostility on Macy's part, and he would quiet down and say nothing further. The boy seemed to be giving up his rigid controls over his feelings. He did not actually discuss his family situation, however. Currently the caseworker was seeing Macy on alternate weeks. Macy was considered "not available for meaningful discussions of himself or his family situation."

The awakening powers and individuation of this boy increasingly came to the fore in all areas, even in his cottage life. This can be attributed to the natural development of personality in a child in a favorable growth-producing milieu, but the cottage mother's supportive role in this process cannot be discounted. She played a significant part in this growth, by giving Macy the sustaining, unequivocal love which he did not receive from his inconsistent, narcissistic, and sick parents. The unchanging, secure, and consistent relation with her eliminated the stress under which he had lived in his own family and freed his ego energies for self-fulfillment and expansion.

The group discussions, though playing a secondary role in this boy's improvement at this point, made him aware of the nature of his home environment, the mother's personality difficulties, and the problems in adjustment he would have upon returning home. His ego was at this juncture still too weak to face these facts. This strength he was still to acquire in the future. However, the group played a significant role in maturing this boy. The status of equality with other, more mature youngsters, the *respect* with which he was treated by the therapist, and especially the significant content of the interviews and the values he incorporated as a result of all these experiences and influences, gave Macy an identity and led to general maturity of personality.

During the next ten weeks (six weeks of the summer vacation and four weeks of group sessions) some significant developments occurred in this case.

The caseworker reported changes in the individual interviews which he attributed primarily to the discussions in the therapy group. He said: "Analytic therapy must really be helping this boy. He is talking about things that he never talked about before." Macy had been bringing dreams to the individual sessions that worried him because he did not know their meaning. One dream, to which he referred as "a funny dream," was that he was riding with his father in a car and they met with an accident. His father, who was driving, and another man who was in the car with him got out. Macy was walking down the street with his father and the other man started a fight with the father. Macy, in his dream, grew very worried because of his father's heart condition. Macy knocked the other man down and continued punching him. All of a sudden Macy saw himself riding on a bus carrying a package, sitting with his back to his father, who was sitting behind him. His father became sick. Macy then said, "I don't know what happened, but I told that man I should have killed him." (Obviously a homicidal intent against his father.)

The caseworker asked Macy to associate to the dream, but not much came forth. Macy did not know what the dream meant and did not know how to talk about it.

The following week, Macy again reported a dream. In this dream he was with his sister-in-law, who was being very nice to him and was making sexual advances toward him. The sister-in-law looked as though she wanted Macy to kiss her. He was very tempted, but then stopped, saying to himself: "If I kissed her I knew I was going to fuck her, and I can't fuck my sister-in-law." (Obviously a displacement of incestuous feelings toward his mother.)

Encouraged to talk about the dream, Macy said, "I remember Mr. Ellery talking to us about dreams and we learned in the group that there is a subconscious." He then added that he learned in the group that "when boys think or worry about other people's feelings, maybe what they were really thinking and worrying about were their own feelings.

We think other people have these feelings because we have them." In this connection the fact must be noted that Macy was the favorite of his cottage mother and she had been "extremely seductive with this boy." Macy, in turn, was extremely conforming and ingratiating with her. In the group, however, he had been complaining about the fact that whenever he attempted to assert himself she always "clamped down" on him. This confused his feelings toward her. Sometimes he felt very angry, but she was so nice to him that he did not "feel right, feeling angry."

The maturing process in Macy became apparent in the appearance and conduct of this boy. About three months after the preceding events occurred, the caseworker voluntarily submitted the following remarks relative to Macy. Macy unmistakably appeared "to be growing, . . . he is more of an adolescent." This was evidenced by "his readiness to talk about things that bother him, such as the behavior of the cottage parents, school matters, his anxiety about the type of friends he will have when he returns to his city community, what life will be like for him in school there, and so forth." This was in marked contrast to Macy's persistent refusal for over a year and a half of treatment to talk about things of a personal nature. Macy now carried himself with greater assurance, but the caseworker was concerned with the fact that the cottage mother was "involved in a real battle with the boy" because of Macy's growing independence. He resisted doing chores which were not rightfully his responsibility, and as a result the cottage mother accused him of not appreciating her, of not being grateful to her for all the things she had done for him. The caseworker was concerned that her reactions would negate the boy's gains he had been making from the therapy.

Inquiry of the child care supervisor of Macy's unit confirmed the caseworker's impressions. The supervisor stated that "from the very way Macy carries himself, from the twinkle in his eye, it is apparent that the boy is enjoying life. He now engages in petty obstreperous things that almost any child would engage in." He felt that "this is a sign of growth in Macy. He is no longer the almost 'obsequious' boy he had been, always doing what was asked of him without ever a murmur of protest." He had planned to discuss with the cottage mother her attitudes toward Macy, since he considered that the boy's reactions in the cottage were "quite realistic." Macy had been doing chores that other boys refused to do "out of sheer rebelliousness." He also pointed out that Macy had become very friendly with him and greeted him with enthusiasm whenever they met. This was a completely new development. He recognized that on the one hand Macy was growing up, while on the other he was being pressed by the cottage mother to conform to her wishes. This situation must have caused considerable confusion in the boy.

Richard

After Thirty-Three Sessions

Cottage staff reported that Richard had changed from "a rather scattered, immature, extremely talkative boy to one who is friendly, outgoing, and more related to others and their needs." More recently, he had been acting preoccupied, as if he had something pressing on his mind. He had had two "seizures" during this period since the last report, and another EEG had been requested. The resident physician felt these were not epileptic in nature but rather "hysterical reactions to the boy's emotional problems." The cottage mother suspected that Richard was masturbating at night.

Otherwise Richard developed well. He had grown at least three inches in the past few months. He "carries himself in a more mature, less slouchy way than formerly." The cottage parents noted that the boy could now easily dissociate himself from antisocial activities in the cottage, whereas previously he was easily led into trouble. One of the most marked changes reported relates to Richard's return to the Village after home visits. Instead of slinking away upon arrival, he had begun to seek out the cottage parents and discuss with them what occurred while he was at home. He would complain of not feeling well whenever he was upset by his parents as though he were asking for leeway since he felt so tense; and that with a little rest and reaccommodation to the cottage, he would be all right again. The cottage parents had the feeling that Richard was trying somehow to find an equilibrium for himself, that something had been stirred up in him, and that he was working on it.

At the end of the term, the school reported decided improvement. In the last tests, Richard scored in reading and arithmetic 9.1 and 6.9, respectively. At the time of this report they were 10.2 and 8.2, respectively, a gain of more than a year in each case over a six-month period. The teachers felt Richard was generally doing ninth-grade work in both shops and trades. His work was neat and well done. A year ago he would sit quietly in class, perhaps act out in a foolish and childish manner, picking on other boys, throwing pencils around the room, and giggling. He was now a constructive leader in the classroom. However, he was still considered an expert "con-man, who can talk his way around and through any obstacle." He did his schoolwork on his own, constantly requesting assignments beyond the regular requirements and appeared well motivated academically. In auto shop his work was above average, and he displayed a keen interest in this area. In the classroom and in the shop, Richard's tendency to align himself with the more aggressive, antisocial boys had greatly decreased. He now laughed at their antics and indicated to them that he would not go along with their obstreperous behavior.

The caseworker felt that Richard was now even more available for discussions of his problems at home. During the past few months he had been describing some of the things his mother did when he was on home visits, of which he disapproved. Among these were her keeping constant watch over him, warning him not to get into trouble, and always asking him where he was going. He was now able to verbalize his anger, which contrasted with his earlier attempts to justify his parents' treatment of him. The caseworker felt that Richard was now manifesting more neurotic symptoms than before. He narrated dreams of falling, and wondered whether these dreams had anything to do with what had happened to him in the past. Obviously, this was a carry-over from the group discussions. At the same time, he had become much more hostile toward, and demanding from, the caseworker, which is a decided change from his previous ingratiating, conforming behavior in his attempt to cover up his rage. But as Richard was expressing hostility, he grew much more anxious. He had renewed his frequent visits to the infirmary on sick call and now went there almost every day. This was a repetition of an earlier pattern that had almost completely disappeared for a time.

At another conference held later, this phenomenon was viewed as a throwback to his former defensive reaction brought on by increased anxiety and neurotic tension. Richard was considered now less alienated from his feelings, though he still had a long way to go in fully recognizing his confused and intense anger toward his family. He no longer took the blame upon himself for everything that went on between his parents and between himself and them, and was now able to say that he felt he had been getting "a raw deal" from his father, as when his father made conflicting demands on him, that is, to stay in the house and watch over his siblings and at the same time saying that Richard should have a good time on his home visits.

The relief that Richard had received from his impulsivity and aggressive acting out in the past was no longer available to him. The emotional tensions, therefore, were now less easily contained, and as is not unusual in neurotic conflicts, they were resolved in somatic symptoms. Having removed or decreased the noxious character aspects of his personality as revealed in his conduct, manner, and appearance, the ego now became preoccupied with his inner conflicts, a preoccupation that was observable in his countenance as described by the cottage staff. Because of this discomfort, Richard now became available to deeper psychotherapy, which could not be carried on in a group of acting-out adolescents. Perhaps the depth, complexity, and intensity of this patient's problems could not be worked through in any group. Richard had to develop and work through a transference neurosis with an individual to resolve his conflicts and confusions. This he had already begun when he made excessive demands on the caseworker and grew hostile toward her. The group could only, therefore, be ancillary to individual treatment in this instance.

However, the group had activated the therapeutic process and could now continue to offer a number of important services in the treatment of this boy. It could further mobilize his ego forces, internalize his identifications, supply an arena for reality-testing, serve as a catalytic agent by reducing guilts and superego censors through universalization, and accelerate the cathartic process in the individual interviews.

The most impressive development in Richard, despite the increase in neurotic preoccupations, was the decrease in his self-alienation mechanisms: his disassociation from the delinquency-prone school and cottage mates, his relatedness to his cottage parents, his capacity to confront his parents' conduct and attitudes, his self-confrontation in recognizing his inner disturbances, and his hopefulness that he would emerge from his depressions. His open criticism of his father, which he could not have verbalized before, signified Richard's decreased dependence upon the parent and the slow ejection of him as an internalized image and identification model. Richard was now well on the way to developing a salutary self-identity.

As the ego energies had been freed from the former intrapsychic anchorages, they automatically became available and were just as automatically redirected for activities demanded by outer realities: personal appearance, school achievement, regulated conduct, and interpersonal relationships.

15

Protocols and Comments:
Sessions 34-55

Session Thirty-Four

ABSENT: Louis, Macy, and Richard, who lived in the same cottage, went on a trip to the local movies with their cottage group.

At the beginning of the session only Leonard, Michael, and Jules were present. About three minutes later, Donald arrived. Before Donald's arrival the boys sat around making small talk. Jules had taken on the responsibility for distributing cigarettes. He informed the therapist that should there be a need for an extra cigarette to equalize the share for the boys, he would contribute one. *Leonard looked particularly relaxed.* He smiled warmly and graciously at the therapist, although he did not talk to him directly. He sat in a relaxed fashion and made easy small talk with Jules about his cottage.

As Donald walked in, it became apparent that he was very upset about something, and he lost no time in telling the group what it was. He started off by saying, "I'll make the coffee," but made no move to do so. He sat down, looking glum, with the other boys focusing on him. Noticing this and addressing the group, Donald said: "They still didn't have the transition conference on me and I still don't don't know when they are going to have it. I talked to my social worker, that goddam fag, today again and he said he doesn't know when they are going to have it. All I know is that they are going to have a meeting with Dr.———— on June 30. My social worker told me that I'm going to be staying, but he won't give me a date when I go home. Shit, I don't want to stay here. I don't want this summer for me to be here. I spent enough summers in this place and I'm going to get out of here even if I got to run away. I called up my mother and she said, 'Don't worry you'll get out.' What does she mean, don't worry? I want to get the hell out of this place." Then turning to the therapist: "Mr. W. [social worker] explained to me something about my doing so well that they want to keep me here, but you know, Mr. Ellery, he also said to me that he's not so sure that if they keep me that I won't get into trouble here. I don't understand at this point. He tells me they are going to keep me here because I'm doing so well, but he also tells me that if they keep me here, I'm liable to get into trouble. I think he's right. I know I'm going to get into trouble. I just feel something is going to happen if I stay at the Village."

From this, he proceeded to narrate something that had occurred to him. He said: "Listen to this. The other night I woke up and the next thing I knew, I picked up the bed and I flipped it." Michael laughed at this. Donald got up, walked over to the couch at the other end of the room, and, without actually overturning it, demonstrated how he took hold of one edge of his bed and completely turned it over. "This was about three o'clock in the morning and I don't remember how it happened. I must have been dreaming, but I don't even remember what I was dreaming." He then described how, half-asleep, he had walked over to the window and tried to reach for something that he saw outside and nearly fell out. A staff member woke him up and put him back to bed. At first he was hard put to describe what he was reaching for, but when the therapist asked him specifically, he said it looked like a burning cigarette that was going around in a circle and he saw it moving on the wall and then moving out of the open window.

Donald went over to the open window to demonstrate how he had reached for it, then, turning around, said: "Shit, I was so scared! This is crazy." He was so upset that he could not sleep. He ascribed his disturbed state to the fact that he did not know when he would be leaving the Village. "It might be a month, two months, three months, it might be a year," he said. Nobody had specified a date. There was inordinate anger in Donald's voice. His resentment was particularly directed toward his social worker. He said: "That's what I get for talking about my problems. Shit, I want to get the hell out of here. I knew I couldn't trust them." The therapist asked Donald: "Who do you mean by them?" Donald: "You know, like Mr. P., Mr. R., all the guys on top. They promised me I could leave in June. Now I don't know when the hell I'm going to be leaving."

Michael said: "They better not do that to me. All I know is that if they try to keep me longer than I'm supposed to be staying, I'll run away and they'll never get me." Donald: "I could run away, but I don't want to do that. I don't want trouble from running away. I know; I learned my lesson. I know what my problems are, but I don't know how to tell any-body." Jules spoke up and said: "This fucking place is like a prison and they don't even give you a cent. All they do is keep you."

The therapist responded to this harangue as follows. He said, "Some-how I get the feeling, fellows, that you still see this place as a place where you are sent to get punished." Michael: "Yeah, I do." Jules: "It ain't exactly that, but they shouldn't keep you so God damn long. Every boy wants to be with his family." Donald: "Right. Every boy wants to be with his family. I haven't been with my family for over two years and I don't know how to get back to my family. If they would only give me some time so I could find out." Therapist: "Suppose they told you that you had to stay another year, Don, and gave you a specific date." Don-ald's instantaneous reaction was: "Shit, I wouldn't stay. I would just run. I can't hang around this God damn place."

Therapist, to Donald: "Was there anything in all the time you've been at the Village that didn't feel like punishment to you?" Donald: "Only this, Mr. Ellery. My being in the group. I remember when we first came here, we wouldn't talk about anything. I learned how to talk about my problems to my own friends. [He pointed to the boys in the room as he said this.] You know why? You never ratted on us. I know that our social workers never found out about what the hell we talk about here. Not only that, but *I never knew what it was like to sit around and tell my problems*. I never told my social worker my problems; and when I talked, other boys began to talk. Take Leonard for instance. He wouldn't talk at all when we first started. Now he talks when he's got something to say." Jules: "I talked too; don't forget me." Michael piped up: "That's right, you talk, Jules, and I talk when I got something to say. I never thought I could sit with a bunch of guys and talk about what happens to me." Therapist: "And what is the purpose of all this talking?" Donald: "So we can get to know our problems better." Therapist: "Like one of the things we can do tonight. This business of you flipping the bed over, Don." Donald: "That's right, I want to talk about that. I want to know what the hell got me to flip the bed, because if I stay here I know I'm going to go crazy. I don't want to go crazy. I want to get out." With this, Donald got up and started to prepare coffee for the group. The coffee project took about eight minutes. It served as an interruption, because every boy joined him in the preparations. It almost seemed as if this punctuated the end of the first half of the session, for what followed was extremely interesting.

With the coffee and cookies distributed, the boys sat about rather quietly. Then Donald said, "If I drink this coffee I'm not going to sleep tonight." The therapist laughed and said, "There goes another bed!" Donald burst into laughter and said: "What does this mean? When I was about four years old I used to like to play with matches. I used to light them and I'd stick them in the couch and then put them out. Once I wasn't fast enough and the couch caught fire and my mother had to come and put out the fire with water." The therapist felt that the narrative about fire-setting was only a prelude to something more that Donald was aiming for. However, the therapist decided to deal with the immediate question as it came up. He asked: "Does anybody have an idea as to what this means, playing with matches?" Jules: "Most boys like to play with matches, don't they?" The therapist indicated that they did, but it also had in addition a special meaning. The boys looked puzzled but could not supply any explanation. The therapist finally said, "Sometimes boys play with matches and try to set fires as a way of expressing anger, and sometimes it is a way of getting their parents to punish them."

Donald thought about this for a while and then said, "I wouldn't be surprised if that's why I did it." Jules: "You mean you want to get punished?" Therapist: "Well, it's not that you know that you want to get punished, but remember we talked about the conscious and unconscious part of the mind and how there is a part of the mind over which you have no control, the part of the mind, for instance, like when you dream at night? The unconscious comes out, it leads you to do things that to the conscious mind are silly, but you do them, nevertheless. What is in this part of the mind, where all the memories of your childhood are stored, you are not aware of." Jules: "Then maybe you can explain something, Mr. Ellery. I remember once I wanted to hit my mother. She did something, I don't remember; but instead of hitting her I put my fist through a window, then I kicked the dog, and I remember kicking the furniture. What gets you to do something like that?" The therapist explained to Jules that "there are times when children get very angry at parents. After all, in everybody's life, there are times when they want to do something and sometimes parents have to stop children from doing things. It is natural to feel angry when you are stopped, but on the other hand, society tells you you are not supposed to be angry, or if you are angry, you are not supposed to hit your parents. So what do you do with your feelings? You take it out on something else, and this is what they call 'displacement.' "

Donald: "That's like when your boss gives you a hard time and you come home and give your family a hard time." He then said: "Okay, now let's get back to this bed. I got to find out why I flipped that bed over." The therapist, addressing the boys said, "Let's see if we can help Don with this one." Everybody sat quietly thinking. They looked like professional crystal-ball gazers. After a while, Jules said, "Maybe you were just sore." Donald: "Yeah. Maybe I was, but why did I do it at three o'clock in the morning?" The therapist asked Donald if he had had a dream at the time. He said no, he couldn't remember any dream. It now occurred to the therapist that when Donald was complaining about his social worker, he kept referring to him as a "fag" (homosexual), and that the incident with the bed had come through immediately after. The therapist began to see a possible connection between the two ideas. However, before the therapist could formulate this fully in his own mind, Jules said to Donald, *"I'll bet you thought your social worker was in bed with you."* Donald laughed rather nervously. Because of the nature of the revealed content, the therapist dropped the subject, and it was evident from the expressions on the boys' faces that they had sensed the possible explanation, and they too did not pursue it.

Leonard said: "I remember, like Jules did, there were a lot of times I wanted to hit my mother. She used to tell me to do things, always yapping at me. I didn't hit her. I used to walk away." Michael: "I never had thoughts like that. I never wanted to hit my mother. My mother was good to me." This was not pressed with Michael (who was a latent schizophrenic). Jules: "Let me tell you fellows about a dream I once had and, Mr. Ellery, maybe we can all figure out what this dream was all about. One night, I don't remember how many years ago, I dreamed that my father was coming after me with a big stick. Just as he was about to hit me, I woke up. What does that mean?" None of the boys seemed to know. The therapist asked Jules whether his father had ever hit him. Jules: "No, my father never laid a hand on me. That's why the dream sounded so nutty." Therapist: "Jules, had anything happened?" Jules: "The night before I had that dream was one of the first times I ever stole anything." Therapist: "Do you think that maybe that dream was a way of kind of getting what you secretly wanted in your unconscious mind?" Jules: "What do you mean?" Therapist: "Well, Jules, you are telling us that you were never hit by your father, and yet when you steal, you dream your father comes after you with a stick and is about to hit you. Maybe you wanted to get hit, punished by your father." Jules leaned back in his chair and thought for a while and then said: "You know, maybe this is it. Do you think it's possible that *the reason I used to steal was a way of getting to see whether my [adopted] parents were going to do anything about it?* Ever since I was a little boy I remember that one thing always bothered me. I had the feeling that my parents didn't care what I did and they didn't care for me if they didn't care what I did. I think maybe I stole just to find out if they cared enough to stop me."

There was dead silence in the room. (This was a very impressive performance by a boy who was withdrawn and detached and would almost "creep" in and out of the meeting room in the early sessions.) The therapist must have shown the effect of this interpretation on his face, for Donald turned to him and asked: "Mr. Ellery, what's the matter?" The therapist "couldn't" answer and Donald repeated his question, now in an anxious tone: "Mr. Ellery, what's the matter?" Therapist: "Boys, I'm not sure I know how to say this, but I am so taken aback and touched by how grown up you have become, to be able to talk about these things." Donald: "Yeah, *and we used to sit around and talk about screwing all the time.*" Therapist to Jules: "You know, Jules, you have just told me the story of your life." Jules looked up and said: "I'd like to know something. Do you think if I had not been adopted, if I stayed with my original parents, this wouldn't have happened to me?" Therapist: "I don't know. Nobody will ever know. But I know a boy can spend a lifetime trying to find an answer to a question like this, for which there is no answer." (The therapist attempted to address himself by this to Jules's repeated runaways, probably in search of his natural parents.)

Donald asked: "What do you mean, adopted?" Jules: "I guess I can tell you now, I'm adopted. My parents were killed in an automobile accident. I don't remember how old I was when I was adopted, but I love my adopted parents. They are the only ones I ever knew and even if I had a chance to go back to my original parents, I don't think I ever would." Jules looked at the therapist for confirmation (support?). Therapist: "Jules, you can't love parents you never knew." Jules: "There's many a time just before I used to go to sleep that I'd lie in bed and look at the ceiling and I'd try to think about what my parents were like, who my mother was, what my father did. I don't know anything about them. Since we've been talking here, I don't think much about them any more. I got to go home to my foster parents; they brought me up." Michael: "If I were in your shoes, I wouldn't worry about who my parents were. I'd love the people who brought me up."

Now Donald felt free to reveal his "secret." He said: "My father isn't my real father. I found that out about a year ago. I think my mother tried to tell me this when I was a little boy, but I couldn't understand then. My mother was married once before, but I treat my father like he was my father, because I have no other father and he gave me money, he raised me, and I love him like he was my own father." (The record material did not reveal this and it was doubtful if it was true. Perhaps because Donald's mother had been married before, Donald evolved the notion that his father was not his biological father.)

Jules turned to the therapist and asked: "What makes a boy steal money from his parents?" Therapist: "A boy sometimes steals money from parents as a way of trying to get affection from them. Money is like a symbol of affection." He proceeded to describe how in growing up in a family where there were other children, every child felt that the others were getting more affection from the parents than he. Jules: "That's interesting, because I remember I didn't start getting bad until my sister was born. I guess I used to feel that I had my parents all to my-self, and now with my sister I couldn't have my parents all to myself." Donald: "And I remember how all the time my mother used to tell me not to hang around with the 'bums,' not to go down the street and hang around with the guys on the corner because they were 'bums,' and I used to go down to the corner and hang around with those guys my mother called bums." Therapist: "I guess hearing it so much you began to think of yourself as a bum." Donald: "Right. I used to think my mother was right. If I hung around with those guys I was a bum, but if I was a bum I couldn't hang around with any other guys."

Jules: "Gee, how did we get to talking about this tonight?" Leonard smiled and said, "Yeah, how come we are talking about this tonight?" Therapist: "Remember, when we started, I told you that in this group we were going to sit around and talk and in talking we were going to gradually start bringing up memories and talk about things that bother us and that get us to do wrong things—and these things, these thoughts, these memories, these feelings, are all in our unconscious mind." Jules said: "And now that we're talking, one thing leads to another, right? And then we remember these things." Donald: "Like last week when we were talking about parents dying, isn't that the same thing?" Therapist: "Yes, Don, these are memories that we have pushed down because we were afraid of them, and this is called 'repressing.' We sit down hard on them so that we won't think about them, but now that you brought it up, every child has had these thoughts. They become real scary because when you grow up you start applying your grown-up ideas of death to your childhood ideas of death. What you wanted when you were chil-dren was to get your parents out of the house for a while, so that they would leave you alone." Jules immediately said: "Yeah, leave you alone. Let them have a vacation so we could do what we want." Therapist: "That's right, Jules. Did you ever hear a child talk about somebody who died? What do they say?" Donald: "They say they've gone away." Jules: "That's right. Like my mother used to tell me about my aunt when I asked where she was. You see, my aunt died. My mother used to say 'She's gone bye-bye,' and I guess that's the same thing." The therapist confirmed this. Michael added, "Like you just want to get them off your back." The other boys nodded their heads.

Jules had gotten up to leave at this point. But before leaving he came over to the therapist, who was sitting, looked down at him, and said, "Thanks, I'll see you next week," and walked out of the room.

Since it was 8:30 this served as a signal for terminating the session. As the therapist was leaving, Donald came over to him and said: "Mr. Ellery, I don't know what I'm going to do if I have to stay in this place. I'm go-ing to go crazy." Making sure the other boys could not overhear, the therapist said: "Look, Don, I want to talk with you privately about this. I know you're upset." He said: "Good, okay, it's a date. Maybe next week?" Therapist: "Yes, Don." Donald: "Mr. Ellery, I don't want to go crazy." Therapist: "Don, I'm with you on this. You won't go crazy." Donald: "Okay. Then I'll see you next week."

COMMENT

It seemed that now censors had been successfully dissolved and the boys unreservedly faced their unconscious. From a psychoanalytic point of view, depth, significance, and value of the revelations and comments by the boys were too obvious to require elucidation on our part. Jules's offer at the outset of the session to contribute one of his (precious) cigarettes to the group was a significant mark of progress for a boy formerly so oral, possessive, and egotropic.

In recent weeks we had discussed during the supervision hours steps to emphasize and consolidate at appropriate junctures, based on the cues from the boys' communications, several points, most of which had come under consideration to varying degrees at different times. These were: *1]* to reorient the boys' attitudes toward the Village as an educational rather than punitive instrumentality and emphasize that in private schools wealthy families pay heavily for the same advantages; *2]* to press toward an understanding of what therapy is, and the therapeutic aim of the group; *3]* to stress the origin and concept of guilt; *4]* to develop greater self-confrontation in their own threat areas; *5]* to promote acquisition of psychological literacy concerning repression, displacement, motivation (as in stealing), death, and so on; *6]* to encourage a hopeful attitude in terms of personality maturing and the ability to deal with problems; and *7]* to heighten reality confrontation.

Note the growing relatedness when Donald referred to the group as "my friends."

Session Thirty-Five

(This session is recorded in summary form.) The session began with Richard raising a question with the therapist as to whether he should run away. His aunt, whom he liked very much and had not seen for some time, recently had had an operation and had now returned from the hospital. He asked permission to go home for the week end and see her, but this was denied. He felt sorry about it and wanted to know whether he should run away. The therapist asked Richard if he would not like to discuss it with the boys in the group. In a facetious manner, Michael advised Richard to run away, as did Louis. As a discussion developed, *Leonard took the lead* and said that Richard might have a harder time than he expected. For instance, if he ran away what would happen? He would have to come back and then he would be denied another week end. Although Donald claimed that he would run away under the same circumstances, he said, "I've had other reasons for running away, but I didn't run." This statement seemed to make an impression on Richard. Jules suggested that Richard discuss this matter again with the supervisor and maybe some solution would be found. Richard thought this was a possibility.

The therapist's contribution to the discussion was to project the situation into the future. He raised the question as to what would happen, in terms of past discussions, when the boys did leave the Village. There would be times when something would seem important, but carrying it out would bring unpleasant consequences. Richard related well to this proposition, indicating that maybe he ought to think more about this, and "not just use runs" as an immediate solution to his problem.

The room was extremely hot, despite the two fans that were provided, since it was situated directly under the eaves and had only dormer windows. This resulted in general fatigue and lethargy. However, the boys were able to start a discussion about cottage parents with complaints that were to a large extent a repetition of earlier sessions, during which Donald turned to the therapist with the critical comment that "this is just like what used to happen in the beginning." The remark had the effect of throwing the boys into a silence.

Macy, in the latter part of the session, insisted that he did not like his "relief cottage father" because he was always "observing" him and "snitches" to the cottage parents. This became the general theme in a conversation that arose among Jules, Macy, and Michael. Donald and Richard engaged in recounting to one another experiences with "relief" men, laughing hilariously at some of them. The therapist interjected the question of what was meant by "snitching." It developed that what the boys called "snitching" was actually part of the relief man's job, namely reporting all that had occurred during the cottage parents' absence. The therapist asked why this was looked upon as snitching.

Macy was growing extremely agitated, and he again began to talk, as he had in preceding sessions, about his being unable to sleep at night. The therapist tried to elicit from him what specifically happened when he went to bed. Macy said that he always thought about his relation to his cottage mother. He was very fond of her, but couldn't stand her screaming. She never spoke in a soft, low voice. He would do anything she asked. He proceeded to describe his feelings of attachment to her and how he could not tolerate any negative feelings toward her on his part.

Macy said he was the "favorite" in the cottage (which was confirmed by the supervisor), and elaborated on his extreme confusion between his liking his cottage mother and at times feeling angry toward her. He was not able to accept his anger or to tell her of it.

Macy now returned to recounting how he lay in bed and constantly thought about this, how he liked her but only wished that sometimes she wouldn't ask him to do such things as extra chores and that she wouldn't raise her voice when he didn't do a chore exactly as she wanted it. Yet he "holds it all in." He then spoke of his fears relative to his feelings and his worries. The therapist highlighted this conflict by verbalizing for Macy the fact that somehow it seems unnatural to him to have two opposite feelings toward one and the same person, sometimes even at the same time. At this point the session ended.

COMMENT

Here we have tangible evidence of the adage that "where the id was, the ego must be." Contemplation, anticipation, and evaluation of intransigent acts are now within the capacity of these boys. Macy reveals ambivalent transferential feelings toward his cottage mother and a new avenue of therapy is opened up.

NOTE

Because the boys requested it and had repeatedly returned to the subject over the past two months, we agreed to continue the group sessions through the summer. However, because of the therapist's vacation schedule, the boys were told that it would be possible for him to hold sessions only through July.[1] We anticipated difficulties in scheduling because of conflicts between the group and other occupations and recreations to which boys in institutions are assigned when academic school is out. The heat in the top floor room where the group met, which was growing increasingly oppressive as summer set in, was another consideration. This latter factor was envisaged as affecting the quality and possibly also the content of the interviews.

Despite our doubts and hesitancy, we felt that the gesture of gratifying the boys' wishes would cement their positive transference to the therapist and create an image of him as an all-giving parental figure, which none of them had experienced before. At the same time, the boys would be placed by this arrangement in a situation of experiencing difficult realities of their own choosing, that had not been imposed on them.

1. Perhaps it should be noted that both the therapist and the present writer, as his supervisor, contributed their services during this month.

The first session in July was the trip to New York, which was the subject of the boys' preoccupations for some weeks prior to its occurrence.

Session Thirty-Six

(All-day trip to New York—Summary.) The following boys were able to go on the trip: Michael, Leonard, Richard, Donald, and Macy. Jules could not go because of a party, held that day in his cottage, that included girl visitors and dancing. Louis had run away the night before, the precipitating cause unknown.

The therapist described the trip with the general phrase "most enjoyable." The group traveled in the therapist's car, rather than in the official station wagon. This gave the ride the quality of *en famille*. The group went to Radio City Music Hall, and afterward ate at a cafeteria. Each boy was given $2.25 to pay his own way into the movie and to buy food. This amount was set by us in advance to prevent the boys from changing the plans they had decided on and going on a "splurge."

The boys' conduct throughout was exemplary. Donald tended to walk a little ahead of the group as they walked from the parking lot to the theater, as though he did not want to be identified with the group. (The therapist's hunch was that he was made uncomfortable by the presence of Macy, the only Negro member. This hunch was confirmed by Donald's muttering something under his breath, which the therapist overheard, about being with a Negro. However, in the theater he sat with the group and joined it without hesitation in the walk to the restaurant afterward.)

Following lunch, the boys asked the therapist if they could go shopping for records. Apparently, some of the boys brought money with them for this purpose. The therapist assented, but indicated that he had to be back at the Village at four o'clock, and asked the boys to meet in front of the restaurant at three. All promised to be prompt and went their separate ways. By three o'clock, punctually, every boy had returned to the car. On the ride back, Donald and Richard told the therapist that they had been tempted to run away, but decided not to because they were with him. "If we were with somebody else, we might have run," they said. The therapist told them that he appreciated their telling him this. (Subjectively, he felt pleased at the boys' capacity to control their impulses.) No more was said on the subject.

In the movie Donald had appeared somewhat restless. It seemed as though staying put for an extensive period was difficult for him. He seemed essentially hyperactive. While the other boys sat calmly watching the movie, Donald was squirming in his seat, looking around, whispering into his neighbor's ear, and so on.

During the rides to and from the city, the boys talked and laughed freely and seemed to enjoy themselves fully. While walking to the movies, they talked mostly about cars they saw on the streets. The discussion was led by Macy and Michael. On the way from the movie, Donald initiated a discussion among the boys about rock-and-roll records.

NOTE

Because of Donald's persistent agitation, his hostility toward his caseworker, and repeated requests that the group therapist become his "social worker," we arranged with the clinical staff for the therapist to see the boy also individually. This was done because of the boy's need, but we also wished to observe the effect of the new arrangement upon his transference attitudes toward the group therapist. Another consideration was that we decided to continue Donald in the institution for another year, and it was felt that his current caseworker could not work this through with him. Donald had an individual interview with the group therapist before the next session.

Session Thirty-Seven

Donald was minutes late. Louis brought with him several magazines which he had taken from the table in the lobby. Macy and Jules helped themselves to a magazine each. The three boys sat quietly reading.

Richard stated, without any connection, that he would like to go home and see his seven-year-old cousin. He said: "The kid is acting like I used to. I always thought that boys of about twelve or thirteen steal. My cousin is only seven, and *he is already following in my footsteps.*" He went on to say that he heard from his mother that his cousin entered stores and took things when he was supposed to be in school. He would sneak out of school. Leonard: "Why is he following in your footsteps?" Richard did not answer for a while and then said: "Maybe because he once saw me steal something. I don't know. I don't know what that kid does. My cousin is a real stupid kid. He's going to have to learn the hard way." Therapist: "Do you have any idea why your cousin does this?" Richard: "Like I said before. I'm not sure. Maybe because he once did see me steal, but that's no reason for him to steal things now." Jules, who was reading the magazine, lifted his eyes and said to Richard: "Maybe he wants to get punished." Richard: "Get punished? At his age? He didn't do anything." Jules: "You remember? Like we were talking." Richard remained thoughtful but said nothing.

At this point, Donald walked in. He had a rather sour expression on his face. He mumbled hello to the therapist, ignoring the other boys, sat down for a few seconds, then got up, walked over to look at the boiling water on the stove, went to the washroom, returned, and sat down again. (This was the first group session after the first individual session between Donald and the group therapist.) Richard still seemed to be thinking about what Jules had said. Then, tentatively, "I remember we used to talk about that thing being in your unconscious mind about wanting to get punished and maybe that's why I did things." Therapist: "What about that, Richard?" Richard kept thinking but said nothing. Leonard: "I bet even that little boy wants this to happen." Realizing Richard's uncertainty about the concept of "unconscious" in the past, the therapist said: "Remember this is not something you are aware of. When you are aware of it, it may sound silly, but this is something you grow up with; it is in your unconscious mind and we call it 'unconscious' because you are not aware of it." Richard nodded his head as if suddenly the idea became clear to him.

A brief silence ensued. The therapist took this opportunity to bring the idea to a head. He said: "Fellows, this idea of punishment is as old as man. There are certain people who go out and pay to have other people whip them, because they carry a sense of guilt for something they think they did or thought when they were kids, but they are not aware of it any more. In olden days there were even religions where people would flog themselves or one another as a way of trying to get rid of guilt." Richard immediately responded: "That was religion?" Then almost as if trying to answer his own question, Richard said: "I heard of religions that used to do human sacrifice. What kind of religions are those? If you kill for religion then you still got the guilt." Jules: "That's why those were stupid religions." The therapist joined the discussion: "And that's one of the reasons there have always been religions, because people do have a sense of guilt." Richard: "That's why there's confession, right?" Leonard: "Yeah, in confession you talk about your sins." This subject was not pursued, and Macy stated that there might be a war between Russia and the United States because of Cuba. "If Khrushchev doesn't watch out, if he keeps shooting his mouth off, there might be a war." Richard and Donald proceeded to discuss war. Donald described how the United States was going to shoot rockets at Russia. Richard reminded him that Russia could retaliate. After a considerable time of this, the therapist decided to turn the discussion into channels more consistent with therapeutic aims, and asked if anyone ever thought that maybe war was another way in which people tried to hurt one another as a way of punishing either themselves or others. Donald: "How can that be? People start wars because they want land." Leonard: "That's not a bad idea."

Donald was becoming quite agitated. He began to roam around again; he prepared coffee just for himself. None of the others had had his coffee. Donald murmured something under his breath, which the therapist did not clearly hear. He turned his attention to Donald: "What's the matter, Don?" Donald: "Nothing. What makes you think something's the matter?" Therapist: "Well, Don, you look as though something is bothering you." Donald smiled, sat down, and said, "No, nothing is bothering me tonight." As he was holding the cup with one hand, he was tapping on the armchair with the fingers of the other. Richard: "I've been thinking about what you said. Where does this all come from?" Therapist: "Where does what come from?" Richard: "Like you were saying before about guilt." Therapist: "All of this comes from what happened between you and your parents when you were a child." Donald explosively exclaimed: "Parents! Parents! Why do you always talk about parents? If you was my father, you'd try to get me out of here, wouldn't you?" (Donald was obviously referring to the individual interview.) Therapist: "Don, if I were your father, I would try to do what is right for you." Richard: *"Mr. Ellery is like a father to us.* He sits with us and tries to help us understand our problems." Donald: "I don't hate my parents! I don't know why people say I hate my parents." (Donald was obviously referring to the individual interview, during which he had asked why he had to continue at the Village. The therapist specifically reviewed with him areas where he had difficulties. One of these was that he had "mixed feelings" about his parents. These were the exact words. Donald was now distorting what had been said to him by using the word *hate.)* He repeated, "Why do you think I hate my parents?" Therapist: "Don, I didn't say you hate your parents, but I wonder what makes you say that I did." Michael laughingly said, "Maybe he says it because it's really true." The therapist decided not to pursue this theme of hate, and dropped the subject for the moment. (The therapist had a feeling of discomfort as Donald brought in the content of the individual interview, since he was the only boy whom he saw individually.)

Addressing the therapist directly, Donald said: "I still don't know what your feelings about parents have to do with it. How can what happened between you and your parents have anythong to do with what happens to you now?" Although there was an element of belligerency in the way he asked the question, there seemed to be curiosity in it. Therapist: "That's a fair enough question, Don. A couple of years ago I had to go to see a psychiatrist, and I'll tell you why. I remember that what used to bother me is that I found every time I was out having a good time, I would nag myself and say to myself, 'Gee, what are you having a good time for, Norm?' You know Don, I had to go to talk out my problems to find out that the reason I was nagging myself was that when I was a boy, every time I was about to do something, my mother would say to me, 'Be careful, something is liable to happen.' Now, I'd forgotten that. But I really didn't forget. It was in my unconscious, and every time I was having a good time, my unconscious mind would bring up this memory and it would make me feel tense, even though I didn't know where it was coming from. I found that from talking about it, I was able to really enjoy myself and not torture myself."

Richard responded to this immediately. He said: "Every time, when I was a little boy, I'd go downstairs and my mother would say something to me, and I'll bet that's what has been giving me a hard time. She used to say, 'Keep out of trouble.' It never failed. As soon as I walked out of the house that was all I heard, 'Keep out of trouble,' and what do you think happened? I got into trouble!" He went on to describe a number of times when he went out of the house, and the next thing he knew, he was shoplifting, hitting girls, or planning some other escapade with friends. He finished by asking: "So what got me into trouble?" Therapist: "Richard, you just finished telling me." "What?" "Richard, I don't have to tell you; you told me. Come on, what put the idea of trouble in your head?" Richard: "Oh, that's right, my mother kept saying I'm going to be in trouble, so I guess I began to feel like all I could ever do was get into trouble."

Jules interjected: "But where does the guilt come from?" Richard: "Well, maybe you get sore at your mother for this and you don't like feeling this way." After a brief silence, the therapist said he agreed with what Richard said. Macy seemed lost in his magazine. The therapist thought it would be appropriate to bring Macy into the discussion on the basis of his feelings toward his cottage mother (see session thirty-five). Saying that he was sorry to interrupt his reading, the therapist turned to Macy and said, "Macy, weren't you talking about something like this a while ago?" Macy: "You mean about my not being able to sleep because I think of going home?" Therapist: "Macy, is that what you told us? You couldn't sleep because you couldn't go home?" Macy: "No. I mean about how I worry about Mrs. G. yelling at me." "And what worries you Macy?" "You mean I feel guilty about the way I feel about Mrs. G.?" Therapist: "What do you think?" Macy shrugged his shoulders and said, "Maybe I do feel the same thing as Richard."

Richard took over and said: "I'll tell you something I never told anybody before. When I was about twelve, I took a can of lighter fluid and sprayed it all over the living room. I was about to take a match and light up the living room. I got the idea from watching a television program at my cousin's house. My sister came in and grabbed my hand. If it wasn't for my sister, I would have burned down the house." Therapist: "Richard, was this the only reason that you did it? You just got the idea from a TV program?" Richard: "I think so. Why should I do something as nutty as all that?" Therapist: "Richard, what had happened just before that?" "I can't remember." "It may not be easy to remember, but we have time." Richard: "Let me think. Oh, yeah! I remember. The day before it was snowing and me and my friend were throwing snowballs and by mistake I hit a man on the side of his face. The man went and told my father. My father said to the man: 'I'll take care of it. When I take my boy home, I'll fix it.' I was so scared, I didn't go home. I was sore at my father, because he wanted to beat the hell out of me and didn't give me a chance to explain. I was so mad! Maybe that's why I used the lighter fluid." As if he needed to defend his father, Richard stopped abruptly and said: "Well, he's my father and he wanted to do good by me. He didn't want me to hurt people." Therapist: "Richard, it's not that your father isn't really a good father. This is not the question. But you know, very often parents will do things not realizing the effect it has on the child. We are not saying that your father is bad, but the same way some things happened to you that make you angry, things also happened to your father." Richard: "Maybe my father used to get beat up when he was a kid. In fact I know he was beat up, *so maybe that's all he knows, is how to beat up his own kid.*"

Donald changed the subject to a narration about "a character" in his neighborhood whom he always thought of as being "rotten," but one day, because this person did him a favor, he decided that the man was not so bad. It was difficult to understand just what Donald was talking about, since he brought this forth *a propos* of nothing that was going on. Donald finished by saying to the boys: "Sometimes you really don't know people. They act nice to you, but they are out to give you a real screwing." (The therapist recognized that Donald was talking about him.) The therapist decided to interpret the transference at this point and said, "Don, I have a hunch that this is what you feel about me." Donald broke into a smile and nodded his head, but didn't say anything. The therapist encouraged him to talk more about it. Donald said, "Naw, there's nothing more to talk about." Therapist: "Don, I know you feel something about me and maybe you'd like to tell us about it." Donald: "Well, I've been kind of feeling that, because of you, I have to stay at the Village for another year," and he explained to the group that there had been a conference which the therapist had attended, that the therapist was his caseworker now, and that Donald now had to stay at the Village for another year, but he was not going to stay. The therapist said to Donald, "If it's all right with you, Don, can I tell the boys what happened?" Donald: "Sure go ahead. I don't care."

The therapist explained very directly that he was asked to attend the conference, the first time this had happened. After the conference it was decided by the administration that Donald was to stay another year because he was as yet not "cured"; he still had many problems that would make for a very difficult adjustment if he were to go home now. The therapist specifically told the boys that he had not made this decision. Donald and the therapist had discussed the conference before it occurred and the therapist attended it only after Donald gave his permission. Following the conference, the therapist was asked by the administration to be Donald's caseworker. He had agreed, since he knew how unhappy Donald was and he felt that perhaps he could help him at this point. The therapist again re-emphasized the point that staying or leaving the Village in no way depended on him. Following this, Donald said: "I know I'm not staying because of you Mr. Ellery. The Village thinks they can help me with my problems. I don't think they can, but they think they can." There was no belligerency in his voice now. It was as if he were just waging a feeble battle. Richard said to Donald: "You ought to be glad Mr. Ellery's your worker now. You're always complaining about your other worker." Donald did not respond to this, but turned to the therapist and said, "How would you feel, Mr. Ellery, if you were in my place?" Therapist: "Don, I would probably feel as angry and frustrated and disappointed as you feel right now. I know, Don, how much it hurts inside." Donald lowered his head and did not say anything.

It was 8:30 now. All the boys got up to leave for their cottages. As the therapist was leaving, Donald and Richard stayed with him. Richard said: "What I was going to tell you, Mr. Ellery, was that I kind of feel that no matter how long I stay at the Village, when I get out I'm still going to get into trouble. I still got problems and I don't see how they are ever going to be solved at the Village." Therapist: "I feel that you are getting much better and that it is not hopeless. You will be able to leave the Village and understand yourself enough so as not to get into further trouble. But before this happens, Richard, there is a lot we have to talk about." Donald didn't say anything. With this, the boys and the therapist parted.

COMMENT

In this session psychological literacy was carried forward and a widening of conceptualization occurred, for example, in the discussion of religion and the unconscious. It was evident that Donald's transference feelings had been affected by the individual interview. He now defended his father against the therapist, for he feared accepting one for the other. The therapist, having become aware of it, was able to cushion the impact of the threat of "disloyalty" and "abandonment" of the father. Placing himself in the same category as the boys—as a patient—the therapist reduced the threat and opened a way for Richard to trace the origin of his delinquencies—his mother's image of him and her expectations from him. His tracing the screen memory of the cause for his nearly setting the house on fire was a remarkable feat of free association, and his recognition that his father was repeating his own father's dealing with his children would help him later to "forgive" his father.

As already indicated, we had been discussing for some time at our supervisory conferences two topics that needed to be clarified by the boys. One of these was that they had to recognize and accept the fact that they were "patients" requiring treatment and that the Village was a place analogous to a hospital (not a punitive instrument), where they could learn to overcome those conditions "inside" themselves that would keep them repeating their past behavior. The concept of the Village as having a nonpunitive aim had been broached in a previous session. Now the therapist took the opportunity to introduce the idea of "cure" before discharge from the institution. These two pivotal ideas would have to be carried forward later.

Session Thirty-Eight

On the way to the session, the therapist met Macy, who told him he was going for a (scheduled) haircut. He, therefore, came to the session ten minutes late.

At the outset of the session, the group agreed to end at eight o'clock, Michael, Louis, and Richard had to attend a party in their cottage, and there was a party also at Leonard's cottage. Both were scheduled to start at about 7:45.

Donald at once busied himself preparing coffee for the group. As a result, and unlike at other sessions, coffee was served early. Though this was accomplished quietly, it delayed the discussion. Donald looked considerably more relaxed than he had in the preceding several sessions. Michael commented that Donald was a "bug on coffee." There was a ripple of giggling, which quickly subsided, and there was silence again.

After a few minutes Louis reported to the boys that he was going on a home visit the following week and was looking forward to it. He then informed the boys that he got his "home visit" because he had run away. (Louis had run away for a day about two weeks before. He had told the therapist when they met on campus that he ran away because he was first promised a home visit, and then it was canceled. Louis returned on his own.) He said that this was the first time he had ever run away. (This claim was checked and found to be true.) He never wanted to run, he said: "But after they kept putting me off, I couldn't stand it any more. I thought I would really show them that I'm not bluffing. They thought I was a goody-goody, I would never run away. I'd warned them that they better listen to me. They didn't, so I ran." After a moment's pause, Louis continued: "I guess they realized I wasn't kidding, so now I got my home visit." He went on to say that he now had "a new sense of power," implying that if he should not be allowed a home visit in the future, he would run away again. Michael asked: "What do you mean, a new sense of power?" Louis: "Like I told you. They ain't gonna bullshit with me anymore. The only way I got any attention was by running away. Now everybody is trying to make it up to me. They should of done that before I ran away." (In this instance, at least, the boy was right. A check on the circumstances surrounding this episode revealed no valid reason for denying Louis his home visit. Someone on the staff "snafued.") In a gloating tone, Louis described how he could get any request he wants right now, " 'cause I got this new sense of power." He knew they didn't want him to run away, but now, finally after two years, "I showed them that I can run away, and now they are going to listen to me."

Silence set in briefly, then was broken by a remark from Donald: "I never ran away." Richard: "Yes, you did. What are you lying for?" Donald smiled, but said nothing. Richard: "I've been here a long time and I never ran away." Again silence. Macy had now walked into the room and sat down. Therapist (to Louis): "What about it?" Louis: "What about what?" Therapist: "What about this feeling of a sense of power, sort of taking things into your own hands?" Louis: "Maybe that's the only way you can do things around here if they don't listen to you," and he began to laugh. Michael: "What's funny?" Louis: "Nothing, I just feel like laughing." Therapist: "Maybe there are other times when you kind of took things into your own hands as a way of calling attention to yourself." Louis: "Like when?" Therapist: "In some of our past meetings the boys talked about taking things, stealing. Isn't that one way to show a sense of power; taking things into your own hands to get attention?" Louis: "I stole just for the fun of it." Richard: "But it wasn't much fun, you got caught." Leonard: "That's right, I remember stealing when my mother wouldn't give me an allowance. I had to go out and get one for myself by stealing." Richard seemed to come alive at this. He said: "That's what happened to me. I used to tell my parents that if they don't give me an allowance, I'm going to have to get one, one way or another. When I said that, they didn't even pay attention to me."

Louis: "Are you trying to say that my stealing was like my running away, getting a sense of power?" He seemed to address this question to no one in particular, but Richard turned to the therapist and asked, "Do you think so Mr. Ellery?" Therapist: "That's a possibility. Let's think about it." Macy: "I didn't steal for that reason. I don't know the reason, but I know I didn't steal for that reason." Nothing was said further. Then Macy: "Mr. Ellery, do you know what made me steal?" Therapist: "I'm not sure, but we can try to figure it out." The boys seemed puzzled, and the therapist presented several reasons why a boy might steal: "a sense of power, we were talking about; wanting to get revenge against certain people; as a way of getting attention; as a way of getting excitement; and in order to get caught, because getting caught would mean getting punished for feelings we're afraid of and try to keep pushing down." Jules immediately reacted to this and said: "Remember a couple of weeks ago I told you why I stole? *That was because I wanted my father to do something about it.* My father never used to pay attention to me, but when I started to steal he came after me." Richard (to the therapist): "Didn't you once tell us that sometimes a boy will take things 'cause he wants to get sent away 'cause he thinks he's done something real bad?" Therapist: "Sometimes it's because he had *thought* something real bad and now wants to push it down, but he still feels guilty for having thought bad." Richard looked thoughtful and Louis began to act up. He walked over to Michael and began to talk to him, and soon both began leafing through a magazine. This attracted Donald's attention and he walked over to them. A conversation arose among the three boys.

Richard moved over and sat down near the therapist and began to tell him a rather involved story of how he and a "couple of boys" had broken into a warehouse. He later told his father about it. His father worked out a plan for locking the other boys in the warehouse and calling the cops. (The story sounded a bit fantastic.) However, Louis and his group were making so much noise that, even though Richard was sitting nearby, the therapist could barely hear what he said. The therapist looked in the direction of the three boys. Louis caught his eye and said: "Okay, Mr. Ellery, I'm sorry. We're making a lot of noise." The therapist said to the three boys, "Maybe you'd like to talk with us." There was no response to this. Richard continued with his story during the therapist's interchange with Louis. His was a rambling tale with no point, and when the therapist asked him what the point was he was trying to make, Richard could not define it. Macy said to Richard: "Why don't you talk louder? I can't hear what you're saying." Richard looked in Macy's direction, but did not continue his tale. He said instead, "I was just telling Mr. Ellery a story." Donald yelled out: "So tell it to all of us!" but Richard would not.

Leonard, as though trying to bring the group back, said: "We were talking about stealing and the reasons for stealing. Is that what you're talking about to Mr. Ellery?" Richard: "Nah, I'm not talking about the reasons. I'm just telling Mr. Ellery a story." Donald yelled again, "Well, tell all of us."

Macy turned to the therapist and said, "Mr. Ellery, what do you think of two guys who are real good friends who are always fighting?" Therapist: "What do you mean, Macy?" Macy, pointing to Donald and Richard: "Why don't you ask them?" Donald: "Shut up! When I want to tell Mr. Ellery something, I'll tell him." Macy: "Go ahead, tell him the story." Donald, angrily: "Look, when I want to tell Mr. Ellery, I'll tell him. I don't need you to tell my stories."

Richard reminded the group that it was eight o'clock and the session officially ended. However, this was not the end. As the therapist was leaving, Richard and Donald accompanied him. Donald proceeded to tell a story of how the other day in the gym he was choking Richard, and described vividly having his fingers around Richard's neck. He said he wanted to provoke Richard into hitting back, because Richard's being his best friend worried him. Donald worried about Richard because other boys picked on him but Richard never hit back. Donald asked: "How come I had to choke Richard to get him to hit me back?" (What Donald seemed to mean was, "What feelings were behind it?") The therapist felt uncomfortable discussing this in Richard's presence, but Donald kept urging him on. In the discussion that ensued Donald described how he felt bothered by other boys' weakness and, surprisingly, sensed that Richard reminded him of his own weakness in his attempts to avoid difficulties.

COMMENT

The therapist took the opportunity didactically to push ahead the boys' understanding of the determinants of their behavior, in this instance, stealing.

Note Louis's responsiveness to an adult (the therapist) when he caught the latter's eye and his awareness of his efforts at disrupting the session; also, note Jules's application of his learnings to his behavior.

Session Thirty-Nine

ABSENT: Macy and Michael, on home visits; Jules, at a dance held in his cottage.

This was the last session before the therapist was to leave for his vacation. Leonard commented on this fact as the session began. Louis said, "This is going to be a sad session." "What do you mean, Louis?" the therapist asked. Louis: "My best friend was sent to Bellevue." He did not elaborate on this, even though the therapist asked him if he would like to tell just what happened. Louis shook his head and said, "No sir, I'm not talking."

Donald took over the conversation, saying that he had planned on running away, but decided against it: He would wait until the therapist returned from his vacation so that he could talk with Donald's mother and father. (The therapist had seen Donald's parents that day. They insisted on Donald's leaving the Village and threatened to institute a suit against the Village if he were not discharged. This was dealt with as reasonably as possible, but they remained adamant.) Donald turned to the therapist and said: "Remember I told you I was going to run away? I'll bet you knew all the time that I wasn't going to run." Louis: "Shit, if it was me, I would run. You know what I did? They wouldn't give me a week end. I ran. Now I'm getting a week end. They're holding a transition conference on me. I may get extra week ends. That's the way to do things!" Donald asked whether if he learned to read he could leave immediately. In a whining, babyish tone of voice, he said: "Am I staying because my cottage parents want me to stay? Well, I ain't going to stay." (Leaving the Village, which was encouraged by his parents, seemed to have become an *idée fixe* with Donald. There was really no way of talking with Donald about this, or at least the therapist did not feel there was.)

Richard, sprawling on the couch, now took up the theme of running away, and declared that he, too, would do it, because he did not know when they were going to hold his transition conference. Every time he talked to his social worker about it, his social worker gave him a different date. He was very upset because he had spoken to his mother recently and found that his social worker had told his mother that Richard was threatening to run away, and if he did, they were just going to add time to his stay at the Village. He didn't know what to do. Louis reiterated that his solution to all this would be to just run away and get people to do what you want them to do that way. Louis: "I got me a weapon, I got; I'm going to use it." Richard and Donald fell to describing how "lousy" the pass system was for home visits; how "they" promised you one day, and on the very day you were supposed to go home, somebody told you they made a mistake. Richard led in these accusations, and Donald kept confirming them: "That's the way it always works." Donald then turned to the therapist and said with finality: "If I don't go home at the end of August, I'm going to run away, too."

In response, the therapist stated that he did not wish to apologize for the pass system, and he could understand their "gripe," but there was another issue here, and that was what happened when one didn't get one's way? "It seems from what you're saying tonight that, when you don't get your own way, you take things into your own hands. Isn't this what happened when you were younger?" Louis immediately said, "I don't know what you're talking about." Therapist: "Louis, don't you?" Louis: "Oh, by the way, Mr. Ellery, I got to go back to my cottage at eight o'clock tonight, because I got to finish scraping the floors. All the boys in the cottage were told that if they don't do their chores, their next week end is going to be taken away." Therapist: "Louis, is it possible that you prefer to go back to your cottage rather than talk about this?" Louis: "Look, Mr. Ellery, I'm trying to tell you this is serious. Frankly, I'd rather be here because I can smoke here and I can talk. The whole cottage is on restriction this week and they won't let us smoke because a couple of guys messed up doing their chores." After a brief pause: "Okay, okay, you're right. I used to steal because my mother wouldn't buy me things. I used to ask her a hundred times to buy me some clothes and she wouldn't give me the money. I went into a store and I just took."

Donald immediately joined in: "That's what happened to me too. You think you're the only one? I took everything off the fucking rack that I could lay my hands on when I couldn't get money from my parents." Louis: "Hey, Mr. Ellery, are you insinuating that when I get out of here, I'm going to steal?" Therapist: "I'm not insinuating that. I'm insinuating that there is a problem every boy in this room is going to face. There are going to be times when you want something and you can't have it and what happens? Louis, you've been telling us how you've decided to take things into your own hands. What I am trying to say is that this goes back to something in your childhood." Louis grinned and said, " I want a definite date when I can go home." Richard: "Aw shut up! Enough!" Donald told Richard that if he said it again, he'd take him outside and "knock the shit" out of him.

Louis got up, walked around the room briefly, and then sat down near the coffee table. Donald left his seat and began to prepare coffee. The therapist had purchased a pie for the boys since this was the last session of the season, and they profusely thanked him. Donald served the therapist a piece of pie and coffee. Louis turned toward the therapist while he was sipping his coffee and said in a thoughtful manner, "You mean that's why I'm taking things in my own hands now, because when I was a kid I used to do that at home?" Donald did not give the therapist a chance to answer as he returned to his favorite subject. He said: "You know this guy Cookie? He ran away. He's working on a job and the Village forgot about him." Louis: "Aw, that's my boy, Cookie! He don't give a shit about nothing. He ain't got a conscience. That's like me." Therapist: "Louis, you don't have a conscience?" Louis thought for a while and said: "I don't know. I guess I do, but this guy Cookie can do whatever he likes and it doesn't bother him. I like that." Therapist to Louis: "And what does your conscience feel like to you?" Louis, looking very serious, said, "Aw shit, it just haunts you." There was absolute silence in the room now.

After a brief silence, Louis addressed the therapist, "I got a headache Mr. Ellery." Richard: "That's funny. This afternoon I was talking to my mother on the phone and my nose began to twitch. What made my nose twitch?" Donald: "In a way I'm glad I didn't run away, Mr. Ellery. You see, if I can get out and the Village lets me go, I'll feel good because I been here a long time and it means that if I run away, I leave in a lousy way and I don't want to leave in a lousy way, not after I've been here all this time. Maybe the Village can help me when I get out. I may want to come back to the Village and talk with the boys. I don't want to come back like a runaway. Do you know what I mean?" Therapist: "Yes, Don, I know what you are talking about. It sounds as though you are making a decision about yourself." Donald: "That's right, I don't want to act like I used to when I was a kid—just run and not give a shit about anybody, because I know I'm going to hurt only myself." (It was obvious that three boys—Donald, Louis, and Richard—were becoming aware of inner [neurotic] conflict. Richard with his twitching nose, Louis with his headache, Donald with his impulse to run and being stopped by "something" from carrying it out, were revealing conflict, an experience quite new to them.)

Louis was the key person in this discussion. He was looking significantly at the therapist as if he were trying to communicate something with his eyes. The therapist addressed him: "Louis, something is bothering you, isn't it?" "How do you know?" "This headache, look when it comes on." Louis said, "I can't snitch," as he looked around at the other boys. Donald to Louis: "You better tell him. You know Mr. Ellery never takes anything out of this room to the social workers." Louis looked at each boy successively as if he were taking a vote. Each nodded assent.

Louis proceeded to disclose the fact that one night he was awakened by a commotion in the middle of the night and saw A. B., a boy in his cottage, attempting to have "sex with other boys." At first Louis wanted to join in, but he stopped and thought to himself: "If I get into this, I'm going to have more trouble than I asked for. I better go back to bed," and he did go back to bed. But he said, "What bothers me is that I could have stopped A. B., and yet I had a hunch I couldn't stop him." Donald: "I know what Louis is saying. A. B. is kind of a dumb kid, but he is a nice guy. I'm a friend of A. B., or I *was* a friend of A. B. Sometimes he does crazy things. You want to stop him but you can't because he's got that crazy look in his eyes and you don't want to get into a fight." Louis: "That's right. That's right. I didn't want to get into a fight. I wanted to mind my own business." Louis looked relieved through Donald's support, and said, "Maybe I could have kept A. B. from going to Bellevue."

A period of silence set in and the therapist said: "Louis do you think you could have watched A. B. twenty-four hours a day? I wonder if what really happens to A. B. depends on your having to watch him." Louis, nodding his head, said, "I guess you're right." The therapist realized from Louis's tone of voice that he had not quite clarified Louis's confusion and said, "Louis, I'm going to play a hunch with you." Louis smiled in a challenging way, almost as if he knew that the therapist's hunch was right. He said, "Go ahead." Therapist: "Louis, I know that you are bothered by the fact that you did not stop A. B. from getting into trouble and being sent to Bellevue and because of what A. B. did. I very much doubt if you could have stopped him, but I think there is something else that's been eating you. Is it the fact that you were tempted to have sex, and maybe you feel you ought to get punished like A. B.?" Louis's head jerked back almost as if he had been struck in the face. The therapist stopped talking, letting his statement "sink in." Louis slouched in his seat, his eyes on the ceiling, lost in deep thought.

After a few minutes of silence, he finally said, "How did you know?" Therapist: "Your headache told me, Louis." Nothing more was said, since every boy in the room was lost in thought. Louis broke the silence. "Why the headache?" Therapist: "What was being said here tonight was talk about what we call 'conflict.' Do you know what I mean?" Donald immediately picked this up. "Like you want to do something and you don't want to do something." Therapist: "Right. Look boys." Using the left hand to represent an urge, he said: "You want to do something, as a child would, but now I suspect that all of you are growing up and there is another part of you that comes in and says: 'Should I do it? what will happen if I do it? [representing this with the right hand and pushing it against the left]. This is what we call the conscience. Where does it come from?"

The therapist went on to explain that the conscience arises from the rules and regulations that society, for its own preservation, sets down. "And now you are taking these rules and regulations inside of you, and as they begin to bang up against the part of you that just wants to do things, there's pain." Richard: "Like tension." Therapist: "Right, and this hurts. I know, fellows, that living the way you are—and this is true for all boys—there is a temptation to have sex with other boys. But why does society not want you to do this? Because in order for society to survive, there must be children born into the world, and it demands that sex be had only between a man and a woman." Richard: "In other words, if only boys kept having sex everybody would die out." "Right. But there is one more thing I want to raise, and I know this bothers every boy here, and that is the fear that if you are tempted to have sex with another boy you will grow up to be a homosexual, or as sometimes you fellows refer to it, a 'faggot.' " Donald stood up and said: "I remember we talked about that, Mr. Ellery, in your office, like when I was trying to choke Richard. Remember when I told you about that, and I told you because he was weak? Isn't it because maybe I thought Richard was going to grow up to be homo?" Therapist: "Yes, Don," but then added the comment: "It does not follow that because you are afraid of it, it is going to happen." Louis: "Wow, I sure got into this one tonight!"

Louis was lost in thought. There was silence in the room. He stood up and said: "I want to ask you a favor, Mr. Ellery. When you come back from vacation, can I see you in your office?" Therapist: "All right, Louis. I'll see you." "Thanks a lot. There is some things I just got to talk to you about." He sat down again and said, "It's eight o'clock, I got to go now." As he began to leave, Donald stopped him and said: "Louis, is that the way to go out of this room? This is the last session, remember. Say good-by to Mr. Ellery." Louis looked embarrassed as he smiled and came over to the therapist, extended his hand, and said, "I hope you have a nice vacation, Mr. Ellery." "Thank you, Louis," and, shaking hands, the therapist said: "I'll see you when I get back. I'll be back August twenty-ninth." Louis then left.

Richard took over. He said, "I'm going to tell you something tonight," and went on to describe a real gang fight which had every element of sadism in it, including the use of chains, belts, and sticks. Richard claimed that he was part of this fight. Extending his arm, making it tremble, he said: "You see how nervous I was. I didn't want to be in that fight, but I was so God damn scared, I didn't know what to do, so I got into the fight." After Richard had continued his narration for almost ten minutes, the therapist asked him about his being "nervous" in the fight. Richard: "I was scared of what my parents would do." Asked to be more specific, he said he was always frightened of his parents' hurting him when they beat him.

From this he then went on to describe one stealing episode from local stores in the neighborhood after another. Therapist: "Richard, I'm a little confused. You were always afraid of getting hit by your parents, but this didn't stop you from stealing." Richard: "Oh, I just steal for the fun of it." Putting up his hand to check him, the therapist said: "Richard, remember what we talked about? Five reasons for stealing." Then he enumerated on each finger a reason: "one—power, two—excitement, three—revenge, four—punishment, five—" but Richard would not let the therapist finish. He said: "That's it, punishment. I was thinking about what you said. I remember that all I ever done was things that got me punishment from my parents. I know it's crazy, I don't understand; but that's what I always do. I know I'm going to get hit and it's like I steal just to get hit, because it never fails." Richard then extended two arms in front of him, and said: "It's like with my left hand, I want to kill myself. They won't let me leave the Village. I feel I'm going to be here the rest of my life. I know it's not true but that's the way it feels. But my right hand says to me: 'No, you can live, you'll get out some day. So you kill yourself. What are you going to get out of it? Nothing!'" Donald: "Yeah live, live. That's stupid, killing yourself. You're not going to hurt anybody but yourself. Don't worry, you'll get out of the Village!" Richard: "I know I will, but it's like Mr. Ellery says, that's conflict." Donald now went on to describe a number of gang fights in which he was involved.

The session was ended after his recital.

Donald stayed on after the others left. He wanted a commitment as to exactly when he was going to be discharged from the Village. The therapist did not feel he could commit the administration in this matter. He told Donald that he did not want to make any promises he could not keep, but that he would be seeing his parents and talking about his leaving the Village. Donald said: "Well, my parents said you told them about your going along with their getting me psychiatric treatment. I'll go to a psychiatrist after I leave the Village." (When the therapist had seen Donald's parents, they had suggested that when Donald was discharged they would arrange for him to have psychiatric treatment in the city.) Donald said, "When my parents see you at the end of August, can I see you too?" Therapist: "All right Don, I'll see you with your parents and we can all talk together." He said: "Okay. I'll be here when you get back," and left.

COMMENT

The boys returned to subjects already discussed in previous sessions, which could be construed as resistive stereotypy, but the general reactions and the very pregnant silences rather indicated absorption, assimilation, or internalization of these ideas. Especially significant was the affect that now accompanied the repetition of the incidents of stealing, guilt, conscience, punishment, and the like.

However, what seemed most significant in this interview were the suggestions that can lead toward *control,* whatever the reasons may be for the deviant or antisocial behavior. For example, Donald told us that he wanted to run away, but decided against it, and, contrariwise, Louis promulgated the idea of acting upon any wish with no consideration of consequences. The need to implant the idea of self-control was a theme in many of our supervisory discussions.

Because ours were acting-out boys and not deeply psychoneurotic, we deemed it advisable to deal with the question of control rather directly and had waited for the opportunity and readiness for it on the part of the boys. At this point we felt the boys were becoming ripe for it, since they had worked on the understanding of causes for their troublesome behavior and the place of impulses in it. They had also come to recognize the differences between infantilism and maturity and had acquired considerable psychological understanding. Therefore, we made use of the opportunities the boys presented for re-emphasizing the importance of self-control and maturity versus impulsivity.

To repeat, such a procedure would be ineffective and even damaging where behavior served to resolve inner conflict or anxiety, as in the case of psychoneurosis. Our boys, while having considerable underlying anxiety and guilt, acted them out. For this reason direct, didactic or exploratory procedures could be effective, but not before resistances were eliminated and the capacity for self-confrontation established. The ineffectualness of the direct approach in the case of psychoneuroses is well demonstrated by Frank (pp. 154-168) and Richard (pp. 736-738), both of whom were psychoneurotic.

From this point on we frequently emphasized the theme of the relation of control and maturity, and made it almost an exclusive topic toward the end of treatment. The resurgence of hostility against the institutional staff could be understood as being a displacement of the boys' resentment toward the therapist for "abandoning" them by going on his vacation.

NOTE

During the two weeks before the group met again after an interval of six weeks, several of the boys, upon seeing the therapist on the campus, inquired when the "group discussions" would start. The boys who were most insistent were Richard, Donald, Macy, and Michael. A fortnight before the group met, Louis came to ask the therapist if he could become his caseworker. He said he was unable to get himself to talk "to her"; though he had "a lot of things to talk about," he would never tell his caseworker. He mentioned leaving the Village in January, looking at the therapist to confirm it. The therapist would not commit himself on either count, saying that he would consult with the authorities and see what could be done, as well as considering the availability of time in his own schedule. As to Louis's being discharged in January, the therapist could not enter into this matter since it was beyond his scope. Louis accepted this, expressing his hope to be out of the Village by the end of December.

In discussing the situation with the caseworker involved, the therapist discovered that while he had been on vacation a transition conference was held, and it was decided to discharge Louis in January. The boy had been informed of this decision and promised that he would be home that month, because, the therapist was told, "he was pushing hard to get out and we felt that the only way we could hold him was to give him a definite promise."

Session Forty

(This was the first session following summer vacation—a lapse of six weeks.) The boys greeted the therapist warmly as they came into the room. Richard and Macy were about four minutes late because they had had to go to the infirmary. The boys sat around quiet and relaxed. After a period of silence, Donald turned to Leonard: "Maybe it's time you began to talk." Leonard looked embarrassed and after a few moments said: "I had a pretty good summer. It went fast." A discussion arose among Donald, Michael, and Jules as to how fast the summer went. For Jules it went "kind of slow." He didn't get enough home visits. Michael had "a pretty good time" at the Village, "no kicks about that." Donald said, "I'm getting out in October, October fifteenth," and looked toward the therapist for confirmation. He continued: "I'll bet you guys know it was pretty slow for me this summer, waiting to get out of here." Jules with a smile on his face said: "You're still here. We expected you to be gone already." Donald just shrugged, but did not say anything.

This interchange was followed by a rather long pause, the boys obviously feeling uncomfortable and too diffident to speak, almost as though they were trying to find a way out. The therapist commented that, just in case memories had grown a little hazy, he would like to go over why the group had gathered. He explained that "we are here to talk about feelings and things that make problems for us, how we get along with ourselves and other people, as well as the feelings that get us to do wrong things that get us into difficulties." Macy quickly picked this up and said: "That's right. It's like we weren't even away. I feel like I was here last week." Jules: "Yeah, isn't that funny? I feel the same way—like I was here last week, like we never stopped seeing each other." Leonard: "I don't feel that. I know it was six weeks that we haven't been in the group." Jules: "Tonight nobody is saying 'I quit.'" Richard, who had come in and sat down rather quietly, said: "Ha ha, remember that shit, remember Jameson?[2] When I was coming over tonight, I saw Jameson, and I told him to come to the group and he said, 'Shit, I'm not going to that group.'" Louis: "I was going to come in here, too, and say 'I quit,' but I thought better of it. I decided to stay; then I found that you creeps ain't such bad guys after all."

Sparked by Donald, the talk turned to the subject of going home. He again announced that he was going October fifteenth. Louis said he was going the end of December "come hell or high water." Jules: "Me too. I'm supposed to go at the end of December, and I'm going to get the hell out of here whether they keep me here or not." Jules slumped in his seat, looking up at the ceiling as though becoming uninterested in the discussion after having made his declaration. Louis turned to Macy and said, "When are you going home?" Macy: "As soon as I can get the hell out of here. They haven't had a transition conference on me yet. Hey, Mr. Ellery, do you remember when my transition conference is supposed to be?" The therapist told him that he did not know and reminded the boys that he had nothing to do with the scheduling of transition conferences. Richard was now telling the boys how his conference kept being put off from one month to the other. He was always given another promise by his social worker. At this point he did not know what to believe, and the hardest part about staying at the Village was the fact that he never really knew that the date they gave him was really the truth. He described a number of incidents in which he was given a date only to look forward to it and then find that the date had been changed with no explanation as to why. Picking this up, Donald reiterated, almost by way of reassuring himself, that he was definitely going to leave on October fifteenth. (There had been a transition conference on Donald at which the therapist was present with Donald's consent. The date set for Donald to leave the Village was October fifteenth.)

Louis, looking at the therapist out of the corners of his eyes and, acting childish in an obvious effort to provoke, said: "This is a fucking place. You just serve your time. They ought to put you in prison to

2. The boy who visited the group once and refused to continue.

serve your time." There was a provocative smile on his face as he said it, as if he were waiting for a reaction. When none was forthcoming, he said: "You don't get anything out of this place. They just teach you to be a bigger crook. You know the adults they got around this place? They're bigger crooks than the kids; that's why they don't get caught, because they are bigger crooks." Macy broke into laughter at this remark, and Richard said: "When I get out, do I have to tell the school that I was at Children's Village? Don't I have a record?" He turned to the therapist and asked for an answer. The therapist explained that boys leaving the Village do not have "records." Donald was not sure of this, and expressed his doubts. He thought "the record will follow me around for the rest of my life." Louis: "I would rather spend my time in Sing Sing. If I'm going to learn 'big things' I might as well learn them big in Sing Sing, not at the Village." Leonard began to laugh and looked at Louis as one who was more to be pitied than laughed at. Leonard asked at what age he could be sent to prison if he got into trouble after leaving the Village.

This question grew into a general discussion about the various prisons such as the Tombs, Sing Sing, Riker's Island, and so on, in which all the boys participated. When the group quieted down the therapist commented that he wondered whether the boys worried about only the date of discharge. Were they not concerned also about what happened after they get out of the Village? How would they adjust? Donald's response to this was immediate. Addressing the boys he said: "That's what's on my mind all the time. If I get out in October—October fifteenth—then I got to think of holding a job, going to school at night. And you know what my father said to me? My father said that he wants me in by nine o'clock every single night." Everybody quieted down at this and looked at Donald, with pity in their eyes. Louis was first to speak. "How are you going to come in at nine o'clock? If my father wanted me in at nine o'clock, he'd be glad to see me at two o'clock in the morning." Donald: "I don't mind if my father wants me in at nine o'clock. He's doing it for my own good." The expression on his face, however, was far from being appropriate to his utterance. He looked sad and depressed.

The therapist said to Donald: "How do you really feel about coming in at nine o'clock?" Donald remained quiet for a moment, looked rather pensive, and then said: "I guess it's for my own good. I don't mind. Maybe on week ends my father will let me come in a little later. You know, like when I go out with a girl on a week end." He was lost in thought. Louis began to act up at this point saying, "When I get out I got to get me some jigjig" (fornication). The boys laughed uproariously at Louis's remark. When the laughter subsided, Donald turned to the boys and said: "You know that crazy Mrs. D. [a specialty teacher]? She's a crazy loon." Donald stood up, stooped over in imitation of her walk, saying: "She's an old loony. They ought to retire her; she's past seventy-eight" (which was not the case). He sat down again and told of how he had come to her class and noticed on the wall a number of paintings he had never seen before. He sat down on a desk and began to examine the paintings, saying they looked pretty good. Mrs. D., according to Donald, ran over and began pushing him saying, "Get off the desk." Donald got very angry and said to her: "Keep your hands off of me! Just ask; I'll get off." Mrs. D. said: "You are a lousy no-good hoodlum. You belong in prison, not in the Village, you lousy hoodlum delinquent."

As Donald was telling this, *his eyes welled up with tears*. He took the therapist's arm and said: "I'm not a hoodlum, Mr. Ellery. Why should anybody call me that? You know what else happened? I walked up to her at the end of the hour and I said to her: 'I'm sorry for the way I acted. I didn't mean to upset the class. I won't do it again.' She said to me: 'You are a lousy hoodlum. I don't have to talk to you. I'm a citizen of the United States.' That's a hell of a way for her to talk, especially when I come up to her to apologize. I felt like killing her, but then I thought to myself, what's the point? I don't have to stay with her long, just a little while, a day, and then I leave." The therapist remarked that he thought that Donald exercised quite a bit of control. Macy: "Yeah, that gal, she's crazy. She's always walking around talking about hoodlums and delinquents. Not only that, but she's always snitching on us."

Louis interjected himself into the discussion and began to take over. He described how he sat in his class and, at an appropriate moment (an appropriate moment being when there was peace and quiet in the classroom), hid his face and let out a shriek. Richard invited him to demonstrate it, and Louis seemed only too happy to oblige. The shriek did have something of a blood-curdling quality to it, but the boys broke into hilarious laughter. In competition with Louis, Richard told stories of outwitting teachers, of tricks boys played on each other, of boys in a "sneaky way" starting a chant going in the classroom and when the teacher looked around he couldn't discover who started it, of a board eraser mysteriously thrown across the room. Donald contributed vivid memories of his "fooling around in the classroom" and of friends who did likewise. Soon Louis and Donald fell to complaining against teachers who "got mad" when all this occurred. The other boys present seemed to sympathize with the two. Even Leonard got in on the act, describing how a few times when the teacher was not looking he had made noises which provoked general laughter in the classroom.

The therapist raised the question with the boys about the teacher's getting angry. He asked: "What did you expect?" and then added, "It seems to me that you are having a hard time giving up babyish ways." Richard said: "It's not that, Mr. Ellery. *We are just talking about fond memories of the past.*" Donald laughingly said: "Fond memories, my ass. You still do it, Richard." Richard: "No, I don't!" Michael turned to the therapist and said, "Sometimes it is a lot of fun being a baby." Therapist: "What do you mean, Mike?" Michael: "It's good to have a laugh once in awhile, like you are with all the boys in the room and you don't want to be left out in the cold." (This statement was important in the light of what transpired later in the discussion, when the boys talked about being called "chicken.")

A discussion about stealing was introduced and all of a sudden Michael began to talk about shoplifting, going into stores with a big overcoat and filling pockets with goods. Louis took the floor and mimicked a boy going into a store and stealing: He is apprehended by the police and, once in custody, he bows his head in shame and in a low, sobbing voice asks forgiveness and pleads with the policeman to let him go; he will never do it again. The policeman releases him. Louis then acts out walking out of the door of the supermarket where he is apprehended, turning around to the policeman and sticking a finger up in the air as he says, "You fuckin' sucker," and runs off. There was a pandemonium of hilarity among the boys. Jules laughed so hard he was pounding both feet on the floor, spasmodically rocking back and forth in his seat. (Louis's mimicry was excellent. In fact, at some points, the therapist had great difficulty restraining himself from bursting into laughter.)

Louis was in his glory and proceeded to tell the boys that sometimes this did not work when he got caught. The cop might say to him: "Never mind the tears, sonny. You were stealing." Louis now attempted the "cool," detached approach, and demonstrated how it worked. He would turn to the policeman and say: "You are quite right, officer; I stole and I realize now that I've done something for which there is no forgiveness. I was with these bigger boys and they asked me to come along with them shopping. I like to be with big boys, officer. I didn't know they had stealing in mind. Well, I went along and I saw they were stealing. Officer, I didn't want them to think I was chicken so I stole too. I realize now that I did a very stupid thing." Louis then described how the officer might say to him: "My boy, I realize you learned your lesson. I'm going to let you go." Louis would bow very politely and say: "Thank you, sir. You will never regret it." Louis would then walk out of the supermarket. At the door he'd turn around and yell to the officer: "You dumb cock-sucker!"

Donald jumped out of his seat and took the floor. He began by describing and using both hands to demonstrate his techniques for shoplifting; how he, like Louis, used to bow his head and weep when caught. He got away with it on three different occasions, but the fourth time the policeman said to him, "Okay, Buster, no more tears, you're going away." Richard now stood up and began to deliver his spiel on stealing, various ways of using hands and fingers to take things off shelves and putting them into overcoat pockets.

This continued for about ten to fifteen minutes. Following the hilarity, the group quieted down and the boys sat in silence. The therapist said, "Are you boys aware of what you are doing tonight?" Richard, looking in the therapist's direction, said, "What do you mean, Mr. Ellery." Therapist: "It seems to me that this has happened before, hasn't it? Even before you came to the Village—standing around bragging, bragging about stealing. Remember we talked about what happens when you are called chicken and how you had to prove that you were not chicken? Isn't something like this happening tonight?" Donald said: "It will never happen to me again. When I get out of the Village, I'm just not going to steal. I told you, Mr. Ellery. By the way, what I said tonight, that isn't going to keep me from leaving on October fifteenth, is it?" Therapist said: "No, Don, what you say here has nothing to do with your leaving on October fifteenth, but there is something here to think about. This bragging about stealing." Louis looked somewhat subdued and said, "We were just talking about old memories." Macy: "Like hell you were. You said before that when you get out of here you are going to steal again." Louis: "I was only kidding. I told you I'm just talking about old memories." Michael: "Maybe we ought to think about what we just said, because we're talking like we're heading for prison again." Richard: "Like we were acting up in school when we were trying hard not to stop being babies. Right, Mr. Ellery?" Jules got up at this point and said, "I got to take off, Mr. Ellery." It was now about 8:27 and the boys got up and ended the session.

The boys had taken their coffee early in the session with little commotion.

COMMENT

As could be expected, this was a "regressive" interview. The continuity having been broken, the boys returned to the original pattern, very much as ordinary boys do on the first day of school. But the significant part of this phenomenon was that, whereas, when they first came to the group their behavior reflected their *actual* personalities, now they re-enacted "fond memories of the past," and were aware of the roles they now played. This could be described as *awareness by contrast* or *derivative insight*.[3] The vicarious re-enactment of stealing episodes by Michael, Louis, and Donald have therapeutic value as mirror reactions that help self-confrontation and serve the emergence of a better self-image, controls, and insight. To some of the boys this re-enactment had counterphobic significance—for Louis more than for the others, as he attempted to convey his need of the therapist and to attract the latter's attention to himself.

The boys further conveyed their emergent maturity by looking ahead: Richard's concern about a "record"; Leonard's query about the age of imprisonment; Donald's projection into the future as to job, school, relation to father, and adjustment when he returned to his community, as well as in his manifest control during his conflict with the art teacher.

The therapist did well to prevent the regression and re-enactment from running its gamut by pointing out to the boys the nature of the discussion and thus bringing them back to reality. This had a good effect, as witnessed by Michael's and Richard's last remarks. Such a step taken too early in treatment might have had negative results, however.

Session Forty-One

The session started by being disorganized, because of an error on the part of the clerk in sending passes to the boys.[4] As a result some of the boys were not certain whether a session would be held, and others came late. Among the latter were Louis, Macy, and Michael. (In fact the therapist had to call on the telephone for Michael, whose pass indicated a wrong date for the session.) Donald brought with him a small dog which belonged to one of his cottage mates, and the boys in the room took turns petting it as the group talked about it. Jules brought a radio with him, and Louis and Jules were busy operating the dial, while Macy had several magazines that he had picked up in the lobby on his way up to the meeting room. Leonard, too, was busy reading a magazine. These occupations continued for almost ten minutes, by which time all the boys had arrived.

When the initial hubbub quieted down, the therapist commented

---

3. Slavson, *Analytic Group Psychother-apy* (New York: Columbia University Press, 1950), Chapter IV.

4. It must be noted that, according to our plan, passes were not required by us and the group therapists never looked at or signed them.

that there seemed to be some difficulty getting started. No one said anything. The dog wandered around the room and finally went over to the therapist. Michael asked the therapist whether he liked dogs.

The question turned everyone's interest to the therapist. All gazed upon him expectantly. The therapist leaned over and patted the dog. All eyes turned away from him. (It was obvious that the boys' watchfulness was prompted by their desire to ascertain his attitude toward dogs.) Following this, Michael started a discussion about a transition conference, saying that he did not know when a conference on him would be held. Louis said, "I got my transition conference already and I'm getting out of here in January." He did not state who specifically had told this to him. Michael wanted to know whether the therapist was going to transition conferences, and was again told that he did not. Jules inquired: "Well, why don't you write a report on how we get along in the group? Maybe we'd get out faster." The therapist smiled and asked, "What would you like me to put into the report?" Jules: "Just put in that we are ready to leave." Michael added: "That's right, Mr. Ellery, write down that I come to the group and now I'm ready to go home." Now Louis picked up a magazine and began to read, as Macy, Louis, and Leonard were already doing. Smilingly, the therapist said, "Gee, maybe when I write a report, I ought to put down that Louis is reading a magazine and Don is playing with the dog." Louis: "Okay, okay, never mind, don't write reports on us." This remark caused general laughter on the part of all the boys, but Louis and Leonard put down their magazines. However, Macy continued reading.

Jules and Louis got into a discussion about what they were going to do when they "get out." Louis spoke about finding a job and having money for himself because *he didn't want to depend on his mother* and to have to ask her for money. Jules said: "I got a job waiting for me already. I think my father is looking into it. When I get the job I got to get me some clothes, because I haven't bought clothes in a long time." Louis: "I know that I can make about $50 a week. I can work. I'm a pretty good worker and I think that I'll get a job when I get out and maybe I could also go to school." Donald looked up and said, "I got a job waiting for me in a luncheonette." Turning to the therapist, he said, "I want to go to night school like I told you, Mr. Ellery" (referring to his individual sessions with the therapist). With this a brief silence descended. Donald started to prepare coffee, which served as a signal for all the others to proceed to do likewise. Richard walked over and asked the therapist whether he would like some coffee. The therapist told him that he would. Richard prepared and brought the coffee to the therapist. Cups in hand, Richard, Donald, and Leonard sat down. Soon the boys were all seated. The silence continued.

The therapist commented: "I know, fellows, that you are all interested in getting out and the time when you will be getting out. But you know one of the things we have talked about here is what happens when you do get out." Donald: "I'm not worried about what happens when I get out. I know I'm going to get a job and I'm going to hang around with my brother and his friends and I'm not going to have any more trouble." Louis spoke up: "What makes you so sure you aren't going to have any more trouble?" Donald: "I learned my lesson. I'm not going to be a jerk and get into trouble, because the next time I can't come to Children's Village; the next time it's prison for me." Richard: "You'd look good behind bars." Donald: "Aw, shut up, will you? If you get behind bars, you're not going to wear a brand new suit and spats." Louis looked very serious. In a low voice that gradually grew in volume, Louis said: "When I go home on a week end, I don't hang around with my old friends anymore. I don't even see them. I don't even want to see them, even though they still live on the block. Many times I just go away from the neighborhood. I know some other people from a church my mother used to go to, and they are not such bad guys after all. Like I used to think they were fags." Michael: "That's like with me when I go to B——— on a week end. I don't look for my old friends. They get me in trouble and I don't want any more trouble and if I hang around with them I'll get into trouble." Leonard: "But it ain't easy making new friends." Richard: "That's right, Leonard." Richard now turned to the therapist: "Isn't that right Mr. Ellery? You just can't go out and make new friends; it's not easy." Therapist: "What's it like, Richard?" He said: "I don't know. I know it just isn't easy."

At this point the therapist said: "I remember we once talked about this, boys. Doesn't making new friends have something to do with the way you feel about yourself? For instance, is it possible that one of the questions is, 'Will boys who don't get into trouble or do wrong things want me for a friend?'" Richard: "We talked about that and I remember the last time I said something about they are not going to be sure whether they can trust me, and maybe I'm not so sure I can trust them." Louis interrupted him and said, "One of the things I found out was that I was a sucker for having my old friends." Donald asked him: "How were you a sucker?" Louis described how he felt he had been "used." He thought he was a "wise guy," to get into trouble, have fun, act real crazy, run around, steal, bop girls, be involved in gang fights (which he described in some detail). He summed up by saying: "One of the things I realize now, I was used. For instance, I'm on the inside [in Children's Village], my friends are on the outside [in the city], so I get nothing out of it." Richard: "That's what happened to me. My mother always used to say to me, 'If you hang around with bad friends, then what's going to happen is that you'll end up behind bars!' Sure enough here I am." He turned to the therapist and said, "Not that I'm saying this is a prison, but I'm not home and sometimes it feels like a prison." Donald: "One thing I found out at Children's Village; if you want to make something out of yourself you can't hang around with a bunch of guys that are going to call you chicken and then get you into trouble. Like, you're still tempted to get into trouble but what does it get you? It's fun for a while and that's it."

During this discussion, Macy continued reading and Richard said to him, "Why don't you put the magazine down?" Macy: "I can read. I'm listening. I hear everything that you're saying." The therapist commented: "This sounds different from what we used to sit around and talk about. I feel as though I'm sitting with a bunch of men who are getting to know what's really right for themselves." Michael smiled at this and said, "Fellows, remember what it was like in October?" Louis said, "Yeah, boffing and banging [sexual intercourse], that's all we talked about." Donald laughingly said: "Yeah, boffing and banging. How come we don't talk about banging girls any more?" Louis stood up and said: "I can still bang, but I don't got to brag about it. When I was home the last time, a couple of the boys from the old gang paid me a visit. They said, 'Hey, Buster, you going to join us again when you come out of that dive you're at?' I told the boys I wasn't at a dive and that I wasn't going to join them. One of the boys wanted to get fresh and kind of threatened me. I told him I'd bust his head open if he tried to push me around." Richard: "If there are gangs in your neighborhood, you can do two things. You can get away from the neighborhood or your parents just got to move because, when these gangs are around, they put pressure on you to join." The therapist picked this up and recognized the reality of this problem of returning to neighborhoods where there were gangs and what it was like for boys when the gang asked them to join. Louis said: "You don't have to. A lot of guys do it just to act big, but you don't have to join. You just stay away from them and you stay away from the neighborhood and you find friends somewhere else."

Donald looked agitated. Although he remained in his seat, his expression suggested that he had removed himself from the situation in the room. He then leaned over toward the therapist and said, "I want to tell you something." Richard attempted to break in, but Donald said, with irritation: "Let me talk, Richard; let me talk first." Richard would not renege and Donald said with disgust: "Aw forget it. I'll tell you privately, Mr. Ellery." With this he left the room. He came back in a few minutes and walked around the room toward the electric plate and prepared himself another cup of coffee; then he sat down in his seat next to the therapist.[5] Meanwhile, Michael got into a side conversation with Macy which the therapist could not overhear. Jules was listening to the radio, which was playing very quietly. Soon Louis took the radio from Jules, and placed it against his ear. The sound of the radio was not audible in the room. The therapist turned to Donald and asked: "Something is bothering you, Don?" He said: "Nothing is bothering me. What makes you think something is bothering me?" Therapist: "Just the way you look, Don." Donald: "I'll tell you when I see you alone, Mr. Ellery. I don't feel like talking about it in front of everybody." At about this point there arose lively side conversations: Leonard was talking with Richard, Louis with Macy and Jules. After three or four minutes, Donald seemed to feel that he could talk to the therapist privately. He leaned over and in a low voice said, "When I go home, there's something strange I can't quite figure out." He then described how when he went home now, he found that it was quiet there; there was no yelling, no screaming, and his father was very nice to him. He said, "My father is always very nice to me, but now he is exceptionally nice." Contrary to his past practice when Donald talked to him in confidence, the therapist now tried to involve the group, and he said to Donald, also in a low voice: "Maybe the other boys would like to hear what you have on your mind." Donald: "I don't care if they hear." Louis: "Then speak louder so we can all hear you." Donald leaned back in his chair and turned toward the group.

He sat quietly for a moment, then Richard said, "Come on, we're waiting to hear." Donald: "Give me a chance, give me a chance. I'll tell you. Don't rush." He then proceeded to tell the boys how in the past when he used to go home his father was "all right." Once in a while his mother would push his father around, and it didn't bother him. But now his father allowed him to come home at any time of the night. He clarified this by saying: "I don't mean I can stay out all night; but, for instance, if I come in at two o'clock in the morning, my father doesn't yell or scream at me the way he used to. When my father used to scream at me, I would do it intentionally." Richard: "Yeah, just like me. When my father would tell me, 'Don't come in late,' and then scream and holler about my coming in late, what do you think happened the next night? I came in late." Donald, interrupting: "Time [stop], huh, fella? I'm talking, I got the floor." Richard leaned back and didn't say

5. It was suggested to the therapist at the supervision conference that the two boys could have acted out the conflict between them in role-playing and thus find the solution. We also suggested that as the boys became still more com- | fortable in discussing their strife with their parents, the therapist should take alternately the roles of the child and the parent, thus demonstrating a so- cially more acceptable way out of a dilemma or conflict.

anything. Donald continued: "When I go to my father now, I say: 'Dad, I need two dollars. I'm going out with the boys.' He doesn't give me a hard time. He doesn't scream and yell, 'What boys you going out with?' or, 'Don't go out with the bums!'" Donald described how his father would give him the two dollars and just say, "take it easy spending the money, Don." Louis: "Well what's the point of the story?" Donald: "I don't know if there is any point. I'm just telling you the way it is when I go home." He said nothing beyond this. Therapist: "Don, somehow this worries you, doesn't it?" Donald thought for a while and said: "I don't know if it worries me. I don't think I'm worried. I'm just happy that my father is nice to me when I go home. One of the things I found out here was when I went home and my parents used to say, 'Don't go out with bums,' 'Come in early,' and always tried to tell me what to do, I would find ways of not doing it. Now I don't think I'm going to have to do that [to be spiteful] any more, because they are nice to me."

Richard: "I got my own room and my sister can't come in. When I go home on a visit and my sister tries to get in, even my mother yells at her and says: 'Leave Richard alone. He can stay in his own room if he wants to.' That sure is different than the way it used to be. When I used to go home all my sister and brother would do was live in my room and if I tried to get them out, they would snitch on me and then my mother would hit me." Louis, with surprise: "Your mother hit you?" Richard: "Well, not hit me. She used to scream at me and get my father after me." Donald quickly spoke up: "Now they treat me like a man. My mother told me that I was always my father's favorite. I once heard my father say, 'If anybody should have been sent up, it's your brother Danny.'"

Donald then proceeded to tell that once recently by accident he had picked up his father's wallet, thinking it was his brother's, and was leafing through the photographs and discovered that his father was carrying a picture of him in his wallet. With a very sad and yet warm expression on his face, Donald said: "My father never carried my picture with him before. I was surprised when I found my picture in his wallet. I thought my father hated me when they sent me to Children's Village. I know I broke his heart." Richard: "I know I nearly killed my parents when they sent me to the Village. I really broke their heart. My mother cried for days after I came to the Village. My mother used to feel that it was her fault because I came to the Village." Donald: "That's the way I think my parents felt. They probably felt that they were the cause that got me to go to the Village." For some time Macy had been interested in the conversation. He had stopped reading the magazine, and although he did not say anything, his face showed intense interest.

Louis got up to leave and the group followed suit. It was now 8:28. As the group was leaving, the therapist turned to Donald and said, "You know, Don, I still have a feeling that there is something bothering you about all of this that you haven't spoken about." Donald: "Maybe there is. I don't know quite how to explain it. We got to talk about it, Mr. Ellery." As the therapist went down the stairs, Donald and Richard accompanied him, Richard talking about all the nice things his parents did for him now when he came home, such as buying him clothes, shoes, socks, and taking him along when they went out.

COMMENT

New self- and social identities made their appearance among the boys in this session. Not only did Donald not wish to depend on his mother for funds, but he, with others participating, planned on a normal place in society, carrying responsibilities. The boys now consciously rejected their former undesirable friends and earlier pleasure-seeking behavior. Their increased capacity for reality-testing was seen in their recognition of the difficulties in dealing with the inexorable neighborhood gangs and in their suggestions of practical plans for evading them, such as moving out of the neighborhood. The therapist was quite right in saying that he now felt he was facing "a group of men." They now recognized that their delinquencies were no more than actions of "wise guys" and "suckers," contemptuous terms applied to their former selves.

The process of inversion the boys had passed through so far yielded a very significant change in values and attitudes. All the boys now agreed that the Village had a beneficent intent and was helpful to them, in contrast to their barrages against it in the past. This change toward more benign attitudes was dramatically verbalized by Louis, who now perceived the boys at church no longer as "fags," but as "not such bad guys, after all," and in Donald's changed attitude toward his family, and especially his father. It is quite possible that Donald's improved personality had given his parents a new awareness of him as a person. Both Donald and Richard verbalized a better understanding of their parents and deeper empathy with their feelings, while the other boys present did so vicariously. "Each must understand his parents and forgive them," and these boys were on the road toward it.

Psychoanalytically speaking the boys had now passed the pregenital, narcissistic stage, with which they came to us, and had now entered into the genital phase, with more mature attitudes toward sex and, therefore, also toward the world of reality.

In the boys' spontaneous analysis of the change in their interests from "bopping girls," and such, to their present realistic and self-controlled aims we see the phenomenon of derivative insight, which is characteristic of activity group therapy, but occurs also in analytic groups. (This is insight arrived at without direct verbalization, but as an automatic result of personality maturity and self-confrontation.)

It is interesting to note to what extent the boys had, on the whole, assimilated ideas and consolidated attitudes during the six-week interval between sessions.

Session Forty-Two

Immediately at the beginning of the session, Michael, then Donald also, began to prepare coffee, which served as a signal for all the others to participate, each serving himself. The cookies were distributed by Donald. As the boys were seated, Donald turned to the therapist and asked: "Can I ask you something Mr. Ellery?" Without waiting for a reply he asked what the therapist would do if he were a certain boy, K. K. was on a home visit and his mother had fallen down and fractured an ankle. K.'s parents were divorced and K. never saw his father. Because of her injury, the mother was confined to bed with a splint on her leg and K. had to do the housework. He decided not to come back and to stay at home an additional day. Instead of returning Sunday, he planned to come back Monday, but a Children's Village custodian came Sunday night to "pick up" K. K. tried to explain to the custodian that he was needed at home to help his mother and that he was worried about her. The custodian reassured K., and promised him that if he returned with him, he would arrange for K. to go back home the following morning. K. agreed, and after having done the shopping and prepared food for his mother, he came back. However, once K. was at the Village, "everybody" denied that any such promise was made to him and K. was not permitted to go home. Donald wanted to know whether the therapist would not under the circumstances "run" home to take care of his mother. The therapist asked Donald if these were all the facts. Angrily Donald replied he wasn't sure. The therapist asserted that he could understand how K. felt, but instead of answering the question he said to Donald, "I wonder what you would do in this situation."

Donald immediately responded that he would run away, go back to help his mother, because he loved his mother. If his mother ever needed him, he would wait on her hand and foot. He said: "I would do all the shopping, clean the house, make sure she was all right. I would go out and work and make sure she had enough money. That is, if I didn't have a father around." Therapist: "How would you feel about doing this?" Donald: "I'd like to do this; she is my mother and I love her." Richard spoke up: "Yeah, me too, my mother was sick a lot of times and my father was at work and I didn't mind taking care of my mother, going shopping and running errands." The therapist raised the question about their use of the words *like* and *love* in relation to doing things for their mothers, saying that he wondered if this described their feelings. Michael: "Well, don't you love to do things for your parents?" Therapist: "Sometimes. But sometimes I do things and it doesn't mean I love doing them, and it has nothing to do with whether I love my mother."

Donald became agitated and very annoyed. Louis: "I guess we just can't agree with you tonight, Mr. Ellery." Donald: "I'm not saying that I hate my mother!" Therapist: "I know you are not saying that, Don. It is possible to love your mother and still sometimes not like having to do certain things." Donald continued to appear agitated. Richard reiterated what he had said previously, namely: "I enjoy doing things for my parents. I never mind it." Michael, who now joined the conversation, said, "I never mind either." Donald picked up his chair and moved it farther away from the group, thus seating himself in the far corner of the room, near the electric plate. However, just before Donald made the move, he had distributed the cookies, which he had in his hand, thus drawing the boys' attention away from the discussion. At the same time, Leonard, Macy, Jules, and Louis, who had been listening, *lit cigarettes, almost in unison.*

The therapist realized that he was getting to a sore spot (threat area) with the boys—their feelings about parents. He therefore attempted to differentiate between such feelings, the sense of obligation toward parents and "love." Donald was now again attempting to disrupt the discussion, and the therapist decided in this, the forty-second session, to deal with these feelings directly. He said, "Does anybody have any idea why Don is distributing cookies at this point?" Macy winked at the therapist, but said nothing. Louis looked very annoyed with what Donald had just done, and was making his annoyance obvious by a grimace on his face. Richard said, "Donald is trying to break up the discussion." Donald: "No, I'm not. I'm just giving out the cookies. I don't want to eat them, so you guys can have them." Therapist: "Maybe we can figure out what just happened with the giving out of the cookies and the lighting up of cigarettes. I notice that whenever we begin to talk about something that doesn't feel comfortable and you begin to get nervous inside, there begins the lighting up of cigarettes, the making of coffee. . . ." Richard blurted out, finishing the sentence for the therapist, "and biting nails, right?"

The therapist agreed and then said: "This happens with most people. When they get nervous and tense inside they go back to doing things they did when they were much younger. For instance, one of the first stages every human being ever went through was eating, satisfying the mouth as a way of getting away from feelings of being tense." Donald: "I know. Like I'm always biting my nails." Macy: "That's right, in school when I sit in class and I don't feel like paying attention and I'm bothered by the class, or I just feel nervous, I start to bite my nails. Is that the same thing, Mr. Ellery?" The therapist said that it was.

Donald: "I don't understand. Are you really saying that I hate my mother?" Therapist: "Don, let me give you an example of what I'm try-ing to say. When I used to live at home, my father was a pretty sick man. In the middle of the night he used to wake everybody up and we had to call a doctor, sometimes get oxygen for him. Do you think I liked being awakened? This didn't mean that I hated my father; but like everybody else—I don't know anybody who likes to be awakened in the middle of the night, regardless of what the cause is." Donald, now less agitated, but with strong resentment, said: "I know something like that used to happen to me. I don't think about it as much these days but my mother likes to take a drink once in awhile. She is not a lush" (at this there was giggling in the room). "She is not a lush [as if to emphasize the point]; she just likes to take a drink and relax. Sometimes she would go out, maybe with her girl friends; then four o'clock in the morning she would call up and tell me to come down and get her, she was at a girl friend's house. Once or twice I had to go down to a bar to get her. When I'd get up and I'd hear her voice on the telephone I used to curse her out. I used to be mad at myself for cursing, but that's the same as what hap-pened to you, Mr. Ellery, right? You don't like to get up out of a warm bed in the middle of the night." Richard rose and left the room, going to the washroom and returning within about three minutes, but Louis picked himself up, went over to the couch, spread himself out, and closed his eyes as though he were falling asleep.

Michael interrupted, commenting, with a smile on his face: "I know what used to burn my ass. Every time I was watching television, my mother would always find a way of getting me out of the house on an errand. Up in B——— it is pretty cold. In the middle of winter, you just don't feel like going out of the house on an errand." Donald (as if he had not heard what Michael had said): "I don't know why my mother always picked on me to go out and get her. She used to tell me, 'Dad is tired, he worked hard, so you better come and get me.' " With a pathetic look on his face, he said that he used to ask his mother why she had to call him out in the middle of the night and she would say: "You're my son. I raised you." Then: "I used to curse under my breath because if I cursed near her I knew she'd tell my father and then I'd get a licking." While Donald was talking, Macy was all attention. (The expression on his face was one that indicated he was pondering every word.) Jules was paying attention, though at the same time leafing through a magazine. From the way he was doing it, it appeared that he wasn't really interested in what was in it.

Richard, at this point, engaged Leonard in a side conversation. Leonard had not said anything throughout the entire session, but he was now talking with Richard. However, Jules recognized the meaning of Richard's act and said, "Now Richard is trying to break up the discussion." Richard became very defensive: "No, I'm not. Why don't you just mind your own business?" Jules did not answer him.

Silence settled upon the group. Donald got up and moved around aimlessly near his seat, still in the corner of the room where he had moved. Jules was looking through his magazine. Macy was staring straight ahead of him, his eyes fixed at a point above the therapist who was sitting directly opposite. Michael squirmed in his chair a bit and then got into a side discussion with Donald. He got up and took the portable radio that Jules had brought with him and listened to it, playing it so quietly that he had to place it to his ear.

Finally Donald said: "Well it looks like I'll be getting out of here soon. You know, I think about what it was like when I came here to the Village. I learned a lot about my problems since I'm at the Village. *My biggest problem is how to control myself,* but I know it now, I never knew it before. If they sent me away a year later, I would have been in real big trouble." Louis, lying on the couch, opened his eyes and yelled out from the other end of the room, "Like what, Don?" Donald: "I don't know. I just know I would have been in trouble." He proceeded to describe how when he left the court to go to the detention center to be "picked up by the Village," his father was angry at him, but broke down and cried. He broke his father's heart and his father was "sore as hell" at him, but then when he was about to leave, his father came over and gave him a pack of cigarettes and 35 cents, saying, "Here, you may need it." The therapist said that though his father was angry, he still had "come across" and given him a pack of cigarettes and money. Donald asked: "What are you trying to say?" Therapist: "You know, I was thinking about what you said last week, Don, about being surprised at your father carrying your picture in his wallet, your not being sure he loved you, and I'll tell you what I thought about. Sometimes when we feel a certain way about ourselves, for instance angry at ourselves, we have a way of putting it on other people." Richard said, "What does that mean?"

Therapist: "Did you ever hear the word *projection?*" There were blank looks all around. Macy was staring at the therapist and waiting for his next sentence. The therapist said: "It's like this. You know what a projector is? It throws a picture against a wall or a screen." Macy, Richard,

and Donald nodded their heads. "Well, sometimes when we have feelings
that we don't want to admit to ourselves or don't like, we kind of project
them or throw them onto somebody else, and then we say the other
person has the feelings, not us. If we are mad at ourselves or ashamed of
ourselves, we don't want to admit it, so we say the other person is mad
or ashamed. For instance, in growing up, all boys go through a time
when they are not so sure how good-looking they are, the kind of impression they make on girls; so many of them think that it is the girls
who don't think they are good-looking or that they are not making the
right impression." Donald immediately reacted to this and said, "That's
what I was talking about with you in your office, right Mr. Ellery?"
(Donald had conveyed to the therapist his feeling of being ugly, unacceptable to girls, and so on.) Louis was now wide awake and yelled out:
"That don't bother me. I just go around screwing. I know the girls love
it. One look at my dick and they are dying for it." Everybody laughed
and Louis returned to his somnolence.

Donald said: "I got to ask something here. When I get up in the
morning, I say: 'This is going to be a good day. I'm not going to get into
any trouble, I'm going to behave myself,' but by the end of the day I
always do something to fuck up. I don't mean to be bad or mean, I just
kid around but sometimes I don't know when to stop, and before I know
it I'm having an argument with the coach or a teacher or even with my
cottage father. I hate myself after it happens but I can't stop. Why do I
do it?" Macy: "Me, the same way. I go to school, I sit there, and I say
I'm here to learn. Before I know it, I'm screwing around. The teacher
gets mad at me, but I get mad at myself, too, because I told myself I
wasn't going to do it. I'd sure like to know why I do it."

Everybody's attention, including Louis's, was riveted on the therapist,
who said, "Maybe we can try to figure this out, fellows." The boys tried,
but got nowhere in their attempts to trace the cause of such behavior
and were looking to the therapist for an answer. Therapist: "Frankly
boys, I'm not sure I know the answer, but I could think of a couple of
possibilities." Donald: "Like what?" Therapist: "Well, sometimes you
kid around as a way of getting people angry; then when you get them
angry, you can say to yourself, 'you see, I knew all along they were no
good.' Another possible reason is sometimes it is hard giving up being a
baby, even though you may want to grow up." There was silence in the
room. Richard got up and left the room. It was evident from the expression on the boys' faces that they did not understand or accept these explanations. Therapist: "There is one more possibility. You can take your
choice as to which one applies to you. The other possibility is that kidding around is a way of getting attention that you feel you can't get
any other way."

This seemed to have struck home, at least with Donald and Michael. Donald said to the therapist: "Remember what I told you in your office about when I used to hang around with my brother's crowd when I was younger. I used to go around patting the girls on the asses, acting like a kid, mooching cigarettes, and then they didn't want me around. It's not that they told me to get away, but I could feel that they were giving me the freeze." (Donald had described this also in earlier sessions. However, in the group he boasted that he refused to "hang around" with his brother's crowd, because they were too "goody-goody" and he didn't want to have anything to do with anybody who just sat around in an ice cream parlor and had no fun. Now Donald was offering a different explanation.) On the heels of Donald's statement, Michael said: "I used to do that when I stole. I was always with a bunch of boys where I would look out for them while they were stealing or I would get in and steal with them. I always felt they liked me because I was as big a crook as they were." Donald: "But sometimes that gets you a shot in the head. So how can you want attention that way?" Therapist: "Remember we once talked about the unconscious? Your conscious mind really doesn't want a 'shot in the head,' but maybe in your unconscious mind a shot in the head is better than no attention at all. Remember how we talked about boys stealing, just to find out if they were going to get any attention from any adult, even if it were only a 'shot in the head'?" Jules confirmed this: "Yeah, I remember telling you about that."

The group became agitated. There was general shuffling of feet, and Richard, now back in the room, was conversing with Leonard. Michael returned to listening to the radio, and Louis was joining in the conversation with Richard and Leonard. Donald started to boast about the girls he had taken out and said that if after he took a particular girl out and spent money on her she didn't want to kiss him, then he hated her. If she wouldn't "fuck" he wouldn't take her out again. The therapist smiled at this and asked quietly: "You mean if you spend money on a girl you feel entitled to have intercourse with her?" Donald: "You're damn right!" Louis backed Donald on this. Donald then said: "But I'll tell you this, if my daughter got knocked up I'd break her head. In fact, if my daughter laid for any boy I'd break her head." This declaration was met with general giggling.

The therapist asked: "How about laying somebody else's daughter?" Laughter broke out from the entire group. Donald said: "What would you do, Mr. Ellery, if your daughter got knocked up? Would you make the boy marry her and take the boy to court?" Therapist: "Don, I think I would try to help my daughter if she became pregnant outside of marriage, or as you say, 'knocked up.' Girls have a reason for becoming pregnant. Sometimes it is their way of getting love or having someone to love, or sometimes having a baby is a way of getting back at somebody." Macy: "I never knew that."

It was 8:30 now, and Louis got up, saying he was going back to the cottage. Everybody started to walk out, except Donald, Macy, and Michael. Donald wanted to know why some girls wouldn't "lay" for him even though he took them out and showed them "a good time." The therapist explained to the three boys that a girl considered intercourse as a means of having a baby, and she wanted to have a baby only when she was married and had a husband who could take care of her and the baby. Girls were raised this way, and that was why girls didn't like to have intercourse without being married, because of the possibility of their being alone, with nobody to care for a girl and her child. Also, intercourse was something girls did with love, not just because they went out with a boy and he spent money on them. Donald thought this wasn't right; he said a girl should "do it" because he gave her a good time. The idea of a girl having intercourse only when she was married and had a husband and raised a child appeared novel to him. However, he took his stand with little conviction. Macy, on the other hand, was nodding his head as if he accepted what the therapist had said.

COMMENT

There was little initial resistance against launching into a significant group interview here. The boys seem to have accepted their negative feelings toward their parents, but were still ambivalent; they still felt guilty over such feelings and sought to deny them, but they were now unsuccessful in this. Their protestations were readily displaced by memories of mothers' and fathers' thoughtless and unkind treatment of them. The superego censors appeared much weaker than in the past; the boys were more receptive and less resistant. All this served the therapist as a signal for entering into the interpretation of resistances. Now, because of their psychological literacy and growing insight, it was permissible to enter into the sources of their resistances and regression. However, these subjects were apparently still too threatening and had to be dropped. Donald introduced the concept of *control*, which was most significant. He now recognized the tenuous strength of his ego, but faced up to injury he had caused his father and could accept the fact that his father loved him.

As a step in the re-education of the boys, we now introduced the concept of "projection." Donald and Macy were introspective as to their conduct. Donald viewed his behavior—"fooling around"—and recognized that *he* caused difficulties for himself and others (self-confrontation, insight). The self-confrontation spread to the other boys, who described their past in stealing and in crime, no longer boastfully as in past sessions. The discussion gave the therapist an opportunity to extend psychological understanding of other persons, girls in this case. Donald's discussion of intercourse with girls no longer had the element of bravado as in earlier sessions, when several of the boys sought to outdo one another in tales of their delinquencies. His introducing his reactions to the idea of sexual acting out by a daughter of his suggested that what seemed like lighthearted treatment of delinquencies was actually a counterphobic strategy on the part of the boys.

Donald's extreme agitation during the discussion of feelings toward mothers and his verbal reaction to it was in line with his schizophrenic character, but his ego was nonetheless strong enough to expose her deviant behavior and his resentment toward her.

Session Forty-Three

Before the session began Donald and Leonard proceeded to prepare coffee for themselves and were followed in this by the other boys. The boys were seated and ready to start at 7:10. The group sat around sipping their coffee and munching cookies and chattering unrestrainedly. Jules was talking with Michael, Donald with Louis across the room, saying something about not having received a pass to see the cottage supervisor. After a few minutes quiet settled in the room.

Donald turned to the therapist and said, "Mr. Ellery, when people get married does everybody go on a honeymoon?" Not waiting for an answer, he asked: "Where did you go on your honeymoon when you got married?" The therapist told him, "To Florida." Donald said that he wanted to ask a personal question, averring: "I'm not trying to be nosy. How did it feel when you 'got into' your wife?" Macy quickly added: "Isn't it true that when you go on a honeymoon, that's when you're supposed to screw your wife?" Louis answered this by saying: "That's right. That's all you're supposed to do on a honeymoon, is to fuck your wife." Donald: "That's not what I'm talking about. I mean why do people go away on a honeymoon? Why don't they just get married and set up a house? What do you need a honeymoon for?" Donald, as he was asking these questions, was looking across the room at Macy, though it was obvious that he actually was addressing everybody in the room. Macy, however, answered that he did not understand why people needed a honeymoon and asked where the idea originated.

There was silence in the room, with every boy looking at the therapist as if waiting for an answer. The therapist said that he was not sure where the idea of a honeymoon originated or where the word even came from, but that the purpose of a honeymoon was to give a chance to a man and woman who got married to be alone together and get used to one another. It was part of the preparation for married life, the purpose of which was to raise children. To do this properly, the husband and wife needed time together in order to learn how to live with each other's good points and bad points, so that when children came they could raise them without fighting with one another. Louis said, "That sounds like a pretty fair explanation." (It was obvious that in these questions there was an underlying curiosity about the boys' own parents' sexual relations, and the therapist did well not to enter into that phase at this stage.)

Donald revealed concern about his own future role as a husband and father. He said: "I want to marry a nice girl, a girl I can trust. Like when my wife and I have kids I want to feel that my wife is pretty responsible with the kids, that she will take care of them and do the right thing for them." Leonard: "That's what you ought to find out before you get married. You talk these things over with your future wife and see how she feels about it." Donald: "If you love your wife and you have a good time with her, I guess you enjoy having *intercourse* with her, right?" As he finished the sentence, he turned directly toward the therapist, as if the question were directed to him. The therapist agreed with what Donald had said.

A period of restlessness ensued. Jules was leafing through a magazine. Louis initiated a discussion with Donald, who sat almost across the room from him. They talked about a boy who was to have a home visit the coming week end and who told Louis that he might not come back, that he would run away at the end of the visit. Donald, in the meantime, got up and helped himself to another cup of coffee. Then turning to the other boys he asked who wanted more coffee. The only boy who did was Richard. Donald brought him a cup of coffee. This diversion lasted about four or five minutes. Then Michael spoke up, asking the therapist whether it wasn't true that if you tried to get a job without much education, you couldn't get a good job. "You have to take less money and take jobs that don't really make you feel like working. Maybe the best you can take is carrying heavy packages around." Richard who had said nothing during the preceding discussion, got up and left the room, and the slamming of the washroom door indicated his destination. Jules slouched in his chair and closed his eyes, and Michael seemed to have forgotten the question he raised, for he picked up the radio Jules had brought and, playing it quietly, listened to it. Suddenly he stood up and began to do a rock-and-roll dance that consisted mainly of shuffling his feet in beat with the music. Richard came back.

After a while, the therapist confronted the boys with their behavior, saying: "I don't quite know what's going on tonight. The minute we start to talk about something, a lot of talking and shuffling around begins. I wonder why all this is happening?" Louis, Donald, and Richard didn't say anything, but they wore expressions of guilt, almost as if they had been caught at something naughty. The shuffling and talking at once ceased, but still nothing was said. Then Macy asked Richard: "Why don't you talk tonight? You haven't talked much lately. You used to talk all the time." Richard did not answer. Donald began to engage the therapist in a side conversation that grew out of the individual interview about his going down to the Board of Education in the city and enrolling in a night school. He had an appointment for the coming Monday.

As Donald diverted the therapist's attention, the others again became restless. Michael raised the volume on the radio so high that, although Donald sat next to the therapist, the latter could hardly hear what Donald was saying. The therapist turned to Donald and apologized for cutting him off, but said he could hardly hear him with all the noise in the room. The therapist turned to the boys and said: "Well, here it goes again! Do you have any idea what you're doing?" Macy: "What do you mean?" Therapist: "Well we started to talk about a couple of things tonight and the next thing you boys cut off from it. You begin to fool around. Is there something about what we're saying that makes you feel uncomfortable?" There was no response. Silence reigned. Therapist: "Maybe we ought to think about this." Macy again said, "I don't quite know what you mean, Mr. Ellery." Therapist: "Well look, do you notice how when we begin to talk about something we reach a point and then 'boom,' everybody pulls back and you start kidding around, talking, shuffling your feet, running out to the bathroom. This is what is called 'resistance.' It means holding yourself back when you don't want to talk about something and trying to change the subject."

A prolonged silence followed; not a word was said. Everybody sat quietly. The therapist finally asked: "Are you upset about something?" No answer. Therapist: "I'm going to ask you something. Is there something you're sore at me about?" Macy said, "We never get sore at you, Mr. Ellery." Jules: "Why should we get sore at you?" Donald: "No, it's not you. I don't know what it is. We like to kid around sometimes." Therapist: "I wonder if you're really being honest with yourselves now. Suppose you are sore at me. What's going to happen? Are the walls going to cave in?" Louis: "You do right by us, Mr. Ellery; we're not sore at you," and Jules: "Yeah, like we said before, we just like to kid around." Therapist: "I hear what you're saying, but I always remember the time you were talking about how people get mad at you and then you get mad at the people because they get mad at you for kidding around—like with your cottage parents." Again there was silence which continued for another few minutes.

Donald finally turned to the therapist and said: "A funny thing happened the night I was home on my home visit. My mother sprained her back. She's not badly sick. She just sprained her back and it's a little hard for her to stoop and pick things up. I noticed that my brother Danny—he doesn't worry too much about it. But I always worry about my mother. I worry more than Danny. I was lying in bed that night and I was thinking to myself, what would happen if my mother died? If my father died? I would have to take care of my little brother. We might have to move out into a cheaper apartment that I could afford. Then I said a little prayer and asked God to forgive me for having these thoughts about my mother and father. I tried to sleep but then I thought about it again—about maybe my mother dying, my father dying—almost like I was trying to find out what it would be like. I worry more about my mother and father than my brothers do. When my father has a cold, I worry about him. I don't see my brothers staying up and worrying about it." As Donald was describing these feelings the shuffling of feet began again and the boys looked somewhat agitated. Michael, who had turned on the radio, now turned it up again. (Apparently Donald had aroused a great deal of anxiety in the boys. His unmistakable death wishes toward his parents struck a resonance and a fear that the boys could not contain. There was nothing to do but allow the boys to abreact to their feelings and the tumult to subside. Since the boys recognized that the therapist would not react, the disturbance died almost at once.)

When the boys had quieted down, Richard said that he had a dream the other night. The dream went like this: He had been discharged from the Village and his father was telling him not to steal. Sure enough, Richard went back to his old neighborhood, met his old friends, and they decided to steal. Where did they steal from? They went to the store where his father worked. Richard turned to the therapist and asked: "What does that dream mean?" Therapist: "That's a good question. I wonder whether we can figure it out." Donald took the initiative and said, "Maybe the dream means that Richard went to steal in his father's store because if he gets caught he knows he would get off because his father works there." Therapist: "That's one possible explanation. I wonder if there are any more." The boys sat back thinking, but it was Donald who spoke up. "I know. I think it means that Richard tries to steal in order to spite his father. Like with me. I remember many times I used to do things just because my father told me not to do them. You know, he didn't even tell me not to do them; he ordered me not to do them."

Imitating his father's gruff voice, he gave an example of how his father warned him not to go to the poolroom and hang around with certain boys. The next thing Donald knew he was down at the poolroom, hanging out with those boys.

Richard said: "I bet that's it. I get a funny feeling now when I go home. My parents don't yell at me. They treat me differently. Like when I'm going down, they just say, 'Try to get back on time.' They don't order me like your father did, Don. *And this gives me a funny feeling.*" Louis: "What's the funny feeling?" Richard: "I don't know. They just aren't the same with me any more. Like I expect them to act tough with me like they used to but they don't any more." Donald: "That's what I've been thinking about. Like, I don't like my father to yell at me. I don't want to be treated like a little boy any more. I'm a big boy and when my father gives me an order, I wish he wouldn't yell. He could ask me something. I would listen to him." Practically raising himself from his seat, Donald told the boys how he was going to tell his father off if his father ordered him around again. Therapist: "What do you mean, Don?" Donald (in a very rough voice): "Don't tell me what to do, Dad! I'm big enough. I'll do it how I want." The therapist, imitating Donald's father's voice and assuming his role,[6] shouted: "I want you in at nine o'clock, Don!" Donald yelled back: "I'm not coming in at nine o'clock and you can't make me!" "I damn well will make you! You be here at nine o'clock!" Donald: "Just for that I'm coming in at three o'clock, and I want to see what you're going to do about it!" "You come in at three o'clock and I'll beat the living daylights out of you!" "To hell with you! I come in when the hell I want. I'm a big boy!"

The therapist stopped the acting and turning to the other boys asked: "How do you think Don handled this?" Macy immediately said: "I think Don's asking for a black eye," and Louis: "If you talk that way to your father, what do you expect him to do but get mad at you?" Donald turned to the therapist: "Okay, Mr. Ellery, let's do it again. Maybe I'll try another way. Yell at me to come in at nine o'clock." The therapist did. Donald, in a soothing voice, said: "Look Dad, I'm seventeen now. I would really appreciate it if you would try to trust me. I'm not going to do the things I used to do. I know better than that now. I would just like to be with my friends, and at my age I don't think it's right to come in at nine o'clock." Michael then said, "Boy, that sure sounds a lot better." Leonard: "You don't sound like such a tough guy any more." Richard (with a smile on his face): "It's about time you wasn't so tough. What do you expect but a black eye when you act tough?"

Louis now proceeded to recount the many arguments he had with

6. See note 5, session forty-one, p. 499.

his mother. Not only would he get in arguments about going down-stairs (into the street), but after the argument was finished, his mother would send him on an errand. He always felt like telling his mother "to go to hell," but he wouldn't do that. He said he found another way of telling her. "I just didn't do what she asked me. Now when I come home my mother doesn't yell at me any more. It's like she trusts me, like she's changed. I know that I changed. I don't go with the old crowd any more. I don't look for trouble. I know what it's like to get into trouble." Then: "Mr. Ellery, there's something I want to ask you. I was meaning to ask you a long time. When I go home I don't feel like coming back. I feel like getting myself a job all day and then going to school at night. I want an education. I know that without an education, I'll never be able to get anything good; but I know I don't leave the Village until January. When I leave in January, then I could go to school the right way; get my high-school diploma and get a job in the evening. In that way I'd get my education faster. But when I go home on week ends I'm so tempted to stay home. I hate coming back to the Village so that I don't know what to do first. You see, if I don't come back to the Village, I can't enroll in school and go full time. But I could make money and go to school at night because at night school they don't ask too many questions." Louis said that he wanted the therapist to give him an answer as to what to do.

The therapist said, "Louis, what would really be right for you?" Louis pondered the question as all the boys watched him attentively. Louis then said: "I think the right thing would be for me to get an education as fast as I can. I know I'm smart. I read at the tenth-grade level. That's pretty good. I could go through high school if I really tried." Therapist: "Louis, isn't this really a question that every boy is going to have to face? To use an old fashioned word, *patience*—putting off something that you feel like doing today for something better, that will really help you if you can really wait a while, such as waiting until you leave in January." Louis: "I know what you mean. When I leave in January, I could really get an education and make some money on the side, but if I leave now I'd just be a runaway from the Village, and I'd always worry about the cops coming after me; so I really couldn't go to school or even work." After a moment's thoughtful pause he said, "I think what I'm going to do is wait." Donald: "That's what you ought to do, Louis, that's what I did. You got to have patience. You can't have everything at once. Now I'm getting out of the Village the right way." Turning to the therapist, Donald said: "You remember when I threatened to run away from the Village? But then I'd be a fugitive. That's no way to live."

Louis: "There's another problem I got. When I go back home I find I'm not friendly with the boys like I used to be. There are two brothers,

Dave and Martin. Martin is a tough guy. He runs around with the hoods. He's always trying to get me to go rob a store with him, even when I go home now. I don't want to go with him. I tried to knock some sense into this guy's head. He doesn't know what it's like to get into trouble and be put away. I can't knock sense into him. Dave belongs to a rock-and-roll group. Every so often they go down and they cut a record. I like Dave. He's my kind and I like brilliant boys. I can talk with them. I can't talk with a guy like Martin." He stopped, lost in thought, and then said that his problem was that he felt a "loyalty" toward Martin. They used to be "real buddies," but now he just didn't have the same interests Martin had and he wanted to be buddies with him and yet he didn't want to.

The therapist asked Louis what it was that made him feel he still wanted to be buddies with this boy. Louis said it had to do with the fact that they used to be buddies, and he didn't feel he could really leave this guy cold. The therapist said it sounded as though he was talking about a feeling of obligation, at which Louis nodded his head. The therapist said, "Can you really be friends with a person just out of a feeling of obligation toward him?" Louis: "I don't know. That's what I'm trying to decide. I think my problem is I'm trying to be this guy's social worker and I can't. Shit, I had enough of robbing and stealing. If I stay that way I'll never be anything but a crook. One of the things I learned at the Village was that I got a good mind. I could really make something out of myself if I tried hard enough." Macy turned to Louis and said: "Then you ought to try hard enough. That's stupid going with a guy just because you used to be friends with him."

At this point Jules rose to return to his cottage, and since the time was 8:27, the other boys filed out too.

COMMENT

The boys, quite on their own, now followed up the explorations of their feelings toward their parents which they initiated in the last session, but this time they proceeded in a disguised fashion to matters of greater intimacy, namely, the sexual relation between them. They also formulated their intention of being better parents than their own had been, and that their wives would be better mothers than their mothers were. Donald, who usually employed profane terminology, for the first time employed the term "intercourse."

Attention to marriage, relationship with wives, and having children brought up by association the realistic matter of jobs and adequate preparation for them, which signified an increased sense of reality and movement toward maturity. However, since these topics were comparatively new in the road toward maturity, they activated anxiety and defensive distractibility. The therapist, being secure in the transference feeling toward him and in the boys' ego strengths, checked them by interpreting the resistance.

The breakthrough of the resistance revealed the reason for the block, namely, hostility and death wishes toward parents, which were communicated by Donald, Richard, and Louis. However, when Richard described his discomfort at being treated with respect by his parents ("Like I expected them to act tough with me . . ."), the therapist overlooked the opportunity to point out how the psyche, when it became accommodated to negative responses, craved them. (It is from this and similar remarks that we derived the concept of *onto-archaic mind*, which we shall discuss more fully later.)

The therapist's utilizing an opportunity to re-enact roles was most valuable as a demonstration to Donald of the inappropriateness of his reaction to his father, as spectator therapy, and as an opportunity for reflection and discussion by the group.

Louis's mature planfulness for his future, his reality awareness, improved self-image and identity, and understanding of his friendships were a far cry from his recitations of rapings, muggings, rumbles, and other violent acts that he indulged in during early interviews. His manner and deliberativeness were on a par with a well-organized adult. The other boys are of great help to him in resolving his false loyalty to his undesirable friends.

The therapist could have pointed out that the provocativeness ("having fun") in which the boys indulged could in addition have an element of disguised hostility against adults which the latter intuitively sensed and reacted to with punishment. These and similar situations were thoroughly discussed and all possibilities explored in our supervisory conferences.

Session Forty-Four

Preparation of coffee, in which all the boys were involved, was first on the agenda at this session. Louis was the initiator in this. It went off quietly and smoothly.[7] Following this and the distribution of cigarettes the boys remained quiet as they sipped their coffee. The

7. Note should be taken of the fact that no difficulties had been experienced for some time in the distribution of cigarettes and cookies and that the preparation of coffee always went off in an orderly and quiet manner. One boy would assume responsibility for distributing cigarettes, which were now supplied in a sealed package by the therapist. There had been no challenge or question as to the fairness of apportioning them.

silence was broken after about a minute or two by Louis calling out to Richard to begin the discussion. Richard merely smiled embarrassedly, but said nothing. When Louis discovered that Richard was not going to accept his suggestion, he commented in an offhand manner that come January he would be out of the Village. Jules contributed the fact that Mrs. D., a teacher, got angry at him earlier in the day because he was drawing a swastika. With genuine unknowingness, he said he had no idea why she got mad at him. Then, after a moment's reflection and in a voice full of contempt, he said, "Maybe she's a Jew." He added that he had heard that Jewish people do not like the swastika and said that the "war was over a long time ago. What are they so mad at?" (Apparently Jules was not aware of what the swastika represented to people generally, nor of what had happened during the war, since he was born after its conclusion.) Michael stepped in and said, "Maybe she had somebody killed in the war and that's why it bothered her." Jules, in an offhand manner, "I guess she's got her reasons."

Donald turned to the therapist and asked, "Isn't it true that the Nazis killed millions of people?" The therapist indicated that it was, and took the opportunity to explain what the swastika represented to people, certainly to those who had lost members of their families in concentration camps. To them the swastika had become a symbol of torture and killings by the Nazis. Such memories, he explained, still hurt, but he could understand that for one who did not live through the period when all this occurred, it might be a little difficult to understand why a drawing of a swastika could be so upsetting. Leonard said he had heard that there were people walking around with numbers on their arms, that they had been in concentration camps. Donald wanted to know where the numbers came from, and Leonard told him that it was a way of identifying them, "like you were in prison and you get a number. The Nazis were supposed to have killed millions of people." Michael: "Yeah, I heard something like that, but we don't study that too much in school." As he was going over to get more coffee, Jules said: "I guess Mrs. D. is all right. She's not the worst. She's kind of an old lady, anyway." Michael to Jules: "Okay, so be careful what you draw in her class next time." Jules did not respond to this.

After Jules took his seat, a brief period of quiet ensued, which was interrupted when Donald turned on the portable radio which Jules had brought with him. Donald played the radio low. Michael took it from Donald and tried to tune in another station. Donald took the radio back from Michael, sat down, placed it on the floor next to him, leaned back in his chair and stared at the ceiling dreamily as he listened to the music. Richard said, "I heard that one of the boys I used to hang around

with has just been sent up to E——— (a custodial reform school). He
got himself a pack of trouble now; something like armed burglary."
There was no immediate response to this statement, but after a brief
silence Michael said: "I hear stories about that in my old gang. Most of
the guys now are either in the army or they are serving time. Just as well,
because when I go back to B——— I don't want to see any of them."
Richard: "That's a good point of them guys being put out of circulation.
When you go back to the neighborhood you don't have to see any of
them." He stretched out in his chair, stared up at the ceiling, and then began to reminisce. He took quite some time to describe one delinquent
escapade after another, including car thefts, in which he had been involved with these boys. (Richard had no known record of car-stealing,
nor had he talked about this in previous sessions.) His reminiscing had
the quality of living in a past which he embroidered for the benefit of
the group. Michael kept interrupting him, and when he finally stopped
to draw a breath, Michael smilingly said, "Them were the good old
days." Almost surprised at what he had said, he looked self-consciously
at the therapist and said apologetically: "Like I said. Them *were* the
good old days. When I get out, them days are going to be gone forever."
Richard now took up his monologue again and narrated how he used
to get his "ass beaten" by his father when he found out about Richard's
truancy and shoplifting. His father used to come after him and really
give him "a beating," but then his father would say to him, "Look, if
you got to steal cars why the hell don't you steal me a Cadillac?" This
was greeted with laughter from the boys. The only boy who refrained
was Donald, who was still leaning back in his chair listening to the
music which he played very softly, so that it was not interfering with
the conversation.

When the laughter subsided the therapist asked Richard what he
thought of his father's remark. Richard did not know what the therapist
meant. Therapist: "You have told us any number of times how your
father used to beat you for the things you did, such as playing hooky,
truanting from school. Now you are saying that even though your
father beat you for supposedly stealing cars he also told you to steal
him a Cadillac." Richard was somewhat taken aback at hearing this. He
did not say anything at first. After a few moments in which he seemed
to be having an inner struggle, he said: "Aw, that didn't mean anything.
My father was only joking. My father can kid around sometimes, but
I sure know he didn't want me to steal any cars." (The therapist thought
that because of the delinquent nature of Richard's father it might be
desirable to hold Richard to this.) The therapist repeated what he had
said before, namely, that on the one hand Richard was told not to
steal, and on the other hand he was told that if he did have to steal, to

steal something "for me." Richard: "Aw, I don't know. Stealing was just fun that's all; that's the only reason I stole." Therapist: "Aw, come on. We've talked about this before. Remember what we talked about?" The therapist put up five fingers. Richard: "I know, five reasons for stealing," and then, "I remember one of them was revenge." He tried to recall others, but could not. Jules blurted out: "Attention! Remember how I talked about how I stole to get attention from my old man?" Richard: "That's right, but I didn't steal for attention." Jules: "Maybe you didn't, but I did; that way I'd make my old man come after me." Michael: "I don't remember why I stole. I always thought I stole because it was a lot of fun to steal, but I guess there were other reasons." Richard laughed and turning to Michael said, "You know there were."

Michael now launched into a narration of his stealing in the manner of an old man recollecting his unsavory past. Donald had turned up the volume on the radio at this point, but soon turned it down again as Michael continued to recount one tale after another of his playing "hooky," his serving as a lookout while other boys did shoplifting, and of others acting as lookouts for him while he did the stealing. Donald had turned up the radio again in an obvious attempt to drown out Michael.

Michael had stopped talking, since no one appeared to be paying attention to him. The boys seemed to be leaving him alone with his memories. The radio was playing quite loudly, and the therapist turned to Donald and said, "Don, I have the feeling you are trying to say something." Donald sat up erect and said challengingly, "No, I'm not." Therapist: "I know what you are saying, but I still get a feeling that you are trying to say something." There was silence for a few moments, and then Donald said, "Well, what am I trying to say?" Therapist: "I don't know, Don, but look how you are trying to break into the discussion with the radio." Donald: "I just turned it up louder so I can hear the music." But he seemed to recognize that he was offering a rather limp excuse. Again nothing was said. Finally the therapist said to Donald, "I know this is the last time you will be coming to the group discussion, Don, and so far I haven't heard you mention this." Donald mumbled under his breath, "I'm going to miss the group." Jules: What did you say?" Donald raised his voice and said: "I said I'm going to miss the group. I've been helped a lot in this group. I only hope that when I get on the outside I'll never have any trouble again. I found out some of the reasons I got into trouble. One of the things I know now is that *I used to be a pretty angry kid*." Richard jokingly to Donald: "Hey, Don, come on, let's go steal a car, huh?" Donald: "Fuck you. That's in the past."

Louis and Michael got into a discussion about their car-stealing and

shoplifting activities. This lasted a few minutes. The therapist interjected the question whether this was not something that was on everybody's mind—not only getting out of the Village, but what would
happen once they did. Michael: "We're only kidding now, Mr. Ellery.
We know that if we get into trouble again there is no more Village for
us." He then turned to Donald and initiated a banter among the boys
which, while humorous, still contained kernels of truth about their stay
at the Village. For example, Michael said to Donald: "Well this is the
end of your three square meals a day. When you get home you're going
to have to wait for your CARE package." Laughter broke out as
Richard continued: "My problem is, I don't know how to send you
your coffee in an envelope. If I put the cigarettes in an envelope with
the coffee, I don't think you're going to like the way the cigarettes
would taste." And Louis said: "Maybe we ought to send the coffee in
powder form. Let's just put the instant coffee and some sugar in an
envelope with some cigarettes and mail them to Don every Thursday."
Macy's contribution was: "Imagine, you're not going to have three
square meals a day. Not only that, but you're going to have to work
for a living." Richard (to Macy with a suppressed smile): "Now don't
say that to Don. If you frighten him you are going to stunt his growth."
Donald laughed self-consciously at being the butt of all the teasing.

Michael said that when his cottage father woke him in the morning,
he would immediately go to the telephone and call Donald in the city
to wake him up. He said, "It's no good when you break up routines."
The boys continued this for quite some time. When they quieted down,
the therapist said to Donald, "Don, I think what everybody is trying
to say is that we enjoyed having you in the group." There was quiet
assent from all the boys and Donald said: "Thanks, fellows. This is one
of the nicest things that ever happened to me. I'll never forget any one
of you. The only thing I hate about leaving is not coming here Thursday
night." Michael, continuing with his humor, said, "If you can get your
hands on a car, that shouldn't be any problem." Donald laughed at this.

Louis stood up, stretched himself, and said thoughtfully: "That's the
way the cookie crumbles. I was going to break out of here before
January, but I guess I'll hang around. I'm going to go to school when
I get back, get a part-time job, make some money, get me some real
sharp clothes." Still standing, he described the kind of clothes he was
going to wear. One gathered from his description that he would look
like a bizarre "sharpie." He then sat down, changed his tone, and moved
into something far more serious. He said that when he got back home,
he knew that his mother would want him to visit a lot of relatives of
his father's. He didn't like his father's people; he didn't have much in
common with them. "My father is a Hawaiian, and his people are

Hawaiians. When I'm with them I don't quite feel right. I don't look like them; they are light-skinned, I'm dark. My mother is Negro and I feel at home with my mother's people. I don't quite know how I can say this, but I don't feel like seeing my father's people even though my mother tries to make me. Even my father, he tries to make me." Louis sat down, thought for a while, and then said: "It's like being outside. For instance, if I went to Hawaii, I wonder how I would feel. I probably would not be taken for a Hawaiian, but I'm part Hawaiian because my father is Hawaiian. I'd rather always stay with my mother's people, because they never ask me what I am. They just take me for a Negro." Looking directly at the therapist, he said, "You know what I mean Mr. Ellery?" Therapist: "I think so, Louis. You are not quite sure who you are." Louis: "Right. That's about it! I'm half-and-half; I feel happier when I'm with my mother and her people, but I don't want to make my father mad by not going to his relatives. It's a pretty rough one to figure out." He stared at the floor with a pensive expression and said, "I got to think some more about this."

Macy got up and said: "I got to get back. It was now 8:25 and the boys left. Richard got up to leave with Macy.

COMMENT

This session was characterized by *1]* counterphobic recounting of past delinquencies; *2]* Donald's nostalgic mood because of his impending departure from the Village; and *3]* Louis's awareness of a confused identity. Note need be taken of *1]* the mature and placid attitude toward the coffee, cookies, and cigarettes during the past several sessions, signaling reduction of oral preoccupation and anxiety; *2]* absence of diffuse and infantile talk about girls, sex, and intercourse; and *3]* reduction in the use of profane and obscene language (which had the significance of anality).

The boys have quite evidently emerged from the remnants of the pregenital phase and have entered the phallic phase, which made it possible for them to examine the realities of their lives. This they had been doing now for a number of sessions. That is, their reality-testing had improved.

The underlying anxiety that pervaded these acting-out boys had been made manifest on numerous occasions when they reacted with resistance and a variety of diversionary tactics as guilt-laden topics were introduced and by repeated turning to talk about their delinquent exploits.

(Because of the advanced stage of the group's therapeutic development, no replacement for Donald was made.)

NOTE

Donald's removal from the group was forced by the parents, who insisted that he be returned home. They had threatened court action should the institution detain him longer. Their attitude stemmed from the caseworker's unwise commitment, without our knowledge and contrary to our judgment, that Donald would be discharged on a certain date, and we believed that even if it were possible to keep the boy in the institution, which probably could have been accomplished in the light of our clinical evidence, it would have been therapeutically inadvisable to do so. Donald's attitude, his realistically justified negativism toward his caseworker, coupled with his intense desire to return home because of his strong Oedipal (incestuous) tie to his mother, would have caused many problems in the group and in the institution.

It was becoming increasingly evident to us that Donald might be a latent psychotic and the effort of dealing with his hostility toward his caseworker would prove too strenuous for his ego. Because of his strong positive transference upon the group therapist, we suggested that the latter continue to see the boy individually *after* his discharge. This we succeeded in arranging with good results.

We also anticipated, because of Donald's absence, a plateau in the group's productivity, which in the sessions since the summer break had been rising in therapeutic effectiveness. He was one "instigator"–if not the major one–at the sessions.

A note on the effect of the therapist's seeing Donald in individual interviews as well as in the group: The obvious result was that his ambivalence was greatly increased. On the one hand, he consistently took a seat next to the therapist during the group sessions; on the other, he displayed antagonism to the therapist, was more irascible and more moody. This is desirable in real analytic psychotherapy, where the therapist should be the object of both love and hate, for when these feelings are worked through they result in affect and personality integration. When transference is divided between two therapists, one or the other therapist may become the object of the patient's hostility. This is demonstrated in session forty-five.

Session Forty-Five

(This session was ten minutes late in starting because Louis, Richard, and Macy–who lived in the same cottage–did not arrive on time because, as Richard explained, they had not received any "passes." However it must be noted that these same three boys had been arriving four to ten minutes late for the past several weeks. It was known that the cottage mother in charge resisted the boys' coming to the group because in her view it threatened her authority. When seen by the group therapist on another matter, she took the opportunity to complain against Richard that he was "quite fresh to her, especially whenever he returns from the group discussions," and she raised the question as to whether Richard should continue, since she had another boy in mind that she would rather have in the group. The therapist explained that removing Richard from the group at this juncture would be deleterious to him, that this was a stage he was passing through and that hopefully Richard would behave more maturely in the future.)

While Louis, Richard, and Macy were awaited, Leonard, Jules, and Michael busily engaged in a conversation about life in their respective cottages: what boys were going on week ends, and so forth. The most noticeable aspect of this was the leading role that Leonard assumed. In fact, the therapist had never before seen him so voluble as he was during this session, and it began while the three boys were absent. (It was possible that assertive Donald's absence served as a boon to Leonard, so that he was enabled to assume a more active role.) With the arrival of Louis, Macy, and Richard the preparation of coffee was started and this took about five to eight minutes. Thus it was about 7:20 when things quieted down and the boys were sitting around quietly sipping coffee, munching cookies, and smoking cigarettes. From one end of the room, Louis yelled out to Macy, who was sitting across from him, that Macy should start the discussion. Macy acted as if he did not hear. After a few moments of silence, Louis raised the question whether he would be able to stay at the Village until January. There was almost a teasing quality in the way he said it. However, he soon indicated seriously that he was thinking about getting a full-time job, but he didn't know whether it would really pay to do so, and added: "Maybe I ought to go to school and get out of school and get a high-school diploma as fast as I can. In the meantime, I can work after school."

Michael said that would be the smartest thing to do. "Boys can't even get a good job without a high-school diploma, so why don't you try to get the diploma?" Leonard chimed in and told Louis and Michael: "The most important thing to do was to get a high-school diploma. Even if you want to get a job as a delivery boy, today everybody wants high-school boys and if you are not a high-school boy, then you are out of luck. You make less money." Louis said, smilingly, that when he got out he wanted to make $100 a week or he wouldn't work. Michael began to laugh and said: "You'll be lucky if you make $40 a week. What do you mean $100 a week? What the hell you got to offer?" Louis: "Man, I got charm, personality, and wait till you see me when I'm all sharped up in my new duds." He got up and began to strut up and down the room, showing the boys how he walked when he had new clothes on. It looked as though he were caricaturing someone in the Easter Parade. This aroused gales of laughter from the boys. Louis finally sat down and the laughter subsided. Louis, too, seemed to subside. The bubbling quality in him, observable earlier in the session, now disappeared. He looked much calmer. The discussion continued about school, with Macy asking the therapist with an air of authority whether it wasn't true that if one wants a fairly good job one should have a high-school diploma. When the therapist responded to this in the affirmative, Macy declared that he was going to try as hard as he could to get through school. With this the conversation ended.

Jules, who had his portable radio with him, turned it on and played it somewhat loudly for a few seconds, but then lowered it and left the room. He soon came back. Michael went over and helped himself to another cup of coffee, asking the therapist whether he wanted one, and then turned to the boys and asked them if they desired more coffee. Leonard was deep in a discussion with Macy, the content of which the therapist could not hear. (As already noted, Leonard had never been so talkative in any other session.)

These diversions lasted only a few minutes as Louis asked the therapist whether he knew about his transition conference. The therapist's response in the negative seemed to spark similar questions from the other boys, especially Michael and Leonard. Even Macy asked whether the therapist would attend his transition conference. At this point, the therapist again made it quite clear that he did not attend these conferences and that he never knew when they were held. Richard complained about the fact that he did not know how much longer he would stay at the Village. His worker was always promising him a transition conference but as far as he knew it was always being moved from one date to another, and he didn't at all know when there was going to be such a conference. He said that they had had a conference scheduled for last April, but at the last minute they canceled it. He never knew why it was canceled. Then they were supposed to have a conference last June. Again it was canceled—according to Richard, with no explanation. Leonard spoke up, saying that if they canceled his transition conference, he was going to do what Louis had done; he would run away. Louis: "Now you are learning the smart way. One of the things you find out about these people, they don't listen to you until you take action in your own hands."

The therapist expressed his wonderment at this discussion and why it was suddenly introduced. No response was forthcoming. Suspecting that it was set off by Donald's leaving, the therapist raised this question by saying, "I wonder how you feel about the fact that Don is not with us any more?" Michael responded saying: "I'll bet he's dying tonight to get back to the group. For all I know he's on the train coming here." Giggles and smiles greeted this statement and Leonard said: "He better make it before 8:30. Otherwise he just isn't going to have any discussion tonight." Louis declared that he missed Donald. He said that when the group started he didn't like Donald, "but now I kind of like the guy and it's kind of funny him not being around tonight." Richard: "We used to have a lot of laughs with Donald around. Donald was my friend. It's funny he shouldn't be here tonight." No other comments were made on the subject, but the therapist decided to explore it further and said, "Maybe you feel that it is somehow unfair that Donald has left the Village and you are still here." There was no immediate response to this, but soon Louis assumed what seemed to be the role of spokesman for the group and said: "We're not jealous. If he could get it, fine for him. Don was here a long time, and at least we know you can get out of the Village, like Don got out." Leonard, looking directly at the therapist, said: "I go along with what Louis said. At least you can get out of the Village, so it means they don't hold you here forever."

The usual moving about and shuffling of feet signifying discomfort ensued. It started with Macy getting up and helping himself to more coffee. He in turn offered it to the boys, but there was no response. Richard got up and went out to the washroom. Jules began to walk around the room, playing his radio. Although it was tuned low, it was enough to serve as a distraction as he moved from one end of the room to the other. Therapist: "There we go again." Macy: "What do you mean?" Therapist: "What's the magic word that describes this?" Jules laughingly said, "I remember, *resistance.*" Leonard added: "Yeah, that's right, *resistance.*" Therapist: "Okay, what's the matter, fellows?" No one commented as the shuffling continued for a little while longer. Finally there was quiet and Richard was back in his seat.

Macy began to describe a teacher, Mr. L., calling him a "nice guy." What made him such a nice guy he said, was that Mr. L. somehow conveyed to them the feeling, "I'm on your side, fellows, so you better listen to me." Mr. L. told the boys about the staff members who wrote reports on them and warned them that they'd better be careful what they said about the Village because people were always watching them and writing reports on what they said. These reports were used in the transition conference. For instance, Mr. L. told Macy that he was always talking about sex, and that this was liable to come up in the transition conference on him. Mr. L. said to him: "You better keep your mouth shut because you never know who is watching you and who is writing what about you." Macy (to the therapist): "Mr. Ellery, do you know who might be observing us?" Therapist: "Macy, are you asking whether I am writing reports on you that are going to be used in the transition conference?" Macy: "No, no, Mr. Ellery. I don't mean you. I know you don't write reports on us." Michael, however, was not so sure. He turned to the therapist and asked: "Don't you write reports on us that go to the transition conference?" The therapist stated with emphasis: "I do not. But since you boys have been told this, I can very well understand that perhaps you feel that I am observing you and writing reports to be used on you." Louis: "No, we don't think so. That's not it." Macy nodded his reassurance that he did not think so either. Michael said that he rather wanted the therapist to write reports, because these might help him at his transition conference.

Louis said that what bothered him was that his caseworker might write reports. "She is no damn good. In fact, how can she write a report when she doesn't know my business?" He then imitated the caseworker's manner of talking and walking and for at least five minutes he kept the boys in stitches as he described how she tried to get an interview going with him. He finally summed up by saying that he and his mother were "enemies" of his caseworker. The therapist asked Louis why. He said: "She doesn't know what she is doing. I just don't like her." He went on to say that she and Richard's male caseworker, to whom he referred as Sister K., were having a secret love affair. In fact, all the boys knew about this secret love affair. He then went into an imitation of Richard's "feminine" caseworker's walk and talk. This was greeted with hilarious laughter by the boys.

The therapist decided to disparage Louis's histrionics and his verbosity and asked Louis directly where he got all this information, especially about this "affair" that he was describing. Louis simply said that everybody knew about it. "Who is the everybody, Louis?" "Well, just everybody knows about it." Richard interrupted at this point and said: "My caseworker has pictures of opera stars hanging on the wall. When I come in for my interview, sometimes I just sit there and look at the pictures. You know what that guy says to me? He says: 'Why are you looking at the pictures? Those pictures are mine. I don't want you to look at them. You just look at me. It's none of your business what's on my walls.'" Richard laughed and said: "Imagine him wanting me to look at him. I got to break out laughing every time I try to look at him." Louis began a forced giggle and said: "They want those people to help us. They're crazy, they can't help us." Richard continued to describe how in the midst of an interview his caseworker says to him, "Just a minute," picks up the phone, dials a number, and says: "Hello, Ann? Don't forget about that party we are having after the opera. You'll be there? Good!" Then he hangs up and says, "Okay, Richard, what were you talking about?" Richard now said: "Why should I talk? I never know when he's going to pick up the phone next."

Macy, directing his remarks to the therapist, said: "I want to ask you something. Why do boys think of certain things?" When the giggling that met this remark died down, the therapist asked: "What do you mean, Macy?" Macy said when he is alone he finds himself thinking about a lot of things over and over again. It took him quite some time before he could even hint at what some of these "things" were. Finally, after talking in vague and general terms, Macy said: "Mr. L. warned us not to think about sex too much, because if you think about it, it is liable to affect your brain. When I'm on the outside I don't have to think about sex. I got plenty of girls and I could—you know, Mr. Ellery—I could take them to bed; but here at the Village it is not the same way, so I find myself thinking about girls and about feeling them, then I find myself thinking about home, what I'm going to do when I get out, go to school, if I can make it in school, whether I can go to school and not fool around anymore." Louis, with a suppressed giggle in his voice, said: "I'm always thinking about sex. It won't bother me. I'll get it when I get out." None of the others reacted to this, however. The therapist encouraged Macy to elaborate, and he said he didn't know, it was just that he did a lot of thinking about it. The therapist asked him: "Do you feel that something is going to happen to you through thinking about sex?" Macy denied that he did: "I don't feel that way. I just wonder why it keeps coming back and back in my mind." From the way Macy described it, there seemed to be a ruminative, obsessive quality to it.

In the midst of this, Richard announced that he had to get back to his cottage. Michael asked Richard to stay a little longer, but the latter said he had a chore to finish and that if he didn't, he wouldn't be allowed to watch television that night. With this, Jules got up, and Leonard followed. The boys began to leave. Macy stayed behind, came over to the therapist, and said, "Let's talk about it next week." Therapist: "Okay, Macy. We'll talk about it next week if you want." Macy said: "I'll bring it up when we start next week," and left.

COMMENT

The outstanding feature of this session was Leonard's release from the evident inhibiting effect on him by Donald. This could be explained by the fact that, since Donald was a borderline schizophrenic, and an aggressive one to boot, Leonard, being extremely sensitive, may have sensed the tenuous nature of Donald's ego and been frightened by him.

The boys' vituperations against their caseworkers, certainly to the extent that they are exaggerations, may be a continued move toward breaking off dependence and show a diminishing need for protection and belonging characteristic of children and the immature. However, to be truly healthy, they must acquire perspective conforming with inner and outer reality, rather than transferring violent feelings from parents to surrogates. This matter needed to be taken up with them, but it could not be done at this juncture without jeopardizing the therapist's relation with the boys. The boys were also probably angry at their caseworkers for not discharging them from the Village as Donald was discharged. This may have further intensified their hostility.

The generally desultory nature of this interview can be attributed to a mourning mood at the loss of one of their number (sibling), but it is important to note that the boys did not regress to physical acting out to any appreciable degree.

The persistently direct dealing by the therapist with the group's resistances and diversional acts in the last several sessions was part of the plan suggested at the supervisory conferences, since we were convinced that the boys had not as yet worked through their deeply ingrained distrust of adults (and probably never completely would), and that they would, therefore, continue to act out toward the therapist, if permitted, both to express hostility and as a testing device. The direct approach, rather than analysis, was made necessary in our judgment by the boys' persistent and intensive denial of their negative attitudes toward the therapist whenever these were brought to their attention. In such instances directness is more effective because it naturally leads to analytical introspection, as was the case here.

Session Forty-Six

Leonard came early, and the therapist and he sat waiting for the others for about ten minutes, during which time Leonard talked about his prospective week end at home—how he wished he had an extra day so he could find a job and be able to put in two full days of work. He liked the part of the city where he lived, since it provided him with a country-like atmosphere. He talked about his having friends, and said that a number of boys who had been at the Village now lived in his borough and he had made friends in his neighborhood. (Though this was "small talk," its remarkable feature was that Leonard spoke distinctly, without hesitation or diffidence or quivering in his voice as in the past. There was a full-bodied quality to it and a bubbling kind of happiness not in evidence before. For some reason, his enunciation seemed to have a combination of western and southern regional accents. It appeared as if he had almost planfully developed this singular accent.)

About a minute before seven, Michael came into the room. He had with him a copy of a newspaper and said he had brought it to cover one of the tables used in the serving of coffee; cleaning up would be easier, he said, because no coffee would be spilled on the table itself. He then proceeded to cover the table with the newspapers and arrange the milk, sugar, and jar of instant coffee neatly on the paper. He lined the wastebasket with the brown paper bag that had contained the supplies and began to straighten the chairs. As he was doing this, he declared that he would bring more ash trays so that each boy could have one. He asked the therapist what he thought of this idea of covering the table top. The therapist said that it was a good one. Michael seemed proud of what he had accomplished and conveyed a genuine feeling of belonging in the room and the group. A few minutes after seven o'clock the other boys arrived in a body. They took their seats quietly, with Macy, Louis, and Richard starting to read magazines they had brought from the lobby.

For a few moments there was silence. Then Michael began by saying, "What were we talking about last week?" There was no response and Michael said, "I think Macy was trying to talk last week when we ended." Macy looked up from his magazine and said: "I was talking about thoughts in my mind, but that's the end of my problem. I didn't think those things this week so I don't have any problem any more."[8]

Michael, however, would not give up so easily. He said, "You sure get rid of those problems fast." Macy did not answer and continued to leaf through the magazine. Then, murmuring under his breath as if he wanted the boys both to hear and not to hear, said: "I was thinking a lot about sex. That's what I was talking about last week, but this week I didn't think much of it so I guess that's the end of it. I'll wait until I go home and then I'll have intercourse with a girl." Louis, who was still leafing through a magazine began to giggle under his breath. There was

8. Two days before the session the therapist had received a telephone call from Macy's caseworker requesting a conference. The caseworker told the therapist that Macy had come to him the day before for a regularly scheduled appointment and told him he "had a problem." Macy then revealed that on the preceding Saturday he had allowed one of the boys to "suck" his "penis." Macy said he felt dirty and guilty because of it and described a sensation of constriction in his throat. During his recital Macy told the caseworker that whenever boys in the cottage had an argument, they generally ended up by calling each other "faggot." Now, since the incident, whenever Macy heard this word he felt "so terrible inside" that he felt like "punching the guy"; he cringed "inside." He complained, "I could have waited until Christmas and had intercourse with a girl. I don't know what got me to let a guy suck my penis." He asked the caseworker if he could help him with this problem.

silence for a few moments; then the therapist commented, "Macy, you have raised this problem a number of times and talked about it, but every time you drop it almost in the same breath." Jules: "Every guy wants to have a girl once in a while; there's nothing wrong with that." Michael: "No, there ain't anything wrong with it. I have a girl once in a while myself. Last time I was home, I banged a girl in my neighborhood. Except around here, when you don't have girls, some guys bang boys." Macy flinched as Jules continued: "I never touch any boys around here." Michael: "There goes the first big lie of the night." The boys laughed at this remark. The tension that was mounting was relieved somewhat by the laughter. Louis, however, did not laugh. As he was leafing the magazine he looked as if he were in a different world, removed from his environment.

Michael leaned over to Leonard, who was sitting next to him, and whispered. Jules turned up the radio a little louder. Richard was busily absorbed in reading his magazine and said nothing. Finally the therapist said, "I bet it would feel better if we changed the subject now." Jules: "How so?" Therapist: "I get the feeling you are all pretty uncomfortable talking about it." Michael again took the initiative and said, "Every boy at the Village has had sex with another boy." Jules: "Not me. I don't do it to other boys; they do it to me." Michael: "That happened to me once when I first came to the Village. I plugged a boy for a pair of pants." Laughter greeted this and the therapist asked Michael to be more specific. He said, "I put it in his ass, because he had a pair of pants I wanted." Jules: "A boy once jerked me off, but I wouldn't jerk off any boy."

Macy spoke up at this point and slowly said, "I once had a boy suck me off." By way of explanation (or expiation) Jules said: "That's the hard part of being with boys where you can't get a girl. You want to have sex but there are no girls around. You try to control yourself and it's hard." Everybody remained silent for more than a minute, when the therapist said, "I wonder how you boys feel about this." Jules: "I don't know how the other boys feel, but I feel like a lump of shit after it is over." Michael: "It feels good while you are having sex but then later, when you think about it, you feel so dirty inside." Macy: "I felt so dirty I went upstairs to take a shower. I was ashamed of myself." Jules described how he lay in bed after he had had a sex experience with a boy and thought about it and wondered why he wasn't able to stop. He knew ahead of time that he would hate himself for it. He said, "Like the other guys say, I take a shower because I feel so dirty for what I did." Macy: "I never want to do it again. I think I had my lesson. I hated the boy who sucked me off, but I can't blame him because I let him."

The therapist tried to explore with the boys what it was that made them feel the way they did feel, "this feeling of guilt you talk about." Jules took the lead and stated, using almost a direct quote from what the therapist had said many sessions before, that the purpose of sex was "to make babies and if nature lets boys fuck boys, then there won't be any babies." Michael agreed with this, saying, "We talked about this, right, Mr. Ellery?" The therapist affirmed it and described briefly how society had set up rules and regulations in order to protect and preserve humanity. "These rules are now inside you, and when you break these rules, it is a feeling of guilt you get." Macy spoke about "urges," how impossible it was to hold in the urge when you were away from girls for such a long time. The others agreed, but did not seem to offer it as a justification, only to let themselves and others know that they had these urges. The therapist confirmed what was said, and recognized their difficulties in trying to control their urges. Yet the fact was that these urges did have to be controlled. For instance, people might have a very strong urge to eat, but what would happen if people ate all the time? Michael said: "You could hurt yourself doing that, eating all the time. Besides, if you have sex with boys the same way you can have syph, or if you have too much sex with girls you are going to get one girl who has the syph."

Jules immediately asked how syphilis was transmitted. The therapist described it briefly. Jules then asked the boys: "You know about C. R. [one of the boys at the Village]? He's had sex so many times that he gets periods." Richard looked up from his magazine and said, "I didn't know that." The therapist asked Jules if he could explain what he meant. Jules said, "He gets periods like girls get periods," and added that a staff member had told him so.

Therapist: "Jules, do you know the purpose of a period?" Jules: "No, I don't." Richard: "We once talked about it here, but I don't remember any more. What does the period do?" Michael: "Where does it come from?" The therapist told the boys about ovulation, "the egg," and the "swelling" of the wall of the uterus by developing a lining and so on. Jules was growing visibly tense. As the therapist came to the description, in very simple and concrete terms, of the function of the "blood" in the uterus and its relation to the growing embryo, Jules's discomfort seemed to be increasing. The therapist stopped and asked: "What's the matter Jules?" He said, "I don't know." Richard intervened and said, "Why does the blood stink so much?" At this, Jules at once became interested. The therapist explained to Richard the decomposition of the lining that was being expelled with concomitant bleeding and about bacteria when there is no sperm present in the uterus. Jules finally said: "Ugh, it's disgusting. I heard that that thing in the woman's body is the dirtiest place in the body." It was not clear what Jules was referring to, but Michael quickly supplied him with the proper word when he said, "You mean

the vagina, right?" Jules said: "That's right, that hole. Somebody once
told me it is a very filthy place. The filthiest in the whole body." Macy:
"I can't stand the sight of scum," then correcting himself, said "sperm."
"I get the feeling it is so dirty that I never look at it." Richard nodded.

Leonard had not said a single word throughout this conversation, but
was avidly interested. Michael said: "Yeah, scum is real filthy stuff. I
hate the sight of it." Jules: "How does scum make a baby?" Louis looked
up from his magazine and said: "What goes on Mr. Ellery? How can you
make a baby out of scum." It occurred to the therapist that the disgust
the boys were verbalizing stemmed from their associating semen with the
excretory process. He, therefore, said: "I have a book in my office that
shows diagrams and explains the whole thing. Do you want to see it?"
The boys in a chorus said yes, they wanted to see the book. The therapist
went down two flights of stairs to his office and fetched the (anatomy)
book. When he returned, he found every boy in the same position as
when he had left.

As soon as the therapist came into the room the boys moved their
chairs closer, making a small circle around him. Louis, who had been sitting on the couch a distance away, came to sit on the arm of Jules's chair.
The therapist sat down and opened the anatomy book to a diagram of
the male reproductive system. Questions came tumbling one over the
other as to what the pictures represented. To bring some order out of a
rising chaos, the therapist told the boys that it would be necessary to
examine the figures step by step and that he would describe each part
and what its function was.

Complete silence ensued, during which the therapist went over the
diagram explaining where sperm is generated, how sperm is released
from the body, what occurs in the penis to create an erection, that is,
how blood is held from flowing back fully from the penis by valves
in the veins so that the penis can stay erect. Macy asked to see a picture
of a sperm. There was a drawing of a sperm in the book and a discussion
arose as to its body and "tail," which made it mobile. Louis was on the
point of becoming humorous, but was quickly hushed by Jules and
Macy and did not say anything further. Macy wanted to know where
"wet dreams" come from. Michael reminded Macy that the group had
talked about that, but Macy said he did not remember. It was obvious
from their expressions that the other boys, too, did not remember what
had been said. The therapist repeated the explanation in terms of "nature's
preparing boys' bodies to become fathers" so that they would be able
to produce children and continue the human race; that sperm was
"manufactured and stored," but when there was no further room for
storage, it had to be discharged. This produced "sex feelings," again
nature's preparation for fatherhood. Macy broke in to say, "Even when

you don't think about sex?" Therapist: "Remember what we talked about once, the unconscious mind?" Richard said, "Yeah, that's right," pointing to the very area that the therapist had once pointed to, "where you got memories that you don't think about all the time." Therapist: "That's right. When you go to sleep these memories come out in dreams and you have a sex dream and the sperm is discharged." Macy exclaimed: "So that's why it happens!" And Michael: "That's what Mr. Ellery told us before."

At this point, Richard began to describe a motion picture that a number of boys (as well as the therapist) had seen on TV. In the picture there was a man who dreamed that everywhere he went there was an umbrella with a hole in it over his head. It was raining around him, but through the hole in the umbrella blood was dripping. As he tried to break away, he found he was surrounded by bars as in a prison. The man went to a psychiatrist, who supplied him with words to which the man had to respond with "the first word that comes to his mind." Then in a flashback the man suddenly remembered how when he was eight or nine years old he "snitched to the cops on his father who was wanted as a criminal. The cops arrested his father and shot him." The man who was narrating the dream later became a criminal and every time he shot somebody, he used to see his father's face. After the psychiatrist had explained the dream to him, the man no longer shot anybody. He didn't feel like killing people. The explanation the psychiatrist gave, as reported by Richard, was that he "felt rotten for having snitched on his father. He felt like he killed his father."

The therapist said, "Well, what does this show?" Richard, pointing at the therapist, said, "I think I know what you're trying to say, Mr. Ellery, but I don't quite get it." Therapist: "Did he want to kill his father?" Richard said: "No, he later thought he wanted to kill his father but when he was a kid he didn't know what he was doing. He didn't mean for the cops to kill his father. I get what you are trying to say. You think when you're grown up you want to do something that you did when you were a kid, even though when you were a kid you didn't know if you really wanted to do it, and maybe didn't even mean it." Jules: "That's right. In other words, when you grow up you think you wanted to kill your father even though you didn't," but he quickly indicated that he was talking exclusively about the motion picture. The therapist evaded at this point relating this thought to the boys and continued to talk about the movie. Richard said, "And all of that is in your unconscious mind?" Therapist: "Right, Richard. In this picture, remember, the man, whenever he tries to run away, runs up against bars. What do you think it means?" The boys thought for awhile. Macy said, "What do you think it means, Mr. Ellery?" Therapist: "I'm not sure, Macy, but I got a feeling from what you told us about it that in the dream the man is punished. You know that is one of the things that dreams can do. They supply you with the punishment you may be unconsciously looking for." Michael said: "Some people end up in prisons to get punished. Remember we talked about that, too, here." Silence ensued.

Louis had picked up the book on anatomy and was leafing through it. He found a picture which he drew to Jules's and Macy's attention. From the boys' expressions, it was clear that it was a picture of the female reproductive organs. When Macy took the book from Louis and handed it back to the therapist, he raised questions about various parts of the diagram, a cross section of the female reproductive system. He pointed to every detail and asked what its purpose was. Explanations were given him of the production of the "egg," its movement through the Fallopian tubes to the uterus, what happened when intercourse occurred. Jules raised many questions about the process of penetration in intercourse. The questions were derived from fantasies of "ripping" and "shredding" of flesh. He could not conceive of the penis being able to enter the small opening of a vagina, an actual photograph of which was in the book. The elasticity of the tissues involved and their capacity for stretching and moving apart, which prevent pain, was explained to him.

A cascade of questions now ensued about "the growing child" in the womb. All were now using words like *womb, uterus, embryo,* and others. As soon as the therapist would say one of these words, one or another boy would repeat it. Macy particularly picked them up extremely well and quickly. The boys were curious about how a baby could pass through such a small opening. The therapist described the position of the baby, its coming out usually head first, the width of a woman's pelvis, and the elasticity of the vaginal orifice. A diagram of a fetus *in utero,* with the umbilical cord attached to the mother's body, was available in the book. Richard was particularly interested in the details of the umbilical cord and the function it served. This information was given him specifically.

Louis asked about the difference between fraternal and identical twins. (He did not use these terms, but explained what he meant.) The therapist told him that the difference lay in the fertilization of one ovum or two. The therapist proceeded to describe the process of cell fission and the process of differentiation in relation to the development of different organs. Jules said that he had heard that in every *sperm* (he used this word) "there are 'certain things' that make you black, white, blue-eyed, brown-eyed. What are those things?" Therapist: "You are talking about 'rods' or 'chromosomes' in the sperm and ovum. They determine the color of eyes, appearance, the shape of the body. That's why, for instance, one looks either like the mother or the father or a little of both, or maybe like a grandparent." The boys then asked how parents with dark hair could have a blond child, or why a redheaded parent did not have a redheaded child. The therapist then introduced the fact of regressive and dominant genes, without using these terms, of course. Jules particularly inquired what happened when a Negro woman and a white man had intercourse and why the baby was of a different color from either of the parents. Macy was able to answer this question and did a pretty good job of it. He said, "Those rods are going to get mixed up and a third color is going to appear." Michael raised the question of artificial insemination, saying he had heard that some men have "scum" that are dead and can't have any children and "they" take some from a man with live scum and inject it into the woman, and she can have a baby that way. Louis: "That's a pretty neat trick."

There was a long pause as all the boys seemed to mull over what had just been said. Richard broke the silence. "That unconscious thing is a pretty neat trick, too. You know people get hypnotized and in that way you can get rid of your problems." Jules: "That's what they ought to do with me, hypnotize me and then I'll get to be able to know all my problems." Michael: "But that doesn't work for everybody." Macy: "You really get to know about them only by talking about them, right, Mr. Ellery?" Therapist: "Yes, right; and that's what we're here for." Richard: "If somebody hypnotized you could they get you to kill?" Michael: "Mr. Ellery won't kill unless he wants to kill. You can't hypnotize somebody to kill." Richard and Michael got into an argument about this that lasted a few minutes, and then Richard said he'd heard of somebody being hypnotized and made to hang from a tree. The man could have fallen and gotten killed. The therapist commented that even under hypnosis, if one's unconscious mind suspects that you may get into a situation where you will be destroyed, you will come out of the hypnotic trance. "Your unconscious wants to preserve you." Louis (facetiously): "My· unconscious wants to preserve me. Boy, I got a nice unconscious." He then kissed his fingers and touched them to the side of his head, as if he were kissing his unconscious. This provoked laughter from the boys and Macy said: "Well, I know one thing about my unconscious. Many times I want to kill a guy in my cottage who I can't stand. I got a real urge to choke him and take the life out of him." Richard: "So what? I feel that way, too, but I'm not going to do it. *I can control myself.*"

It was now 8:35, and the therapist felt quite tired. He told the boys they could continue with this discussion next week. There was a chorus from Leonard, Louis, and Jules that they should. All the boys except

Louis seemed reluctant to leave. Louis had left immediately. Jules, Leonard, Richard, and Macy remained seated. Finally, after a minute or two they too got up, cleaned up the room, and left, bidding the therapist good night.

COMMENT

This was a significant interview from many points of view. The advance into the genital phase (and consequent personality maturity) received a boost. Macy's reaction to his recent homosexual experience was clear proof of his growth. He had had such experiences before, but this time he reacted with aversion and guilt, and the therapist's introduction of the social roots of guilt should lead to valuable developments in the future.

For many months we had stressed the importance and the approaching readiness of the boys for a more factual understanding of sex and intercourse and the essentiality of control of appetites and its place in the maturing personality. We had outlined to the therapist, as a preparation for this development, the three basic appetites in nature in the service of survival of the individual and the species—eating, evacuation, and sex—and their strongly cathected endowment to assure the discharge of these functions. We also pointed out that the abstract discussions of sex on a moralistic or para-moralistic basis needed to be concretized by visual aids. Following these suggestions, books containing illustrations had been obtained from the medical staff on the campus as a preparation for what spontaneously transpired at this session.

Some important facts about our boys and about adolescents generally were uncovered in this interview. First, all the boys said they had participated in homosexual intercourse. This we found to be true in all groups at the Village. Though we doubt that Leonard was among them, he unquestionably had witnessed it and certainly knew all about it. Verbalization of fantasies about and aversions to the female sexual organs, latent in all males, was rather extraordinary. These fantasies could not but generate hostility, contempt, guilt, and the need for self-punishment. It was therefore essential that these pathological attitudes and feelings be dissipated, and a telling step in that direction was made at this session.

Richard's associating to the predominantly factual discussion of the dream about patricide can be understood in terms of unresolved Oedipal attitudes: sex related to the mother; hence the father has to be eliminated. Jules's self-consciousness when he checked himself in his recital and the boys' general mounting anxiety would be indications of this. The fate of the hero in the film is punishment for Oedipal incest wishes. The bars could be interpreted as the inner constraints, inhibitions, and censors that prevent acting on impulse in humans, and indicated that the man could not overcome his problem without *talking* to a psychiatrist. Toward the end of the discussion the concept of control was again introduced. This would soon become the center of our attention in the interviews.

On the surface, at least, Louis still remained the least affected of the boys, especially in matters of sex as a defense.

Note need be taken of some minor phenomena significant as indicators of the allotropic development in the boys and their growing maturity: Leonard's comfort with the therapist; Michael's concern with, and arrangement of, the room; awareness of the need for control of the sexual "urge"; the use of scientific terms such as vagina and sperm, instead of the obscene words used by them in the past and common to their culture.

A significant strategy that the therapist employed effectively in this session was to support the group's resistance when he said, "I bet it would feel better if we changed the subject." This was the first time he had employed a paradigmatic strategy because he was certain of the boys' interest in the subject under discussion, and the boys did reject his suggestion.

Session Forty-Seven

Leonard came at ten minutes before seven, the same time that the therapist arrived. Leonard told the therapist about a job he hoped to get when he returned to New York, working in a grocery store. He had worked there on his week-end visits home and found that he enjoyed the work—putting goods on the shelves, sweeping the store, running errands. At the end of the day there was a lot of money in the cash register and many times he had felt tempted to take some of it, but resisted the temptation. As Leonard put it: "I don't want any more trouble. I've had enough, and the woman [owner] trusts me."

At seven o'clock sharp Michael came in and soon he and Leonard were engaged in a conversation about various friends they had in common at the Village. Michael, who was from a distant city, asked Leonard many questions about New York, its movie houses, shows, and so on.

The session began at 7:15 instead of 7:00 because the three boys from R. cottage—Louis, Richard, and Macy—came late. They had not received their passes. In this instance it was a "relief" man rather than the regular cottage parents who was responsible for this. (Our conviction still held that behind these delays was the cottage mother.) Jules, who lived in another cottage, also came late.

By 7:20 P.M. the boys had taken coffee and the cigarettes had been distributed by Michael. The boys sat around in an easy, lounging fashion. Louis opened the discussion. He said that he had nearly run away the evening before. Richard first asked why, but caught himself and said, "Oh yeah, I know." Jules said: "I don't know. Why did you want to run away?" Louis: "I can't tell you. It's very secret." No one reacted to this, and Louis said: "Okay. You want to know?" Macy: "Go ahead, tell them. There's no secret." Louis launched into a rather lengthy enumeration of the events of the preceding night. It seemed that Louis had a hat of which he was proud. On occasion, he lent it to boys when they asked him and they had always returned it. "I trust most of the guys in my cottage," he said. However, on the evening in question he discovered that his hat was missing. Since he had not lent it to anyone, he asked each boy in the cottage whether he had seen his hat. They all said they had not. Finally, Louis undertook an investigation of his own by examining with a friend every boy's locker. Sure enough, he found his hat in a locker owned by a boy named B. It was obvious to Louis that the hat was stolen because it was very carefully hidden under a pair of trousers. Macy was nodding his head in confirmation of what Louis was saying, and from the look on Macy's face it seemed that he knew at first hand what had happened.

Louis continued describing how, following this incident, he went to the boy B. and asked him why he had stolen his hat. Mimicking the boy, to the glee of the others, Louis repeated how the boy swore on the Bible, his mother, his father, his sisters, his brothers, and so on, that he did not steal the hat. Louis told B. not to swear, that he did steal the hat and he had better admit it. B. would do no such thing. Louis was very angry, and went to his cottage parents and told them what had happened. Both cottage parents made light of the incident. They merely told him not to get excited. Louis now averred that B. was their favorite and that was why they did nothing about the matter. Having received no satisfaction from them, he went back to B. and again accused him of stealing. Again B. went on a swearing rampage, claiming that he had done no such thing. Even when Louis confronted him with his friend who had helped him find the hat, B. continued to claim that he had not stolen it. Louis finally "resolved" this problem by punching B. in the ear. B. began to scream bloody murder. The cottage parents ran down and verbally assaulted Louis. "I was so mad, I just felt like running. Just as I was about to run, I thought what's the point. In two months I get out. Why should I get in Dutch now?"

After a brief silence the therapist said, "I can understand that you were very angry, and you were able to control yourself from running away, but I wonder what you think you solved by using your fists?" Louis immediately said: "I got revenge. Mrs. K. doesn't take my part. When I step out of line she is always ready to lam me out." Jules, in Louis's defense, said: "Sometimes when you don't use your fists, they'll steal from you all the time. Some guys don't understand anything but getting hit and if you don't stand up for yourself, then you're a punk and everybody pushes you around." Silence continued for a few moments.

The therapist again raised the question whether one can survive only by using fists. Where does this idea come from? Louis: "That's the way it always was here at the Village. For instance, when you are new, boys walk up to you and they test you out. They push you around, take your things, want your food, want your money. If you don't stand up to them with your fists, cottage parents don't help you. You are going to get a beating. They'll leave you alone only when you show them that you aren't afraid." Macy stood up and demonstrated to the boys what happened when he came to the Village. Boys came up to him and began to ask for and take things from him, and only when he couldn't hold in his anger any more and used his fists, did they leave him alone. Michael added: "It was like that in the beginning, but no more. Boys know that I can't be pushed around. I never push anybody else around. One thing I know, if I want to get out of the Village and learn not to fight any more I got to practice that—not fighting. I don't think it's right to push a little boy around and I'm the biggest boy in my cottage."

Louis: "Mr. Ellery, you remember Bill [a boy who left the Village and subsequently, while fleeing from the police in a stolen car, collided with a station wagon, killing a mother, father, and child]?" The therapist nodded, and Louis went into a very prolonged narration of Bill's exploitive and cruel conduct toward other boys in the cottage and his unfairness in dealing with them. He ended by saying: "Bill just had to be king and anybody who wouldn't recognize him as king was in for trouble."

The therapist asked: "How did you feel about Bill?" Louis: "How did we feel about Bill? There wasn't a boy in the cottage of the Village that didn't hate him. What made it even worse was that we knew that Bill couldn't have done it if the cottage parents had stopped him. They just didn't want to mix in. Bill really made life easier for them. He ran the cottage so that they wouldn't have to get their hands dirty." Richard said the boys knew of the fear in R. cottage when Bill was there. "When Bill got into trouble we kind of felt sorry for him [referring to the auto accident], but we were glad that he got into trouble, got put away." Michael: "Look what happened to the king. Now he's locked up until he's twenty-one, and he'll probably be a criminal for the rest of his life."

The therapist agreed with Michael saying: "Yes, look at the boy who had to live by his fists, but I'm interested in this word *king*. What do you think made Bill feel that he had to be king?" There was silence for a few minutes and then Richard said, "It's like we used to say here [in the group] if you got to be king so bad, it's only *because you are so small, you got to show you are a big shot.*" Louis: "That's the trouble with little guys who feel they have to be king. They got to make everybody miserable to be king."

Therapist: "I wonder what Bill was fighting all his life. From what you tell me, I feel what it was like to live in R. cottage with Bill, but Bill seemed to be like a boy who was driven to do what he did. What do you suppose drove him?" Momentary silence, then Richard: "I think I know what you are trying to say. He was fighting back at somebody. Do you think maybe he was trying to get back at his parents? Maybe he was just trying to go after his father." The boys turned to look in the therapist's direction, and he said: "Maybe. What do you think about it?"

There was no immediate response, and in a somewhat detached way, the therapist said: "Gee, I wonder. It's just a sheer accident: Bill gets out, and the next thing that happens he crashes into a car with parents and children in it." Richard: "Maybe he saw his father's face when he was running from the cops." Macy: "Naw, maybe it was just an accident." Richard: "Accident, my ass!" Louis: "I sure hope that it never happens to me." Richard: "I wonder what my chances are about going straight when I get out of here." Michael: "I know I'm going to go straight," but there was doubt in his voice. Michael said that he would go to school, not get into any more trouble, that he wanted to have an education, and so forth. He then asked about Donald. How was he doing? (He knew that the therapist was seeing Donald on "after-care.") The therapist said he was doing all right. He would like to come up and sit in with the group. There was immediate response to this on every boy's face. Richard: "Why doesn't he? He knows he's welcome." Louis: "I'd sure like to have that cat back in the room here. He was a lot of fun. Is it really okay if Donald comes up again to the group meetings?" The therapist said: "Yes. The only trouble is that Donald has a problem about transportation." Louis: "I'm glad Donald is doing all right." And Michael: "Let's not talk about what we are going to do when we get out," and with this he lay down on the couch, as if to remove himself from the discussion. However, this was not the end.

Louis said: "I don't know; I just don't know. I want to get out of here. I don't want any more trouble. What happened in the past is over. I want to go to school. I know I got a good mind. I know I can get me an education. I can amount to something. Bill could have amounted to something.[9] He was a bright boy, but all he amounts to is being an inmate at E——— [prison]. I don't want that to happen to me, but I got to go back to schools which are filled with jitterbugs and bopsters [slang for gangs]." Louis, walking in front of the group, imitated the tough gait of a bopster as he went up to a boy and offered membership in his gang. "And what happens if you don't accept membership is that they beat the hell out of you," said Louis. "How can you win? You got to move out of the city to get away from this." Richard: "I hope when I get out I can go to Holy Cross High School. In a Catholic school the brothers beat up anybody who bothers you. You got half a chance in a Catholic school. You don't have it in public schools." Louis: "If I can get away from my neighborhood, if the Board of Education will let me go to a school outside of my turf [slang for gang area], maybe then I can get me an education, get a job, and grow up the right way." He leaned back, and there was a very sad look on his face as he mumbled under his breath, but loud enough for the therapist to hear: "I guess it just can't happen." Jules was nodding his head in agreement with Louis.

The therapist said, "I kind of pick up tonight a feeling of doom, that there is no way of changing your destiny." Nothing was said for a while and then Louis: "That's the feeling, doom. I'll tell you why I tell you this tonight, Mr. Ellery. Mrs. K. [cottage mother] said to me, 'I give you two weeks after you're out of the Village and then you're going to be in trouble.' Mr. Ellery, every boy that Mrs. K. ever said that about was in trouble. Bill was told by Mrs. K. that in a month after he's out he's going to be in trouble, and sure enough it happened." Macy supported Louis in this, mentioning a few boys to whom Mrs. K. had said they would be in trouble, and sure enough they did get in trouble. Controlling his anger as best he could, the therapist said, "Louis, Mrs. K. is not God, and I know Mrs. K. said this to other boys who never got into any trouble after they left the Village."

Louis's eyes welled up and he refused to believe it. Louis: "She's right. She's always right. Before a boy leaves, Mrs. K. tells that boy just what's going to happen to him. She's like a fortune teller." Therapist: "Louis, even fortune tellers are wrong and Mrs. K. is just not God." Louis: "Are you saying that you feel that I can stay out of trouble?" Therapist: "That's what I'm saying. I'm saying, Louis, there is no law that says that you or any other boy in this room has to get into trouble

9. By this remark Louis reveals considerable perspicacity, for Bill had a good intellect and a strong character.

again." Louis, drying his eyes, said, "It's really like learning to handle yourself." Therapist: "What do you mean?" Louis: "Well like you tell us, Mr. Ellery, you can't always get the thing you want. You got to control yourself even though everybody around you tempts you into trouble." Therapist: "Right, Louis. This is the difference between being a child and a grownup. You come into manhood when you learn to know when you are tempted and learn to control yourself against giving in to temptation." At this point the therapist reviewed the various ideas the group had talked about in past sessions: temptation to steal, to play hooky, to engage in sexual activity, masturbation, and so on, and ended by saying: "You don't go to hell because you are tempted. The important thing is to know that every time you give in to temptation, you are remaining a little infant, and you rise above being an infant by controlling yourself against temptations and remembering that there is a time and place for everything."

Leonard, acting as spokesman for the group, said: "I think that's what we learned here. There is a time and place for everything." Richard interjected, almost cutting Leonard off: "I remember things now I never used to think about. For instance, my father always used to treat me like I wasn't there. Whatever I did, he never did anything. He spoiled me; he didn't teach me to stop doing things. When my brother started getting older he did the same thing with him. He paid him almost no attention, but then later he started having it in for me. One day I wake up and I find everything I do is no good. I just can't do anything right with my father. He starts to slap me around. Even when I used to steal, my father really didn't give a shit until he started slapping me around. I don't remember when this happened, but I do remember when my father got a new car in 1958. I wanted that car to be destroyed. I wanted to get revenge, like we used to want to get revenge on Bill. I used to dream about a truck hitting my father's car, and what do you think happened one day? When I came home from school my mother tells me my father was in an accident; a truck hit my father's car. I felt sorry for my father and I know I also felt glad."

He looked at the therapist as if to gauge his reaction to what he had just said. Then: "You don't blame me for wanting revenge, do you Mr. Ellery?" The therapist shook his head in the negative. Richard then said: "I know two brothers. One brother is spoiled. Whatever he does his parents say, 'you are a nice boy'; he can't do anything wrong. The other brother loves his parents. He wants to do everything for them, but whatever he does is no good. If he washes the car, they yell at him because he didn't wash it right. If he goes out to help his mother shopping, she makes fun of him because of the way he carries packages." Richard described extensively the difference between the two boys. The one boy, who even stole cars, was protected by his parents; the other, who wanted to go straight, wanted to show his parents that he loved them, got nothing from them. Richard summed up by saying: "With some parents there is just no justice. Both boys are going to get into trouble—one for never being stopped, and the other one for being stopped too much." He leaned back, and there was silence.

Michael reminded the boys that it was time to go. The therapist looked at his watch and discovered that it was 8:38, but no one moved to go. Louis finally got up slowly and started cleaning up the room, and the session ended.

COMMENT

For some time we had been aware of the boys' readiness to examine three lines of thought: *1]* the differences between psychological infancy and maturity; *2]* their feelings of being doomed to a fate of criminality and ultimately prison; and *3]* the self-fulfilling prophecy. We discussed these on many occasions in our supervision conferences, and waited for an appropriate opportunity to expand on these topics, since they had already been touched upon in a number of previous sessions. In this session the opportunity was presented to us by the boys.

In this session, also, the opportunity was offered to the therapist by Louis's episode to attack the "jungle law" rule of life by which our boys lived in their neighborhood cultures. Although we did not make much of an inroad in this direction at this time, we did open the area for future consideration. The fact that the boys were living under a dome of doom was re-emphasized. The concept of the witch mother in the person of Mrs. K. was dispelled.

Mrs. K.'s "powers" were obviously an extension of the magic powers of the boys' witch mothers. The boys' religious and superstitious backgrounds supplied fertile soil for their fears. Despite all this, however, the incorporation of psychological insights was demonstrated at two significant points: one was when Richard interpreted Bill's need to be cruel as a reaction-formation to his basic weakness, and the second when he recognized that Bill's diffuse aggression was displacement of aggression toward his father.

The boys' growing capacity for relatedness was touchingly displayed by their joyful hope that Donald would come to the group. Perhaps at once the most surprising and most hopeful development was the change that occurred in Louis. This hardened, resistive, and difficult-to-reach boy had uncovered striking awareness of his inner struggles and the place of environmental factors in the genesis of his problems. His striving for a socially more useful life was touching in its pathos and genuineness. His ruminations had a strong curative effect upon the other boys. The therapist's pointing up the relation of control (of temptations) to maturity could not but have salutary effects. The boys were ready for this, as witness their alluding quite on their own to controls on three different occasions in this session (as well as in some of the preceding sessions). Richard, who now seemed to have taken over the role of "instigator" formerly held by Donald, had come a long way from his former defensiveness where his father was concerned. He now could confront himself with his death wishes against his father. His insights were of a high level in his analysis of the two brothers, both of them would be in difficulty for completely opposite reasons.

Session Forty-Eight

ABSENT: Leonard and Jules, who attended a dance of their unit.

Richard, Michael, Louis, and Macy arrived late together. Louis, acting as spokesman, said that they were late because they had encountered other boys from the dance and stood around talking with them. Louis went through some dancing motions which brought laughter from the others. However, the therapist overheard a conversation between Richard and Macy about stopping off to talk with the boys in the other (therapy) group that had been meeting at the same time in another building. Michael then told the therapist that he was talking with some boys "in the other group" and told them, "we are the original Thursday group."

There seemed to be an air of hilarity among the boys. Richard was again holding a side conversation with Macy. Louis began to prepare coffee for the group, and Michael distributed cookies. These activities proceeded quietly and took about four minutes. Footsteps were heard on the stairs. Everybody stopped what they were doing and listened. Louis said, "I'll bet that's Jules." Suddenly, Donald, who now lived in the city, appeared in the doorway. The moment the boys caught sight of Donald, a wave of enthusiasm swept through the room. Louis ran over and pumped his hand. Macy yelled out, "Yaa, Don." All the boys gathered around him and entered into a lively conversation. Donald was attired very neatly in a black suit and a green sport shirt, making a very presentable appearance. He walked over to the therapist and shook hands. Richard repeated: "It's good to see you. We were hoping you'd come back." Donald looked slightly embarrassed, but managed to say: "Thanks, thanks a lot. I wanted to come back for a long time."

Donald was bombarded by a host of questions from everyone. Macy wanted to know how he was doing. Richard asked: "How are things on the outside? You want to come back?" Donald had taken a seat directly opposite the therapist and answered Richard's question in a weary voice. "I don't know. I might not mind coming back. Things ain't so hot on the outside." This remark seemed to dampen the boys' enthusiasm. They quieted down, and Donald said, almost by way of correcting himself: "Not too bad outside. I'd rather be outside than here at the Village, that's for sure." Louis immediately informed Donald that he was leaving in January so he would soon know what it was like. Richard: "Well, what's the matter, Don, what's happening?" Donald: "I got a little trouble at home. Me and my father—we don't get along. But he's all right. He loses his temper once in awhile, that's just the way he is. I can't spend my time worrying about him." Michael: "Why don't you come back then?" Donald: "I thought about it, but, naw, I'm going to stay home. I don't want to come back." Louis: "I'll bet the guys in your cottage would like to see you again." Donald: "I know they would. I'm only going to stay here a little while and then I'm going over to my cottage to say hello to the boys." Louis: "How did you get up here?" "I took the train. I fell asleep on the train and landed up in T. I had to take a train to come back and used up all my money." Then, looking at the therapist, Donald asked: "You going home tonight, Mr. Ellery?" "Yes I am, Don." "Could you give me a lift to the Bronx? You live in the Bronx, don't you?" The therapist said, "Yes, Don, I'll give you a lift."

Louis and Donald got into a conversation about whom they knew "on the outside," who was doing what, and so on. This continued for a while and then Donald, looking at the therapist, said, "These guys are happy to see me." Therapist: "We're all happy to see you, Don." Donald stood up and bowed very deeply, saying: "Thank you, thank you one and all. It's good to be back with the old bunch." There were a few moments of silence. Donald got up and made himself a cup of coffee. Louis ran over and offered him some cookies. When Donald was seated again, Louis told him what he had said in the preceding session concerning what it would be like when he got "outside." Louis told the boys that although he was getting out in January, he still wasn't too sure about his plans for school. "Like I was telling you last week, a lot is going to depend on the kind of school I go to." He then described at some length the various schools he could attend, and the problems in each. They all had gangs, and the gangs would approach him and force him to become a member; if not, they would test him, pick fights with him until he fought back. He said, "I don't want trouble, but I know trouble is going to happen." Michael said: "That's the way I've been figuring. I just know when I go back, I'm going to get into trouble. It may be three months, it may be

six months, it can even be five years from now, but I got a real hunch
that I'm going to land up doing something bad like maybe murdering
somebody."

Louis appeared to be annoyed with Michael as he tried to tell the
therapist that he had to get himself into a school where there were no
gangs. Michael, however, continued to talk about the same subject,
almost oblivious of what Louis was saying. As a result, there was a sort
of crossfire of conversation. Donald stepped in and said: "I wouldn't
worry if I were you. If worse comes to worst you can come back to the
Village." This seemed to focus Louis's and Michael's attention on Donald, with Michael asking the latter: "Do you really want to come back?"
Donald: "No, no, I'm not saying that. I'm just saying you know that if
things don't go right there is always the Village. You can come back."
Nothing more was said for a while. Donald rose and said: "I'll see you
later, fellows. I want to go over to the cottage and see the boys there."
Then, turning to the therapist, he said, "I'll see you at 8:30, Mr. Ellery,
okay?" Therapist said, "All right, Don."

With Donald gone, Louis, Michael, and Richard got into a discussion
of what "a grand old fellow" he was and how nice it was to see him
again. This did not last for long, because Louis got back to discussing
what he considered his problems with school. He said: "I got a good
chance of getting me an education, getting out of here and not really
getting into trouble again. But it is going to depend upon the kind of
school I go to, who my friends are." Louis said that he had learned that
if he went back to his old friends in the neighborhood he did not stand a
chance; they were going to try to tempt him into trouble. "How much
will power can you have before you get into some kind of trouble?" he
asked. When he left the Village in January he planned to stay with an
aunt who lived in a "better neighborhood." He would register at a school
in that neighborhood, giving his aunt's address as his own. He had not
told this to his social worker because if he did, she would be liable to
"louse up" his leaving. He narrated how he came upon this plan as a
result of discussing the problem with his mother, and even his mother
told him not to tell this to his social worker. They (meaning Louis and
his mother) did not quite trust what the social worker might do with
this information. The therapist faced Louis with his plan and wondered
if it would not be possible to make these arrangements through the education office at the Village. The Village might be able to help him get
into a good school, but could the Village help him if he already had a
compact with his mother not to discuss it? Louis said: "You are right in
a way, Mr. Ellery. I know that maybe I'm kind of screwing things up
for myself, but I'm so close to going home I just don't want to louse

things up." Then after a moment's thought added: "I ought to think about it."

Richard again elaborated on how he was going to try and "get out" in January.[10] He told how when he went home on visits now he avoided many of his old friends, and this way he found he didn't get into trouble by hanging around and doing what his old friends used to tell him to do. In fact, many of his old friends were no longer at home. A lot of them were either in a training school or prison.

Michael hardly allowed Richard to finish. He broke in and said: "I wish I could say I was not going to get into trouble. I got a feeling that when I get home one of these days I'm going to murder somebody. I'm not going to want to. Like I remember when I first came to the Village, I used to get into fights. I didn't pick the fights, somebody was always picking them with me to test me out; but what would happen? I hit the guy hard, then I felt rotten for hitting him so hard. I know I'm a pretty strong guy. If somebody picks on me I lose my temper; I see stars. Before I know it, I start to swing and—boom, I can kill somebody that way."

Silence ensued as Michael was lost deep in thought, staring at the floor. Finally Michael said, "Ah, that's the way it goes!" "What goes?" the therapist asked. "I don't know. Just a feeling, a hunch I got." "Let me ask you something, Mike. How do you feel about walking away from a fight." Michael: "That I could never do. I go to school, boys pick on you, girls are around, they watch you. You think I'm going to walk away from the fight? Then your life isn't worth a plugged nickel. They keep after you. They call you sissy, fag, fairy. That's no way of staying out of a fight, by walking away from it." (Without saying a word, Richard walked out of the room.)

The therapist said: "Mike, you've been at the Village for some time now. You say you don't get into fights any more. Somehow you are able to control yourself." Michael: "I control myself because I know I'm getting out soon and that one of the ways of getting out is to control myself. But what happens when I'm on the outside? When the Village is just kind of a memory?" Therapist: "This is the same feeling of doom we talked about last week. I wonder where it comes from?" Louis answered, "I don't know," and Michael added: "I don't know either, Mr.

---

10. During the preceding week Richard's caseworker had called the therapist to inform him that Richard's parents were going to make an active attempt to remove Richard from the Village. Richard had not been committed through the court. He had been placed by the Department of Welfare, and the parents claimed that they could bypass the courts, which was true. The caseworker indicated that the parents felt that Richard was "okay now." He no longer was a problem at home, and they wanted him home in January, rather than June, the planned discharge date for him.

Ellery. I just know it's there." Again silence. Therapist (speaking to the boys as a group): "I wonder whether when you were growing up you used to hear that you were going to get yourself into trouble and maybe this has become a part of you." Michael's immediate response to this was: "I don't know who used to say that to me. Maybe it was my grandfather, but I don't even remember my grandfather too well; but what you say kind of sounds right. Like I don't remember where I heard it, to tell you the truth." Louis: "Naw, I never heard it." Then halting, he corrected himself and said: "I think I used to hear that from my father. But my father—he doesn't have much to do with me. He's like you say, on the outside. My mother, she's the one who used to beat me, used to tell me not to go with bums, to watch out, stay out of trouble, and not go to the poolroom. My father used to say it, but he never did anything about it when I did get into trouble. In fact, me and my father, we don't have much to do with one another." He suddenly changed the subject and said: "I would like to go to college. I think I can make it in college, but again it depends upon the kind of school I go to."

Macy, who had been silent throughout this discussion, spoke up. He began to describe how difficult it was to stay out of trouble in his cottage. He always found himself in trouble with the relief man. For instance, he felt the relief man was always watching and reported on him to his cottage parents. Why did he report on him? Because Macy fooled around, and when the relief man told him to stop, Macy would get mad and say: "Why should I stop? I'm just kidding around." The therapist asked: "Macy, what about this business of kidding around?" Macy: "What about it? Boys are boys, they just kid around." Therapist: "You are saying something important; namely, that you have a part in what happens to you and you are not at the mercy of people and outside forces alone. For instance, do you have an idea, Macy, what kidding around means?" Macy: "No, what?" Therapist: "It means generally that you are trying to get somebody mad. Remember we talked about all things having a reason. Well, when boys fool around this is a way of provoking people and getting them mad." Macy: "I always thought kidding around was just kidding around." Michael spoke up: "In other words, you can start a fight even though you don't realize you are starting a fight." Louis said to Michael, in almost a condescending tone, "You mean you didn't know that yet?" Michael: "Well, I can look out about those things. I mean I don't have to go pick fights. I'm just still worried about people picking fights with me."

About this time Richard and Donald crawled into the room through the window. (This unusual entry was made because the cleaning man, on leaving the building, had locked the front door and the two boys had to come in through the fire escape.) It was 8:30, and the group broke up.

(The therapist drove Donald to his home, although originally he had planned to let him off near a subway upon arrival in New York. Once on the highway, however, it seemed just as easy to take him to his home. All Donald had in his pocket was a single token for the subway.)

COMMENT

Donald's return to the group brought the boys face to face with the reality with which they had been struggling in recent weeks. He became the representative of that reality, and the boys' doubts and fears of returning to their homes were reactivated or enhanced. The significantly manifested onto-archaic attitudes of dependencies reappeared, but what was striking was that now the good, protective mother was the Village, which they saw as a haven in case of failure or distress. This attitude was a far cry from the views they held when they first came to the group and signified a growing maturity, decreased projective distortions, and a more sanguine sense of values.

In his struggles with reality, Louis occupied the center of the stage in this session. He had a shrewd understanding of the sources of his difficulties and viewed his problems practically and realistically. His stubborn hostility to the Village staff had given way to the possibility that he could enlist their help in rearranging his life in the city.

Richard, too, had become aware of the need to avoid his friends as a preventive. We recall that he recognized in a previous session his suggestibility, but at this point he is dealing with this difficulty in the best way he can. Michael, however, was of great concern to us. Michael was obviously schizophrenic, and when he said that some day he would kill someone even though he would not want to, he evaluated correctly the weak controls of his impulses. The group had helped to bring this to his awareness and at present his impulses were under better restraint, but we could not be too sanguine about him and his future. We could only take this as a warning that he would bear clinical watching after his release from the institution.

The violent reaction to the term "chicken" is common among delinquent and acting-out youths (and among adolescents generally), and we made note of it for future discussion. There already had been a preliminary to it in session forty-seven, when the concept of being "king" was analyzed, and we were to push it forward some time later. The theme of "doom" was repeated and was correctly emphasized by the therapist. Such ideas and concepts need to be repeated over and over again until they are lodged in the psyche and counteract the onto-archaic attitudes. The etiology of "kidding around" (provocation), which had been discussed before, needed further consideration in the future to prevent avoidable interpersonal conflicts.

Note need be taken of the ease with which the boys discussed themselves and their difficulties and the mature understandings and objectivity with which they confronted themselves.

Session Forty-Nine

ABSENT: Louis, in hospital with a bronchial condition.

Jules was first to arrive. He came about five minutes before the set time. Being alone with the therapist seemed to be disturbing to him. After a few embarrassing moments, he began to tell the therapist that he was planning to run away and wanted to know what his penalty would be. He said that he had been denied a Thanksgiving week-end home visit because of a sex attack that he was accused of attempting on a boy about a month before and his purportedly threatening the boy with a knife. He said: "It's unfair. That happened a month ago. The Village is carrying a grudge against me, and they won't let me go home on my week end." Jules was full of rage. He had heard that, at the transition conference on him, it had been decided that he would leave December fifth.[11]

He stated that the "coaches" who attended the conference had already told him that he would be leaving on that date. However, when he raised the question with his caseworker, the latter told him that he would not be leaving, that there was some mistake. The coaches had already dropped Jules from the varsity team and he was upset about being eliminated from basketball varsity. He was looking forward to participating in it.

During Jules's recital, the other boys filed in quietly and he was not deterred from finishing his complaint. There was a slight interruption, however, when Michael began to prepare coffee and found that there was no instant coffee on hand. (The evening before the therapist had investigated the coffee supply and had found the jar half full.) The coffee jar was empty, and since the room was accessible to the clinic staff, the coffee might have been used by them. The therapist explained the situation to the boys. Macy, speaking for the group, said: *"That's okay, Mr. Ellery. We'll do without it tonight."* There was some milk which the therapist had brought for the coffee, and as an afterthought the boys decided to have milk. Leonard distributed cups of milk and cookies to each boy.

---

11. This decision was reached in consultation with staff. It was possible for us to reverse it later. Jules was continued at the Village until the termination of the group.

The interruption lasted but a few moments and Jules continued with his complaint. However, before he could get far into it, Richard asked him what he was talking about. Jules briefly recapitulated what he had already told the therapist, and then turned to him again, saying he was not sure what he should do. If it was true that he'd be leaving December fifth, and he ran away, it might mean that he wouldn't be discharged on that date. But he was not sure that he would be discharged then, so he didn't know what to do. Michael said to him: "Why don't you wait and find out instead of just planning to run away?" Jules thought about this a little while and then asked: "Mr. Ellery, what do you think about my running away? What would you do if you were in my place?" The therapist said, "Jules, what do you expect to accomplish by running away?" Jules: " I don't know, but at least I'd get home to my family for Thanksgiving. That's important to me. I don't see my family often [Jules lived in a city distant from the Village], and Thanksgiving is a pretty big holiday in my house; I would like to have dinner with my family." Therapist: "Jules, I can understand that, but I kind of wonder how you will feel being 'on the run.' Could you really be with your family comfortably?" Jules said: "That's what I am thinking about. I don't want to be a fugitive and it doesn't feel right being on the run, but what am I going to do? I don't know when I'm going to leave and it feels to me like the Village is just sore at me and kind of pushing me around. I want to get even with the God damn Village for this."

Jules immediately began to describe how, now that he was at S. cottage,[12] he no longer had any difficulties. In fact, a funny thing had happened just the other week, he said. He found out that one of the boys had a concealed knife on him which he was going to use on another boy, and Jules took the knife away and turned it over to the cottage father at S. cottage. The cottage father said to him that he knew that Jules would never use a knife, and Jules told the cottage father, "but that's why I'm here, because they accused me of using a knife." Jules described that this cottage father was using him "almost like a monitor." He helped the cottage father make sure that the other boys went to bed and he kept order in S. cottage. He felt that, because of his good behavior and doing whatever he was asked, the Village ought to try to understand and give him his Thanksgiving week end. The boys were listening closely to Jules's recital.

Michael said to Jules, "Would you really use a knife if you had a chance?" Jules: "Well, I once did," and he described how a few months

12. Following the incident for which his home visit had been denied, Jules was transferred to S. cottage, which was being used at that time to isolate boys. Though he was still in "isolation," we arranged for him to attend the group session.

before someone had hit him and Jules, having a knife on him, attempted to stab the other person in the stomach but was restrained from doing it.[13] Jules now took on a façade of real toughness, speaking in an appropriate voice. He said he would "cut up" anybody who frustrated him. Although he was obviously "putting on," the striking fact was that by contrast he appeared to be a rather weak, "soft" youngster and now was struggling hard to present a façade of toughness.

The therapist decided to face Jules with this episode and explore his reactions to it. The therapist asked Jules how he felt about it. He said that he was glad he had been stopped, because he realized now he could have gotten into "some very bad trouble." He added: "I was scared shitless. I guess I would have used the knife, because I lost control of myself, and I'm glad there were people around to stop me." Richard spoke up and said: "I don't blame you for wanting to get even. They are sure giving you a rotten deal." Michael agreed, and then Macy chimed in, repeating almost exactly what Richard had said. Leonard said nothing, but appeared extremely interested in the discussion. Jules continued the theme of "vengeance," and the therapist raised the question as to who would really get hurt from attempts to "hurt back." Jules said: "I know what you're trying to say. I realize that I may be the only one hurt in this, but there are times I just don't feel like giving a shit."

Silence ensued for awhile. Suddenly Michael, as though he were initiating the discussion, asked: "By the way, what were we talking about last week?" (One did not get the feeling that Michael was trying to change the subject.) He answered his own question by saying, "Yeah, I remember; we were talking about school and going back to school, and Louis was talking about going back to school in his old neighborhood." Jules quickly said: "Well I'm not going back to school. I didn't work out in school. I don't like it, and I know if I go back to school I'll have trouble." Macy: "I know I may have trouble in school, too, but what the hell, I got to go back to school, I want an education." Michael: "What are you guys so worried about getting into trouble? I'm not worried about it. I know I'll do good outside." Macy: "But last week you were talking about all the trouble you were going to get into." Michael: "So what? I don't think I will. Oh, yeah, maybe five years from now I'll get into trouble, but I don't think I'll have trouble as soon as I get out of the Village." Jules said he knew he would not make out in school, and he was not even going to try to go back.

---

13. Though this sounded like fantasy, an inquiry from staff confirmed it. Although all the details of the incident were not known, it was reported that Jules did have to be restrained from using his knife. The staff questioned whether Jules would have actually done the stabbing, but there was little doubt of his impulsivity.

The therapist raised the question with Jules of his tendency to quit when he felt he was not doing well. Jules thought about this for a while and then said: "Well, I got a bad temper and I know that in school my temper's pretty bad and when a teacher says something to me I fly off the handle. So what? I don't go back to school." The therapist persisted, and asked whether there was some connection between the two things he was talking about: this need to get even and his bad temper in school. For a few minutes there was absolute silence in the room. Then Jules said: "Well, I remember this. When I had a fight with my mother at home, or when my mother picked on me, I didn't say anything at home, but the next thing I knew I go to school, the teacher says something, and boom— I fly off the handle. When I had a hard time in school, sometimes I wouldn't even say anything in school. But I go home, my mother starts to pick on me and boom—again I fly off the handle."

Interrupting Jules, Michael spoke up: "That's what happened when I went to school. I remember I used to want to get even with the teacher because my mother had just finished bawlin' me out." Richard now joined the discussion and described how a number of times when he was in the classroom he would hear his mother's voice as she had yelled at him when he was about to leave for school. "Sure enough it didn't take much to get me angry with the teacher," he said. Many times he wouldn't even bother to get angry with the teacher. When he was asked to do something, he would run out of the class and stay out that day.

Now it was Macy's turn to describe a number of incidents in which his father had "pushed him around." His father would not give him a chance to explain why he came home at eleven o'clock when he was told to come home at ten. There now arose an exchange among Jules, Macy, Richard, and Michael of incidents on the same theme, namely, troubles with parents that gave rise to trouble in school. Jules said: "One of the things I like about being in S. cottage [to which he was transferred] is that I don't have to put up with Mrs. G. Mrs. G. [his former cottage mother] reminds me of my mother. She's always watching what you do. Whatever you do she's got a comment to make about it, and she's always picking on small things and I can't stand her voice. I don't know how to describe it, but I just can't stand it." Richard supplied the words for Jules. He said, "You mean she screeches at you." Jules: "That's right. All she does is screech her head off at you. I don't mind her bawling me out when I really do something wrong, but Mrs. G. can come down at you at the craziest times, even when you're not doing anything. It's like something is eating her and she's got to take it out on you."

At this point Macy went off into a long explanation of something that had happened to him at home. He had gone with several of his friends to see someone off at the airport. While there, he and the friends decided to go to a restaurant. While in the restaurant they got talking and "kidding around," and before they knew it, it was late. He rushed home and arrived out of breath. His father immediately asked him for an explanation as to why he got home late. Macy was trying to catch his breath and was panting. Demonstrating with his hand, Macy reproduced his father's slapping him, even before he could get a word in. He then said: "I was so fuckin' angry that I swore come hell or high water I'm going to get back at him. I did get back at him. 'Cause a couple of times my father would go lookin' for something like cuff links and, guess what? They just weren't around. I'd walk around the house lookin' kind of innocent as if I knew nothing about it, and my father couldn't say a word to me 'cause he never caught me stealin' 'em. But then I cut it out 'cause I figured enough is enough."

Jules: "Well, I haven't come to figure that enough is enough yet. I'm going to get back at this fuckin' Village for what they're doing to me." Therapist: "I understand how you feel, Jules. And yet we're also talking about how this feeling of getting back at people has something to do with what happened to you when you were younger." Jules: "Yeah, that's so. Like what we're saying tonight, right, about getting back? For instance, my mother, because of all the things she used to do." In a pathetic tone of voice, Jules said, "I don't really want to mess up around here, but I hate being treated like shit and that's what I feel they're doin' —treating me like a piece of shit." After a silence Jules said: "Well, I'm going to think about this some more. I don't want to do anything to hurt myself." This sounded almost as if he were making a "last ditch stand," as he added, "But I still think I'm going to run away if I don't get my Thanksgiving week end."

It was time to end now. The therapist announced that the following week being Thanksgiving, some of the boys would be away. Macy and Michael announced that they were not going home; they lived too far away and would be having a long Christmas vacation instead. The therapist asked the boys if they would like to meet the following week on Wednesday instead of Thursday since the holiday fell on the regular day. Michael and Macy were enthusiastic, and agreed to meet. The therapist turned to Jules and asked: "What about you, Jules?" Jules looked at him with a smile on his face and said: "I probably won't be here. I'm going to run away." Then he added, still with a smile: "But I'll tell you what. If I am here, I'll show up for the discussion on Wednesday night."

COMMENT

The absolute confidence the boys had developed in the therapist was made apparent in many ways in a number of sessions, but it reached its ultimate in Jules's confiding that he would run away and the freedom with which he reported on his intransigent act. Jules had not achieved as much inner change as some of the other boys; nonetheless he did confront himself with his acts and recognized his uncontrollability. The ease with which Michael moved into the discussion and the continuation from the previous session of examining the reality of school and life outside the Village, and especially the participation of other boys in the Village, revealed mature efforts at anticipating and finding a *modus vivendi* in the larger community. The boys now understood and accepted the therapeutic purpose of, and process in, the group, and of the Village. During the discussion that ensued, they displayed singular insights into their feelings and behavior mechanisms, which would eventually emerge as self-control. All the boys showed newly evolved and much healthier self-identities.

The boys now freely narrated without any projective defenses their attitudes and misdeeds and recognized the origins of these in the home without defenses or injury to self-esteem. Jules's associating his cottage mother and his natural mother is a sign of his psychological literacy; his recognizing of the identity of his feelings toward them shows insight. This gave the therapist an opportunity to elaborate on the mechanisms of transference and substitution which were operative in these boys' lives and which got them into conflict with the community.

The boys' awareness could have been tied up with the displacement patterns they so eloquently and vividly described in relating their conduct at school, which they recognized to be substitutes for the home and vice versa. This was the first time the boys afforded so clear an opportunity to the therapist and of which he did not take advantage. Understanding of displacement feelings is particularly important for antisocial, acting-out persons, since the predominant source of their conduct is displacement of hostility from one object to another. Also, control of displacement as part of emotional maturity could have been pointed out.

Of special note is Macy's equanimity in the face of frustration by the absence of coffee.

Session Fifty

ABSENT: Richard, Leonard, and Louis on Thanksgiving home visits; Jules had run away.

Michael was the more active of the two boys in the discussion. They were both somewhat uncomfortable at first. The absence of the other boys, to whom they were accustomed, seemed to generate a degree of discomfort for both Michael and Macy, as evidenced through their body movements and posture. The strain gradually disappeared,

however. Michael busied himself preparing coffee and seemed to make
it a rather elaborate procedure. He first covered the table with newspapers, which had been done only once before, washed the pans, and
then carefully measured the powdered coffee before he placed it in
each cup. This slow and prolonged activity was accompanied by an
incessant stream of talk. Michael discussed the weather, who went where
for Thanksgiving holidays, and other current topics. He then told Macy
that when they went home for their Christmas holiday, maybe they
ought to meet in B———, where both boys lived, and have "a ball"
there.

Macy and Michael appeared to compete with each other for the
therapist's attention, vying in describing the various sections of B———
they knew or had visited and the movies they had seen. Michael appeared
to be exceptionally interested in motion pictures and asked the therapist
about a number which the therapist had not seen. All the movies he mentioned were of the horror genre. Then Macy took the stage away from
Michael and said that that day there had been a great deal of discussion
about such things as atomic energy, planets, constellations, and such, in
his science class. He asked a number of questions, which the therapist
answered, on matters of scientific fact, such as whether it was true that
the "evening star" was the planet Venus; had the therapist ever seen the
constellation the Big Dipper, and what did it look like? Michael displayed a surprising store of information on these matters, such as the
constellation Orion and how an atomic explosion occurs. There was a
pleasant and quiet back-and-forth conversation between the two boys. In
fact, they no longer competed with each other but were absorbed in their
conversation.

Macy prepared coffee for himself, Michael, and the therapist, and a
long silence ensued as the three drank the beverage. Macy began an
enumeration of the many chores he was responsible for at his cottage. He
had to clean and buff the living room floor, wash dishes, help set out
food in the cottage dining room, and many others. The therapist inquired
why he had so many chores, but Macy did not answer immediately, as if
he were trying to reflect on something. He then said that somehow he
always had additional chores added to what he was doing, because he
was Mrs. K.'s "favorite boy." Michael greeted this with loud laughter,
but Macy went on to explain to Michael and to the therapist how he
remembered having had very simple chores before, but because he had
done them so well, Mrs. K. praised him and said she always had wanted
him to do other things. Other boys, she said, did not do so well as he.
Now when Mrs. K. needed someone to help her do things in a hurry,
she always picked him. Then Macy discussed his feelings relative to this.
He did not want to do these chores, he said. His face grew red with anger

as he said that Mrs. K. had promised him that he would be leaving in January. She said that should it be necessary, she would go to his transition conference and make sure he got out at that time, and for this, he said, he was grateful.

Another period of silence set in, after which the therapist pointed out to Macy that he could tell from the way he looked that something bothered him. Macy began by being evasive, but it did not take long before he launched into a general tirade against Mrs. K. He described her angrily as "very contradictory" with him; sometimes for no reason at all she started "yapping" incessantly about something she claimed he had neglected to do. He would much rather "get hit any day of the week" than have Mrs. K. "yap" at him. However, as soon as she began to sense that he was getting angry, she became friendly and would tell him: "I was only kidding. I'm only doing this for your own good, because I am interested in you." (From the manner in which Macy described these episodes there appeared to exist a rather seductive relation between the boy and his cottage mother.) Mrs. K., Macy said, tucked him into bed on occasion; she was always ready to give him extra food, and sometimes, because she did it in the presence of other boys, they resented him. He never quite knew how "to add up" Mrs. K. She was never the same way twice. He knew now that since he no longer was trying to be "the best boy in the cottage" Mrs. K. yelled more and more at him. In fact she told him that he was going to go "the way of all the other bad boys in the cottage"; that is, within two to three weeks after he was discharged, he would get in trouble again and would probably be "locked up."

The therapist asked Macy how he felt about this. He became enraged at Mrs. K. On the one hand, he said, "she tries to be a friend," she made him the favorite boy in the cottage; and on the other, when he tried to "be himself" and not "like a baby" with her, when he wanted to go where he wanted to go, or sometimes to stay up late, she became very angry.

The therapist asked what Mr. K.'s role was in this. Macy said that Mr. K. used to be very antagonistic toward him. In fact, very often he found himself being blamed by Mr. K. for many things that he never did. More recently, however, Mr. K. appeared to have become "more tolerant" (which seemed to the therapist to coincide with his wife's becoming less tolerant of Macy). Macy said Mrs. K "wears the pants" and Mr. K. just "disciplines" the boys. "He doesn't fuck around with Mrs. K. He doesn't get near her. I don't think he can stand her either."

Macy spontaneously referred to his own home and said, among other things, that in many ways his own mother "used to do what Mrs. K. is doing." She'd hug him, take care of him, and then when he wanted to go out with friends, she always warned him against them. At this point, Michael cut into Macy's monologue and said that the same thing happened in his home, too. But this was the extent of his participation. He remained pretty much in the background while Macy was talking. Macy returned to discussing his family. He described his father as being a rather weak person who "brings home the pay, sits down at the table, eats his meal, never says a word," while the mother "harps" at Macy about the way he eats, his table manners, and so on. He summed up by saying that he might just as well have stayed home rather than getting in with Mrs. K. However, he found it very difficult to take a stand against her. Nor was he sure as to how he really felt about her. Even when he felt angry at her, "there is a part" of him that felt she was doing it for his own good and he could not stay angry.

COMMENT

Because of the size of the group, this session resembled an individual interview. The significant character of Macy's cottage situation was that it was a replica of his own family and served the end of working through his Oedipal feelings. The fact that he drew the parallel himself signified his psychological literacy and capacity for self-confrontation.

Session Fifty-One

ABSENT: Leonard reported at a dance given by his unit.

This session was held after the boys had returned from a three-day home visit. It started promptly at seven. Louis was in the lead as the four boys came into the room and was in a playful mood. He entered imitating a "hipster," which he often described in the interviews. He nonchalantly waved to the therapist and took a seat. The boys giggled for a while, but this soon subsided. Michael put water on to boil for coffee and then distributed cookies and cigarettes. Following this the boys sat for a time without uttering a word.

Finally, Macy started the ball rolling by picking up where he had left off at the preceding session. He said he had thought he would be late for the session because he had a great many chores in his cottage. In fact, he wanted to go back at eight o'clock, because he had not finished his chores, and he had to finish them, he said. When the therapist inquired why he had to return, since he had a pass until 8:30, Macy said: "I don't know if that means anything with Mrs. K. If I don't finish my chores tonight, she is liable to hold me up for Christmas by reminding me that I didn't do a chore. Things ain't going so well between myself and that woman." Louis turned to the therapist and by way of explanation of what Macy had said, declared that Mrs. K. had been "riding" Macy, because he was no longer the "little boy" in the cottage, and Mrs. K. was "pushing a little hard." Also, if one did not do a chore, Mrs. K. "stays on your back. She keeps a grudge and she keeps after you until you got more work to do than you started with."

Louis strutted around making fun of Mrs. K. He mimicked her voice, her speech, how she called boys, and so forth. His antics brought much laughter from the others. Richard, too, got up and joined the act. He mimicked Mrs. K., in much the way that Louis had done. After this, Louis and Richard became more serious. Richard said that he wished he didn't have to live at "that cottage." He would be "damn happy" when he got the hell out of there. Louis immediately took over and said, well, he had only another month or so to put up with it, because he'd be leaving in January. Acting as spokesman for himself, Richard, and Macy—the three boys from Mrs. K.'s cottage—Louis said that, whenever any of them did something that Mrs. K. did not like, she immediately "throws up" to them the fact that they were getting "fresh" because they were members of the "discussion group." Louis and Richard took turns describing, mostly for the benefit of the therapist, how, if Mrs. K. ordered that dishes be washed immediately and they said they would do it in "a few minutes," Mrs. K. would at once say, "You're acting up just because you are in that lousy discussion group." Louis turned to Macy for confirmation of this. Macy nodded his head, but did not say anything. Louis then reported that Mrs. K. had on a number of occasions threatened the boys with being removed from the discussion group.

Being aware of the boys' exaggerations, the therapist tried to explore as to when and how this occurred and, more especially, what their feelings were about it. Louis, still acting as spokesman, said that recently Mrs. K. had not been saying these things. She had acted as they described until about a month ago. Louis: "I would just like to see her try to stop me from coming to this group! I learned more about my problems here than anywhere else in this lousy Village, so she can't tell me where I can go and not go." Richard: "This is the only place you can talk, and nobody cuts you down for saying what's on your mind, and yet Mrs. K. doesn't like the fact that we come here to talk. She must think we are always talking about her." Louis added, "She's a nut and we just make believe that she don't know what the hell is going on and we just try to get along with her."

Macy had a very sad, forlorn look on his face. The therapist asked him whether something was bothering him. Macy shook his head and said nothing. Richard to Macy: "Go ahead, if there is something bothering you, tell Mr. Ellery." Macy: "Naw, there's nothing bothering me.

Aw, forget it—just the same old crap, Mrs. K., the cottage . . . I'll be getting out of here soon so what the hell is the point?" Louis said, "Well talk about it, man. I'm talking, you can talk, too." Macy: "Well I did a lot of talking about it last week when you guys were home. I don't know—I don't feel like talking about it tonight. Maybe later I'll talk some more about it." Louis: "That's okay. You know you are always welcome to open your mouth here."

Standing up in front of the group, Richard began to orate at some length on a number of fights he had had with a boy in his cottage. Much of this was delivered in a very quick, rapid-fire fashion. It was difficult to determine whether what he was narrating had actually occurred. He had not mentioned the boy's name and kept referring to him by a nickname, "the eel." However, the therapist gathered from the looks on Macy's and Louis's faces that they knew the boy about whom Richard was talking. Richard gave a number of reasons why he hit this boy: He always snitched to Mrs. K. on other boys, he acted like a little "mama's boy," he was a "goody-goody," also a "fag," and so on. At the end of this long recitation the therapist bluntly raised the question about Richard's physical aggression. He asked: "What is this business with the use of hands? This pushing around of boys?" Louis: "Well, man, like once in a while you just got to use your hands on a boy. Otherwise, you know, some of them just get your goat and if you don't use your hands they are going to keep getting your goat. They keep asking for it by the way they act, like little namby-pamby." Michael: "That's right. Some boys just kind of provoke you; they look for fights with you, and you got to use your hands.

The therapist said that it was difficult for him to understand what the group had been talking about in the last few sessions. For example, "there has been a lot of talk about how not to get involved in further difficulties, and yet tonight Richard, Louis, and Macy are saying it is all right to use your hands with boys when you feel like it to push them around and beat on them."

Louis became somewhat apologetic, but also extremely playful. In fact, for a while he was reverting to the Louis of old. He proceeded to describe one incident after another in which he personally took part in gang fights and beatings of boys in his neighborhood. "The boys were the kind of boys who always get you mad because when you do something they go squealing on you to their mothers, to your mother, to the teacher. They are always watching and observing you so they can get medals for squealing and be goody-goody boys." He went through rather elaborate mimicking and exaggerated motions to demonstrate how he would walk up to a boy, accuse him of "snitching" on him, and then "take a sock at him." He and the other boys in the group laughed up-roariously during this performance. It continued for quite some time, and then Richard got up and began to prepare coffee, inviting the boys and the therapist to partake in it. This provided a five-minute recess as the laughter died down and quiet descended on the group.

Richard gulped his coffee as if he wanted to get it out of the way so that he could continue with the talk. He stood up and started to describe a boy at the Village, whom he named, who was Richard's personal enemy. In fact, every time Richard met this boy he "takes a swat" at him. He described fights, mostly in the auto shop, between the two of them. Louis wanted to interrupt, but Richard shushed him and Louis accepted the rebuke. This was unusual, for in the past Richard generally had de-ferred to Louis, the toughest boy in the group. Richard, still standing in front of the group, narrated one incident after another of his seeing this boy "walking around like a fag." He went through exaggerated motions of an effeminate person to illustrate his point and mimicked the boy's voice. "The God damndest thing about that guy is that he does it just to get hit," said Richard. Macy: "You're not kidding. There are times I could take that guy's face, just put it in my hands and I could bash on it." Michael: "I know how you feel. I know a lot of guys like that. I don't beat on them. They're real jerks." Louis: "They may be jerks, but when they try to get you mad, I know they do it just to get you mad, and it's like they get other boys to always do what they want, to beat on them." After Richard's exposition and declamation, which continued for a while, silence reigned in the room.

The therapist asked what it was about this boy that made them so mad. Richard said: "Like I told you. It's because he's a fag. He is always crying like a little crybaby and I just got to punch on him." Therapist: "Richard, suppose as you say the boy is effeminate, a fag, as you call it. What is there about this that gets you so mad?" Richard, Michael, and Louis looked completely nonplused. The expression on their faces seemed to say, "It's the most natural thing in the world to beat on a person be-cause he is a fag." The therapist persisted: "What is there about this that gets you so mad?" The question was met by completely unsuitable hilarity, led by Louis, which continued while the therapist remained pas-sive. However, the hilarity did not appear to be malicious.

Louis took the floor and for at least five minutes launched into a description of all the "characters" he had met when he was "back home" (on home visit). He narrated one incident after another of going to a dance and meeting "faggots." He observed that "these guys were pretty good dancers, and the only way you could tell they were queer was from the way they walked and the way they dressed and also the way they talked." Louis wound up the discussion by saying he was "disgusted" with them, he "hated" them, and if he ever got a chance he'd "knock the shit out of a couple of them."

At this point the therapist attempted to explore actively the feelings that had been stirred up in the boys. He said: "Here there is talk about using fists, beating on these people. Maybe these people stir up fears about ourselves since one of the very first fears that I know every boy in Children's Village has is whether he might become homosexual." The therapist soon discovered that he was on very thin ice. Michael took most vociferous exception to what the therapist had said. So did Richard. Macy said nothing, and Louis, half-joking and half-acquiescing, giggled and said, "Hey, Mr. Ellery, I can go back and tell you about all those girls I screwed, remember?" The therapist said that what confused him was that there were complaints about a cottage mother and, granted, there might be something to complain about. But "now we switched off and are talking about ourselves, how we, in order to settle something or to express our feelings, have to use fists and beat on people to do it. What do you think of this?"

Louis's response to this was: "Well to tell you the truth, I don't think that I would do it again. What's past is past. I can go to dances, I can see people I don't like. I get along with them. I can talk to them; they don't bother me too much." Richard looked puzzled. When asked for his view, he said: "Nothing. I was just thinking that once in a while I use my fists. . . ." He broke off and began to laugh as if it were a big joke. (Richard was not a pugnacious boy. In fact, one of his problems was his excessive need for adult protection against other children, since he was always picked on and beaten by them.)

Therapist: "Well, Richard, let's look at it. You talked tonight about using your fists. What do you think of it? How does this fit in with your talking about being ready to leave the Village and wanting to stay out of trouble once you leave?" Richard said: "When I leave the Village, I know I got to control myself. I think what I'm trying to say is that it's okay to use your fists sometimes when you are a kid. But I know, like growing up now, I got to keep my hands in my pockets when I feel like beating on somebody." Macy spoke up: "Maybe people get mad at you when you start throwing your weight around because you can really hurt somebody, and that's why they come down pretty hard on you when you use your fists." Before Macy could finish, Louis stood up and began describing a number of his "punchy" friends, as he called them. He referred to them as "former friends" and demonstrated through exaggerated motions and mimicry how they went to dances and walked up to girls and asked them for a dance, at the same time implying that they would like to have intercourse with them. Louis continued on this topic for quite a while, and when he finished the time was at hand to end the session. (It should be noted that although Macy had planned to leave at 8:00, he stayed until 8:30, the end of the session.)

C O M M E N T

During the supervision conference, the therapist commented on this session that there was "something unreal" about it; he and the boys "were not quite *together*." He felt that there was a "playful quality in the boys," as though "they decided to take a vacation from anything meaningful."

The boys' reaction at this, the first session after a three-day visit to their homes and former haunts, *would be* regression. They reverted to the subjects and gripes that appeared in the first interviews. However, there were two important contrasts between this and previous sessions that signified progressive development. One was the "playful quality" to which the therapist referred. At the early sessions the boys actually *believed* in the justice of their complaints. Now these complaints were half-hearted. At first their defensive projections were necessary for them to sustain their self-esteem; now they showed the results of having worked through many of their feelings. They had become cognizant of their own and their parents' attitudes and motives, and their defenses were less rigid and of lesser need. What they were saying no longer carried the earlier conviction and reality. It is interesting that the therapist had intuitively caught this quality, when he employed the term "unreal" to describe the boys' attitudes. Whether they knew it or not, they were only half-serious.

Another significant remark by the therapist was that there was a "playful quality" about the session. The playfulness may have stemmed from the boys' reliving almost in fantasy their earlier behavior as a testing maneuver, much as small children test themselves and others around them. There was evident here an almost "teasing" quality in re-experiencing an earlier phase of their lives, and the three boys who had visited their homes infected the two who had stayed behind.

On the other hand, the home visits may have caused real, though temporary, regression in some of the boys. Louis, especially, sustained a considerable return to his old self. His acting out might have been a reaction to feelings of guilt about his behavior at home, or an act of revenge against the therapist and the Village as being responsible for his involuntary abstention from the old pleasures with his city friends.

The initial regression displayed by the boys and the later developments in this interview suggested to us that they had been experiencing a struggle between their old patterns and inclinations and the new perceptions they had acquired through the therapy group. We had on reflection formulated the terms *onto-archaic mind* (to describe their former attitudes and cravings) and *new perceptions* (to indicate the new values they had acquired). We therefore suggested to the therapist that he again introduce these concepts at the right time to the group, indicating that these two forces struggle with each other for ascendancy, and that each boy would have to decide for himself which should predominate.

Some of the other significant steps taken by the therapist in this interview were his bringing to the fore the boys' distortions when he asked them to pinpoint Mrs. K.'s attitudes (and they admitted that they had been speaking of the past); when he confronted them with their acceptance of physical force, contrary to earlier declarations against it; when he attempted to explore the reasons for the boys' hostility toward an effeminate colleague—but made the very serious error of giving the reason for it as their own latent homosexuality, for such a statement could have proven disastrous were it not for the strong positive feelings the boys had for the therapist. The therapist had apparently failed to grasp the strong anxiety when his repeated question "was met by completely unsuitable hilarity."

The therapist capped the interview appropriately when he called attention at the end of the session to the boys' pugnacious trends and the reality of keeping out of trouble upon return to their homes. It was significant in this connection that Louis referred to his friends as "former friends."

Macy's preoccupation with Mrs. K.'s treatment of him (after he had been her special favorite) and his depression signified that he was working through transferential Oedipal feelings toward her, which, if he was successful, would prove of considerable maturational value to him.

Session Fifty-Two

Jules arrived about five minutes early. After greeting the therapist he sat down quietly for a few moments, and then said that he had run away. He had left in the evening and came back the morning after Thanksgiving Day, staying away two days. He said that he stayed at home only one hour, and now wondered whether he would be allowed to go home at Christmas time for good. He had been told different stories about it. The coaches told him that he would be leaving, and because of it, he was "thrown off" the varsity team. However, his caseworker explained to him that the rumors he had heard about leaving were not true, that he would be staying at the Village. Jules then described in some detail his having arrived home just as the family was finishing Thanksgiving dinner. The therapist asked Jules how he felt about what he had done. Jules said he was glad to be home and see his family. However, the tone of his voice seemed to suggest that he really had not had a pleasant time of it. The therapist asked whether Jules really felt "it was worth it." He responded, tentatively, "In a way it was." He was thinking of staying away, of getting a job and working, and then maybe "the Village" would not look for him. But he did not want to be a fugitive. "I'd always be worried that they're looking for me and that any minute they may come and get me, so I came back. I didn't feel like coming back, but I came back."

At this point the other boys came into the room, with Louis in the lead. He appeared to be again in the "playful mood" of the preceding session. However, the moment he sat down the playful expression disappeared from his face. He grew serious. The other boys, too, sat down, taking their accustomed seats. Leonard, on the other hand, appeared quite lively and asked the therapist in a friendly, outgoing manner how he was feeling. Macy said that he was cold and meandered over to prepare a cup of coffee for himself. Richard asked Macy to give him one, too. Macy did so. Michael undertook the destribution of cigarettes. Now Louis went over and helped himself to a cup of coffee. Finally there was quiet in the room.

Louis said: "I'm going to tell you something tonight, Mr. Ellery. Mrs. K. is beginning to sound on the discussion group again. Like she keeps saying whenever we don't do what she wants that we are learning all of this in the discussion group." Richard attempted to break in to confirm what Louis was saying, but Louis held up his hand and Richard stopped talking. Louis continued: "Let me tell it, huh? Remember we talked about it? Now I'm going to tell it." He then described in detail how if a chore were not done properly by one of the boys who attended the group, Mrs. K. made a comment about the fact that if he did not belong to the group, he would not be "messing up on his chore." He narrated an incident about the preceding evening that involved Macy. Mrs. K. had made the remark that "Macy used to be such a nice boy, but he isn't that way any more." Richard again tried to interrupt, and this time was successful. He told of the boys in the group being "pretty mad" at Mrs. K., and they were going to start fooling around and really "give her the business" if she did not stop "sounding on the group." The therapist asked Richard what he meant, but he would not continue. After a self-conscious pause he said: "I'm only kidding, Mr. Ellery. We don't want to make more trouble than there has to be." At the same time,

Macy, who sat next to Leonard, was talking to him. The conversation seemed to revolve around Macy's playfulness in the cottage, which may have provoked Mrs. K.'s outburst.

Louis, repeating his complaints, now launched into a rather lengthy description of how Mrs. K. picked pretty insignificant things to yell about. When asked to describe these things, he couldn't. He said they were so silly he just couldn't remember them. "If it was something big, I'd tell you Mr. Ellery, because we know when we mess up. But sometimes she doesn't like the way we make a bed. We make the bed the best way we know how and we think it's pretty good. One day she will say, 'That's a nice bed'; the next day we make it and she changes her mind. Now it's not a nice bed any more. Things like that, Mr. Ellery."

The therapist said he could understand their feeling sore about it, but there was one question he just had to ask because he was wondering about it. Was there anything that they did that sort of set Mrs. K. off? "Remember, boys, we once talked about provoking people." Louis stood up and said: "No, we are not provoking her. We know we ought to lay off her and we try to, but it's like I said—one day it's good, the next day it's bad. For instance, I know that to get out of the Village I got to behave myself in the cottage. I got to play it cool. But sometimes that ain't no good, because when you're good and she asks you to do something and you do it even though it's not your chore, she'll never stop asking you to do it even though another boy should be doing it. For instance, this guy C., he always goofs off on his chores so Mrs. K., she comes to me and she says, 'why don't you help C.?' So I help him. What do you think happens the next day? The next day she comes over to me and says, 'I want you to do C.'s chore.' I say: 'But Mrs. K., I did mine. Why doesn't C. do his?'" Louis began to gesticulate wildly as he quoted Mrs K.: "'But you should do it! I asked you to do it. You are talking back! D., D. [calling her husband], the boy is talking back to me!'" They tell you at the Village that you are supposed to assert yourself, not to be afraid to be a man. Well, I dare you to try it in our cottage." Richard jumped to his feet and seconded what Louis had said. Richard: "That's right. I dare you to just try it when the K.s are around. If you assert yourself they always think you are trying to fight them. We don't want to fight, we just want to be grown up. We're sick and tired of constantly being told to do this, to do that, and then be made fun of when we don't do it."

At this point, Jules moved his seat up closer so as to hear better what was being said. Michael was attempting to involve Jules in a side conversation. Though he sat next to the therapist, the latter could barely overhear what Michael was talking about, though it had something to do with going home. Louis yelled at Michael to shut up, but Michael acted as though he did not hear.

Silence ensued for a little while. Louis appeared tired from the exertion of telling his tale. The therapist said: "Look, I can understand what you are living with, but I wonder this: Is Mrs. K. the only person you ever met like this? What was it like when you were home? Had you ever encountered anything like this before?" Louis immediately said: "No. Like when I had trouble with my mother, I had trouble because I know I did things at times and I didn't blame my mother for yelling at me. I knew that if I didn't do these things, my mother wouldn't yell at me. All right. We talked about it here. When I go home I'm just not going to do these things. Maybe my mother is right; maybe she is wrong. I'm just not going to do these things at home. At least I knew where my mother stood. But you tell me how we can ever find out where Mrs. K. stands. When she feels she can't handle it, she gets Mr. K. on us." Richard: "Yeah. I feel like bashing Mrs. K. in the mouth, and maybe if her husband wasn't around I would bash her."

Suddenly Richard changed the subject. He reported that he had been "tested on psychological" by Dr. M. that afternoon. Louis looked at the therapist with a gleam in his eye and said, "You know Dr. M., don't you?" The therapist said that he did, and Louis observed, "Boy, she's a real piece of ass." Richard then described Dr. M. as having two swell tits he would love to get his hands on. He said that during the test she started asking all sorts of "crazy questions." (It sounded as though Richard was referring to either the Rorshach or the TAT.) Richard described the examination as if he were engaged in a game with Dr. M., because he intentionally gave "ridiculous answers." There was one picture he was shown and Dr. M. asked him what he saw, and he said he saw a young girl. Richard knew that it was obviously an elder woman. He went on to narrate how this girl was pregnant, "got all knocked-up," had a lot of children, and so on. (The therapist was unable to determine whether Richard was describing this solely for the benefit of the boys or whether this had actually occurred during the test.)

The therapist asked Richard what had made him do this. Richard laughed the question off, but then said, "Well they just try to find out if you are crazy." Michael, and then Macy, seconded this; these tests tried to show that you were crazy. The therapist interjected an explanation to the effect that this was not really the purpose of the test. He pointed out that the boys had talked about these tests in the past, and obviously they had not been found crazy, because somebody thought enough of their responses to get them to Children's Village, which did not take crazy boys.

Macy asked: "You mean somebody thought we could be helped by Children's Village? We didn't have to be put in an asylum?" Therapist: "Right." Richard: "I always knew I'm not crazy." The discussion turned again to Dr. M. Louis described how he'd love to take her out, put his arm around her, and say to her: "Come here, baby. I got something for you." Hilarious laughter broke out at this. (The therapist was tempted to explore this reaction to the woman psychologist and parallel it with their behavior that provoked Mrs. K., but he felt that this might be dangerous, considering the mood they were in.) The therapist said, addressing all the boys: "Well look, where are we now? What were we discussing?" Richard: "We were discussing Mrs. K. and the hard time she is giving us." Therapist: "Okay. Let me ask this question: Is there any way that you can handle Mrs. K.? Can you find a way to live with this?" Louis stood up and said: "No. You never know what is going to happen next, where you are going to get hit from next. So how can you handle her? If you're good, she makes a sissy out of you. So you don't want to be good all the time, you just want to be yourself. Then she yells and screams and then we really start fucking around. When she screams at us, we really get going on her." "How, Louis?" "Well, we laugh back at her." Richard: "Yeah when she gets my goat, I don't do things just because she gets my goat." "And then what happens?" the therapist asked. "Well, the same old story, it keeps going," Louis said, "like a snowball rolling down a hill." Therapist: "I want to see something."

The therapist walked over to Richard and yelled at him as Mrs. K. might: "I don't like the way you did your chore! You can do your chore much better!" Richard screamed back: "I don't want to do my chore!" Therapist, screaming: "You better do it or I'll get Mr. K. after you and then you'll really get it!" Richard yelled. "The hell with you! I'm not going to do my chore!" Therapist: "You're no good! You're just no good, Richard! You won't do as I tell you!" Richard gazed straight at the therapist: "Fuck you, I'll do as I please!" The therapist now returned to his seat, a smile playing on his lips. He turned to the group and said: "Okay, fellows. How do you think Richard handled it?" Leonard was first to speak up. He said, "He got mad at you, and when somebody gets mad, they are asking for trouble." Michael: "Richard should have punched you in the nose." Laughter from the group, in which the therapist joined. When it subsided, Louis said: "If you were in the cottage, Mr. Ellery, if you were the cottage father things would be different. We wouldn't have this problem." Therapist: "But Louis, what do you think of the way Richard answered me?" Louis: "I don't know. I guess he answered you all right." Therapist: "Is that all right? To get so hot under the collar? And what happens when two people are hot under the collar with each other?" Macy advocated punching Mrs. K. in the nose and was almost ready to introduce it as a "resolution" for the boys to vote on.

The therapist said to the boys: "There's something I want to tell you. I've often admired how you boys who have had to put up with so much in your life have managed to get by. I've always felt that you are made of pretty good stuff. Maybe a lot of other guys who had to put up with less didn't even go as far as you boys have gone. Don't you think there comes a time when you've got to kind of say to yourself, maybe I'm above getting mad and cursing and ready to use my fists because maybe some people just aren't worth it? Maybe sometimes you have to allow for other people not knowing what they're doing and not knowing that they have hurt you and sometimes you need to walk around with the feeling inside that 'I'm better than all of this.' " Michael spoke up: "Better? You think we did so good in our lives, Mr. Ellery, even though many of us are going to spend the rest of our lives in prison?" Louis: "That Mrs. K.! When she tells you something, it's going to happen. Bill leaves the cottage, she says to him 'in less than a month you're going to be in prison.' Sure enough, he is in prison. Me—she gives me two weeks."

Therapist: "I think I hear this business of doom again. How can I think much of myself if my life is doomed? Isn't that it, fellows?" Michael suddenly jumped up, clapped a hat on his head, and proceeded to run wildly around the room in a helter-skelter fashion. Therapist to Michael: "What is the matter?" Michael (still running): "Nothing." Therapist:"Well, what do you call it, Mike?" Michael, with a smile: "I guess I'm just trying to provoke you, to see if I get you mad." Therapist: "Why do you want to do that?" Michael: "I don't know. You're the only guy around here that doesn't get mad." Louis, soothingly to therapist: "Don't pay any attention to him, Mr. Ellery. He's nutty tonight." Therapist (to group): "But what about this always having to make somebody mad at you?" Richard: "Aw, there are always some people like that trying to get you mad. Don't pay any attention." Therapist: "In other words, there is a way of handling yourself when something like this happens?" Louis, assuming the role of spokesman for the group: "We got to talk some more." Richard: "Well, it's time we broke up tonight, because I got to get back. There is something I didn't finish doing in the lousy closets in the cottage and I want to get them cleaned out so that I can go home for Christmas. Otherwise somebody is going to start telling me that I don't go home for Christmas." This ended the discussion.

COMMENT

We were aware that the struggle at Mrs. K.'s cottage would continue, since we had had reports from other sources of her resentment against the group. We therefore anticipated developments in this direction by conveying to the boys the idea of the need in life to accommodate oneself to the inevitable, which might be done through 1] resignation,   2] rising above pettiness and annoyances, and   3] increased frustration tolerance as a result of ego enhancement. It was on the basis of these and similar supervisory discussions that the therapist raised the question as to whether one could find a way to live under adverse conditions. We also suggested that some of these abstract ideas might be incomprehensible to the boys due to their intellectual and spiritual impoverishment, and would have to be demonstrated or acted out. The therapist did well to grasp the opportunity to "role-play" and demonstrate dramatically the behavior of a boy under stress.

However, the boys, except perhaps for Leonard, did not get the point of this re-enactment. Here the reversal of roles, which has been common in all parent-child relations since time immemorial, could have been profitably employed. Had the therapist taken the role of the boy being attacked and responded with reason and equanimity, that is, demonstrated "rising *above*" a situation and exercising self-control, the value of the byplay would have been immeasureably enhanced. Instead, even when the point was made by the therapist later that one could rise above getting mad, and the like, it was much less tangible and less convincing than it would have been had it been played out. If the boys had witnessed a demonstration of a mature way of dealing with a difficulty, and had the opportunity to compare it with Richard's reaction, a much clearer outcome would have emerged. Michael's irrational dramatic play acting later in the session (probably to test the therapist's frustration tolerance) may have been a sequel to the role-playing episode.

An important development worthy of observation is the insight the boys have acquired without any discussion of the subject in the past that they no longer wish to be little, dependent boys as the price of receiving kindness and protection from a substitute mother. Their self-image (identity) had changed, as had their Oepidal strivings. They were now desirous of being independent entities with a status of equality and with respect. These are most convincing evidences of growing maturity. We note that the expectation of doom was still present in the boys and needed to be dealt with again in the future.

The therapist laid the foundation at the end of this session for a therapeutically significant exploration for the future when he raised the question why some people have a need to make others angry at them, another subject we had repeatedly considered in our supervision conferences, for we were aware of its being an impelling need in our boys that created many difficulties for them.

This session was a telling experience for the boys. So much so that, through their leader, as it were, they found that they "got to talk some more" about it.

The boys' resentments at being sequestered from their homes still lingered after their recent visits to their families and were enhanced by their nostalgic expectations of the prospective visit for Christmas. Nonetheless, a backward look at the earlier sessions cannot but impress one with the salutary changes in them. Their self-respect, grasp of reality, insights and understanding, controls, and language had dramatically changed. Though these were marred from time to time by regressive outbursts, we felt that the boys were unquestionably on their way.

Session Fifty-Three

ABSENT: Macy and Michael on home visits for nine days for Christmas.

The session began on time. Louis, Jules, Leonard, and Richard came together. They seemed in good spirits as they came up the stairs; they were laughing and joking. The good spirits continued after they came into the room, but they grew somber as they took their (usual) seats.

In a very friendly and cordial manner Louis asked the therapist how he was. The therapist told him that he felt fine. In a friendly voice Louis said "good," and proceeded to distribute cigarettes to the boys, while Richard busied himself with coffee for the group. All of this proceeded very quietly, as did the distribution of cookies that followed. In the meantime, Louis was telling the therapist about difficulties he was having in the new cottage. (Macy, Louis, Richard, and Jules had been moved with their cottage mates to a newly rebuilt building with the same cottage parents in charge.) The relief man was "giving everybody a hard time," Louis said. After he had distributed the cigarettes, he sat down and in almost a monotone described incident after incident of this man's constant "picking on boys." (It sounded very much like the complaints the boys had voiced in the preceding sessions against the cottage mother.)

Louis said that once you had finished a chore this man immediately began to find fault with it. "You can't please him nohow. He's always looking for dirt, even if he has to get down on his hands and knees and poke his head way under the bed to find it." Richard interjected the comment: "He's a real stickler. He drives you crazy. You break your back, you think you done okay—do you ever get a good word from him? No! He comes along and right away he finds what's wrong. Not only that, but he also talks to you in a pretty crazy way. He says, 'get your fucking butt into bed.' It's not that you're lazy going to bed or taking your time, but he talks to you like a kid might talk to you." Louis and Richard alternated, with each supporting the other in describing the things that were going on in the cottage. The man kept a list for reporting boys to Mrs. K., they said. When he could not handle a boy he went yelling for Mrs. K. Richard said he did this because he was a sissy; he started something and he couldn't finish it. Jules: "Maybe we ought to jack him up." No one took up this suggestion, however.

The therapist observed that the boys had placed their coats in a pile, whereas in preceding sessions they had always laid them rather neatly on an empty chair or hung them on the hooks provided. He also noticed that first Jules, then Leonard, then Louis got up, walked behind the heap of coats, and seemed to be doing something there which the therapist could not make out. Louis must have become aware of the therapist's puzzlement and said, by way of explanation: "We're wrapping a package for one of our teachers. We want to give him a Christmas present." This statement was accompanied by furtive glances among the boys. Finally, Louis got up, went behind the pile of coats, and brought out a Christmas card, which he handed to the therapist. Handwritten below the greeting was the following: "Thanks, Mr. Ellery, and we appreciate all you have done for us this past year. God Bless You." Each boy present had signed it. Even the signatures of Macy and Michael, who were absent were attached. (They must have signed the card before leaving.) The therapist read the card and told the boys that he was very much touched by it, and ended by saying, "Thank you very much." Richard: "That's funny, you thanking us. We're the ones who should be thanking you." Louis quickly said: "That's right. We should thank you. Thank you for all the good advice you gave us during the year and thank you for letting us come together every Thursday night." A few moments of silence followed. Recalling the incident, the therapist remarked later: "I couldn't help but say to the boys, 'You are a pretty grand bunch of boys.'"

A sentimental and uncomfortable silence ensued, which was broken by Jules, who said, "Is it true we are getting a new boy into this group?" Therapist: "No, it's not true." Jules: "Well G. said he's got a pass for the group and he's going to come." The therapist said there must be some mistake because he knew of no plan for having boys added to the group. Jules: "If he comes, we throw him out." Louis: "That's right. We don't want any more boys here. This is just enough. It's nice the way it is now." The therapist raised the question, "How would you feel about having new members in the group?" Richard: "Nothing doing, nothing doing, not in our group. Let them go to Mr. S.'s club.[14] We're the original Thursday Club. Mr. S. is just a poor imitation of us." Louis seconded this, saying: "We have enough boys now and, when a new boy comes in, he'll sit around for a couple of weeks saying nothing. He won't know what to say. He won't talk. We talk, and if you join our club you got to talk. We don't want to break in anybody new." Even Leonard, who had not said anything until now, chimed in. "I go along with the boys. We got a nice club going, don't disturb it."

In an offhand manner the therapist commented that maybe accepting a new member into the group would be something such as one felt when a new baby was born into one's family. A newcomer gets more attention. No one really picked this up, though Louis said: "Well my sister, she is married now, she is out of the house and guess what? I got the place all to myself." He said nothing more, and asked if he could elaborate on it, he would not do so. Richard broke in to say: "Let's go back to talking about this Mr. G. [relief man]. I got to finish telling you about this guy." Richard launched into a rather lengthy story of how this man, by one means or another, abused the boys. Louis interrupted to tell of a man who used to say, "get off your mother-fucking ass" and do this and that, and kept repeating the phrase. "Imagine talking to boys like that? A long time ago when we came to the Village, we used to talk like that, 'mother-fucking this' and 'mother-fucking that,' but we don't talk that way any more and there are grown-ups who talk worse than kids."

The therapist said to Louis, "Louis, is there some possibility, no matter how slight, that maybe there is a way of getting along?" Louis thought for a short while and then said: "If there is I don't know it. I'll tell you what I do. I slurp him." When he said the word *slurp* Louis had a look of disgust on his face. (Slurp is a slang expression meaning to be obsequious in an effort to buy off someone.) Louis said he knew that if he got into a fight with either one of the cottage parents or this relief man, he would lose a week end. So, as the free week end approached, "it's 'yes, Mrs. K., oh no, Mrs. K., thank you, Mrs. K.' And now I got to do the same thing with Mr. G. I don't want to slurp him but if I want to get out of here, if I want to go home and see my folks, how the hell can I do it without slurping?" Therapist: "Louis, I'm interested in that expression you use, 'slurp.' You say and describe it like a pretty rotten thing, and yet maybe you do have something there. Isn't it a way of kind of sizing up a situation and instead of just fighting

14. The therapist in another group that met
the same evening in another building.

it endlessly when you know you can't win, you think it out and then say, 'What can I do so things won't get worse for me?' " Louis: "Well that's what I do. I size up the situation. I got to think of my own interest and protect myself." Therapist: "Then why is that slurping, Louis? Maybe you are taking the only course possible, since just fighting it and getting vengeance, as you used to say here, would be the childish way of handling it?" Louis thought a while and then said, "You mean maybe I'm not really a slurp?" Richard broke in and said: "We always call it 'slurping,' but maybe we are doing the only thing we can do, even though we hate it. We are looking out for ourselves."

All of a sudden, footsteps were heard on the stairs outside the room. The boys seemed slightly startled by this unusual sound. Louis asked: "Who the hell is that coming up?" Suddenly the door opened and a boy appeared. Richard said, "You see, I told you he is in our club." The boy came over to the therapist and handed him a pass that was made to be presented to him stating that the boy was to attend the group. The therapist asked him where he got the pass and was told that the cottage mother had given it to him. Therapist: "I think there is some mistake," and telling the boys that he wanted to check on it and would be back in a minute, the therapist went downstairs, accompanied by the boy, to inspect the receptionist's master sheet. The boy's name was on it. Obviously the receptionist, in making out a pass, had made one for him by mistake. As required by regulations, the therapist called the security officer on the telephone and explained to him the situation and sent the boy to the latter's office. The therapist told the boy that he was sorry he was inconvenienced. When the therapist returned to the room, he found the boys rather quiet, and Jules and Louis were now sitting on the couch playing cards. The therapist explained to the boys the error. Nothing more was said about it.

Though playing cards, Louis was talking to Jules about having to be a slurp, and how he didn't like it. However, the therapist sensed a distinct difference in the tone of his voice now. Instead of the former derision and disgust when he used the term, his voice now had a contemplative quality as though he were grappling with the idea that maybe he was not "slurping," but acting more like a mature individual under the circumstances, trying to make the best of a situation.

The therapist picked up this feeling and raised the question of not fighting fire with fire. How did the boys feel about it? No immediate response was forthcoming. Instead Jules lodged a complaint against another staff member. The therapist said: "I sympathize with what you are saying, boys, but there is the question we've been batting around for the past couple of weeks, and that is what should we do when there are others around who are sick—who are childish. How can we show them that we are worthy of better treatment than we get? This is important because this is what we'll come up against every day of our lives." Richard's reaction to this was: "Aw, the hell. You beat the shit out of them." Louis, however, said: "But like we say, we got to show we're better. There's a teacher in the school who told us one day that he was walking down the street and he had his girl friend with him. A guy ran up and screamed 'What are you doing with my girl friend?' Then this guy punched the teacher right in the nose and knocked him to the ground. The teacher told us that he was about to get up and haul off on this guy, but his head cooled off and he thought to himself, 'I shouldn't hit him; he's nuts, you don't hit nutty people.'" After a brief moment of silence, Louis continued: "What the teacher told us was that one of the things you have to learn as you become a man is 'control'— how to control yourself. When you learn this, that's when you're a man. I guess he's got something there, because you told us the same thing, Mr. Ellery." Leonard said, "Mr. Ellery told us that's when we will stop being babies, when we learn to hold on to ourselves." Jules: "Boy that's the fucking hardest thing in the world to do, to hold on to yourself and not haul off. If I were that teacher I might have wanted to kill that guy." Richard: "And then what would have happened? You would have been in the chair before you knew it." Richard then said that he knew a man who wouldn't let other people pick on him—not that he went around fighting these people, but he would hold his head so high, stick out his chest, and walk away from them. Louis laughingly said, "That's what you call a 'cool cat.'"

Since the time was up, Louis said that he was going back to the cottage, where a Christmas party was in progress. All rose, exchanged Christmas wishes, and left. As the therapist was walking toward his car, Louis yelled out after him to drive carefully, because there was ice on the road.

COMMENT

The two major themes of this session were dignity and control. Louis, for one, recognized his so-called "slurping" as a *modus operandi* for preventing difficulties and to attain ends. He no longer impulsively reacted with violence and vengefulness but adapted to the inevitabilities of a situation. He began to doubt his characterization of his conduct as "slurping," seeing it rather as "doing the only thing we can do," as a mature individual meeting the demands of circumstances.

For some months we had discussed at our supervision conferences the fact that one could not always alter the conditions of one's life, nor change the conduct and manners of others toward one. It is necessary to rise above these, become aware of one's own dignity by not reacting or becoming involved. As a result, this matter was touched upon lightly by the therapist in the preceding sessions. He now took the occasion to elaborate on it further. The episode quoted from the teacher was very apt and demonstrated that the significance of the therapist's thought was fully grasped, which would serve the boys in good stead in the future when they were called "chicken," or when others attempted to provoke them into a fight. The boys recognized that control, growing out of a sense of dignity, was the mark of a man, as contrasted with being a "baby."

A new trend in the recent discussions of the group needs to be observed at this point. The boys seemed to have abandoned self-analytical topics for discussion of interpersonal relations. The meaning of this was not clear. It may have been an outcome of *1]* new pressures in their environment; *2]* greater awareness of others; *3]* greater recognition of the importance of improved relations with the world around them; or *4]* the social structure of the group life in the institution. It was more likely, however, that it proceeded from our change of emphasis to one which was more suitable for these boys. Whatever the reason, it reflected a growing maturity, diminished narcissism, and a rise in allotropic attitudes and reactions. Had these boys been psychoneurotic, this trend would have had to be checked as a form of resistance; but in view of the fact that they had been aggressively acting out and fell largely in the category of character and behavior disorders, therapy needed to follow and encourage the road they were taking toward social adaptation. This phenomenon was part of their newly evolving social identities. ·

NOTE

There was no session the following week because of weather conditions.

Session Fifty-Four

ABSENT: Macy, on home visit; his father had died.

The session began on time. Louis was first to arrive and informed the therapist that Macy would not be at the session because his father had died. The therapist said he was sorry to hear it. Louis also said that Richard would be late because of a chore Mrs. K. wanted him to finish before he came to the group. Richard was the last boy to arrive. By this time the other boys had helped themselves to coffee, which had been prepared by Michael and Jules. Jules had informed the group that he

was now working in the Village canteen (PX) and that he was happy
about it. He brought with him candy which he had paid for with money
given him by the boys in advance. The one boy who had no candy
was Leonard. It seemed that he had not been able to get to Jules to give
him money before the session. Jules, noticing that Leonard had no candy,
offered him a bar of chocolate, which Leonard accepted.

While drinking coffee, the boys carried on a conversation about
their home visits, with Louis and Michael taking the lead. Louis asked
Michael whether he had had a good time in B——— during his Christmas
vacation. Michael said he had, but he did not appear very enthusiastic.
Louis, talking to Michael, but in a voice loud enough for everybody
to hear, stated that just another twenty days or so and he would be
getting out of the Village. He did not want to do anything at this
point that might "mess up" his chances. Louis said, "If I had a chance
and it would not hurt my chances to get out of the Village, I would
tell that lousy relief man in my cottage where the hell to get off." He
was talking about Mr. G.

He proceeded to describe at some length what had happened the
night before. There was a boy in the dormitory where Louis slept who
snored. Louis asked the boy many times to stop snoring, but "sure
enough," the boy did not stop. At one o'clock in the morning Louis
"rapped the boy in the head." He demonstrated how he had done it
by making two fists and gently knocking the knuckles against each
other. The boy woke up and started to scream. Louis warned him
again about his snoring and the boy went back to sleep. The next day
the boy told Mrs. K. that Louis had beaten him during the night. Louis
insisted that it was "a dirty lie." He did not beat him; he just woke him
up so that he, Louis, could get some sleep. However, "Mr. G., who
was around at the time, grabbed my hands and Mrs. K. started slapping
me. That son-of-a-bitch [Mrs. K.]! If I live to be a hundred years, I'm
going to get Mrs. K. for that."

He went into a rather lengthy and heated recital about Mr. K., saying
that he really was "a fairy and a woman," and that Mrs. K. was awfully
weak. She needed somebody to sneak up on Louis and hold his arms
in order to slap him. He got even with the other boy. He started to
"beat on him" later, but he was stopped by other kids. Louis seemed
quite "hot under the collar" at this point. Michael stepped in and said,
"who asked you to beat on this guy?" Louis: "That lousy bum. Who
told him to go around snitching on me? How would you like to sleep
someplace where somebody snores all night and drives you crazy?"
Michael: "But he couldn't help snoring." Louis seemed to cool down
and said: "I know he couldn't help snoring, but Mrs. K. doesn't want
to change my dorm. She knows it bothers me, and it is like she is getting

satisfaction from it bothering me. I don't think she wants me to sleep at night." Jules: "If it was me, I would have beaten the shit out of that boy. I would have kicked him in the fucking stomach and broken his guts." Michael: "Are you crazy? Why the hell do you want to do that? You're going to be the only one who will get in trouble." Jules smiled as though he had been caught red-handed. Embarrassment spread over his face and, looking in the therapist's direction, he said: "I'm only kidding. I wouldn't do that, especially not if it meant I'd have to stay at the Village or not get out of here." The therapist asked Jules if that was the only reason he would not do it. Jules again smiled somewhat embarrassedly, and said, "I don't know. I guess I just wouldn't do it because I would just make a lot of trouble," then added, "for myself."

Silence ensued, during which Jules went to get himself another cup of coffee. Louis joined him. The silence continued while the two boys were getting the coffee. When they returned to their seats, Louis initiated a discussion about vengeance against Mrs. K. He was thinking of doing a number of things: When he left the Village, he would call Mrs. K. and tell her that she was "a no-good fuck." He was going to call her and pretend he was various boys' fathers, start a conversation with her by asking Mrs. K. about "his boy," and then make obscene remarks, such as: "Is dick still up your cunt? Why don't you give some more ass to Mr. K., because he don't look so hot any more?" This was greeted with great hilarity by all the boys except Leonard, who sat in his chair smiling rather feebly, looking quite uncomfortable and out of place.

This recitative continued for almost ten minutes. When the hilarity died down and Louis looked as though he had unwound himself, the therapist asked: "Louis, what is it you're trying to accomplish by all this?" Louis: "Like I told you. I'm just going to get revenge." Michael immediately spoke up and said: "I think Louis is crazy tonight. I never saw a guy itch for trouble like this." Louis: "You're full of shit, Mike. And why don't you mind your business?" Jules: "Yeah, maybe Mike ought to mind his own business sometimes." Michael, however, would not be provoked and said nothing. Now Richard began an interminable description of his endless life of trouble with Mrs. K. He told of incident after incident in which Mrs. K. was wrong.

When he was finished with this, the therapist pointed out to the boys the contradiction in what they were talking about. On the one hand they were complaining about all the injustices meted out to them, which understandably would make them angry—but the question was: "How do you handle yourselves? Remember this is what we were talking about. Do you make things better by going out and getting revenge?" Richard felt there was no other way but to get revenge. Jules said that if he had a chance he would sick Mrs. K.'s dog on her, but pulled back, looking at the therapist (even though the latter had not been looking at him) and said: "Naw, that won't work. I want to get out of the Village. I'm not going to do much by getting revenge on Mrs. K. I'll just take it easy and not make things worse for me." Michael, with the manner of an adult, said, "Jules sounds like the only smart boy in the room tonight." Louis burst out laughing at this, and Jules asked him, "What are you laughing at?" Instead of answering, Louis again launched into a recital of how he would call Mrs. K. on the phone and tell her to "go fuck herself" and other similar expletives. Again he indicated that he would pretend to be the father of some of the boys and make ridiculous requests of her.

The therapist asked Louis directly if he had any idea of what he was saying. Louis said no. Therapist: "Louis, in the past few meetings, we talked about how to be above acting childish. Do we really make life any better for ourselves if we act as childish as some of the people we are angry at? What you are showing tonight, Louis, is that when you are mad at somebody, you want to get even so badly that you are ready to become a little child." The effect of the statement was as if the therapist had slapped Louis in the face. He sobered up and became very serious. Richard thought that Louis was right, for when he, Richard, left the Village, he was going to get even with Mrs. K. In fact, Mrs. K. had already told him that soon after he left, he would get into trouble. He was going to stay out of trouble, he declared, "just to prove to Mrs. K. that she is wrong." Louis said he was going to do the same thing. Mrs. K. had given him two weeks, and reminding the boys again that Mrs. K. had given Bill a month, he said, "I'm going to come up here to Mrs. K. [holding up the middle finger of his right hand] and say 'You were wrong, screw you.'"

Richard broke in to say that if he could have his way he would go to the Director of the Village and explain to him that he was ready to leave the Village. The therapist asked Richard how he would tell this to the Director. Richard groped for words and for a mild way of expressing himself. At first he said, "Hey, Mr. P., it's about time I got out of here," but then quickly corrected himself and quietly said, "Mr. P., I would like to speak to you about my being at Children's Village." He would tell Mr. P.: "I know my problem. Children's Village helped me and I believe I am ready to go home and I would like to discuss this with you, Mr. P." He would then tell Mr. P. that he had been there over two years; he was "doing good now," and he would like to leave. The therapist asked Richard about his statement "I know my problem." "Suppose I, as Mr. P., would say, 'Richard, when you say you know your problem, could you tell me what you mean?'" Richard's response to this was: "I learned that one of the reasons I got into trouble was because I was trying to get vengeance on my parents. My mother would accuse me of doing things and I would try to get even with her by really doing them. The same way, I ran away when my father hit me and he had no good reason to hit me." Richard then said, "I guess that's what I had to come to Children's Village for and that's what I learned at Children's Village." Richard then turned to the therapist and asked whether he felt that Mr. P. might listen to him. The therapist said, "Yes, I think he might, Richard." Richard, looking rather self-satisfied, said, "I think I can talk good now."

The therapist was puzzled as to the appropriate manner of dealing with this regressive mood in the boys and decided to recapitulate the events that had started this discussion. The therapist reminded the boys how Louis had described hitting a boy and then "everything began to snowball from there on in." Michael's comment was, "That's what happens when you gotta use your hands." He asked Louis whether he had gone up to Mrs. K., told her about the boy who was snoring, and really asked for a change in dorms. Louis did not respond to this, but from the look on his face, it appeared that he was trying to beat a retreat. Jules said: "I think that the way to win was to stop. That way [continuing to fight] I'm going to be either at the Village or in some other place like the Village for the rest of my life." Nothing further was said.

Although it was only 8:10, Leonard got up and said that he had to go back to his cottage. He had promised his cottage mother to help her do the silverware and told her that he would come back a little earlier from the group to help her, so that most of it could be done before he went to bed. The therapist did not respond and Leonard left. Following his departure the tone in the group seemed to change. The discussion was changed by Michael, who narrated that he had gone out with a number of his friends during his home visit and had a good time. They had gone to a movie and to ice cream parlors, and nothing more. Richard joined Michael in the conversation and the two boys talked about their activities when they were out of the Village, Richard indicating that he would sometime like to go to B——— to see Michael. Louis silently listened. Jules was getting himself a second cup of coffee and asked the others whether they wanted any. They said no. Jules now reverted to describing his work in the PX, and again announced that he was happy about it. He said, "I have a chance to make some money and I could use this money for clothes when I get out of the Village." (This was the only job that Jules had ever held at the Village.) He seemed for more relaxed than he had ever been at group sessions.

At about 8:25 Jules put on his coat and said that he was going to the PX so that he could put in another half-hour of work before it closed. At this, the other boys left also.

COMMENT

The regressive trend continued, as did the resistance. The group obviously lacked an adequate "instigator" at this point. Since Donald had left the group another had not come to the fore. There was nothing for the therapist to do but to observe developments, continue probing tactics, and maintain as much of a therapeutic climate as possible. There had arisen in the last few sessions a considerable degree of cohesion in the group. This is partly a result of the fact that three or four boys lived in the same cottage and were activated by the same hostilities. The cohesiveness and resultant interpersonal relatedness was well demonstrated when Jules gave a bar of chocolate to Leonard, which was in considerable contrast to their ungenerosity and food-grabbing practices of the past.

However, the aspect of this interview that required special attention was the revenge theme and the almost reflex response of beating up people when dissatisfied. This pattern and jungle principle seemed deeply ingrained in the boys, and its exercise had caused much difficulty to them and others around them in the past. The therapist attempted to highlight this, but with little success. In the supervision discussion, therefore, we again suggested the reintroduction of the concept of the ontoarchaic mind, which we had formulated, that is, the idea that the boys tended to act on their old "habit"—direct action. While they seem to *understand* intellectually other and better ways of reacting, when something they did not like happened, they reacted as they had before they acquired the new understandings. It was a conditioned reflex action. Here Pavlovian psychology needed to be explained with vivid illustrations and some principles of neurology given, such as the synapse and neuron paths (engrams). This was to be followed by an explanation of how there was always a struggle going on between this old (archaic) mind and their new understandings, and that it was up to them to decide which should take precedence; also, that as they practiced new ways of reacting, these would eventually displace the old. It is such conceptualizations and the didactic role of the therapist that differentiate paraanalytic from purely psychoanalytic therapy.

Note need be taken that the boys did not exhibit the same type of infantile regressive behavior as was the case on their return from the previous home visit, indicating that their character changes have been to a degree internalized and had structurally become part of their personalities. This growth was further revealed by some of the boys' disapproval of Louis's striking the boy (to which all would have acquiesced in the past) instead of seeking a more amicable solution. Louis, the toughest boy of the lot, himself became aware of his error, as he sought to terminate the discussion in obvious embarrassment.

Session Fifty-Five

ABSENT: Jules, Richard, Macy, and Louis, who had gone with their cottage group on a roller-skating trip to New York City.

Only Leonard and Michael were present. Leonard said that he would like to "hang around" despite the absence of the others. Michael expressed an interest in having a session, but he said he must return to the cottage at eight o'clock. He served as host. He prepared coffee for the therapist and Leonard, distributed the cookies, and then sat down, remaining rather quiet. Leonard was also quiet and looked a little uncomfortable, perhaps due to the unusualness of the situation. His discomfort seemed to last but a few moments. He soon launched into a discussion about his going home and now he felt that he was ready to take a job, maybe in the candy store he had talked about in the earlier sessions, or as a delivery boy. His mother knew some people in his borough and he thought he might do well as a delivery boy. Michael joined the discussion and said that he would be going back to school. He had recently been tested at the Village school and felt he did "very well." There were "tough words" to read and to understand in the tests and he tried to understand them by "breaking the words apart" and understanding their individual components.

Michael told at some length how he enjoyed reading, that when he came to the Village he used to read comic books, but he got "some good books" in school which he now read. Leonard said: "What I like about the Village is that it's done my mind some good. I think it strengthened my mind." Michael: "How so?" Leonard: "I don't get tempted to run away from the Village. I used to. I never really ran from the Village, but now I don't even feel the temptation. I had a lot of cottage parents in my cottage and I seemed to be able to get along with them even though sometimes I have to tell them off when they try to get me to do things I don't want to do, or I think they are taking advantage of my good nature." Michael: "At least I know I am never going to come to the Village again and I'm just not going to have trouble any more when I get outside."

The therapist asked whether they could recall from previous discussions anything about the situations that "had gotten them into trouble." Michael said: "I was just an easy follower. Boys used to lead me. I was gullible." The therapist glanced at Michael with a faint smile on his face and asked: "Is that what you got out of it?" Michael smiled back and said "Oh, yeah, I remember when I told the boys about how my mother didn't think I could do anything good and maybe I became a good shoplifter to prove that I could do things good." Leonard was staring rather intently at Michael. Michael did not continue and the therapist said to Leonard, "You look as though you want to say something." Leonard: "My trouble was not with my mother, but with my father. I had always been sore at the guy. He used to beat me with his fists, so I'd run away from home. My mother and father are separated now and I don't have to put up with him, but I guess I like him," and pointing to Michael, Leonard described how many times he would not come home at night on time because he knew it was important to his father that he be prompt. Leonard finished by saying, "I guess I'm the only one who really got into trouble, not my father." Leonard evaded any discussion of his mother, and the therapist felt it best not to involve him in it at this point.

Leonard and Michael then talked about how much they would like to meet sometime, either in New York or in B———, where Michael lived. Michael said, in a voice of self-importance and with some feeling of dignity, that when he got back to B——— he was going to be "busy pretty much of the time," because he would be attending school and trying to finish high school so he could get a "good job." Michael described at some length the positions he held before he came to the Village. All of these seemed to be delivery or messenger boy's jobs he got on the "spur of the moment to get some money in my pocket." The therapist commented that Michael seemed to be a pretty resourceful person in this respect, and Michael indicated that he knew what the therapist meant when he said, "You can take care of yourself when you have to." Leonard proposed that there should be some kind of agency that would help boys find jobs, and all three discussed together a number of the agencies of which they might avail themselves when they get back to the community. At this point Michael leaned back in his chair, looking very comfortable and with a strong sense of "belonging." Leonard got up to brew some more coffee. There followed a rather lengthy discussion between Leonard and Michael about the car that one of the staff members had purchased recently. At eight o'clock all three left.

COMMENT

Despite Leonard's silences during the group discussions, he had obviously gained considerable insight into his situation and his reactions.

This is not unusual in analytic therapy groups, where vicarious catharsis and spectator therapy are common phenomena. The boys' practical planning for the future was rather impressive, and now it seemed to ring true, as did also their capacity for relatedness when they wished they could get together after they left the Village.

NOTE

The session was canceled the following week because of a heavy snowstorm that made walking at night hazardous. The boys who met the therapist on the campus during that week invariably stopped him to inquire why there was no session.

16

Third
Intermediate Progress Reports

Donald

After Forty-Three Sessions

IN COMPARING the clinical picture obtained by the psychologist at this time with one reported a year before, it was noted that the boy's intrapsychic conflicts were intensified: "They were now more in focus, and his intrapsychic discomfort and stress had increased." The decrease in emotional impulsivity appeared to be the most significant gain, which may have represented an "emotional tightening up and a constructive step toward the establishment of stronger inner controls." He felt less submissive and solicitous, and tended to adopt a more active and independent role, a change in attitude which is generally associated with a better perceptual integration.

While Donald still found considerable difficulties in his masculine identification, he was significantly less guilty over sexuality and seemed more assured of his potency. "He still perceives women as more adequate than men; however, he is now able to express his resentment and antagonism more openly and consequently expects to be rejected. Since he has internalized his conflicts he is suffering more, a suffering which is particularly difficult for him to tolerate, because at the moment he does not know of any means of alleviation. He still has no model to constructively canalize his increased anxiety and is greatly in need of developing a positive transference with a supportive, reassuring, unequivocal male authority figure. With less emotional impulsivity, more inner discom-

fort, and increased anxiety the neurotic elements dominate the clinical
picture even more than the previous examination indicated, and Donald's
amenability to further treatment has consequently improved. Also, the
fact that this boy has much of a creative potential for which he has
found no adequate outlets strongly suggests that treatment be continued." The trend in the test results was toward a loss in functional
intelligence, which was definitely related to increased anxiety.

The psychiatric report at this time indicated the boy's greater ability
to control himself; ". . . perhaps through the group therapy process he
has developed these controls." Bizarre behavior noted before was no
longer present during this interview. The psychiatrist now described
Donald as "a borderline schizophrenic, whose underlying psychosis can
give rise to violent temper outbursts and resultant loss of contact with
reality." He also noted "poor judgment," which made the prognosis even
less hopeful than before. He felt "it might be possible to reach this boy
if he were to be seen individually by the therapist who works with him
in the group."

The cottage staff felt that Donald had displayed impressively greater
control than ever before. While he still needed firmness, Donald seemed
to be aware of, and to seek out, limits. He now asked the cottage parents
what he was permitted to do, whereas previously he had just acted without restraint. The cottage life supervisor said: "You can talk with this
boy now. Before, he was always ready to act first, and think later." There
had been a time when Donald's sleeping habits presented a problem. He
often used to wander around the dormitory at night, and, although it was
not known whether he had engaged in sex play, he was always "up to
something, such as starting a pillow fight, throwing water around in the
bathroom, and so forth." Such was no longer the case.

In reviewing the entire work done with this boy by the casework
department, the caseworker reported that "Donald has shown an ability
to control himself that we never thought possible. At one point he was a
very confused, very tenuous kind of person who was explosive. One
never knew what would trigger him off. Donald shows an ability to think
for himself, plan for himself, and evaluate his future."

The teachers reported that Donald was "a much happier boy, relaxed,
and not jumping out of his seat as in the past." His education counselor
stated, "Donald was of no use to anybody before he got into the group."
Now, he was "no longer a sulking, isolated youngster who fights at the
drop of a hat. He now approached his teachers and talked to them with
ease and was amenable to class discipline. He is a socially acceptable boy,
whereas previously there was something of a wild animal about him."
Donald now asked realistic questions and seemed genuinely trying to
learn, instead of viewing school attendance as an imposition by adults.

He was reading at fourth-grade level; in arithmetic as well he was entering the fourth grade.

The overwhelming anxiety under which the boy operated when he came for treatment was greatly diminished, largely because of his psychological separation from his mother, now that he was able to view her objectively. The hypercathexis of his mother, the associated libidinal urges toward her, the repressive forces that operated on this complex, and the bound-up anxiety produced the defensive, schizophrenic-like withdrawal from reality observed by the cottage and clinical staff. The physical separation from the mother and the counter-cathexis engendered by the group's acceptance of his feelings, the encouragement of catharsis through it, and the catalytic activation purged the boy and diminished the anxiety in him. Once freed of its crippling and constraining forces, his capacity for reality-testing and objectivity went forward, and ego forces became available and were employed in general development and personality growth.

Donald left the Village after forty-three sessions in group therapy. Consideration was given to his readiness for returning home, and, on the other hand, to the pressure from staff and, particularly, his parents to have him discharged as soon as possible. Both the group therapy department and the psychiatrist considered this undesirable and recommended that he continue in the Village another year. The group therapy department also disagreed with the caseworker and the psychiatrist, who were of the opinion that Donald was psychotic. The psychologist who had examined Donald four months earlier (the same person who had tested him previously) also indicated that the boy did not appear to be psychotic; rather "he has an impulsive character and has considerable violence in his make-up." It was this impulsivity that seemed a threat to various members of the staff.

Since there was this difference of opinion as to diagnosis as well as on future planning for the boy, it was decided that a conference would be held to present the divergent views. In view of the fact that it was the policy of the group therapy department not to become involved in administrative discussions—for we did not wish our boys to feel we were either "reporting" on them or participating in decisions as to their remaining in or leaving the Village—we hesitated to attend the conference. However, we realized the importance of this in relation to the boy's continuing treatment. Therefore, we decided that the group therapist would first see Donald individually and tell him that he had been asked to participate in the conference and request Donald's permission to do so. The group therapist told Donald that this was the first time since he had conducted groups that he was to attend a conference. Donald said it was all right with him, and added spontaneously that the therapist could say anything he wished about him, "even what I said in the group. I know you want to help me."

Participating in the conference were the psychiatrist, the caseworker, the casework supervisor, the group therapist, the director of the child guidance clinic, and the child care supervisor. Each person present substantiated the fact that Donald had made considerable progress since he joined the group. The cottage life supervisor, for example, noted that Donald was much better controlled, and able to withstand frustration. "During this period when there has been some question about his leaving, Donald has not acted out explosively; he has talked about running away but has not done so. When he feels upset now, he comes to people like me to talk about his problems, after which his anxiety seems to subside." The supervisor characterized this as "a remarkable change." This was substantiated by the caseworker, who pointed out that Donald, though very upset, was now able to sit still in an interview and engage in conversation. He added that Donald's teacher had reported that the boy was no longer a management problem in the school. He got along well with the teacher and the boys. Whereas previously he would be the initiator of trouble in class, he had now taken over positive leadership of the group.

The group therapist reported on the boy's movement from the time he entered the group as a very depressed youngster. At that time, Donald was bringing in incidents related to his antisocial behavior inside and outside the Village, including his bizarre sexual behavior. Gradually he had been able to bring to the group free material, his anxiety about himself, about being at the Village, his worry and concern about leaving, what was going to happen to him, and so forth. He had also been able to talk about his mother, his feelings of guilt for his thoughts, as well as his behavior at home.

The psychiatrist indicated that he was convinced that basically Donald was a "psychotic personality," that the evidence for this lay in the concreteness of the boy's thinking, his lack of impulse control, his very poor judgment, and his difficulty in comprehending reality situations. The psychiatrist felt that perhaps in group therapy too much had been opened up for this boy and that this might account for much of his current anxiety. The psychiatrist felt that this youngster was in a homosexual panic. He recommended that rather than opening up feeling with this boy he should be worked with as a psychotic child rather than as a neurotic.

In a supervisory discussion by the director of the project and the group therapist it was decided to communicate our disagreement and to ask permission to continue with the boy on an individual basis through the ensuing summer. It was our conviction that the impulsivity in this boy would be decreased only when he developed a transference relationship with a controlled, calm person, and as he gained insight into his behavior and recognized his impulsivity he would acquire control over it. It was also our conviction that he was neurotic and not psychotic and that we should, therefore, proceed with him as a neurotic. Permission to see the boy individually was granted by the administration. We planned to continue with the boy through the summer months, rather than discharge him before the summer, so that we could work through the idea of his continuing in the Village for another year. However, for various reasons this was not possible, and Donald was discharged early in the fall, with the group therapist continuing to see him on occasion in the city.

Donald was not told the results of the interdepartmental conference for some days, the reason being that no definite decision was made as to whether Donald should be retained at the Village. The final decision was to be made by the director of the child guidance clinic, who wished to discuss the matter further with the caseworker's supervisor. The group therapist, therefore, saw Donald later on the day the conference was held to tell him of the outcome and at the same time set up another appointment for him two days later when he might have word of a definite decision.

At this later interview the group therapist told Donald that he had something to tell him which he knew would be upsetting to him. It was decided that he was to remain at the Village for another year, because everybody felt that although he had shown rather good progress, there still remained many problems that needed working through. Were he to leave the Village at this point, he would find himself unhappy at home, since these problems would continue to interfere with his getting along in school or in a job, and with his family. The therapist told Donald that everyone at the conference had faith in him and in his ability to overcome his difficulties and for his own good wished he would remain, and that the group therapist would be his caseworker.

Donald grew visibly and increasingly more agitated during the therapist's statement. His agitation was manifested by tightening of his jaws and by his left hand, clenched into a fist, being banged into the open palm of his right hand. He grew restless, moved about in his chair, and then repeated audibly: "I will not stay. I will not stay at the Village. I'm going home. Nobody is going to keep me at the Village." When he grew calmer, he said that he was sorry that the therapist was the one to give him this news, because the therapist was the one person whom he liked in the Village. Donald seemed to struggle with his feelings of anger toward the therapist. As he got up and paced up and down the room like a caged lion, the therapist half-expected that momentarily Donald would start pounding at the wall with his fists. Donald finally declared that he would run away. He had controlled himself up to now, but there was no point doing it any longer. The therapist agreed that he could run away any time. "Would this really solve anything?" he asked. Donald became slightly less agitated, but kept repeating that he would run away.

The therapist noted that during the three individual interviews he later had with Donald concurrently with the group sessions he found the boy seriously blocked, so that he seemed unable to comprehend words of more than one syllable. He did not seem to understand simple concepts and displayed very little ability to think abstractly. The therapist had not noticed this in the group. The therapist also noted that Donald seemed to have a very difficult time remembering things, and would return to a subject which seemed to have been already settled. Donald would raise questions about it as if he did not remember discussing it only a few moments before. This pattern did not strike the therapist as a deliberate maneuver. Rather, it seemed to be the result of real obsolescence.

During these interviews Donald told the therapist that by remaining at the Village he felt like a "traitor" to his parents. His mother was in the process of securing "working papers" for him and had been making arrangements for his discharge with the child care supervisor. The therapist encouraged Donald to talk more fully about his feelings of disappointing his mother by remaining at the Village, but he did not seem to grasp what was said to him. Instead he kept repeating how much his mother and father wanted him home, that they had been waiting for him to return. Judging by the tone of Donald's voice, the therapist was convinced that the boy did feel he was a traitor to his parents.

The therapist made it clear to Donald that he would see him as often as necessary during the coming weeks (while the boy was going through this travail). Donald's most acute struggle seemed to center around his feelings of anger toward the therapist, which were very threatening to him, although the therapist reiterated Donald's right to have these feelings and that he could understand why Donald felt as he did.

After Donald left this interview, the therapist called the child care supervisor to inform him that Donald was very upset and to anticipate some acting out on his part. The therapist also advised the coach at Community Center of how Donald was feeling. About two hours later Donald returned to see the therapist and seemed less agitated. He asked the therapist for ten cents so that he could call his mother and let her know what had happened, and to tell her to proceed engaging a lawyer to force his removal from the Village. (The therapist thought the request of the dime was in part a test of the therapist.) The therapist gave Donald the dime (which Donald later returned with thanks).

Before he left the interview with the group therapist (described above), Donald asked for cigarettes, which the therapist gave him. He then began to talk about the trip the boys in the group were planning and asked whether he could handle his own money. (Funds for the trip were supplied by the Village.) Donald asked in a "very testing way" where the group would eat, what movie they planned to see, and so on. He was assured that these arrangements would depend on the group's decision. Donald grew increasingly more relaxed at this point and talked freely about the trip and that he would take on the responsibility for discussing plans with the other boys and help them decide where to eat and what movie to see. Before leaving, Donald and the group therapist made an appointment to meet again the following day at nine in the morning.

The child care supervisor reported that Donald did not come to see him and appeared less agitated than had been described.

When the group therapist arrived at his office exactly at nine o'clock the next morning, Donald was already waiting in the lobby of the child guidance building. The group therapist reported that he made it a point not to pick up the telephone when it rang while this boy was in his office. (This was one of Donald's major criticisms on numerous occasions, of his previous caseworker, namely, that when he was being interviewed the worker spent much time on the telephone.) Donald was much more relaxed than on the preceding day. Though not quite his usual self, he was visibly much less agitated.

Donald told the therapist that his mother had told him that she was going to get a lawyer, and Donald assured the therapist that he would be going home. However, the therapist noted that Donald did not seem to be completely convinced, and his feeling of urgency was lessened as compared to the preceding day. He said that now that he was going to remain at the Village, he found that people were "being very nice" to him. For instance, for the first time his cottage parents began to call him "Donald" instead of referring to him by his last name only. The child care supervisor and the cottage parents had spoken to him about why he should remain at the Village, and it was obvious that he was very much touched by their interest. Again in a very teasing and testing way, Donald said that when the group would be away from the Village on their trip (which was scheduled for the following day), he might consider "taking off." When told that he would be unconditionally trusted and that the therapist would not be watching him, he said: "You don't have to worry about me. I wouldn't do anything to mess up. I could have run away a number of times but I didn't do it." The therapist admitted that Donald could have got home easily, but this was not the point because it would not solve the problems they were dealing with at this time. (It was the therapist's feeling that Donald was less agitated because he was sure as to what his parents were going to do—that they were going to take legal action for his release.)

The therapist tried to explore with Donald his feelings about the other boys knowing that he would have to remain at the Village. While Donald denied it, the therapist felt sure that there was a certain degree of loss of face, which is normal in the peer culture at the Village. Donald again expressed anger toward the therapist and wanted to know what the therapist had said at the conference, indicating that perhaps the therapist was the one who was responsible for the decision to have him stay. The therapist raised the question of his anger openly with Donald, but Donald drew away from this and denied it completely. During this interview, the therapist suggested the possibility of his talking with Donald's parents. The first time this was mentioned Donald categorically refused to give his permission. When this question was now again raised, Donald said he would think it over and let the therapist know later. Another appointment was set for the following week. The therapist told Donald that he would be seeing him twice a week during the next month.

Approximately a week after the interview described above, Donald's father came to the Village to see the group therapist. Prior to this the father had telephoned to inform the caseworker and the latter's supervisor of his intention to engage counsel to remove his son from the Village. Instead, the group therapist, who now acted as Donald's caseworker, had agreed to see the father and explain to him the decision to retain Donald for another year.

The father looked unkempt, unshaven, "like a truck driver who has been on the road for some time." The father was making a very strong effort to control his anger, but his cracking voice and flushed face gave him away. (The therapist was struck by the similarity between father and son—not so much in physical resemblance, because they did not really look alike, but in the kind of explosiveness he detected in the father and which had been all too evident in the boy.)

The father focused his anger on the fact that he "had been lied to." He said the caseworker had definitely committed himself to Donald's return home at the end of the school term. No one had advised him of the change. It was Donald who had illegally telephoned to tell his family of the new development. The father needed and was given a great deal of repeated assurance that he had a right to be angry about the manner in which the situation was handled. However, unfortunate as it was, the purpose in seeing him was to let him in on some of the thinking that led up to the decision. While the father's anger seemed to subside at this point, he became defensive of his son, and the therapist got the impression that the father seemed to be "a saturated delinquent himself." The father considered the boy's problem as being primarily due to the colored boys in the neighborhood, "who were constantly picking" on him. The police in the neighborhood, too, were "picking" on Donald, while actually Donald "had not done anything" to warrant his having been sent to Children's Village. Later in the interview the father did mention his awareness that Donald had been doing "some wrong things such as truanting, riding in a stolen car, and others, but there were hundreds of kids in our neighborhood who did the same thing and were never sent away." It was evident that, though he denied it, the father considered Donald's being sent to Children's Village only as punishment.

The therapist explained to the father that all who had been working very closely with Donald felt that if he were to return home now, he would have a great deal of difficulty adjusting to school, to a job, or even to his parents at home. Donald was still at the mercy of strong feelings that were very confusing to him. He did not always have control over what he did and was "pushed into doing things first and then feeling sorry about it later." If Donald were to go home at this point, he might do something very serious that would be of real concern not only to the boy but also to his family. The group therapist explained that it was out of interest in Donald and feeling that he did show evidence of growing understanding of himself and an ability to control himself that the Village wanted to invest another year in him.

The father responded to this by saying, "I feel very, very confused now," but much of his anger had subsided. "Much like a subsiding storm," noted the therapist. The father said while he did not want to get a lawyer—"It would not do anybody any good"—he did not know what else to do. The therapist recognized his feelings at this point and his right to proceed legally if this should be his ultimate decision. The father then stated that he wanted to talk this over with his wife. He said this with an air of a man who was "pretty much at the mercy of his wife."

The therapist suggested the possibility of an interview with him and his wife together. This Donald's father eagerly grasped at, and an appointment was set for the following week. Immediately preceding the joint interview with both parents the group therapist saw Donald for a short time. The boy was resistant to talking, and therefore the two sat for a while in silence. Then, after a brief chat about the program at the Village, the therapist raised the question of how Donald felt about his parents coming to see him. Donald denied having any reaction, so the therapist took the initiative to explain that he wanted to talk to Donald's mother and share with her what he had told the father the previous week. It was evident that the father had recounted to Donald everything that was said in the interview, although the therapist had requested the father to be judicious about it.

The therapist described the mother as "a short, heavy-set, bosomed, rather attractive white-haired woman who gives the appearance of being well scrubbed and clean." She was extremely angry. Her face was flushed, her manner brusque, and the movements of her hands nervous. Because she seemed to have difficulty in beginning, the therapist initiated the interview, recognizing that she had not had an opportunity to talk with the therapist and that she must have some questions about what was happening with her son. Throughout the interview, the mother was the dominant person, with the father somewhat cowed by his wife.

In very well-controlled tones, the mother repeated the same complaints the father had offered and that the caseworker had made a definite commitment for their son's leaving the Village at the end of the school year, or as soon as the parents could get working papers and a job for him. She was very angry because she had learned about the new developments in the situation from Donald, rather than from the caseworker or someone in authority. However, through all of this harangue, the mother expressed an interest in the therapist's opinion about Donald. The father apparently had not shared with his wife the content of the previous week's interview, so the therapist went on to tell the mother what he had told her husband about Donald's current adjustment and the potentials for the future. He used the hypothetical illustration of Donald's having pneumonia and the doctor at the hospital telling them that their son was not ready to be discharged. What would they do? asked the therapist. Spontaneously the mother retorted that she would let him remain at the hospital, but this admission seemed to be too much for her, because she immediately added, "I'm going to get a lawyer!" The therapist told the mother that she was entirely within her rights to do so and that the Village would make no attempt to oppose her, since the only person who would suffer through such a conflict would be Donald. Rather than have Donald get hurt, she could take him home, but as parents they should know what they could expect.

Both parents remained silent for some time. Then they began to talk about Donald's readiness for a job. The therapist asked about what type of job they were planning for him, and they proved unsure and very tenuous. The mother spoke of the possibility of Donald's working for an uncle, but the exact nature of the work seemed unclear to them. The therapist asked her if she knew anything about Donald's reading, and she responded that she was aware that it was "not good." The therapist then asked if she had any idea what would happen if Donald obtained a job and could not read. What kind of job could he hold and for how long? Here the mother looked at her husband and became very reflective. She admitted that this had been worrying her and raised the question as to why Donald could not read, but answered it herself by saying that perhaps if she got Donald a tutor he would learn. The therapist said that if it were purely a matter of teaching through a tutor, there would be no problem. This had nothing to do with Donald's brain. He could not learn to read because he was "very upset inside and very confused and was using all his time and energy to control himself." This prevented him from having enough energy left over with which to learn.

The mother seemed to understand, and the therapist tried to hold her to this understanding of Donald's problem. What came out in the ensuing discussion were the parents' strong ambivalence and their own fear of the boy. If they were to agree that Donald might stay at the Village, they would not know how to deal with him. The therapist emphasized that this, the fear of Donald, was one of the very things the staff at the Village was concerned about, for they discovered that they seldom knew what Donald might do next. Both parents admitted that this greatly concerned them. The mother was worried that "he is liable to be very angry, to run away, and we may never see him again." The therapist tried to help the parents by suggesting that Donald might feel very upset about staying at the Village because he felt his parents wanted him home so badly and perhaps he felt almost like a traitor toward them. He asked what they thought might happen if Donald felt that his parents supported his remaining at the Village, rather than being against the decision. The mother indicated that this had never occurred to her, and now terrible confusion displaced her former anger and she did not know what to do.

The father, who kept looking at his wife throughout the interview, as if to try to guess her attitude and almost as if seeking permission to have his own opinion, had said very little. He now spoke up, saying, "Maybe we've just got to face facts with Don." The mother threw an angry glance at him, as though he were reaching a decision without her participation.

Since both parents were quite confused and could not resolve the problem, they agreed to set up another appointment for the following week. Unfortunately, this appointment had to be canceled and was not held until two months later, after the summer vacation. When the parents were seen again, their anger toward the Village seemed to have been reinforced and hardened, so that they once more insisted that Donald be returned home. It was because of their renewed attempts to get Donald out of the Village, as well as the pressure from child care staff and the boy's caseworker to have him sent home, that the decision was reached to let him go home. The director of the study had decided that, with the boy's attitude and the climate created by the staff and the parents, Donald's membership in the therapy group would be untenable. Even if he were retained in the Village, he could not be assimilated by the group any longer.

It was decided in consultation with the director of the study that Donald would need sustained contact with the group therapist on after-care to insure the boy's adjustment in the community—to home, school, and job.

During the first six months following Donald's return home, he was seen by the therapist eight times; the parents were seen once. During that period Donald canceled two appointments. Telephone conversations were held twice each month.

Louis

After Forty-Four Sessions[1]

Louis was discharged from the Village at this juncture and re-ferred to after-care. This was a routine referral for casework supervision and treatment of boys who resided in New York City and their families. Boys in other towns were usually referred to available local family and guidance facilities.

The cottage supervisor described Louis as still being somewhat hostile, but no longer participating in any antisocial or destructive acts. It was also evident that he was able to control his rage. His anger now was appropriate and he could talk about it instead of acting on it. He still found it more difficult to relate to female staff members than to males.

The teachers reported increasing ability to reason and to discuss his reactions, which he did intelligently. He had good relationships with male teachers. The one female teacher of whose class Louis was a member reported that she could not motivate him to study. However, his over-all achievement record indicated good educational motivation. He functioned above the eleventh grade in reading and arithmetic, which was appropriate to his age and somewhat better. He presented no dif-ficulties in the auto shop, but preferred reading to doing shopwork. His voracious reading was commented upon by other staff members as well.

Louis still remained relatively uninvolved with his female caseworker. Outside of expressing his persistent wish to be returned home, he re-sisted discussing anything relative to his home and family. The case-worker felt, however, that Louis was far less hostile and much less demanding of special privileges than he had ever been before. He was seen by her approximately once every two weeks.

The psychological examination administered before he left the

1. See p. 321, first paragraph.

Village revealed no significant change in intellectual status. He appeared to be well motivated. Rapport was easily established and maintained throughout the examination, except for a few minutes during the Rorshach inquiry when he became evasive, flustered, and somewhat withdrawn. His appearance and presentation were more appropriate, and he was better related than before. There were signs of gains in ego strength and impulse control. The heroes of his stories were now more guided by the reality principle. Whereas in the preassignment test the pleasure principle was predominant, Louis now appeared capable of more differentiated perceptions of the world around him, and his tendency to withdraw had lessened.

The pervasive anxiety experienced in relation to the maternal figure is still present but more circumscribed, and its effects have less impact. The unsatiable orality on a more unconscious level—the wish to return to the mother—may always be a problem to Louis. The pervasive feelings of frustration, besides leading to depression, also provoke much rage and hostility. The paranoid position is maintained, and under continued stress, thinking disorder and delusional tendency can manifest themselves. There has been an improvement in this area, however. Louis does not become so rapidly disorganized, and the impulses do not fragment the ego as much. He can now tolerate more intense conflicts and turmoil, but his (basic) ego is not resilient enough to sustain long periods of stress, and the acting out of strong hostile and destructive impulses remains quite probable. The anxiety experienced in relation to the father image is associated with feelings of inadequacy and phallic insufficiency. In spite of these feelings of inferiority, he has developed more heterosexual interests, and he now experiences less hostility and fearfulness in relation to his sexual impulses. There are signs of increased responsivity, but there are also indications of increased wariness, suspiciousness toward others. While there have been gains in ego strength and impulse control, the inner disorganization based on his experience with an unpredictable, destructive mother persists. Mistrust of others, aggressive stubbornness, lability of affect, potential for aggressive active acts still characterize the present clinical picture. In summary, while the neurotic elements have receded (less sexual conflict, less anxiety), the psychotic elements remain (ranging from depression to agitated acting out with paranoia as a constant feature).

It is probable that, had Louis continued in group treatment, further inroads into his pathology would have been made, and it is certain from the above that he would require skillful and intensive postinstitutional care to prevent recidivism. His intentions, as verbalized in the group, could not be sustained by his psychic resources without help.

Leonard

After Fifty-Five Sessions

Steady though not too dramatic changes were noted. Leonard had at this point relatively new cottage parents. He adjusted to the change rather well. He was described by the cottage life supervisor, who had known Leonard since he came to the Village, as "a more solid boy in appearance and able to assert himself adequately. His demands and interests were realistic and in keeping with a boy of his age," but he was still somewhat of an isolate. He did not seek out boys, but they came to him. The pattern was true also to a large extent in his relation with his new cottage parents. Recently, Leonard said that he was aware of the kind of personality he had and that perhaps he would always be like that. He now rebelled, as he had not previously, at the slightest move by others to exploit him, and refused to do any chore unless it was within his own area or responsibility.

His social adjustment in school continued to be "excellent." However, academic progress was almost at a standstill. His reading grade was 3.5 and his mathematics grade, 3.5 (as compared to 3.0 and 3.1, respectively, three months before). While Leonard had been working hard in the remedial reading class, his eagerness outstripped his abilities. The school personnel planned to extend the remedial reading sessions from one to three times a week in the hope of speeding up progress.

The caseworker felt that Leonard was not reached by individual interviews. He remained uninvolved and refused to discuss his home situation. Interviews centered mainly on reporting daily activities. He was more assertive, however, in his demands to go home. The caseworker felt that "this was a vastly different boy today than when he arrived at the Village. Now he walks erect, no longer gives the appearance of being a hunchback and is much better able to express his feelings and his anger. Currently, Leonard is beginning to raise some very realistic questions and to evaluate what returning to the community may hold for him. He described his fears for a job, in being accepted by an employer, and his ability in holding down a job."

The discussions in the group of the realistic problems the boys would face upon returning to their communities and seeking jobs had helped Leonard to mobilize his ego forces and bring to his awareness the actualities of life that in the infantile, dependent state in which he came to us did not exist for him, or only vaguely so. This realization of the conditions and actualities of the larger world furthered his maturity and called upon his newly acquired strengths. But instead of withdrawing into his protective schizoid shell, which he was wont to do in the past, he now faced difficulties and sought out help.

His assertiveness in resisting all semblance of exploitation, of which he was an abject victim in the past, clearly revealed his ego strength and the reduction, and perhaps elimination, of his self-alienative structure, which was so prominent at the time he joined the group. He was now on the road to acquiring an identity apart from his mother.

Jules

After Fifty-Five Sessions

In the seven months since the last progress report, Jules had sustained two transfers in cottage placement. For some weeks he lived in the cottage that housed the infirmary. Because he was the only boy there, with only the supervisory staff, he was the recipient of more attention than usual, and he made a satisfactory adjustment. When he was returned to a regular residential cottage with a group of older boys nearer his own size and maturity, he reacted at first with visible disturbance, but was soon able to settle down. This cottage was equipped with individual bedrooms rather than dormitories, and this seemed to meet Jules's needs.

The cottage parents reported that Jules easily accepted direction from them and was getting on well with the other boys. In fact, they said, boys looked up to Jules, but not as a leader. Rather, they "somehow admire him for having made such a good adjustment." He was no longer so defiant toward staff, but displayed an attitude of self-confidence. He appeared to feel at ease with his cottage parents and with staff members and no longer withdrew or isolated himself, displaying an air of independence.

Jules's progress in school slowed down during this period. His current reading score was 8.8 and that in arithmetic 8.0, as compared to 8.6 and 7.3, respectively, six months ago. His behavior in school, however, had greatly improved. He was more courteous and amiable, accepted supervision gracefully, and had grown more concerned about his appearance. The teachers considered this latter development as "most significant." The boy was no longer "sloppy" in his dress; he paid attention to his clothes. He looked well groomed and "more appropriately a teenager." Jules was "a most attentive student" and had shown "great interest" in the music class. Science, however, was still beyond his depth. Although he tried hard, he seemed unable to understand it. The teachers suggested in their reports that "while the grade scores may not reflect a rate of improvement as great, since the last report, his concentration had improved significantly. Jules no longer wandered around the room, he was far less restless, and needed far less supervision in the classroom than before."

His new caseworker, who had seen Jules only three times preceding the writing of this evaluation, was able to give only a vague impression. He felt that there were "many loose ends about the boy" which suggested to him a "psychotic core," though there had not been any indication of this in previous evaluations. In the most recent psychiatric interview, on the other hand, the psychiatrist found that Jules had "greatly benefited from group therapy." But he opined that while favorable changes took place, they had not as yet been "deeply integrated into Jules's character," though he was far more reality-oriented ·and the delinquent trends were significantly reduced. The boy's conduct and response to relationships clearly indicated the "tightening up" of psychic forces and his inner ease. The dichotomies and inconsistencies prevalent in the preceding evaluation were less evident, or not at all apparent. He operated now as an integrated, "solid" individual. His mature and reality-oriented reactions dominated all areas of his life, and the noticeable gaps of six or seven months ago were no longer present. Of interest was the leveling off of his academic progress. He was still academically retarded about a year-and-a-half. This had to be viewed in this case as consistent with his native capacities. There had been a consistent gap in all three psychological tests held until this time between his performance and verbal capacities and his full-scale results indicated a low intellectual potential.

What was of greatest significance in this case was the impressive strengthening of his ego forces as through the group he achieved a self-identity, and the fact that his self-alienative processes had been greatly diminished, which led to a diminished social alienation.

Michael

Because of shifts in staff, no reliable progress report on Michael could be obtained, for the new staff people were not equipped to evaluate his progress at that time. A final progress report was, however, compiled at the end of the therapy sessions and appears on pp. 732-733.

Macy

After Fifty Sessions

The cottage life supervisor described Macy as no longer so intensely dependent upon the cottage mother as he had been. He no longer sought her approval or acceptance, nor did he expect her to gratify his infantile emotional needs. He had become reliant and assertive and was calmly able to withstand criticism from her. The cottage mother, however, was still strongly attached to the boy, and sensing his growing away from her, became more demanding and highly critical of him. One of the significant developments was his refusal to walk the cottage mother's dog, which to him represented being considered a small child, unable to resist impositions and express his wishes. In reporting these developments, the supervisor stated: "Group therapy has helped keep this boy together during this trying period."

Macy had recently gravitated toward the cottage father, rather than the cottage mother as in the past, consulting him on his problems. Macy became one of the "constructive leaders in the cottage group." Even his voice had grown in timbre, and he projected it with inner security. He now walked erect, and did not bow his head when talking with adults. "We are now dealing with a real teenager," the supervisor said. His requests were now "very reasonable," both in content and manner, and he made no excessive demands.

Up to six months before it had been rumored that Macy had been engaging in homosexual activities, but of this no further evidence was forthcoming. The cottage parents reported that Macy was getting other boys in his cottage involved in discussions of heterosexual sex activities.

The school reported a remarkable "spurt in Macy's reading (11.1) and arithmetic (8.5)." In English, social studies, and science, he functioned at a tenth-grade level without difficulty. He made noticeable improvement in his attitudes and behavior. Macy was now able to function independently, though at times he allowed himself to be drawn into obstreperous behavior. However, he now "stops to think about it and has displayed control." He had a free and easy relation with teachers and conversed with them frequently and fully. They planned to be less firm with him as a way of testing the boy's ability to function independently.

In casework, too, Macy had made significant gains. The caseworker reported that "group therapy must really be helping this boy. He is more spontaneous and talked about things that he never did before." He gave the impression of being a more normal adolescent, exhibiting a readiness to talk about matters that were bothering him. He continued to discuss his cottage parents, school, anxiety about friends, and life at home. He seemed to be more sure of himself now than ever before. More recently, he had revealed his guilt feelings upon the death of his father a few weeks before; also, about having engaged in homosexual activity. He said he felt "dirty, maybe going crazy." The caseworker stated: "There is more superego formation in the boy now. Although Macy was ingratiating to all adults when he first came to the Village, he really did not take them seriously. He felt it was all right for him to do anything he wished. Now Macy stops to think and talk about whether what he is going to do is right or wrong." He verbalized his pride in being able to control himself and had an awareness that he would have problems in re-adjusting to community living. "This was rather different and unusual for a boy who previously would deny problems or any need for help."

In a psychiatric review at this time, the psychiatrist felt that the boy had a better-integrated ego, and that he was far more reality-oriented than in any previous examination.

The emotional maturational process had continued very satisfactorily in Macy. His self-assertiveness and insisting on his right as an individual were indices of increased ego strengths; his detachment from the cottage mother in defiance of her opinion of him, indicate improved self-identity as a result of being freed of Oedipal involvement with her and the intellectual understandings he had gained through the group discussions and the individual interviews with his caseworker (who, fortunately, remained on the staff throughout Macy's treatment career). The unmistakably benign relations with peers and the cottage father, the spontaneous discussions of heterosexuality, indicated a masculine orientation and acceptance of his biological destiny. The sundry corrective developments begot a diminution of self-alienative operations and instead generated self-alliance; they integrated the psychic forces, on the one hand, and directed them toward more auspicious outcomes, on the other.

Richard

After Fifty-Five Sessions

Richard continued to show good improvement in the cottage. He had developed a noticeable sense of humor and could take kidding from both staff and the other boys without becoming angry and feeling personally injured. He struck everyone as a much more matured boy, not only in the way he carried himself physically but in his behavior as well. He no longer acted foolish and inappropriately, showed a good sense of responsibility, and had no need for constant supervision, as was the case before group therapy started. "He seems to try to stop himself and evaluate the consequences of his acts and is not impulsive as he was."

His school level had risen to the tenth grade. His work in mathematics was at the 9.5 level. Richard was studying algebra at this time and seemed quite capable at it. He was working up to grade in all other subjects. In auto shop he continued to do well, completing all his assignments, and got along well with his peers. He became more independent both in the classroom and in the shop, and no longer needed intensive supervision or structured settings as was the case before.

The caseworker reported "a big change" in the home situation. The parents were no longer in open conflict. Richard seemed to enjoy himself more on his home visits and no longer came back upset as he had previously. The caseworker noted a "marked decrease in restlessness and an increase in the seriousness with which Richard discusses his future." The psychiatrist who re-evaluated Richard's situation at this time felt "there is a good chance Richard would not get into further difficulties at home and in the community." He suggested, however, that many of the observable changes "have not as yet been integrated into the boy's personality."

Richard was retested by the psychologist as well at this time. The psychologist found that "there was a notable change in the patient in that he showed a more casual approach to the projective tests, less inhibition, and more willingness to comment on, and examine, his own responses."

> Intellectual functioning remained at high average, close to the superior range (full-scale IQ 116). The productivity on the projective material increased and there was less constriction. The energy which was previously wrapped up in responding to things in the environment was now directed toward people. His previous reluctance to get involved in interpersonal transactions was related to his lack of masculine identification and to the intense conflict experienced in the maternal relationship. He is now able to deal with his Oedipal fears and his conflicts are more toward the surface. Thus the trend is toward normalization; the anxiety has lessened, and he is able to get closer to his conflict without panicking. The conflict also appears less intense. He is moving away from preoccupations with the primal scene and from sexuality involving the mother figure. While there was previously a complete blocking in the sexual sphere, he is now able to tolerate and explore some of his sexual problems. The defensive system is not as tight; anxiety and painful affect, like grief and sadness, have

lessened somewhat. He still has great fear of masculine authority figures, which are perceived as sadistic, a perception which is linked to his sexual conflicts, in which oral aggression—perhaps a fear as a wish for oral incorporation—appears to be of some significance. Under stress Richard is yet unable to integrate affective promptings. He is more responsive to the environment provided the situation is not too emotionally loaded. However, when strong affective demands are made of him he still reverts to his main defensive mechanism, somatization.

In summary, improvements are noted in various areas: the maternal relationship is no longer overpowering, an element of distance has been introduced and a more casual attitude toward the mother is apparent. There is a beginning of differentiation in sexual role instead of the previous emotional blocking over sexuality. Generally, progress has been made toward masculine identity and increased relatedness.

17

Protocols and Comments: Sessions 56-75

Session Fifty-Six

BECAUSE OF WEATHER CONDITIONS, this session was held at 4:00 P.M. instead of the usual 7:00. All the boys were on time. They came in rather quietly. Richard asked why the time of the meeting had been changed and the therapist explained that there was a possibility of a snowstorm in the evening. Louis said it made no difference to him when the group met as long as it met. He was glad that there was a meeting. Jules busied himself making coffee for the group, while Louis was working on a book of crossword puzzles. Judging by the questions he was asking the other boys, the therapist felt that Louis knew how to do the puzzles rather well. He was working on rather difficult words, and the other boys were of little help to him, but he was able to formulate most of the words himself and called out each word before he wrote it down. Jules was serving coffee and cookies while Richard proceeded again to narrate a problem he had been having with Mrs. K. Exactly what this was escaped the therapist. He talked loudly across the room to Michael, who wore a bored expression on his face. Michael did not seem to be listening but was trying to attract Louis's attention by snapping his fingers. Louis looked up momentarily and returned to work on his crossword puzzle. Richard turned to Leonard and asked him whether he had received a scholarship. (Being assigned to a "work group" for which payment was received was known as a "scholarship.") Leonard said rather proudly that he had been "placed in the scholarship group." Nothing further was said about it.

There was a rather lethargic quality to the group. Conversations would begin and end abruptly. The therapist wondered to himself whether the fact that the group as a whole had not met for almost three weeks had something to do with this reaction. (The change of time from evening to daylight may have had something to do with it also.) As the therapist was thinking about this, Richard said: "It's been a long time since we've been here, right Mr. Ellery? Well, a lot of things are happening now. Things are a little quieter in the cottage. Mrs. K. isn't saying anything about the club." (The child care supervisor for the cottage in question, following a consultation with the group therapist, had discussed the group with Mrs. K. and explained its value to the boys; also that they must have absolute freedom to talk there. Mrs. K. agreed to this "somewhat reluctantly.") Richard added that the other day there had been "a fight" between Mrs. K. and a number of boys. He, too, became involved, because she was picking on a lot of boys and he thought that she was picking on him also. When he realized that Mrs. K. was not attacking him, he kept his "mouth shut," although he felt tempted to say something to her. However, she later "bawled" him out for the way he had done a chore. Richard said that he was very angry with Mrs. K., but did not say anything, since she "let it slide." Richard said: "If she can let things slide, maybe I ought to keep my mouth shut, because this way she is not going to come after me when I have to get out of the Village. Also, I think it is better that way because then I don't get mad at her all the time if I just let things slide and don't pay attention sometimes."

Michael said, "It's about time you said that because all you used to talk about was how you were going to fight with Mrs. K." Richard, however, as if to justify himself, went into a tirade against Mrs. K., but now it had a different quality: The complaints were so picayune that it was obvious he was trying to save face. For example, Mrs. K. didn't like the way floors were done, cutlery wasn't done right in the cottage, and so forth. There was an empty quality to his recital as he rattled off his complaints. He seemed to be trying for attention rather than complaining. Michael must have sensed this, for when Richard stopped Michael applauded him derogatorily and said: "Okay, Richard, you talked enough. We heard this before." He was supported by Louis who said: "Yeah, shut up already. We heard all of this crap before." Richard looked very hurt, but said nothing.

Louis said that this was his last session with the group. He was starting school the following week in the city, and "I guess this is the last time I'll be with you guys." This statement met with dead silence and a rather depressed mood on the part of the group. After a rather prolonged silence, the therapist asked the boys how they felt about Louis's leaving. Macy was the first to speak up: "Louis, I'm kind of sorry you are going, but I wish I could go with you. I wish I could get out of here." Jules laughed and said: "Boy, I wish I could get out of here, too. If I don't go soon, I'm going to run away." There was a hollow ring to Jules's voice, however. He seemed to be aware that he was not leaving soon, but had to believe that things were still under his control. Louis acknowledged the boys' statements by saying: "Thanks, boys. Thanks. I appreciate that a lot. Maybe I'll come up and visit you on Thursday nights. We can sit around and talk about old times." Leonard asked Louis what he was going to do, and Louis described how Mr. T. of the education department would go with him to the Board of Education and get him enrolled in an appropriate class. He would enter the tenth or eleventh grade. Louis thought he could get into "a pretty good school" and would be having a "pretty good time in school." Michael asked: "Do you think you are going to have any more trouble?" Louis: "Naw, I don't think so. Maybe I won't have trouble any more, just to show Mrs. K. that I'm not going to have any more trouble. I don't care what Mrs. K. thinks any more. I'm not going to have trouble. I'm going to be with the right fellows when I get outside."

Michael: "I wish I could say that. I'm not so sure. I know if somebody gets me mad, calls me a name, I'm going to bop them. There are a lot of times I talk about not having fights, but I think about it sometimes, like after I leave, you know, our meeting tonight, and I'm not sure." Michael stopped, and the therapist asked him if he could talk more about how he felt in this area. Michael: "I don't know what to say. I know I got a bad temper. If somebody gets under my skin, I'm liable to let them have it." Jules: "I don't want trouble, but when somebody sounds on me, I can't walk away from it." Then turning to the therapist: "But you say, Mr. Ellery, you can walk away from trouble." Therapist: "The question I raised is who is really the better man, the guy who has to start letting his fists fly first?" Jules: "But suppose somebody starts to beat on you?" Therapist: "We're not talking of having to defend yourself when somebody beats on you with their fists, but that isn't the way the fights start. The way the fights seem to start is that somebody says a word, you take offense and right away your fists start to fly." Jules laughed and said, "Yeah, that's what happens a lot of times!" The therapist said that maybe fists started flying because when somebody uttered a nasty word it reminded them of their own feelings, that they were not so sure about themselves. If one had respect for oneself inside, then people couldn't push one around with words. Jules asked: "Didn't you fight when you were a kid?" Therapist: "When I was a little kid, but I also grew up and in growing up I found out that part of being a man is standing up with dignity even when people who don't have dignity have to sound on you."

This set off an intense and prolonged discussion among Richard, Jules, Macy, and Michael as to whether they could act similarly. Michael was very unsure. The tone of his voice implied the wish that he could do it (be able to ignore unfriendly remarks about him, resist the temptation to steal, and not react when called chicken). Richard said, "I know I got into trouble because I'm easily led," and Michael made a remark to the same effect. The therapist interjected: "Come on fellows, we've talked about this before. What do you remember of our talking about why we got into trouble like stealing and playing hooky? Remember the words *revenge, getting back?*" Michael: "That's right, we talked about getting back at your parents." Richard immediately picked this up and said: "That's right, your parents. But I don't have to get revenge on them any more. What happened, happened; it's over." Louis: "I think my parents can kind of make room for me now. They don't push me any more. Maybe it's because I'm not a little boy with them." Leonard: "Maybe it's because you are not a kid any more. I don't have to get even with my father any more; he's not around also. I kind of feel sorry for the guy now. I can't expect too much from him." Richard: "I don't feel sorry for my father. He's old enough to know what he's doing, but as long as he knows not to keep picking on me for nothing, things are going to be okay."

Jules stood up and invited the boys to another cup of coffee. The response was in the positive, and each boy went up to the table to get himself a cup of coffee. (The therapist did not call attention to this maneuver as resistance. He felt the boys actually needed a respite from the feeling aroused by what they had been talking about.) The boys quietly returned to their seats.

Michael asked how one went about getting a job. What did one do? This sparked an immediate interest in all of the boys. Macy asked: "Where do you go to get a job? What do you do?" The therapist described in detail the steps for consulting employment agencies, how these agencies operated, how to fill out an application, how to dress when one went to an employment agency or to see a prospective employer for an interview. Louis raised numerous questions about agency fees. He and Richard tried to compute whether it was worth consulting employment agencies, because one had to pay a portion of one's salary to them, and whether it would not be better to try to get jobs on their own. Michael thought that he would try to get a job at the supermarkets in his neighborhood as a stock clerk. Louis thought of trying department stores, saying that he did not think he would have too much trouble getting a job, because he could read and write "pretty good." He said, "When I dress up I look real cool, and if anybody ever got a job through looking cool, I'd be the one." This was greeted with laughter. Talk about getting a job continued for a long period of time. It was now 5:25, and Jules said he had to get back to the cottage, because he wanted "eat quick and work in the PX tonight."

This ended the session as the boys left. Before he left, however, the therapist said to Louis on behalf of all the boys that they were going to miss him, and that all were very glad that he had been in the group. Macy said: "That's right, Louis. Mr. Ellery said it." Louis looked somewhat embarrassed, and then said: "Thanks, thanks to all of you. I'm going to see you again."

COMMENT

This session was marked by two themes: personal dignity and self-control, two topics which we decided to concentrate on because the boys we were dealing with were acting-out patients.

Richard's resolution of his conflict with Mrs. K. and his self-control demonstrated a growing capacity in that direction which could not have been possible without his first having dealt with his former tendencies to project. With the decrease of his paranoid-like reaction, resulting from his therapeutic experience in the group, his ego was able to deal with his hostile and pugnacious impulses toward Mrs. K. He gave as the reason for his self-control the desire to leave the Village. Being able to check himself, if only in the service of self-preservation, was an achievement for a boy like Richard, who had acted on impulse in the past.

There was a fleeting period of mourning when Louis announced his termination with the group, which was observed also after Donald's leaving. In the latter case it was verbalized at the session that followed.

A display of self-control was evident also in Louis's plans for his future and his unequivocal desire and confidence that he would do well in the community to which he was returning. Michael's recognition of his lack of controls employed the same theme, though in a negative way. He recognized his "temper" and confronted himself with it—a step toward ego strength, but considering Michael's clinical problem, one could not expect very radical changes.

The therapist planfully led the boys into an examination of self-control, personal worth, dignity, maturity. Jules's question demonstrated to what extent the factor of identification with the therapist as an ideal played in psychotherapy. The fact that the therapist was given a chance to describe his own developing controls was of immense value. However, the therapist seemed to display impatience and irritation when he almost chided the boys for forgetting the previous discussions of causes for negative behavior. In addition, this matter was inappropriate at this juncture, for this was not what occupied the boys' minds at the moment. They were, rather, interested in self-control and not causes. A therapist must always follow the principle of relatedness.

Richard, as well as other boys, became aware that as he acted more maturely, his parents treated him with greater deference and respect, and Richard's emotional objectivity toward his father (as well as Leonard's; see session fifty-five) further reflected maturity. The boys' hostility and guilt and resultant dependence had abated, and they could now view their parents really objectively.

However, the boys still had narrow limits for emotional tension, and this was clearly shown in their universal interest in coffee when the emotionally laden topic of fathers was discussed. The thread of the discussion was thereby broken and Michael turned the group's attention to the practical problem of job-hunting. But in this, too, a change can be noticed from indulgence in id activities (acting out) in the past to ego-oriented preoccupations. Attention need also be given to the absence of obscene language, which had been gradually diminishing for some time.

NOTE

To reinforce Louis's confidence in his successful adjustment after he left the Village, and to counteract the effect of Mrs. K.'s predictions of his failure, we decided that the group therapist should see the boy individually and reassure him that Mrs. K. did not hold the key to his destiny. A detailed rehearsal of the actual conversation was held with the therapist. Louis was scheduled to leave before the next session, but his departure was delayed until the day after so that he was able to attend it. When the therapist encountered Louis on the campus between the sessions, he had invited the boy to come to his office for a chat. The interview lasted fifteen minutes, since Louis had to go around to see a number of staff to get signatures for his discharge papers. He was very much pleased to have been asked to come and that the therapist spared the time to talk with him. The therapist told Louis that he wished to talk with him about the matter he raised in the preceding sessions about Mrs. K.'s telling him that he would "stay out of trouble for only two or three weeks after he left the Village."

The therapist explained that everyone was to some extent superstitious, but in Louis's case he was perhaps a little more superstitious about Mrs. K.'s prediction about him. The therapist said that he knew this was quite upsetting to him and that there was "a part" of him that believed it. Louis agreed, but said that he was going to make it his business to come up to the Village to see Mrs. K. after three weeks and show her that he could stay out of trouble. He further stated that he no longer believed her as much, and reminded the therapist about one of the boys in his neighborhood who he had been afraid would involve him "in trouble." This boy currently was in prison and would no longer be around. The therapist re-emphasized to Louis that he knew and respected his ability to stay out of difficulties and that he could do well because in many ways he had far more in himself than most other boys. The therapist mentioned his intelligence and his ability to think things out, which were superior to those of most boys, but wondered how this all registered "inside" of him and how he felt "inside about it." Louis said he was aware that there was "something different" about him. "I can even go to college, if I want to, because I got pretty good brains. I want to make something out of myself. Before, I didn't think I could make something out of myself. I'm glad I came to the discussions on Thursday nights, because you always seem to respect me and what I have to say, and now I believe I've got something to say." The only reason he would like to remain at the Village was the fact that he could come to discussions on Thursday nights. "I got a lot out of it. I don't know how to say thanks, but I'm goin' to say it anyway. Thanks."

The therapist told Louis that he was very happy that he had been part of the group and that he was aware of "the big decision" he "carries inside him" now: the difference between acting like a man and the way he used to act; the ability to decide for himself what was right and what was going to be part of his future, as opposed to doing things just to get in good with certain boys. Louis agreed with this, and said that he had been giving it a lot of thought. The therapist and Louis then discussed the fact that now he didn't have to think that putting up with people and not answering or fighting back was just being a "slurp," that he had to decide, as everybody did, when it was worth fighting back and when it was not and would only get one into trouble with people. Louis reminded the therapist that he was thinking about this also because "we had discussed this business of slurping in the group." His not saying anything to Mrs. K. when he was angry was his way of knowing that he "could keep his mouth shut," if "opening his mouth" was just going to make more trouble and keep him from getting what he wanted for himself. He had learned that "by figuring out what you do and what's going to come out from what you do, that maybe you don't have to worry about landing up in prison later."

Session Fifty-Seven

Leonard arrived five minutes ahead of time; the others were five minutes late save Richard, who was ten minutes late. The therapist overheard the latter say that he had visited "the other group." During the time that Leonard was alone with the therapist he first silently leafed through a magazine, but soon began to talk about his plans for "getting out." He said now he knew that he was going to leave in June, and was happy about it. Leonard actually looked happy. He was smiling— which for him was unusual—and was not wearing the frown that used to appear on his forehead from time to time. He went on to tell the therapist that he felt the Village had done a lot for him. "My mind feels much better," he said, because he did not think about a lot of things he used to. He did not specify what these were. He said, "My mind is stronger than it used to be when I came to the Village," and reminded the therapist of how he looked physically when he came to the Village. (The therapist had interviewed him on admission in the capacity of intake supervisor.) Leonard said that he walked "much better," wasn't "hunchbacked any more." (When Leonard first came to the Village, he did appear to be hunchbacked. His chest caved in, which was no longer the case.) The therapist asked Leonard if he was aware of the change in his voice. Leonard immediately smiled and said: "I know what you mean, Mr. Ellery. I can talk loud and I say what's on my mind." The therapist agreed. (There was now a much stronger quality to Leonard's voice, in contrast to his feeble, apologetic tone when he first came to the group.)

Jules was the first of the others to come into the room. No explanation was offered for his lateness, but the therapist overheard Louis saying something about the custodian not being in his office to sign the boys' passes. (The boys were required to be checked by the custodial office before they came to the group and have their passes signed, which was not done in our case.) Michael began by asking the boys what the group had been talking about the previous week. No one answered, and he turned to the therapist. The therapist commented that some of the things the group talked about included fighting, getting jobs, and the like.

In a very sketchy and nonstructured way he tried to review some of the topics discussed: Michael: "That's right. Okay, who's going to start tonight?" He then pointed to Leonard and said, "You start, Leonard." Leonard did not respond. Jules turned to Louis and said, "Last week you said you weren't going to be here, but you're here again." Louis said: "That's right. I don't mind being here. I got one more day. I'm going to be leaving in the [next] morning." Jules: "Mrs. K. has already put the hex on you?" Louis: "That's okay. I don't give a shit any more. Mr. Ellery gave me some good reinforcement this morning." He looked in the therapist's direction, smiled, and said, "Mighty grateful, Mr. Ellery." Macy took up the subject and said that Mrs. K. did this with a lot of boys, so why worry about it? The therapist caught an expression on Jules's face he could not understand at first, but then it suggested he was responding to Macy's being worried about Mrs. K.'s "mystic" powers. The therapist picked this up and said, "I think a lot of you boys have been thinking about this." Jules said tentatively: "I used to think about it, but I'm not thinking about it any more. She's crazy. She can't tell what's going to happen to me when I get out. My own father and mother can't tell, psychiatrists can't tell, so how can Mrs. K.?" Macy: "Well, she's been right so far. You remember Bill?" A discussion now arose again about Bill and what he did (stealing an automobile, crashing into a station wagon, and killing a family). Jules: "We talk about Mrs. K. too much. Let's change the subject. It's not fair to Mike and to Leonard—they're not in the same cottage. Why don't you say something, Leonard? You're always quiet." Leonard looked embarrassed but did not respond.

Despite the frequent reappearance of this topic in the past, the therapist, in conformity to the supervisory discussions, decided to re-introduce the theme of "doom" that seemed to persist in the boys' unconscious. (It should be kept in mind that all the boys in the group, with the exception of Leonard, were reared in family cultures of intense superstition and fear of the supernatural.) The therapist, therefore, raised the question of whether the boys were trying to merely avoid discussing Mrs. K. or was it some feelings that were stirred up in them that life could not be better "on the outside." Jules's response was to get up and brew a cup of coffee for himself and invite the others to do the same. All the boys joined in, but this was done expeditiously, as was also the distribution of cookies and cigarettes. The boys sat down again. Richard, who had arrived some minutes before, saying that there was "general cleanup" in his cottage every Thursday night, said that Mrs. K. was mad at the boys for coming to the group because she thought they were evading "general cleanup." Jules said with emphasis that maybe they were, but they still had the group and they would come, "general cleanup or not." Richard said that he was glad to come, because he could get out of general cleanup that way. (This may have contributed to the disapproval on the part of Mrs. K. toward the boys' attending the group.) The therapist, who had not been aware of the conflict in time, raised the question whether they could arrange for cleaning up earlier. Louis, serving as spokesman, said that the boys had already talked with Mrs. K. about it, but they had to eat their supper, and by the time they got ready to start cleaning up it was already late, and they had to stop and go to the group, and by the time they returned the "cleanup" was finished. Mrs. K. did not want to arrange "general cleanup" for any other night, he said. As if to reassure the therapist, Jules said that getting away from general cleanup was not the only reason the boys came to the group; they really liked to come.

Louis again proposed to the therapist a number of questions about how one went about getting a job, very much along the lines he had the previous week. This time, however, he was most concerned about income tax. As a result a discussion arose as to why income taxes were important. Jules said: "How can the government run? They need money for ammunition, to have a president, to have congressmen, to pay salaries, and it has to come out of our money." Macy wanted to know what would happen to him if he did not file an income tax return when he had a job, because he did not know how or when one files such returns. After the discussion had progressed for a time, the therapist suggested he would try to bring income tax forms to the next session and all could go over them together. With the help of Macy, Jules, and Michael, Louis was now trying to figure out how much money he could earn on a part-time job and realistically came up with $20 per week. If he worked a year, this would be $1,000. The therapist had told the boys that earnings of less than $600 did not have to be reported, and they would get a refund of the taxes they had paid. Louis discovered that this would not help him, because he would probably make more than $600 in a year.

Michael wanted to know why the government just couldn't print more money, since they already had the printing presses, and Jules inquired where money was made. The therapist gave them this information and some economic laws that govern the fiduciary affairs of a country. Despite the therapist's explanation of the gold standard, Michael still insisted on asking why the government did not go on printing as much money as it needed. Louis was curious as to how money bills were identified. Jules, pulling out a dollar bill from his pocket, explained the serial numbers on each bill and how the government "keeps track" of them.

Michael commented that when he got a job, he would "hang on" to his money, and he would make sure to try to spend it wisely. He knew a lot of boys in his neighborhood who, as soon as they got paid, went out and splurged; either they drank or they spent it on girls. He was not sure he would not splurge, but he knew that if he had to buy himself clothes and take care of himself, he had to "look after his money." Louis affirmed that this was exactly what he was going to do, too. When he got a job, he would ask his mother to save for him or he would go to a bank and put a "little bit" away each week, so that if he was ever out of a job, he wouldn't have to go hungry and "looking for money" or go to his mother, who did not have too much money anyway. Jules began bragging how he was going to "take out" all his friends, buy them liquor, and so forth, but Michael immediately stopped him by saying: "What are you bragging for? If you haven't got anything smart to say, just shut up!" Jules did not continue and did not appear angry at the interruption. He seemed to retreat, not saying anything further. Michael then said to the therapist: "You remember you were talking with us about being called 'punk' and getting into fights? Well, me and Louis were talking about it this week." He then reported how he and Louis happened to meet each other on the campus and somehow got to talking on this subject. Louis had said to him, "Maybe Mr. Ellery has something when he says the better man walks away from a fight, without using his fists." Louis (to the therapist): "That's right; I think you really got something there."

As if to reassure himself, Michael asked the therapist whether the latter walked away when somebody wanted to fight him. The therapist told him that he did, because he felt that he was better (superior) than anyone who tried to solve any problem by force or would be picking on him. Michael said that he realized that he had been doing this sort of thing at the Village and thought he did so only because he wanted to get home quicker by refraining from fighting. Maybe he was; "but," he added, "it's not so bad. Maybe I can make a habit of walking away when people try to beat on me." Jules still stuck to his code: Nobody was going to "beat his brains in," and if somebody started punching him, he would have to punch back. Michael: "We're not talking about defending yourself and of a case of self-defense. But when somebody challenges you to fight, and they don't hit you yet, you can walk away. There is still time." Jules: "Oh, that's what you mean? Well, yeh, that makes kinda sense!" Leonard now spoke up: "I try to do that all the time. I know I'm not the best fighter in the world and I'd rather walk away than get a black eye." Michael: "Well, I know I can get a black eye, but I also know that I can give somebody a black eye, and just knowing it makes me feel better, so I don't have to prove it all the time."

At this point, Richard, who had been relatively quiet throughout the session, said he had to go back to the cottage. This was the signal for termination. It was 8:25.

COMMENT

The special significance of this session was the increased sense of reality concerning the management of money and the provident plans for spending and saving it. Others were the mature and more secure feelings indicated by renunciation of fighting as a means for securing status and self-worth. Apparently, there occurred a strengthening of ego controls, but perhaps more importantly, self-identity had been established, as a result of which the boys did not feel the need to win fights. This was well-formulated by Leonard, though with him this may have been largely fantasy. Nonetheless, Leonard's awareness of the change in him and the therapist's observations on the improvement in this boy were very significant signs of strengthened ego and self-image.

Rising maturity among the boys was also demonstrated by their giving up their need to continue the talks about Mrs. K. They had worked the problem through; it was now behind them. She no longer exerted the same influence on them. The emotional separation from the mother figure was apparently accomplished.

NOTE

Because of the advanced stage of the group, no replacement was made for Louis. We continued for the next five months until the termination of the group with the five remaining members.

Session Fifty-Eight

(The therapist had been unable to obtain federal income tax forms as planned. Inquiry in a number of banks and the local post office brought the information that these would be available in two weeks. The therapist informed the boys of this fact at an appropriate time during the session. Jules, Michael, and Macy informed the group that during the week their class in school worked on state income tax forms.)

There was a delay of about ten minutes in getting started because of the bad walking conditions due to snow and sleet on the roads, and the need to check on passes at the "security office." Jules and Leonard, who came together about five minutes after the set time, told the therapist that they had left their cottages a little earlier than the others and were therefore able to have their passes checked sooner.

There was little communication between Leonard and Jules while they were waiting for the other boys to arrive. When the boys did come, it was obvious that there would be little discussion of significance at this session. There was a lot of chatter about the Community Center, the various coaches, and games and activities in which they had engaged during the past week. This was followed by a long discussion between Macy and Michael concerning their trip from B———, where they both resided. Michael described how the last time they had gone to B——— the train was packed and both he and Macy had to sit on their suitcases most of the way before they got seats.

When these subjects were exhausted, Michael turned to Leonard and asked him to start the discussion tonight. "Why don't you start? You don't talk much here." Leonard did not respond, but this time he did not seem so embarrassed as he had in preceding sessions under similar circumstances. Not receiving any responses from Leonard, Michael said: "Okay. What were we talking about last week?" Richard reminded Michael that the group discussed going home and what it was going to be like in "the community." Michael declared that he had it "all figured out." He was going to school and work on a part-time job. Macy and Michael now engaged in a lively conversation about the various part-time job possibilities in B———. Both boys agreed that the jobs they would probably get were as messenger boy or in a factory as shipping clerk. Both decided that they would go back to school. Michael's voice conveyed conviction and determination as he described his plan of entering high school, even though when he first came to the Village he was only in the seventh grade. He could now read above tenth-grade level, he said (this was confirmed by the educational staff), and he felt he should go to high school.

Macy changed the subject at this point to talk about a basketball game that the Village boys had played. He had forgotten the name of the school against which they had played. One of the boys mentioned one and Michael said, "That's the place the Jews come from." Macy described how the boys on "the other team," who seemed older than the Village boys, were playing "very dirty," and there was nearly a riot in the gym because boys in the bleachers wanted to jump on the opposing team. Jules said they must have gotten scared. When the therapist inquired as to why they thought "the boys were playing dirty," Jules said: "They thought they had to beat us come hell or high water. We played clean because we knew we could beat them and did not have to beat them by playing dirty like them." Michael reported that the coaches had asked the boys on the Village team "to try to play as clean as possible, just to show the other boys how a basketball game can be a fair-and-square deal." Suddenly Michael interrupted and said: "Let's get back to what we were talking about. We're changing the subject again," but Macy wanted to continue talking about the basketball game. Michael persisted. He repeated: "Let's get back to talking about what we were supposed to talk about, about going home and what we're going to do in the city. Come on Leonard, you start talking." Leonard said in a rather feeble voice: "I know what I'm going to do." Michael, however, turned his head away from Leonard, almost as if he expected to lose interest in what Leonard might say.

Jules started to prepare coffee, which, with the distribution of cookies and cigarettes, drew the boys' attention away from the discussion for about five minutes. These activities were carried out quietly and the boys were soon back in their seats.

Richard broke the momentary silence as he said: "I know what I'm going to do. I got a good deal waiting for me when I get out. All I want to do is to get out and I can't wait until June." Macy wanted to know what Richard was talking about, referring to the phrase "good deal." Richard remained rather secretive about it, however, and did not explain. He began to giggle and said: "I ain't worried about getting out of this place. I'll be okay. Everything's going to get fine as long as I get out. My stupid social worker won't tell me anything. I ask him questions about what to do—he doesn't say anything. This sister, he's a real fag." Michael interrupted to say that he was told by a boy that one of the (female) caseworkers at the Village "was laid" by him, and added teasingly: "I'm not going to tell you the name of either the boy or the social worker." However, he leaned toward the therapist, as he was sitting directly next to him, and whispered Michael's own case-worker's name, asking aloud, "You're not going to tell anybody, are you Mr. Ellery?" Therapist: "No, Mike, I will not, but I want to know what makes you so sure this happened?" Michael could not support the rumor. He merely stated that the boy had told him, and from the details the boy had given him, he was pretty sure that it actually happened. Therapist: "Mike, I just have a great deal of trouble believing it. It is not true." Michael: "You know the social worker I am talking about." Therapist: "Yes, I do, and that is why I can't believe what you're saying. Maybe the boy is not really telling you the truth." Michael laughed: "Well I believe it," but his voice lacked conviction. (This fantasy may have been the product of the boy's own projected sexual impulses toward the woman worker.)

Macy interjected: "Well, come on, Richie, tell us what you're going to do." Richard smiled nervously and with a brief laugh said: "I know what I'm going to do. Don't worry about it. I'll be all right once I get out of here." The therapist picked this up and said: "Richard, from the way you laughed, I get the feeling you're not sure. You sound a little worried." Richard did not say anything, but his smile quickly disappeared. Jules: "I got the same feeling that Richard is worried even though he's laughing." Richard: "I'm going to ask you something now. I always get the feeling that there is no point in worrying because I'm going to die soon anyway. I don't know why I say that, but I get the feeling. Oh, let me tell you a dream I had Mr. Ellery. I dreamt that I'm grown up and a big man and I'm sitting behind this big desk. There were a lot of telephones on the desk. The telephones keep ringing, people keep asking me questions, everybody wants to know what I think. I sit there with a big cigar in my mouth, my feet up on the desk. The next thing I know in the dream I see a coffin being carried and I know that it's me in the coffin. Gee, that's a real crazy feeling, to be at your own funeral."

Macy began to laugh very nervously at this. Richard said, "What the heck do you think that kind of dream means?" There was silence. Finally the therapist, addressing the boys, asked: "Do you think we can help Richard with this?" Macy, Michael, and Leonard were straining as though they were trying to unravel the meaning of the dream. After a suitable pause, the therapist asked Richard, "Do you often think about death?" Richard: "Not too often, but more and more I've been thinking about it. I know I'm going home and I want to have a good time and yet I don't know, I got a feeling that it's wrong, isn't kind of worth while, because I'm going to die young. I really worry about that." Therapist: "It sounds to me as though you feel it's almost impossible for you to have a good time; that nothing good can happen to you, something bad has got to happen." Richard: "That thing occurred to me, too. Just as I finished telling you the dream I kind of thought of that." Nothing more was said for a while. The therapist tried to continue with this topic. He said: "I wonder if there isn't something else. In your dream you seem to show that either you're all the way on top in what you got or . . ." Richard interrupted and finished the sentence: "I know, I'm all the way on the bottom. Either I'm on the top of the heap or I'm on the bottom of the heap." Then, with desperation in his voice: "I can't think any more! I can't think any more! I'm so fuckin' confused." There was now dead silence in the room.

Macy said to Richard, "What are you trying to say?" Richard's response was as follows: "When I get out of Children's Village I want to take a job. I want a good job," though he did not exactly know what job was a good job. "My father tells me I should take any job I like, even if it doesn't pay much money. The important thing is that I work at something I enjoy. My mother, she don't think like my father. She wants me to take a job where I make a lot of money but where I don't get dirty, like I wear a suit, a white shirt, and a tie for the job." He then proceeded to say that in the Village he had been working in the auto shop and found that he was very much interested in auto mechanics. When he got out he would like to learn more about it and maybe become an auto mechanic. He tried to talk to his mother about this, but he gathered from her expression that she was not keen on his becoming a mechanic, whereas his father did not care. The father said if he liked it, he should try to learn the trade and his father would help him. The father said to Richard, "Maybe you can make a career out of this." "But my mother wants me to go to college. I'd like to go to college." Michael interjected: "Sure, you get yourself a good education." Richard: "Yeah. I could get a good education, but I'm not sure yet what I want to be. I don't want to feel I got to go to college."

Leonard: "You don't have to go to college if you don't want to." Richard: "Suppose my mother wants me to go to college. If I go to college I can't be sure it's because I want to, or because my mother wants me to go." The therapist commented: "Sounds as though you've got to please three people." Richard at once recognized the implication of the statement and said, "Yeah, my mother, my father, and myself." Jules seemed sympathetic to Richard in his dilemma. He said: "Shit, that's a pretty rough one. How can you please three people at the same time? But you should respect your parents and do what they want you to do." Richard, perplexed: "What do you do if your parents don't agree on what they want you to do?" Jules insisted that one should respect one's parents. Richard: "Well, yeah. They gave you life. I owe my life twice to my parents. First time they had me born, the second time—remember how I told you once how I fell off a roof, or out of the window rather —my father caught me in his arms and saved my life. I owe him a lot." The therapist at this juncture decided to introduce an examination of the feeling of obligation toward parents (and resulting submission and guilt). Therapist: "What was your father supposed [expected] to do?" Richard stopped short and looked at the therapist perplexed and very serious: "I don't know what he was supposed to do. I guess he was supposed to catch me. I would do it to my kid." Jules repeated: "But shouldn't you respect your parents? Be what they want you to be, because you owe your life to your parents."

This question was addressed directly to the therapist, who said: "I have another question maybe we could kick around. That is, did you ever think of what parents owe to children?" Jules: "No, I never thought that way." Macy derisively: "Parents owe to children? Parents don't owe anything to children! It's children who owe everything to parents." Therapist: "Boy, that sounds like some bargain!" Michael, turning to the therapist: "If you had a kid, wouldn't you feel that he should do everything you ask?" Therapist: "I would feel that in becoming a parent, in creating life, I take on a big obligation and my obligation as a parent is that I have to help my kid become whatever he is capable of becoming, the thing in him we call *potential*. I feel I should help my kid to find out what he wants, what he can do best, and even though it may not be the same thing I can do best, to help him find the way to become that." The eyes of all the boys were riveted on the therapist, and he continued. "Look boys, I'm a social worker and I like being a social worker, but I know that I can't be a mechanic because I don't have the talent. There are a lot of other things I can be, and can't be. Now it doesn't mean there is anything wrong with me because I can't be a mechanic, and it doesn't mean that a social worker is better than a mechanic or vice versa. It just means that I can only become what I have a talent for becoming. Now if my mother said that I have to be a doctor and forced me to be a doctor, I might become a doctor, but I would be pretty miserable at being one if I didn't really want to be one. So I figure, if I feel that way it means that other people, too, can't be what they're not." Michael broke in: "That's what Shakespeare said, ain't it? 'To be or not to be . . .' " Jules quickly finished the quotation: "That's the question." A very deep silence pervaded the room. After a while Michael said, "Then, what does it mean, that all people should be equal?" No one answered this and the therapist said: "It means that all people have the right to discover what they can be and what they are good at, and should have the opportunity to become that. That might include the right to go to school, the right to get an education." Richard interrupted and said: "There's nothing wrong with being a mechanic if you want to be a mechanic. I got a hunch I could be a pretty good mechanic."

It was now 8:35, and Leonard began to get ready to leave. Michael and Jules asked Leonard to sit down, Michael adding, "Every time it comes to half-past eight I hate it, because I want to stay." Leonard said he had to go back to his cottage, and the session ended at this point.

COMMENT

For several sessions now one or another of the boys had been taking the initiative in starting the discussions. In this session, Michael took the first step as he invited Leonard to start. Richard's effort at concealment of his doubts and insecurities relative to his future and his feelings of failure was recognized by the boys, since they were now more psychologically insightful. Their prodding him brought forth his dream, which led to a very fruitful reality-oriented discussion and conclusions. Of particular value in the onward movement toward maturity was the disturbing discovery of their basic submissiveness to parents (of which they must be freed). The therapist utilized the opportunity that was offered him to discuss the "basic neurosis" in all humans, namely, submission to parents, especially the mother. It was to this unconscious problem that the boys had largely abreacted to by social and delinquent behavior. Further elaboration and repetition of the topic was in order for the future.

Session Fifty-Nine

ABSENT: Macy, who attended about eight minutes of the session.

The boys arrived on time. Macy came in dressed up. He told the therapist that he had to go on a roller-skating trip, but wanted to come even if it was only for a little while. He wanted to be told when it was seven o'clock. When it was time, he appeared very reluctant to go. Jules commented: "You really don't want to go; you want to stay." Macy laughed briefly and said, "Yeah, I would like to stay tonight, but I better go because I promised I'd go." Whereupon he left to join the roller-skating trip, arranged for his class by the chaplain.

About ten minutes were then spent in preparing and distributing refreshments and cigarettes and in small talk about cottage events. The group seemed "unsettled," though not nervous or fidgety. Richard told the therapist that he had talked with Louis on the phone, and Louis said he might visit the group sometime next month. Louis would not tell him the exact date, since he wanted "to surprise" the therapist and the boys. Michael said he looked forward to seeing Louis again, and Jules commented that Louis "was a lot of fun while he was in the group," and that maybe when Louis came they could "throw him a party." Michael wondered how Louis was getting along "on the outside," and asked whether the therapist had heard from him. The therapist told Michael that he had not.

The boys now settled down and Michael asked: "Where did we leave off last week?" When no one responded, he turned to the therapist and asked him the same question. The therapist said that he thought the group had talked about obligations to parents and the like. Michael: "Oh, yeah! That's right. Maybe we ought to talk about this some more." Leonard stirred in his seat and said, "Okay. If we want to talk about it, let's start talking about it." Michael invited Leonard to initiate the discussion, but Leonard did not take him up on it, remaining silent.

Jules stretched himself out in a lounging posture in his armchair. Richard, instead, launched into a report about the preceding week end, on which he had visited his home. He and his father had gone out for a ride on the highway when all of a sudden he noticed that the speedometer in his father's car was not working. Richard felt that his father exceeded the speed limit. "I started to get scared, because since the speedometer wasn't working, I didn't know how fast the wheels were going; I had a hunch we were going too fast. We were passing everybody. In fact, my father when he would see somebody in a lane going a little slow would zoom around him like crazy." Richard described how he felt that his father "didn't know what the hell he was doing." Richard had asked his father to slow down. He demonstrated how his father had turned to him with anger and told him to mind his own business. "What are you, chicken?" asked the father. Richard said to his father, "Hey, dad. I'm just asking you to be careful; don't get mad." Richard, now standing up, went on to describe examples of his father's speeding and inconsistent way of driving. Once when a car passed them, Richard asked his father jokingly: "How come you let everybody pass you?"

Following this remark, his father "zoomed on." Jules: "You stupid idiot. You started it all." Richard: "Maybe I did." Richard continued to say that it didn't make sense to him. His mother wanted to drive the car, but his father would not allow her to take instruction so that she could get a license. He told her that she would never be a good driver. In fact, when Richard asked his father whether he would teach him how to drive when he got older, his father said, "I'm not so sure you could ever be a good driver."

There was a faint smile playing on Richard's face as he was relating these incidents. It was almost as if he were making an effort to divorce himself from having feelings about them. When he had stopped this narrative, Jules and Michael began to talk about Richard's father, Michael saying the father was "just trying to act like a big shot, zooming down a highway with a car where you can get killed. If I had a car I wouldn't drive like that. I'd be careful because I want to live." Jules said, "Me too, why should I drive crazy and want to get myself killed?"

The therapist raised the question about the inconsistency in Richard's father's conduct, and said: "I feel slightly confused about all this. I remember you telling us that your father is always trying to get you to obey the law, got mad at you when you didn't go to school, when you played hooky, when you didn't get good grades, when you used to lift things from shops, and he somehow doesn't show any respect for the law himself. What do you make of this, Richard?" Richard did not react to this. Instead, he proceeded to describe some of the things his father did. When he went shopping with his father, for example, his father would buy twenty-five cans of beer and ask Richard to carry the package to the car. There was something about the way his father behaved that gave Richard a feeling that his father tried to conceal from Richard that he had the beer. Richard and his father seemed to engage in a cat-and-mouse game, with Richard pretending that he did not know what was in the package. When they reached home his father stealthily placed the beer in the refrigerator. "Who he hides it from I don't have the slightest idea," declared Richard. Richard just as stealthily went to the refrigerator and "stole" a couple of cans of beer and drank them. When his father discovered the missing beer, he would chide Richard in a semihumorous vein, half-angry and half-proud of him. Richard then stated that his father did not appear to be too upset when he saw Richard in a semidrunken state. The therapist attempted to explore how Richard felt about these goings on and specifically put the following question to him: "Doesn't this leave you a little confused? You are expected to be a good boy, follow rules and regulations, on the one hand, and there is a kind of flaunting of rules and regulations on the other."

Without waiting for Richard's answer, Michael interrupted and asked the boys their religions, and from this arose a discussion of Ash Wednesday, with Jules wanting to know how come he hadn't gotten his ashes yet? This continued for a short while, then Jules started to prepare coffee. With Michael's participation, he served coffee to everybody in the room, and handed out cookies. Jules was still in the process of brewing his own coffee at the end of the room, when all of a sudden he said, "I remember having some pretty crazy dreams a long time ago." He went on to say that he did not remember how old he was, maybe about ten or eleven, but it happened twice that he had a dream in which he was lying in bed and his father came over to him, put a shotgun right between his eyes, and was about to pull the trigger when Jules woke up. He screamed with fear and his mother came running. She sat on the bed next to him and comforted him. A moment later he said: "I had a second crazy dream, and that was I was lying in bed and I was kind of half-awake, half-asleep, and all of a sudden I see my father coming after me with a club like he's going to bash my head in. I woke up again and screamed, and my mother came in the room again and said, 'Shh, shh, it's just a dream.' " Uncomfortable laughter rippled through the room when Richard said, "There goes the unconscious mind again." The therapist asked Jules what he thought the dream meant, but he did not know, nor did the others. (The therapist remarked in his report: "Something warned me that the latent content in this dream had better remain untouched, that it might prove to be too upsetting. It appeared like an Oedipal dream, but I could not be certain of it. In fact, I felt blocked as to the meaning of it, so I let it slide.")

Jules's dream spurred Richard into describing how he had recently begun to tell his mother his dreams. He said, "You remember about the dreams I told you in the group?" When he told them to his mother, she asked, "You still having those nightmares?" This got him very angry. (It seemed that it was her disdain that disturbed him.) He had always had nightmares as a child, and when he would wake up at night agitated, his mother would come into the room and call him "dopey." He said: "After we talked about it here, Mr. Ellery, I know that all the boys have dreams and sometimes have nightmares and you are not dopey [because of that], but I couldn't tell my mother about it. I told her that I don't think I'm dopey any more, and that I can have dreams if I want to just as everybody else can have dreams." Suddenly he switched to talking about his cottage and the chores. The change was as complete as it was surprising. The minute Richard did this, Michael chidingly said: "There you go, Richard, changing the subject. That isn't what you were talking about."

Michael, who was sitting next to the therapist, nudged him with his elbow as if he were in league with the therapist. Then, to Richard: "Why don't you get back to tell us how your father shows you how to be a crook?" Richard's face reddened with anger, but he did not say anything. The therapist said, addressing the group: "I wonder, did this happen only to Richard? I mean, this being told to be a good boy, follow rules and regulations, and all of a sudden you find that the people who tell you these things are not doing them themselves." Michael: "It happened to me. Once my mother had a TV man repair our set and she owed him $25, which she paid him. When the man left the set broke down. The man refused to fix it again. My mother threatened to kill him. I don't remember how she threatened to kill him—with a knife or something else—but she spent the night in jail. I was sorry it happened. She shouldn't have threatened him. She should have taken the guy to court. I didn't like the idea of my mother having to go to jail."

Michael continued, saying that when he stole it was because he didn't have anything in the house like the many things other boys had and he just decided "to take them." Richard said he had stolen because his parents never stopped him. They didn't seem to know what he was doing and he wanted his parents to stop him, but they didn't. Jules spoke up and said: "Aw, come on. You know you stole for revenge. You're always sore at your parents." Michael said: "That's right, admit it, Richard. You stole because you wanted revenge on your parents." Richard thought for a while and then said, "There are times when I get so mad at those parents of mine. Like the last week end when I was home on a visit. My father gave me $35 to go buy a suit. I went out and I couldn't find anything I really liked for $35, so I came back and gave the money to my mother. Then my father accused my mother of taking the $35 and using it for herself. Before I knew it, there was a fight between the two of them." As Richard was narrating this incident the same faint smile described earlier played on his face. There was a quality of forced detachment in his attitude.

Therapist: "Richard, how did you feel when this fight was going on?" Richard: "What do you mean?" Therapist: "Well, I see a smile on your face. Did you really feel like smiling when all this happened?" Suddenly Richard's expression changed. His face grew a deep red, his jaw set, and clenching his fists he shook them, exclaiming: "I'll tell you how I felt! I felt like jumping in there with my two fists and just start pounding away at my father. He's a crazy bastard. He's always looking for a fight with my mother. I came into the room and tried to explain to my father how my mother happened to have the money, that I gave it to her. All of a sudden, my father turns on me and he says, 'Who the hell asked you?' He was going to punch me, but I got out of the way." His father threatened that, if he did not mind his own business, the next time he tried to interfere he was going to get "the fucking shit kicked out" of him. Richard sat back in a state of complete physical and emotional exhaustion.

Nothing more was said by anyone. After a pause, Michael asked Richard if he was an only child. Richard said: "No, I got one sister and a kid brother. That's also the trouble. My sister is always taking my things, breaking my records. I come home I don't know what records are going to be there and, I don't know, she brings friends up to the house and when I'm home it's like I don't belong there." Michael then asked Jules if he was an only child and Jules said: "No, I got an older sister. She's pretty good, but sometimes she can't keep her hands off my things." A three-way conversation sprang up among Michael, Jules, and Richard, with each complaining of how his sister took his things. The therapist's attempts to explore their feelings in terms of sibling rivalry and the need for attention from parents fell flat. (Obviously, the boys were not ready for it, or were preoccupied with other subjects.) The discussion about siblings bogged down into just a listing of complaints which began to grow to gigantic proportions, but the therapist had the feeling that the boys were very little emotionally involved in the topic.

The discussion seemed to peter out and the therapist changed the subject in response to an earlier inquiry by Jules whether the therapist brought along income tax forms. Each boy was given a short form and, led by the therapist, all studied the various items on the forms during the remaining ten minutes of the session. The therapist was impressed with the fact that every boy in the room was able to read with ease. The boys asked questions as to the meaning of terms like "dependents," "exemptions," and such. These were explained to them. Jules took out a pencil from his pocket and filled out each question and then showed it to the therapist. He had filled out the form rather completely. The others did not fill them out; they rather discussed the various items on the forms.

COMMENT

Louis had emerged as the "leader" (instigator) of the group after Donald had left, with Macy ranking second. The absence of both Donald and Louis made the boys anxious and fidgety. (A similar reaction occurs also in flocks of birds and herds of mammals in the absence of the "leader.") The expectation that Louis would visit settled the group down somewhat, and the boys continued with their discussion of parents where they had left off the previous week. Note need be taken of the fact that the boys again initiated the interview, in which Michael took on the leadership role. In the conversation that ensued, Richard con-

tinued to be critical of his (delinquent) father, whom he had staunchly
defended in the past, thereby displaying his newly acquired individuality (self-identity), which would help him break through his delinquent pattern now that he had a more wholesome frame of reference
—the therapist and the group mores.

The therapist made the error of reflecting on Richard's father, which
Richard could not accept. The "new father" attacked the old one, and
this Richard could not sustain. Therefore, he ignored the therapist's
statement. Unfortunately, the therapist did not register Richard's discomfiture and followed the same line again, at which point Michael
"rescued" both the therapist and Richard. This is a rather important
point in psychotherapy. The therapist should not reflect negatively
upon a parent, even if the patient is violently engaged in attacking him.
It is one thing for the patient to disparage his parent, but quite another
when the therapist joins in. The patient's guilts are aroused by this.
The therapist's conduct also set up anxiety in the other boys: Michael
interrupted to speak of Ash Wednesday and Jules began to prepare
coffee.

However, the discussion of fathers brought to Jules's mind the dreams
of his adoptive father's assaults on him. Here the therapist exercised better
judgment as he followed the basic rule of psychotherapy: "When in
doubt, don't." Richard's telling of relating his dreams to his mother
set up anxiety in him and he suddenly changed to a neutral subject—
the chores in the cottage—though the theme was "mothers." Michael,
who had assumed leadership, pointed out to Richard his resistance
maneuvers.

Unfortunately, the therapist again returned (countertransferentially)
to degrading parents, and Michael, sensing the therapist's interest and
trying to please him and be in league with him, narrated the incident
between his mother and a TV repairman, and her incarceration. There
is little value in debasing parents as had been done in this session, and
apparently the line taken resulted from the confusion between recalling
and living through traumatic experiences with parents, on the one hand,
and exposing them, on the other. After all, the boys would have to live
with their parents; while their relations needed to be less of dependency
and less emotionally charged, they did not need to be those of disdain
and contempt.

What followed pointed up the boys' gains in psychological literacy
and objectivity. They recognized the revenge element in their stealing.
The therapist did well to activate Richard to relive his rage at his father
for his fighting his mother and thus divest himself of this feeling. This
was followed, through free association, with feelings of anger against

siblings. By contrast to their hostility toward their parents, this topic was anticlimactic, but it served as an escape from the tension created by the former topic—parents.

Session Sixty

The session began promptly at seven o'clock. Macy and Jules proceeded at once to prepare coffee and passed it and cookies to everyone in the room. Macy appeared depressed. From bits of the conversation among Jules, Richard, and Macy, the therapist gathered that Macy was having a very rough time of it in his cottage. (The day before the session the therapist had received a telephone call from the cottage supervisor to say that Mrs. K. was complaining about Macy's assertiveness, lack of promptness, and similar matters. The supervisor felt that Macy "was just being himself for a change" and was less submissive and tame than formerly. Mrs. K. was again blaming the group for this change in Macy. Though the supervisor had not mentioned it, the group therapist suggested that Macy might be reacting to the death of his father.)

Macy began by saying he did not want to talk about his cottage any more, he was very tired of the subject. Yet he looked concerned. The therapist remarked that Macy looked upset. Jules immediately stepped in and said that something had happened that he wanted to ask the therapist about. Mr. K. called the boys together and told them that he was aware that they had been talking against him in the group. He told them: "I don't mind if you talk about me as long as I'm there to defend myself." What Jules wanted to know was, how did Mr. K. know that there had been talk about him in the group discussions. He added: "Somebody here is talking to Mr. K. about it." After this the boys were silent, and the therapist asked whether they thought he had talked to Mr. K. There was no immediate answer, and then Richard, serving as spokesman, said in a very hesitant but unconvincing tone that he did not think that the therapist had been speaking with Mr. K.

Sensing the boys' suspiciousness, the therapist told them that he would give them his word that he had not spoken to Mr. K. about what the boys had said in the group discussions, Macy said reassuringly: "That sounds all right with us, Mr. Ellery. We believe you. I think Mr. K. was just trying to fish to find out what we talk about here." He then went on to explain that he and Mrs. K. were "just not getting along." He felt that one of the problems was that he did not "snap to attention" any more. Macy snapped his fingers as if to demonstrate what he meant. For instance, when she wanted him to do a chore he did it, but he did not jump and say, "Yes, ma'am."

Looking very despondent, Macy continued, saying about Mr. K.: "He's a pretty nice guy." The other boys who lived in the same cottage nodded their heads in assent. The therapist tried to help Macy verbalize his feelings, and asked him if he could specifically describe exactly what was bothering him. Macy: "*I am trying to not be a baby any more,* but they make it so hard in that cottage not to be a baby. I don't want to be a goody-goody, and now everybody tells me they are disappointed in me." He then went on to say that Mr. K. had slapped him just the other day. This, according to him, did not arise out of anything that had happened between himself and Mr. K., but Mr. K. appeared to be very disturbed at seeing his wife upset because of Macy, so Mr. K. took it upon himself to slap him in the face. Jules continued to defend Mr. K., saying: "He is just a nice guy and what can he do? Mrs. K. is his wife." (This theme had appeared in several other sessions.)

The therapist tried to explore whether the boys really felt so positive toward Mr. K., since he seemed to let Mrs. K. run the cottage instead of his doing it. Richard: "If I was Mr. K. I wouldn't know what to do either. Mrs. K. is such a bitch, what can he do but kind of knuckle under to her? She wants everything her way. She's got him wrapped around her little toes and she's going to see to it that everything goes her way. He ain't going to buck her in that cottage." Macy murmured: "But I get mad at that bastard, too" (referring to Mr. K.). Previously all his anger had been directed toward the wife. Macy said, among other things, that Mr. K. "just doesn't have balls. He gave his balls to Mrs. K., so he is the weak guy there."

Having divested himself of some of his anger, Macy now voluntarily revealed that he "fools around a lot" and that he "gets hit for fooling around" when all he's doing "is having fun." He described a number of incidents of playfulness involving other boys. He always did this, he said, when some staff member was present. However, he could not understand why they should get so irritated with him. Michael quickly said, with finality: "Ain't any such thing as fooling around." Macy did not seem to hear this and began to describe an incident in which the entire cottage group had been punished because several boys had "stepped out of line," which included throwing snowballs at the associate cottage father. While the group was in the dining room, Macy had begun to hum a religious song. When the associate father objected to this, Macy's response was: "Hey, what do you want from me? I'm singing a religious song. Mind your own business!" Everyone in the group broke into loud laughter at this. Macy, in surprise, asked: "What are you laughing at?" When no one answered him, Macy, too, sat quietly. Finally the therapist said, "Did you sing that song because you were feeling religious?" Macy laughingly said, "No, I just wanted to get him mad." Jules: "So why can't you say so? You wanted to get him mad. That's what we're talking about. You fuck around to get people mad." Then, turning to the therapist: "But Mr. Ellery, that's crazy. When we fool around we're trying to have fun and people get mad at us. We don't want to get them mad, and yet you said we do get them mad. How come?"

The therapist reminded the boys of a previous discussion about this subject, and pointing to his head said: "Remember—conscious, . . ." Jules immediately finished, "Unconscious mind." Therapist: "Okay, what did we say fellows? There is a part of you that forces you to do things for reasons you don't understand, and it has to do with your feelings that are buried inside of you. It is possible that, although with your conscious mind you see fooling around as having fun, with your unconscious mind having fun really means getting somebody, an adult probably, mad at you." Michael said: "This makes sense. Go on, Mr. Ellery, explain." Macy: "Why should I want to get people mad when I'm not really mad at them? I don't feel mad. All I think is that I'm fooling around with somebody but I know I'm getting them mad anyway." Therapist: "Everything you do has a reason for it. I know it sounds strange to you now, but when you understand the reason it won't sound so strange. Did you ever hear of the word *transference*?"

Richard: "Yeah, I heard it." Reflecting a while he said, "It means taking something from one place and putting it in another place." Therapist: "That's right, Richard. That's exactly what I mean. Transference means taking your feelings that have developed in you ever since childhood about the people who are close to you and then putting these feelings on other people and treating them just as you learned to treat the first people when you were a child." Jules: "Give us an example, Mr. Ellery." Macy: "How does that work?" Richard immediately stepped in and said: "You mean when I'm sore at my father, maybe sometimes I take it out on my mother. It is easier to take it out on my mother than on my father, even though I'm really sore at my father." Michael: "You hate somebody because they remind you of somebody else." Therapist: "That's right." Jules: "Go ahead, Mr. Ellery, you give an example."

Therapist: "Okay. Let me see. Look, I've had a hard day at the office. My boss screamed at me, and yet I'm afraid to answer him back. I'm afraid that, if I answer back, he'll fire me, I'll lose my job. So I keep my feelings in, and go home. I open the door, and as I step in my wife says to me, 'Would you mind wiping your feet?' and I say:

'Who the hell are you to tell me to wipe my feet? This is my home!' "
The boys began to laugh at this, and Jules said: "I get it. You're really
talking to your boss, but you take it out on your wife because you're not
afraid of your wife." (Although this was displacement and the explanation was technically incorrect, the therapist thought that he had nonetheless gotten across the *idea* of transference and did not contradict it.)
Jules then said: "But I'm not afraid of my mother any more; she treats
me nice. I'm not afraid of my father."

Michael said to him: "Are you crazy? Remember that dream you
told us about last week?" Jules said, "What dream?" "That dream where
your father put the shotgun up between your eyes." Jules, looking at
the therapist, said: "I'm not afraid of my father. I stand up to him.
When he gets sore I yell at him." Gazing directly at Jules, the therapist
said, "If you're not afraid of him then why are you yelling at him?"
Jules broke into laughter and said, "That's a good question." Michael:
"Damn good question; medal, Mr. Ellery! If you are not mad at people,
you don't yell at them. When I used to get mad at my mother I used
to go out at night and forget to come home." Richard: "Well, that's
what I did, and then my mother would really burn. I knew she would
burn in her stomach. I couldn't yell back at her. I couldn't even answer
her. She would talk me down, but I knew that by staying out late I
really fixed her wagon."

The therapist added by way of explanation: "The way you learn
to handle your parents as children is the way you handle all adults."
Jules: "We never did that to you, did we Mr. Ellery?" Michael: "We
always liked you. We never tried to get you mad." The therapist smiled:
"Remember what it was like in the beginning when we first started
together?" Macy: "I remember. Somebody here once tried to play
basketball in the room." Michael, kiddingly: "Yeah? Who? Who? (It
was Michael who had once tried to break up a session by playing basketball with a wad of paper and a wastepaper basket.) Jules: "I remember
when Michael and Louis used to play cards. I'll bet they did that just
to see if they could get your goat!" Richard, reflectively: "So that's the
way we get people mad!" However, he backtracked and began to talk
about the "relief man" at his cottage and how unfair he was with the
boys. This was a transparent, though feeble, effort and the therapist
did not react to it.

It was now closing time and the therapist ended the session.

COMMENT

In working through their attitudes toward their cottage parents,
the boys were actually attaining emotional clarification in relation to

their natural parents. The reversed roles of Mr. and Mrs. K. and their differential attitudes toward the boys in many respects resembled conditions in the boys' homes, and as the boys learned to deal with the problems in the cottages, they were preparing to deal more adequately with their families when they returned home.

The boys' becoming aware now that their "fooling around" actually represented acts of hostility had significance and obvious importance, both for psychological literacy and ego-strengthening. It was particularly valuable that they were here able to reflect, in the light of their new awareness and controls, on the aggressive and disturbing way they behaved in early sessions of the group.

Session Sixty-One

ABSENT: Jules, in the infirmary with a chest cold.

The session began promptly at seven o'clock. About ten minutes were consumed at the outset in preparing coffee and passing around cookies and cigarettes. Richard and Michael carried on a dialogue about transition conferences. Then Richard asked the therapist whether he attended these conferences. This perennial question had not been asked for some time, and now it made its appearance again. The therapist again said that he did not attend these conferences. Richard reported that his cottage father, Mr. K., had told him that he should "behave himself" if he wanted a good report. It was important that he show he was worthy of such a report. Richard's understanding from Mr. K.'s statement was that he was expected to behave himself at least during the period before the transition conference, just for the sake of getting a good report. Richard said: "If that is all they want from me, that's not so bad. But why should I behave only during that time? I can behave most of the time now." Michael commented that that was pretty silly, to ask you to behave just to get a good report. He thought you were expected to behave well most of the time.

Richard reported at some length on his interview with the psychiatrist. He repeated the conversation he had had with the doctor. The psychiatrist, according to Richard, kept asking him, "How do you know you are not going to steal when you get home?" Richard told him that he felt that he did not have to steal any more, that he understood many of the reasons why he got in trouble before, and that some of the reasons had to do with getting back at his parents. When the doctor asked Richard where he had learned this, he said that he learned it through the group discussions. The doctor asked Richard who helped him most at the Village. Richard said Mr. Ellery helped him most in the group discussions, because in these discussions the boys sat around discussing their problems, and he found in this way that he wasn't the only one who had problems. "I told the doctor I now know where some of my problems come from and that's because for a long time I couldn't tell my parents what I really thought about them and how I felt about certain things they would always ask me to do."

Richard was very wary of the psychiatrist. "I kept feeling that he was trying to catch me," he said. To support this, he said the doctor had repeated the question about stealing ten minutes later. Richard felt angry and wanted to say: "Why are you asking me this question again? I thought I answered it before," but he withheld this response because he did not want to antagonize the doctor. He felt that the doctor would have a great influence in the transition conference. In a rather amusing way, at least to the other boys in the room, Richard described how he gave answers to the doctor other than those he would have liked to give. This brought a thunder of laughter. It seemed that the psychiatrist and Richard had played a game of cat-and-mouse.

When Richard finished, the therapist asked him why he had tried to be so funny with the doctor, *funny* being the word Richard himself had used. Richard thought for a while and then said that the psychiatrist was trying to find out if he were "crazy" and indicated that he had to be cautious with the doctor on this score. Then, looking directly at the therapist, Richard asked: "You don't think I'm crazy, do you Mr. Ellery?" Therapist: "No, I do not Richard." Richard then stated that in previous interviews with the same psychiatrist, the latter had asked him all sorts of "crazy questions." "He once asked me if I ever slept with my mother." Michael immediately popped up with: "That's a damn crazy question to ask! It's none of his business, and he's got no right to ask those kind of questions." Macy said that this psychiatrist had once asked him, too, something like that and that he lost his temper with him. On one occasion, Richard said, the psychiatrist said to him, "Did you ever feel like doing it to your sister?" Richard had asked: "What do you mean doctor, by 'doing it to your sister'?" The doctor said to him: "You know what I mean. Why don't you want to talk about it?" Richard said he didn't know what to say, he was very angry inside when this question was asked of him, so he just shut up and he didn't answer. "You can't trust him because he asks you these real crazy questions that are none of his business—and besides, what is he trying to do, drive you crazy?" There was a long pause after this point. Richard got up to refill his coffee cup.

Nothing was said during a long interval. Richard then said he "can't wait to get out of here." As far as he knew he would be going late in June, early July, or in September. The psychiatrist had asked him:

"Suppose you don't get out in June, are you going to run away?" Richard had told the doctor: "I'm not going to run away. It is not going to do me any good. If I have waited this long, I can wait a little longer." The doctor didn't say anything in response.

Michael repeated he could hardly wait to get out of the Village and get back to B———. However, Richard seemed bent on continuing to talk about his interview with the psychiatrist. He had mentioned in the course of that interview, in response to a question as to whom he missed most in his life, that he was not sure, but said something about his grandfather. His grandmother, his mother's mother, was still living, and sometimes when he looked at her he got a very funny feeling. Sometimes he saw his grandfather's face in place of hers. Richard described an incident of about a year ago when he was home and was sitting at the table, eating. His grandmother was there and she called him by his name. For a minute, Richard said, he looked startled, and his grandmother asked what was the matter. When Richard recovered he told his grandmother, "Nothing grandma, nothing's the matter." Richard said, "The matter was that from the way she called me, for a moment I thought I heard my grandfather's voice calling me."

In response to the therapist's question about the "funny feeling," Richard tried to be more specific. He said that he was not sure what it was, but as he thought back he really liked his grandfather. In fact, when his mother and father used to give him a "hard time," his grandfather would always give him candy and sometimes extra money that made it possible for him to go to the movies after his parents had punished him and denied him money for this purpose. His mother and grandfather always used to fight about this, and his grandfather would say to his mother: "Look, he's just a little boy. Don't be so hard on him."

Macy said: "It's nice to have grandparents. Sometimes they can help you when your own parents don't have the money. Sometimes they can even buy you clothes when your parents can't buy them." Richard: "Yeah, that's what used to happen to me, and that's why I still kind of miss my grandfather. When my grandfather died I was so upset I cried for a couple of days." Michael: "That's a pretty long time to cry, Richard." Richard: "Maybe, but I still get a very funny feeling about him dying, and I don't know what that feeling is." Nothing more was said on this subject, and the therapist asked Richard if he could talk more about "this feeling." Richard: "I want to, but I don't know how to put it. It is something I just can't put straight into words. I guess you have a lot of feelings when people die, right?" The therapist agreed. Michael turned to the therapist: "Do you know what some of these feelings are?" Therapist: "Maybe I do, Mike. I know what everybody feels when someone close to them dies, no matter how old they are. This feeling is guilt." Richard seemed to echo this in a somewhat questioning tone: "Feeling guilty, Mr. Ellery? I had nothing to feel guilty about that I know. I just know I missed my grandfather a great deal. Could there be another feeling?" Therapist: "Well, sometimes there is another feeling, as when somebody you like and are close to dies. You feel angry because you feel they have left you and you want them back." Richard nodded very slowly and thoughtfully.

Immediately Macy said: "I know what that feels like. I was reading *The Reader's Digest* in my cottage the other day, and they tell a story about a man dying and how the doctors would put their hands on the man's chest and they would rub the man's chest. I think it's something like you are supposed to massage the heart and this brought the man back to life. Since I read the story I had the feeling that if I were home when my father died maybe I could have saved him." (Macy's father had passed away a month before, it will be recalled.) Macy said that maybe he could have massaged his father's chest and could have prevented his dying. He described how he was very angry at the doctor, who did not save his father, even though his father was already dead when the doctor arrived.

Michael said to Macy: "I don't think you could have saved your father. I think you are blaming yourself for something you couldn't have done." Macy looked inquiringly at the therapist as if seeking confirmation. The therapist told Macy that what he had in mind was massaging of the heart. For this the chest has to be cut open and this requires very special surgery which Macy could not have done, and even then the chances of reviving someone are very small. The therapist was rather definite that there was not a thing in the world that he could have done, aside from the fact that he was not even at home when it happened. Macy: "I know, I know. It's just something I was thinking about, and sometimes you wish you could have been home and done something about it. I know I was pretty angry because my father passed away. My mother was left alone, she was pretty upset, and I couldn't be with her right away." He then described at some length how he had found out from Mr. K. about his father's death. Mr. K. had apparently told him very sensitively and had helped Macy pack and get off to B——— for the funeral.

The therapist commented briefly that what Macy had said confirmed the theory that there was a factor of guilt present among the survivors of the dead. Macy looked very solemn and tears welled up in his eyes. He said: "It's not easy when you love somebody, somebody who sometimes gave you a hard time and was good to you at the same time and they pass away. It leaves you feeling kind of mixed up." Then, almost as if to reassure the therapist quickly, he said he did not want his father to pass away. This seemed to be an extremely sensitive area for Macy, and the therapist did not continue with it beyond commenting that sometimes people feel mixed up because at times in the past they may have had angry feelings toward those who passed away and feel that they should not have had these feelings. Richard: "Yeah, I guess in a way that's it. Maybe that's what's bothering Macy. It's kind of unfair; nobody lives too long anyway. There's not enough time to do all the things you want to do in life and then you die. I wish I could live for a thousand years, but I know I can't, so I'm going to try to make the best out of my life for the time that I'm going to be here."

A brief silence ensued; then Michael asked if the therapist had read in the papers about the man who had killed the little girl. (Michael was referring to the case of rape and murder of a four-year-old girl by an elderly man which filled the headlines for some days at the time.) Michael wished he could get his "hands on this guy." He would "hang him by his balls." This now became the topic of conversation among Richard, Macy, and Michael: getting hold of "this guy and killing him." Richard thought they ought to give a medal to the executioner who pulled the switch when this man was electrocuted, but Leonard said, "Nobody has the right to kill anybody, even if he is an executioner." Richard thought about it for a while and said: "I've begun to think that way, too. It ain't going to bring this girl back if they kill the man. He's just psycho and you're not going to make him better by putting him in the chair." Richard described the reaction of the people in the crowds as he had read in the newspapers and seen it on television. He wanted to know why these people were so angry, since it was not their child. Therapist: "Does anybody have any idea about this?" Nobody seemed to have any notion as to why the people were so angry. Richard: "Do you know the answer, Mr. Ellery?" Therapist: "I'm not sure I do, Richard, but I'll throw this out for what it's worth and maybe we can sort of kick it around. Would it surprise you to learn that everybody is afraid of their feelings of anger, their feelings of wanting to hurt and maybe even murder sometimes?" Michael immediately said, "Not me; because I don't have those feelings." Richard: "You're talking about the unconscious now, aren't you?" The therapist said he was.

Richard: "What I don't understand is, suppose you have the feeling of wanting to murder. Doesn't that mean you are going to murder?" Therapist: "No. It does not mean that. It means that if you know you have this feeling, you can then control it. If you have it, but don't know it, how can you control it?" Richard: "That's sensible." Macy: "In other words, you can have the feeling and there is nothing wrong with having the feeling as long as you know about it and take care of the feeling." Leonard, who had been silent during most of the discussion, spoke up at this point and said: "When you find out about your feelings then you can do something or not do something. I'll bet this man who killed the girl thought he was the sweetest guy in the world." Richard laughed and said: "Yeah, I bet he thought he was the sweetest guy in the world that couldn't harm a hair on anybody's head. Like me. I always used to be ashamed of being angry. In fact, when the doctor asked me if I was angry I told him no. I'm not sure why I told him no, but I know that's the answer I gave him. Maybe I'm more ashamed of it than the doctor would have been."

The group had overstayed its allotted time and the therapist terminated the session. As Richard was rising to go, he said, "Let's talk more about this next week."

COMMENT

The objectives toward which we worked were beginning to be realized. Here now was a group of boys who calmly and maturely examined their feelings, honestly and without fear, and convincingly manifested inner controls, objectivity, tender sentiments (of which they were completely incapable when they came to us), and eagerness to understand themselves and the world around them. Though the retaliatory impulse to which they had been exposed all their lives raised its ugly head for a moment, their inner balance soon made it possible for them to suggest that there would be no gain in taking the life of the sex offender.

Richard's parrying with the psychiatrist and the exercise of aim-directed self-control fully justified our efforts in this direction. He and the other boys now recognized that behavior with an ulterior purpose was not enough, that one had to behave (be social) most of the time. This seemed to be their objective now. Richard's seeming auditory and visual "hallucination" relative to his grandfather had to be understood rather as a mechanism of residual infantile wish-fulfillment rather than psychosis, and this should have been explained to him. Michael's consoling Macy as to his inability to save his father was a touching manifestation of empathy and affection. Though the therapist's explanation of the cause of mourning was incomplete and the reason given for the mob reaction toward the rapist was inaccurate, they served the purpose of assuaging the boys' intellectual curiosity. What was most striking was that the boys had grown curious about subtle matters that few in their social and cultural environment ever attempt to explore.

Session Sixty-Two

The session began on time, although Jules, who was working at the PX, was five minutes late. He sent word by Macy that he would be delayed. Michael began by asking what the group had been talking about in the preceding session. The therapist asked if anybody remembered. Leonard said, "I think we were talking about Macy's father dying." Michael: "That's right; that's what we were talking about." He leaned over, turned toward Macy, and asked: "You want to talk more?" Macy said, "Jules must be thinking about dying, because when we were sitting at the table at the cottage, Jules said to me, 'Hey Macy, what would you do if I died all of a sudden?'" Macy had laughed and said, "What I'd do is burst out laughing." Macy added that Jules did not seem to like the answer, and called him "a cold-hearted bum." Richard commented to the effect that Macy liked to "razz" people sometimes, and Jules sometimes looked for a "razzing." Macy added that on two separate occasions the same evening Jules had tried to provoke him by pretending to "steal" his food, reaching over for bread at the dinner table, with his sleeve brushing against Macy's victuals. Macy said it was "accidental on purpose." Michael, in the meantime, invited the boys to have a cup of coffee, which he prepared for them. He also distributed the cookies. This activity took up about two minutes, after which Jules came into the room rather silently, sat down in his usual chair, and greeted the therapist in a very friendly manner.

Upon entering, Jules asked for a cigarette, and Richard told him not to smoke because he had been in the hospital last week with a cold. Jules said: "Fuck it. I got to smoke," and added that Mrs. K. had warned him that if he continued to smoke, he would die. Macy immediately said, "There he goes again, talking about death." All the boys laughed, and Jules joined in. After this he grew serious, as he said, "That's not so funny, because all of a sudden tonight I found myself thinking about death, since Mrs. K. told me what she did." He then explained that Mrs. K. had a relative who was a doctor and who always told her about people who died of lung disease from smoking. Jules wondered if this could happen to him, too. He said that Mrs. K. had told him that he might get an abscess in the lungs. Jules began to laugh at this, as if he were making light of his concern. The therapist picked this up and asked Jules whether it was bothering him and wondered how he felt about the matter. Jules confessed that he did not know; it just felt funny, because he had never thought of death before. He then corrected himself that on one or two other occasions in the past he may have thought of it, but tonight he "kinda thought of it in a row." However, he did not expand on the subject. Michael (to Jules): "Come on, it's on your mind tonight." Jules: "I don't know what to talk about. It's not bothering me too much. I don't think it's too important."

Jules got up to put more sugar into his coffee. This seemed to signal that this discussion was at an end. Michael had brought a small radio with him and Jules asked him for it. Michael immediately said: "I know what you're trying to do. You're trying to get away from talking." Jules sat down blushing, as if he had been caught red-handed, and said: "I don't know what to talk about any more. I just think it's kind of screwy." (It occurred in a flash to the therapist as he looked at Jules at that moment that he was much calmer, much more mature and stable, and much less anxious and "jumpy" than he had been when he first came to the group.) The therapist decided to pursue the discussion, and asked: "Jules, do you feel that you're changing?" Jules looked up, almost as if caught by surprise. He thought for a moment, and then said: "It's funny you asked that, because everybody keeps saying to me that I have changed a great deal. I remember when I used to come here, I used to feel jumpy inside and very nervous. I couldn't sit still. Now I know I can come here and I don't feel nervous any more inside. Mrs. K. told me that I'm doing very good, that she likes me, but I remember when I was always a big problem in cottages. The funny thing is, I listen to what people say to me. I remember when I never used to listen to what anybody said to me. I pretended like I was listening but I didn't." Then, after a momentary pause, "How come you asked me that, Mr. Ellery?" Therapist: "I'm not sure, Jules, but when you were talking about the feeling that maybe you're going to die, it occurred to me that maybe what you're feeling is that some part of you is dying." Jules immediately said, "You mean the part that didn't listen to people and used to be nervous all the time?"

Michael thoughtfully remarked: "Jules is more mature now, like all of us." Macy, just as thoughtfully, repeated: "Like all of us. Me, I still like to fuck around [act up], but I think when I fuck around, I don't feel right doing it like I used to." Macy accounted for this by saying that it was because of the transition conference that "they are going to have" on him, and his fear that everybody was watching him and making reports on him, because Mr. K. warned him that if he wanted to get a good report, he'd better behave himself. Michael said, "The same for me, and I'm not sure I behave myself now because of the 'transition' or because I really want to." The boys became restless at this point. All the boys, with the exception of Leonard, rose to replenish their coffee cups. This lasted but a few minutes, however.

Michael now introduced the subject of his being on the boxing team and that there was to be a match next week. Macy told Michael "to beat the shit" out of his opponent. Michael: "When I fight, even boxing, I get mad and, boy, I could give a good fight to whoever I'm fighting." Jules said he hoped he could be on the boxing team, too, and then laughingly added: "If I can't find somebody who would put me on the boxing team, then I'm going to have to find somebody I can knock around." The therapist picked this up: "A little while ago we were talking about changing and how you felt about it. Now, all of a sudden, we are talking about fighting. What's this all about?" Michael: "Well, I don't mean regular [hostile] fighting. I just mean boxing, being on a team. I don't want to talk about it tonight, because my boxing match isn't till next week. If we talk about it tonight, I'm going to sleep and I'm going to think about it, and tomorrow morning I'm going to feel like fighting somebody just from talking about it. Then I will have to go over to the coach and ask him to put gloves on me and I'll·have to find somebody to fight with." (Apparently talk about fighting was too stimulating for Michael, and he recognized and confronted himself with his poor ego controls and defenses. Because of the psychotic base of his personality, this required cautious handling.)

Fortunately, Macy stepped in at this point and asked: "What do they mean when somebody is punch-drunk?" Richard answered this by saying that punch-drunk means that somebody walks around "hearing bells all the time and every time they hear a bell, there really isn't a bell, and they come out fighting." Macy then wanted to know how this came about. When no one seemed to know the answer, the therapist explained that the term referred to a person whose brain was damaged as a result of the head having sustained a great deal of punching. The details of this process seemed to attract a great deal of attention from the boys, for all eyes were on the speaker. The therapist took advantage of this concentration and elaborated with some gory results of fighting, such as broken jaws that needed wiring, brain concussions, even death and its frequency following prize fights. Richard immediately picked this up and said, "Well, that's one good reason not to fight any more, because you could really get banged up pretty bad and maybe sometimes you don't recover any more."

Macy told of someone he knew back in B———, a young man, who used to be a fighter when he was younger. Now, in his late twenties, "this guy is finished because he always acts as if he's got something weird on his brain." Leonard: "You mean his brain probably got damaged." Macy: "Yeh, that's what I mean. If that's what can happen to you from fighting, then that ain't for me." Suddenly the boys began to grow restless again. At first this was not obvious; there was only a slight increase in physical movement. But soon Richard began to act rather silly, saying he had to go back to his cottage to get his "opium shot," which was met by uproarious laughter; then there was shuffling of feet while the boys still remained in their seats. After a brief interval of this, the therapist asked: "Fellows, what's happening? I feel you're kind of restless. Every time we start to talk about something, you're beginning to get jumpy." Macy: "It's probably nothing, Mr. Ellery. Don't pay attention to it." Brief pause, and then: "Maybe. I don't know. All right. I'll tell you Mr. Ellery, I was thinking about what we talked the other weeks about getting people mad. I think you've got something there. Like tonight, I was eating macaroni and meat. I looked at Mr. G. [associate cottage father], and when he wasn't watching me I'd slurp with my mouth. [Macy made a "slurping" sound to demonstrate it.] I knew what I was doing, and then I kind of stopped and said: 'What the hell am I doing this for?' And then I thought what we talked about." Jules: "That's right. Me and Macy were talking about that, and I guess you were right. We do fuck around when somebody is around to get mad."

Richard took over, and with humor, which to the therapist seemed to disguise a great deal of hostility, said: "I don't know. I got a hunch Mr. Ellery is a robot. I bet if we walked over and peeled the skin off him we would find a robot there who is taking down dictation for Mr. P. (director of the Village). He is really a spy planted in this group." There was nervous laughter, in which the therapist joined. Michael said, "Oh, come on, Richard, you're not going to make Mr. Ellery mad." Richard said, "I'm not trying to get him mad." Therapist: "Maybe you're wondering why I don't get mad, Richard." Richard: "You don't get mad because you're a nice guy. We can talk here and sit around and do what we feel like doing. I used to wonder why you didn't raise your voice to us. We used to fuck around a lot here to get you mad, but you never raised your voice. You were always nice and calm and you talked to us like we were gentlemen. I guess you figured out that by being nice to us, we would be nice to you. You were right." Jules: "Mr. Ellery, you don't get mad, and I know we fucked around. How come you didn't get mad?" Therapist: "Remember you used to ask me what would you do if somebody picked on you and tried to get you into a fight? Well, I showed you boys, didn't I?" Silence fell upon the group, then Jules said, "In other words, you didn't get mad at us because you understood what we were trying to do to you."

Suddenly Richard began to rock back and forth in his chair like an infant and made all sorts of weird sounds. Jules turned on him with anger in his voice: "Why in the hell don't you stop acting like a two-year-old!"

Richard was brought up short by this exclamation. He sat back in his chair and didn't say anything. Macy: "Sometimes I feel I got a split personality. I act different in the cottage than I do when I'm outside in B———." Jules: "That's right, the same thing happens to me." Therapist: "Well, try to remember when you, as you say it, start fooling—is there always an adult around?" Jules thought for a while and then said, "Most of the time, I guess there is, but I don't understand why they can't let us fool around and why they get so upset." Therapist: "Well Jules, you just said somebody was acting like a two-year-old and that bothered you. How do you think it feels to an adult to see boys fourteen, fifteen, sixteen, and even seventeen acting like two- or three-year-olds?" Jules did not answer and there was silence in the room. The therapist continued: "Don't you think that maybe when they see you boys acting like little kids that this can be pretty upsetting, as it would be to anybody?" Michael, as if he were joking, said, "If I saw a four-year-old come in and act like that, I'd jack him up, and I'd punch him even if he was a four-year-old." This remark brought laughter from the boys.

Jules said, "The other thing I'm not so sure about is that many times we fool around when an adult isn't even there." The therapist wondered whether some of this fooling around might not be playing to an audience, namely, other boys. Jules didn't think so, because when he was back in the city he had many friends and he didn't fool around. The therapist was at a loss as to how to answer this, and invited the other boys "to kick this around to see if we could come up with an answer," but no answer was forthcoming. The therapist then said: "The one thing I wonder about is this, fellows. When I didn't get mad at you, even though you were trying to get me mad, what happened to you?" Jules: "I don't know, tell us?" Therapist: "It seems to me that you stopped trying to get me mad. In other words, when I was treating you decently, you boys were able to respond in the same way." Macy: "Well that's all we ever wanted. Somebody to treat us nice," and Michael added: "I never tried to get Mr. Ellery mad." Richard: "Oh, you're so full of shit!" Michael laughed at this, and Richard added: "But I never tried to get you mad, right Mr. Ellery? I think I'm the only one who never tried to get you mad." The therapist broke into loud laughter and said, "What do you think you were trying to do when you tried to lead a symphony orchestra here in the room?" Richard now began to laugh too, and said, "Yeh, I remember." Jules turned to Richard: "So don't act stupid like you don't know from nothin'."

Time was up and the therapist called attention to this fact. Macy and Jules said to one another they wished they could "sit around until ten o'clock and talk." They didn't feel like leaving, but all soon returned to their cottages.

COMMENT

Jules's awareness of the change in him and the therapist's interpretation is bordering on true psychoanalytic procedure, as were a great many other episodes in the course of the interviews in this group, but this one seemed to touch upon metapsychology. The session could be characterized as one of recapitulation by the boys of their growth from uncontrollable, irascible, pugnacious, and unreasonable individuals to vastly more mature persons. The fact that they singled out one trait in the behavior of some of them, namely, teasing ("razzing") is an indication of their self-awareness and a desire for self-correction. Macy's becoming aware of his intent against an adult by "slurping" his food was uncontrovertible proof of the fruits of the discussions. This was true also in the matter of fighting. The boys all revealed understanding of themselves, and Michael indicated it also by his remark that talking about the boxing match would interfere with his sleep. His mature attitude was seen in his refusal to talk about it, so as to prevent having a restless night. Thus he applied the tenets of mental health to his own life.

The discussion confirmed the importance of the therapist as an identification model, as an ego ideal, and as a force in the maturation of his patients, which was amply demonstrated by the boys' reminiscences of his response to their provocations in the past.

Session Sixty-Three

Richard was last to arrive. (From the very outset, there was an air of restlessness among the boys that had not been noted now for some weeks. It manifested itself at times as silliness, difficulty in beginning, and transilience in the discussions.)

The session opened with preparation and distribution of coffee and cookies. When Richard arrived, about four minutes late, there was a kind of "giddiness" in his attitude. As he came in he made "a funny face" to no one in particular, and Michael, who happened to see it, broke into laughter. Richard seated himself in his usual chair, looked restless, got up, helped himself to coffee, sat down again.

A discussion arose between Jules and Macy about a basketball game they had witnessed in the gymnasium some days before. Jules was describing what he would have done had he been playing and how he would have sunk a number of baskets. Following this, Jules asked Leonard to open the discussion, but Leonard did not respond. In fact, Leonard did not say anything throughout the session. Jules then tried to enlist Richard's and Macy's help in getting Leonard to talk, Jules saying to Leonard: "Come on, you're always quiet. Why don't you say something tonight?" Leonard just smiled with embarrassment and said nothing.[1]

Michael had brought candy which he had purchased at the PX. (This was the evening when his cottage group went to the PX to spend some of their monthly allowances.) After eating it, Michael pulled a paper cup of ice cream from his pocket and began to eat it, too. He did not offer any of it to the other boys, and no one seemed to pay attention to him. Suddenly, out of the blue and for no apparent reason, Richard asked the therapist whether he thought Richard was "crazy." Therapist: "What makes you ask?" Richard said that he had met someone in the "guidance [clinic] building" in the afternoon whom he described as "a psychiatrist" who had given him a test. (Earlier that afternoon an applicant for a job as staff psychologist had apparently examined Richard as part of his test for the position. This was an oversight insofar as all the boys in the group had been tested at periods by a specific psychologist attached to this project. The unscheduled test seemed to confuse the boy.) Richard proceeded to say that he had seen the psychiatrist only recently and was tested not long ago and now he was tested again, and he wondered whether the "Village thinks" he was "crazy." The therapist assured Richard that this did not mean he was suspected of being crazy, nor did the therapist think that he was crazy. However, he said: "Richard, you brought up this business of being crazy last week, too. I wonder if there is anything to it."

Richard looked somewhat disturbed by this question, but unhesitatingly said: "Naw. There's nothing to it, Mr. Ellery. I don't think I'm crazy." Therapist: "But it seems to bother you even though I've given you reassurance before." Richard then stated that Jules sometimes fooled around with him in the cottage and called him "crazy." Jules: "That's nothing; I call a lot of other guys crazy. That doesn't mean you're crazy." Michael spoke up: "I don't worry about things like that. I know I'm not crazy so why should I worry about it?" Richard did not say anything for a while and then: "That doctor asked me today what I would do if somebody called me a punk and I was holding a gun in my hand standing right up against him. I was going to tell him I was going to shoot, but then all of a sudden I heard your voice, Mr. Ellery." (From what Richard said next it appeared that he actually did hear the therapist's voice from the adjoining room.) "You were in the next office.

1. Note must be taken of the fact that the reports and tests on Leonard showed that the progress he had made was among the most impressive in the group, a good example of "spectator therapy." (See the various reports on individual boys.)

And then I remembered what you told us, so I said to this doctor, 'If somebody called me a punk, rather than shoot I would walk away.' The doctor said, 'You'd walk away?' 'Yeah, I'd walk away.'" Therapist: "How did you feel when you said that Richard?" Richard: "I don't remember; I don't remember how I felt." The therapist smiled and said, "But your first impulse was to pull the trigger, huh?" Richard: "Yeah. It was. But I kinda knew what you were talking about when we talked about how sometimes you got to walk away from a fight." Michael said: "It's about time you learned. You know nothing can happen from a fight but you getting hurt."

Jules was beginning to tear at some of the threads on the covering of the easy chair on which he was sitting. The therapist asked: "I wonder what's making you do that, Jules." Jules smiled embarrassedly as if he had been caught by surprise and said: "Nothing in particular. Everything's okay with me tonight." Michael: "Then why are you ripping the chair?" Jules appeared angry and exclaimed: "Because I feel like it! You want to make something of it?" While this interchange was taking place, Richard was making sounds like a baby talking. Apparently he was trying to get the boys' attention by acting in an infantile way. Jules said to Richard: "Why don't you knock it off? I told you last week you're acting like a baby." Richard pretended that he had not heard Jules and persisted with the baby sounds, but only for a brief moment, and then began to tell a story of how he had started to "fool around in the cottage" that evening making noises, and when the relief cottage father called him down for it he pretended that he was not the one who did it.

At this point the boys had got up to refill their cups and again restlessness set in. (It was rather striking that Richard, who just a few minutes before had talked about being crazy, now acted as though he were crazy.) The therapist decided to explore this with him. When the boys had sat down and quiet was restored, he said: "Richard, there's something I'm wondering about. Just before you said that maybe people at the Village think you're crazy, and yet from the way you're acting tonight, I get the feeling that you're trying to put on an act as if you are crazy." Richard abruptly: "What do you mean?" Therapist: "Richard, I get a feeling that you're trying to get my goat tonight." Jules: "That's what I've been thinking. Richard's been sitting here and acting strange and he fools around like that sometimes in the cottage, too." Richard pretended to be falling asleep as he slouched in his chair. He tilted his head back and closed his eyes. From that posture he announced: "I'm not trying to get your goat, Mr. Ellery." He got up, went over to the table at the other end of the room, helped himself to a few cookies, and whispered something to Macy, who was near him, before he sat down again.

Macy turned to the therapist and said, "Richard wants to know if you're mad at him." Therapist: "No, I'm not mad. I'm just trying to understand what you're doing, Richard." Macy: "Don't pay any attention to him, Mr. Ellery. Some people just have to act like they are crazy. They act crazy so they can get you mad." Richard turned on Macy and angrily said: "That ain't so! I'm not trying to get Mr. Ellery mad." Michael (to Richard): "Come over here." Richard went over to where Michael sat. Michael: "Lie down on the couch." Richard, seemingly going along with the gag, lay down on the couch. Michael sat himself down at the head of the couch and said, "Okay, sonny boy, now tell me all your problems." Richard began to giggle and Michael said to him: "Now this isn't a laughing matter. You're going to have to tell me your problems if you want to get any better. If you're not going to talk when you're sitting up, then maybe you'll talk when you're lying down." The situation was so comical that the therapist could not restrain himself from joining the boys in laughter. This byplay lasted only a few moments. Richard got off the couch and returned to his chair, and the group calmed down.

Jules narrated that while he was working on his job at the PX, the art teacher came in and sat down at the counter. Some money fell out of her pocketbook and she left it lying there, apparently unaware of it. Jules said that this was not the first time this had happened. On previous occasions, too, when she had come into the PX she had somehow carelessly placed her pocketbook on the counter in such a manner that money would protrude from it. On this occasion, while she was eating the sandwich she had ordered, the money was there "to be stolen." "Man, how much temptation can a guy stand?" he asked. Macy: "What would you do?" Jules: "If she does it again, I think I'm going to steal it. One day I saw two hundred bucks sticking out of her wallet while her pocketbook was on the counter." Michael: "I couldn't stand all that temptation. I would just have to take that money. I know that when I get out, it's going to be a real problem for me to stand up against temptation. If anybody ever puts money like that near me, boy, I'm going to have a rough time." Jules: "Well, that's what I'm talking about. To have all this temptation—I think I would take that money."

A few moments later, Jules was talking about wanting to get out of the Village, complaining that he had been there too long. All of a sudden, he started to complain about his caseworker who never gave him a definite answer as to when he would be discharged. As reported by Jules, his caseworker said to him, "What are you going to do when you get out?" and Jules answered him, "When I get out I'm going to get myself some hobbies so I can stay out of trouble." The caseworker then told him that if he needed hobbies that proved that he couldn't stay out of trouble, so maybe he'd better not leave yet. Macy agreed that this was unfair and said: "How does the caseworker know that you're not going to get into a good job so you don't get into trouble any more. That's the trouble with some of these caseworkers. They just don't trust you that you know how to stay out of trouble by this time."

The therapist pointed out to Jules that on the one hand he was complaining about the caseworker, while on the other he had just said that he could not resist temptation, that his first instinct when he saw the money was to take it regardless of whom it belonged to. Jules began by defending himself: "So what? I'm not going to look to steal, but if I see it on a counter, then I think it's fair for me to take it. People ought to look after their own money." Michael to Jules: "It's about time you knew why you stole." Jules: "What do you mean, know why I stole? I still don't know why I steal." Michael: "You don't know why you steal? What do you think we've been talking about all this time? About getting even on your mother." Jules: "What are you talking about?" Michael got up and, imitating role-playing (see pp. 516, 566), approached Jules and began to upbraid him, saying that all Jules wanted was vengeance, he wanted to get in trouble as a way of punishing his parents. Jules: "You're crazy." Richard, pointing at Jules: "Come on, come on, you know the unconscious. We talk about the unconscious here." Jules, angrily to Michael: "If you're so smart, why don't you talk about your own problems? Why are you talking about my problems for?" Michael: "I talk about my problems. The only thing is you don't want to admit you got problems. I admit I got problems." Jules to Michael (who was still standing near Jules): "Why don't you sit down and just mind your own business?" (It must be noted that during this entire interchange between Michael and Jules both boys were smiling.)

Jules became more serious and Michael returned to his seat. Jules turned to the therapist and said: "I been thinking about that, but I'm still not sure why I stole. You still think it had something to do with my parents?" The therapist asked Jules what he thought. Jules said: "But my parents are nice to me. When I go home now they are very nice. I have a good time. I don't fool around any more." Therapist: "But I also remember that when you used to go home you got into trouble. I had the feeling that you're full of anger at your parents because you sometimes look like you're full of anger at everybody." Jules: "It shows, huh?" He then added: "Honestly, Mr. Ellery, I can't see it yet." He was very serious and seemed to be really working hard on the idea. He said,

"I get along with my father." Therapist: "Why are you afraid of him?" Jules: "How do you know I am afraid of him?" Therapist: "Remember that dream with the shotgun up against your eyes?" Jules: "But I don't feel afraid of him any more." Therapist: "We're trying to understand what you *used* to feel." Jules: "I wish I could remember, I wish I could remember. Give me some hints, Mr. Ellery." Therapist: "Jules, I always felt that although your mother gave you things she always asked a lot in return." Jules thought about it for a while, then said, "No, I don't think so." (It was obvious that regardless of what the therapist might say to him at this point, he would negate it.) Jules asked, "Do you think it might be something else?"

Therapist: "Since you're asking, Jules, I want to raise one matter that you once raised in the group and that's why I will talk about it." Jules immediately said, "You mean my being an adopted child?" Therapist: "Yes. You never talked about that really, except to tell us that you were." Jules: "I don't know how old I was when I was adopted. I think I was six. My mother knows everything about my real mother, but she never told me about her. I know one time I used to go looking for her, but I don't look for her any more. I don't give a shit about her. I think she's still living with my father somewhere but I don't know where. She rejected me. When I was a little boy she put me in an orphanage. If she don't give a shit about me, I'm not going to give a shit about her." As he was saying this, Jules's voice and face reflected tremendous anger. The therapist commented, "Although you say you don't give a shit, your voice has a lot of anger in it, Jules." Jules denied this. "I don't think about her any more. She's not part of my life. I don't want to see her. I love my own parents now because they are the only parents I have ever really had. Even if I had a chance to go back to my real mother, I wouldn't go back." Macy: "I think it had something to do with this, Jules." Jules: "What do you mean, Macy?" Macy: "Well I think you got a lot of memories buried that you don't know about yet, and you're not talking about yet." Jules looked very intense and appeared sincerely trying to assimilate this thought.

Michael interrupted to say he was going back to the cottage. As the group was getting ready to leave, since it was 8:30, Jules came to the therapist and said: "Could you see me every week in your office, Mr. Ellery? My caseworker can't help me with this. I think maybe you and I can find the answer." The therapist told Jules that he would have to "check" on it. He didn't know in terms of all the work he had to do and whether the Village would permit it. "But," he said: "I'll do it, Jules. I'll try to see you next week and send a pass for you." Jules said: "Okay, I'll talk to you then."

Thus ended the session.

COMMENT

We were unable to establish the reason for the boys' restlessness and regression beyond hypothesizing that the approaching Easter vacation and plans for home visits might have been the cause. An additional factor may have been the spring weather.

The therapist did well to have brought out Jules's feelings concerning his adoptive status in the family, which is a core problem with this boy. This subject should be pursued further and worked through.

The dialogues among the boys clearly revealed a high level of psychological understanding and self-awareness and their struggles to overcome their impulses. As a group, they were at the threshhold of societal morality.

NOTE

There was no session the following week, because the therapist attended a professional conference.

Session Sixty-Four

ABSENT: Macy and Michael, on home visits to B——— for Easter vacation.

Jules and Richard were about five minutes late in arriving, and Leonard had arrived about five minutes early. During the ten-minute interval, Leonard was telling the therapist about the "scholarship program" he was on. He was earning about $25 a month helping the painter and was quite excited as he spoke of it. He seemed to be getting a lot of satisfaction from this occupation. Leonard described the various cottages he had worked at with the painter, and how he was saving money so that he would be able to buy clothes for himself when he left the Village.

Jules and Richard arrived and greeted the therapist warmly, Jules telling him that Macy and Michael had sent regards and wished him a happy Easter. Jules reported that the two boys would not attend the session because they had gone to B——— for home visits. After making himself comfortable in a chair, Jules picked up the discussion where he had left off two weeks before, saying to the therapist that he wanted "to talk about the thing you talked about last time—why I stole, and the feeling you had that it had something to do with my parents." He asked for a summation of what had been said, but Richard interrupted and said, "You remember, don't you?" Jules: "I remember what we talked about, but I still can't see that my stealing had anything to do with my parents."

He then abruptly changed the subject and asked whether the therapist had attended "the conference" on him that had been held during the past week. Jules's caseworker had told him that there was to be such a conference.[2]

From the manner in which Jules put the question, the therapist gathered that somehow he had learned that the therapist had attended the conference. He also suspected that since so many people were involved, it was inevitable that the therapist's presence at the conference would have become known. He therefore decided to tell Jules that he had been at the conference, because the Director had instructed him to be.[3] Jules wanted to know what was discussed and the therapist indicated that everybody agreed that he had made progress. A smile of satisfaction spread over Jules's face, and he said: "That's nice. At least they are saying nice things about me now." He then reported that he had talked with his caseworker as to when he would be going home and it was his understanding that it might be at the end of June.[4] Jules said that he did not want to stay until June; he wanted to go in April. He had always thought that he had been promised he would go in April, and every time they kept shifting the date. Jules said he felt like running away; then he fell silent. From the manner in which he said it, however, it appeared as if he were debating with himself whether or not he should run away. He seemed very undecided. As the silence continued, the therapist said to him directly: "Jules, it sounds like you are not sure whether you want to run away." Jules: "That's right. I feel very tempted to run away, but I don't want to louse myself up any more."

Jules looked very tense as he said that he was not able to decide

---

2. This conference was called by the agency in another state which had referred Jules to the Village. They had sent a memo stating that because of lack of funds, Jules would have to be removed from the Village within a week. The conference was attended by various staff members from both agencies, including their psychiatrists as well as the probation officer and the group therapist. The referring agency was very impressed with the gains Jules had made. The visiting psychiatrist indicated that Jules had told him in a recent psychiatric consultation when Jules was on a home visit that he had got a lot out of group discussions. The Village psychiatrist stated that Jules was far less hostile, less delinquency-oriented than he had ever known him to be before. However, controls had not as yet been sufficiently internalized and it was questionable as to whether they ever would be, since Jules was an extremely traumatized boy. The psychiatrist felt that the boy had been reached by therapy.

3. This was an error in judgment. The boy should have been told in advance. The group therapist had consented to attend the conference because the group was the pivot in this boy's treatment.

4. The staff of the placement agency agreed on the basis of Jules's improvement that they would attempt to raise the necessary funds and keep him in the group therapy program at least through the second week of June. The group was scheduled to terminate at the end of June.

whether he wanted to run or not. Therapist: "It sounds to me like you are now beginning to feel the change in yourself—the part of you that has grown up, that thinks about what it does and the consequences, the part that is more able to control your impulses—and that part which wants to run away from any situation when it is not to your liking, to take things into your own hands even if this means hurting yourself." The therapist further described to Jules that this was the part of oneself that everyone carried around. It could be called "the childhood part," or, to use a new word, "the *archaic* part"—the part that wanted to do what we pleased regardless of what happened as a result. Jules repeated that he was not sure what he was going to do. He would hate to stay here beyond April. Then added: "I know my problems. I found out about them." As the therapist concentrated on Jules, Leonard sat quietly listening.

The therapist raised the question as to what Jules meant by "I know my problems." Jules thought a while and then said: "I'm not so sure. I just can't talk about it yet." Now Richard spoke up. "Go ahead, Jules, you can speak about it. Mr. Ellery is trying to help you. Why don't you try to tell him, and maybe you can find out even more about yourself. I found out about myself by talking here, so you better talk, Jules." Jules looked very troubled and said: "I just can't talk about it. I don't know what it is!" Then he said, "I still want to know what made me stop stealing." Then after a moment's hesitation, added: "Oh I know. I played hooky, but I went from worse [stealing] to better [hooky]. But why did I steal? What did it have to do with my parents, Mr. Ellery?" At this point, the therapist decided to be direct. He reminded Jules of the dream he had had some time ago when he dreamed his father was coming after him with a gun. He asked Jules, "You remember what you said at that time?" Jules: "I remember, it was a nutty dream because my father never hit me and you said, maybe I wanted my father to hit me and that's why I stole, but I don't know if that's it, Mr. Ellery. Maybe it has something to do with my real parents before I was adopted, but I never think of them any more. I don't want to know them. I don't talk about them and I forgot all about them." Therapist: "Maybe you do think about them in the part of you that we call the unconscious mind even though you are not aware that you think about them." Richard: "That's possible, Jules. Maybe you think about it but you still don't know that you think about it."

Jules grew extremely tense and screamed: "No! I don't think about it! I don't want to know about them!" Therapist: "Jules, how do you feel about your mother never having told you about your real mother?" Jules: "I don't know. I don't think about that either, but I think she does know about my real mother but I don't want to ask her. I don't want to find out. I don't want to think about it!" Jules thought for awhile and then: "Something just came into my head, Mr. Ellery. I can't remember whether I was in an orphanage or not before I was adopted." Again he fell to thinking and then said: "Yeah. I think I was in an orphanage. I don't remember what my own mother looked like." He thought some more and then: "That's funny, the idea that she is a blonde woman just came into my head." Richard: "That's not so strange, because you got blond hairs on your head." Jules leaned back in his chair and said: "Something else just came to me. I'll bet when I was adopted [at six years] I must have hated my own mother [who deserted him at four-and-a-half years] for giving me up. Also, I don't know why I stole. I don't think it is just because I hated my own mother. I could have done other things. Why did I have to steal? Even though I may have been sore at my mother who adopted me, I didn't have to steal. I don't think revenge had anything to do with it."

Having gone this far, the therapist decided to reveal something he had known about Jules, namely that his mother had rebuked him frequently about besmirching the family name in the small New England community where they lived, and said: "Jules I think what you did depended on the way you felt at that time. You must have been pretty sore and mixed up, and you did the most brilliant thing you could have done." Jules: "What do you mean?" Therapist: "Jules, did you want to get even with your mother for adopting you and what you did was to attack the family name?" Jules smiled and said: "Boy, have I heard that one before! My mother [referring to his adopted mother] always told me that I would throw mud at the family name by stealing. Come to think of it, maybe I'm another Einstein. I was mad at my mother for adopting me, but I also was afraid even though she told me, 'I love you,' that I might get adopted again, that she would give me to somebody else, and maybe what I wanted to do to my real mother, I took out on my other mother."

Richard interrupted and said he was not sure sometimes about the way his parents felt about him. For instance, many a Sunday his parents did not come to visit him. There was a part of him, he said, that talked like this: " 'Well, my father has got to work; my mother may not have the money to come up [to visit him],' but inside I feel mad and even though I say this to myself, I still feel mad. Once I was sitting on my bed near the window on a Sunday, waiting for my mother to come. One of the boys in the cottage began to tease me, saying, 'Your parents don't like you; they don't love you any more; they aren't going to take you back; they aren't going to come up to see you.' " He tried to laugh it off, he said, and then added: "But I wasn't laughing inside. I felt hurt. I tried not to think about it. I tried to sleep but I couldn't sleep.

I kept thinking about it, even though I didn't want to. I felt so mad I wanted to scream. It hurt so bad inside." Richard said that when he went home now, his parents were so nice to him, they gave him almost anything he wanted. In fact, he got better treatment than his sister ever got. He described incident after incident of how much better treatment he now received than did his sister. On the other hand, he was worried about it. He said, "I don't know what I'm so worried about, Mr. Ellery."

The therapist asked him if he felt that he could not believe that his parents really cared for him and he was not sure what might happen. Richard thought about this and said: "I think that's it, but my stupid caseworker told me that when I really go home and stay home, not just a home visit, it is going to be back to the same old business. My mother and father are going to scream at me, my sister is going to get better treatment than I will get. How does my caseworker know, Mr. Ellery? Why doesn't he keep his big mouth shut?" The therapist commented that maybe his caseworker was not God, and maybe there *was* some difference in the way his parents treated him now. Richard: "That doesn't mean I don't get mad at them any more, but at least they like me more. I think so, but I'm not sure." Jules, sadly: "I know what it feels like, Richie—when your parents give you love, can you feel it as love or do you think they are going to take it away from you the next day?" Richard agreed with this, but he could not be sure after all the trouble he had had with his parents. "How can you trust that when things are so nice for you now that this is the way it is going to be?"

The therapist asked him whether it felt almost like waiting for the ax to drop. Richard agreed, saying he did not know how he was going to get hurt again. Now his parents listened to him and they took into consideration what he wanted and what he said, but how long was this going to continue after he left Children's Village? The therapist commented that somehow he felt either he had to be at one end or the other, he got nothing or he got too much, and was he trying to find for himself a middle point? Richard said he thought he was trying to find a middle point but didn't know what that would be like, whether when his parents didn't always hug him, he was going to feel as though he was being "rejected" again. Jules said he thought of talking to his mother to find out about his "real mother." He didn't know what to do; he was not sure. He said when people asked him about his real mother he told them that she was dead and that his real father was dead. "I don't know why I do it. It's like I don't want to believe they are still alive. I might find out that they are living right next to me. I'd go to see them. They may not want me, or they may want me, and then I won't be sure who I'm going to stay with." Richard: "Aw, come on. You know who you are going to stay with!" Jules thought a while and said: "I guess you're right, Richard. I'll stay with the mother who adopted me. She is the only mother I have really known."

Time was up and Leonard had to return to the cottage to wash and iron a shirt for the next day, so the boys left.

COMMENT

Apparently the discussion of the preceding session touched off deeply affecting areas in Jules, for a two-week interval did not pale his interest. He spontaneously introduced the subject of his adoptive state and revealed intense affectivity around it, which he attempted to work through. His ambivalence and confusions were bared, as were also those of Richard.

The group had now moved from the realm of ego-therapy to analysis of intensive libidinal involvements with various members of their families. This was a promising development, and should the group continue to meet much longer, this direction would lead the boys to affect-laden suppressed memories and feelings that would be truly reconstructive. The transition would then have been made from para-analytic to analytic group psychotherapy.

Two considerations deserve note as revealed in this interview. One was that the smallness of the group probably favored the depth of the material produced. The other was the unmistakable demonstration of the fact that a transference neurosis cannot be worked through in a group, partly because of the interference with free association. Note how Richard broke into Jules's monologue and ended his free association at a critical point.

Session Sixty-Five

ABSENT: Macy and Michael, still on Easter home visits to B———, because of the long distance from the village.

Because of a special Easter program the boys were about eight minutes late. Leonard was the first to arrive, followed by Jules and Richard. The boys experienced initial difficulty in getting a discussion going, though the therapist did not recognize an unusual degree of resistance on the part of the boys. Jules wandered about preparing coffee, distributing cookies and cigarettes. Richard sat by himself looking rather tired. He told the therapist that he had run from the gymnasium where the program was going on and he wanted "to catch his breath." These diversions lasted but a few minutes.

Having relaxed a bit, Richard reported that when he was on home visit the preceding week, he took the therapist's advice and spoke to his parents about how they felt about him. (Note: No such advice had been given to Richard by the therapist.) He had asked his father: "Dad, do you care for me?" Richard said that his father was somewhat taken aback and said to him: "Of course, Richard, I care for you. Why do you ask?" Richard had said to his father: "I just wanted to know, Dad." Later on, Richard approached his mother, saying to her: "Mom, I kind of wonder if you love me," and Richard's mother had said, "Richard, of course I do; but what makes you ask?" Richard's response, as he described it, was that he was just wondering about it and wanted to ask. It appeared to the therapist that these inquiries were carried on in a sort of mechanical way, and Richard's report of them had the same detached, mechanical quality, as reflected in his tone of voice. He apparently did not wish to discuss it further, for he at once rose and proceeded to help Jules with the refreshments. He and Jules got into a brief conversation in low voices and Richard then returned to his seat.

Having settled down, Richard turned to the therapist: "Mr. Ellery, I got a problem I want to talk to you about. I got to make a decision." His problem was that when he left the Village in June, he could get a job working on a Good Humor wagon selling ice cream. On the other hand, he was not sure whether he wanted to do this or would prefer working with his father. His father was a superintendent for a number of buildings; there was a lot of work to be done on them during the summer, and he was wondering whether he should help his father with this. Richard sat back, thought for a while, and then went on to say that his father worked days for a bread company, as well as acting as superintendent of buildings, so he was sometimes called "at all hours of the night" by various tenants requesting him to do repairs on plumbing, faucets, and the like. Richard might have wanted to help with these chores, but he did not know how to fix "these things." Richard said his father made himself available at almost all hours of the day and night when he was not working at the bread company, whereas Richard could not possibly do this; he would not interrupt his sleep to fix faucets. Besides which, he would be going to school in the fall; he would have homework to do and would really have to sleep at night if he were to get to school on time the next day.

Richard said nothing further, but looked at the therapist with intensity. The therapist said, "Richard, I wonder if you want me to make the decision for you." Richard said he did. Jules turned to Richard and said: "Mr. Ellery can't make the decision for you. You got to make it for yourself." Richard: "I know. But I still would like somebody to make the decision for me. What should I do, Mr. Ellery?" The therapist told Richard that he would be glad to discuss it with him, but Richard apparently wanted a definite answer and asked: "What would you do if you were me?" Therapist: "What I might do, Richard, may be right for me . . ." Richard interrupted and finished by saying, ". . . but it might not be right for me, huh?"

The therapist added that one of the things one faced as one grew up was the making of decisions even though one could not be sure what would happen after the decision was made. Richard said that this was always the hard part of making a decision. "You can't be sure of what's going to happen later." Jules said to Richard: "If you can't work at night, and people need you at night, what are you taking the job for?" Richard: "I thought of it and yet I want to help my father." The therapist raised the matter of how Richard felt about working with his father. Richard indicated that he did not anticipate any problems in this respect; he did not at all mind working with his father. He held that it might be easier for him to work with his father than on a Good Humor wagon: He could take it easy; he wouldn't have to rush to get there at a set hour; and so forth. Richard now made himself another cup of coffee, following which he leaned over and talked to Jules for a few moments, and the therapist could not overhear. Then Richard returned to his seat and changed the subject. He talked about going out on dates, maybe sometimes traveling cross-country with his family on their vacations together. He then returned to discussing some happenings in his cottage. None of these topics, however, had any significance.

Addressing Richard, the therapist commented that "somehow we were going all over the map tonight. How do you feel about sticking to one thing?" Richard looked at the therapist very pleasantly and said, "Of course, Mr. Ellery, let's kind of finish talking about this." The therapist said that Richard had started off by saying that he had gone to his father and his mother to ask them how they felt about him. Richard: "I wanted to know; I wanted to be sure. After we talked about it last week I thought that when I go home for Easter I would talk to them about it." Following a supervisory suggestion that emotional dependency be reviewed with the boys, the therapist asked how he felt after his talks with his parents. Richard: "I felt pretty good. I felt good about myself." Therapist: "When your parents tell you that they love you, you feel pretty good about yourself. Now suppose, sometime, for one reason or another, your parents may be tired, or for some other reason they're not able to say this to you. Or, in fact, they may be kind of bushed and they might act angry with you. How would you feel about yourself then?" Richard thought a while and said, "I don't know if I know the answer." Therapist: "Well it seems, Richard, that how you feel about yourself depends to a great degree on what your parents say about you." Richard reflected again and said: "Yah. That's right."

Jules stepped in and said, "That means yourself." Richard, thoughtfully: "I guess that's right"; then he added that his parents had been very nice to him during the last week end. In fact they had talked with him and he was able to talk with them; there was no fighting. The past few week ends when he had been home, he had noticed the same thing. Even his sister was nice to him. She didn't break his records as she used to or take them without first asking his permission. As a result he volunteered to give her some of his records as presents. Therapist: "Richard, do you feel that maybe some of this has happened because you yourself have changed?" Richard: "Oh, I know I changed. I don't come home with a chip on my shoulder any more. I'm scared what's going to happen when I get home, but I don't know, I feel a little better inside. When I go home I don't worry so much about what's going to happen and I find that things go along pretty good."

Jules left for the washroom. Therapist: "Have you ever thought, Richard, that maybe since you've changed, you go home and greet your parents differently and they in turn greet you differently? It's the same way as when you walk up to somebody and have an angry look on your face, and even though you may not know you're angry the other person may get angry at you and then you wonder why the other person got angry." Richard immediately picked this up and said: "Oh, I know that. If you walk up to somebody and you look like you're itching for a fight, the other person's going to strike first before you do. If you walk up to the other guy with a smile on your face, the other guy wants to show you that he can smile as good or better than you, so he's going to smile back at you, right?" The therapist agreed. Richard continued: "I guess this is what happens when I go home because I don't look as tough as I used to. I don't look scared any more, either; but I walk in, I say hello to my mother and father. I'm nice to my kid sister and everybody is nice to me. I seen that happen a lot of times around here at the Village, where one fellow walks up to another guy and he looks tough and before you know it there's a fight. I always used to think, how did that fight get started? I heard what you said, Mr. Ellery, and maybe that's how fights get started. One boy is probably itching for it, and the other boy knows that this boy was itching for the fight, right?" Again the therapist agreed.

At this point, Jules came back. Richard did not say anything further. However, the therapist felt that what had just transpired was important enough for Jules to know and he asked Richard whether he would mind if he repeated it for Jules. Jules expressed interest and the therapist began to review the discussion for Jules. However, Richard took over and explained to Jules in even greater detail what had been said, supplying many illustrations of how sometimes fights occurred in cottages and with cottage parents only because of the way boys looked at the cottage parents. He said among other things: "When you itch for a fight, you get one, even though you're not the first one to throw a word or a fist." This discussion seemed to settle something in the boys' minds, as manifested by their facial expressions and the way the two settled back in their seats. Throughout the discussions, Leonard appeared intensely interested, but he did not say anything.

Jules now launched into a description of the "very nice home visit" he had had with his parents, who had called for him at the Village and driven him home. When they got outside the New York State line, Jules took over the driving of his father's car. He had a permit for driving in his own state and his father let him do it. Richard interrupted Jules and began telling of once being in his father's car when it was standing still, and in "fooling around" he inadvertently shifted the transmission. When his father got into the car he asked Richard: "Richard, did you drive?" Richard said, "No, I didn't do anything." His father asked: "How come the transmission is in first?" Richard laughed and his father took it "good-naturedly." Later his father allowed him to drive. He described driving the car on a highway and speeding. His father told him not to speed but Richard took "a couple of fast corners," once doing almost 50 miles an hour.

The therapist raised the question of Richard's father's allowing him to drive a car. "Richard, it sounds almost like your father encouraged you to act in a delinquent way." Richard: "What do you mean, Mr. Ellery?" Therapist: "You don't have a license to drive a car. [Richard was fifteen years old then.] By driving a car without a license you were breaking the law, aside from the fact that this was a very dangerous thing to do." Richard did not accept the fact that it was dangerous. In fact, one of the things he enjoyed about going home was that his father permitted him to drive the car when there was not much traffic, and added, "I didn't get caught, so what's the fuss about?" Therapist: "Richard, something you do does not become legal only because you don't get caught." Jules: "That's right. You should know that by now. You could have killed somebody." Richard: "But I was driving the car on an empty highway. It was night; there was nobody around. There's nobody I could have killed." Jules: "That doesn't matter. You didn't belong in that car behind the wheel. When I drive the car, my father is next to me. I have a permit and the law says that I can drive a car if I have a permit [in his state]. I don't drive the car in New York State because the permit isn't good in New York."

Therapist: "Richard, this is what we were talking about last week. Remember that word I used, *archaic*." Richard nodded, signifying that he remembered. "I was talking about the little boy, the little infant, that does things when he wants to do them and doesn't give a hoot about the consequences," said the therapist. Richard now admitted that he was really very nervous when he drove the car, demonstrating as he talked how his hands shook on the wheel. "I knew I could control my feet on the gas and on the brake, but I wasn't sure I could control my hands on the wheel because they shook so much. I was really scared stiff when I drove that car." He then added that he wanted to think over what he had done and maybe he ought to talk some more about it. The therapist agreed.

COMMENT

Reality-testing, a major characteristic of maturity, was displayed by Richard in his ability to consider the relative merits of the two jobs as they related to his schooling, his understanding of the reasons for the increased harmony in his family, and the part one played in interpersonal conflicts. These recognitions stemmed from the discussions at the group sessions, but they seemed now to be more than conceptualizations, as witnessed by their relevance and the clarity with which they were presented. They were now incorporated as *attitudes* and had emotional significance, as revealed by the relaxed state of the boys after the discussion. The doubt that was engendered in Richard about the propriety of his driving a car unlawfully was an effective maneuver on the part of the therapist to counteract the "delinquent" trends in the boy, which, as we know, had been encouraged by his father. As a result of our supervision discussions, the therapist did not press the latter point, namely, the father's delinquent character.

Of no small significance was Richard's self-confidence in initiating a discussion with his father about the latter's feelings about him and the mature way with which he could now converse with the parent.

Session Sixty-Six

There had been no meeting during the preceding week because the therapist was on vacation. As the boys walked in, Macy (who had been away for three weeks) said, "It's good to be back to group discussions." The absence of two out of five boys for two weeks, and the cancellation of the session on the third week, created some difficulty in getting started this time. Jules and Leonard prepared coffee and distributed cigarettes and cookies. Leonard and Michael got into a private discussion about their respective cottages, the Easter home visits, and trivial incidents around the Village during the past few weeks. Richard had stretched out on the couch and appeared removed. Jules held a conversation with Macy about their home residences. After a period of this desultory activity, Michael commented, "Maybe we ought to start talking about something instead of just bullshitting," but nobody seemed to pay any attention to him. It seemed the boys needed a period of reacclimatization.

The therapist overheard Michael saying to Jules, "Mine is bigger than yours," and Jules countering that his was bigger than Michael's. (They were obviously referring to their penises.) Jules looked in the therapist's direction, and although the therapist was not observing Jules, he was aware that Jules was embarrassed. This discussion was quickly dropped. However, a few minutes later Michael took a seat next to Jules. This was the one ordinarily occupied by Richard, but it was vacant, since Richard was lying on the couch. Jules asked Michael: "What the hell are you coming over here for?" Michael, seductively: "I just feel like being near you." Jules said nothing. (This seemingly sexual byplay had never before occurred in the group, and the therapist was puzzled as to its meaning. Jules and Michael were not living in the same cottage.)

There was silence while the boys were drinking coffee. Soon Michael got up and returned to his own seat, which was next to that of the therapist, and began to tell the group about the good-looking teacher in the school whom he would like to get his "hands on." Jules picked this up immediately and said, "She's got a beautiful butt," and looked to Michael for confirmation. Michael said, "How could you see her butt today in class?" Jules: "She was sitting in a chair and her ass was hanging over the chair and I just felt like putting my hands on it." Michael now regaled the group with a mass of incidents involving "good-looking female teachers" in the school. There was one teacher by the name of H. whom the boys were constantly touching. She must have liked it, because she never screamed at the boys or fought with them, and guys used to come to the room just to look at her. When she walked in the hall someone would always put his hand on "her ass." Jules told of a boy by the name of S. who once grabbed this teacher and put his arms around her, and she said to him: "You mustn't do that. It's not good for you."

This conversation ended, and another silence set in that lasted for quite some time. Leonard and Macy went up to refill their cups of coffee, took the cookies, and passed them around again. After this, the two boys sat down. The silence continued for another moment and then Jules asked: "Why don't we start talking about something tonight?"

Richard immediately said that his caseworker had told him that his parents had a surprise for him when he got home, but the caseworker is not going to tell him what the surprise was. Richard thought this unfair, because he was sure that the caseworker knew what it was. Richard thought that the caseworker must have seen his parents, who must have told "something" to the caseworker. Richard said, "I wonder if he's trying to torture me." Jules: "Well, why don't you wait until you go home next time and see what the surprise is? Or why don't you just write your parents so then you don't have to be wondering all the time about what the surprise is."

Jules turned to the therapist and said: "Mr. Ellery, I spoke with my caseworker about what we were talking about here, you know about my being adopted and all that. My caseworker told me that the reason I stole was because I was angry at my mother who gave me up for adoption. He kind of feels the way you do, Mr. Ellery, that a lot of what I did was because I was angry. I kind of wonder though why I gave up stealing, because I didn't steal all the time. Later I went to playing truant. Why did I do that?" Therapist: "Jules, that sounds like a very good question; maybe we ought to talk about it." Jules said he didn't know the answer. He had been thinking about it the past week, but he still did not know the answer. He then said: "It's hard for me to remember feeling mad at my mother now. I know I feel mad at my real mother but I don't feel mad at my other mother [his adoptive mother]. My caseworker told me that you've got to understand all your feelings and then you'll never steal again. How do you understand your feelings?" The therapist commented that one began to understand them by talking about them, as they did at the group, and through talking one got to know more and more about the things he felt inside. Jules: "I don't know what to talk about any more. If I'm still mad, why don't I feel it?"

The therapist explained that sometimes people bury feelings in such a way that they don't really feel them any more. Macy immediately added: "You mean in your unconscious mind you still got the feelings even though you can't feel them?" Richard: "That's right. We always talk about that, like what's in your unconscious mind." The therapist explained that even though things are buried, what remains is a symptom and at this point explained to the group what is meant by a symptom. "For instance, when you run a fever it means that there is something wrong with the body. You may not know what it is, but the symptom is a warning that something is not right. In the same way, you've known people who always act as though they are happy, as though there is nothing wrong at all, and yet they do things that hurt other people." Richard: "Well, that proves they are not really happy, that something inside is wrong. When they do things like hurting other people, it's like running a fever." Jules continued the explanation: "It's like having a sore and that sore may be cancer and you have to find out what the sore is all about. In other words, stealing is really what is called a symptom." Michael quickly added: "That's the thing I always wonder about myself. When I leave Children's Village, I know I'm always going to steal small things, nothing big. I don't want to get into trouble again, but I got a hunch I'm always going to be stealing small things. I guess I can never change. I used to worry, remember Mr. Ellery? We'd talk about it, about killing people when I get mad, get into a real fight. Now I kind of think maybe I'll steal things." Richard to Michael: "You ain't finished yet, Mike. We got to talk some more here." Michael did not say anything further at this point.

Macy: "Something I got to ask you about. When I sit in the class-room I daydream what it would be like if I climbed out on the ledge of the window and threatened to jump and what would I do if anybody, like the boys in the class, tried to stop me from jumping." He wondered why he had such thoughts and whether it proved he was "crazy." "If you think of suicide, does that prove you're crazy?" Therapist: "No, that does not mean you are crazy." Michael: "I used to think I was crazy for thinking that way. Many times when I felt very miserable I kind of felt like doing away with myself. For instance, I know that if my mother were to die, my sisters were to die, I would be left all alone. I'd be so miserable that I might want to kill myself. Why do people sometimes want to kill themselves when they are feeling miser-able?" Therapist: "It's because people sometimes need to feel that they can stop the misery and don't have to go on feeling miserable. But there is another way, and that is trying to find out what makes you miserable, just as we are doing here." Michael: "Do you think I would kill myself?" Therapist "No, I don't think so." With a smile on his face, Michael said, "I'm going to prove you're wrong." He went over to the window and began to climb onto the fire escape. Richard ran over to him and said, "Come on, Mike, I'll join you." Michael turned around and said: "The hell with you. You're liable to push me," and climbed back into the room. Macy to Michael: "Why don't you stop acting like a horse's ass? Sit down in your chair and let's talk." Michael seemed to sober up. He sat down and nothing more was said on this subject.

Macy described how sometimes, while lying in his bed before he fell asleep, he thought of what it would be like to lie in a coffin, and have people milling around looking at him. He asked the therapist what he thought about this. The therapist said he was not sure, but he won-dered whether it had anything to do with getting attention. This did not feel quite like the correct explanation, and Macy indicated that he, too, was not sure as to what it meant. He said that he thought about it all the time, that is, not all the time, but like before he was going to sleep or while he was in the classroom. He was always afraid that this proved that he was crazy, and again he asked if the therapist thought he was crazy. Therapist: "No, it does not prove that you're crazy, Macy, but it does prove that there is something bothering you." After a silence that followed this interchange Macy said, "I don't know what it could be." It occurred to the therapist to ask the boy: "Macy, I wonder if this has anything to do with your father dying?" (Macy's father had passed away about two months before, and Macy in previous sessions talked about his guilt concerning it.)

Macy said he wasn't sure and asked: "What do you mean, Mr. Ellery?" Therapist: "Macy, do you still feel guilty for your father's dying?" Macy remained silent for a few long moments. Then he said: "I still feel that if I was home I could have saved him, like I told you, remember, about reading in *Reader's Digest* how you can massage the chest and the heart will start working again? I think maybe if I was home I could have massaged the chest of my father and he might still be living. Do you think I might have saved him Mr. Ellery?" Therapist: "It is more than just massaging the chest. It takes a very skilled doctor to open up the chest and massage the heart, something you certainly couldn't have done. But let me ask you this, Macy. Supposing you were home, do you think you could have stayed near your father twenty-four hours a day, especially since nobody had any idea that your father might be sick or was going to pass away?" Macy thought and then said: "No, I don't think I could have been with him for twenty-four hours a day. I have to go out of the house and I have to be with my friends and do things around the neighborhood." Therapist: "Macy, you are making a pretty tall demand on yourself—that you should have been there at the exact moment when your father had a heart attack and passed away." Richard spoke up: "Suppose you were there, Macy, and suppose you did massage your father's chest and suppose your father still didn't live, then you'd really be blaming yourself." Macy: "Yeah, I guess I would be kind of blaming myself." Therapist: "Macy, from what you are telling us, I get the feeling that what you are doing is trying to punish yourself for what happened to your father." Macy: "Maybe you got something there." He thought for a minute and said: "It's funny, I never wanted to die. I always was afraid of dying, but now I'm not afraid any more, because I know I'll go to heaven and there's somebody waiting for me in heaven" (referring to his father).

Michael asked why people were embalmed before burial. Jules answered his question by saying, "So as to preserve the body." The therapist refrained from encouraging this discussion. Michael wanted to know why the body "rots in the grave." The therapist explained in terms of the action of bacteria. Michael talked about worms and insects "eating into the body." Macy joined in this, saying he had heard that the body "decomposes." A discussion sprang up among Jules, Macy, Michael, and Richard about embalmers putting powder on the face of the corpse, dressing it, and keeping it in a refrigerator so that "the body wouldn't rot." The therapist wondered if the boys were trying to understand what death was all about. Macy said he never wanted to think about death: "But I guess you have to sometimes. You can't always keep pushing it away because you think about it in your unconscious mind anyway."

It was 8:30 at this point and the session had to end. As the therapist was leaving, Richard approached him and told a dream he had had the night before, about a huge, seven-foot Indian in the basement of his cottage who was going around beating up boys. Any boy that came into the cottage basement was beaten up by the Indian. Richard had gone into the basement and as the Indian approached him, he ran away. Richard concluded by saying: "Maybe we ought to try to find out next week what the dream meant." The therapist assented.

COMMENT

Macy's spontaneous assertion, "It's good to be back to group discussions," reflected the emotional significance of the sessions to the boys, though one could question whether it was the "discussions" that were missed or the total climate and relationships in the group. Without interference from the therapist the boys themselves now pressed for inauguration of talk and restrained their mates who interfered.

Psychological literacy and self-confrontation were unerringly demonstrated by the boys: Jules on the causes of his stealing; Michael on the replacement of impulse to steal for that of killing and his doubts as to his sanity and suicidal fantasies; Macy on daydreaming in school, and death (lying in a coffin), including his guilts concerning his father's death.

Preoccupation with pathology (self-destruction, decomposition of corpses, being eaten up by worms) is characteristic of the self-doubt and violence fantasies of adolescents generally, and particularly in boys who have been exposed to the pathogenic climates in which the members in this group had lived. This was equally true of the homoerotic and heterosexual urges displayed early in the group session, which had been reawakened during the boys' visits to their former haunts (in their home settings). The boys' openly bringing up verbally and acting out these preoccupations leads to improved mental health.

Session Sixty-Seven

Leonard came about five minutes ahead of the set time and while alone with the therapist talked about his plans for getting a job helping to take care of the horses at a raceway, where he would be living away from home. He was not certain whether this plan would work, but he hoped it would. This was only one of several jobs he was considering, he said. Another job that was waiting for him was in his neighborhood, making deliveries for a grocery store. Leonard indicated that as the result of his "scholarship" at the Village (which provided boys with an opportunity to work with a maintenance crew and earn money), he might get a job as a painter's helper, with the eventual possibility of learning the painting trade.

At this point, the other boys came into the room. Michael stretched himself out on the settee immediately upon arrival. The boys moved the chairs to form a somewhat smaller circle than was usually the case. Richard was the first to pull his chair in, and the others followed. There was an exchange of pleasantries among the boys, Michael asking whether it would be possible for the group to take a trip "like last year."[5] (It was now spring, the end of April.) The therapist told him he would "check with the Club Department" whether this could be arranged. Michael repeated the request, as if to reassure himself and the other boys that the therapist would attend to this matter. The therapist reassured him that he would.

Following this, there were a few moments of silence. Richard began to narrate an incident that had occurred in his cottage just before he came to the session. He talked calmly, without emphasis or emotion, about his attempt to "get an extra week end," "bargaining" with the associate cottage father. The latter had told him that he did not have the authority to grant him this special privilege. Macy suggested to Richard that he check with his social worker about this. Richard said that he intended to do it, but had little hope for it. He did not mention the purpose for which he wanted this special privilege.

Michael said that he was very upset. "I just came from track and I came in second. I got a bum foot and my foot was bothering me, but I hate coming in second." Macy asked Michael how he could expect to win with a "bum foot." Michael said with emphasis that he *"had* to win." He hated coming in second. What seemed to bother him particularly was that the boy against whom he was running was one whom he ordinarily could have beaten. Michael continued: "I ran against this

5. See session 36, pp. 471-472.

boy last week and I beat him hands down. That guy's a punk; he stinks!"
Macy: "You can't win them all. Sometimes you just don't win, so why
don't you get used to it?" Michael did not respond. He lay quietly on
the couch for a few moments, seemingly mulling over this statement.
After a while he said: "I know you can't win them all, but I'm still
pretty sore that I lost this race. If it wasn't for this lousy foot of mine,
I could have beat him." Therapist: "What do you think about what
Macy just said?" At first Michael didn't say anything, and then: "I
know you can't win them all, but that still don't stop me from feeling
that I got to win them all." He then went on to describe that this was
a feeling that he always had. For instance, a couple of weeks ago, he was
in a boxing match and didn't win; the coach who was refereeing the
match ruled against him. He was very upset about it, because he felt
he should have beaten the boy who was his opponent. He then commented out of context that he had altogether forgotten about this boxing
match and only now that he had lost the track meet, did he recall it.

Therapist: "Mike, how do you feel when you lose?" Again there
was silence for a few moments and then: "I feel kind of shitty; like I'm
not good. Like I can't win anything." Jules: "Everybody gets that
feeling once in awhile, it doesn't mean you can't do anything. Right,
Mike?" Michael: "What do you mean right? That ain't the way I feel.
I feel like I—I don't know how to tell it to you, but I feel crummy
inside and then I get sore. I think what I'm really sore at is thinking *about*
myself." Richard (in a very professional tone of voice): "You're sore
at yourself?" Michael said, "That's right. What do you think I'm trying
to say?"

Jules and Macy were trying to start a side conversation. Actually
it was more glancing and whispering under their breath than loud talking. This died down very quickly; then there was silence in the room.
Michael, who was lying on his back on the couch turned on his side
toward the group, propped up his head with his arm, and said: "I guess
that's the way it goes. The next time I go out on track, I'm going to win.
I'm going to practice, practice, practice, and then I'm going to win!"
The therapist referred back to his feelings about himself. He said, "Mike,
when you said you feel crummy inside when you can't do something,
something started going through my head." Michael: "What was it, Mr.
Ellery?" Therapist: "I remember a long time ago when we were sitting
here and talking, you mentioned something about your mother asking
you to move some furniture. You tried your 'best' but she told you it
wasn't good enough. I remember your saying that somehow you never
were able to do anything good enough to please her." As if he were
pondering this Michael said, rather quietly and in a questioning tone:
"My mother?" He remained quiet for a while then said: "I didn't think

of my mother. That's funny you should mention it. What the hell would she have to do with this?" He then added that his mother *was* satisfied with what he did. She never criticized him. But then he corrected himself and said, "She did criticize." Macy: "I remember your saying something about moving furniture and she didn't like the way you did it. In fact she made fun of you."

Michael, gazing directly at the therapist: "I'm not sure. What do you mean?" Therapist: "I was just wondering, Mike, from the way you were talking and from what I remembered about what you once said, whether you were still trying to kind of please your mother in everything you do. You've got to come out on top. For instance, tonight you said you had a bad foot; you had sprained it; and then you ran a race and couldn't win. You're upset because you couldn't win a race with a bad foot. Well, I remember your telling about moving furniture when you were a very little boy, and it was pretty heavy furniture and yet you couldn't please your mother." Michael: "That's right. I couldn't please my mother." Michael then turned onto his back again, looked up at the ceiling, and reflected. He put a hand up to his forehead as if he were deep in thought. Then he said: "I don't know if this has anything to do with it; maybe it does. I'm not sure. I'll think about it." He turned back on his side, facing the therapist and said: "Sometimes you like people better than your own mother. I never knew, for instance, that boys could like their grandmother better."

He went on to describe how when he was a child he had lived for some time with his grandmother in the South. She was very nice to him. In fact, she used to like everything he did. She used to kiss and hug him a lot, gave him food and candy, always took him with her wherever she went, and he always wished he could stay with his grandmother. Then his mother took him away. He was not clear as to why his mother took him away, but he remembered that he enjoyed being with his grandmother more than with his mother. "Is there something wrong with liking your grandmother more than your own mother?" he asked. Therapist: "From what you say Michael, I certainly can understand it." Yet Michael seemed to remain unsatisfied. There was an expression of guilt on his face. Macy very actively and quite obviously tried on a number of occasions to steer the conversation away from Michael (or the topic?). He, Richard, and Jules got into discussion of the numerous happenings in their cottages, about going to the movies, and similar trivia. However, Michael, who was now deeply involved emotionally, quickly stopped this. He said: "Look fellows. I'm not finished talking yet." After a silence Michael said: "It's different now, Mr. Ellery. I think my mother really likes me. You know when I go home, my mother lets me go out. She doesn't always ask me where I'm going. She kind of trusts that I'm not getting into trouble any more. Now, how do you explain that, Mr. Ellery?" The therapist asked Michael if he had any explanation for it himself. He said he didn't. Therapist: "Maybe it's because you are different. Remember we once talked about it here. Maybe now you approach your mother differently. You don't look angry. If you look nice, she'll treat you the same way." Richard said: "I remember we talked about it. If you go up to somebody expecting a fight and look like you are expecting a fight, they are going to get into a fight with you." Jules: "Yeah, I remember we talked about that." Jules said this in a tone of annoyance.

Nothing more was said. Macy again began to talk about the cottage: the fact that the cottage parents and his caseworker did not let him go home yet, that he felt ready to go home as soon as possible. The therapist directly raised the question with Macy of why he was trying so hard to steer the discussion away from what he and Michael were talking about. He asked: "Macy, do you know what you were doing?" Jules: "He knows what he's doing. He's trying to talk about something else." As he said this Jules got up and began getting some coffee, and Macy joined him. A short period was taken up with coffee-making and distributing of cigarettes and cookies. Drinking coffee and chatter among the boys lasted for a longer period than in previous sessions. It seemed like a long time, but the therapist did not feel that he should break in at this point, for there seemed marked resistance in the group. (The therapist was not clear as to what brought it on; perhaps it had something to do with the discussion about parents.) Finally (after about ten minutes), the therapist said: "Does anybody have any idea how come there is so much restlessness here tonight?" No answer, but the boys seemed to quiet down and Richard said, "Okay fellows, let's kind of calm down." Jules said he was talking with his caseworker about going home and his caseworker said that he would probably be leaving sometime in June. Jules remarked: "Boy, I can hardly wait to get the hell out of the Village. No more trouble for me once I get out."

Therapist: "By the way, I was thinking about what we were talking about last week. Remember Jules? Why you gave up stealing and went to playing hooky?" Jules appeared interested and nodded his head. Therapist: "Jules, tell me, when you stole did your parents always know about it?" Jules: "No, I don't think so. Half the time they never knew about my stealing." Therapist: "When you played hooky, did they always know about it?" Jules: "No. But nine out of ten times they found out because the school either sent a letter to my mother or called her. What are you trying to say, Mr. Ellery?" Therapist: "Couldn't you more easily hurt your family by playing hooky than by stealing because when you truanted they always knew about it, and remember we talked about how important it was for your family to keep a clean name in G——?" Jules thought about this a while and said, "Doesn't make too much sense to me *yet*." (The therapist noted a faint expression of annoyance on Jules's face and decided that perhaps it was premature to proceed with this line of uncovering. However, Jules himself stayed with it.) He thought for a while further and then said: "Nope, it don't make any sense. What the heck! That's the past. I don't think I'm going to go to school, but if I do, I'm not going to play hooky any more. I know I'm not going to steal when I get back."

All the boys were listening intently as Macy broke in: "Yeah, the past is the past. Once in a while me and the boys just sit around and we talk about the good times we had in the past, but that don't mean we are going to have the same kind of good times. They weren't even good times, because we got to pay for what we did." Richard: "Yeah. We're at the Village. What's the point in stealing any more? Just to come to the Village again? We aren't even going to come to the Village. They'll probably put us in prison if we steal again." Michael: "Hey, Leonard, how about you saying something? You're always quiet here." Leonard looked somewhat embarrassed, but did not say anything. Jules prodded Leonard: "Go ahead, say something. We're always talking here." Leonard remained quiet and for a moment looked as if he were going to say something, but remained silent.

Macy called attention to the time, and the boys got up and left.

COMMENT

Leonard's initiative in making plans for himself without his mother's dominating interference was a mark of his growing self-identity and maturity. Whether in the final stages his mother would permit this independence was questionable, but the fact that he had mobilized power to cut the silver cord was a good omen.

The general reaction to Michael's compulsive need always to be the victor was very helpful both to him and to the other participants. Its value was enhanced by the therapist's relating this to his self-image engendered by his mother's consistently downgrading Michael and his efforts, and tracing it to its infantile origins. Michael now no longer relied on magic or overconfidence, but accepted the fact that he needed to practice to succeed—displaying a growing sense of reality. This growth was further in evidence when later the conclusion was reached that fun which led to disaster was not worth while.

Michael had become aware of his mother's liking him now. Similar reactions of parents were reported by all the boys in their family relations, and they were helped by the therapist to tie this up with the changed attitudes in themselves (the self-fulfilling prophecy).

At this stage it was possible for the therapist without incurring negative reactions to face the group with their distractibility, which led to their voluntarily calming down.

Session Sixty-Eight

The session started on time. The boys came singly, Leonard coming in first. After they had seated themselves quietly, Jules proceeded to prepare coffee for everyone in the room. Some pleasantries were exchanged, during which Michael inquired about the proposed group trip. The therapist told him that the Club Department had approved it and that the tentative date set for it was May twenty-fifth. As the boys had requested, it would include a ride to New York, a movie, and lunch. Jules asked whether it would be possible to go to a dance, since the Y.M.C.A. in a nearby town held dances on Thursday nights from six to eleven o'clock. He wondered whether the therapist could get permission for the boys to attend such a dance. There was general assent to this suggestion. The therapist informed Jules that he was not sure that he could get permission for it, but he would certainly inquire. Jules also stated that the movie trip would conflict with an R.O.T.C. parade and review set for the same day. The group discussed this and decided on the same day of the week, which was the day of the regular meetings, either the week before or after May twenty-fifth.

Having disposed of this piece of business a silence ensued that lasted a considerable time, until Michael suggested that someone start the discussion. He first turned to Leonard, asking him to begin: "You don't talk here, Leonard, so come on. You've been here a long time. You know you're supposed to talk. How about talking tonight?" Leonard hesitated for a long moment then said, "I'll talk when I feel like it." He said this in a tentative tone of voice, as though surprised at his boldness. Michael did not challenge him, but Jules, insistent, said: "Yeah, do like Mike says. Talk here." Leonard did not answer.

Richard essayed a report that when he had seen his social worker recently the latter had said he was starting a group for discharged boys in the city, and invited Richard to join it when he left the Village. Richard was laughing as he narrated this, saying: "I think it's very funny, him wanting to start a group. What does he know? He's just a faggot." Michael added: "Yeah, Sister W. is just a faggot." Richard went on to say that the caseworker had told him that there would be a group of boys who would sit around talking about the problems they had. Richard told the caseworker he was not sure he wanted to join such a group, and the caseworker told him to think it over. This was the only group he wanted to belong to, he said. He liked it here, and added, "I found out a lot about the things that used to bother me and they don't bother me so much any more." Jules: "That's right. This is the only group we want to belong to, and Mr. W. isn't going to compete with us." Michael broke into laughter and said: "Remember when Jameson came to the group. I still remember and I still laugh every time I think of it. He walked in the door and said: 'I quit. I ain't coming!' " Richard recalled it too, and said: "It's too bad Jameson didn't come. Maybe he could have learned something.

The therapist decided to try something at this point. He said to the boys: "Most of you, when you first came to the group, said either that you wanted to quit or that you didn't want to belong to the group. How come you stayed?" There was no immediate response to this. Michael, with a smile, finally volunteered: "I guess I stayed because of the food." The therapist reminded him that there was no food in the beginning for at least a month or six weeks. Michael thought about it and said, "I still stayed for the food." Richard: "I stayed because I could get out of the cottage; that's the reason I stayed in the group." Jules: "I don't know why I stayed around this place. I just decided maybe I'd give it a try and find out what all the jazz was about." Richard supplemented his original statement with: "That's right, me too. I wanted to try out what this jazz was all about." Macy entered the discussion at this point, saying that he didn't know what had made him come to the group, but he was glad that he had, because: "You can sit around this place, you drink coffee, smoke cigarettes, you can talk about anything you feel like talking about. That's pretty good. You can't do this anywhere else in the Village. I'm glad I could do it here. Sometimes I hate leaving the group when the group is over at night. I wish we had another half-hour or an hour just to sit around and shoot the breeze."

Macy, clearing his throat, then said, "Funny thing happened to me this week," and went on to say that he had received a letter from a girl who wrote to him quite often. In this letter the girl told him that he was crazy, she didn't want to write to him any more, and she was going out with another boy. Macy said he was very upset when he read the letter. He had shown it to Jules. Macy said that what upset him so much was the fact that up until then, this girl had written him pretty regularly, telling him that he was the only boy in the world she liked, that she was crazy about him, that she wanted to marry him, and such. All of a sudden, he got this letter. It made him very mad. If she were nearby, he would have "torn her apart." Then he sat down and wrote her: "You are crazy. The only difference with some people when they are crazy is that they know it. You are the kind of girl that doesn't know it." He then elaborated, giving other choice phraseology he had used in the letter, in which he indicated to her, among many other things, that he had never really loved her, that he was just playing around with her, that he didn't care for her, and so on. Macy added, however, that he still liked this girl, but he was so mad at her that he was glad he was not near her because he might beat her up.

The therapist asked Macy if he could tell some more about what it was that had got him so mad. At first he found it difficult to formulate his ideas, but then he said: "I don't know. I didn't like losing the girl, not after she led me on and told me that I was the only boy in the world for her and all that. You don't blame me for being mad do you, Mr. Ellery?" Therapist: "No, Macy, I don't. But it just occurred to me what Mike said last week and what you said to him." Macy said, "What do you mean?" Therapist: "Remember when Mike was talking about how he hated losing the race? What was it you said to him?" Macy: "Oh I remember. Something like you can't win them all. I guess that's the way it is, you can't win them all the time." Macy then added: "But I'd sure like to. What I do is I go out with more than one girl at a time, so if I lose one, I always got another girl."

Michael, who up until this time had been rather quiet, became playful, seemingly trying to divert the group from Macy. The therapist asked Michael what was it he was trying to do. Jules: "Don't pay him any mind. He's trying to bust things up tonight." Michael denied this rather vehemently, and then got up and left the room. He was gone about ten minutes. Jules meanwhile said: "If any girl called me crazy, I would punch her in the nose. I'd knock the shit out of her." There was no response to this and the therapist asked Jules: "Jules, do you have any idea what would make you do it?" He said: "I don't know, I hate being called crazy. No girl is going to call me crazy and get away with it. I'd punch her in the nose." Then, almost as if suddenly becoming aware of what he was saying, he smiled and said: "Naw, I don't think so, Mr. Ellery. I don't think I'd really punch her in the nose." (From the way he said it the therapist had the feeling that Jules was trying to propitiate him.)

The therapist became involved with the boys in a discussion as to what it was that made people angry when others crossed them, reminding the boys of previous discussions about the feelings people "bury" (suppress) because they do not like to face them, and that when someone calls these feelings to their attention, they fight back. Using Jules's situation specifically, the therapist said: "For instance, the word *crazy* bothers you, and it has come up in our discussions before. Maybe the doubt you have about yourself and the doubts that are buried are 'started off' when somebody calls you this word." Jules seemed thoughtful, but said nothing. Macy: "I don't got any doubts about me. I know I'm okay. I ain't got a doubt in the world and I'm still mad at this girl." Therapist: "You have any idea what the word *adolescent* means?" Almost every boy in the room nodded his head. Therapist: "One of the meanings of adolescence is that it is a period when you have a lot of doubts about yourself: the way you are growing; what is going to become of you; how you are going to be; what you are really like. This is what hurts so much when a girl kind of jilts us. *She reminds us of all these doubts.* We want to be liked so much that when a girl jilts us it makes us kind of feel that we will never be liked." Macy immediately picked this up and said: "That's what I was angry about. I felt like I was a piece of shit when she wrote that thing in the letter about me." Richard thoughtfully added: "This is the time when we all think about ourselves and where we are going to go, who we are going to be. Right, Mr. Ellery?"

A spontaneous discussion arose among the boys as to how Macy should have written the letter. Jules said that maybe the girl still loved Macy, maybe she was "mixed up, wasn't sure." Macy said now he was feeling a little sorry about sending the letter. Maybe he "still could have had her" if he had answered her the right way. Richard said: "Aw, why don't you forget her. There are a lot of other girls. You can always find another girl, Macy." Macy: "I know, but that's not the point. I got to admit I still like this girl." He remained thoughtful for a while. (By this time Michael had returned.) Macy then said, "I like her, but I'm still sore at her." He went into a long account of all the girl friends he had had, and that most of them liked him. In fact, one girl whom he hadn't seen in a number of years told his sister, who in turn told him, that she was "crazy" about him, that Macy was the kind of boy she would like to marry. Macy: "I don't know how she could feel that way." Therapist: "What do you mean?" Macy: "I don't know. This girl doesn't really know me any more. It's been a lot of years since I saw her, or she saw me, for that matter." Therapist: "Maybe there's another part to the question, Macy. Maybe you are also saying, 'How can anybody like me?'" Macy thought a while and said: "Well, that's what we were talking about before, the doubts you have about yourself when you are—what do you call it—oh yeah, an adolescent. But you got to learn how to control your temper. It's like you get mad sometimes when a girl doesn't say the right thing to you and then you get into trouble with girls. That way, you don't have any girl friends."

Therapist: "Maybe there is a reason for your feeling that way." Macy: "Like what?" Therapist: "Well, before we were talking about those buried feelings, remember? Maybe your getting mad when a girl says something you don't like has to do with those buried feelings. For instance, every boy who ever lived got mad at his mother at one time or another when he was a little boy because of the way she talked to him. But a boy is afraid of telling his mother he's mad or angry, so what does he do? He pushes the feelings down. That's his way of bury-- ing them. But they don't stay pushed down. They come out the rest of your life. You grow up, a girl says something you don't like, and un- consciously it seems like your mother talking to you again—and boom! Your feelings jump out." Richard: "That's pretty interesting. You mean in your unconscious mind you still want to get [fight] back?" Jules rapidly interrupted, as though he were personally offended, and said: "Naw, I don't think that's so, Mr. Ellery. I just don't think that's so." Macy: "Well, maybe it is so. You can't swear what's in your uncon- scious, Jules."

There was a silence, interrupted by Macy, who changed the subject to speak about his cottage, but this lasted only a few seconds. He switched to talking about his sister-in-law, who was an extremely jealous person. His brother always had to put up with a lot of "crap" from her. She wouldn't even let his brother talk to his mother. From what Macy said, his sister-in-law was always on the prowl looking for someone to whom her husband might be attentive and feeling herself robbed of his attention. Macy finished the story by saying he wasn't sure why he brought it up, but then said, "Maybe she's got a problem like this" (apparently the one described by the therapist).

At this point, Jules stood up and said he had to return to the cottage. It was 8:25. Michael, too, rose and left with Jules. Richard, Macy, and Leonard remained. Macy continued to talk about his sister-in-law. "She's a pretty funny kind of person. Maybe she didn't get enough attention as a kid and she's trying to get it now. Isn't that right, Mr. Ellery?" Therapist: "It sounds like it. It just goes to show what your unconscious can do." Richard told Macy, as if it needed telling, he had a "queer sister-in-law." Macy said that he didn't pay much attention to her and "what the heck, I only see her once in a while."

It was 8:30 at this point and everybody left.

As the therapist was going down the stairs, Richard approached him and engaged him in a rather innocuous conversation about week ends, his cottage, and the like. He then said that on his last week end home, his father and he were in the car, his father driving. "A funny thing happened to me. I didn't want to talk about it in the group. We were driving down a highway and my father began to speed up. Remember I told you how my father speeds down the highway?" Richard then described a new type of reaction in himself to it. He did not enjoy it. He remembered what the therapist had said about his father teaching him how to break the law, and Richard said this made him feel "crummy" about what his father was doing. He then wanted to know why he felt so different, almost. He seemed puzzled about feeling different now about things than he did before. The therapist did not want to get involved, but did mention that perhaps Richard was different inside. Richard said, "Maybe so." He then said that he did not really want to come back from the week end, but he did come back. One of the reasons was that his mother began to cry when she realized that Richard had thought of not returning to the Village. He said that he did not want to break his mother up. From the way Richard described it, and from his tone of voice, it seemed somehow he had found himself doing the right thing almost in spite of himself.

COMMENT

As in some of the preceding sessions, the therapist concentrated on expanding the boys' self-understanding and psychological literacy generally. They now responded to it with alacrity and participated with ease. They again proved unafraid of self-revelation and were once more hospitable to psychological insights. The boys were now also aware of, and were ready to verbalize, their pleasure at attending the group and the values to them of the discussions.

Jules's questioning of the therapist's explanation of the reasons why a boy felt hurt at being jilted by a girl revealed also sound perceptiveness of human feelings on his part. The therapist's explanation was inadequate, for it is narcissistic injury, doubt of potency, and deflated ego ideal that are involved here rather than only the repetition of childhood experiences with mothers, even though these experiences contribute to the formation of the difficulties. Macy's associations to the conversation with his sister-in-law's jealousy was interesting, for her reactions also stemmed to a degree from self-doubt and insecurity, though there might be present in her also the element of homosexuality.

Macy, in calmly reporting on the girl's letter and his feelings in the matter, displayed a high degree of control. There was no outburst of rage or vituperation with which he would have responded in the past, and the boys' reasonable evaluation of his conduct further illustrated their general maturity and controls.

It was an error for the therapist to have faced the boys with a *fait accompli* relative to the trip. Both destination and date were set by him. These should have been matters for decision by the boys.

Session Sixty-Nine

The session began promptly. Leonard, however, came about ten minutes early, and he again talked about plans for a job on leaving the Village at the end of June. He had been working on this with both the educational director and his social worker. He hoped he could work either at the raceway or on a farm where he could take care of horses. He appeared happy about the possibilities for these jobs. The main objective of these was that Leonard would not be living with his mother, he said. This was his own decision, and despite his strong attachment to his mother in the past, he was now prepared to live away from home. He said he had some money saved up with which he would buy new clothes and other things. To a question by the therapist, Leonard affirmed that he had always been interested in animals. Even when he was small he had liked dogs and cats, and took care of them, and he now felt he would be very happy looking after animals. He thought this was a very responsible job.

Jules, Richard, Macy, and Michael arrived together. All greeted the therapist in a friendly manner and took their usual seats. Michael tried to get the discussion going by asking, "Where did we leave off last week?" Macy: "I think we were talking about girls." There was no response to this. Richard immediately got up and began to prepare coffee. For some reason this took an inordinately long time. When the coffee was ready to be served, Richard from time to time called each boy's name to ask how much sugar he wanted. This process began to generate a degree of restlessness.

In the midst of this Jules announced that he was thinking of running away. He looked in the therapist's direction with a half-smile, as if he were half-teasing and trying to get a reaction from him. The therapist asked Jules what this was all about, but Jules merely repeated his statement, adding: "I know there is something queer about this. I know I'm going to leave in June, at the end of June. The date is set, but now it seems so far away, I'm really thinking of running away." The therapist attempted to explore the matter with Jules. Richard interrupted by walking around the room distributing cookies. There seemed to be almost a deliberate effort at disruption on his part, but the therapist decided not to enter into it but to await further developments.

Having been thus interrupted, Jules got into a cross-the-room conversation with Michael about who failed to do a chore in their cottage. He then said: "I know that I'm beginning to louse up at the cottage. I don't finish chores and I don't feel like doing them." This didn't seem to continue, however, and as Richard seated himself, a quiet of brief duration ensued. Michael broke the silence. He said: "I'm dying to get out of here, but the other day I felt something, well, like the word Jules used, *queer* inside. Like if they postponed my leaving for a couple more weeks, I don't think I would be too upset." He smiled, looked around, and said: "That sounds queer. Here all the time I have been talking about leaving Children's Village and now—Oh, I know what it is! Maybe I'm not sure what it's going to be like on the outside!" Jules quickly said: "I'm not going to school when I leave the Village. I know that my big trouble is when I get to a school. If I find the work hard, or if I don't understand the work, I'm kind of tempted to fool around. I'm going to work, have some money; and I know if I have a job I'm not going to get into trouble." Richard: "The only thing that bothers me when I get out is that I might be tempted to steal my father's car. If he ever leaves the keys and he is not around, I might take the car out."

Jules, looking in the direction of the therapist with a smile like the cat who'd swallowed the canary: "The other day I drove my father's car alone. I broke the law and I knew it. I wasn't supposed to break the law." (It seemed to the therapist that the boys' statements reflected anxiety about leaving the Village, the fear as to what it might be like on the 'outside.' Jules's claim seemed like a fantasy or pretense. The transactions in the group were now of a counterphobic nature.) Richard was beginning playfully to annoy Jules. Jules had pulled up a chair, placed it in front of him and put his feet on it. Richard, who was sitting directly across from Jules, extended his feet and began to push Jules's feet off the chair. Jules, understandably, pushed back. At this Michael spoke up. He said that one of the things that bothered him was that he knew he might "give a girl a baby" when he got out. He spent some time talking about the fact that he was preoccupied with a desire "to give a girl a baby." He ended by saying, "I think of going inside and giving her a baby." Jules: "If you give her a baby, you got to marry her and support her. You can't do that." Michael: "But I've got to fuck around. I know I'm going to give her a baby." The therapist was not quite clear as to what was transpiring in Michael's thoughts and the meaning of this rather unusual pronouncement and had begun (erroneously) to expostulate on the use of a contraceptive, but quickly realized from the expression on Michael's face that this was not meeting his need. (This fact became clear as the session progressed.)

Michael said: "I'll feel like a man. I want to live like a man. I don't want to get in with the gangs any more in my neighborhood." Macy: "Yeah, that's what worries me, about getting into fights again. I know it's going to be hard to walk away from a fight like we talk here, especially when there are girls around."

After Macy had spoken, the therapist pointed out that what he and the others were talking about was "control." "Now that you are faced with the real possibility of leaving the Village, you are scared as to what it is going to be like." Jules: "Yeah, that's right. We're scared, but I'm not scared." From Jules's smile it was obvious that he did not expect anyone in the room to believe him. Richard and Jules began to "fool around" at this point again. It now seemed like a battle of feet, with Richard doing the provoking. Having attempted to disrupt the session a number of times, Richard seemed ready to be faced with his conduct. The therapist, therefore, turned to him and asked: "Richard, do you have any idea what is making you do this?" Richard: "I'm not doing anything. I'm just fooling around." Therapist: "Exactly, this is what we talked about, remember? Remember our discussion of the meaning of fooling around and how you always wonder what it is that gets people annoyed?" (To bring home to Richard the consequences of his behavior, the therapist was ready to tell him that he was very much annoyed with his acting out. In fact, he felt quite irritated with Richard.) Instead, the therapist said, "Do you think that Michael and Jules are the only boys in this room who are scared about leaving the Village?" Richard did not answer, but he became quiet and settled down. The group (possibly sensing the therapist's unaccustomed irritation) fell silent.

After a while a discussion arose, sparked by Macy, about "walking away from a fight." Macy thought that he was still not sure whether he could do it. He described an incident on his last week end home. One of his friends was discovered in bed with a girl by her father. The father "beat him up" and threw him out of the house. The boy came to Macy and asked him to go with him to beat up the girl's father. Macy demurred saying: "I'm not going to do it. I've had enough trouble, and I'm just not going to do it anymore." The friend said to Macy: "I thought you were my friend. Big friend you are!" Macy's retort was: "I'm your friend, but being your friend ain't going to mean that I'm going to join you in trouble and maybe get sent away." Jules suddenly interrupted to say that he had heard that Louis was in jail. He was caught in a gang fight. Richard supported this by quoting one of the science teachers who had announced this to the boys. Michael said: "I guess Mrs. K. was right. She gave him just a couple of months after he left the Village to get into trouble."[6] Though a bit stunned by this news, the therapist attempted to elicit the boys' feelings about it. There was no response, but a shuffling of feet that lasted a few seconds was heard.

6. It was inappropriate for us to trace the origin of this gossip, but inquiry of the caseworker in the city and the parents brought a denial of this. In fact, Louis was doing well in the community.

Then Jules, referring to his statement at the outset of the session, said: "I'm not going to run away. I know it. I'm just kidding around." The therapist commented that the "two parts" of him were fighting: "You remember how we talked about the grownup self and the little baby inside that fight each other." Jules: "You're right. They still fight. It's not easy to stop fights like that unless you punch yourself in the mouth."

Michael: "Isn't it queer to be scared of leaving the Village? All the time you wanted to get the heck out of here." Therapist: "No, it's the most natural feeling in the world. After all, you've been in a place where people have taken care of you. You've been fed, you've been looked after, and now you have to take the plunge into a world where you are not sure what's going to happen and you are responsible for what happens to you." Michael: "I know, you got to control yourself. I don't know if I can do it, Mr. Ellery. I don't know." Jules immediately stepped in and said, "I always thought it was strange to feel scared about leaving the Village." The therapist deemed that it would be helpful to describe a reaction of his own in a similar situation and said: "Once I was in a hospital for a month and felt weak. When I had to leave the hospital I was frightened, even though all the time there I was dying to get out. When the time came to leave, I wondered whether I would be all right, whether people would still take care of me because, in the hospital every time I needed something, all I had to do was to push a button and a nurse would come. It's not easy to give up something like that."

Michael's response to this was: "I guess everybody feels that. I used to think that everybody was glad to leave the Village, but I had never seen a boy walking around with discharge papers who wasn't scared inside. I wish I knew I could control myself. I have a hunch I'm liable to kill somebody someday. My life has been full of trouble. I don't know what it's like to live without trouble. I wish I could go down south. When I was a kid it was nice in the South. All my relatives were there, but I now got so many problems." Michael leaned back and fell into a thoughtful silence. Therapist: "Talk about it, Mike." Michael looked longishly at the therapist and finally said, "When I go back to B———, my mother, she doesn't want to go south, I've got to stay with her and I know B——— is the worst place for me." Richard broke in with an air of self-disapproval and blurted out: "I got this urge to steal my father's car. When I'm tired, I'm tense. I sleep at night or I don't sleep at night. I kind of keep thinking about driving a car." The therapist said to him, "Richard, now that you know you have the urge—and that's very important, knowing what you are tempted to do—maybe you can control it." "You mean it's not much [not serious] to have the urge?" Therapist: "No, Richard, it's not. You will have temptations to do many things.

The important thing is to know it, figure out what would happen to you if you did do it, and then you'll be able to control yourself."

It was at this point that Michael more clearly expressed what he meant by "giving a girl a baby." He said that by "giving her a baby," he would literally be forced to marry the girl, a decision he could not make without getting in such difficulty. If he were responsible for a wife and child, he would be able to "stay away from trouble." He burst out: "All my life I wanted to sit down and talk to somebody, a man, to tell him everything I've done in my life, everything I feel." Tears began to well up in Michael's eyes as he continued: "I can't tell my social worker, I don't think I would tell a man because I think—I don't know what I think. I'm not sure. I might tell him, but then I'd never want to see him again. I couldn't see him again. I couldn't face him again." Dead silence settled over the group for quite some time. No one spoke.

Richard broke the silence: "It's funny," he said, "I thought I was nuts for being scared about leaving the Village." Michael looked as though he wanted very much to communicate with the therapist. Ignoring Richard, the therapist said to Michael: "Mike, in this room you've told the boys, and me, a great deal about yourself. How do you feel about having said all this to me?" Michael did not answer. Therapist: "Now that I know something about you, Mike, maybe you are wondering how I feel about you, whether I don't like you any more." Michael: "I don't know. I don't know, Mr. Ellery. I know it's hard for me to sit down and tell everybody my whole life. If somebody was to show a movie of my life you know what they would see? One trouble after another. I think I'm the only boy in the world who ever had so much trouble."

Jules: "What do you mean, you're the only boy? What the hell do you think it's like being raised in an orphanage? What do you think it's like to get thrown out by your own parents? What the hell do you think it's like not to be loved when you need love?" Michael: "Okay, but that happened to you in the past. Your life is okay now, you got nice parents, they got money." Jules: "What difference does that make? It may be better now; it'll be better for you, too. My life was a whole load of shit." Jules leaned back and said: "Maybe I got something out of the Village. Like Mr. Ellery said, now there's a fight [intrapsychically]. *I'm not a little boy any more.*" Macy: "We all got a lot out of the Village. At least we can sit here instead of a prison and talk about our troubles."

Michael said: "Life isn't easy. I always wanted life to be easy. Why can't it be easy?" Therapist: "Mike, what law says it has to be easy? Do you think I wake up every morning feeling like going to work?

Don't you think there are days when I walk around feeling like I'm dragging my behind, when I don't feel like doing anything, when I got worries, when I'm nervous inside? There is no such thing as having everything easy." Michael: "I don't know. I don't know any more. How many times I wanted to take my life! I lie in bed and think about putting a gun to my head and killing myself. Sometimes I think of jumping off a roof, but I'm afraid I'm liable only to get hurt and not die right away." Jules: "Why don't you try gas?" Michael: "No, no. I'm scared of gas! Hell, I don't want any gas." Jules: "Well some people hang themselves." Michael: "Well, that's not for me, that's not for me." The therapist mentioned to Michael that the one thing he hadn't heard him talk about was the fact that he was an intelligent boy: "We both know you can read well, do well in school, and academically could do very well and get yourself an education." Michael: "I know, I know Mr. Ellery; but if boys pick on me in school, I know I'm going to fight back. It's going to be hard for me to walk away from a fight. I'm going to try, but I don't know whether I could do it." Macy: "You'll just have to. You've just got to. You can't get into more trouble."

Because of Michael's weak ego, the therapist deemed it necessary to continue to be active. He said: "I'll tell you what just came to my mind. I once had a dream about standing in a doorway. Behind me was a long road; in front of me, a pool. I didn't know what to do. I remember thinking about the dream and it sort of reminded me that I knew the road that I had come down, but I didn't know what it would be like to jump into the pool and swim, whether I'd sink or swim, whether I could get across the pool." Michael immediately said: "Oh, I can interpret that dream for you. It means you are not sure, you are not sure what's going to happen to you. I had a dream; listen to this one. Ten guys were chasing me with knives. They wanted to kill me and I was running. I ran into a poolroom. The guy who owned the poolroom chased these guys out and I was free. What do you think the dream meant?" The therapist asked the boys to interpret the dream but no one would. The therapist said he was unsure, but the one feature of the dream that struck him, was that a minute ago Michael was talking about dying and getting killed, and yet in the dream, he was running away from death. He wanted to live. "Like a big part of you, Mike, is fighting to stay alive." Michael thought about it and then said: "Maybe, maybe. But the dream also shows I'm afraid of gangs, that they are liable to come after me."

Richard stepped in at this point and said: "Remember that dream I told you about snakes I once had? About them coming after me and I was scared? I remember when I go to the zoo with my father, I always want to go to the snake house. I'm not ascared of looking at snakes, but in the dream I was scared. How come?" Therapist: "Remember we talked about 'symbols.' You were scared of the symbol the snake was." Richard immediately said, "You mean like the snake might have been the devil?" Therapist: "Could be. Remember we talked about the punishment dream at that time?" Richard: "That's right, those snakes were out to punish me for stealing." Michael interrupted: "Remember the dream I told you about, the devils in my room and one little devil hitting me in the side? I'm not even sure I dreamed it. I think I was awake when that happened." (The therapist avoided this topic with Michael.) Jules came to the therapist's rescue: "Remember that dream I told you about, about my father with the shotgun. I think my eyes were open then. I'm not sure it was a dream. I know my father didn't put a shotgun to my eyes. I can't explain it. It was like I was sleeping and wasn't sleeping. How can that happen?" This was dealt with intellectually and objectively: "Jules, there's a big word for this, they call it a *hypnagogic hallucination*. It's the twilight zone, being half-awake and half-asleep, and sometimes you can have such 'dreams' even though your eyes may be open." Jules: "Oh, that's what it is." Michael: You think your father really came after you with a shotgun?" Jules: "Naw, I know he didn't come after me with a shotgun." Michael: "I can't figure my life out. I just can't figure it out. I don't know what to say any more."

The group overstayed the allotted time, and as they were leaving the therapist spoke to Michael aside and asked him to come for a talk in his office. Michael said that when he got the chance he might; he did not know whether he wanted "to talk yet." The therapist said he would always be available whenever he wanted to see him. At this point, Richard came over and said to the therapist: "When I leave, I'll want your telephone number, Mr. Ellery. Before I ever get into trouble again I'm going to call you and talk to you."

(Later that evening the therapist called the cottage supervisor to tell him that Michael was agitated and that the therapist was concerned with his state of depression as a result of his excessive introspection and suggested that Michael might need watching. Arrangement was made for someone surreptitiously to "keep an eye" on the boy during the evening and night.)

COMMENT

Michael's suggestion that the group continue with last week's discussion indicated aim-direction and mature interest, which appeared increasingly more frequently now. The boys returned to their feelings of dependency and fear of the rigors of the large community which they were to face. This problem was the subject of many of our supervisory conversations: The boys had to be prepared for these new adventures, and one of the suggestions was that everyone had to reconcile himself to the fact that living involved suffering, that pain was inherent in living. The boys gave the therapist an opportunity in this session to introduce this concept when he talked about his own difficulties and resistances and his struggles with them.

This session was replete with counterphobic ideas and feelings, to the extent, with Michael, of a desire to have an illegitimate child as a means of controlling his behavior. Michael, who was a borderline schizophrenic, was seeking to bolster his ego by diverse means, and this was one of them. He was afraid of losing control and doing bodily harm to someone, a fear which he had brought up many times, and he now sought escape by suicide. The therapist did well to build up the boy's ego by enumerating his strong points. Avoiding further discussion on the presence of devils in Michael's room was also good strategy.

Again one of the themes of the discussion was control, a subject of paramount importance to these boys, and they showed an excellent grasp of it and its place in their lives. The boys now appreciated the value of their sojourn at the Village, and Jules recognized the inner struggle within himself of his ontogenetic archaic mind and his newly evolved perceptions. He climaxed this with the statement, "I'm not a little boy any more."

The content of the group's interviews in the last ten sessions had been characteristic of psychoneurotic patients, rather than of acting-out delinquents, as had been the case in earlier sessions.

Session Seventy

Leonard was first to arrive, about five minutes early. Before the arrival of Michael, who was next, the therapist and Leonard sat talking about his jobs and his living away from home. Leonard was thinking about the clothes he was going to buy for himself. The boys from Mrs. K.'s cottage—Jules, Macy, and Richard—were eight minutes late. Jules explained that the boys had had no time to finish their chores and had been kept after dinner to complete them.

The therapist opened the session by telling the boys that he had checked through on the report of Louis being in prison. He had called Louis's mother, and she had told him that Louis was attending school and doing well. Macy turned to Richard and said, "You're the one who started the rumor here." Richard: "But the teacher told us." Michael: "Well it ain't true then, because Mr. Ellery checked." Very little more was said on the subject. Michael asked the therapist whether he had cleared with the Club Department the plans for the group's trip. The therapist informed the boys that the trip was planned for June first. Jules initiated a discussion as to what movie the group should see. Michael suggested that the week before the trip, the group peruse a newspaper or magazine to check on available movies. Definite arrangements for the time and place for gathering were made by the boys.

After an extended period of silence, Michael, who appeared buoyant, reported that he had had "a couple of job offers"—as shipping clerk, stock boy, and messenger—but that he had decided to go to school instead after he left the Village. He asked if any of the others were planning to return to school. Leonard was the first to respond with, "I'm not going to school." Michael: "Boy, you're wasting your life not going to school. Why the hell don't you go back and try to get an education? What do you think is going to become of you later?" He said he was going to live in B——— and a Mr. H. there would get him a part-time job.[7] Richard began to prepare coffee for the group, and Jules joined him. The serving of coffee, cookies, and cigarettes was carried off quietly and expeditiously, which had been the case at a number of past sessions. There was little or no conversation. Finally, Michael said: "Let's get back to talking. Nobody is saying anything tonight." However, the silence continued for a while longer until Jules said to Leonard: "Come on, Leonard, your turn to talk." All the boys except Leonard laughed. Michael: "That's right, you're always quiet. Come on, open your mouth; say something." Leonard, with an embarrassed smile, said, "I'll talk about my cottage parents." Richard: "Never mind your cottage parents. There is too much talk around here about cottage parents." Michael: "That's right, we're sick and tired of hearing about cottage parents. For a change, let's change the subject." Macy: "Yeah, that's right. Who the hell wants to hear about cottage parents!" After this, a brief silence. Then, Macy: "Come on Leonard, you must have something else to talk about." Leonard did not say anything. Jules: "Leonard, he's always keeping his mouth shut around here. All he does is listen, never talks, never joins." Richard: "Maybe he's a spy. He's trying to find out things about us." Leonard's not talking was bandied about for an-

---

7. After last week's episode, the therapist talked to a member of the Community Center Department at the Village who knew Michael well. This staff member also came from B———, and he had told the therapist that about a year ago a Mr. H. from B——— had worked in the department. Mr. H. and Michael "warmed up to one another" and Mr. H. promised that when Michael returned to B———, he would look after him, and invited him to the community center which Mr. H. now directed in that city. Mr. H. was called on the telephone during the week. He promised to speak to Michael without revealing that this was arranged by the Village staff.

other few minutes as Leonard sat with an embarrassed smile playing on his face, but he did not say anything. Another momentary silence ensued.

The therapist took the initiative and said: "In the past you have asked me what to do when somebody sounds off or picks on you. I think maybe Leonard is showing you [how to deal with it]." Jules: "Good old Leonard. He doesn't get into trouble." Michael: "Yeah, that cat is cool. He knows when to keep his mouth shut." Michael: "But, Mr. Ellery, the big problem is [how] to keep quiet when they push you real hard. I mean by pushing real hard, like when they sound on your mother. I can't take that." Richard immediately joined Michael in this and said, "That's right, fellows can call me names, but when they sound on my mother, boy, I get into a fight." Macy, too, joined the chorus saying that he could take practically anything but "sounding" on his mother. "Those fucking boys better keep their mouths shut." Michael admonished Macy: "What are you using that language in front of Mr. Ellery for?" Macy caught himself, looked in the therapist's direction in embarrassment, and said apologetically: "I'm sorry, Mr. Ellery. I don't mean to curse any more." Michael: "Mr. Ellery, suppose somebody sounded on your mother and called her names. Wouldn't you get mad and fight them?" Therapist: "No." "You wouldn't? You wouldn't defend your own mother?" Therapist: "What's to defend? Should I get into a fight with somebody who says things about my mother? It seems to me that there must be something wrong with a person who would just go around 'sounding' on my mother." Michael: "Suppose you came home one day and you found someone beating your mother with a baseball bat. Wouldn't you get into a fight?" Therapist: "Well, I would have to defend my mother and pull the person away." Michael did not let the therapist finish: "Well," he asked, "what would you do? What would you do?" Therapist: "I would call the police . . ." Michael again interrupted: "But suppose the guy took a swing at you?" Therapist: "I would have to defend myself the best way I could, but that isn't the issue. I don't think that's what we're really talking about. What we're talking about is using fists as an answer to words." Macy: "That's what I've been talking about all the time. Lots of times I get mad inside now, but I don't want to fight any more. I try to control it, especially with Mrs. K. Oh, I don't want to talk about her any more." Richard: "Yeah, let Mrs. K. alone. Let's not talk about her any more."

Michael still wanted to know what the therapist would do if a boy "sounded" on him (that is, called him names or made fun of him). The therapist told the boys that he was once a cottage parent in a correctional school, mentioning its name. (This school was known to the boys.) Some mornings he would come down to the group and one boy would say "fuck you." Jules, abruptly: "Did you hit him?" Therapist: "No, I didn't hit him. I felt sorry for such a boy. After all, just think about it. You come in and say 'good morning' to somebody and they say, 'fuck you.' Isn't there something really wrong with that person? Do you think that by using my fists, I could improve the situation or make that person better?" This statement seemed to bring on a long silence from the boys; all of them seemed lost in thought. The therapist decided to take advantage of this mood and said: "What I'm talking about is try-ing to figure out for myself what is right for me. You know in my work I come across people who say things to me that could make me mad. If I were to go around fighting with them, where do you think I'd be? What I'm talking about is the difference between being a little baby that does whatever it wants to do without thinking of the consequences, and the young man or adult who has to begin to think: 'If I do some-thing, what is it going to get me in the long run? What's right for me in the long run?' This is what I think you boys are fighting with—the part of you that is still the little baby and the part of you that doesn't want to be the little baby any more, that's the growing man in you. If you are on a job and somebody says something to you that you don't like and you get into a fight, how long do you think you're going to have the job? Well, I'm faced with such problems all the time. Before I do something I've got to stop and figure out what will eventually happen. This is the advantage of being able to control yourself. In the long run, I come out ahead, because I can hold a job, make a living, have money, do what I want, go where I want."

Macy said that this made " a lot of sense" to him and yet he wondered whether the therapist thought there was something wrong with any-body who always wanted to fight. The therapist said that it showed that such people haven't yet grown up inside. Macy proceeded to tell the therapist what happened in his cottage. He said: "I don't want to keep sounding on the cottage or Mrs. K. I'm tired of talking about her, but I got to tell you what happens." He went into a long description of how he was often told to do work that other boys shirked and Mrs. K. picked on him. When he tried to explain to her that the jobs were not his and therefore he didn't want to do them, Mrs. K. grew very angry and would say to him that he was not the same boy that he used to be, that he would "come to no good." Macy explained that even Mr. K. was fed up with this. On a number of occasions he told his wife to keep quiet, but she did not heed him. Macy began to boil inside; he began to have fantasies of yelling and screaming at her to leave him alone, but he bided his time, bit his lips, and walked away.

Turning to the therapist Macy asked: "Do you think there is some-thing wrong with me for getting mad?" Therapist: "No, I don't think there is anything wrong with you for getting mad. The important thing is how well you are able to control yourself, because what would happen if you started to scream or yell back?" Macy: "She'd hold up my discharge. She'd get me into more trouble and I don't want any more trouble, but it's not easy to keep things inside." The therapist agreed that it was not easy, but wondered if he ever tried to figure out what made Mrs. K. do what she did. Macy said he didn't know and sometimes he just didn't care. The therapist said (and this the therapist knew through Mr. K., who had mentioned it to the therapist one day) that Mrs. K. was going through a "change of life" and proceeded to explain to the boys what it was and how it made a woman "nervous and tense," which at times accounted for her behavior toward the boys. Jules's comment was, "She must have been going through a change of life all her life," and began to read a comic book, first cautioning Macy against getting too involved with Mrs. K., saying: "Just don't pay her any mind. You've lived long enough with her already. You know what she's like." Macy: "I know what she's like, but it still gets me mad. It's hard for me to control my temper, but I try to control it. I don't want any more trouble."

Macy then described an incident that had occurred a number of weeks before, in which a boy who had been teasing him, provoked him into a fight. The boys in the cottage rushed in and tried to hold Macy back and said, "Watch it, you're losing your head." Macy demonstrated with an expression of fear how he had "lost his head" and said: "That's why I don't want to get into fights. You can't tell what's going to happen." Jules: "That's right. You lose your head and you can't tell what's going to happen; that's why you got to stay out of fights." Richard, who had listened intently, launched into a description of a situation in which he had to control himself. His caseworker was seeing his mother and Richard wanted to sit in on the interview, because he knew they were going to discuss after-care and what Richard would be doing after his discharge. The caseworker agreed to let Richard be present. Although the caseworker did say some nice things, such as, "Richard will be able to stay out of trouble; he'll do all right," he also said, in Richard's presence, that Richard would probably go back to fighting with his sister. Richard became very upset about this negative evaluation of him. Furthermore, because the conference was held in New York, he wanted to spend some time with his mother after the interview, but the caseworker insisted that Richard immediately return to the Village despite the fact that his pass did not expire for several hours. Richard, in anger, felt like running away; he was with his mother in New York, had some time and wanted to spend it with her, and he was being ordered back. Richard's mother said she would travel on the train with him. As a compromise, Richard asked her: "Why do you have to travel so far?" His mother said, "All right, at least let me take you to the station." Richard recognized that his mother wanted him to return to the Village and was going to make sure that he did not "get into any trouble" now. But she said: "Look, you're my son and I want to be with you. I'll go with you to the station," and she did. Richard again described his intense temptation to run away, but he thought it over and said to himself: "I will only get in more trouble. Here I am close to getting out. I'll be getting out in June, and what's the point of having any more trouble in my life?" So he returned to the Village. He summed it all up by saying, "It's not easy to always try to figure out what's going to happen to you next."

At this point the session ended.

COMMENT

Further evidence of emotional maturity of the boys was revealed in their objective attitudes toward cottage parents (as substitutes of their own parents) and the freedom from affective involvement with, and dependence upon, them. This process can be viewed as vicarious working through of the Oedipal struggle in their family settings and the point to which the boys had now arrived is that of maturity and constructive individuation. This maturity was in evidence during this session also in the boys' refusal to continue complaining about cottage parents, apparently accepting this situation as inevitable and adapting to it; by recognizing that the less one says the less likely one is to get into difficulties; in Richard's self-control in resisting the impulse to run away, and his recognition of his mother's subtle strategy in seeing him to the train (to prevent him from doing it). In this, Richard displayed empathic understanding of his mother's motives, which is rather rare among adolescents.

The fly in the ointment, however, was still the inclination toward the jungle law of physical combat in anger. This remnant of atavistic propensity is still present, though much less intense than it had been. The boys now recognized the consequences of "losing one's head." The instinctive association of rage and attack had been consistently reinforced by the boys' microculture and now operated as a conditioned reflex, but this mechanism was now becoming accessible to examination and ego control. The therapist again pointed out, with profit, the inner struggle between the onto-archaic mind and newly acquired values, and emphasized the importance of making a choice through self-control.

However, the motivation for it was laid by the therapist entirely to personal advantages, "not getting into trouble." As previously stated, we repeatedly emphasized in our supervisory conferences the importance of making palpable to the boys the *social* aspects of behavior, rather than exclusively expediency and self-advantage. To refrain from committing acts only because they might bring disadvantage to one actually encouraged vandalism, delinquency, and crime: They were permissible as long as one was not found out. Unsocial conduct needed to be eschewed also because it brought discomfiture, damage, or suffering to others. This moral view needs to be brought to adolescents' attention along with personal gains when allotropic feelings had been evolved in psychotherapy.

Session Seventy-One

This session was marked by restlessness on the part of all boys in the group, and the discussion in no way related to what had been discussed in the preceding sessions. At first this was quite puzzling, but when the therapist put the problem to the boys, asking them for the reason, Macy explained that tonight they "just feel like sitting around and talking." This had been a hectic day for them. Macy explained that he, Michael, Jules, and Richard had participated in the R.O.T.C. parade and were tired. (The therapist was aware of a rather heavy program that had been arranged for that day. During the morning and early afternoon there was a review parade of members of the R.O.T.C. corps. Boys were generally very excited and tense prior, during, and after such reviews, and it was likely that the session was the first opportunity for them to relax and overcome some of their tensions. The therapist, therefore, decided to let the boys carry on in their own way.)

During most of the session the boys sat around discussing plans for going home. In essence, they all agreed that they wanted to go home. Macy stated that he would probably return to school. He had spoken to the education counselor (principal) at the Village, who had told him approximately how well he could expect to do in school. Macy appeared gratified to learn that he could enter school in the city at his grade level and do well. Jules reaffirmed that he would not be returning to school. His uncle had promised to have a job waiting for him and the social agency in his town (which had placed him at the Village) had agreed to his taking that job.

Michael, who seemed in good spirits, talked with Macy about returning to school and said he hoped to have a rather "good time" of it. When the therapist asked Michael what he meant by a "good time," he said that he would try to look for new friends. He would avoid going with the friends he previously had had, who led him "into trouble." He knew he could find friends, both boys and girls, with whom he could have a good time in school. He again referred to the fact that after school hours he might have a lot of trouble in the community because his neighborhood was filled with gangs who might try to force him to join them. He said that they would threaten him that either he join or get beaten up. Jules countered Michael, saying that he need not have such difficulties, but Michael insisted that Jules did not know what he was talking about, because Jules (who came from a small town) did not come from the kind of neighborhood he did. Richard told Michael that he had to take his chances like everybody else, referring to himself, and saying that he was going to try his best to "stay out of any trouble," because he could not get an education and at the same time run around late at night with boys in his neighborhood.

Richard, looking perturbed, turned to the therapist and in a quiet, conversational tone, without the pressure that had characterized his speech before, reported that his mother had written him about an accident his father had had with the car. He said this was the second time his father had been in an accident within a year. Macy, who overheard this, asked: "What are you so worried about?" Richard said that his father would not tell anyone where the car now was. He did let on, however, that the car "is a wreck"; but when the mother asked who was at fault for the accident, the father did not respond. Richard then said that in the first accident, almost a year ago, the father was also very secretive. The boys gave Richard's narration sympathetic interest. (It should be noted that Richard did not participate in the talk by the boys about going home and their plans.)

The therapist tried to encourage Richard to talk further about his concern, but Richard remained noncommunicative. (There is the possibility that Richard used this incident and exaggerated it as an attention-getting device.) He was unable to specify just what was worrying him. His main concern was that his father was so secretive about what had happened. Remembering Richard's statement some months ago that he had once wished that his father would sustain an accident with his car, the therapist attempted to explore possible guilt feelings in relation to the current accident, but Richard merely shrugged his shoulders and said, "It's possible," and said nothing further. Macy told Richard not to worry about it so much, and advised him to go home and try to talk to his father about it in person. Richard said that that would not do much good.

Jules introduced a conversation about the proposed trip to New York which was to be held the following week. He presented a plan that the therapist drive the boys to New York (as on the preceding trip) and that each boy then "go wherever he wished" and then all meet at a prearranged time and place to return to the Village. Michael seconded this suggestion. Jules assured the therapist that "the Village can trust us" and, speaking for the boys said, "everybody would return on time." The therapist raised the question whether the purpose of going to New York was just for the therapist to drive the car or whether "we are going in, and wanted to stay together, as a group." Jules said, "Oh, if that's what we want, then that's what we'll do." Richard said that all should stay together as a group, since they had been "a group all the time." Michael asked if the boys could "do the same thing we did last year," that is, allow some time for the boys to do individual shopping after lunch and then meet to go back (see session 36). The therapist agreed they could if that was what they wanted. Jules: "That's okay," but Leonard said he would prefer that all "stick together as a group, rather than each one going off on his own."

COMMENT

After a period of understandable restlessness, the boys did get down to rather mature exploration of their future, recognizing the community impediments to their desire to meet the responsibilities that lay ahead of them. Richard, however, avoided entering into this conversation because the painful memories of his father had been reawakened by the news of the car accident in which the father had been involved and his strange behavior following. The other boys were sympathetic with Richard and tried to allay his concern, evidence of their allotropic feelings.

Session Seventy-Two

Trip to New York.
ABSENT: Leonard, who was included in a trip with his class to the Bronx Zoo.

Prior to starting on the trip, the boys were each given $2.25, so that they would feel that they were on their own by paying their own way and spending their money as they preferred. Since the boys were required by the school authorities to remain in their classes until 10:30 A.M., this hour was set for departure.

The ride with Jules, Richard, Macy, and Michael was "a most pleasant one." While initially there was some scrambling for seats in the therapist's car, with Michael insisting that he sit next to the therapist, the boys soon settled down and behaved well after that. Macy sat to the right of Michael in the front seat, with Jules and Richard sitting in the back. The boys agreed beforehand that on the return trip the seating arrangements would be reversed. The boys were rather quiet at the start, as if there were an uneasy feeling about leaving the grounds and driving with the therapist in his car, and seeing him in a different role than the accustomed one. However, once the parkway was reached, Jules and Richard scanned the theater section of a newspaper they had brought with them, trying to involve Macy and Michael in a discussion as to what movie they should see. There was no agreement. Richard and Macy wanted to go to Radio City Music Hall; Michael and Jules did not want to see a stage show. Jules did not even want to see the film that was being shown there. Richard, therefore, suggested that the decision be made "when we hit New York."

Jules, Richard, and Macy struck up a discussion of their plans for returning home. Jules took the lead, saying that he had the prospect of a good job, working for his uncle either as a messenger or as a stock boy. Richard asserted that he was pretty sure of going home and said: "I'm kind of surprised I stayed this long at the Village. I could have sworn I would have run away." He then reminded the therapist that he had said on a number of occasions that he was going to run away. Michael asked Richard what was keeping him at the Village. Richard looked at Michael with surprise: "What's the point of running away? I lasted this long. Why should I spoil everything now?"

The general conduct in the car on the ride to New York was "most exemplary." On one occasion a number of boys in an open convertible car cut off the therapist's car, obviously to start a fight. Michael said: "Don't mind them, Mr. Ellery, they're nuts. They're going to have an accident." When the boys in the convertible did not succeed in evoking a response, they went on their way. Jules referred to them as "a bunch of jerks." Michael asked for permission to turn on the radio and the rest of the trip was devoted to discussion by the boys of the various rock-and-roll and pop songs being played.

When the group reached New York, they walked along Broadway for about five blocks trying to decide what movie to see. The boys, among themselves, seemed to reject every movie they passed. The therapist had the feeling at this point that the boys were trying to end up on Forty-Second Street.[8] There was a lot of huddling and whispering among the boys. Although nothing was said, it seemed that though the boys wanted to see the nearby pornographic movies, they were not quite

8. Forty-Second Street is usually filled with all sorts of "strange characters." However, the therapist could not be certain that this was the aim; it was only a hunch. There was also the pos- sibility that the boys were trying to approach the small movie houses on Forty-Second Street, where the films shown often tend toward pornography.

sure how to get the therapist to go along with them. Finally, Richard suggested that the group go to the Paramount Theater, which was showing *Return to Peyton Place*. The group accepted it. Each boy purchased his own ticket and bought candy inside the theater. All this was accomplished quietly and expeditiously. The group went to the balcony because the boys wanted to smoke.

(The therapist found the film rather interesting, although within it were overtones of incest, rape, and so forth. However, it could not by any stretch of the imagination be considered lewd or pornographic.) The boys seemed to be very interested in the movie. However, the following was observed: After a half-hour Richard seemed to become restless. He talked with his neighbors, Macy and Michael, who were sitting on either side of him. None of the conversation could be overheard by the therapist. Jules, who was sitting on the far side of the therapist, was also engaged in conversation. However, none of it was loud enough to annoy anyone. (The theater was rather empty during the morning hours). Richard went out, presumably to the washroom, on at least three occasions, but the therapist suspected that he probably telephoned to his family and friends. The group had come in while the film was already in progress, and during the intermission between the showings all the boys left, the therapist remaining alone. The boys were gone the ten minutes of the intermission and returned with new batches of candy as the showing began.

Although at some points the boys seemed to become restless, as evidenced by their talking with one another, they did not miss anything of the content of the film. From their comments, it was obvious that they were following the story very closely, but like all persons with emotional disturbances, they had a short span of concentration. The therapist observed repeated movements among the boys, though not enough to annoy anyone nearby.[9]

The movie ended. Jules, as spokesman for the group, asked the therapist whether they could have lunch in Y——— (a town on the way to the Village). The therapist was surprised at this request and asked: "Why Y———?" Jules said that he and Michael wanted to see some girls they knew there, and then added: "You can trust us, Mr. Ellery. We

9. Perhaps what added to the restlessness was the fact that the boys were in one another's company. The therapist remembered from his own days at that age that going to movies with a number of friends was somehow different from being alone. With friends there was always the temptation to talk, to share impressions, to wisecrack, and the like, and in this respect these boys were not different from ordinary adolescents. Throughout, the therapist was impressed with a feeling of camaraderie among the boys. There was friendship and warmth for one another. No teasing or name-calling appeared at any time during the trip.

just want to say hello to the girls and then we'll come back and meet you." The therapist agreed to this. After the car was parked, Michael and Jules went off by themselves. All agreed to meet at 3:30 P.M., having reached Y——— at about 2:40. Macy said he wanted to do some shopping in the "five-and-dime," and that he would meet Richard and the therapist at a certain cafeteria, where they were to have lunch. Through a misunderstanding, Macy did not join them for lunch; he had gone to another cafeteria. Richard and the therapist had lunch by themselves. During lunch alone with the therapist Richard seemed rather silent. The therapist engaged him in a conversation and he quickly responded, but again began to talk about going to school and asked whether the therapist, who had known him so long, thought he could "make it in school." The therapist answered in the affirmative. Richard was reading on the level of the eleventh grade, which was far above most boys at the Village, and the therapist told him so. Richard now felt he could "get a good education" if he just tried hard enough. He had learned at the Village what it was like to do homework, something he never did before. He said almost confidentially: "I never talk much about this, Mr. Ellery, but I think I really got something out of the Village. That's why sometimes when I think about leaving, although I sound like I'm in a hurry to get out, I ain't too much in a hurry to get out." Then almost as an afterthought he added that he hoped that nobody tried to stop him at this point from getting out of the Village.

Richard mentioned briefly in passing that he had spoken with his father about the car accident (see session seventy). His father told him that it was one of those accidents where two cars came to the same spot almost at the same time at a cross-section and it was hard to know who was to blame for it. Richard felt better now that he knew, since he no longer felt that his father was all at fault. His father was having the car repaired. As the two left the cafeteria, Richard said that he enjoyed having lunch with the therapist.

At 3:30 Macy came to the car, but there was no Michael or Jules. At 3:45 the two were still not there. Richard and Macy volunteered to go hunt for them, although they did not know where to go. They went off, but came back in ten minutes and said they could not find the missing boys. Richard said: "Don't worry, Mr. Ellery, they'll come back. They won't run away." At 4:00 Jules and Michael were seen walking with two girls. They stopped at a distance, said good-by to the girls, and came up to the car. They looked very guilty for being late. When they approached, Michael said: "I'm sorry, Mr. Ellery. We forgot the time. We didn't know what time it was." The therapist looked at Michael and asked: "Is that what happened?" Jules: "Well, we just couldn't say good-by to the girls. We wanted to talk to them a little longer." Richard: "You better say sorry to us, too, because you kept me and Macy waiting." Michael and Jules apologized to the two boys.

The ride back to the Village was uneventful. After ariving at the Village, each of the boys individually approached the therapist and thanked him profusely.

COMMENT

The demeanor of the boys on the trip shows significant changes in ego functioning and integration: They did not accept the challenge of the "hot-rod" riders and failed to become angry or provoked; they were capable of group decision in regard to choice of theater and program of activities; they were entirely responsible relative to their activities and gathering on time; they were *genuinely* grateful to the therapist for his participation in the trip; they behaved well in the theater and related to each other and the group in a warm and mature manner; and they were not hilarious, hyperactive, or foolhardy.

Note need be taken of the fact that the therapist (as was our strict policy always) treated the boys with respect, with an attitude of trust in their responsibility and capability of making constructive use of their freedom and money.

Session Seventy-Three

ABSENT: Leonard, unable to attend because of work at the cottage which he had to finish prior to his going home for the week end.

Richard and Macy were first to arrive. Jules came in a few minutes later. Jules at once proceeded to report on what had transpired during the trip to New York when he and Michael went off to see the girls in Y———. First he stated that he was sorry that they had been late.[10] He felt that the therapist had been angry. The therapist asked Jules why he should be angry. Jules: "I know we did wrong. We lied to you, Mr. Ellery; wasn't that it?" The therapist said that this was not the question, and reminded him of the discussions concerning considering others and the consequences of our acts. The therapist had instructions to return to the Village at four o'clock, but returned at nearly four-thirty. "Now supposing there are other groups who in the future will want to take trips. Isn't it possible that by not keeping our promise, we may prevent other groups from getting permission to take trips?" Jules said that he and Michael did not even think about such consequences.

10. The error was really the therapist's, in expecting that the boys could visit girls, including travel, in forty minutes.

He added: "Yeah, I understand, Mr. Ellery, we didn't realize it. Again, we are pretty sorry it happened." Therapist: "Did it surprise you that I could feel mad about things?" Jules: "No, you're only human. But I think you were nice to us anyway. You didn't bawl us out."

At this point, Michael came half into the room. He opened the door, looked in, and said to Jules, "Aren't you coming?" Jules: "No, I don't feel like coming." Michael then walked into the room. Jules now changed his mind and said, "Okay I'll go with you." Turning to the therapist he said: "Mr. Ellery, Mike and me are going to be gone just for a few minutes. We'll be back right away." Jules and Michael left, returning in about fifteen minutes. When the two boys left, Macy asked the therapist, "Did you like the picture we saw last week, Mr. Ellery?" The therapist said he had liked it. Macy: "That was a real good picture. Remember that part about the mother who wouldn't let her son get married? Gee, that reminded me of my own mother. I remember when I was a kid, my mother wouldn't let me go out with girls—like she was jealous of me. I think it was like in the picture. My mother couldn't share me with anybody." Richard did not let Macy finish what he was saying, but launched into a description of a number of incidents that had occurred to him over the week end while he was on a home visit. The therapist was unable to discern any point to the jumble that poured forth from the boy. His extensive recital seemed to have as its aim to hold the center of attention.

Richard told of having seen the car that his father had "banged up." Richard's father had finally told him how the accident occurred. The cause of it was a broken rod, as a result of which he had lost control and the car went into the opposite lane of the road. An oncoming car smashed into his car. Miraculously, no one was hurt. Then Richard proceeded to describe how his sister was in the car at the time, and his father pushed her to the floor of the car so she would not be injured. Following this, hardly catching his breath, Richard described going to his aunt's house and having a "nice dinner" with his aunt and uncle. From this, Richard jumped to describing what had happened between him and his social worker.

Richard had seen his social worker in New York and told him that he had found a job through a friend in a tailor shop. The owner was willing to teach Richard how to do pressing and other tailoring chores. The man promised to pay Richard $20 to $30 a week during the summer months. The social worker told Richard that he was worth more money. Richard countered that he wanted the job nonetheless. The social worker then told Richard that he would contact Richard's mother and try to get her to talk Richard out of taking that job. Richard said he was enraged by this interference and proceeded to walk out of the office. He even thought of not returning to the Village, but, Richard said: "Why should I run away because I'm mad at him? Why should I take it out on the Village?" The therapist asked Richard what it was he was so angry about. Richard responded that he felt that the social worker was trying to "louse" him up. After all, he had a right to make a decision about the kind of job he wanted. Besides, why should his mother be called in on this? He was old enough to take the job he felt was right for him. The therapist said to Richard that he had no need to defend the social worker, but he wondered if he could not be right in saying that Richard was worth more than $20 or $30 for a 40-hour week. Richard said there might be something to this, "but I know maybe I can learn something in the tailor shop. It's going to be for the summer, and maybe I could have a permanent job out of this, so I want to try it."

Jules and Michael returned at this point. They were no sooner in the room than a strange boy came in to call for Jules. Jules had a brief talk with the boy just outside the door; then Michael and Macy joined them. The boys soon returned. Jules asked: "What were we talking about before?" Macy briefly recounted what Richard had been talking about, mentioning also the film they had seen the previous week. Jules asked whether the therapist liked it and was told that he did. The therapist then brought up what Macy had said about the part in the film where a mother could not let her son get married and said, "Do you remember that remark in the picture about the only love that has to lead to separation is the love between a parent and a child?" Macy: "Yeah, I remember that," and mentioned the character in the film who said it. He then asked, "What do they mean by that, Mr. Ellery?" The therapist explained how in the love relation between a parent and a child, eventually the parent has to help the child live his or her own life and to separate himself from the parent and the home. Macy responded to this by saying: "That's a pretty good way of putting it."

Jules associated to this by the following remark: "In the past few weeks I've been kind of 'messing up.' What's nutty about it is here I'm ready to leave and I find that I'm messing up. Why do you think, Mr. Ellery?" The therapist asked Jules if he had any ideas on this. Jules: "I'll bet it has something to do with my leaving the Village soon. I don't feel afraid to leave, but maybe in my unconscious mind I'm kind of afraid. Maybe I'm trying to do things so that they would keep me here longer." Richard: "That's like me, or I think it's like me, because more and more as I think about leaving the more scared I get, because I want to be sure that things will be all right for me on the outside." The therapist commented that separation from any place or person that one has known for some time is always painful and one is always frightened about what's going to happen next. Jules: "Mrs. K. has already given me the works. She told me that I am going to be out of the Village three weeks and will get into trouble again." Richard: "She's given me the curse too, the same thing." Therapist: "Remember, Mrs. K. gave Louis the 'curse' and Louis is doing fine." A brief conversation ensued here about the rumor that Louis was in jail. The therapist again informed the boys that Louis was doing well in school, and he knew this for a fact since Louis has been seeing his after-care worker, so he could not be in jail.

Jules asked the therapist what the therapist would do if someone gave him a fifth of whiskey. The therapist asked Jules, "Why the question?" Macy said that Jules had a fifth of whiskey hidden away on him. The conversation was taking place while the boys were drinking coffee which had been prepared and distributed by Jules only a few minutes before. The question gave rise to a discussion of drinking whiskey and the meaning of it. Jules said, "It makes you feel big," and Macy averred, "You're a small guy if you got to feel big through whiskey." Jules asked querulously: "What's wrong with drinking?" Therapist: "You remember our discussions about what it does to your brain, your nervous system." All of a sudden the therapist noticed that Macy was offering his coffee to Richard, saying, "Would you like to take a sip?" From the way he said it, the therapist began to suspect that there was more than coffee in the cup. He asked Macy directly: "What are you drinking?" Macy became embarrassed and began to laugh. He said: "I can't lie to you, Mr. Ellery. There's a little whiskey in my coffee." With an embarrassed expression on his face, Jules told the therapist that he had "a bottle" hidden under his shirt. Now the therapist was able to discern a bulge in Jules's shirt. Jules: "If nobody catches you, there's nothing wrong with it." The therapist said, "But Jules, here we're all talking about going home, 'making it on the outside,' and still we don't seem to have caught the idea that there are things that are wrong whether you get caught or not." Macy: "That's right, like when Richard was in a car speeding down a highway—that was wrong even though a cop didn't catch him."

Jules: "I know, I know it's wrong, but I don't know what's making me do it tonight." And then, with an air of self-justification: "I feel like having a snip of whiskey." Jules, Macy, and Michael, who obviously had whiskey in their coffee, were beginning to show its effects. Therapist (to Jules): "I really wonder what the meaning of this is." Jules became defensive and appeared ready for an argument. The therapist said calmly: "As in the case of everything else that happens here, we try to find a reason for it. There must be a reason why tonight whiskey was brought to the group." A long silence ensued that lasted for at least three minutes. Finally Jules said: "I think I know, Mr. Ellery. We're trying to take advantage of you. You're a nice guy and this is the only place we could think of doing it." No other comment was forthcoming from the boys. Then the therapist said: "But there is still a reason why you are trying to take advantage tonight. You're trying to find something out?" Jules: "You once promised us that you would never snitch on us and you never have, but I still am not sure that you're not a snitcher on boys." Macy: "Jules sounds like he's trying to prove you can be a rotten guy." Therapist: "I wonder why Jules has to prove this." Jules: "Do you know why, Mr. Ellery?" Therapist: "I think I do, Jules. I think all your life you've gone about trying to prove that people can be rotten to you and you constantly try to force them to treat you that way." Jules: "But why do I want them to be rotten to me?"

The therapist explained to the boys that when in early childhood one experienced unpleasantness and unhappiness at the hands of parents, he grew up believing that all people were like that, and when he found this not to be true, it bothered him, it made him nervous and tense until he could prove people were rotten. "In your case, Jules, I think that you are trying to force me into doing what your real mother did. You want me to turn my back on you." Jules seemed to sober up quickly enough at this. He said, "Is that why I'm always fighting with people even when they don't really give me a reason to fight?" Richard: "Yeah, you probably are fighting for that reason." Macy: "So what's my problem? What got me to drink tonight?"

Therapist: "I'm not sure Macy, but there's one thing I do know. You have a way of saying yes to people when you really mean no, and maybe drinking is a way of thumbing your nose at them, because you don't like yourself for saying yes when you mean to say no." Macy bowed his head and said: "That's the story of me and Mrs. K. I used to take all the shit: walk her dog, do everything, do all the chores. I could never stand up and say I didn't want to do something. Then I got filled up with hatred inside and now I want to tell people to their face what I really think. I still find it hard, but I tell you, Mr. Ellery, more and more I'm doing it." Therapist: "Maybe what we can pull out of this tonight is to see how what happened in the past still drives you now; how you're willing to do the wrong things and to hurt yourselves and others because of your feelings inside." With utter sincerity, Jules said: "How do you stop?" Therapist: "By control, Jules. All of life is filled with temptations. The thing that separates an adult from an infant is controlling temptations and not doing things that are wrong to do." Jules, thoughtfully: "What a battle; what a battle. I want to grow up, but it's sure hard."

The session ended on this note, but as the therapist was leaving, Jules, Macy, and Michael came up to him and profusely apologized for what they had done. The therapist said, "Maybe what's more important than being sorry is knowing the reason for doing these things."

COMMENT

Michael's and Jules's repeated apologies for delaying the group's return the previous week might be understood as indicating a growing social awareness and sense of responsibility, but the developments in this session threw a cloud of doubt over it. The question arises as to whether they were not "softening up" the therapist for their drinking escapade. Were they attempting to gain his confidence so that he would not suspect them of their collusive act? The motive for the blatant transgression could stem from a number of strivings. It was undoubtedly related to the boys' impending separation from the Village, which was several weeks off; but the intrapsychic intents were more obscure. The act might have been a hostile move toward the therapist, to serve notice on him that they had not changed through his efforts: He had failed. Or it may have been a challenge to his authority, or a strategy to defeat him. Jules's explanation was also possible, namely, an effort to defeat himself by preventing his discharge from the institution as a self-punishing strategy. It might also have been a test of the therapist's tolerance and integrity, for did not Jules make it rather easy for the therapist to detect their connivance? Or was it a declaration of independence?

On the other hand, the therapist might have been correct in attributing the transgressive act to a neurotic "repetition compulsion," that is, the need to be treated as the boys had been treated by their parents. The therapist's remark that more important than being contrite was to try to understand behavior was an effective way of concluding this session.

NOTE

During the day of the next session the therapist met Macy on the grounds of the campus. Macy said that after last week's "meeting" he and Jules felt "pretty crummy" for what they had done (referring to the fact that they both had had some whiskey in their coffee). Macy said that he and Jules had talked it over and that they both wanted to apologize for what they did. The therapist again told Macy that what was most important was to understand what made them do it. Macy said that Jules told him that he was trying to find out "how far he could go" with the therapist, and added, "In any case, it was a pretty stupid thing to do and we're sorry, Mr. Ellery."

Session Seventy-Four

ABSENT: Macy, on a trip with a group conducted by the chaplain.

Because of a basketball game in which they participated, Jules and Michael were a half-hour late. They had informed the therapist of this in advance. The session started with only Richard and Leonard present. Both boys informed the therapist that the date for their discharge had been set—about ten days away. Richard complained again about the fact that his social worker told him that he should be working for his father, saying: "How would you like it if you had a son and your son didn't want to work with you even though you needed help from your boy? How would you feel?" Richard felt pretty upset by it, but said: "I don't want to work for my father this summer, because I think I can make more money working for that presser [tailor]. I think I can make enough money to hold me while I go to school next year. You know when the autumn comes, then I won't always have to go to my parents and ask them for money."

Leonard reported that his job of working with horses at a racetrack "had fallen through," then restated that he wasn't sure whether he would get the job or not. The education counselor, who had been working with him on getting the job, would try to get him another if this one did not materialize. Leonard said, "I thought this job would give me a good chance to live away from home and make some money and be kind of independent." Richard: "It's pretty good when you can be independent and make some money on your own. Then you always know how much money you have and how you are going to spend it and you can kinda keep a budget." He then proceeded to talk about his cottage mother, Mrs. K., who was "going around giving everybody the curse." (By the "curse," Richard meant that she was telling the boys how long it would take after they left the Village before they got "into trouble.") He said that she gave him three weeks. Then he said: "After you told us about Louis, I don't think the curse means anything any more, like that word you used, you know *superstitious*. I don't want to be superstitious. Maybe what we all ought to do is all the boys who got a curse on them come back after the time has gone and tell Mrs. K., 'Look, your curse don't work.'"

With nary a breath between topics Richard reported that his father was getting his car fixed; the insurance company was paying for the body work on it. Suddenly he changed the subject. "Remember that time we used to talk about dreams? Well you know, I'm still getting those nightmares." He described how "every single night" he was subject to some sort of nightmare. When asked by the therapist if he would describe these nightmares, Richard told of one in which he saw himself on a ship being chased by pirates. They captured him and tied him up, and one pirate swung his sword and cut off Richard's head. In another nightmare he was walking down a street and suddenly a building collapsed and he found himself trapped in the rubble. Still another took place in a forest and the trees seemed to be moving, coming toward him. There was also an animal, something like a bear, moving through the woods, and just as the bear was about to pounce on him, Richard woke up. Richard narrated with appropriate affect the fear he sustained during such nightmares and complained that they "just don't seem to go away." He asked what their meaning was. (The therapist was unable to establish whether these nightmares occurred every night or only occasionally. He was also impressed by the fact that Richard had not introduced the subject before this.)

The therapist turned the question back to Richard asking him if he could recognize what was happening in all his nightmares. Richard quickly said that in all of them he seemed to "get attacked by something or somebody." Then: "There's a lot of nightmares I had that I can't remember. I guess if I tried hard enough maybe I could remember, but tonight I just can't remember every nightmare."

(Having become aware from the supervision discussions that theoretically nightmares stemmed from incestuous urges, the therapist decided to explore Richard's nightly visitations, since he didn't feel he had anything to lose by such an inquiry.) The therapist asked Richard about a complaint of his at a previous session. "Richard," said the therapist, "didn't the psychiatrist once ask you about having sex thoughts about your sister?" Richard confirmed it and said that the psychiatrist asked this question of a lot of boys. He recalled that Macy, too, was asked about it. The therapist wondered what Richard thought of it. Richard said: "Ah, he's crazy. Nobody has sex thoughts toward his sister." Then, as if correcting himself, he said, "Anyway, they *shouldn't* have those thoughts toward their sister."

Richard fell to thinking for a while and then said: "I think a long time ago—you know my sister who is about a year younger than me—I once thought what it would be like to screw her, but I thought that because I was a kid. I had a dream once. I dreamed that I had gone into the bathroom and my sister was there. She was naked. I started to go at her and just as I was about to touch her I woke up. I was pretty scared about the dream and I went to my father and told him about the dream. My father told me: 'Forget it. It's just a dream; it doesn't mean anything.'" Richard continued: "If any of my friends try to touch my sister, I'd break their ass. I wouldn't go around touching anybody else's sister, and I won't let any of my friends touch mine." Richard recalled that he had a "friend at the Village" who had met Richard's sister once and asked him: "Do you mind if I go out with your sister?" Richard told him, "It's okay if you go out; but if you get fresh with her, I'm going to tear you apart." Richard then said, "You shouldn't think about these things." When the therapist picked him up on this, asking if he felt that "thinking and doing were the same thing," Richard became rather vague, but insisted that "these things nobody should think about." The therapist commented that it was still hard for Richard to believe that thinking and doing were two different things.

At this point, Jules and Michael walked in and Richard immediately stopped. (He was probably grateful for the intrusion, though the therapist could not be sure of it.) As soon as Jules came in, he walked over to the corner where the electric plate was and began preparing coffee. Michael distributed the cookies. These activities took only a few minutes. Immediately after this was accomplished, Jules said: "Well I got the word. Next Saturday I take off for home." Michael: "I think I'm going to leave next week, too." The therapist commented that this was the next to the last session of the group. Next week would be the last. Jules: *"The only thing I hate about leaving the Village is that we won't have a group any more."* Michael: "It would be nice if we could meet 'outside,' and every week sit down and talk like we've done for over a year now." He was silent for a while, then said: "Too bad. I guess I live 500 miles away from the other boys in the group."

A discussion arose among Jules, Michael, and Richard as to how long the group had met. Giving dates to corroborate his claim, Michael said that it had been meeting for almost two years. Jules, with surprise: "Hell, it's been that long? I don't believe it." Michael: "You remember that first meeting when that jerk came in and screamed, 'I quit!' That guy was a royal idiot. He could have gotten a lot out of our talks together." Jules turned to the therapist and said with tenderness: "You're a pretty great guy, Mr. Ellery. It was worth knowing you."

Michael: "We should thank you, Mr. Ellery, for the opportunity for this gregarious group of young men to get together on a weekly basis in order to ventilate our problems." The therapist looked at Michael with surprise. He wasn't quite sure that he had heard correctly. Michael seemed to have caught the expression on the therapist's face and burst into laughter, as did the others. Michael then told the therapist that he, Jules, and Richard were in an English class where for the past few weeks they had been "building vocabulary." Michael: "I bet you never thought that I could be so voluble." Jules: "You're not being voluble, you're being really superfluous." Michael looking at Jules: "Your intense jealousy is beyond my comprehension." At this point the therapist laughed louder than anyone else in the room.

From here on there ensued a sort of contest between Richard, Jules, and Michael as to who could use the biggest word. Jules topped everyone in this, having used one that neither the boys nor the therapist knew the meaning of. After this banter had continued for some time, Jules said that even though he was leaving in about a week, he still felt the urge to do something "screwy." He could not be specific about this, but said: "Why should I feel this urge? Like I want to 'mess up' just to prove I can." The therapist said, "You're probably going through a struggle between the thing we called, you remember, the onto-archaic mind, or the little child in you, and the new part of you that is growing up but is still not fully grown." Jules: "I guess that's it. I sure hope that fight stops soon. I'm sick and tired of it." Richard: "Don't worry about it. It'll stop. Just give it a little time. Like I feel like running away still, and I know how crazy it is now. Here I'm going home in about a week and still I get the urge, so I know it's got to be something nutty in me. What do I do? Stop paying attention to it." Then with a very philosophical expression on his face, he said, "This too shall pass."

Jules described at some length how he was going to get work with his uncle who was a union machinist. He would be learning about machines, and he added, "Maybe I could go into the trade in machinery." This sparked the other boys, including Leonard, to discuss their former friends at the Village who were now back "in the community." Every boy mentioned seemed to be doing well; not one boy was mentioned who had got himself into further difficulties. Michael said: "If I can do good in school, then I'm going to have it made. The only problem is if I can stay away from some of those gangs that are going to try to get me to be a member." Jules: "I think I can do okay. As I think about it, most of the tough boys who I used to hang around with I just don't go near. I wouldn't have them for friends even though they might want me for a friend." Richard said that he wouldn't mind really staying at the Village during the summer. "The Village is a pretty nice place. The only trouble with the Village is that during the summer the program is boring. They got a program for little kids. Us big guys ain't interested in the program." Michael: "It would have been better if we stayed here while there was school but during summer they let us go home and then we came back for school." He then added: "I got a hunch I'm going to miss the Village. It's been pretty good to me."

It was now about 8:30 and the session ended.

Session Seventy-Five

This was the final session. It began on time with all the boys present. Jules, Leonard, Macy, and Michael arrived together. The boys entered looking somewhat solemn, as though they had come for a wake. They seated themselves very quietly, as each boy, one by one, said good evening, somewhat stiffly, to the therapist. Richard came in at this moment with an expression of urgency on his face, walked over to the therapist, and handed him an envelope. Jules, addressing Richard, exclaimed: "Hey stupid, that was for the end of the session." Macy said to Richard: "We got to rehearse you some more." Then, turning to the therapist, Macy said, "Read the card, Mr. Ellery."

The envelope contained a card showing a multicolored vase of roses. On the left side was printed the phrase, "Thank you so much." The verse printed on the inside of the card was the following: "No one could be any nicer than you. Thank you so much and so gratefully, too." A handwritten message read: "Thank you very much for everything and great appreciation." This was followed by the signatures of all the boys.

The therapist was greatly moved and it took him a few moments to collect himself as all eyes were on him. He lifted his head and addressing the group said, "Thank you very much." Macy: "What the hell are you thanking us for?" Michael chimed in: "You got to thank us, Mr. Ellery? We thank you, we thank you, we thank you for everything." After a moment he added, "Mr. Ellery, you made the Village a home for us." There was deep silence for at least two minutes. Not a word was said as every boy stared at the floor. The silence was finally broken by Richard: "Well it happened. I got my discharge papers and I'm ready to go." However, his voice had a strained quality, as if he were trying to break the uncomfortable silence. Now Macy said, "An hour ago they gave me my discharge papers and I'm going home, too." (Richard and Macy were scheduled to leave two days after the session.) These remarks seemed to relieve the tension, and the next half-hour was given over to talk about going home. Richard described in his usual detail all the steps he went through getting his discharge papers and having them signed by the various officials of the Village. He then told his "audience" about his going to work in a tailor shop during the summer and returning to school in the fall.

Macy said that he was going to school in the fall and hoped he could pick up some job in B——— for the summer months. In any case, he would be "happy to get back to his family." Michael stated that the date of his discharge was still not set, but he expected it to be soon. Michael's voice conveyed hesitancy and he bore an expression of sadness. The therapist said to him: "You look upset, Mike." Michael ran his hand over his face, but said nothing. He leaned back in his chair, staring at the ceiling, and remained silent. Leonard said that the job he hoped to land "working on a farm" had "not come through yet." The other job that he was aiming at might come through in September, or at least he hoped it would materialize in September. (This was the job taking care of horses that would enable him to live away from home.)

Macy: "I think I'm going to do pretty good [in school]. You remember, Mr. Ellery, when I used to worry about if I can behave in school? I think I can. I took some tests here at the Village and they showed that I'm pretty smart." Michael chimed in with: "I'm going to try my best. I swear by Jesus, I'm going to try my best!" He turned to the therapist as if he were seeking confirmation. The therapist said: "Mike, I know that you can read above the tenth-grade level and that you can do well in school. I think you will do well." Michael smiled a smile of gratification and said, "It's nice to have somebody have confidence in you once in a while." Jules quickly stepped in and commented: "I always used to think that I had to grow up to be a wild one. I can fuck around"—looking directly at the therapist he apologized for using the word, then smilingly continued—"I guess the Village didn't do me any harm. I don't know where I'd be if it wasn't for the Village." Michael turned to him: "You know where you'd be. You'd probably wind up in prison if they hadn't been good enough/to send you to the Village."

Macy: "I remember when I came to the Village, the judge in B——— told me that not every boy can get into the Village. When I came here I used to think, 'What's the big deal about being at the Village?' The last time I saw my mother I told her I'm glad the judge gave me a chance to go to Children's Village. He gave me a chance to grow up the right way. No more fooling around and hooky-playing for me. I'm not going to steal. I'm going to try to make something nice out of my life." Then turning to the therapist he said: "Mr. Ellery, it's kind of hard knowing that the group ain't going to be together any more. Michael and me live up in B——— and that's pretty far away. I'll tell you what: Maybe if you have some more groups next year, maybe Michael and me can come down to the Village and visit the group and tell the boys what we learned from it."

Richard: "This morning I had to go to Mr. J. [casework supervisor] to sign my papers because my caseworker is on vacation. Mr. J. asked me who was the person I would go to if I was in trouble. You know what I said? I looked at him and I said, 'I'd go to Mr. Ellery.' Mr. J.

then asked me what I think helped me most at the Village. I told him that it was the group; that every boy in the Village should be in a group, because this way we can sit around and can talk and if we talk long enough, we're going to talk about ourselves and our problems. Mr. J. then said, 'You think every boy should be in the group?' I said: 'Yeah. I think every boy should be in a group.'" Macy then said protectively: "Well we don't want any tough guys in the group. I mean you remember when Jameson came to the group, he walked in and he said, 'I quit!' He's a stupid jerk for doing something like that. He could have learned something had he sat down." Then, almost as if to warn the therapist, he said: "Take guys in the group that can really learn. You don't want stiffs in this group who are just going to give everybody a hard time and not learn anything from it." Macy now stepped in: "You know we've been doing all the talking tonight. We haven't given Mr. Ellery a chance to open his mouth yet. I bet you don't want to see the group end, do you Mr. Ellery?"

For a moment the therapist was not quite certain what to say. He was greatly moved by the attitudes and the maturity of the boys, and their conversation brought into relief the realization that this actually was the last session. He decided to convey his thoughts and feelings with naked honesty devoid of "techniques" and "therapeutics." He said: "I don't like to lecture and I don't want to make a speech, and yet I feel like doing both of these things just now. I find it kind of hard to talk, almost as though I've lost my tongue, but I really want to tell you what I feel inside. I think you know that I enjoyed meeting with you and looked forward to it every week. It's hard for me to accept and realize that this is really the last time that we will be getting together as a group. I hope every one of you knows how I have felt toward you and what, from the bottom of my heart, are my deepest wishes for you." Jules murmured half under his breath, "I know, Mr. Ellery, I know."

The therapist continued: "I really feel that each one of you can go out from the Village and make something of his life. I said before that I don't want to make a speech, but I guess I'm doing it anyway. If there is anything you have learned from the group, I hope it's the fact that we all live in one world together, and what we do affects somebody else. You've learned of a thing called *society* and its need to set rules and regulations so that we can all live with some peace in what is at best a very troubled world. I hope you are at the point now where you can really stop and think and feel whether what you do is right or wrong and in thinking this way you will have begun to really think of yourselves and what is right for each one of you. In my heart of hearts I truly hope and wish that each one of you never never gets into trouble again. I'm not going to tell you that life is a bowl of roses. It isn't, for you or for me. However, we don't have to make it any harder for one another or ourselves than it already is. For myself, I have had the satisfaction that few people have in life, and that is to see a group of boys try to struggle from being little babies into grown men, the hardest struggle that life has for anybody. For some time you will go on feeling the struggle, but I think each one of you can make it."

As the therapist was speaking, Michael lowered his head and covered his face with his hand. The therapist then realized that he was sobbing. A deep silence ensued. Not a word was said by anybody, and Leonard murmured to himself: "*We're men. We're men.*" Richard again was the first to break the silence. To the therapist he said: "When I was home the last time I was talking to my mother about Children's Village and about my leaving it. My mother stopped me from talking. She called in my sister and said to her: 'Richard is coming home from the Village. He was away for two years. I think we all ought to forget it. The Village was no good for Richard. Don't anybody mention the Village in this house. Let's let Richard forget about the time he spent at the Village.' I told my mother: 'Mom, I'm not ashamed of where I was. I'm not ashamed any more of what happened to me. Did you ever think of what would have happened to me if there wasn't a place like Children's Village? Would you have liked to visit me behind bars instead of coming to a place where I had a social worker, where I had a group where I could talk about my problems, where people were nice to me, and to you, and where people taught me how to be an educated man? You think I could ever go to school if I was sent away to prison? Do you think anything good could have happened to me if I had gone on truanting and stealing and running away from home?' "

Richard added that he didn't know whether he could convince his mother about this. She still said that she didn't want his sister to mention Children's Village, since this might hurt him. Michael, who had stopped crying, looked up, and wiping his eyes said: "I'm not a gangster today because of the Village and because of you, Mr. Ellery. You know what, I love each bum in this room." There was loud laughter that broke the intense tension.

At this point, the group broke up. Jules approached the therapist and said that every boy wanted him to sign their "passes," which they were not going to turn in. They wanted to have the therapist's autograph. The therapist agreed to do this. (This was the first time in seventy-five sessions that he had signed a pass.) The boys lined up and he signed the passes. As the group was leaving, profuse good-bys and "I'll be seeing you" filled the air, and Michael came up grabbed the therapist's arm, squeezed it affectionately, and said, "I'll see you around, Mr. Ellery."

COMMENT

The outstanding feature of this session was, of course the changed attitude on the part of the boys toward the institution (transference toward the institution). They had begun their group treatment with intensely hostile feelings toward it as the cause of their being sequestered from their families and friends. Their oral dependence and infantile strivings had been marked. As they rose in the levels of maturity, the separation anxiety diminished, self-sufficiency increased, and the boys were able to recognize and accept without demurral the benefits they derived. Such objectivity and absence of defensiveness are unmistakable indications of ego integration and maturity of the total personality.

The feelings the boys evidenced toward the therapist were both touching and significant, but still not devoid of traces of dependence. The transference had not been dissolved, but this could not have been achieved in seventy-five sessions under the conditions in which the therapy took place.

We have stressed in our "comment" on each of the sessions the changes in the boys in clinical and psychodynamic terms. However, to assess their growth fully from the psychosocial vantage point, the changes that occurred in them ought to be viewed also with an eye on their psychomoral aspect, or better still, the *personality quality* they had attained through the group therapy experience. Not only had their values been transformed from egotropism to a degree of allotropism, and the apparent sense of responsibility they had acquired, as is further demonstrated in their social adjustment after leaving the Village (to be described later), but there also emerged an aestheticism and spiritual quality that were entirely alien to the personalities of the boys, with the exception, perhaps, of Leonard. Their rough, bullying churlishness and toughness began to take on an unmistakable polish and even a degree of refinement which would undoubtedly have grown more trenchant, more apparent, and more deeply ingrained in the characters of these boys had the group treatment been extended beyond the short period of the demonstration.

This "refinement" was demonstrated by the language they now employed, but even more thoroughly by nonverbal expression, such as bodily stance, manner of walking, use of language, modulation of voice, and the numerous more subtle and less describable aspects and behavioral mannerisms that distinguish the cultured from the uncouth. These results are undoubtedly the outcome of the relaxed climate in the group, the therapist's deep respect for the boys and their identification with him, the enrichment of their intellects and deeper feelings for things and people evoked by the discussions, and the relations among the members of the group and with the therapist.

NOTE

Relative to Richard's mother's attitude toward the Village, the following incident may be of interest. About a month after Richard had been discharged, the group therapist met her and her daughter on a street in New York. She was most cordial and profuse in her gratitude for what was done for her son and she especially mentioned the group and what it had done for Richard. She said that he often spoke of it and made a point of the therapist's contribution to his development and adjustment. She thanked the therapist for his interest and his part in Richard's improvement and adjustment in the city. The therapist was impressed with Richard's sister's attractive appearance, physical development (though premature), and her sexual appeal. After this encounter, the therapist could better understand Richard's dreams and nightmares.

18

Final Progress Reports

IN THIS CHAPTER are given the final reports on the progress of the boys after seventy-five sessions (about twenty-one months of group therapy), at the termination of demonstration groups. Louis and Donald left the group before it ended and their progress is recorded on pp. 596-599 and 585-595, respectively.

Leonard

The cottage supervisor described Leonard as the "social worker of the cottage." Boys come to him with their problems, and he seemed to have a very soothing, supportive effect upon them. The cottage parents noted that more than at any time before Leonard seemed comfortable with himself. He smiled more often, reflecting an inner satisfaction. He was well liked by all, and status and recognition came to him without his seeking them out.

The teachers reported that Leonard had made some small progress in reading and math. They noted that he was currently more at ease with himself and no longer berated himself for not reading so well as the other boys in his class. He frequently approached teachers to discuss with them his academic work and sought individual attention.

The caseworker reported good progress, particularly during the past few months. While the main focus of the interviews was getting a job in preparation for leaving the Village, Leonard had been voluntarily discussing the possibility of living away from his mother. He expressed a desire to remain and work at the Village and had in addition initiated efforts on his own at seeking a job and made plans for his future apart from his mother. The caseworker felt that Leonard was no longer as dependent on his mother as he had been before and was eager to try himself out. "There is some striving for identity and reaching out into the environment. . . . Leonard's defenses are strong and he has succeeded in exposing or undermining his resistances."

The psychological test, the third within twenty-one months of group treatment, pointed up that Leonard was still easily intimidated and frightened, but, while still inclined to self-doubt, he was not as overpowered as previously; and these characteristics did not interfere as much with his performance. Intellectual functioning significantly improved: full-scale IQ was 91 as compared to 81 a year and a half ago. Leonard could now perform better when dealing with things than interacting with people. Leonard's inability to relate and his fear of being hurt still determined his maintaining himself at a safe distance from people. At times he felt somewhat depressed, isolated by the impact of his deficiencies. However, he had gained much strength and was now more capable of controlling his impulsive reactions. His relationships to paternal and masculine figures had much improved, involving less guilt and much less dissatisfaction. He had become more frankly masculine in his identification and self-concept. Previously, there was much ambivalence and obsessive doubting about sexuality. While there had been much growth and much more assertiveness, fears of frustration were also in evidence. He had acquired more of a masculine identity, but still was in a tentative operation with much indecision. His dependence, conflict, and desire for security were still present and he might perhaps be inclined to give up his masculine strivings to adopt a passive role through which all his dependency needs would be fulfilled.

"In summary, the comparison between present and past data shows a higher intellectual level with a significant rise of 10 IQ points, as well as a steady gain in ego strength and impulse control. The changes and improvement noted concern mainly rational aspects of ego-functioning. His emotional life, although somewhat revitalized by his experience in the group, remains limited and crippled by guilt and by a basic powerful fear of losing control. It is perhaps to counteract his own destructive impulses that he maintains his schizoid position, preferring to stay away from really close relationships and in a relatively neutral emotional climate."

The psychiatrist who saw Leonard at this time commented: "The group experience has given Leonard some knowledge of interpersonal relationships in other families and he has gained understanding of his peers. He has found some of the material threatening and has needed to emphasize the difference between himself and others in order to maintain his defenses.

"In spite of the fact that he finds it threatening to hear other boys admit their fear of leaving the Village, the group experience seems to have helped Leonard to contain his separation anxiety."

While the psychological findings may be correct in reflecting the deficiencies in Leonard's psychic structure (and possibly constitutional structure, which could not be altered in the brief course of treatment), his function as a person had vastly improved. The offspring of a psychotic mother and a schizoid (and possibly schizophrenic father), his constitutional assets of necessity have to be inadequate for the struggles that a *complex* society presents. Hence, his interests in horses.[1]

However, Leonard's potentials, as limited as they may be, had not been tapped. The conflicts and tensions in the home, which at first frightened and later enraged him (feelings that served to frighten him further), and the mother's parasitic attachment and demands on him throughout his life, impotenized him so that he could not mobilize ego strengths even for the simplest responsibilities of daily living or academic effort. His fears of people, stemming from the pathological relations in the home, blocked him off from any sort of interpersonal relations. Leonard was devoid of any degree of self-identity and was almost completely socially and self-alienated.

Under these conditions, removal from the home was definitely indicated, but that by itself, as valuable as it may have been as a preventive for further pathogenesis, could not solve his problem. He needed help to break through his inordinate psychic incapsulation and discover safety in the actual world. He needed a milieu in which he could project emotional pseudopods without being hurt. This an individual relation with a feelingful, understanding adult could have supplied him, but he would not accept such a relation. His fears and defensiveness would not permit it. He needed a *neutral* field for operation where no demands would be made on him and there would be no need for him to react or relate. The group was such an environment which "opened him up" for further exploration of life. It supplied him, in addition, with models of identification and with security.

This fact was recognized by his fourth and last caseworker at the

---

1. In this connection see the case of Paul in S. R. Slavson, *Re-Educating the Delinquent through Group and Community Participation* (New York: Harper and Brothers, 1954; Collier Books, 1961), pp. 46-48, 196 (pp. 57-60, 201 in Collier edition).

time of Leonard's discharge from the Village after a stay of three years. The caseworker wrote: "Through the participation in group therapy, he has acquired some knowledge of interpersonal relationships in other families and has gained some understanding of his peers. The group experience also helped Leonard to contain his separation anxiety from Children's Village."

However, throughout his life, Leonard would require a mediated environment, where demands would not exceed his limited psycho-organic resources.

Jules

The cottage staff were impressed with Jules's "real effort to exercise control over his impulses and conduct and his growing ability to respond to reason." He had not run away from the Village in more than a year, despite the fact that there were situations which in the past would have prompted such acting out. He had taken up a hobby, breeding and caring for pigeons, and had devoted a great deal of time and responsible effort to it. He took the responsibility for buying food for the birds, for which he had to save from his allowance. The cottage supervisor felt that Jules "still had a great deal of adolescent rebellion" and among his friends in the cottage were the disturbed boys, but "he had shown marked improvement in getting along with his cottage mates." Jules was now far less isolated from group activities and was "no longer prey to his impulses but rather struggles with them and arrives at independent conclusions."

Quite unexpectedly, he now was at the top level in his science class in school and seemed to have made the greatest progress in this subject. He was respected and liked by his schoolmates. However, he still needed direction in the classroom. Though his placement in school was the ninth grade, the teachers felt that he could easily be advanced to the tenth grade in a regular school, which would place him on par with his chronological age. Jules was described as "mechanically inclined," having good comprehension in the auto shop and able to apply what he was taught in school. The teachers expressed surprise that Jules was now "able to accept the fact that he was a good worker and was talented in mechanics." They thought that this increase in self-confidence resulted in greater relaxation in school, with a corresponding decrease in motility and restlessness.

In individual casework, similar progress was noted. Jules talked freely about his natural and adoptive mothers and had recently expressed a desire to see his natural mother, saying, "If I were to walk down the street I wonder if I could recognize her." He questioned whether he would want to live with his natural parents, and resolved this dilemma by saying that he thought he could get along with his adoptive parents, since he now understood them better. Jules raised questions as to what the future held for him, and he no longer needed prodding to bring his problems to interviews. The caseworker indicated that what seemed to have happened with Jules was that he recognized that in order to get along with anyone one does not necessarily have to like him, which had been his conviction heretofore. In the past, Jules had difficulties with everyone whom he did not like. This seemed natural to him. Now, however, he showed a greater degree of tolerance toward people and their limitations as he perceived them. He was now able to stop and evaluate the consequences of impulsive acting out and had "a real desire for internal controls."

The psychological tests administered at this time indicated a rise in Jules's IQ from 88 (the last test) to 103. The psychologist stated: "In considering the three sets of projective material (tests done at intervals of about six months) it appears that at first a pattern of avoidance and withdrawal was predominant. Six months ago there was much acting out, the emotional effervescence being perhaps precipitated by a homosexual panic. Presently the issues and conflicts are clearer and closer to consciousness and their impact is less intense. There is now more poise and calm in Jules's attitude. The beginnings of reality-oriented preoccupations have replaced the childish wish-fulfillment and materialistic orientation of the deprived psychopath. Although he has developed some of the tact and sensitivity of a person more mature emotionally, he is not capable of becoming really involved with others, and interpersonal relations are not very close. The dread that he experienced in relation to a destructive, unpredictable mother figure is now more adequately defended against, but still persists."

The psychologist's report proceeded to state that it appeared that Jules has made his most definite progress in the area of sexuality. Previously he had refused to admit his sexual impulses and experienced them as chaotic and very threatening. He now accepted his sexual role, although an aggressive, somewhat sadistic element was retained. He was now faced with his ambivalent feelings: while he had matured emotionally and was capable of more nuanced, varied responses, he was also capable of psychopathic reactions. In summary: "Improvements are noted in several areas: gain in intellectual status, improved self-esteem, acceptance of masculine role and sexual impulses, and a gain in emotional maturity.

Personal relationships are still limited and precarious. Strong hostility and elements of psychopathy constitute the weak points in the present clinical picture."

The therapeutic dynamics that served in the improvement of this patient have been substantially indicated at the different stages in the recounting of the process. One important contributing factor, however, was not dealt with. This is the element of sex, which though not evident in behavior, played an important role in the reconstructive process, which was revealed in the final psychological retest. While the malignant identifications that this boy had unavoidably established and the effects of the adoptive father's inadequacies as an object of male identification were pointed up, the less obvious libidinal development and strivings had not been brought to view.

In the construction of the history of the patient, an important phase in his development—up to six years of age—was unavailable for exploration. Practically nothing was known to us of his life and the nature of the influences to which he had been subjected during this period, and there were no means at hand to elicit such information. However, some of the interpersonal dynamics may suggest the content of his psyche in relation to sex and his possible fantasies. It was the adoptive mother who was the effective parent, who controlled and threatened him, to which as a small child he had to submit without adequate protection from the father. His identifications, therefore, had of necessity been of a feminine nature, and this was associated with cruelty, fear, and dread. This may be the reason, at least in part, for Jules's avoidance of relationships and the tension between him and the cottage mother at the Village. By avoiding class relations and battling with the new mother (female) figure, he sought to avoid the feminine image he had of himself and the destructive, sadistic fantasies that were associated with it.

A significant incident occurred in this connection early in Jules's group treatment career. A violent struggle took place one night in the dormitory when Jules threatened with a knife a boy who refused to participate with him in a homosexual episode. The boy extricated himself and was escaping from the dormitory when Jules threw the knife at him, barely missing him as the latter ran through the door. Jules then sat down on the bed of another boy and similarly demanded sexual gratification from him, threatening him with the knife. This boy, as well, somehow evaded Jules and ran out screaming in terror. "Security officers" were summoned by the cottage parents and Jules was placed in the "detention cottage," which was then still in operation. It was here that sex was discussed with him by the adult in charge, which sparked the sex discussions in the therapy group. At our request, Jules was permitted to attend the group even though he was excluded from all other activities.

This episode confirms the assumption of his basic feminine identification and the sadistic fantasies associated with sex which was revealed in the projective tests by the psychologist. His intimate functioning with a group of boys, the identification with the two male therapists, and his generally relaxed state and conscious awareness and acceptance of his background and current relations, all served not only to reconstruct his psyche but to redirect his sexual strivings in conformity with his biological potentials. The above episode was the last of a homoerotic or homosexual genre in the life of this boy. Having achieved a new image of himself, he was able to function adequately in his environment.

Michael

Cottage staff reported "real improvement in this boy." He had become something of a "superego" for the boys in his cottage. This development can best be illustrated by the following incident related by the cottage life supervisor: A boy who resided in same cottage confided in Michael that he had stolen money and was either very frightened or guilty and asked Michael what he should do. Michael unhesitatingly advised the boy to report to the cottage parents and tell them exactly what had happened. This the boy did. This rather unusual line of action was in striking contrast to what he would have done in the past and is even more significant in view of the fact that Michael had himself stolen money in the early stages of his group therapy career.

Michael was now far more accepting of set limits and was under better inner controls. He was no longer underhanded, and he did his chores with responsibility, not trying to evade them as he had previously done and requiring far less supervision. The cottage parents reported that he seemed "to show more positive leadership and had a quieting effect upon the more obstreperous boys." Michael now seemed to be concerned as to how people felt about him, and when he sensed someone was displeased with his actions, he desisted from the annoying behavior. The cottage parents described him as "friendlier and much less isolated from his cottage group." He talked freely with the boys and interacted with them in "an easy and natural way," and was "under better internal control." In recent months, Michael had acted less like an isolate, participating in the cottage life with relative ease. However, he was still self-defeating in athletic competitions.

Progress in school, as well, continued. Michael now functioned at least at tenth-grade level. He made a greater effort to approach his teachers and on occasion asked for extra assignments. He was described as being "very proud of his work and achievements." Michael continued to help other, slower boys and displayed a considerable knack for explaining mathematics to them.

The caseworker reported essentially the same minimal involvement in that relation as before. A psychiatric examination revealed that while Michael was "still essentially a psychotic child, he has managed to hold together quite well. His reality sense is still operating and he would probably be able to function adequately if he did not come under undue stress situations." The psychiatrist noted that Michael "was more understanding of what people expected of him and was far less rebellious and more realistic." The prognosis remained "guarded."

In the psychological examination given at the termination of the group by the same psychologist, it was found that Michael's intellectual functioning had risen (full-scale 93 to 99 in 1½ years), and that he had become more integrated. "Compared to previous productions, his projective material is more limited and impoverished. He is more evasive, cautious, perhaps even holding back some of his percepts. His mode of thinking, however, is less primitive—not as autistic and egocentric—and the pathology is not so blatant. His struggle to seal off his pathological thinking is so intense that he becomes overly cautious and guarded. The interpersonal disorganization has settled down in favor of much watchfulness and less paranoid constriction. The thinking disorder has diminished and there is much less turmoil and hostility. However, if overwhelmed by fright, he is still apt to fight and react violently. The fear of thus losing control over his destructive impulses is quite great.

"Sexual stimulations are far less powerful and less indiscriminate. The whole drive system has been modified: there is less crude aggression and less psychopathy. Homosexual orientation is no longer preponderant, and this particular change is very probably related to the decrease in schizophrenic symptomatology.

"Another important change consists in the different relationships to the mother. The maternal figure is now more vague and distant and has lost her previously great powers of sexual attraction. Castration fears are still present, but their impact is limited.

"In summary, there are sizable gains in ego strength along with a reduction and neutralization of the underlying schizophrenia. Thinking disorder, contaminations, and circular reasonings have receded."

Macy

After Sixty-Three Sessions

Macy had become "one of the most respected youngsters by his peers in the cottage. By the very way he carries himself and through his tone of voice, he seems to have a calming effect on other boys." He evaluated situations realistically, and showed exceptionally good judgment, whereas previously he might have acted purely on impulse. When the cottage mother said something to him that he did not like, rather than lose his temper he approached her with calm and attempted to be reasonable with her. Other boys, witnessing this, began to follow Macy's example. Macy "performed all his chores with a real sense of responsibility and made no attempts to evade them as he had done in the past, though he did this very subtly. He now looked relaxed, smiled, joked and seemed to enjoy life." He freely acknowledged to the cottage personnel that he had been helped at the Village, which was in striking contrast to his insistent and prolonged complaints against it and the demands that he be returned home.

In school, he had advanced three years in a one-year period, functioning now at eleventh-grade level, whereas a year ago he had been functioning at eighth-to-ninth grades. He approached the learning situation "in a methodical manner, with a great deal of effort and extra work, showing exceptionally good motivation and a very real desire to return to and finish school after discharge." He was exerting constructive leadership in the classroom and had maintained very good peer relationships. He continued to seek out teachers for extra help and additional assignments. While his primary assets appeared to be in the academic subjects rather than in shop, he nevertheless completed all his shop projects on time and did them skillfully.

The caseworker stated that Macy was now "truly ready to benefit a great deal from individual treatment." As at no previous time, at this point Macy had become much freer to talk about his feelings and his conflicts. He was capable of "feeling his anger," but "doesn't blow up at such times," and the improved frustration tolerance which was observed by the psychiatrist some months ago was now described by the caseworker as exceptional. Macy verbalized his fears about leaving the Village, and what the future in his home community might hold for him. He was able to view his cottage mother objectively and recognize her limitations and assets, the capacity for which obviously originated and materialized as a result of the group discussions. The caseworker concluded with the remark: "Macy has shown marvelous growth in therapy."

In the psychological examination following termination of group therapy by the same psychologist, Macy showed a gain in his IQ of 10 points over the previous score (103 from 93) one and one-half years earlier. Several changes were noted: "Self-esteem has risen and feelings of inadequacy have diminished slightly. His percepts are more structured and he is somewhat more mature. He has gained some ego strength, is increasingly involved with the world around him, and is more reality-oriented and controlled. His narcissistic preoccupations are not so intense.

"One of the major changes concerns his relationships to parental figures, and more particularly the father image. The latter, previously inaccessible, is now more in focus, though still inadequate. It seems that the boy has come to examine his relationships with his parents and has realized their limitations and failures (reality, objectivity). He feels very guilty about this essentially correct perception of them. He is starting to assume the masculine role, but experiences great guilt over it and over his sexual impulses. Generally, Macy responds more quickly to the human environment than he did, but the noted improvements are seen to be limited." (The psychologist further remarked: "Except for [Macy's] characterological passivity and lack of drive, his difficulties are essentially neurotic.")

The supervisor of the unit of cottages in which Macy lived reported the following at the termination of group therapy: "Macy seems to have finally worked out many of the problems he had had with his cottage mother. The group experience must have been exceptionally helpful to him since he has not continued to be the quiet, submissive 'child' he used to be, in danger of remaining such for life."

NOTE

It must be observed in this connection that in session thirty-five, Macy talked about his insomnia due to conflicts with his cottage mother. Since, for administrative reasons, the cottage situation could not be altered, it was determined that this problem would be pursued and worked out in the group therapy sessions. There was evidence of the cottage mother's hidden sexual provocativeness toward the boy and, on his part, unconscious conflict duplicating that in relation to his own mother. It was decided after a prolonged exploration in a number of supervisory conferences that the latent difficulty should not be explored. but the boy, supported by his cottage mates who were also members of the therapy group, would free himself of his dependence on, and need for, the cottage mother, which would automatically dissolve his sexual strivings toward her. In other words, rather than dealing with his libidinal strivings toward the cottage mother as a displacement of his strivings toward his own mother, the problem was dealt with on an ego level. This plan proved successful, as shown in the group interviews that followed. The value of this experience to our patient was that by working through his attitude toward the cottage mother, he had also altered his attitudes and relations with his natural mother.

Richard

Richard's steady progress, as noted before, continued in almost every area. The cottage parents found him a "much more pleasant boy, quite relaxed and friendly." He developed "a charming manner, no longer ingratiating or manipulative." His emotional reactions were now always appropriate to the situation. He was now "one of the most accepted youngsters in the cottage, having changed from being a clown to a boy who can now give and take with the others without the need to be the center of attraction." Richard had formed a very good relationship with the cottage father. He appeared able to discern other people's problems. For example, recently he knew that the cottage mother was under stress because of a personal problem and he made sure not to make unnecessary demands on her. He had allied himself with the adult staff in the Village, steering clear of the antisocial elements among the boys. He told the cottage staff that he felt he had gotten much help from, and was "very glad that he had come" to, the Village. Richard was given a room of his own, as was true of all the other boys there, in a cottage that had been recently rebuilt, and took excellent care of it and his possessions. He no longer needed special supervision and had been rather neat and wellgroomed. Now, more than ever, he seemed to care how he looked and has become "a real adolescent with adolescent interests."

The school personnel reported that Richard could function adequately in a regular school. He was described "as a very bright boy who learns quickly and [unlike formerly] retains information easily." The teachers felt that Richard's most impressive achievement was an increase in frustration tolerance as he worked on very difficult projects. In this area, he seemed to be above the level of other boys in his class. He developed "an excellent sense of humor and was extremely well liked by his peers." They seemed to admire the fact that Richard had made good academic progress, and he served as a model for some of them. Richard could now work independently, displaying good judgment, and he handled his tools in the shops appropriately. He no longer tried to evade work. The report contained a prognostic statement that "given favorable conditions, Richard will make a good adjustment when he returns home."

The caseworker likewise reported good progress. Richard verbalized his feelings and attitudes well. Stimulated by the group, he had brought to the interviews the ambivalence he felt about returning home, his anxiety about whether he would be able to succeed while living with his family, about going to school and holding a part-time job. He was aware of, and discussed, his reactions toward his cottage mother as they related to his feelings toward his mother, and drew a parallel between the two. He could now examine his reactions to people and his expectations of them and recognized his tendency to side with his (delinquent) father. He was seeking a way out of being a delinquent and adopting more healthy social attitudes. He seemed to accept the fact that he had problems and did not try to blame everything on the outside world. The caseworker also felt the prognosis was good for a satisfactory adjustment in the home and in the community.

The psychiatrist noted that "certainly a real improvement has occurred [in Richard], but one wonders how deep this improvement is. . . . Conflicts continue particularly in relation with the mother figure, but in spite of these conflicts, there is some evidence that the boy has been able to move in the direction of making more constructive and helpful decisions for himself, and in the ability to set more appropriate goals for himself that are aligned more securely with masculine strivings. . . . Even his speech seems somehow more cultivated than when he was first seen (about two years before), with a rougher quality . . . demonstrating the . . . 'masculine sheen' of his associates. . . ."

PART THREE

Conclusions

19

Outcomes, Reflections, and Recommendations

AS THE TERMINATION of the boys' stay approached we became increasingly concerned with their futures. Our awareness of the pathogenic home and neighborhood milieu to which they were to return and the still tenuous nature of their ego strengths and general maturity made us uneasy. We doubted the boys' readiness to cope with the tensions that their homes would continue to create, the temptations to which they would be exposed, and the pressures that would be exerted on them in their immediate microcultures. We were not misled by the apparent behavioral improvement in the institutional community, nor by the boys' verbalized intent and comprehensions. We knew that these were skin-deep and might prove ephemeral under the load the boys would be called upon to carry. The brief period of therapy reached only the surface of their characters and the cognitive areas of their minds. We feared that the unconscious conative, the onto-archaic mind, was only touched and that it might reassert itself in the climate of their new life.

However, the institution's administrative management of the boys was beyond our purview, and following our original policy of detachment within this area we took no steps to influence decisions. This policy we adhered to also during the life of this study relative to any aspect of the internal organization, policy or management of the institution, its staff and departments. The rigid adherence to this self-imposed regimen was actuated by our wish to test the acceptability and effect and effectiveness of group psychotherapy in an unaltered setting. Although on the whole we found the policy and practices of the Children's Village liberal and patient-centered, some modifications in routines and relationships would have favored our work. We, however, eschewed them, for we did not wish to test our methods in "ideal" circumstances, which are generally unattainable in actuality. This attitude was maintained also after the boys' return home. The advantage in refraining from manipulating the postinstitutional life of the boys was to test the tenacity of the carry-over of the attitudes and character changes acquired through our therapy into the rigorous circumstances of the boys' lives.

Although every one of the boys who remained with the group left it with an improved identity and a higher level of social values, a sense of direction in his life, and a valid, realistic plan and purpose which he had acquired in the group, we were not certain as to how many of them had the psychic strength to carry out their intentions. Therefore, for two years we followed up the adjustment of the seven boys who had participated in demonstration group C, which, as noted, extended through two school years instead of one.

We experienced considerable difficulty in this respect. The difficulties arose predominantly from the parents' resentment at the interference in their lives, but also were due to the migratory nature of these families, as will become clear from the individual case studies to be presented. However, despite these difficulties reliable data were obtained from various dependable sources.

Outcomes[1]

Donald

Donald, a schizophrenic, loquacious, and overaggressive boy (whose mother was inordinately sexually seductive with him), had been involved in many and serious delinquencies. In their customary delinquent fashion, his parents induced a relative to forge a certificate assuring him of a job, thus making it possible for him to obtain "working papers" on his discharge from the Village. Donald wished to return to school, but his anxiety around his inability to succeed (even in an evening program) was so great that he actually could not bring himself to enter the school building. Because of Donald's seemingly severe pathology and because of his hostility toward his social worker, we arranged for the group therapist to see the boy for a brief period after his return home. Essentially, Donald continued to be a highly impulsive youngster; his ego was extremely fragile and he was unable to focus meaningfully

---

1. It is suggested that the reader review the case material on all boys at time of referral in Chapter 10 before continuing with the follow-up reports in this chapter.

in an interview. His agitation and hyperactivity were now more in evidence and he displayed little confidence in his being able to hold a job. During a period of some months he changed jobs three times, claiming that the pay was inadequate or the employer did not treat him properly. Donald's inner turmoil, in addition to his basic pathology and the Oedipal incestuous urges, was enhanced by his awareness of his psychic debility and reality demands, which he came to recognize through the group discussions. Instead of supporting him and allaying his anxieties, the parents nurtured them. They pressed Donald to go out and work, berating him when he failed to do so, but at the same time they kept engaging him in work around the home and giving him the responsibility for the younger children.

The mother continued to drink heavily and persisted in her openly seductive maneuvers toward her son. She continued coming home intoxicated late at night, slapping him on the buttocks while he was asleep, and ordering him to get into bed with his father, while she crawled into Donald's bed. Despite his fragile ego, Donald had to be faced by the therapist, though gradually, with the question as to whether his was a home in which he could continue to live. Initially, Donald evaluated the possibility of quitting his home, but this was beyond his ability to face. His infantile dependency upon the parents and the material security they supplied for him without any effort on his part outweighed his feeble acquiesences in the casework interviews to leave home.

As is characteristic of such patients, Donald continued to be extremely sensitive and would feel slighted and hurt when a girl with whom he went out refused to "neck" in the movie house. He felt rebuffed and immediately broke off the relationship. (This mechanism, coupled with his reactions toward employers, raised the question as to the presence of a mild paranoia in this boy, which was observed also in his father.)

On the one occasion when the parents came for an interview they presented a rather hazy picture of what was going on at home. They tended to condemn Donald for not holding jobs, but, on the other hand, refused to say anything meaningful about what was happening at home to prevent it. They either denied problems or made light of them. The therapist remarked, "Discussing the situation with them was like trying to put stockings on an octopus."

We did not anticipate that Donald would retain the evident and rather impressive (transference) improvements he had shown in the group and in the protected Village milieu unless he was given adequate support and continued psychotherapy. Our view seemed to be well-founded. But despite the discouraging developments, Donald did maintain some of the progress he had made during his career in the Village. The group therapist, continuing as his individual caseworker, reported about six months after Donald's discharge from the Village that Donald "has not returned to his former delinquent friends (as he said he would not in the group interviews). He defended himself against them by attaching himself to, and going out in the company of, an older brother, who, he considered, had a good influence on him. When the older brother planned to join the navy, Donald talked about doing likewise, but was not entirely certain that he wanted to enter the armed services." Donald spoke with fondness about the Village and on a few occasions expressed a desire to return, but he immediately indicated that this would constitute a loss of face and status for him.

During this period, Donald struck up a friendship with a girl with whom he "went steady," and talked of eventually marrying her. About a year after he had left the Village, Donald discovered that the girl was pregnant, and he panicked. It was evident to the therapist (who saw the girl once with Donald) that, to escape from an extremely unpleasant home situation replete with tension and social pathology, she had maneuvered the pregnancy and then insisted that Donald marry her. Donald now again planned to join the navy to avoid the responsibility for which he was far from ready, but he apparently was in great conflict about it since he felt guilty toward and attached to the girl, who insisted on marriage. He came to see the therapist, bringing his girl friend, and in the discussion, they came to the conclusion that they would be wed; the girl's family later supported this decision and the wedding soon took place. Donald discontinued his visits to the therapist. The couple went to live with Donald's parents (of all things!) while they were looking for an apartment. Donald found employment on a building construction job, where his duties were to fill the truck tanks with gasoline from a pump and act as a general helper on the trucks. In a telephone conversation with Donald's parents a year and a half after his discharge from the Village, they reported no difficulties of any sort.

In our attempt to learn of Donald's adjustment two years after his discharge from the Village, we asked the group therapist to telephone the boy's parents, who had since moved to another part of the city. The mother answered the phone, saying that her son was just outside the house parking his father's car. When the boy came in, the therapist could hear her raucously screaming at him for driving the car too fast as he backed it. She upbraided him violently, using vulgar terms and cursing him. The therapist could also overhear Donald's defending himself, in a childlike screeching voice, that he did not drive the car too fast, but to no apparent avail. The therapist described the boy's voice as for all the world like that of a small child.

Donald informed the therapist, during the ensuing phone conversation that he had one child and another was on the way and that he was soon to be admitted to a city treatment facility for drug addicts. An appointment to see the therapist was set for a few days later but Donald did not appear for the interview.

Louis

Regarding Louis, our toughest boy, who had decided to continue to get "an education," an inquiry ten months after discharge yielded the information that he was attending high school in the city and was doing well. No difficulties were reported at home, in school, or in the community. The social worker in the Children's Village city (aftercare) office wrote: "The most striking thing about Louis has been his good adjustment and his continuing in school. He attends the ——— High School and gets along well there. There has been no incident of his being involved in delinquency.

"Over all, one could say that this youngster seems to be much more outgoing and talks rather meaningfully and with great affect of the fact that there is no togetherness in his home, and that he must rely entirely upon himself. His hobby is singing, and he was referred to ——— House for musical training. He seems to be able to strike up a rather spontaneous, free relationship with the worker. He often came to the office out of loneliness, just to sit and talk with someone on appropriate subjects, such as the fact that his mother and father do not get along, that there is no warmth in the home, and that his family seems to relate to him only when he is in trouble. . . ." The caseworker planned to see the mother on alternate weeks, but she never turned up for her interviews.

However, either because his parents would give him attention only when he "got into trouble" or because of the tensions in the home and absence of constructive guidance and his own still weak ego, he began to get into difficulties in which he became involved with the police. But instead of sinking deeper into the mire of crime, Louis had enough strength and awareness to extricate himself by taking refuge in the army. It will be recalled that Louis was discharged from the Village after forty-four sessions, contrary to our advice and through an error by his social worker. However, he seemed to have acquired enough awareness and purposefulness to take a step toward his own rehabilitation. Two and one half years after his discharge from the Village, he was still in the army, serving as clerk for his company after a course of training. He tentatively planned to follow a military career.

Leonard

Leonard, our withdrawn and silent boy, who had presented so comic a sight and was the butt of his peers' derision, contempt, and exploitation, partially succeeded in breaking away from his mother, which he so fervently desired. Shortly after termination of the group, Leonard had a job on a farm work-camp for the summer. He worked in the kitchen, where he did well. In a letter, the camp director congratulated Leonard on his good services and asked him to return the following year. As expected, Leonard's mother was dissatisfied with this arrangement and about his staying away from home. She made many long distance calls to the camp, as well as to the Village, threatening to "go to the police and get my boy back." She sabotaged every plan to have Leonard work on a "horse farm," which he so greatly desired, and insisted that he return home when the summer job ended. Our repeated efforts to make contact with Leonard after his return home, were completely thwarted by the mother, however.

About two years after discharge from the Village, and with great difficulty, we were able to locate Leonard's father where he now lived with his new wife and children, but we failed in our repeated efforts to speak to him on the telephone. However, the stepmother informed us that Leonard was living with his mother and was holding a job. The father had no contact with Leonard and was being sued at the time by his former wife for nonsupport.[2]

Jules

Five months after termination of the group, and four months after discharge from the Village, Jules, the adopted boy who frequently ran away from home in search of his natural parents and stole and truanted as a means of punishing his adopters and testing their love for him, re-returned to his adoptive home. The probation officer, who continued his contact with the boy and his parents, reported that Jules "has made an excellent adjustment at home and on his full-time job as a salesman at a discount store selling merchandise." His leisure time was spent

2. It is the present writer's opinion that youngsters with Leonard's potentials, despite their having been psychologically maimed by their families, should continue as legal wards of the state indefinitely so that their rehabilitation can be completed and made permanent.

either at home or at the local Y.M.C.A., where he was a member of the Hi-Y Club, and he had not fallen out with the law. At about the same time, Jules came to pay a visit to the Village, in a car which he drove himself, to see his former group therapist.

Jules had grown in height and was now a little over six feet and appeared very neat. He bore himself with evident self-confidence and his general appearance was good. He said he wanted to see the therapist, to let him know how he was doing. He was earning $70 a week working in a department store in two capacities—selling and as a stock clerk. He was living at home and had "no trouble at home whatsoever," and was quite happy. He had acquired a girl friend whom he planned to marry the following year. He had had no difficulties with the law and, most important, he said, he no longer associated with his friend of the days prior to his admission to the Village.

In the course of the conversation Jules said that the most important thing that had happened to him was being in the group while at the Village. He recalled that his former cottage mother in a fit of anger, had predicted that he would get into trouble a week after he left the Village, and he felt very proud of the fact that this prophecy had not come true. Jules was trying to get the addresses of all the boys in the group, because he wanted to write to them. Before his discharge the boys in the group had discussed the possibility of having a reunion (at the Village), and he considered arranging such an event.

Jules turned over most of his earnings to his parents, who saved it for him so that he could get married. He kept a small amount as "pocket money," he said, and already had "a few hundred dollars in the bank." Next year he would have enough money to make a start in married life.

Jules did not continue to attend the mental-health clinic in his community, because he wished to find out "how things would go" for him without any help. When he left the Village he had taken a job with "an uncle" in the machinery business. However, the uncle was not doing too well. There were a number of trained, older people working for this uncle, and they were being dismissed from their jobs because of poor business. Jules said that he had gone to his uncle and volunteered to resign, since he was the least trained and, in addition, "the others had families to support." He said he realized that he would have to take care of himself and wanted a job where he did not feel beholden to a relative. He went out and found the job in a discount department store, which proved to him that he was able to get and hold jobs on his own.

Jules said that he would from time to time be in touch with the therapist. In the meantime he wanted to say hello to some of the other people at the Village, including his former cottage mother.

In a conversation with Jules's uncle a year and a half after the boy's return, a member of the educational staff was informed that Jules was "doing very well on his job in the department store." The uncle reported that because of Jules, the (family) name was "once synonymous with terror in the area" where they lived. Now Jules seemed to be "a changed boy." He held his job and made a "pleasant and outgoing appearance in the community." He was still going out with the girl he was planning to marry and was an "accepted member of the community."

Michael

Because Michael's family's whereabouts could not be traced, no information was available as to his adjustment two years after discharge from the Village. However, the fact that no inquiry had been received by the Village from the police or a court would indicate that his criminotic pattern did not reappear during this period.

Five months after termination of group treatment, and his return to his native city B——— a month later, Michael sent a Christmas card to the therapist; inside he had written the following: "Merry Christmas and a very happy New Year. God bless you, Mr. Ellery. Mike."
On the back of the card the following appeared:

> Dear Mr. Ellery:
>   How are you doing? Fine I hope. As for myself, I'm coming along fine. Well I'm going to school now, in the 10th grade. I've been looking for work ever since I've been home, but no luck. If I do find a job I'm going to quit day school and go to night school. P.S. Will write more next time.
>
>   MIKE

The therapist answered Michael's card with a letter expressing his pleasure at hearing from him and saying that he recognized that it could be difficult finding a job but he was happy that Michael planned to continue with his education.

Less than two weeks later the following letter from Michael was received:

> Dear Mr. Ellery:
>   Just a few lines to let you know that I received your letter and was glad to hear from you. How are things in the Village? I miss the group, and wished that we could get together again.
>   Mr. Ellery, I haven't forgotten about the things you talked about and the advice that you gave all of us.
>   Some fellows I go with have asked me to get into trouble with

them, but I remember when you said to the group and myself, "fellows before you do anything think what you're doing and it takes a man to say no." I will always remember that until the day I die, and I have you to thank. If it wasn't for your group I don't know what I would be doing now.

I miss having to discuss my problems with someone, and I know that everyone has problems, besides me. I used to think that no one has worser problems than myself.

Mr. Ellery why don't you continue having groups. I know a lot of boys would appreciate it.

I don't think other teachers are as good a teacher as you are.

Macy told me that he has been writing you. He told me to tell you hello. I have to close now.

Yours Sincerely,
MIKE

A year and a half after Michael was discharged from the Village a member of the Village staff received information that Michael was afraid to continue living in his old neighborhood in the upstate New York community lest he "kill someone" in the neighborhood gangs who attempted to involve him in criminotic activities. For reasons that could not be ascertained, the family moved to New York City and "Michael and his mother" were living there. From the reports obtained from former residents of the Village who were in contact with Michael, it was learned that Michael was working and had not been in any difficulties with the legal authorities.

It will be recalled that Michael during group interviews frequently expressed concern over his uncontrollability and fears that he might kill someone who would provoke him. Our observation of him convinced us that, though this was not definitely clinically established, Michael was a borderline schizophrenic. The fact that he was removed from his pathoplastic social environment and moved away from his neighborhood could be attributed to the awareness of his condition he derived from the group discussions.

Macy

Macy, of an inordinately pathological family background and destructive mother, did not fare so well as the others.

Five months after discharge, a report on Macy from the local social service agency indicated that he was doing very well, attending high school on a full-time basis, and working at a part-time job, and that he was "getting along fine" at home, despite the extraordinary pathology of the family. In a letter to the group therapist several months later, Macy wrote:

> Hi Mr. Ellery,
>   Just a few lines to let you know how things are going. As for me every-thing is o.k. and I hope the same for you. Have you started any more group discussion? Me and Mike[3] were talking about it the other day, some of the good times we used to have there. Like the bad times too. I'm in school and it's pretty hard. Sometimes I get so that I just want to quit and get out of it all. I drive now. I got my license. How has the other guys been? Have you heard from them? I still got the last pass that we got, to see you [the signature] in the wallet of mine. Well, I can't think of anything else to say. So I'll close for now.
>
> Your Good Friend,
Macy M.

However, about a year after discharge, Macy, as he had foreseen, got into a fight with a boy at school over a girl (fifteen years of age) with whom he had had sexual relations, and seriously injured him. He was arrested, but later exonerated. In response to our inquiry on the status of the case from the social service agency in the city where Macy lived, which worked with him and his family, the following report was received:

> The family to which Macy returned must be described as a multi-problem family. Everyone in this family appears to be suffering from a severe character disorder. When Macy came back, he appeared to have gotten tremendous emotional gains from his residence at the Village. This immediately threatened the entire family. The mother became extreme in undermining and sabotaging whatever gains Macy had made. An example might serve to highlight this. Macy has a younger brother John; the mother used to say to Macy in John's presence: "I bet you think you are so great because you were helped by the Village. Well, I think John, who is much younger than you, can beat the living daylights out of you." The mother would actually provoke fights between Macy and his younger brother. Further, there is a sister in the family who recently made a suicidal attempt by taking sleeping pills. The exact circumstances of this are not clear.
>   Macy returned to school upon coming home, and seemed to be doing well, but here the mother again very actively sabotaged. Somehow, the mother was able to manipulate the school authorities and get Macy to quit school. She wanted Macy to go to work and become the breadwinner of the family. This clashed with Macy's very real desire to continue school and finish his

---

3. Michael and Macy lived in the same city, some distance from the Village.

education. [It will be recalled that Macy's father had died while Macy was in residence at Children's Village.]

Currently, Macy is living with a brother-in-law under court order. The social worker who was present when Macy appeared in court, indicated it would be extremely detrimental for Macy to continue living with his mother and the court ordered that Macy reside with the brother-in-law, the husband of Macy's eldest sister. The court directed the mother to pay for Macy's keep and informed the mother that this man was to have full jurisdiction and sole control over the boy. So far things are going well, but this brother-in-law is very involved with the mother and it may not be too long before there is more trouble. Macy is very much aware of how he has been provoked into fights at home but felt completely helpless to do anything about it while he was living at home.

Macy later telephoned his former therapist, long distance, and the therapist reported the following:

Macy had just seen his girl and she had given him "the gate." He was very upset, feeling extremely guilty about the whole relationship, and as I tried to clarify this with him, one of the elements of guilt was that he felt she would now turn into a prostitute because he was the first boy to have had intercourse with her. He was feeling extremely hurt; his ego had obviously taken quite a setback. He has discovered that the girl was not pregnant.

I talked with Macy about this and pointed out how unrealistic it was for him to take all the blame upon himself. I recognized how terribly hurt he must feel at the moment and reassured him that this will ease up with time.

After further discussion, Macy agreed that maybe it would be best for him to share all of this with his local social worker. He did not want me to talk to her about this, however, because he wanted to be the one to communicate it to her. He told me the reason he had not told her about all this before, was because, "she's a woman and I always feel very funny talking to a woman." He reassured me, however, that the next time he sees her he will talk to her about it, rather than continue living with this unhappiness.

Later I called the social worker to prepare her for Macy's discussion with her and also to urge her not to share with him what I had revealed to her. She was quite understanding and the question arose whether Macy might better use a male caseworker. She said she has been considering this and it is possible that they can assign Macy to a male caseworker, since Macy's experiences with women have been so devastating.

The social worker was very much aware of the feeling of doom that Macy carried with him and his need for her support and help to feel that he was not fated for destruction. Essentially, she was going to try to help Macy to become self-supporting and is trying to find him a job. If he does return to school, it will be a part-time job. She felt Macy might be amenable to this plan.

Richard

Following a review of Richard's case in the after-care department six months after his discharge, the psychiatrist at the after-care clinic in the city wrote as follows about Richard:

> This boy, who will be sixteen in January, was discharged from Children's Village six months ago. He is not doing well. Since return to his family the inner conflicts engendered by the parental relationship seem to have immobilized him. He is not functioning in any area. He is described, both at home and at school, as "lazy," "dazed," "absorbed in his thoughts and won't help with the work at home." He truants from school, does not keep his appointments. He had a job for the summer, obtained for him before he left Children's Village, but quit it after eight days, and since then has made no effort to do anything else. Superficially, Richard is reasonable and apparently cooperative. When he has discussed the situation with his caseworker, he agreed with the worker that he is behaving foolishly and insists that he wants to finish school and promises to attend; but his behavior does not change.
>
> This is a boy who verbalizes well and can easily make one feel that he is participating in therapy, but whose underlying conflicts have remained untouched. This technique has probably served him well in dealing with his dominating, ambitious mother whose standards he outwardly accepts and verbalizes, and his resentful, delinquent father with whom he identifies. He talks like his mother, but acts like his father. Perhaps his stay at the Village has made this conflict more nearly conscious and more disturbing to him, for since its reactivation by his return to his parents, it seems to have brought him to a dead stop.
>
> Since he will not keep his appointments here, there is little we can do for him. However, it looks as though the situation would soon inevitably come to a head. The father is stealing money from the rents which he, as (part-time) building superintendent, collects, and the mother has had to make up for it, for which she has taken out a loan. This obviously cannot continue indefinitely, and when she is unable to replace the money he takes, the father will be apprehended. She recently talked about leaving her husband. (The truant officer who visited the home

several times decided that little can be done with the family. Neither Richard nor the mother cooperated.)

Richard has been told by the principal of his school that if his truancy continues through the present term, he will be transferred to a special school for problem pupils in January. The mother has said that she would withdraw him from school rather than have him sent to a special school. Either of these events would precipitate a domestic crisis which might penetrate Richard's defenses of withdrawal and denial, and enable us to intervene therapeutically. All we can do now is to wait and be ready to offer help when he will accept it.

Diagnosis: Passive-aggressive personality; neurotic reaction reactivated by his return home.

Prognosis: Guarded.

We had anticipated difficulties with Richard after his return to his home and the community. We were aware that despite his impressive behavioral improvement, his overriding neurotic problems could not be worked out in a group. To reach his difficulties, he would have to develop a transference neurosis toward his therapist in individual treatment—required in the therapy of a psychoneurotic—which he had begun to do while in the Village. However, the duration of the treatment was too brief to work through the complexities of this pathognomic personality. There was also the question whether a disturbance such as his could benefit from casework treatment on a once-a-week basis.

An added factor, which contributed to the deterioration of this boy's personality more than any other, was the unsuitable treatment he received at the hands of the caseworker in the agency to which he was referred by the authorities in the city where Richard resided. The line the caseworker took was one of authority, pressure, and censure, in the belief that this procedure would mobilize the boy's ego energies. The same approach was also used with Richard's family; it only served to antagonize the mother, whom the caseworker pursued with demands. The final straw in this case was the caseworker's suggesting to Richard that he live in a "residential club" away from home before the mother was prepared for this step. As a result, she broke off contact with the agency. She moved away from her quarters, leaving no forwarding address and obtaining an unlisted telephone. By this strategy she and her son cut themselves off from further contact.

The coarse, insensitive treatment by the caseworker left no refuge to Richard from the vortex of his inner conflicts and tensions. He now carried an emotional load vastly heavier than when he entered the Village. To a much larger degree his compulsive delinquent behavior and that of his father proved less tolerable to him than before, when his conduct was considerably more ego-syntonic. The discussions in the group and his increased self-alliance and the emerging self-identity rendered his impulses and his father's conduct much less tolerable. This increased his conflicts and tensions. Since he had no one with a sympathetic ear and a desire to help him, he felt trapped. Hence, the "dazed" aspect of his being, to which the psychiatrist in the follow-up study in the city referred.

Reflections

While the outcomes of the boys' participation in the group by and large confirm the validity of the use of para-analytic group psychotherapy with delinquent adolescent boys, it can be expected that the results would have been more impressive had we used for our demonstration a group selected by tested criteria. However, as already indicated, we decided on a group consisting as nearly as possible of a sampling of the run-of-the-mill delinquent. We were convinced *ab initio* that analytic psychotherapy would be effective with selected patients (a conviction that was justified by our experience with observation groups), but the utility of a rehabilitative technique and its social values lay in its applicability to a maximum number. We must emphasize here, lest misunderstandings arise, that this blanket principle does not hold for psychotherapy. In psychotherapy, procedures have to be suited to the specific *clinical* category of patients and the needs of each individual involved.

We can also assume that had the boys been exposed to para-analytic group treatment for a longer period, better and more tenacious outcomes could have been expected. A brief period of seventy-five sessions is obviously insufficient to counteract the effects of the deep imprints during impressionable and formative years. Before placement in groups, the boys had been in the institution one or two years. Had they received therapy such as we have described through their entire stay, more salutary and more lasting results could be envisaged. As it was, three of the boys left us in midstream. Because the pressure from parents for release of their sons had been increasing with the passing of time, the boys themselves had become restive under the circumstances. In one instance, a boy was due for return home.

If we are to judge from the samplings in our four groups, para-analytic group psychotherapy is suitable for nearly all delinquents. (The exceptions are active, full-blown psychotics and constitutional psychopaths, though we are not too certain of the conclusion respecting the latter.) The universality of its effectiveness can be traced in the first place to its appeal to all adolescents because it does not involve too deep intro-spection and confrontation of the unconscious. But the factor that carried more weight with our groups was that this procedure touched them midway in their psyche, as it were. Para-analytic therapy concentrates primarily on behavior, the major concern of our boys, since it was for their behavior that they were being "punished," as they viewed their commitment to the Village. At the same time, we threw the light of understanding upon their acts, and they recognized this as the source of their salvation. This hope involved them on the conscious level, and once the recognition became apparent to them, they readily participated and invested their libidos in the process. This was our opportunity to involve also the unconscious, which led to the inversion technique.

Adolescents are notoriously poor psychotherapeutic risks. They re-spond to psychotherapy only perfunctorily if at all; they universally offer great resistance to it. Reasons for this are well known and do not require repetition here. What is of interest, rather, is that once the initial distrust of the therapist was overcome, our boys threw themselves wholeheartedly into the therapeutic maelstrom. While there appeared, as the protocols reveal, periodic flashes of regression and inevitable group resistances, by and large the boys' participation was fullhearted. Their feelings toward the therapist and the group, their eagerness not to miss sessions, and their requests for more frequent "meetings" indicate a rare and unexpected enthusiasm and involvement.

The fact that the para-analytic type of group (or individual) inter-view involves the intellect, learning of scientific facts and self-under-standing, makes it palatable to youngsters and arouses their interest. These characteristics of the group discussions enlist *natural* curiosity and supply it with the ingredients from which the adolescent finds a purpose and direction for his life, with the emergent certainties and securities of which he is desperately in need.

The loyalty to and enthusiasm for our groups at the institution far exceeded, in our experience, those in urban out-patient clinics. Two explanations which can be offered for this seemed to be suggested by some of the boys' own statements in the group interviews. One was the fact that in the group they found a haven from the pressures from which they could not escape in the institution, while the larger com-munities offered a variety of such escapes. The other reason was that in the group the boys were *unconditionally* accepted. To them this meant being trusted and respected, which was not the case in families and ordinary schools. Our group climate met the boys' urgent needs for acceptance and ego support, and it was in this climate that they were able to achieve a state of relaxation, and thus become receptive to the educational and reconstructive efforts of the therapy.

If this diagnosis is correct, penologists and criminotherapists may need to revise some of their theories and practices.

A significant outcome of our observations was that, underlying the aggressive acting out characterized by seeming indifference and unconcern for the boys' own welfare and that of others, there was a reservoir of overwhelming anxiety, characteristic of nearly all delinquents. This anxiety they suppressed within themselves and concealed from others. Through the inversion technique, we succeeded in reaching the founts of this anxiety, which led to uncovering the unconscious and deeply repressed virulent feelings and malignant attitudes. It is not uncommon for criminals and delinquents to talk to social workers, psychiatrists, parole officers, and others in authority of their feelings of contrition, guilt, and remorse. These are usually maneuvers of evasion or atonement that in most instances "come off the top of their heads," as it were; they do not recognize the sources of their conduct, the deeply suppressed onto- and phylo-genetic urges lodged in their unconscious. The confessionals, if they are not intended to mislead, proceed from socially derived frames of reference and the ethos, as well as from fear of punishment and sometimes even from fleeting guilt feelings. The confessionals are not made in an *analytic mood*, which we succeeded in generating in our boys, thus clearing the psyche for assimilation of new feeling-attitudes and concepts. As a result, paratoxic distortions, defenses, and rigidities gave way to flexibility, receptivity, and more benign dispositions. This process was confirmed by the boys' communications both in the group and to their social workers. All the boys remembered after discharge from the Village the values and the guidelines for living that had been arrived at and discussed in the group sessions. Even the few who succumbed to the exigencies of their impoverished milieu quoted them regretfully in their statements. The majority held fast to them. Such results cannot be attained by tutorial or punitive techniques. They can emerge only when the way for them is cleared in the psyche, and only then can they become part of the mental structure of the individual.

The outcome of our work with our boys was their unmistakable advancement in maturity. Because of the bound-up anxiety and the absence of adequate self-identity, all the boys, with no exceptions, were fixed on the infantile level, which in our opinion is characteristic of all criminotic persons. As long as the criminotic individual remains with his inner turmoil he will remain unchanged, no matter what ideals and probity he will mouth and for whatever reasons he may do so. Only when his hidden anxieties are allayed or eliminated will it be possible for him to advance in maturity, namely, to grow less dependent, less narcissistic, less self-indulgent, and more advanced in reality-testing and awareness of the relation of act and causality. These characteristics and capacities have their roots in an adequate self-identity (which comprises in its structure social identity and loyalty). For identity is the individual's frame of reference datum line, from which flow his mode of life and his value system. It was, therefore, our task to induce or generate a corrected identity in each of our boys which would be compatible with a wholesome social pattern—and, therefore, responsibility.

That we have succeeded in this is made evident by the boys who managed their lives out of an awareness of self and reality. Even those who were less successful in this still retained memories of the life-criteria and values derived in the groups, though because of inadequate ego resources they could not hold up so well as others under the inordinate burdens imposed on them. Their identities remained on a rudimentary level; but the significant fact is that despite handicaps and deficits in some of our boys, inroads had been made, and one can only speculate what greater outcomes could have been achieved had the therapy been extended.

The severest failure of the boys' parents (and this is probably true in the education of all criminotic persons) is that they had not given purpose and direction to the lives of their offspring, largely because they did not possess them for themselves. Schools and other supplementary educational and community instrumentalities may substitute, in some instances, for the parents' failures in this regard. However, where the damage is too severe, these agencies are of no or little avail. Where the youngster was not helped progressively to acquire an identity commensurate with his age and native capacities, these agencies could not be effective, for there is no fertile soil for planting the seed. Purpose and direction stem from the individual's self-identity and self-reliance. Socially derived aims are selected, usually through unconscious determinants, stemming from various identifications and one's own identity. A complex society, such as ours is, offers innumerable possibilities for choices, and choices are determined by what the individual *really* is —his identity, which comprises his native powers, his predilections, and his identifications. Psychotherapy helps the individual to establish an identity, the center of which is identification with the therapist, a fact to which our boys' statements in the protocols and their later communications testify.

In any discussion of the nature and genesis of identity, the somato-constitutional factors need to be considered. First are the infant's and child's somatic needs and tensions, such as hunger, pain and discomfort, kinesthenic imbalance, and awareness of the *self*, which is followed by and extended to awareness of the nonself: the mother and later other persons in the environment, who become objects of identification that are absorbed into the identity complex of the individual. An inclusive view of self-identity must take into consideration the "self" which is the resultant of somatic sensations, all awareness, tensions, pains, pleasures, discomforts, feelings, strivings, and relationships. Of no small importance are the state of health, the metabolic, neurologic, and kinesthenic balances and imbalances, and the hereditary structure of the ego and its potentials. These were to us objects of special concern and observation. Medical reports, even psychological tests and psychiatric impressions, do not always adequately furnish full information. Much is revealed of individuals in a group situation, especially when it is emotionally charged, that cannot be observed in any studies and tests. The impact of a group activates much which does not come through in a one-to-one situation. We recall in this connection that individual therapists in urban clinics frequently remarked, after conferences with group therapists on patients in parallel treatment, that they never understood their patients as fully before these conferences. The observations by group therapists of patients' behavior and reactions under the impact of others reveal characteristics that do not come through in individual interviews.

In this respect social workers and therapists in an institution have an advantage over therapists in outpatient settings. The contacts with their patients outside interviews and the continuous exchange with other staff members concerning them yields a vastly fuller picture than clinical interviews alone can supply.

Two major observations suggest themselves from the differentials in the postinstitutional adjustment of the boys whom we studied here. The common factor present in Neal's and Jules's entirely satisfactory adjustment was the guidance and support they received—one from a substitute father in the person of his former teacher, the other from an uncle and a job which served as a transition from the institution to the community. Leonard also did well while he was in the protected environment of the summer camp and would have continued to do so within the limitations of his potentials. Louis, who found himself torn between his striving to live up to his new-found values and identity and the reality of his milieu, sought out support in calling upon the after-care social worker when the pressures, turmoil, and strain within his family circle built up in him stresses he could not sustain at the time. He resolved the impasse by flight into the protective setting that the army offered, instead of succumbing to the adversities of circumstance.

If we were to identify a common element that might account for the comparatively lesser improvements by Donald, Michael, and Macy, it would be their intense involvement with their mothers. These involvements in the cases of Donald and Macy were strongly tinged with mutual incestuous strivings between the mothers and their sons. Of note is also the fact that these two boys were the only ones in our group to become sexually involved with girls. This can be understood as a neurotic defense against their prohibited sexual strivings toward their mothers.

To return Richard to his criminogenic home environment was to court trouble. However, as in other instances as well, the parents' insistence and their legal rights to their children made these exigencies unavoidable. Whether Richard would escape the life of crime, despite the mother's efforts, remained in the realm of speculation. However, what is significant is that at this writing almost three years have elapsed since his return to the community without any report of his involvement with the law.

Note must be made in this connection that despite the severity of pathology and the personality problems in the seven boys under study, none returned to a life of crime, though a few bordered on it. If they had not achieved complete recovery, all seemed to have established more salutary societal frames of reference for their lives and conduct. It would be difficult to speculate how much better results could have been achieved had the boys participated in para-analytic group psychotherapy for the one or two years they were in the Village prior to joining, or had it been possible to extend their stay after they had joined the group.

Recommendations

The above observations lead to a number of suggestions as to the residential and postresidential treatment of acting-out delinquent adolescent boys.

In the first place, where individual therapy is clinically indicated, it should be conducted by therapists trained *specifically* for work with delinquent teenagers and should be conducted on a much deeper level than is usually the case in institutions and at more frequent intervals than once a week. Turnover in the treatment personnel ought to be prevented, so that the relationship with therapists might not be interrupted, since in the case of the emotionally deprived this relationship forms the center of the therapy even more than with other types of patients.

In view of the fact that no training for psychotherapy in residential treatment specifically is available elsewhere, the agencies themselves need to provide, in addition to experience, such training for the clinical staff and for all others who carry management and coordination responsibilities within the institution and with the residents' families and community resources.

Psychotherapy needs to be extended not only in the dimension of depth, but also in the dimension of time. In cases in which this is indicated, psychotherapy needs to be continued after discharge from the institution. However, even where psychotherapy is not a part of post-institutional follow-up, the youngsters need help in adapting to their homes and communities, as was the case with Neal and Jules and to some extent with Leonard and Louis. Naturally, postinstitutional psychotherapy and guidance are more reality-oriented, since the patients are confronted with a more complex actuality which, in most instances, formerly wayward youngsters find beyond their capacities to deal with on their own. At this juncture, the relationship between the therapist, the (hopefully) psychologically oriented probation officer, and the social worker needs to be one of mutual awareness and supportive of the adolescent, who now faces life with a somewhat altered personality and, perhaps, a newly acquired awareness, which his parents and others closest to him may not adequately appreciate or understand. The adolescent needs help in adjusting to his new condition, and the persons who exert an impact upon him should support him in carrying his new inner stresses. Essential also are friendship, guidance, professional understanding, and fullhearted empathy in these circumstances. In this parents and teachers as well should be involved. The frequently impersonal inquisitorial, and authoritarian supervision accorded the dischargee do not meet his needs or allay his unavoidable anxieties. What is needed is a firm but warm friendship. Trust and respect will more readily turn a youngster from his deviant path than will harshness and persecution.

In another rehabilitation institution for delinquent boys, financial provision was made at varying times for twelve of its former inmates to pursue a college career. This exemplary feat was accomplished not officially by the institution, but rather by one staff member, who succeeded in enlisting the interest of various organizations and individuals of means in boys who had shown promise in academic pursuit.[4] Contact with them was maintained by this interested staff member and his wife for years after they had severed connection with the institution.[5] It is this type of relationship that sustains damaged personalities and weakened egos of young people until they are strengthened by life to carry their burdens and withstand life's stresses. The institution in question had for many years maintained a "scholarship fund" to be used for boys in various ways to aid them in their rehabilitation after discharge. Neal and Louis were "college material," had they received encouragement

---

4. Of interest and perhaps of curiosity is the fact that at this writing one of the former residents of that other institution was a classmate (working for a doctor's degree in psychology) of the group therapist who conducted the demonstration group at the Village described in this volume.

5. Both were on the present author's staff in the project described by him in S. R. Slavson, *Re-Educating the Delinquent through Group and Community Participation* (New York: Harper and Brothers, 1954; Collier Books, 1961), to which reference has been made elsewhere in this volume.

and aid. Only one boy of the sixty-three in all our groups went on to college; he had been a member of one of our activity therapy groups.

To achieve maximum results from residential treatment requires "indeterminate" stay in the institution to accord with the corrective and rehabilitative indications of the specific individual. Psychotherapists and other effective personnel, such as teachers, cottage parents, recreational workers, and all others who come in direct contact with patients in residential and in extramural guidance and treatment, need to be aware of the multi-causality of the delinquent life-pattern. Even our brief discussions of the boys brings to light the variety of sources of the generic phenomenon of delinquency. To be effective, it is essential here, as in all psychotherapy, that the psychodynamics generating the specific behavior and the nuclear problem of each individual be identified and the direction of the total therapy planned to suit corrective needs.[6]

Psychotherapists working with delinquent adolescents, and to a lesser degree also with adolescents generally, need to extend their armamentaria beyond generic and ordinary clinical concepts and understandings. It is not sufficient to classify the youngsters by clinical categories and proceed to treat them accordingly. Actually, the majority in the delinquent population do not strictly fall within blanket and inclusive categorizations. As revealed in the spontaneous communications in the protocols, the presence of the doom motif; the deeply buried feelings of cupidity, self-contempt, tendencies for denial and self-delusion, self-hatred; and the generalized attitude of worthlessness (disguised as it may be) need to be revealed and dealt with by the therapist as the interviews progress and the defenses give way to reality.

If this procedure were applied in individual therapy with this type of patient (and adolescents generally), it would be felt by the patient as rejection and criticism, and he would react with hostility, resistance, and angry flight from the therapeutic relation. In a peer group, the dynamics of interpersonal reactions, such as universalization, mutual induction, catalysis, empathy, mutual identification, the rescue fantasy (and many others) take the edge off feelings of self-debasement and of narcissistic injury: The group is, therefore, recommended as the treatment of choice with adolescents generally and with the vast majority of delinquents particularly.

Symptom and conduct improvement may reflect basic intrapsychic change, but this is not always the case. Observable improvement, when

6. Although our comments on the group session protocols were directed toward the group interactions and the common problems of the boys, in our supervision conferences stress was laid on identifying the nuclear and peripheral problem of each member of the group and on the means of dealing with them. An example of this is the case of Neal.

it is not conscious strategy intended to mislead adults, can be due to temporary absence of provoking circumstances, transferential attitudes, or, hopefully, an actually strengthened ego. The last, however, cannot occur in the psychoneuroses (as was the case with Frank p. 154 *et seq.* and Richard). A *neurotic residue* remains with such patients, which by the principle of repetition compulsion impels the "improved" delinquent to resume his antisocial life-pattern. Such patients require prolonged psychoanalytic therapy and, if possible, a standard psychoanalysis.

The specific content of the delinquent's psyche, as revealed by our boys when they were placed in an analytic state, requires correlative training in the clinic staff so that its members may be able to elicit it in the interviews (examples of which are replete in the protocols) and to deal with such content therapeutically as steps in building new identity and strengthened egos. To illustrate how far short from these aims in-service training in the field falls, we reproduce the list of topics in a seminar of 17 sessions given by a staff psychiatrist for caseworkers who conducted psychotherapy in a residential treatment institution for delinquents.

The topics (each with recommended reading) were: the essence of casework relationships; a theory of personality; the worker-client relationship; the impact of clients' unconscious on caseworker reactions; the contributions of ego psychology; the casework relationship—individualization, purposeful expression of feelings, controlled emotional involvement; the casework relationship—acceptance, the nonjudgmental attitude, client self-determination, confidentiality; therapeutic considerations of the borderline personality structure; learning through recorded material basic concepts in diagnoses and treatment of borderline states; personality diagnosis in casework; the concepts of casework—situation, the person, the problems, the place, the process, the caseworker-client relationship, the problem-solving work; person, problem, place, and process in the beginning phases; content in the beginning phases; method in the beginning phases; diagnoses: the thinking in problem-solving, the client workability and casework goal, the balance expression of Oedipal remnants; some problems of delinquency and their treatment by a casework agency; character analysis.

The seminar for supervising caseworkers was conducted along strictly psychoanalytic lines by a visiting psychoanalyst with no antecedent contact with adolescents or experience with institutions and the problems the staff have to cope with.

While a number of the seminar topics listed above have some bearing upon the nature of delinquent character, the sessions were purely theoretical with no relevance applicability or evocation of the judgments essential for transforming theory to experience. Unlike academic teaching, in-service training needs to draw on the experiences with patients and staff derived from the workaday life in and out of the clinical sphere. Much of the theory encompassed in the seminars had already been part of the prepractice generic professional education of the caseworkers. They also had had clinical "field-work" training as graduate students, and many had held positions as caseworkers and therapists in various clinical settings before they came to the institution. What they needed at this point, in preference to theory, was the *understanding of the mind* of the adolescent and training in how to use this understanding in the special endeavor in which they were currently engaged, namely, reconstructing the personalities of *delinquent* adolescents. We consider that the overriding value of our present volume lies in the delineation of the *process* by which this can be achieved, as reflected in the group session protocols.

Beyond the institution in the lives of the young people are their homes and their communities. Some suggestions have already been made elsewhere in these pages with regard to this problem. More specifically, the homes to which the young people are to return need to be of special concern to institutional staff. To permit the homes to undo the corrective work of the institution and erase its effort and effect is social waste and a personal tragedy. Homes need to be thoroughly scrutinized before dischargees return to them. While it is conceded that ideal homes would not produce problem children of the type requiring social sequestration, some may be tolerably suitable to the reconditioned personalities of the dischargees. In others, the pathoplastic effect of the milieu may have been decreased either by professional guidance of parents or removal of a pathogenic member of the family; or with his newly found strengths, the adolescent may be able, with continued supervision, to sustain the negative pressures of the family circle. Dischargees can be returned conditionally to such homes.

However, there are many homes to which a former resident of a rehabilitative institution should under no circumstances return. Once an individual has succumbed to a set of negative influences, he becomes allergic to them, and over-reacts to these influences as an alcoholic does to a drink. Allergy is over-reaction to substances to which one had been previously exposed with negative results. Similarly, an individual exposed to a repetition of a situation usually reacts more than one who had never experienced it before. (One reason may lie in the fact that the anxieties weaken the ego, rendering it less able to bear up under the repetitive stress.)

Our experiences with parents of delinquent children, and of others in difficulties, make it palpably clear that these parents are either indifferent to their children, actively reject them, or unconsciously approve and encourage their delinquencies. Either foster homes or residence clubs, preferably the former, are indicated for such youngsters.

The needs of delinquent youngsters for continued postinstitutional guidance and thérapy may require alterations in the juridical structure for dealing with them. It may be necessary, for example, to declare legally some of the less promising as temporary wards of the state so that no impediments may be placed by relatives to the therapeutic plans deemed necessary by clinical staffs. Some punitive measures may have to be provided for those of the relatives who offer active resistance to these plans. The general guiding principle needs to be established that parents' rights to the management of their children cease once they have failed in their responsibilities to the extent that community intervention is rendered necessary. This principle in no way contravenes the individual's democratic rights. Society, too, has the right to safeguard its integrity and health. In fact this is currently the guiding principle in penology. What is suggested here is only an extension of that principle.

Our boys' own awareness of the effect on them of the neighborhoods in which they lived, as evinced in the therapy group interviews, makes palpable the importance of the neighborhood in rehabilitation efforts. The need to be accepted, to belong, rather than ostracized by one's peers, the allergic over-reaction to social pathology, and the psychic hegemony of the onto-archaic tendencies, combine to lead the former delinquent back to his haunts and way of life. If the exposure to therapy and the comparatively more wholesome living in the institution are extended for long periods and fall on fertile soil, the adolescents could acquire the strength to cope with pressures and resist temptations they encounter on their return home. But this occurs now only fortuitously and cannot be relied on in the vast majority of the returnees. Exhaustive study and appraisal of the milieu is, therefore, essential before the delinquent is discharged to his family. It is necessary to appraise among other things the likelihood of his re-establishing former associations either voluntarily or through threats and pressures, and what effects these would have.

One of the conditions for returning a boy to his family, for example, may be its moving to a more favorable neighborhood as well as a better located and appointed dwelling. Hopes and sincere wishes for improved order in their lives were verbalized by the boys in our groups on many occasions as their awareness emerged and striving assumed a more mature quality. Some of our boys acted on these, as, for example, Michael quitting his neighborhood after his discharge and Louis joining the army, a step that was largely motivated by his nearly becoming involved in delinquencies with his former cronies. However, these voluntary self-chosen solutions may be beyond many of the returnees to criminotic neighborhoods.

The importance of the institution as a therapeutic and rehabilitative community is too frequently overlooked in the plans of residential treatment. As we demonstrated in 1934, personality reconstruction can be achieved in many delinquents, though not in all, exclusively through the instrumentality of communal participation and group status without the benefit of clinical services.[7] The impelling need to be "trusted" and respected and to have status is universal among all young people, and delinquent youngsters are no exception to this. This topic was one to which the boys in our groups repeatedly returned. Since character change and ego strength grow out of the satisfactions of felt needs, these yearnings on the part of residents in correctional institutions must be satisfied in order that the young people may return to their communities as stronger and more socially oriented individuals. We have shown in the records of our group that needs have to be satisfied to varying degrees, even if they are infantile and regressive, as first steps toward budding maturity. When maturity is attained, these needs automatically evanesce. Immaturity feeds on denial as much as upon overindulgence. But because strivings favor growth through group participation and status via constructive effort, they need to be nurtured and encouraged by every possible means.

The four basic dynamics of personality development in a democratic culture are acceptance, status, participation, and responsibility. *Re-Educating the Delinquent*, to which reference has been made, is a report of group activities and community life in a corrective institution for delinquents that operated on these four principles.[8] In our work with the boys at the Village, as well, we have shown that the only way in which we could have made inroads into their minds and feelings was by initially accepting them unconditionally as they were, and tolerating their conduct and their values. This spelled not only acceptance, but also status. From the very start, the boys were made to feel by every means, subtle and direct, that the groups were theirs and their responsibility. We were careful, however, not to verbalize it. We did not wish to hand it down as a code; it rather had to evolve from, and be perceived by, the participants; controls had to emerge from them and them alone, rather than be suggested or imposed by an adult. Had the latter been the case, the boys would have rebelled and nullified our effort at advancing their maturity. The protocols amply demonstrate how free group participation established identity and begot responsibility.

What was done in the microculture of the therapy group in this regard is applicable to the larger institutional community, as described in the volume referred to in the previous paragraph. A therapeutic community in a correctional or re-educative institution includes *1]* cottage

7. See Slavson, *Re-Educating the Delinquent through Group and Community Participation.*

8. See Chapter XIII of that volume, entitled, "The Democratic Basis of Corrective Re-education."

life under the guidance of dedicated and sensitive personnel; *2]* schooling adapted to the capacities and interests of each learner; *3]* encouragement and full expression of talents in a great variety of pursuits to engage the many predilections of young people, and not only formal schooling; *4]* a variety of flexible social and special interest groups; *5]* participation in the planning of life in the cottages and the institution as a whole, and assuming responsibilities voluntarily for carrying out plans; *6]* assuming many of the duties in the conduct of the community life usually carried by paid adult staff; *7]* making and carrying forward plans for holiday, seasonal, and social mass celebrations and events; *8]* extending activities into, and establishing contact with, the general community as a transitional phase for resuming life in it in the future.

These and other activities, as well as the steps that were taken in actualizing them, are described also in the volume referred to.[9] Any effort to set them forth, no matter how briefly, would extend the present volume immoderately, and the interested reader is referred to the previous work. However, one cardinal principle needs to be reiterated: a therapeutic community must be flexible, mobile, devoid of unnecessary external controls, free of authoritarianism and of motivated aims for results; rather the motive must flow from the inner process of achievement in the Director and all of his staff. All staff members must be sensitively dedicated and feel a call for the strenuous but most rewarding effort of rescuing children from the tragedies that the future may hold for them.

The effectiveness of a therapeutic community lies less in its content than in its spirit. Emphasis on administrative rigidities conducted with impersonal detachment prevents the emergence of those intangible qualities from which all worthwhile human relations and the richness of life flow. "Programs" and "controls" that characterize all too many homes, schools, and all re-educative facilities deal a deathblow to spontaneity and spiritual expansion. Orderliness must flow from purpose and aims derived from self-discipline. In the absence of free, fullhearted, and truly motivated participation, imposed order becomes necessary, but evolvement of personality and character growth require inner motivation. Motivation can and should be activated by the environment and its expression must be voluntary and spontaneous.

This type of education (as contrasted with academic learning) and reconstructive process requires a staff of persons with flexibility, free of prejudices and personalized aims of their own—persons with sensitivity, imagination, spiritual richness, unbounded inner security, respect for the individuality of others, and faith in human capacities and potentials.

9. A list of such activities and detailed techniques can also be found in that volume.

Index

Page numbers in boldface type refer to comments on individual boys interspersed among the protocols in Part Two. The material on those pages will enable the reader to trace quickly the therapeutic progress of any individual boy.